MW00783701

THE FLETCHER JONES FOUNDATION

HUMANITIES IMPRINT

The Fletcher Jones Foundation has endowed this imprint to foster innovative and enduring scholarship in the humanities.

The publisher gratefully acknowledges the generous support of the Fletcher Jones Foundation Humanities Endowment Fund of the University of California Press Foundation.

Mediterraneans

THE CALIFORNIA WORLD HISTORY LIBRARY

Edited by Edmund Burke III, Kenneth Pomeranz, and Patricia Seed

Mediterraneans

*North Africa and Europe
in an Age of Migration,
c. 1800–1900*

Julia A. Clancy-Smith

UNIVERSITY OF CALIFORNIA PRESS

Berkeley   Los Angeles   London

University of California Press, one of the most distinguished university presses in the United States, enriches lives around the world by advancing scholarship in the humanities, social sciences, and natural sciences. Its activities are supported by the UC Press Foundation and by philanthropic contributions from individuals and institutions. For more information, visit www.ucpress.edu.

University of California Press
Berkeley and Los Angeles, California

University of California Press, Ltd.
London, England

First paperback printing 2012
© 2011 by The Regents of the University of California

Library of Congress Cataloging-in-Publication Data

Clancy-Smith, Julia Ann.
    Mediterraneans : North Africa and Europe in an age of migration, c. 1800–1900 / Julia A. Clancy-Smith.
        p.   cm.
    Includes bibliographical references and index.
    ISBN 978-0-520-27443-3 (pbk. : alk. paper)
    1. Europeans—Tunisia—Tunis—History—19th century.   2. North Africans—Tunisia—Tunis—History—19th century.   3. Immigrants—Tunisia—Tunis—History—19th century.   4. Tunis (Tunisia)—History—19th century.   5. Algeria—History—19th century.   6. Europe—Emigration and immigration—History—19th century.   7. Africa, North—Relations—Europe.   8. Europe—Relations—Africa, North. I. Title.
    DT269.T8C53   2011
    304.8'611—dc22   2010019718

Manufactured in the United States of America

19   18   17   16   15   14   13   12
10   9   8   7   6   5   4   3   2   1

This book is printed on Cascades Enviro 100, a 100% postconsumer waste, recycled, de-inked fiber. FSC recycled certified and processed chlorine free. It is acid free, Ecologo certified, and manufactured by BioGas energy.

For our Tunisian family, friends, colleagues
and in memory of my brother, Martin Joseph (1951–2004)

CONTENTS

ILLUSTRATIONS

FIGURES

MAPS

ACKNOWLEDGMENTS

In the summer of 1973, a chartered plane landed in the Tunis-Carthage airport on the last leg of its journey from the United States to North Africa. On board were scores of new Peace Corps volunteers, recent graduates from American universities intending to teach English as a foreign language. I was among the volunteers, unaware at the time that this first encounter with Tunisia would grow into a lifelong friendship. A teaching post at al-Qayrawan in the interior made it feasible to travel though the south and the oases stretching from the Mediterranean coastline into Algeria. But much time was spent in Tunis, with its seductive madina as well as in nearby coastal villages—La Marsa, Sidi Bou Sa'id, Carthage, and La Goulette—whose hold over my imagination proved the most enduring. The present book has allowed me to write about the places and peoples that welcomed and intrigued me so long ago and that represent home and family even today.

As is often true of scholarship, this study came about by accident rather than design in a series of footnotes; those familiar with my first book will detect its influence. Years ago, more than I care to admit, I chased after Saharan rebels operating along the limits of the nineteenth-century Algerian and Tunisian states where a trans-Mediterranean traffic in contraband had sunk its runners deep into the desert, a trade that proved key to anticolonial resistance. As I excavated the tangled networks of exchanges contained in the documents, I confronted major problems in the secondary scholarship—missing persons, floating frontiers, unsuspected mobilities, and unexplored connectivities. A range of people—expatriates, deserters, adventurers, and labor migrants—from all across the Mediterranean appeared in the primary sources but did not figure, at least not prominently, in that older historical narrative still structured around binaries, "the French" or "Muslims" and so forth. Directly related, the nation-state framework and nationalist narrative undergirding research on the modern Maghrib did not suffice. This earlier scholarship searched for, and found, a unique Tunisian (or North African) political identity and cultural personality solely grounded in Islam and Arabic and constructed against France and the French. But who were all these folks who kept popping up in the record and clearly belonged in the story as well? And what did their presence, permanent or transitory, in nineteenth-century North Africa mean for state, society, and local communities as well as for the Mediterranean world? Hopefully I have done justice to some of them, the historical subjects, as well as to the spaces through which they moved—despite the fact that their lives more frequently than not were reduced to a scribal notation, chance encounter, terse police or consular reports, or a long-forgotten ship's manifest. Tracking people in motion for long stretches of time required generous patrons and substantial largesse.

My gratitude goes to the following institutions for financial support and/or for providing safe havens to write combined with intellectual camaraderie. First and foremost, the American Institute for Maghrib Studies and the Centre d'Études Magrébines à Tunis (CEMAT), which saw this project through from start to finish; the American Philosophical Society; the Council for American Overseas Research Centers; the Getty Research Institute, Los Angeles; the Institute for Advanced Studies, Princeton; the National Endowment for the Humanities; the National Humanities Center; the Rockefeller Center, Bellagio; San Diego State University; the Spencer Foundation; University of Arizona, College of Social and Behavioral Sciences Research Institute; University of Arizona, Morris K. Udall Center for Studies in Public Policy; and the Virginia Foundation for the Humanities

This work benefitted immensely from talking about it much too long. Colleagues from the following institutions, who are no doubt relieved that this is nearly over, graciously offered critiques of work in progress: the American University in Cairo; Center of Modern Oriental Studies, Freie Universität, Berlin; Institut de Recherche Magrébin à Tunis; Duke University; the Getty Research Institute; Harvard University; Johns Hopkins University; Marquette University; Massachusetts Institute of Technology; New York University; School of Oriental and African Studies, London; Princeton University; San Francisco State University; St. Antony's College, Oxford University; Stanford University; University of California, Berkeley, Los Angeles, and Santa Cruz; University of Chicago; University of Copenhagen, Carsten Niebuhr Institute for Oriental Studies; University of Illinois, Champaign-Urbana; University of Leiden and University of Amsterdam; University of Maryland; University of Michigan; University of Minnesota; University of Navarra; University of North Carolina; Université de Provence/

CNRS/Maison Méditerranéenne des Sciences de l'Homme, Aix-en-Provence; University of Texas, Austin; Université de Toulouse; University of Virginia; and Washington University. In addition, research in many different places has incurred large debts to those who make our work possible but which are too numerous to fully inventory here. The reader is referred to the archives, libraries, and other collections noted in the List of Abbreviations; my heartfelt thanks to the tireless members of their staffs.

At the University of Arizona, large-spirited colleagues exchanged ideas and work in progress with me: Bert Barickman, Anne H. Betteridge, Michael E. Bonine, Gail Bernstein, Linda Darling, Richard M. Eaton, David Gibbs, Leila Hudson, Ute Lotz-Heumann, Amy W. Newhall, Laura Tabili, Susan Karant-Nunn, and Miranda Spieler. The History Department's heads were particularly solicitous: Helen Nader, Richard Cosgrove, Karen Anderson, and Kevin Gosner; as was the dean of the College of Social and Behavioral Sciences, Ed Donnerstein. Two computer wizards, Lucas Guthrie and Rachel Aquilar, saved me from self-destruction on frequent occasions. At the university library, Ruth Dickstein and Jennalyn Tellman greatly aided my research; Scott Cossel provided desperately needed help with images. I thank them all. It has been an immense pleasure to work closely once again with the University of California Press. My heartfelt appreciation to history editor Niels Hooper, Nick Arrivo, Eric Schmidt, and Suzanne Knott for their good cheer, forbearance, and professionalism during the process; my friend of many years, Lynne Withey, director of the press, offered unstinting encouragement. Suzanne Knott's and Julie Van Pelt's meticulous editing deserve special mention as well. Appreciation is also due the press's manuscript evaluators, who not only expended considerable energy reading carefully through a work of forbidding size but also submitted detailed reports (in timely fashion) that greatly improved the outcome: Edmund Burke III, Laurence O. Michalak, Nancy E. Gallagher, and an anonymous reader.

This book is the product of years of conversations and exchanges with scholars interested in histories of the modern Mediterranean, notably Edmund Burke III and Randi Deguilhem, as well as others working on related questions, among them: Ali Ahmida, David Bond, Marilyn Booth, L. Carl Brown, Zeynep Çelik, Mounira Charrad, Fanny Colonna, Alice L. Conklin, Miriam Cooke, Sarah E. Curtis, Karima Direche, Ross E. Dunn, Joanne Ferraro, Israel Gershoni, Eric T. Jennings, Jonathan G. Katz, Habib Kazdaghli, Dalenda Larguèche, Abdelhamid Larguèche, Bruce B. Lawrence, Patricia M. Lorcin, William Roger Louis, Nadia Mamelouk, James McDougall, Laurence O. Michalak, James A. Miller, Susan G. Miller, Odile Moreau, Kenneth J. Perkins, Anne-Marie Planel, David Prochaska, André Raymond, Eugene Rogan, Joan W. Scott, Bonnie G. Smith, Christelle Taraud, Frances Terpak, Mark Tessler, Lucette Valensi, John Voll, and there are many more.

Of course, much of this could not have happened without families, friends, and colleagues in Tunisia. Alia Baffoun, the Ben Achour family, William Granara, the Mrads, Francesco Paterno, and Ridha Saied helped with the crucial matter of housing as well as being good company over the years. The Rostems—Noura, Mohamed, and the rest of the clan—have opened their home in La Marsa to us for over two decades, becoming in the process like kin. Hasiba Agha welcomed me for tea on a number of occasions and answered my persistent questions about family history. Dalenda Larguèche and Abdelhamid Larguèche brought us into the circles of both household and of the historians from the University of Tunis whose intellectual collaboration has proven so enriching. Anne-Marie Planel, at the Institut de Recherche sur le Maghreb Contemporain in Tunis, generously shared her work with me, as did Père David Bond of the Institut des Belles Lettres Arabes. Mention should also be made of research assistance from the bishop of Tunis, His Excellency Maroun Lahham, as well as the White Fathers, White Sisters, and the Sisters of Saint-Joseph.

In the last frantic years of archival research, the CEMAT directors and staff were especially critical to my endeavors: James A. Miller, Laurence O. Michalak, and Riadh Saadaoui. Just before I returned to Tunisia in the summer of 2009, Jeanne Jeffers Mrad, who had served CEMAT so admirably for so long, passed away. I regret that Jeanne, who was also a dear friend, did not see the completed work, as her enthusiasm and support were boundless. Family members are inevitably pulled into the wake of research projects, getting more than they ever bargained for, but they nevertheless provided deeply appreciated comfort. My mother, Elizabeth Cecilia Clancy, pored over several chapters and offered sympathetic readings. Charles D. Smith and daughter Elisabeth Anna patiently endured years of familial displacements to scattered archives in many places. However, my spouse did not only serve as an agreeable traveling companion—he read the entire manuscript several times, something that can sorely test any relationship. The marriage held firm and the book is much the better for his wise counsel; but the mistakes are mine alone.

Julia A. Clancy-Smith
Dar Khadouja, La Marsa, 2009

NOTE ON TRANSLITERATION

Consistent transliteration for modern North African history poses a number of problems because there is no single agreed-upon system among scholars. Proper names, place names, and terms for institutions come from a range of languages— classical Arabic, dialectal Arabic, Berber, Ottoman Turkish, French, and Italian. To complicate matters, proper names and place names often came into English or other European languages through French transliteration, which was not consistent and frequently deformed the originals. Therefore, transliteration in this volume is the product of compromise as is true of all published work on North Africa for this period. Plurals of Arabic words—for example, *wakil* (agent)—are rendered simply by adding "s."

For the most part, a modified version of the transliteration system in the *International Journal of Middle East Studies* for Arabic is employed. However, only the ayn (') and hamza (') are indicated. Turkish words, such as *bey* or *dey*, which refer to Ottoman political offices or titles, are used instead of the more accurate Arabic transliteration, *bay*.

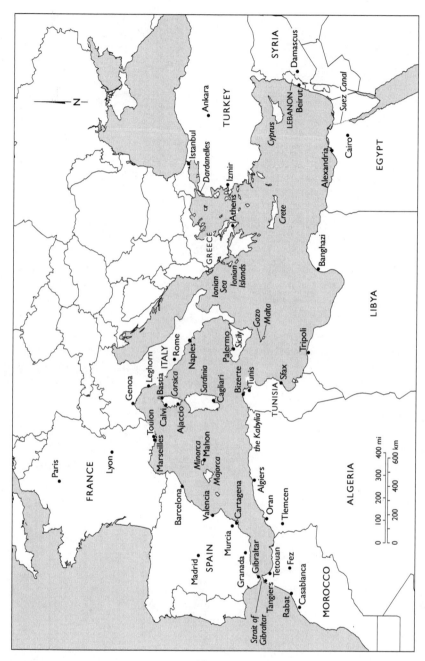

MAP 1. The Mediterranean Basin.

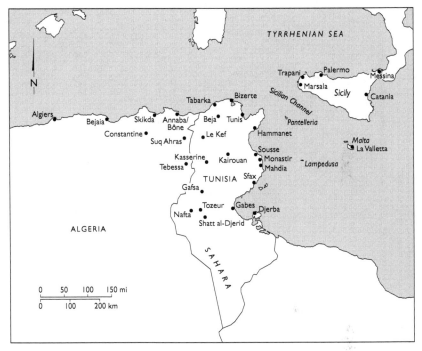

MAP 2. Eastern Algeria, Tunisia, and the Central Mediterranean Corridor.

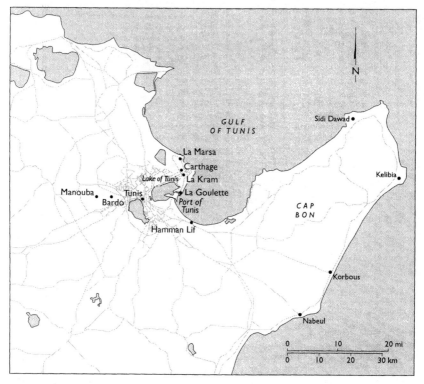

MAP 3. The Tunis Region.

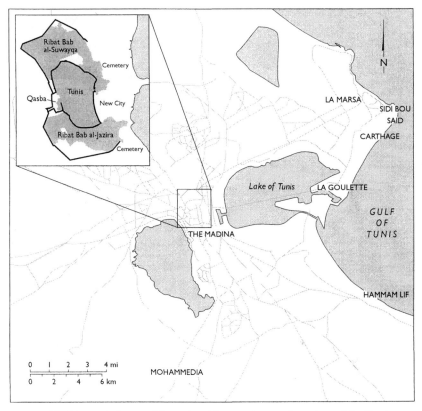

MAP 4. The Tunis Madina and New City. The map is a modern view of the Tunis region; the inset is from c. 1860.

Introduction

Peoplings

PRELUDES

A colossal Anglo-Dutch naval force assembled at Gibraltar under the command of Admiral Sir Edward Pellew, Lord Exmouth, and set sail for the so-called Barbary Coast in the spring of 1816. The expedition first anchored off Algiers, where Exmouth obtained the release of Christian captives; subsequently the fleet moved on to Tunis and Tripoli. By April 1816, agreements were reached with the local rulers of the three Ottoman regencies over the ostensible objective—the abolition of corsairing and the trade in enslaved Europeans. Nevertheless, the armada returned a second time that summer to Algiers, where the commander of the British flotilla, composed of the *Queen Charlotte* and fifty-four gun, mortar, and rocket boats, sent additional demands to the Turkish *dey* (regent). His refusal to accede unleashed a devastating bombardment on August 26 and 27. In the dark of night, barges and yawls crept close to the port, setting it afire and destroying the Algerian navy as well as part of the city. More captives, mainly from Mediterranean islands, were released. Christian slaving and corsair raids had come to an end, at least theoretically.[1] In many ways, the expeditions to Algiers in 1816 constituted a reprise of Napoleon's 1798 invasion of Egypt as well as a dress rehearsal for France's occupation of Algeria in 1830.

Tunisia's encounter with Exmouth differed radically, however, from Algeria's. After leaving Algiers the first time, the fleet had next put in to La Goulette (Halq al-Wad), the port for Tunis, on April 10, 1816, with eighteen warships whose hoisted flags signaled readiness for hostilities. It stayed in port until April 23, but the cannon remained silent. Tunis was spared. After intense negotiations,

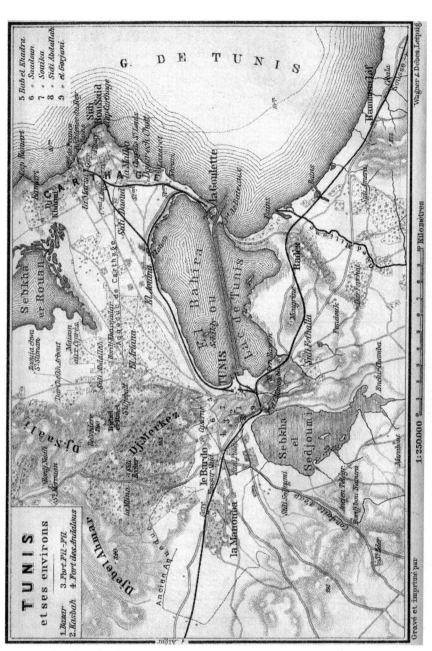

FIGURE 1. Tunis and its environs, 1900. (Karl Baedeker, *Handbook for Travellers: Third Part; Southern Italy and Sicily, with Excursions to the Lipari Islands, Malta, Sardinia, Tunis, and Corfu*, 13th rev. ed. [Leipsic: Karl Baedeker, 1900].)

Mahmud Bey (r. 1814–1824), ruler of the Husaynid dynasty (1705–1957), freed hundreds of Sardinians, Genoese, and Sicilians from bagnios scattered around the capital city. While many released captives returned to Europe with the fleet, some former slaves elected to stay on.[2] As importantly for the peaceful denouement of the affair, Exmouth arrived in Tunis to find to his utter astonishment that Caroline, Princess of Wales (1768–1821), wife of the heir to the British throne, was touring the country's classical sites. As the bey's honored guest, the princess and her entourage were lavishly wined and dined. Caroline's presence rendered bombardment somewhat delicate and may have saved the Tunisians from naval attack. (We will return to the footloose princess a bit later.)[3] If the 1816 expedition signaled the royal navy's supremacy and thus fundamental shifts in power between the northern and southern rims of the Mediterranean, between Ottoman North Africa and European states, its long-term significance emerged a mere two decades later in a curious, contradictory postscript.

In 1836 another British fleet, this time dispatched from Malta, appeared in La Goulette. But now, the royal navy sought not to liberate Christian captives but rather to force the Tunisian ruler, Mustafa Bey (r. 1835–1837), to accept British protégés—Maltese laborers—into his realm.[4] In twenty years, the politics of population movements in the central Mediterranean had been utterly transformed. British gunboat diplomacy no longer rescued captive Christians but instead dumped impoverished island peoples deemed "surplus" onto a Muslim state. The *renegados,* ransom captives, slaves, and freewheeling border crossers of earlier centuries were rapidly being transformed into labor and other kinds of migrants. As social actors, they participated, often unwittingly, in complex population displacements and peoplings then taking place on a global scale.[5]

PEOPLINGS

From the Napoleonic era to the Great War, tens of thousands of people, many of humble social status, crossed the sea from north to south to settle in North Africa, Egypt, and the Levant. Languishing ports were transformed into boomtowns. Alexandria, whose population counted no more than 6,000 in 1798 when Napoleon's army invaded, had swelled to 231,000 by 1882 when the British army occupied Egypt. While much of the increase resulted from internal population shifts within Egypt or from Syrian Levantine immigration, a significant percentage of Alexandria's newcomers came from southern Europe and particularly the Mediterranean islands—Sicily, Sardinia, Corsica, the Balearic Islands, Greece, and Malta.[6] These same islanders settled in Beirut, Izmir, Tunis, Algiers, and Tangier, where many resided for generations.

Some realized dreams of fortune in not too distant places, but many failed. Others came and went, moving elsewhere in the Mediterranean or to the Americas and even Australia. To follow the continuous, largely undocumented departures of men and women for North Africa is to track from "below" the grand rhythms of the long nineteenth century: nation-state construction, imperialism, industrialization, boom-and-bust capitalism, world market consolidation, war and violence, Great Power rivalry, and the indefatigable advance of ecological and environmental degradation, particularly on the large islands.[7] For the Muslim states and societies on the Mediterranean's southern shores, these displacements were neither inconsequential nor benign.

Population movements constitute the bedrock of world history and assume a wide range of guises: epic wanderings, pilgrimage, pastoral nomadism, transhumance, voluntary relocation, forced expatriation, trade diaspora, travel, tourism, slavery, and labor mobility of many kinds. The critical elements in taxonomies of motion are the relative presence or absence of force, the motivations and objectives of those favoring departure over staying put, the duration and patterns of expatriation, and whether the place of exile became over time a space of belonging. To these considerations must be added variables such as gender, age and generation, social class, family structure, religion, and race, all of which determined how individuals or groups perceived their subjective situation at home and responded to the idea of temporary or permanent expatriation, however alluring or frightening that prospect might have appeared. These diverse manifestations of human mobility were not necessarily distinct; yet no matter how or why they departed, the people in motion brought wide-ranging social changes to their host societies and to those left behind.[8]

Fundamental to the nature, velocity, and direction of migratory processes in this period was the modern state's expanding regulatory reach. States and ruling elites around the Mediterranean rim assumed new positions regarding population movements from about 1815 on. Keeping people in, or conversely keeping them out, through compulsion or coaxing (or a range of strategies somewhere in between) turned into major preoccupations enshrined in law, institutions of coercion, methods of identification, and the practices of daily life.[9]

This work re-creates a borderland society—or societies—forged by migrants and mobilities in the central Mediterranean corridor. Its focus is precolonial Tunisia, especially the capital city, in the period stretching from the eve of France's conquest of Algeria until 1881 when the French Protectorate was imposed. Population movements of various sorts into nineteenth-century Tunisia triggered profound social permutations that endured into the colonial period, powerfully marking, I argue, the nature of the colonial state. These changes ranged from different uses of urban space, new sounds or noises in the city, novel ways of organizing households and leisure, worker competition, housing crises, and perceived increases in morally reprehensible acts, such as public drunkenness, prostitution, smuggling, and street fights. Many newcomers, but not all, in Tunis were diplomatic protégés of European states, although often they did not fully comprehend—nor even care much about—their legal or political status as they moved about, driven by a wide range of motivations.

Nevertheless, they presented intractable problems of legal jurisdiction and thus of social order for the ruling dynasty, the inhabitants of the capital, and for the coastal towns where many immigrants eventually settled. When Exmouth's imposing fleet moored in port, perhaps two to three thousand "Europeans," or "Crypto-Europeans," resided in Tunisia; most clustered in the Tunis region, whose population can be estimated at 100,000, and many were slaves or ex-slaves. (While estimates of Tunisia's total population at midcentury range widely, one million inhabitants seems a reasonable figure.) By 1880 the percentage of Europeans and/or those not recognized as subjects of the ruling dynasty, including groups that defy jurisdictional pigeonholing, had climbed to 15 percent or more of the capital city's total population. This contrasts with Cairo, where the percentage of foreign residents never reached more than 6 percent.[10] And it is essential to emphasize that these waves of implantation occurred long before the advent of the French Protectorate.

The selection of this particular port city as a site for studying mobilities and displacements before colonialism requires explanation. French Algeria was transformed into a settler colony soon after 1830. Therefore, Algeria—not Tunisia—would seem to offer a more compelling story. Among nineteenth-century Ottoman port cities, Algiers suffered the most drastic demographic shifts, the result of military occupation, ceaseless warfare, violence, and settler colonialism. With fewer than 100 Europeans, out of a total population of 40,000 before 1830, Algiers counted over 100,000 inhabitants by 1847, of which 69,000 were Europeans of one sort or another. By 1881 French nationals and Europeans far outnumbered native Algerians in a city of nearly 200,000.[11] In view of these dramatic transformations, it is hardly surprising that most work on immigration to North Africa has focused on post-1830 Algeria. Yet, neither the impact that population flows into, and out of, colonial Algeria exerted upon neighboring Tunisia, nor the consequences of the ceaseless "comings and goings" between the two countries have been systematically investigated.[12]

France's invasion of Algeria eventually reoriented the political economy of immigration in the Maghrib and the Mediterranean generally, but those changes resonated with the greatest initial force in Tunisia. Given the demographic overshoot then taking shape on adjacent Mediterranean islands, Tunisia would have attracted subsistence and other kinds of immigrants—although perhaps not on the same scale—had the French monarch not embarked on a disastrous foreign war in 1830. While many of the migratory streams coalescing in Tunisia were interlaced with those at work in Algeria, critical differences existed. This case is more convoluted because religious refugees—Algerian Jews and Muslims—relocated to Tunisia, one type of forced migration not found in French Algeria.

In addition, the state structures into which newcomers were inserted (or rejected like failed organ transplants) displayed features absent from the French colonial state. Before 1881, Tunis and other Mediterranean towns were places where mobile people could reinvent themselves in ways akin to, but also dissimilar from, French Algeria. Finally, the rate, nature, and particularly timing of immigration and settlement made *colonial* Tunisia a different place from Algeria.

Labor migrants, cunning entrepreneurs, travelers, shipwrecked sailors, missionaries, women in distress, and a whole host of others showed up in precolonial Tunisia largely as "uninvited guests." They had to learn to navigate, and manipulate, how things were done locally, notably for consular and beylical legal cultures specific in many ways to Tunisia in the period, although parallels with other Ottoman ports existed. In addition, how people came to Tunisia and how long they stayed or intended to are critical to explaining why they fitted into urban society, were relegated to its margins, or, in some cases, were expelled and dumped on a passing ship. The patterns of migratory movements—return, circular, seasonal, or some combination thereof—are significant because they shaped implantation and social insertion. For example, labor transhumance— seasonal work performed by Sardinians in North Africa during specified months of the year—generated exchanges distinctive from those of labor migrants who came and stayed on, although temporary work often created the preconditions for permanent settlement.

My objective is not merely to salvage these life stories but primarily to understand how Tunisians, defined roughly as subjects of the Husaynid dynasty, as well as other city residents viewed, lived in close proximity to, and interacted or coped with the immigrants. Another aim is to trace how a borderland society came into existence and what that meant for Tunisia's history in the long term. We know precious little about how inhabitants of the capital, which received the lion's share of immigrants, viewed the Maltese or Sicilians who moved in next door and opened a family-run tavern or shoved their way into trades traditionally reserved for designated social groups.[13] Therefore, if one purpose is to piece together the social universe of migrants from "below"—wherever that below may lie—the major emphasis is upon Tunisia, above all, the capital city region. Of necessity, elites, indigenous and otherwise, figure prominently in the story because they compiled most of the documentation on the subsistence migrants, railed against undesirable newcomers, and managed the larger political and economic context framing population movements. As importantly, the immigrants inadvertently, if gradually, undermined much of the political culture of the Husaynid state.

The huge Husaynid family—beys, princes, princesses, retinues of mamluks, courtiers, servants, slaves, and hangers-on—represented a major site of production, consumption, and distribution that spawned various types of networks of which patronage was the most critical. The right entrée into the political class

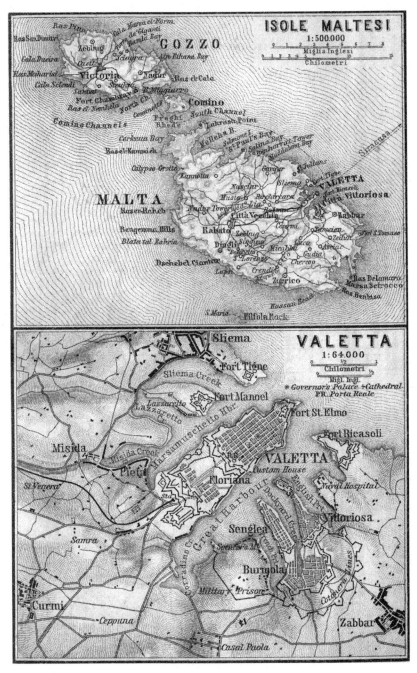

FIGURE 2. The Maltese Islands and Valetta, 1900. (Karl Baedeker, *Handbook for Travellers: Third Part; Southern Italy and Sicily, with Excursions to the Lipari Islands, Malta, Sardinia, Tunis, and Corfu,* 13th rev. ed. [Leipsic: Karl Baedeker, 1900].)

opened up employment opportunities, mainly for Europeans with scientific or military knowledge. At times, ruling elites acted as powerful backers for ordinary people who were fortunate enough to insinuate themselves into princely favor, principally through household service. Nevertheless, the Tunis notables who figure in this story did not constitute a homogeneous class by any means; their origins betray older patterns of trans-Mediterranean emigration, settlement, acculturation, and integration.

Overlapping to varying degrees with dynastic/state elites was a critical interstitial group, the cultural creoles. These long-term residents, mainly but not exclusively "Europeans," served as intermediaries between the increasingly numerous, diverse communities established in Tunis from the 1830s on and the society of the capital city. Some creoles—we might call them Euro-Tunisian *a'yan* (notables)—enjoyed intimate ties, including kinship, with those at the top of the pecking order, the beylical family. Some creoles filled vice-consular posts in Mediterranean ports for European governments and/or worked for the Tunisian state. Most were involved in "private" commercial interests bleeding into diplomatic duties that were inevitably enmeshed with the political economy of the Husaynid state and its household bureaucracy.

By Husayn Bey's reign (1824–1835), the country sat at the convergence of three empires: French, British, and Ottoman. Slightly later, a fourth wannabe empire, the Italian, came into play. For half a century, Tunisia shared a fluctuating border with a European colonial state and was perilously close to Great Britain's Mediterranean outpost, Malta. In response to the unpleasant realities of location where "empires meet," the political class embarked on modernizing reforms similar to those undertaken in Egypt and Turkey: the organization of a modern army after 1839; the establishment of a municipal council; the creation of a police force patterned on the Paris police; the 1857 declaration of a "fundamental pact"; and promulgation of the constitution in 1861. As elsewhere in the Ottoman Empire, the nineteenth century's version of the IMF and World Bank pashas arrived in Tunisia to exploit its growing financial vulnerability—or to encourage collapse. European creditors ultimately claimed most of the country's resources through forced "structural readjustments," culminating in the 1864 revolt and bankruptcy in 1869—a drearily familiar chain of events at work throughout North Africa and the Middle East in precisely the same period whose human cost was high. Nevertheless, we need to slip through the nets thrown by empire and state, if only momentarily, to find out what was going on elsewhere.

QUESTIONS

The big questions are: How and why did precolonial Tunisian society, particularly the capital-city region, "make room for the newcomers"—if grudgingly—and who exactly was a migrant, stranger, or foreigner? How did the quotidian experience of in-migration shape self-views, religious, cultural, or social practices, and institutions? How did North African migratory frontiers and the societies that coalesced along them transform, divert, or stabilize other migratory currents in the Mediterranean world—and beyond? How did the momentous events of nineteenth-century Tunisian and Maghribi history—the 1864 revolt, for example—shape immigration, and what roles did migratory forces play in these seismic shifts? How does the Tunisian case illuminate the intersections between mobilities and imperialisms? Where did Europe begin and end in the nineteenth century, and who was a European? Finally, what does this borderland society tell us about modernities?

Migration should not be confused with permanent settlement and thus we need to understand how immigration resulted in diverse types of implantation—or conversely in forced or voluntary departures back home, to other ports, or to more distant lands. An underlying problem therefore is the definition of a migrant. Among the peoples who debarked in Tunis, we find the Italian woman Giovanna Tellini, accused in 1868 of concubinage and contraband, as well as the saintly founder of a Catholic female missionary order, Emilie de Vialar, who was thrown out of French Algeria and welcomed in a Muslim state. Subjects or servants of the beys returning after long absences, such as the Tunisian 'alim Shaykh Qabadu (d. 1871), are considered, as are individuals, such as the Circassian mamluk Khayr al-Din (c. 1822–1890), brought to Tunis around 1839, who was one type of immigrant and, later in life, a seasoned Mediterranean traveler-scholar. Thus the meanings assigned to the notion of "migrant" are generous enough to comfortably accommodate merchants and mamluks, saints and shaykhs, lumpen proletariat and high rollers. Capturing people in motion raises the question of approach and method. Which approaches best lend themselves to the task of recreating a borderland society (or congeries of societies) over time?

A multisided historical ethnography, with its attention to fleeting facts, ostensibly trivial events, petty detail, the mundane, and experienced, offers one such approach. Ethnography makes sense of recondite shards of evidence generated by migratory peoples and processes because one of its methodological principles is that the story, like the devil, is the details. A fact of no great importance—that Greek residents were distinguished in the streets by their clothing's special hue of red—opens onto much larger social worlds. As a model, Chiara Frugoni's *A Day in a Medieval City* comes to mind.[14] Directly related, my approach draws on spatial theory because catching people in motion means scrutinizing the diverse places that they passed through briefly, or that they gradually came to regard as home, to understand how locality and situation modulated interactions. The built environment and uses of social spaces at a particular historical juncture governed insertion, marginalization, or rejection and conversely the cityscape was profoundly transformed by the newcomers.[15] Taken together these approaches help to vocalize silences in the sources, if only partially.

In addition, I eschew an ethnoscape perspective that tracks a "single" ethnic group, for example, Maltese in Tunisia, which the sources greatly favor, but that fails to translate the social realities of recurring settlement.[16] Nor is a stratigraphic optic, stacking up phenomena in a multilayered cake, equal to the task of understanding how things, people, ideas, words, and behaviors circulated or why older circuits petered out or were forced into blind alleys. Port cities, the principal envelope into which trans-Mediterranean migrations are conventionally inserted, should not be treated as isomorphic or self-referential entities—a tendency in the atomized port-city literature where the local becomes too local. The issue of how circuits of movement and varieties of networks converged, thickened with increased exchange densities, or gradually became uncoupled is the heart of the matter.[17]

One challenge faced was the frame of the Mediterranean itself which, as an imagined, constructed space, tempts the unwary into lyricism, romanticism, or essentialism; indeed "Mediterranean" means something both generic and uniquely specific.[18] To contemporaries, the sea was many things—"beautiful wretch" in one traveler's mind, a sentiment echoed by many people living on, or traveling upon, the Mediterranean at the time.[19] Prior to steamship transportation, and for long afterward, the sea was frightening, a place of peril and mortal danger. "Throughout the age of sail . . . geography had absolute power to limit what man could do at sea. By comparison, culture, ideas, individual genius or charisma, economic forces, and all the other motors of history meant little."[20]

With the nineteenth century's partial taming of the sea, perceived by bourgeois Europeans through the lens of a mythologized antiquity, its peoples and cultures, paradoxically, were increasingly vilified. The purportedly defective nature of "Mediterranean" social structures—an ill-fated combination of religion, flawed family relations, and clientalism—rendered them morally inferior and irredeemably backward. By the late nineteenth century, a deeply entrenched racial bias against Arabs and Muslims excluded them from constructions of a Mediterranean identity, indeed from Mediterranean history *tout court*. Scarcely better are contemporary nostalgic depictions of the "good old days of colonial Tunisia," allegedly characterized by working-class solidarity between Sicilians, Maltese, and Tunisians, a product of social memory and forgetting that influences some scholarship.[21]

Another problem is how to write a history of trans-Mediterranean migrations to, and settlement in, North Africa but not churn out yet another account of Europeans in foreign or not-so-foreign lands. Directly related, narrating subjectivities from an ethnographically local perspective holds the danger of obscuring the Mediterranean's deep history. And the temptation to fall back upon comfortable binaries or taxonomies of religion, civilization, empire, or nation is ever-present. In its time, the scholarly notion of a nineteenth-century Muslim Mediterranean world represented a conceptual advance but carried the potential for resurrecting an older historiography that tended to find only "Muslims" out there.[22] True, the successive settlement of Tunisia (and Algeria) by mainly Catholic folk meant that an increasingly visible nonsubject Christian community took root whose presence was signaled by new religious edifices, schools, and public processionals, which were manipulated by various imperial interests. Nevertheless, social interactions, however fraught or friendly, involved people who were also neighbors, workers, competitors, or illicit lovers and not just "Muslims, Jews, and Christians" or "North Africans and Europeans." Last, but by no means least, women and gender raise problems of methodology.[23] An earlier version of this work devoted a separate chapter to women as immigrants and city residents but was ultimately rejected because it confined women to a sort of narrative quarantine rather than integrating them into the fullness of the story.

BORDERLANDS

Conceptually, the notion of a borderland offers an alternative to binaries or monolithic constructs. As layered zones of contact, borderlands are characterized by fluctuating degrees of internal social coherence forged by high exchange densities, while remaining subject to "pushes and pulls" from larger, external forces.[24] From my search for fresh ways of thinking about the problems of mobilities emerged the idea of a "central Mediterranean corridor," which can be imagined as a series of linked, intersecting borderland regions. The corridor's contours ran roughly from Tunis to the Algiers region, Marseilles, and Leghorn, then to Sicily, Malta, and back along the Tunisian coastline. Like a sentinel, Tunisia commands one of three strategic choke points in the Mediterranean Basin; its positioning in relation to Sicily and Malta makes it the Gibraltar or Dardanelles of the central sea. Between 150 and 300 miles separate the Cap Bon peninsula (or Ra's al-Dar) from Sicily and Malta; stepping-stone islands like Pantelleria are even closer. Incipient transformations in migratory behaviors from about 1820 represented one vital element in the borderland society that grew up in Mediterranean Tunisia. Other factors played into the mix: older and new commercial patterns; demographic and resource structures; transport technologies; and the ecological baseline of prevailing winds, currents, and other natural phenomena that facilitated or inhibited travel.[25]

This part of the sea has nurtured intense communications for millennia, but sometime around 1820 things began to change, slowly at first, then with greater velocity as people abandoned the islands and the Mediterranean's northern edges to settle in majority Muslim lands. In earlier eras, the fluctuating limits between something called Europe and the Ottoman Empire—always moving and permeable—had been located on the big islands of the corridor; after 1830, those limits came to rest along the North African littoral.[26] As Italy, Sicily, and Malta moved closer thanks to major advances in the technologies of transport and migratory displacements, the interior—arid steppes, desert societies, and oasis cultivators—became more remote from the political center. Another compass reading reveals that proximity to Sicily and Malta placed Tunisia along a demographic frontier; the islands' extremely high population densities contrasted starkly with the Maghrib, "a thinly populated land."[27] Finally, the routes that increasingly facilitated population movements along a north–south axis— whether openly or furtively in the dead of night—have remained the same. In the early twenty-first century, tiny Pantelleria just off Tunisia's Cap Bon is a Mediterranean version of the Rio Grande for undocumented people traveling north by island hopping.[28] Nearly two centuries ago, migratory currents began to move in the opposite direction.

Fortuitous location made the Gulf of Tunis and the Sahil (coastal villages) into a giant lint catcher, a finely meshed net snagging a never-ending assortment of down-and-outs, oddballs, and curious types, sometimes by accident, at other times by volition: Italian anarchists and Masons, renegade priests, counterfeiters, scam artists, sailors, and deserters. These people rarely appear in conventional historical treatments, and if they do, play but a minor role. Moreover, historians have turned a blind eye to the social landscape beyond the ports—on the decks of ships and on the high seas—thereby neglecting arenas that shaped the course of events on terra firma; not infrequently, shipboard conflicts spilled over into adjoining ports, engulfing their heterogeneous inhabitants.[29] And the stories of people whose living came from the sea—boat captains, crews, fishermen, and smugglers, to name but a few—are still largely absent from the historical narrative, despite the increasing emphasis in today's Tunisia upon its *longue durée* Mediterranean identity, a political agenda linked to relations with the European Union.

LITERATURES OF MOTION

Over the long nineteenth century, more people left home than ever before in world history but, until very recently, most of the theoretical work on population displacements drew upon documentation from the transatlantic currents or the expanding European empires in Africa and Asia.[30] While representing a crucial chapter in global migration history, the countless local exoduses from Europe and the islands to Mediterranean Muslim states did not garner much scholarly attention until now.[31] In part, this was because older scholarship on modern Middle Eastern history tended to marginalize demographic shifts when working out master narratives. This is curious, since the region has often been characterized as a cultural mosaic produced by complex population dispersals, layerings, and sedimentations. Early Islamic history opens with a cosmic migratory event—the seventh-century movements of Arab Muslim tribesmen out of northern Arabia and into the Persian and Byzantine empires. The classical age of Islam closes with a more somber migratory episode—the Mongol destruction of Baghdad in 1258—one phase in the enormous outpourings of Turco-Mongolian steppe peoples often led by warrior nomads that eventually led to the creation of the Ottoman Empire.

Paradoxically, the modern era has benefited least from historical analyses of migrations to, or from, the area stretching from Morocco to Turkey, despite the fact that in the course of the nineteenth century an estimated two million Muslim refugees from the Russian Empire and eastern Europe were forced out and relocated in Ottoman lands, mainly Anatolia.[32] The relative lack of interest in migration as a central problem in humankind's history stemmed from an earlier tendency among historians of Islamic societies to prefer the "bona fide" Muslim, while slighting the culturally promiscuous Mediterranean port cities populated by multireligious, polyglot communities marked by indeterminate identities and protean allegiances. Blind spots created by the older area studies approach to the Mediterranean Middle East "constantly sought the regionally authentic and consequently marginalized the hybrid Euro-Oriental cities and their mobile inhabitants."[33] Today research on port cities has grown into an international academic industry, although one dealing mainly with the eastern Mediterranean.[34] Some scholars have placed nineteenth-century Ottoman migrations in a world historical perspective by investigating the local forces that, for example, pushed Lebanese peasants from their villages to the cities of the New World or Africa.[35] However, the connections, direct and indirect, between slightly earlier relocations of Mediterranean peoples from southern Europe to the Levant, Egypt, and North Africa and subsequent out-migrations of Ottoman subjects to the New World have yet to be fully explored—even less so integrated into conventional historical narratives.

ENTER THE MAGHRIB

Why was the story of Mediterranean immigration to Algeria and Tunisia from about 1830 to the Great War excluded from older accounts, for the most part? Earlier scholarly disinterest in the North African migratory frontier can partially be explained by the imperialism of statistics.[36] Compared to the earlier migrations to the New World and the vast transatlantic displacements of the late nineteenth and early twentieth centuries, the Maghrib appeared less dynamic in scope because it was not a question of millions but rather of a steady drip of thousands, then tens of thousands of people, relocating over decades. Yet migratory flows from north to south after roughly 1830 represented the largest trans-sea dispersal of peoples since the Iberian expulsions (the so-called Reconquista) of centuries earlier. Moreover, the nature of the archive promotes investigations that take a single national experience as object of inquiry and not multinational or imperial displacements to a single place. And as mentioned earlier, Algeria's turbulent experiment in settler colonialism overshadowed precolonial Tunisia's encounter with immigration, while the abundance of colonial documentation after 1881 privileged that period. Then, too, the sheer knottiness of population flows—at a strategic choke point in the central Mediterranean—may have dampened scholarly ardor.

What other elements—political, intellectual, and otherwise—conspired to make this migratory subsystem less visible than others until about a decade ago? The ideology of colonial North Africa overwhelmed the facts "on the ground" because the official transcript held that North Africa became French at some point in time. However, popular local literature, films, and the lives as well as testimonies of the Maghrib's inhabitants (of whatever social, religious, cultural, or ethnic status) unmasked French North Africa, revealing it for what it was—a collection of borderland societies, some of whose populations bore very lightly the mantle of civilization as imagined in Paris.[37] And as Gerard Noiriel argued in 1988, the French had long suffered a "denial of memory" regarding immigration in the making of the nation, although this denial has been shattered in spectacular fashion over the past twenty years. Since the Maghrib was a special preserve of French scholarship, it is hardly surprising that migration as a historical problem was marginalized. Because of the Algerian trauma, present even today, the denial of memory extended to the study of French colonialism in North Africa, ignored during the decades following decolonization and the end of empire, which created a double erasure.[38]

To the extent that colonial North African history was studied in France after 1962, it was the preserve of scholars on the left. Charles-André Julien and Charles-Robert Ageron viewed the Europeans as illegitimate occupiers and tended to footnote non-French colons in historical narratives, even if colonial officials and the metropole received their due. In their massive two-volume *Histoire de l'Algérie*, less than 10 percent was devoted to the settlers. After forced "repatriation" to France, many ex-colonials supported Jean-Marie Le Pen's extreme right-wing Front National, which rendered them unappealing as historical actors, even less so as objects of scientific inquiry for older generations of historians on the left. The terrible dislocations of decolonization and subsequent south–north worker migrations to France conspired to make the nineteenth-century migratory streams semi-invisible. During the nationalist upheavals from 1954 to 1962, culminating in Algerian independence, nearly 1.75 million people abandoned the Maghrib, one of the largest population movements in postwar European history.[39]

But there were other reasons for previous scholarly indifference to large-scale immigration and immigrants. Nationalist historians writing after independence ignored the hundreds of thousands of Europeans who called North Africa home—they had all left (or most had)—so why study them? The closely wedded tales of imperialism and nationalism conceptualized around mutually exclusive binaries—"the colonizer, the colonized"—offered little space to talk about these people. "Not-quite-Europeans," who became "not-quite-French" by about 1900, represented the history that nobody wanted—like the story of Algerian *harkis* who served France during the war for independence or North African soldiers fighting under the French flag in two world wars. Some writers eventually reclaimed some of this history, but at first it tended to be in the genre of heritage accounts by writers from communities or families exiled from North Africa to a France they knew little or not at all.[40]

The past decade has seen a hefty spike in scholarly investment in migrations and mobilities, with North Africa as its primary focus; needless to say, the current hysteria in Europe and North America about "foreigners in our midst" partially nurtures this reawakened interest. Noteworthy in this new research is Italian work on the highly diverse Italian communities in colonial Algeria, precolonial and colonial Tunisia, and Tripolitania/Libya.[41] On a larger scale of analysis, Edmund Burke's arguments that the Mediterranean rim, including Muslim states ringing the sea, constituted the first recipients "of the liberal reform project in its political and economic forms," which assumed fullest expression under the French Third Republic, suggest where scholarship is heading.[42]

CHAPTERS

The nature of the documentation and questions raised demand the combined skills of the muralist and the miniaturist, which greatly shaped this book's structure. My methodology is to follow people around on their daily rounds—to shadow them, tail them, imagine where they might be, what they might be doing and why—in other words, train the ethnographer's beady, if sympathetic, eye on the archival table scraps and shreds of life stories. Given the unusually recondite primary sources, most migrants' trajectories can only be reconstructed once they landed in Tunis or more frequently when they faced some difficulty—lack of housing, unpaid debts, violent conflict with neighbors—that brought into play local authorities, either Tunisian, or consular, or both. Regrettably the kinds of records that might enlighten us about initial decisions to strike out, to leave home, wherever that may have been—in Malta, Sardinia, Tuscany, or Gibraltar—

for North Africa generally are wanting for earlier decades of the nineteenth century.[43]

Conceptually, the chapters follow a problem-centered exposition rather than linear progression, since the fragmented sources do not allow for a systematic or sustained chronology, even less so for credible quantification. Each grapples with theoretical problems in migration history but fans out to intersect with issues addressed in other chapters. As such, the book forms a latticework of vertical, horizontal, and diagonal linkages that capture the realities of multiple displacements occasioned by the persistence of older patterns, dramatic ruptures, or slow-moving changes. We start somewhere around the 1820s, which furnishes a baseline for appreciating the transformations of later decades. The story's end is a sort of moving benchmark because one argument weaving throughout is that 1881, when France invaded Tunisia from Algeria, did not necessarily introduce the abrupt disjuncture that informed previous scholarship and its dominant periodizations, which distinguished sharply between the precolonial and early colonial eras. In plotting out the chapters' sequences, the frame of an ethnographic voyage, or ethnography of movement, seemed best suited to capture migratory processes and their social consequences for the peoples involved.

Migration is, simply stated, about everything, and the range of potential topics is limitless; thus different chapter arrangements could be imagined, many more questions could be posed. Nevertheless, the available primary sources and secondary literature dictated the selection of problems. While the record is not generous for reconstructing labor markets, for example, some ways of making a living are better documented than others. The inner, intimate workings of urban households, whether elite or humble, Tunisian or not, represent a door only slightly ajar for historians. And the precise networks undergirding the recruitment of laborers either locally or transnationally can only be partially reconstructed. However, since smuggling violated treaties and commercial regulations, more data exist—ironically—for the contraband trade than, let us say, for the mundane realities of domestic service or petty trade. As always, limited time and resources also dictated the topics addressed; in consequence, I was only able to consult some collections—and then not to the degree that one would desire—while potentially important archival and other sources had to be left for future researchers to mine. Therefore, rather than a full or final statement about nineteenth-century North African or trans-Mediterranean mobilities, my study represents an initial journey, a beginning not an end, intended to suggest avenues for research in the years to come.[44]

In sum, this is a tale about how people became migrants, protégés, and then Tunis city residents, how proletarians turned into property holders or remained paupers, how some newcomers in Tunisia climbed to the top of the heap or failed to realize dreams of social betterment after leaving home. Intertwined with these tales are the multiple stories of how subjects of the Husaynid dynasty consorted, conspired, or fought with successive waves of newcomers only to have their world fall apart after 1881, a direct consequence of the people on the move. As a history of trans-Mediterranean displacements in a small place, Tunisia before colonialism stands in for many parts of the globe experiencing similar and in some cases interlinked processes during the long nineteenth century. Because of the problems posed by the sources, the first six chapters tend to fall into the genre of prosopography, while the last three chapters trace individual life stories more fully.

Chapter 1 takes the reader by ship to the Tunis region in circa 1830. We start with the port, Halq al-Wad, or La Goulette, and then proceed to the capital city, where diverse city folk and the spaces they inhabited are introduced. One issue is that of the cultural creoles, longtime residents of diverse origins who had lived and worked in Tunisia prior to the migratory surge partially unleashed by France's invasion of Algeria. But most important is the social geography of Tunis, whose neighborhoods, markets, and places of work and worship correlated to a degree with religious affiliation. In a city on the cusp of large-scale immigration, how did individuals and communities discriminate between "us" and "them," and what roles did religion, language, dress, occupation, and place of residence (to name but a few elements) play in calibrating or affirming identity or conversely difference?

How and why did North Africa turn into a place of permanent or temporary evasion for so many people from across the Mediterranean? Chapter 2 unravels the multiple forces that induced subsistence and other kinds of migrants to abandon the sea's northern rim or the islands to settle in Algeria and Tunisia. It first considers long-standing traditions of travel and movement in the central Mediterranean corridor, including the social forces and cultural norms that governed women's displacements. Theoretically, it revisits some of the scholarship on migrations and migrants to determine how this case study contributes to, or challenges, that literature. It offers a truffle hunter's view and a hang glider's perspective of the processes—large, small, and in-between—at work in North Africa, Europe, and the eastern Ottoman Empire.

Work lies at the heart of the migratory experience. Chapters 3, 4, and 5, form an ensemble as all are devoted to making a living in one way or anther. But what kinds of employment did a preindustrial, precolonial state and society offer? How did "strangers in the city" nudge their way into the existing system of production, distribution, and resource allocation in Tunis and how did abolition and the end of slavery influence labor markets and the search for a livelihood? Domestic work in elite households and employment by local consulates are emphasized because they offered possibilities for men and women of modest means, generated patronage and, if fortune smiled, some capital to start small businesses; these sectors are also the best documented. The theoretical issues addressed revolve around the different kinds of networks, shaped by such elements as social class, gender, ethnicity or national origins, which created work for newcomers or local city denizens.

Newly arrived immigrants with few resources and without patronage most commonly filled unskilled or semiskilled jobs in carpentry, carting, or masonry, engaged in street commerce, or ran small family business, such as inns or bakeries. Women participated in the local economy as tavern or hotel maids, or in petty trade and commerce. When tourism took off after the middle of the nineteenth century, it offered expanded employment as well. Chapter 4 concludes with a consideration of those who did not make it and why they failed to secure stable work. Illness, trouble with the law, or bad luck plunged families into extreme want, particularly after social networks unraveled, frequently leading to forced expatriation or departures for other lands that seemed to hold more promise. At the same time, it is argued that the social universe of the immigrant "down-and-out" in Tunis should not be seen as distinct from the world of the indigenous poor.

The growing contraband economy that operated in the central Mediterranean corridor during the long nineteenth century invites us to consider population displacements in tandem with extralegal commodity flows and various kinds of work. Chapter 5 engages the scholarship on global labor movements that correlates the development of "underground economic sectors" with mobile populations but takes issue with some dimensions of that literature. It argues that contraband depended upon certain kinds of migrations, upon occupations tied to the sea, such as fishing, and the persistence of older forms of sea transport as well as dramatic advances in maritime transportation. In addition, smuggling was often integrated into the legitimate household economy of tavern keeping, transport, fishing, or farming, which blurred distinctions between legal and illegal. And while the archival record is surprisingly scarce, the sex industry constituted smuggling in another register, since "contraband desire" represented one way of making a living in the underground moral economy. The implications of prostitution—or merely love with the wrong person—and its significance to the construction of religiosexual borders meant that when the Husaynid state could no longer effectively police those borders it lost considerable moral capital. Activities or exchanges branded as extralegal, illegal, or illicit drew individuals of different religious or ethnic backgrounds residing in precolonial Tunisia either into a complicit "republic of thieves" or into communal strife that brought disorder to streets and neighborhoods. Thus the social universe of contraband networks and bargains constitutes a perfect vantage point for probing intercommunal relations in a precolonial Muslim state.

This chapter, the last of the work trilogy, forms a bridge between the issues posed by making a living and the next chapter on regimes of legal pluralism. As a way of earning one's bread, smuggling and other proscribed trades led to conflict with neighbors, state authorities, or consular officials, triggering long drawn-out quarrels over legal jurisdiction that became increasingly embroiled in international quarrels.

Within the crucible of Great Power struggles over North Africa, trans-Mediterranean immigration to Tunisia posed intractable problems of law, justice, and social order; legal pluralism raises an inexhaustible range of questions, only some of which are addressed in chapter 6. What unwritten norms or rules structured the older culture of beylical and consular justice at their points of intersection? In what ways did Tunisia's positioning in the central Mediterranean corridor, together with migration, transform that culture? What kinds of punishments and sanctions were available to those in power? How did the people who petitioned the beys or consuls, submitted depositions, stormed the consulates, and leveled or denied charges involving family, friends, and foes live the daily reality of a multicentric legal order and contribute to its ever more baroque configurations? Who were the losers and who were the winners in long drawn-out battles over jurisdiction?

Theoretically, the chapter addresses recent thinking on legal pluralism. It analyzes the disputes that pulled city residents, beylical subjects, expatriate Europeans, and other foreigners into an increasingly tangled legal culture through an ethnography of physical spaces where city inhabitants sought justice as well as the beliefs, rituals, and practices associated with those spaces, notably the right of sanctuary. Algerian subjects claiming French protection in Tunisia constituted an especially knotty jurisdictional case as did another type of border crossing—switching religious affiliation, which was deeply gendered in motivations and consequences. Conversion from Christianity to Islam confronted European consuls and their governments with thorny issues of law, national identity, and religious affiliation. The final section forces us to cross beyond the temporal boundaries of conventional periodizations to ask: Did 1881 or 1883 provoke a rupture in the culture of legal pluralism or did rupture come later? Due to the undeniable weight of past practices as well as the presence of thousands of non-French nationals with a personal stake in the old legal order, to what extent was the colonial state successful in establishing a unified legal system?

Among the myriad groups relocating from Algeria to Tunisia during the 1840s were Catholic female missionaries. Chapter 7 delves into missions in relationship to migration but pays close attention to one French congregation, the Sisters of Saint-Joseph de l'Apparition, as they sought patronage from the Husaynid state and assimilated into local society. It argues that the welcome afforded the Sisters of Saint-Joseph in Tunis by Ahmad Bey (r. 1837–1855) was tied to social order during expanded Catholic settlement as well as the outbreak of cholera on a massive scale. On a theoretical level, the chapter reexamines the literature on global missionary societies with specific attention to gender and empire. Since one of the volume's underlying arguments revolves around questions of temporalities, the chapter extends into the early colonial period (post-1881) to explore continuities and their consequences for the colonial state.

How did immigration affect local and creole or expatriate elites? Examining sociabilities from the perspective of households, women, and gender, chapter 8 argues that princely harims, enclosing numerous, highly diverse individuals, were fundamental to a state organized as a "household bureaucracy" for much of the century. Palace visits, sea bathing, and leisure, in which European and Tunisian notables participated, were managed by women and generated transversal relationships that were often political in nature. One critical site for international diplomacy was the summer palace or villa by the sea; the kinds of sociabilities generated by sea bathing are examined for elites and nonelites. At the same time, tourism brought Europeans in steadily climbing numbers to North Africa for water cures in hydrotherapy sites long used by Tunisians and resident creoles. Not far behind were scheming promoters, the vanguard of the modern tourist industry, seeking to transform thermal stations into spas segregated by religion, social class, and "race." Nevertheless, earlier collective manifestations of leisure, taking the waters, and sea bathing exerted a powerful influence on the colonial state, limiting what it could and could not do.

The final chapter recreates the life story of Khayr al-Din Pasha, a migrant of sorts. Born in the Caucasus during the 1820s, Khayr al-Din was sold into slavery, educated in Istanbul, sent to Tunis around 1839 as a young mamluk, returned to the Ottoman capital in 1877 to serve a prime minister, and ended his days in a palace on the Bosporus in 1890. He is best known as the author of a political treatise advocating the reform of Muslim states that appeared in Tunis in 1867. But he also established one of the earliest institutions for modern education in the Maghrib, Sadiqi College founded in 1875, as well as drafting the Arab world's first constitution proclaimed in 1861. Seen from this perspective, Khayr al-Din, the statesman-intellectual and immigrant of a special kind, becomes a metaphor for the age of migrations. His journey from slavery, to state service in Tunisia, to recognition as one of the most original Muslim thinkers of his generation encapsulates the transformations at work in a borderland society of the central Mediterranean corridor. Revisited and reinterpreted, Khayr al-Din's life reads as a parable for how the Muslim Mediterranean became modern.

We start the ethnographic journey in chapter 1, tracking travelers, city residents, or immigrants as they first arrive in port and then make their way to Tunis "the well-protected." After rounding the verdant Cap Bon pierced by jagged mountains, Jabal Zaghawan and Bu Qarnayn, ships made their way into the Gulf of Tunis guarded by twin islets, Zembra and Zembretta. There an enchanting sight awaited passengers, which the well-traveled compared favorably with the Gulf of Naples in splendor and physical beauty. The cubical village of Sidi Bou Sa'id was the first thing espied from onboard before approaching the port, Halq al-Wad, some ten miles distant from the capital city. Communications between the city and its port were assured by small skiffs that laboriously crossed the shallow lake sheltering Tunis from the open sea. Situated on a slight incline, Tunis, a white city, climbed up to the highest point where the Qasba, a sixteenth-century Ottoman fort, stood watch. With the *buhaira* (lake) in front, abundant gardens and orchards, and the surrounding hills planted in dark green olive groves, the panorama impressed first-time visitors, particularly during the calm summer sailing season when tempests were less likely.

Arrival

Tunis the "Well-Protected"

*Plato thinks that those who want a well-governed city
ought to shun the sea as a teacher of vice.*

HORDEN AND PURCELL, *THE CORRUPTING SEA:
A STUDY OF MEDITERRANEAN HISTORY*

Farid Boughedir's 1994 film *Un été à la Goulette* (A Summer in La Goulette), set
on the eve of the 1967 war, depicts the residue of a culturally striated landscape
still found in many Mediterranean port cities even after the end of empire. The
annual festival to honor Santa Maria de Trapani, transplanted from Sicily before
1881, remained a collective celebration. As in the past, Muslims and Jews took part
in this most cherished of public processions for Maltese and Sicilian Catholics. In
Boughedir's film, religious affiliation presented few barriers to residential cohabitation, socializing, or employment, although cross-religious sexual relations or
marriages rarely occurred, and if they did, social uproar ensued.[1] Yet La Goulette's
populist cosmopolitanism should not blind us to the petty jealousies, daily struggles over work and resources, and moments of communal contention or violence
often (but not always) following the shifting fault lines of national belonging,
legal protection, religious identity, and social class. Indeed Boughedir intended to
critique the nostalgic notion of a Mediterranean cosmopolitanism free from local
strife and intolerance or the passions generated by distant political upheavals.
The La Goulette that Boughedir offered up to filmgoers constitutes the end of our
story and is needless to say a very different place from its early nineteenth-century
avatar prior to large-scale immigration.

Ports are situated at the ragged interface between the legal and moral wilderness of the open water, on the one hand, and the political order of the city and
state, on the other. Passengers disembarking entered a new or at least different sociopolitical system. And because the sea operates as "a teacher of vice,"
ports have been regarded as spaces of danger and promiscuity.[2] After 1830, North
African ports were rapidly peopled by foreigners so that physical expansion was

associated with outsiders or familiar strangers, although definitions of "outsider," "foreigner," or "stranger" differed from place to place and according to the observer. Older understandings of outside/in, of margins and center, often changed dramatically, in some cases more subtly. In keeping with our multisided ethnography, this chapter raises the following questions: How did La Goulette resemble or differ from other northern African ports? What kinds of vessels landed, what did they carry, and how did passengers disembark? When travelers, immigrants, visitors, merchants, or city inhabitants finally made it to Tunis proper, after crossing the lake in small craft, where was home in the city and which community welcomed them? Who was a "native" of the city and how were taxonomies of belonging or difference constructed? And who exactly were the resident Europeans or the cultural creoles that had long regarded Tunisia as their homeland and looked askance at the newcomers pouring in from across the sea?

THE RIVER'S THROAT

The port's Italian name—La Golétta—translated accurately the Arabic, Halq al-Wad, "the river's throat." Located ten miles to the northeast of Tunis proper, La Goulette sat on a narrow spit of land adjacent to a channel connecting the fetid lake to the Mediterranean. This geography sheltered the capital from the perils of the open sea—from whence came one of Tunis's sobriquets, "the well-protected." In 1830, the sullen, frayed remains of a once imposing Ottoman-Spanish fortress still stood then as now.[3] Constructed by the Turkish sea commander Khayr al-Din Barbaroussa after his 1534 victory over the Spanish, the fort fell the next year to Charles V, who greatly expanded its fortifications. After the Ottomans retook the port and Tunis in 1574, they dismantled the fortress, or most of it, for reasons of security.

> La Goletta inconvenient both for commerce and for military purposes . . . must be considered a part of the capital, being intimately connected with it by daily and hourly intercourse. This is nothing but a little channel, called in Arabic Halaq al-Wad or 'throat of the river,' and is the communication between the sea and the Lake of Tunis. . . . The fortifications on each side were built at various times . . . [and] are kept in tolerable repair, and well mounted with cannon, being by their nearness to the level of the water, and their position, admirably adapted both for the security of this narrow passage, as for the roadstead to the east and south-east.[4]

The peculiar topography of the Tunis region deeply inflected relationships with the Mediterranean and other maritime powers because the capital city enjoyed spatial distance from the open sea not found in many other ports, which may have paradoxically made it more amenable to sustained relations with Europe and Europeans.[5] Until Napoleon's 1798 invasion, Alexandria's contacts with Christian

states were restricted, since ships were frequently prohibited from directly entering port because of propinquity to the city center and thus fears of attack; when
the French fleet sailed into Alexandria, no more than seventy or so European merchants resided there. Only after 1805 did Muhammad 'Ali Pasha restore Alexandria
to its rightful status as a great Mediterranean port by importing skilled labor,
notably from islands such as Malta. And until the radical port modifications of
the 1850s, warships could easily approach Algiers's massive outer fortified walls—
which Lord Exmouth did during the 1816 expedition with such destructive force.
La Goulette, however, had remained "open to all Christian vessels" from nations at
peace by treaty with Tunisia's rulers, which attracted Europeans and merchandise
from French and especially Italian ports, above all Leghorn, in great quantities.[6] In
about 1830, resident foreigners in Tunisia numbered over three thousand, although
many were slaves, ransom captives, or formerly enslaved persons; this contrasts
with late Ottoman Algiers where, before the "fly-whisk incident," only a handful
of Europeans permanently resided there, and many departed after the 1827 French
blockade preceding the invasion.[7] Thus geography and the relatively open status
of Tunis help to explain the comparatively larger expatriate community relative to
other North African port cities.

By the early nineteenth century, La Goulette's centrality was undisputed vis-
à-vis the country's other ports. Ghar al-Milh (Porto Farina), thirty-one miles to
the north, had been an active naval base, along with Bizerte, as well as a corsair
hub in the seventeenth and eighteenth centuries. But Ghar al-Milh's maritime
star faded as the nearby Majarda River changed course, dumping silt into the
harbor, which could no longer accommodate large draft vessels. However, Porto
Farina remained a smuggler's paradise as we shall see. With the decline of her
rivals, La Goulette welcomed most of the labor migrants and handled the bulk
of the trade with the Ottoman Empire and Europe, although Sfax was important
for the export of olive oil and other commodities. Tunisia's political neutrality during the Napoleonic Wars made La Goulette a thriving commercial node
and place of transit for colonial goods, such as sugar and cotton, imported into
the Mediterranean by the British, although after 1815 its commercial place in
Mediterranean trade was transformed. In addition, Tunisia (and Tripoli to a
lesser extent) had always supplied Malta and other islands with foodstuffs. For
the 1830 expedition to Algeria, Tunisia furnished the French military with critical
quantities of horses, grains, and supplies.[8]

Traditionally, exports fell into two categories: raw materials, such as esparto
grass or hides, and foodstuffs, when harvests permitted, such as olive oil,
grains, honey, wax, and cattle. Second were luxury items, perfume essences,
finely wrought handicrafts, and luxury textiles; for example, the Jewish prayer
shawls produced with fine Spanish wool, worked by master craftsmen in Tunis,
shipped to northern Italy, and traded to Poland. In addition to olive oil exports,

always first in importance, the most valuable manufactured item giving rise to the largest volume of foreign trade was the round red cap, or *shashiya* (a wool cap worn by Muslim males), produced in the Tunis region and exported over a wide swatch of territory—to Morocco, Algeria, sub-Saharan Africa, and the Ottoman Empire, including the Balkans. As cheaper French and Italian machine-made imitations began to compete with Tunisia's share of the shashiya market in the nineteenth century, the country's most remunerative industry and the capital's most prestigious guild were undermined.[9] Openness and accessibility to trans-Mediterranean currents of trade came with a high price.

ARRIVAL

Most ships arrived in La Goulette during the summer sailing season, when central Mediterranean winds are, for the most part, northwesterly and less treacherous. In winter months, winds known in the period as Kara Yel (Turkish for "black wind") blew savagely from the northeast, smashing moored vessels and destroying life and property. Storms blocked the flow of supplies and correspondence for weeks on end as well as the movements of ships, travelers, merchants, or migrants: "all news and information from London comes through Malta . . . if very long continuous winds blow, no vessels can come into port in Tunis or Barbary."[10] Complex local wind patterns and inclement weather delayed messengers, envoys, and delegations, shaping to no small degree the conduct of trade and international diplomacy. When Ahmad Bey sent a representative in November 1843 to the French captain of the *Jemmapes* anchored off La Goulette to discuss diplomatic matters, the Tunisian official found it impossible to board due to huge seas and gale-force winds that forced him to wait for days on the quays.[11]

Before the advent of steam, passengers experienced delays, discomfort, and great uncertainty. Depending upon the vessel and season, journeys from Valletta to North Africa took six to ten days or more; from Istanbul or Smyrna to La Goulette, between seventeen and twenty days. When the Catholic missionary Emilie de Vialar booked passage in the winter of 1843 with a "bad Sicilian sailing vessel" in Marseilles bound for Tunis, she anticipated an eight-day voyage, bringing along provisions only sufficient for a week. Instead, shifting, violent winds transformed the journey into a two-week ordeal. Several years later, the captain of the *Saint Anne*, Antoine Moresco Roch, left Ajaccio in March 1846 "with a load of oak wood, cheese, dried fruit, and a case full of women's clothing" and six passengers destined for Tunis, Bône, and Philippeville, but his small vessel was blown from island to island for weeks until it mercifully landed in Tabarka, where a Tunisian ship and *ra'is* (captain) provided assistance to crew and passengers.[12]

For trans-Mediterranean communications, the steamship was revolutionary, as indeed it was elsewhere in the globe. In the early 1840s, French and British

FIGURE 3. Portrait of Ahmad Bey. The ruler is dressed in the new military uniform of his modern army; some of the decorations may have been bestowed by European monarchs. (Institut National de Patrimoine, Tunis.)

steamships began arriving in La Goulette, drastically reducing the voyage from Egypt, Malta, Algeria, or Europe from weeks to days to hours. By 1877, Tunis was thirty-eight hours from Marseilles on the fastest steamer. That year, 447 ships entered port of which 207 were steam driven, indicating that more than half continued to be sail powered, although ships could not yet draw up to docks.[13] A wide range of ships dropped anchor: from small fishing vessels, to low-draft *shabbak* (small three-masted vessels), to large commercial or warships—brigantines, frigates, corvettes, schooners—which increased in number as the nineteenth century wore on. A partial list of local ship names from the early nineteenth century— *Baya, Fatima, Gamba, Kara Mabruk, Kara Soliman, Mabruka,* and *Sa'ad,* of Arabic, Turkish, and Italian origins—communicates Tunisia's intimacies with various parts of the Mediterranean.[14]

Even after the advent of steamships, older ways of conducting business prevailed. A typical example occurred in March 1842 when a small Maltese vessel loaded with wheat from Egypt finally arrived in La Goulette after selling off cargo for weeks in various ports along the way. Many, perhaps most, transactions were conducted this way, since small sailing vessels hawked goods like maritime street vendors and transported undocumented travelers who paid modest fees to be deposited here and there along the coast, often in violation of treaties and/ or regulations regarding immigration.[15] For smaller vessels, cabotage (coastal navigation and trade) was the preferred, indeed the only, feasible method for making a living from the sea, but this form of commercial movement means that statistics for who, and what, were transported where are almost impossible to come by. With regular steamship service, record- keeping improved somewhat. But we are getting ahead of our story.

THE PORT AND PORT OFFICIALS:
KAHIYA, QUARANTINE, AND VICE-CONSULS

After savoring the striking beauty of the Bay of Tunis from shipboard, first-time visitors expressed disappointment at Halq al-Wad's lackluster appearance, as it was a place of no great distinction in the early decades of the nineteenth century. La Goulette's facilities dated from the late eighteenth century, when Hammuda Bey (r. 1782–1813) improved dredging operations, constructed jetties, and restored the arsenal as well as shipyards; docks, ships chandlers for supplies and provisions, customs houses, and storage facilities for goods awaiting entry or export lined the shore. In calmer weather, goods, passengers, and the mail were arduously unloaded into small boats; the port was situated near dangerous shoals, forcing ships to anchor a distance from the docks. Small flat-bottomed boats ferried them to the quays lined with the offices of the *gumruk,* or customs house.

Travelers landing in La Goulette first encountered local port authorities and consular agents, although not all nations maintained vice-consuls there in the early part of the century; the same agent might serve several nations, either permanently or temporarily. The most powerful Husaynid official was the *kahiya*, or governor, who as *amin al-tarsakhana* oversaw the arsenal, naval affairs, and the prison. He verified captains' papers and examined merchandise being sent to Tunis, assuring that items, such as spirits, were not introduced as contraband. Because of his functions, the *kahiya* sustained ties with foreign traders, vice-consuls, or the *wakils* (agents) who represented the interests of Ottoman and Moroccan subjects. Importers paid duties to the *gumruk* and frequently had to store their goods in warehouses until the contents could be properly ascertained and weighed. Exporters had to furnish a *sarah khuruj*, or license, for commodities subject to state monopoly and/or export restrictions—notably for olive oil and grains—which required the ruler's permission to ship from the country.[16]

In Tunis–La Goulette, as was true elsewhere, rigorous formalities were connected to quarantine. From the middle of the eighteenth century, the Husaynids had adopted stringent maritime health regulations; a small island, al-Shikli, in the Lake of Tunis, and another off Tabarka, served as quarantine facilities, however inadequate to the task. Ships without valid patents of health were denied permission to disembark in La Goulette and vessels suspected of "foul bills of health" were ordered to depart immediately for ports endowed with large-scale quarantine facilities, such as Mahon or Valletta. Leghorn boasted the first modern lazaretto, constructed around 1590, and by the late eighteenth century Malta's facility had grown into a 323,000-square-foot complex. During Mediterranean-wide epidemics, ships suspected of carrying diseased crews or passengers were refused permission to disembark and theoretically were required to return to their country of origin; even ships with clean bills of health were only to put in to La Goulette where precautions could be taken.[17] When the Englishman Godfrey Feise headed to Tunisia in 1812, he left Valletta on a Maltese *rebecque* whose passengers included "a mixture of various religions, Christians, Turks and Jews." Due to contrary winds, the ship put in at Trapani in western Sicily, where passengers were forced into quarantine. Upon reaching La Goulette, the captain and his *serviano* (mate) immediately went ashore, but passengers, including Feise, had to remain onboard until an order came from the bey for disembarkation.[18]

The epidemics of 1816–1821, followed in 1831 by an unfamiliar and terrible disease, cholera morbus, that provoked panic around the Mediterranean, moved Tunisian officials to establish more effective sanitary policies.[19] By 1824, La Goulette boasted facilities for disinfecting contaminated goods; local quarantine agents were stationed along the coast from Bizerte to Djerba.[20] Alarmed by newspaper reports of cholera devastating England, Husayn Bey established an observation system requiring thorough examinations of vessels before granting permission to communicate with shore. As Husayn Bey strove to implement quarantine restrictions, a Tunisian vessel from Alexandria with returning hajjis anchored in Sfax in 1831; some pilgrims and sailors had already succumbed to cholera. Worse still the rumor mill had it that the qa'id of Sfax had allowed the ship to take on provisions in violation of quarantine. After ordering the ship to immediately depart for Leghorn, the bey threatened to severely punish his official, should the story prove true. When cholera was confirmed in Genoa, Leghorn, and Algiers in 1835, the bey determined not to receive "any vessels from these ports, and . . . likewise established regulations in the quarantine department of the most rigorous kind, for ships which may arrive from any other places whatever, not excepting Malta." In the British consul's estimation at the time, "If it [cholera] should unhappily make its appearance here, the consequences would be frightful, principally on account of our being almost destitute of medical aid."[21] Tunisia was largely spared the first outbreak of cholera, although it was less fortunate during later episodes. With heightened ship movements into La Goulette, the public health danger grew, inducing Ahmad Bey to impose more stringent regulations, notably during the cholera epidemic of the 1850s.[22]

After clearing quarantine, nationals or protégés were authorized by respective consuls to debark in port; it appears that passports or papers, if required, remained in the possession of consular agents until the individual, whether permanent resident or not, left the country.[23] Husaynid subjects returning home had to go through formalities as well. However, rudimentary record keeping in the port, together with the consular system of counting principally nationals or protégés, means that credible statistics on arrivals and departures from La Goulette are lacking for the most part. "I . . . transmit herewith answers to the questions which had been received at the Colonial Office from the Board of Trade. . . . There has been great difficulty in answering these questions precisely owing to no commercial returns of any nature being kept by the Tunisian Government at their Customs House and indeed being so totally devoid of any commercial institutions whatever."[24] Passenger manifests were supposed to be closely scrutinized to ascertain that passengers debarking matched the numbers and names on the manifests. However, the coastal trade was rarely subject to this kind of surveillance because crews were multinational, constantly changing from port to port. In 1858, the British ship *Carmela* arrived from Bizerte after fourteen days of trading with six sailors and a cargo of butter. The owner and master, Paulo Darmania, from Senglia, Malta, made this declaration to the British agent:

[That] he has been in this port for about ten days but that he was not aware of the necessity of presenting his papers at this consulate; he further declares that having left Malta more than a year since, and having been engaged in the coasting trade between Tunis and Tripoli and Algeria, he has, since he left Malta, disembarked

three men named Lorenzo Buttigieg; Palonia Xuereb, and Michele Cassar, at different ports and has taken on board four others named: Giachino Zrafa, Paulo Avela,
Manuele Azzupardi, and Mouhamed Ben Abd Allah.[25]

While improvements were made in identifying, counting, and tracking passengers after the introduction of steam transportation, still the system left much
to be desired, as seen in this 1873 report: "the English steamer, the *Lamefield*,
arrived yesterday in the evening from Malta with forty-three passengers on
board, thirty-five Maltese carters and day laborers, three Greeks who left Tunis
some time ago and are returning; five Muslims . . . if you want to know the names
of the three Greek passengers, which I wasn't able to obtain here, you can get this
information from Mr. C. Foa, who is the boat agent and who is the only one to
whom a passenger list was given."[26] Naming was more important for some social
groups than others. Middle-class male passengers were listed by name, nationality, and profession; wives, servants, and children might be recorded but not
named. Subsistence migrants, many barely tolerated protégés, elicited the least
interest on the part of port or consular officials, unless they posed some social
danger. However, single women were more likely to be identified for purposes of
sexual supervision. Quarantine, passports of various types, and gendered travel
restrictions raise a larger question of women at sea.
    If male travelers theoretically could not disembark until cleared by port offi-
cials, health agents, and/or consuls, women faced an additional impediment;
females traveling alone, unaccompanied by male relatives or escorts, were subject
to special formalities, irrespective of nationality or social class, imposed by the
Tunisian state until Ahmad Bey's reign. These represented a local expression of
older Mediterranean-wide restrictions on women's displacements, notably those
from the "common classes."[27] Women could not leave a ship until recognized
male guardians obtained written permits, which was required each time "women
without men" arrived. In 1829, the English consul petitioned the palace for a
"*teskera* [permit] for the disembarkation of the wife of Vella [the Maltese] and
five children Maltese." Responding positively, Sidi Hassuna al-Murali, the bey's
interpreter, seized the opportunity to complain energetically about the increasing
numbers of Maltese in the country during a period of great distress occasioned
by "the failure of the crops of oil and grain."[28] The same restrictions applied to
the members of other nations, even well-known, longtime residents. In 1824,
Madame Monge desired "to disembark from her ship in port" but she had to have
permission. "I went to the son of the *kahiya* to get his help; he was disposed to
allow her, as she is a resident, to go on to Tunis before procuring the bey's permit,
just in time the order came from the bey."[29] Although the port official was willing
to bend the rules for Mme. Monge, from a respectable family established in the
capital, the consular officer insisted upon observing procedures.

Naturally, subterfuge countered efforts to deny entry to undesirables. A French naval officer, Beaussier, brought his mistress ashore in 1822 disguised as a sailor so that—dressed as a man—she could sightsee and visit the suqs in Tunis. When discovered, the deception provoked a great hue and cry; from La Goulette, Pierre Gaspary, the French vice-consul, warned the consul in Tunis of a serious breach in the system of control:

> I hasten to inform you by express pouch that I have just learned that the *woman in question* disguised as a man just left for Tunis accompanied by Mr. Beaussier. It is certain that I never would have allowed her to leave if I had known before. I should inform you that Mr. Beaussier came the other day to ask me to allow this woman to debark in La Goulette and I refused to allow it in accordance with the order that I had received from you. It appears that Beaussier then took the expedient of disguising her as a man and that Beaussier had given his word to the captain of the ship not to land the woman in port. Monsieur Beaussier accompanied the woman to Tunis.[30]

Whether she was able to shop in the suqs before being apprehended and hustled back to port is unknown. (Since navies forbade females onboard ships, the ruse of dressing like a man was not uncommon for women sea travelers.) In addition, the vice-consuls put up outbound families in distress and provided hospitality and sometimes lodging for ship captains and officers. Shipwrecked or seriously ailing seamen were sent to Tunis, where consulates served as short-term shelters or primitive hospitals.

With sailors from around the Mediterranean putting in, violent clashes erupted on ships or the docks and spilled over into the port, mirroring larger international struggles for mastery of the sea. Vice-consuls mediated disputes involving captains and/or crews, as jumping ship was a frequent occurrence that provoked quarrels; in the 1840s, disgruntled Greek crewmen abandoned their vessel to board another under France's flag, unleashing bitter recriminations between the captains and long negotiations. In September 1842, a spectacular free-for-all erupted onshore, pitting sailors from the British ship *Snake* against a French war steamer's crew. While a French sailor was charged with initiating the brawl, it was concluded that both sides were at fault because the officers had "encouraged the fight"—a fool-hardy act since English sailors outnumbered the French four to one.[31] Increased ship traffic through Tunisia's busiest port after midcentury only confirmed the collective view in Tunis that La Goulette was a space of quasi-permanent moral disorder.

The port functioned as a communications nerve center for news coming from all over. Agents reported ship movements, assembling statistics of monthly traffic for home governments, and served as postmasters for mail. Before steam transportation became widespread, correspondence took weeks, even months, to reach its final destination. The "Diary of Official Proceedings," kept by the British consulate for a six-month period in 1828, and dispatched to London by the first available vessel, was not logged into the Foreign Office until nearly five months later.[32] Of course, bureaucratic inefficiency in London caused delays—in addition to the vicissitudes of transportation in stormy winter sailing months. Dispatches from the central government were most frequently sent to La Goulette via Malta, although not necessarily on British ships. But travelers provided by far the most information about trans-Mediterranean events. When the English ship *Maiden* finally arrived from Valletta in February 1839, with the British consul, Sir Thomas Reade, and his family, the consul shared "abundant news" gathered while in Malta with Gaspary, including French fleet movements about which the French vice-consul was unaware. After 1830, Algeria functioned as another informational web for Tunisia. French warships or small vessels sailing under different flags, running shuttles between Algiers and La Goulette, brought tidings that were not always glad; the news of the devastating cholera epidemic in Bône's military hospitals first reached Tunis via this channel.[33]

FROM BARBARY PORT TO ITALIAN TOWN

Who called the port home in the early part of the century? A small, heterogeneous population of beylical subjects, twenty "European" families, consular agents, customs officials, boatmen, and shipyard laborers resided in La Goulette. Some sixty French nationals worked in state-owned arsenals as engineers or skilled artisans. Inns, taverns, and cafés were few and usually run by Sicilians or Maltese, although expanded immigration resulted in a hefty increase in places of sociability. By 1830, the former bagnio for Christian captives awaiting ransom had been transformed into a vast prison, the *karraka,* one of the main incarceration centers for criminals condemned to forced labor, notably smugglers and petty thieves. Lacking their own prisons, European consuls often confined protégés in the *karraka,* employing it either as a pretrial detention center or for short-term punishment. A resident described Halq al-Wad this way in 1835: "Ships supplied their [the inhabitants] general needs with wine, spirits, tobacco, and vegetables in the numerous storage shops which surrounded the port and were run by Italians and Maltese. Adjacent to the city walls were offices and residences for the governor, diverse Europeans, and the French vice-consul, Gaspary."[34] Until 1848, a small chapel in Gaspary's private residence served as the sole place of worship, but that year Ahmad Bey donated a small piece of land for a church, which later boasted a special altar consecrated to the Virgin of Trapani.[35] Surrounded by walls, the older houses of wood gradually gave way to modest one-storey stone constructions; a monumental gateway, the "Tunis door," provided access to the outside. Ahmad Bey built a summer palace on the site of an older construction on the southern shore of the canal, established a mosque, and expanded the arsenal and the mole. As was true in Tunis, drinking water came from underground cisterns fed by the winter rainwater.

Until the surge in immigration, La Goulette's European community was "too small for members of the community to be able to hide any of their activities."[36] Keeping tabs on the whereabouts and displacements of protégés demanded vigilance, which in turn depended upon access to the kinds of social networks that provided needed information. Despite the fact that everyone more or less knew everyone else in the port, the critical consular functions of naming, identifying, and locating were becoming increasingly difficult. Gaspary vainly tried in 1837 to find an individual named Papaolo Borjé by consulting those in the know about who lived or worked where at any given moment in the day: "I did my best to discover the whereabouts of Papaolo Borjé and I am assured that this individual is not presently in La Goulette; neither is he onboard the Tuscan ship which is leaving for Malta and for Bône. But I did find aboard someone named Paolo Borj, a mason, who is going to Bône . . . he is carrying a passport which bears a French visa."[37]

Expanding settlement, trade, ship traffic, and creeping colonialism triggered the port's physical expansion. As its population spilled outside the older city walls, more residential houses were constructed, facilities were enlarged, and places of popular amusement thrived, especially with the opening of the light railway in 1875 linking La Goulette with Tunis. By the eve of the Protectorate, the town boasted two-storied neo-Moorish balconied houses built by Italian architects and painted various shades of ochre. Decades of immigration gradually transformed the port into a "Sicilian town."[38] At the same time that La Goulette became a space of heightened intercommunal intercourse, it acquired a reputation as a tough place where drinking, brawls, knife fights, and smuggling were common. Or so it seemed to the prim notables of Tunis in whose eyes the port was not a fashionable address.

Until La Goulette was connected to Tunis by a newly dredged seven-mile canal and rail, the journey's next leg entailed crossing the shallow, noxious-smelling *buhaira* in small flat-bottomed boats; Maltese and Sicilian boatmen increasingly shoved their way into this occupation.[39] But it wasn't all bad. During the ride, flocks of bright rose-colored flamingoes migrating from West Africa might be seen as well as the fortress of al-Shikli "a castle built on a small island, rising prettily amidst the soft green waters" of the lake.[40]

When weary passengers reached Tunis, they were deposited on a quay and promenade adjacent to Bab al-Bahr, the Sea Gate; those bringing merchandise into the city dealt with a second, larger customs house. Elite native travelers would probably make their way to the *madina* proper, where notables tended to cluster together. Tunisian Jews headed to the *hara* (Jewish quarter); men without families often stayed in the numerous *wakala* (temporary lodging places) in the more popular quarters of the city's two suburbs, or *ribats*. For centuries, European diplomats and traders had lodged in *funduqs* (large, walled compounds combining residence and commerce) of their nation in the lower madina near the Sea Gate.[41] Later, when they became too crowded, Europeans rented rooms or houses from Tunisian proprietors in the streets adjacent to the funduqs, thereby transforming entire neighborhoods. The Sea Gate constituted the physical limits of the walled city nearest the *buhaira* until after the middle of the century, when land reclamation in the lake's marshy edges furnished terrain for buildings extra muros—houses, workplaces, and shops—to accommodate the newcomers. Thus a gridlike more or less "modern" city existed long before colonialism.

TUNIS "THE WELL-PROTECTED"

What did Tunis represent in the collective mind as human traffic from across the Mediterranean began to transform it into a mini Ellis Island? Its sobriquets, *al-hadhira* (the city as civilization), *al-khadra'* (the verdant), *al-mahrusa* (the well-protected), suggest a conflation between the refinement characteristic of illustrious Islamic centers and notions of "garden" or "paradise" with subtle connotations of salvation. Thus, Tunis constituted the Ifriqiyan prototype of *al-madina*, the city of the Prophet Muhammad and exemplary urban core. With nearly twenty congregational mosques, illustrious *madrasas,* and two hundred *masjids* (smaller mosques), the city had long been a major religious, intellectual, and commercial hub for the Maghrib and sub-Saharan Africa as well as the political capital, associated in the modern era with a ruling dynasty, the Husaynids (1705–1957). With the fall of Constantine to the French army in 1837, Tunis acquired even greater importance for Algerian Muslims as an Islamic haven for refugees unwilling to live under infidel rule.[42]

The wood famine that had plagued the Mediterranean rim for centuries molded North African cities; Tunis was mainly built of *tub* (baked bricks), tile, dressed or carved stone, and marble, the last two for the wealthy, as well as *spolia* from Carthage or Utica that had been incorporated into urban structures and seaside pleasure villas for centuries. The ecological fact that the Maghrib and many islands were especially wood poor had some tangible benefits, as cataclysmic fires were infrequent and so too opportunities for drastic urban reordering. Istanbul, where wood residential structures were found in abundance, suffered a series of devastating fires in the nineteenth century, clearing the way for extensive, at times brutal, modern urbanization. By the early nineteenth century, Tunis's architecture combined Ifriqiyan, Ottoman, and Moroccan influences; Italian spatial organization, materials, and decorative elements were increasingly in evidence and included furniture, objects of daily use, and material culture,

FIGURE 4. Worshippers leaving the Zaytuna mosque-university, Tunis. The oldest mosque in Tunis, the Zaytuna was a place of worship as well as an institution of higher learning that attracted scholars from throughout the Maghrib and Africa. (Library of Congress Prints and Photographs, LC-DIG-ppmsca-06043.)

which reflected the growing clout of Italian mamluks in the political class and the importance of the Leghorn merchants. But that influence was not confined to private residential structures. One of the last congregational mosques constructed, the Sahib al-Tabi' jami', built in 1814, and the Dar al-Bey, employed Italian materials and craftsmen.[43]

Considered among the dynasty's most magnificent structures, the Dar al-Bey impressed even the most jaded visitors with its exquisite interior spaces—marble patios, fountains, and courtyards—and rich décor, with ceilings in hues of vermillion and blue inlaid with gold sequins. The site was originally chosen due to proximity to an important mosque, the city's most prestigious guild, and to the Qasba, where the army was quartered. Decorated in a quasi-Italianate style, the Dar al-Bey enclosed within its vast structures civilian, military, and administrative functions. It had served as Hammuda Bey's principal residence but by the nineteenth century was sometimes used as a palatial residence-hotel for VIPs, such as the English Princess Caroline, whose sojourn during 1816 may have spared the city from bombardment.[44] The court only resided there for part of the year, notably for religious festivals such as Ramadan, but the palace complex also boasted a hall of justice, *bayt al-diwan*, and a throne room. Ahmad Bey installed the prime minister's offices there and Muhammad al-Sadiq Bey (r. 1859–1882) added salons and reception halls for official ceremonies built in the European mode of the period.[45] (A section of the Dar al-Bey served until very recently as the Tunisian National Archives.) The nearby Qasba enclosed the principal janissary barracks until their disbandment in 1811 after a revolt. By the mid-nineteenth century, the Qasba boasted an arsenal with a factory for fabricating canon and gun powder, overseen from 1826 on by a French Polytechnique officer, de Bineau.

Let's inspect the principal streets, structures, and neighborhoods, since the built environment shaped the city's social architecture and in turn opportunities for newcomers from across the sea or rural folk from the provinces seeking a better life. Residential patterns were determined by a combination of religion, kinship, profession, and ethnicity; those from outside the capital city region, from other parts of North Africa, or eastern Ottoman lands tended to cluster together. The absence of indigenous Christians meant that predominantly Christian quarters, like those in Cairo or Damascus, did not exist, although a small, but growing, largely European neighborhood occupied the quarter near the Sea Gate. The *hawma* (neighborhood) represented a key spatial construct understood by its inhabitants as a sort of semipublic, semiprivate domestic space characterized by intense, day-to-day exchanges; waves of settlement gradually transformed the older configurations of some neighborhoods.[46]

Until Ahmad Bey's urban renewal program was launched in the 1840s, the city was entirely surrounded by walls with two adjoining suburbs (*ribats*), Bab al-Suwayqa and Bab al-Jazira. The axis mundi of Tunis was the madina, whose core boasted the eighth-century Zaytuna mosque-university, hundreds of guilds or artisan corporations producing a wide array of goods, state buildings, palaces housing wealthy merchants and 'ulama' families, and countless religious edifices or shrines. Indigenous notables (*a'yan*) preferred certain neighborhoods in the madina—the *nahj basha* quarter or the nearby Qasba district—as residences. Descendants of Turkish officials resided in these quarters, although intermarriage had caused the lines of demarcation to fade somewhat by this period; and because the city was not spatially segregated by class, the madina was home to ordinary people and their humble abodes. Nevertheless, the *ribats* were more popular in composition; less prestigious than the madina, Bab al-Suwayqa enjoyed more esteem than its sister suburb, Bab al-Jazira, since the former abutted the Dar al-Bey, government offices, and the Qasba. In the collective city consciousness, the inhabitants of Bab al-Suwayqa occupied a higher social rung than those unfortunates with an address in Bab al-Jazira, associated with rural, and thus imperfectly civilized, newcomers and reprehensible activities due to the presence of temporary shelters for poor or transient people. Increasingly these were inhabited by impoverished Mediterranean immigrants, first single Maltese male laborers, and later down-and-out families.[47]

An ancient, well-delimited Jewish quarter had been in existence for centuries. The hara's origins lay in the late tenth or early eleventh century, when tradition had it that a powerful Muslim saint, Sidi Muhriz, gave the Jews permission to live within city walls in their own neighborhood. For the most part, Jews of the capital resided and worked in a separate neighborhood, the *hara al-yahud,* which corresponded to the Moroccan *millah,* although it was never surrounded by physical enclosures; some Jews resided in the hara but worked outside its precincts. In terms of city spaces, *suq al-Grana* (market of the Leghornese traders) was a major market as well as a thoroughfare cutting through the middle of the madina's Jewish quarter adjacent to Bab al-Suwayqa. By the 1830s, the hara was appallingly overcrowded and suffered grievously during outbreaks of epidemics.[48]

City quarters had olive oil presses, communal ovens, fountains providing pure drinking water holding the status of *habus* (or *waqf*), and suqs as well as small mosques or prayer rooms. As was true in other Ottoman cities, the noblest professions—dealers in perfumes, silks, and shashiya—were grouped around the principal mosque, the Zaytuna, or the Dar al-Bey. Trades considered noxious or polluting, such as tanning or butchering, were located on city perimeters. Food from the countryside was sold in markets scattered about the madina and suburbs; the *suq al-ghalla* (principal food market) was not far from the Sea Gate where the present *marché central* of Tunis stands. The city's monumental doors were situated to facilitate communication with the fertile Majarda plains, the Cap Bon, and the Sahil, regions producing the country's prized crops, wheat and olives. Many families owned gardens outside Tunis proper, some as far away as the plain of Mornag (Murnaq) nine miles to the south, then renowned for its olive and fruit orchards. And the intricate, multiphased production of the most esteemed export item, the shashiya, took place in Tunis *and* in hinterland satellite villages.[49]

A critical issue revolves around how urban space was gendered. Ethnographic evidence comes mainly from European (mainly male) writers, who inevitably commented upon native women's relative absence in the streets, although an account from the turn of the century described a women's market *(suq al-nisa')* in the madina, near the former slave market: "The souk ... like many others is a white tunnel lined with shops. It is very crowded in the early morning, and is almost the only place where many women are seen together. Some sit on the ground and sell their handiwork, others are busy bargaining for veils and embroideries. All are of the poorer classes and are heavily veiled."[50] Aside from the women's suq, about which little is known, Muslim women tended not to shop daily in the markets. Instead vendors visited regular clients in their homes, calling out to alert buyers that coal, water, sweets, fruit, and cloth were to be had. "Each vendor sang his own peculiar, but familiar melody; his established female clientele knew well the sound of his voice."[51] For the most part, urban women ventured out of households with family members to go to the baths, make social calls, or visit the cemetery; upper-class women left home under the cover of night or in special curtained carriages, guarded by eunuchs, concealing the occupants from strange gazes. "None but the most abandoned prostitute can venture to be seen in the streets, and even then it would be a crime to walk publicly with the face uncovered."[52] Jewish women moved more freely about the streets as did resident Christian women. Since streets were not paved until later in the century, torrential winter rains turned passages into mud-encumbered thoroughfares; when attempting to navigate flooded streets, some women fastened wooden and metal *trampini* (small stilts) to their shoes to protect them from the muck.

Until the mass arrival of largely Mediterranean Christians, the madina was a bustling commercial, administrative, and religious center by day under the supervision of the *shaykh al-madina* (city manager), one of city's the most influential offices. By night it was a relatively quiet area whose shops closed at sunset, and inhabitants rarely left home after the authorities sounded the sundown alert when the gates were closed. European travelers often noted with approval that street idlers, beggars, and vagabonds were few compared to Naples or Marseilles and attributed urban calm to the absence of theaters, pubs, or concert halls.[53] The most ubiquitous space for (male-only) sociability were the hundreds of cafés scattered around the city, owned either by Turks or by Tunis natives, although Maltese, Greeks, or Sicilians ran a few establishments serving alcohol in the early decades of the nineteenth century. As immigrants and others arrived from the Mediterranean, more taverns, hotels, and inns sprang up and newcomers began to compete with native café owners. In 1826, an Italian built the first standing theater, and after 1832 Italian comedies, operas, and ballets were performed. Street entertainment took place during religious feasts or annual festivals whose boisterous excesses the Husaynid state increasingly circumscribed as the century wore on. Nocturnal Ramadan celebrations offered amusement to all city inhabitants who wandered the gaily-lit, decorated streets during the holy month.[54]

PEOPLE

Self-Views

The notion of *twansa,* the allegedly "authentic" inhabitants of Tunis, best translates figurations of "us and them." Long-established residence in the capital city measured social worth, marking urbanites off from provincials, peasants, and small-town nobodies, and complicating the vaguer classical distinction between *al-khassa* (elite) and *al-'amma* (commoners). To this first cut must be added a second, the *baldis/baldiya,* or haughty city notables, who disdained the rough denizens of the popular suburbs and scrupulously observed behavioral norms—a reserved demeanor, moderation, and circumspection in public. "A baldi did not sing, eat, or in any other way call attention to himself while walking through the streets of Tunis. The sure mark of a hayseed was a man who conversed in a loud voice which could be overhead by passers-by; among the leading notables it was even considered improper to be seen in public cafes."[55] For the Tunis aristocrats, status was safeguarded by marriage and residential preferences. A Maliki jurist's *kunnash fiqhi* (notebook) from the late nineteenth century detailed a family dispute over whether a woman from Tunis could be obliged by her husband to reside outside her natal city. Drawing upon earlier opinions, the learned jurist responded that it would be a great inconvenience for such a woman to be forced to live in a provincial town, like nearby Sousse, but not in Alexandria or Fez.[56] While this might seem curious, one need only think of the citizens of Manhattan who feel more at home in Paris or London than in Camden, New Jersey.

Insiders conjure up outsiders regarded as socially distant and thus inferior. Being one of the *barrani/barraniya* (outsiders), people from other parts of the country or the Maghrib, was often tied to livelihood, since many performed tasks considered menial, even repugnant or suspect. The *shaykh al-barraniya* administered the "outsiders," who monopolized specific professions and belonged to certain ethnic or regional groups, such as workers from Gabes who were carters; many barraniya resided in the Bab al-Jazira *ribat.*[57] Needless to say, these niches were permeable and far from stable. Over time, an ambitious "non-*twansa*" could move from the outside in through perseverance, cagey marriage strategies, the right kind of fortune, social recognition of insider status, loss of collective memory regarding origins, and the ability to observe subtle codes of conduct. Despite the tenacious myth of the "authentic" urbanites whose way of life, behavior, and superior culture were immutable, people from Tunisian or North African towns, villages, oases, or tents constantly nourished the capital city region, as did those from across the sea.

Numbers

What was the population of nineteenth-century Tunis? This question has provoked decades of scholarly debate, but it is safe to defer to Paul Sebag's estimates of 100,000. Muslims numbered between 65,000 and 70,000, a figure including about 5,000 from other North African states or the Sahara. Jews numbered about 20,000 in the entire country, with some 15,000 residing in the Tunis region. Until the 1840s, an estimated 1,000 African slaves entered Tunisia each year but not all remained; after abolition in 1846, manumitted slaves and their descendants counted between 6,000 and 7,000 in the capital. If they tended over time to assimilate to local society, nevertheless names, professions, places of residence, and forms of religiosity signaled former servile status and roots in western Sudan. The most visible Ottoman subjects were the Orthodox Greeks, who, while never very numerous, benefitted from the largesse and patronage of Husaynid rulers as well as enjoying considerable autonomy in their religious and communal affairs. In 1830, resident European Christians numbered over 3,000, but all figures are controversial because the first systematic census was only conducted in 1906; moreover what "European" meant was a sort of floating benchmark.[58] A credible account stated that "many Maltese of the greatest respectability... have been established here for 20 years with their families," which suggests that labor migration began in the era just after Admiral Exmouth's 1816 expedition.[59]

In 1848, the English vice-consul tallied 5,800 British subjects, of whom 35 men, women, and children were nationals; less than 200 were Greek protégés from the Ionian Islands under British rule and thus Maltese were the majority by far. Another report from 1847 put the "Christians" at 9,400 of whom the Maltese numbered 6,000. About 60 bourgeois French families called Tunisia home as well. Estimates of the Italo-Sicilian population, from a slightly later period, vary widely; by 1870, at least 9,000 Italians resided in the country permanently, to which another 2,000 seasonal fishermen and sailors should be added.[60]

Muslims and Jews

Sunni Muslims of the Maliki *madhhab* (legal school) were overwhelmingly the most numerous. The most prestigious clans claimed ancestry with the Prophet Muhammad, thus *sharifian* status, and filled the upper ranks of the Islamic legal and teaching establishment, for example, the Zarruq and Ibn al-'Ashur families. After the 1574 Ottoman conquest, a second Sunni legal school, the Hanafi, rivaled the Maliki and received preferential treatment until Ahmad Bey's reforms.[61] A distinctive group of Maliki Muslims were the Andalusians, distinguished by lifestyle, craft specialization, and shared memory of Iberian origins. During the long Reconquista, Spanish Muslims and Jews had sought refuge in North Africa; tens of thousands settled Tunisia in the early seventeenth century, many in villages in the northwest, notably Qal'a-t al-Andalus (Galaat el Andeleus), characterized by special architectural and cultural forms. But the elite preferred Tunis, where they developed the art of shashiya manufacture, still monopolized by their descendants in the nineteenth century; those claiming Iberian ancestry officiated over the city's most powerful merchant or guild councils.[62] Some Muslim notables claimed Moroccan origins, as in the case of the Jallulis, whose ancestors settled in Sfax in the fifteenth century where they prospered in the corsair economy and later acquired powerful government posts and palatial residences in the capital. But Algerians, admittedly an anachronistic term, had always formed the largest North African community, in part because the Tunisian state had recruited Berber Zuwawa (Zouaves) tribesmen from the Kabylia for auxiliary troops. The French occupation of Algeria dramatically inflated the numbers of resident Algerians, particularly after major rebellions.[63]

Jewish communities were distinguished by origins, legal status, and, increasingly, social class; some were Husaynid subjects, others protégés or citizens of European nations, notably the Italian states. The majority lived in the capital city region or in coastal towns such as Nabeul, celebrated for its learned rabbis. But others resided in the far south near Jabal Matmata, the Gabes oases, or on the island of Djerba. Arab or Berber Jews regarded themselves as indigenous but evolved their own vernaculars and wrote in Judeo-Arabic. The synagogue was the center of communal life; boys were sent to rabbinic schools for primary education and to the yeshiva for advanced studies warranting entry into the rabbinical elite. However, customs, food, attitudes, and lifestyle hardly differed from those of Muslim neighbors; superstitions, such as the belief in the evil eye or in jinn (spirits), were shared by both.[64] The veneration of holy persons or saints and collective pilgrimages honoring the "very special dead" were prominent features of Jewish and Muslim religiosity; the tombs of pious rabbis or Jewish sages reputed to possess miracle-working powers attracted Muslims followers.[65]

As Husaynid subjects, the Jews benefited from a large degree of autonomy and, while the bey nominated their qa'id, he respected communal consensus. Yet in accordance with Islamic and local practices, they held a markedly inferior status, paid special taxes, observed sumptuary laws, and could neither bear arms nor possess a mount. At times, native Jews were the targets of humiliation or violence perpetrated by the local Christian as well as Muslim population. Until the 1850s, during Holy Week in Tunis, it was customary for Catholic boys to deliver the *bastonnade* to Jewish youth unlucky enough to be found in the streets. Nevertheless, some Tunisian Jews, like the qa'id Nessim Samama (1805–1873), achieved influence and wealth through state service.[66] Tunisian Jews remained deeply religious, clung to local beliefs, used amulets, and visited neighborhood Muslim soothsayers, which horrified bourgeois and educated coreligionists, especially recently settled European Jews.

In the late seventeenth century, Jews, mainly from northern Italy but of diverse origins, settled in Tunis, where they joined the older communities of North African and Spanish Jews. Known as Grana (from Leghorn), they assumed pivotal commercial and financial roles facilitating trade between Europe, particularly northern Italy, and Tunisia; they chartered ships to export grains, oils, wool, and leather and imported a range of commodities, notably New World products, such as sugar. Some of the Leghorn Jews worked in the redemption business by ransoming North African Muslims held captive in Italy. By the nineteenth century, many enjoyed middle-class status and some maintained patron-client ties with the Husaynid court because of international connections. The medical profession represented another entrée since the beys preferred Tuscan Jews as personal doctors; sometimes, physicians acted as translators for their princely patients, translating documents from Italian or French into Arabic, or even as diplomatic representatives. By this period, families, such as the Lumbrosos, Valensis, and Castelnuovos benefited from European legal protection, which conferred no small advantage. In 1871, the Italian consulate recognized over one thousand Jews under Italy's jurisdiction.[67]

The Grana had their own synagogues, rabbinical courts, and councils, but, as they became increasingly European from the 1820s on, the cultural distance from Tunisian Jews grew. Since the Italians occupied high socioeconomic niches, while the Tunisians were among the least privileged strata working as small shopkeepers, artisans, or peddlers, intermarriage was rare, although not completely unknown. In the older urban cartography, the Grana had resided in or near the hara, but as the Jewish quarter burst at the seams the Leghornese took up residence in adjacent streets, such as Rue Zarkoun, which figures in Albert Memmi's autobiographical novel, *La statue de sel*; bourgeois Tuscan Jews found housing in the Christian quarter, near Bab al-Bahr.[68] Nothing symbolized more concretely the growing legal, social, and cultural distinctions between Arab and Italian Jews than the cemetery wall dividing the tombs of indigenous Jews from those with roots across the sea. However, after 1857, the situation of native Jews improved markedly as discriminatory legislation was lifted and they acquired the right to purchase land and property. Nevertheless, some indigenous Jews sought the formal legal protection of the various European powers as an insurance policy against future troubles.

The Political Class

Tunisia had long made room for outsiders—indeed granting privileged places to some—although the meanings attached to "foreignness" must be calibrated according to the historical period. The origins of the Husaynid political class lay neither in Spain nor the Maghrib but for the most part in the Levant, western Asia, or the Black Sea region. Some arrived in the late sixteenth or early seventeenth centuries as Ottoman military officers, administrative cadres, seamen, and soldiers. Others were Christian adventurers, corsairs, or captives from across the Mediterranean who entered into state service after "turning Turk," converting to Islam. Some had been seized by slave traders or forcibly enrolled in the Ottoman military before being brought to North Africa. Yusuf Sahib al-Tabi', originally from Moldavia, had been taken from his home during one of the periodic levies, the so-called boy tax *(devşirme)*, that the Porte imposed upon the Christian Balkans. Once in Tunis, Yusuf rapidly ascended the political ladder, becoming chief minister by the end of the eighteenth century.[69] As elsewhere in the Ottoman Empire, Georgia and Circassia furnished mamluks (military or state personnel)—young men seized during raids, or purchased by slavers, and sold throughout the empire, including the North African provinces. The few identifiable Georgian or Circassian lineages left today retain only the vaguest memories of their roots. According to Agha family lore, their ancestor Mustafa, was playing in a garden outside his home somewhere in Georgia around 1800 when horsemen seized him and his brother; they were taken to Istanbul, where Mustafa was given to an Ottoman family for education until being sold to the Husaynids for palace service as a mamluk. (The story of the horsemen slavers constitutes a recurring trope in these family histories.)[70]

The dynasty's founder, Husayn ibn 'Ali (r. 1705–1735), was the son of a soldier from Crete who had risen in the Ottoman military establishment that ruled Tunisia. After successfully defeating an Algerian invasion, which earned the gratitude and support of urban notables and tribal leaders, Husayn took the Turkish title of bey and concluded tactical marital alliances with local Arab families, including marriage with women from the provinces in Le Kef near the Algerian border. His descendants, however, pursued Mediterranean and western Asian marriage strategies by often marrying Christian slave women from Genoa, Sardinia, Georgia, and Circassia—unions that over time produced the distinctive Ottoman-Tunisian ruling establishment.[71] In a society prizing kinship, where genealogy represented the principal social map, to come from "somewhere else," bereft of kin, as was true of the mamluks, might have been a serious disadvantage. Yet through palace or household service and marriage, outsiders were absorbed into the ranks of the political class. What were the politics of marriage?

Mamluks who proved loyal, excelled in statecraft, and earned the ruler's favor might be rewarded by marriage to a Husaynid princess—sister, daughter, or niece of the bey. Of Georgian origins, Mustafa Khuja married one of Hammuda Bey's sisters and proved particularly useful because he spoke Turkish, Arabic, and Italian. Another Georgian, Mustafa Agha, held one of the highest military posts in Tunisia under Ahmad Bey and married the ruler's sister. When he wed Lilla Sisiya in 1829, Mustafa built a summer palace, Dar Agha, near Carthage on the dunes overlooking the Gulf of Tunis, a verdant area with vineyards and fruit trees known as Kram (or *karm,* "orchard"). One of the last Circassian mamluks to enter state service was Khayr al-Din, who wed a princess in 1862; it appears that as long as marriage to a Husaynid woman endured, it was to remain monogamous.[72]

The baldis, especially religious notables, were loath to give daughters in marriage to the palace because of the Husaynid practice of taking many wives and concubines of diverse religious and ethnoracial origins, including unions with women of ordinary status from *outside* Tunis; leading 'ulama' families regarded the court's sumptuous atmosphere with restrained opprobrium. The reverse— the wedding of women *from* the Husaynid family—was less distasteful; for example, Ahmad Bey married a sister to the aristocratic Mrabit family. At times, the beys acted as patriarchal matchmakers, involving court favorites and the city's great lineages; refusing a marriage arrangement from the ruler himself was a delicate matter. High-ranking Hanafi lineages, such at the Bayrams, were less reluctant to wed daughters to the palace or court and thus claimed three sources of social esteem: kinship with the Husaynids, prestigious religious positions, and state office.[73] Changing relationships between the palace and the capital's aristocratic Arab Muslim families, the Maliki a'yan, can be gauged by the willingness—or aversion—to exchange women in marriage, an aversion that lessened somewhat with the "Tunisification" of the political class in the nineteenth century.

HOUSEHOLD BUREAUCRACY AND
MEDITERRANEAN EMPORIUM

By Hammuda Bey's reign in 1782, the Husaynid dynasty and its ruling institutions enjoyed virtually unquestioned legitimacy. Until the later reforms, the state functioned as an elaborate household bureaucracy constantly fed by social elements that might have been judged "foreign" at one time but that were folded into local ways of doing things through service, marriage, fictive kinship, and patronage. After a bitter squabble over the throne in 1814, the principle of succession was definitively settled; rule passed to the oldest male. This political pact, largely unchallenged until the dynasty's demise in the twentieth century, came to pass through the intervention of Amina, wife of Mahmud Bey. During her husband's investiture in December 1814, Amina convoked her two sons, Husayn and Mustafa, and bade them take an oath on the Quran to respect each other's rights to the throne.[74] By then, the Husyanids had secured the kinds of political and religiomoral capital enjoyed by independent regimes, such as the 'Alawis, although in contrast to the Moroccan dynasty, the Husaynids never claimed kinship in the Prophet's family. Nevertheless, Husaynid governance played a primordial role in state formation, indelibly marking the country's modern history.

Legitimacy sprang from intersecting sources, above all, assiduous observation of Islamic law and practice, public expressions of respect for the 'ulama', and the inclusion of subjects in the symbolically charged performance of investiture played out in two bay'as (professions of allegiance), one private, the other public.[75] Rulers presided over religious celebrations, the two 'aids, and the ra's al-'am (first day of the New Year), events marked by acts of largesse from princes and princesses alike. Carefully orchestrated processions through the streets of Tunis represented public relations campaigns, since the reigning bey formally received the leading 'ulama', the heads of the guilds, and other corporate groups with great pomp. With Ahmad Bey's reign in 1837, favored members of the European diplomatic corps were invited to attend religious or state festivals.[76]

The location and physical spaces associated with the exercise of power were significant. Under Husayn ibn 'Ali, the court and government were transferred from the Qasba to abandoned palaces of the older Muradid dynasty (1628–1705) situated three miles outside city walls in a stretch of land surrounded by orchards. That palace complex, known as the Bardo, from the Spanish *prado* (field), became the Husaynids' principal residence. With each bey's ascension to the throne, a new palace was built so that the Bardo was in a state of continual construction well into the nineteenth century. After the main gate into the complex stood a vaulted corridor that served as a ceremonial vestibule *(saqifa)*; behind it the palace guard stood watch before the entry to the harim, or women's quarters. A library filled with rare manuscripts brought back from Istanbul and Cairo and a mosque graced the complex, as did numerous tiered marble fountains and luxurious gardens. Other buildings included military barracks, parade grounds, stables, vast kitchens, the *zandala* (prison), and the *mahkama* (tribunal), a spacious, lavishly appointed hall where the beys rendered justice.[77] By the 1830s, the Bardo had the character of a small town, with high-end residences for court notables; modest lodgings for slaves, servants, and retainers; and workshops for producing needed commodities. A chapel to celebrate mass and the sacraments was located there for the small group of resident Catholics in service to the palace.

Thus the political elite resided and worked at a distance from the capital, although some court notables maintained residences in the Tunis madina. Smaller, but elegant, summer palaces were scattered along the coast from La Marsa to Hammam Lif, since both political and religious notables spent the sweltering summers there. With the reign of Muhammad Bey (r. 1855–1859), La Marsa became one of the principal beylical residences by the late 1850s. Surrounded by olive groves, vineyards, and luxuriant gardens, La Marsa had served as a princely pleasure capital since at least the Hafsid époque—indeed since pre-Islamic times.[78] In the nineteenth century, European creoles and consular families resided in seaside villas often loaned by the palace or court dignitaries.

At the level of the territorial state, a sort of royal progress, the *mahalla,* both conferred and confirmed legitimacy. Long before the Ottoman conquest, indigenous Maghribi states had flexed their muscle and collected revenues through this mobile military-camp-cum-tax-collecting expedition, which dispensed justice as it laboriously made its way around the country in two annual forays timed for the harvests. During the course of the seventeenth and eighteenth centuries, the Ottoman office of bey was combined with this reinvigorated local institution. Leadership of the multifunctional mahalla became the principal mechanism for transmitting sovereignty from ruler to designated heir, which the 1814 pact on succession further stabilized. If the reach of political elites in Tunis remained tenuous among pastoral societies at the state's limits, still the mahalla endowed the dynasty with a remarkable longevity and an equally remarkable ability to expropriate the country's resources and producers.[79]

The rulers carefully managed the intersections between the subsistence economy of the peasantry and Mediterranean commerce by naming agents to strategic centers of international trade, notably Malta, Gibraltar, and Marseilles. In addition, where Tunisian merchants resided in sufficient numbers, *wakils* were appointed, mainly in Morocco, Algiers, Tripoli, and Alexandria. Isaac Cardozo, a British subject and a Jew, served as Husaynid agent to Gibraltar in 1836; after 1810, Mahmud Jalluli, and then the Farrugia brothers, oversaw commercial interests in Malta, furnishing information on market prices for wheat as well as the military and political news so critical during and after the Napoleonic Wars. The voluminous correspondence from Malta attests to the Husaynids' keen interest in the island fortress, with its commanding position in trans-Mediterranean and global affairs.[80] Outbreaks of epidemics, for example, the news of yet another terrifying appearance of plague in Alexandria in April 1841, figured prominently as do health conditions and quarantines, since they negatively affected trade.[81] The arrival of ships from Constantinople or Alexandria in Valletta, famine, or crop failures in key agricultural regions of the Ottoman Empire were systematically noted, as were the passages through Malta of Ottoman dignitaries or provincial rulers.[82] Since the dynasty controlled most of the country's resources through a system of state monopolies, its rulers conducted foreign affairs in the manner of quasi-independent sovereigns, concluding bilateral treaties with major trading partners among the European states. This dimension of Husaynid governance raises the question of Ottoman-Tunisian relations.

THE SUBLIME PORTE AND HUSAYNID TUNISIA

An Ottoman province from the late sixteenth century, the Regency of Tunis was both dependent upon, yet increasingly independent of, the Porte, particularly by the early nineteenth century. This is not to deny that the most powerful Muslim sovereign in Dar al-Islam, the sultan, did not hold sway—far from it.[83] Ottoman influences shaped domains ranging from architecture, cuisine, and clothing to financial, administrative, and military institutions to religious and legal practices. And the Husaynid court imitated the Ottoman court but on a scaled-back level of luxury, so as not to offend sensibilities in Istanbul. The sultans always confirmed after the fact the ascension of a new ruler, with letters of investiture and emissaries bearing precious gifts that reaffirmed ties for which there was always a political price to pay. Soon after Husayn Bey came to the throne in 1824, the Tunisian representative to the Porte, Ahmad Qabtan al-Murali, returned with the anticipated *firman* of investiture as well as the ceremonial robe of honor.

As always, this event was the cause for lavish celebrations in Tunis involving state officials, city notables, the 'ulama', and populace.[84] Whenever Istanbul appeared determined to reestablish direct control over the regency, as in 1835 when the local rulers of Tripolitania, the Qaramanli dynasty, were deposed, the Husaynids made haste to proffer rich presents to their overlords.

> The Sahib at-Tabi' takes with him [to Istanbul] presents to a very large amount-nearly two millions of Tunis piasters, consisting of Spanish douros, the conveyance of which from the Bardo to the Golita [La Goulette], occupied forty-two mules; a vessel loaded with upwards of thirty very fine horse with rich caparisons; another vessel with negro slaves; two hundred thousand red Tunisian caps; a great supply of the eau of jasmine and roses; a quantity of jewelry; swords, some of which were magnificently ornamented with large diamonds, guns and pistols and an enormous quantity of Tunis butter in jars which is much esteemed in Constantinople.[85]

Previous to the nineteenth century, the dynasty had relied upon Ottoman military or administrative cadres often recruited from the margins of the empire; but after 1820, supplying Tunis with mamluks from Georgia or Circassia became more difficult and increasingly mamluks hailed from Sicily, Sardinia, or the Italian peninsula. (Some Italian court mamluks maintained ties with birth families and may have convinced countrymen to try their luck in the regency.) At the same time, the native Tunisians entered into state service with Ahmad Bey's reign, which, together with the gradual assimilation of previously identifiable Turkish groups to local society, changed the older Ottoman system of governance. When European states appeared less menacing, the Husaynids used the Porte as a sort of superfund of distant, if convenient, legitimation; but as international political conditions worsened, they petitioned the Porte for recognition of hereditary rights to rule, a pattern seen in Egypt. With Istanbul's proclamation of the Tanzimat (reordering or restructuring of the Ottoman realm) starting in 1839, Tunisian political elites participated in a "three-cornered" conversation on state reform running from Istanbul to Cairo to Tunis. Nevertheless, Ahmad Bey and his successor declined until 1857 to implement these decrees, not from opposition to the principle of legal and social reordering per se, but rather from a desire for change on their own terms.[86] Tunisian state reforms— the Fundamental Pact of 1857 and proclamation of a constitution in 1860—as well as the last-ditch efforts by Prime Minister Khayr al-Din to alter the legal and political configuration of government during the early 1870s, were intimately connected to "strangers in the city." The steady influx of mainly Catholic Mediterranean subsistence migrants skewed older patterns of social insertion, positioning, and order not only for a Muslim dynasty, state, and society but also for European notables long-established in the country, a community aptly described as cultural creoles.[87]

Creoles

The privileged heart of the resident Euro-Mediterranean expatriate community was made up of several hundred merchants, skilled craftsmen, and military personnel linked in divergent ways to the ruling family. Marriage patterns, Mediterranean travels and travails, employment in posts from Istanbul to Tangier meant that their identities lay as much in North Africa or the Ottoman Empire as in Europe. Families, like the Gasparys in La Goulette, tended to monopolize vice-consular posts over generations and shared a polyglot system of communication that marked them off from the newly arrived from Mediterranean islands or Europe. But the key element was their enduring, if labyrinthine, relationships with the Husaynid family and court dignitaries who acted as great patrons—indeed who had transformed captives or people of modest origins into high-ranking state officials. These Euro-Tunisian "old-timers" looked askance at the "uninvited guests" pouring into the country after the 1830s so that the very fact of rapid in-migration caused this small, but critical, interstitial community to close ranks, at least for a while.[88] How can we talk about these people?

The notion of "creole" arising from New World encounters has spawned somewhat contradictory definitions. In racialized understandings, it designates persons of "mixed race" (as race was locally defined) in slave or former slave societies. In another scheme, "creole" names individuals born in slave colonies but considered "white" who assumed the behavioral traits characteristic of racially mixed societies and cultures.[89] In short, creole is as difficult to pin down as Moor, hybrid, or cosmopolitan. One definition suits, to an extent, our case—individuals born in Tunisia of parents from somewhere else, mainly although not exclusively Europe, who sank roots in the country over generations of residence and came to see the place as home. Thinking about them as creoles distinguishes them from recently arrived people, or from those who came to Tunis but moved on, and operates as ballast to the idea that religion and/or "nationality" constituted the sole source of identity and belonging.[90] This represents a major advance because it problematizes the notion of "European" and moves the discussion away from freighted constructs such as Islam, Europe, and the West. It beckons us to enter the in-between spaces forged by people in motion and to consider the range of displacements—spatial, social, mental, and cultural—that underlay continuous local adaptations.

What brought this assortment of people to North Africa? The original Christian community in Tunis went back to the twelfth century, when Venetian merchants set up shop and were later joined by traders from Genoa, Leghorn, Marseilles, and England. From the sixteenth century on, the heads of the Christian "nations" assumed the triple task of administering expatriates, assuring justice for nationals in an Islamic state, and attending to personal business interests.

The core of the early French nation were Huguenot families, first and foremost the Chapeliés. Originally from Nîmes, the family spawned a "dynasty of traders" culled from Reformed Church members who, after the 1685 revocation of the Edict of Nantes, created permanent commercial establishments in Tunis. This resonates with numerous cases of Europeans, including monarchs, who were afforded refuge in the Ottoman Empire.[91] By 1814, a descendant of the Huguenots, Jacques-Henri Chapelié, fifty-two years old, had resided in the country for thirty years and served as the elected deputy of the French nation.[92]

Another dynamic nourished the ranks of the Tunis creoles. The Husaynids intervened on behalf of resident foreigners, offering protection in return for technical, military, or scientific expertise—a harbinger of the nineteenth century. The French Revolution sent waves of people to Tunisia (and elsewhere in the Mediterranean world), where some placed themselves under the protection of Hammuda Bey, who went so far as to attempt to arrange for one family's sequestered possessions to be delivered from France to Tunis.[93] In 1819, Mahmud Bey received a letter from Admiral Jurieu complaining that the ruler had extended his protection to French nationals too frequently and reiterating the principle that only "apostasy" transformed the Bourbon into beylical subjects.[94] The real bone of contention revolved around the tangled, unresolved relationship between religious affiliation, allegiance to the monarch, and emerging forms of national identity; without conversion to Islam, an individual could not abandon France's legal embrace. This question repeatedly arose in the nineteenth century as Christians under European protection converted, seeking to substitute beylical and Islamic jurisdictions for European consular jurisdiction. As vexing for French jurists and diplomats were the ambiguities implicit in the notion and exercise of *nationalité*. Complicating matters was the fact that some individuals switched legal protection because they were at odds with their own consuls or community.

Small acts of defiance by individuals refusing to obey expulsion orders swelled the members of the Tunis creole community. In 1723, a French national, Bernard, and his wife arrived without proper permission from the Chambre de Commerce in Marseilles. Threatened with forced repatriation, the couple placed themselves under English protection and took up residence in the English funduq. They made their living thanks to La Goulette's *kahiya,* who granted the couple the right to operate a small tobacco *fabrique* in the port. Despite a legal ouster in 1743, the French hotel keeper, Guillaume, remained in Tunis by placing himself under Swedish protection. This practice, by no means restricted to North Africa, was frequent enough in Levantine Ottoman ports to move authorities to repeatedly forbid it.[95]

Yet another current feeding the creole community was the Husaynid practice of receiving a fortunate few of the Christian captives seized in raids into the heart of the palace bureaucracy, if they possessed special talents. The biography

FIGURE 5. Portrait of Count Giuseppe Raffo, 1795–1862. The son of a watchmaker taken captive by Tunisian corsairs, Raffo poses in military uniform and wears the era's new headgear, the fez; he was ennobled in 1851 by the King of Sardinia. (Institut National de Patrimoine, Tunis.)

of Ahmad Bey's minister of foreign affairs, Giuseppe Raffo (1795–1862), or Joseph Marie Raffo, offers an example of how the system worked.[96] Raffo, like so many of his fellow "Europeans," had climbed the social ladder thanks to intimate connections to the palace with its multifarious networks. Born at the Bardo, Raffo was the eleventh child of Marie Terrasson and a Genoese artisan, Gian-Battista, from Chiavari, captured by Tunisian corsairs in 1771 and later attached to the court in his capacity as a master watchmaker. Thus began his son Joseph's engagement in palace service at a young age to Husayn Bey, for whom he served as first interpreter prior to being named minister of foreign affairs. Another critical tie was that one of Raffo's sisters, Elena-Grazia (b. 1779), converted to Islam and wed Mustafa Bey, the father of Ahmad Bey.

Raffo remained a devout Catholic as he served five Muslim rulers; he was even granted an audience with the Pope during one of his frequent visits to Italy. Raffo's residence in the Bardo was adorned with Catholic iconography and he acted as a great patron for the Church as well as for the first female Catholic missionaries in Tunisia, the Sisters of Saint-Joseph. Through beylical largesse, Raffo amassed a personal fortune, including the right to exploit the rich tuna fishery at Sidi Dawad on the Cap Bon, a thriving business owned by the family until 1905. He assiduously courted marks of distinction and decorations from leading European states, including the British Crown, and was elevated to minor nobility by the Italian government, which also extended protection. For outside observers, the astonishing social mobility enjoyed by individuals such as Raffo was incomprehensible. Indeed, the American consul to Tunis, Nicholson, barely contained his amazement at Raffo's good fortune in life, characterizing him condescendingly in 1860 as "originally a common servant."[97]

The Cubisol family's trajectory differs from the Raffos because the mechanism that landed them in Tunis was not capture on the high seas but rather the search for a better living. Joseph-François Cubisol (1752–1822) hailed from a family of architects originally from Nîmes, although he was born in La Ciotat in 1752. A master carpenter, Joseph-François had come to Tunisia voluntarily to serve the beys in his capacity as a skilled craftsman; he died and was buried in Tunis. Cubisol's son, Charles (1817–1868), was born in La Goulette and served as French attaché in the port between 1843 and 1854, before being named vice-consul in 1855.[98]

The widow Gibson's life story provides a contrast both with Raffo and with Cubisol. She was the wife of John Gibson, the British vice-consul who died in 1833 after "imprudently exposing himself to malaria on a shooting party among the marshes some distance from Tunis."[99] Burdened with eight children, Mrs. Gibson chose not to return to England, remaining in La Marsa in the family home until her death and burial at the age of seventy-three. Her eldest son, a reputed wastrel, served as the paterfamilias from 1833 on until he expired a decade later from "wounds received while defending himself against a gang of thieves who attacked his house."[100] Their tombstones remain in Saint George's cemetery in Tunis today.

Another group of creoles were Franco-Italian traders, artisans, and workers originally attached to the coral and fishing industries around the small island of Tabarka in the north, from whence their name; others resided in Ghar al-Milh, or Porto Farina, until the port silted up. The Tabarkans were at times considered indigenous Christians because they had resided in the country for decades and were well-acculturated, but the English traveler James Richardson (1806–1851), had only harsh words to say about them: "Upon the whole I would rather trust a respectable Moor than a native Christian. There is a vulgar saying here: 'God defend me from a Algerine Turk, a Tripolitan Jew, and a Tunisian Christian.' The low character of the Tunisian Christians may be traced to their principally originating from the Genoese colonists of Tabarca [sic], for after this island was ceded to the Bey, all the Tabarchines settled in Tunis. Now the Tabarchines were little better than a convict settlement."[101] While the Tabarkans had practiced endogamy, which preserved their distinctiveness in earlier periods, by the mid-nineteenth century intermarriage with other Christians of Tunisia represented less of a *mésalliance* than previously.

Critical to the creole community were marriage patterns and the fact that family dynasties monopolized offices or vice-consular posts for generations. Where and how they lived, with whom they socialized, and the languages they employed operated as yardsticks of local and transnational connectedness. Also significant was where they educated children, the frequency and duration of visits to Europe or elsewhere in the Mediterranean, and where they died and were buried—if fate offered the choice. Due to their command of Mediterranean languages and, as importantly, intimate knowledge of Tunisian as well as European ways of doing things, Raffo and others like him served as cultural mediators and political brokers for newly stationed diplomats, and for the steadily climbing number of speculators, investors, travelers, and tourists, by introducing them to the unwritten norms and codes of local society.[102] Therefore, the concept of creole aligns with other categories of identity and belonging in port cities, such as the polyvalent designation "Moor."

Property rights were central to relationships between creoles and the Husaynid political class. Theoretically, resident foreigners could not own immovable property until beylical decrees later in the century enshrined those rights in law, but in reality some palace insiders, as seen in the Raffos' tuna fishery, gained various kinds of property, although whether rights devolved to descendants was subject to negotiation.[103] One of the major processes at work throughout the Ottoman Empire in the nineteenth century was the concerted effort by resident European traders, financiers, and speculators to establish secure property rights whether by treaty, force, or subterfuge. During the eighteenth century, the Husaynids had been relatively adept at managing the interface between the productive sectors of the economy and the outside world, but the political and fiscal challenges of the second half of the nineteenth century represented something wholly new.[104] Growing insolvency was the consequence of expensive modernization programs, spectacular cases of treasury fraud, usurious European loans, the palace's growing predilection for imported luxury goods, and relentless foreign pressures for commercial and other concessions, above all property rights.

Consuls, Diplomats, and Floating Others

Consuls tended to remain in the post for extended periods, particularly in the early part of the century when transportation was slow and dangerous. Lengthy stays acculturated them and facilitated the transmission of customary ways of doing things so critical to the administration of justice. Until at least midcentury, the consular elite shared a common culture forged by years in North Africa, the Ottoman Empire, or in the Mediterranean world. Success in managing daily relations between protégés and local Muslim society depended upon several factors. The more culturally attuned to North Africa's Arabo-Islamic-Ottoman civilization, the more effective a consul was in calming troubled waters—or stirring them up. Most were conversant with the principal languages, first and foremost Arabic, followed by Italian, and later French, employing them regularly in official and personal communication. As important was the balance of power within the bey's ruling circle at any given moment and the play of forces among states with a stake in Tunisia.[105]

Sir Thomas Reade served for nearly a quarter of a century as British consul, from 1824 until his death in Tunis in 1849. Reade's son Richard, born in La Marsa in 1829, later assumed his father's functions in 1879, after earlier postings in Morocco, Egypt, Spain, and Smyrna. Not all British officials were as upright as Reade, who won guarded praise from the period's principal Arabic chronicler, Ahmad b. Abi al-Diyaf, who was a contemporary of Reade. Another English agent had incurred the bey's wrath on a number of occasions for his outrageous public behavior before succumbing to a fatal illness, leaving substantial debts unpaid. But most consuls were quite chummy with the ruling family. Reade's successor, Louis Ferriere, did an oil portrait of one of the rulers that hung in the Bardo's interior apartments; he must have spent considerable time at the palace to execute the painting.[106]

Ferriere's successor, Sir Richard Wood (1806–1900), had a rather different background from his two predecessors. Consul general to Tunis from 1856 to 1879, he not only mastered Arabic, Italian, and French but also Turkish and Greek, the felicitous result of birth and upbringing in Istanbul, where Wood's father, George, had served as a high-ranking dragoman to the British embassy. Educated in Exeter, young Wood was sent to Syria in 1831, ostensibly to learn

Arabic and garner support for British policies among Lebanese chieftains, but he may well have been a spy. Appointed in 1834 as dragoman in Istanbul, by 1841 Wood held the important post of consul in Damascus, where he became a local *za'im* (local big man, boss) as well as personally acquiring local properties under shady circumstances. His linguistic prowess, together with generations of familiarity with Islamic-Ottoman culture, made him the perfect diplomat, although at times he tended to identify too closely with Ottoman or Tunisian interests. When Wood retired in 1879, he left for Nice, where he died and was buried in 1900; but he spent summers in La Goulette with his eldest daughter, Farida, who had married into the Raffo family.[107] In short, he was both a transimperial actor and a not-quite-creole whose offspring joined the ranks of the Tunis creoles.

Wood's French counterpart, Léon Roches (1809–1901), held the office of consul general to Tunis from July 1855 to October 1863 and boasted an adventuresome life as well. After a time in Morocco, Roches went to Algeria, where he served as Amir 'Abd al-Qadir's secretary in 1837; his perfect command of Arabic rendered him an invaluable interpreter and double agent. Subsequently he was named to Trieste, Tripoli, and then Tunis. (Some sources claim that Roches converted to Islam.)[108] The life trajectories of Wood, Roches, and many others render the label "European" problematic; perhaps "Crypto-European" (as suggested by Edmund Burke III) is more appropriate. Monopolizing diplomatic postings over generations in the Levant, Malta, Greece, and North Africa, these clans forged other networks through shared commercial interests, the patronage of local Muslim elites, and intermarriage. The degree of endogamy within the Tunis consular corps was noteworthy, although Protestants and Catholics did not marry; for example, the Dutch vice-consul wed his daughter to an English Protestant but Wood, a Roman Catholic, gave his eldest daughter in marriage to the Catholic Raffos.[109]

As steamships and other forms of modern communication became widely available and the exercise of diplomacy was bureaucratized, the consular corps remained in-country for shorter periods of time and were less integrated into local society. Unlike the Raffos and other Christian families residing in the Bardo palace complex, creoles and diplomats mainly lived in Tunis (a few in La Goulette), but they shared in the summer rituals of the palace as the Husaynid family and court relocated to the sea.

FROM FUNDUQ TO MEDITERRANEAN VILLA

Until the early nineteenth century, city spaces and buildings allocated to foreign residents were regulated by local interpretations of the Capitulations, bilateral treaties, and custom. The *droit de résidence* (right of residence) was one of the fundamental concessions that the Ottoman Empire conceded to European states under the *imtiyazat* (or Capitulations). The Ottoman governors of Tunisia, and their successors, the Muradid and Husaynid dynasties, granted buildings within city walls and land for cemeteries extra muros, such as Saint George's Anglican cemetery constructed around 1640 but now in a different location.

In 1660 a French funduq was constructed adjacent to the English complex at the edge of the madina on Rue de l'Ancienne Douane near the Sea Gate, where Europeans and other foreign Christians, whether resident or *de passage*, were concentrated in the "quarter of the Francs."[110] Until 1760, the largely Italian Capuchins lived in the French funduq, where they conducted Catholic services in the consular chapel dedicated to Saint Louis. However, in 1767 the Husaynid ruler constructed another building nearby, which became the Church of Sainte-Croix.[111] Placed under France's protection, the church was administered by French and Italian Capuchin monks, who registered births, marriages, and deaths as well as caring for the Saint-Antoine graveyard dating to the early seventeenth century. Other consulates had chapels within their extensive compounds for resident nationals, travelers, merchants, or sailors. From 1769 on, the Maltese Capuchins administered a chapel in La Goulette whose placement proved advantageous in the following century when the port came to be heavily populated by Sicilians and Maltese. During the nineteenth century, Italian Capuchins and French diplomats were often at odds as were different Catholic missionary orders; local tensions reflected struggles in Europe and poisoned the well of interfaith communal relations.[112]

Paradoxically, the presence of cemeteries is most revealing of the attitudes of a Muslim state toward nonsubject Christians, since the existence of visible non-Muslim religious and residential edifices in Ottoman cities signaled the "willingness on the part of Muslim society to ensure an architecturally-appealing residence for European traders, diplomats, and visitors."[113] The relative absence in European cities, such as Marseilles, of commensurate spaces for Muslim, Jewish, or Ottoman Christian traders and travelers to live, store goods, conduct business, worship, and lay to rest those whom death found far from home, stands in stark contrast. The swell in the urban population of Tunis due to trans-Mediterranean immigration rendered buildings and city space a scare resource and contentious issue. Already in 1831, Reade, by then in-country for more than six years, decried the housing shortage:

> With respect to the Consulate House in Tunis, I beg to inform you that it is absolutely uninhabitable. It has been built upwards of one hundred and fifty years ago, and has not been kept in this state of repair which I conceive it ought to have been. The rain penetrates into every room, and the foundation has in some places given way, endangering the upper walks so much that if it is not very soon taken down there is every apprehension of some part giving way. It has been held from this [Husaynid] government by the British government . . . from the period the

Consular establishment was formed here ... I was obliged to hire one [house] in the country [on the La Marsa road] upon my arrival, not being enabled by any means whatever to procure one in the Town, at least in that part where the Christians live.[114]

Two decades later, a full-blown crisis had developed: "In Tunis there is a [residence] called 'Arisha' that shelters about thirty Maltese families and is too small. . . . This is because it is difficult to find habitation in the city."[115] The movement of people out of the funduqs' confines and into adjacent neighborhoods, or later to the newly reclaimed land between the walled city and lake, held momentous consequences for social life in the capital as did the installation of impoverished Maltese and Sicilian families in *wakala* in the madina or its suburbs. For the fortunate newcomer, family contacts, neighbors, communal networks, or informal associations provided a place to stay and work. The poorer Europeans lived crowded together, eking out livelihoods as casual laborers, bakers, butchers, carpenters, peddlers, carters, prostitutes, and beggars. Gradually hotels, cafés, and boisterous taverns were established; small shops sometimes illegally sold spirits, kif, tobacco, and gunpowder in the emerging "underground" economy. Neighborhoods associated with particular immigrant communities became the favored haunt for clandestine, often nocturnal, wheeling and dealing in contraband goods, in which many city inhabitants actively participated. Certain types of work, whether in Tunis proper or the port, allowed some actors to organize black market exchanges. In La Goulette, Sicilians increasingly worked as dockers unloading vessels, porters hauling merchandise to the customs house, and boatmen transporting goods and human cargo across the lake to the Sea Gate. The Maltese moved into carting and the carriage trade, shuttling people around city streets in small wooden vehicles and, in the process, became messengers and purveyors of information and rumors as well as forbidden items. Since local, regional, and trans-Mediterranean smuggling operations were combined with family-run trades, it was difficult to discern where legal and illicit exchanges began and ended.[116]

Small wonder that the city's bourgeois inhabitants, above all the baldi, viewed quarters like Malta Saghira (Little Malta) as inherently disorderly, unsafe, and morally blameworthy. Not far away from the "street of the Maltese," Italians and Sicilians settled on Rue de la Commission, which followed the lower madina's outer walls and gradually came to be lined by coffeehouses, taverns, and a bit later ice-cream parlors. By the eve of the Protectorate, these two streets, plus Rue des Glacières (street of the ice makers), formed the nucleus of Maltese and Italian neighborhoods still perceptible by their distinctive architecture, though now in a state of disrepair.[117]

STRANGERS OR FAMILIAR FOREIGNERS?

How did city natives "name" old-timers and newcomers, whether labor migrants, traders, travelers, tourists, and adventurers? State records and chronicles drew upon a range of descriptors: *al-ra'iya* (subjects, literally "flock"), *nasara* (Christians), or *ajnabi/ajanib* (foreign, foreigners). Ahmad Bey's response in 1845 to resident Christians regarding the shortage of urban space referred to petitioners as *al-afranij* (Franks), *ahl uruba* (people of Europe), and *al-millat al-masihiya* (Christian millets); Church leaders were designated *a'yan*. Another term used by the populace was *rumis* (Christians), which had negative connotations. But geographical markers, such as *ahl Malta* (people of Malta) or *ahl Sisilya* (people of Sicily), were employed as well. Tunis natives probably placed northern Italians and French at the top of the social hierarchy; at the bottom were Maltese and Sicilians whose work, lack of education, and behavior conspired in inferior positioning.[118] Depending upon the observer and context, social designations might be fluid based upon (assumed) place of origin, rank, profession, and, of course, religion.

The nature and tenor of daily relations among religious communities are dealt with in subsequent chapters. Suffice it to say that street conflict or communal quarrels tend to be better documented than mundane quotidian social exchanges, which should give us pause; and perceived religious and/or national differences, when invoked as the root of social strife, need to be carefully scrutinized. Nevertheless, tensions or clashes along confessional lines were most likely to erupt in two instances. Transgressions of laws or implicit codes forbidding sexual contact between Muslim women and non-Muslim men provoked uproar, as did some instances of "love with the wrong person" within different Catholic communities; even prostitution theoretically was to obey sexual boundaries based upon religion.[119] In addition, hostilities between European states and Tunisia, for example, the Sardinian crisis of 1832–1833, or between the Ottomans and European nations, such as the Greek wars of the 1820s, triggered confessionalism. The 1830 invasion of Algiers stirred up animosity toward resident Christians, as did the relentless flow of news detailing atrocities suffered by the Algerians, which inevitably reached Tunisia with refugees. The proclamation of the 1861 constitution, ostensibly erasing legal distinctions based upon religion and nationality, sparked street demonstrations suffused with anti-Christian sentiment. During the 1864 revolt, lines of demarcation followed confessional and national lines; many European residents fled their homes to take refuge onboard ships anchored at sea.[120] Predictably, the French invasion and occupation of 1881 provoked attacks upon Europeans and native allies in the city and countryside.

WEARING DIFFERENCE: CLOTHING IN THE CITY

In the press of the crowd on busy streets, how did city inhabitants, whether "authentic" baldi, creoles, or recent arrivals, identify one another? Here the old saw that "clothes make the man or woman" rings true, because clothing situated individuals precisely in the urban order of things by visually communicating social distinctions and hierarchy. Clothing has always operated as marker and symbol of profession, ethnicity, class, religion, and gender: "as both material and metaphor for the social question."[121] Differences might be subtle, suggested by the quality of cloth in a *jibba, qaftan, ha'ik,* or *burnus:* "a man's rank was judged by the shape, the folds, the color, and the material of his turban."[122] Or, since certain colors were permitted for some but forbidden to others, clothing could be visually resonant, in some respects alarmingly so. Pascal Gandolphe made the mistake of leaving the French funduq in 1781 sporting a bright green cravat, which attracted the wrath of an unidentified, perhaps deranged, assailant who stabbed him to death for blaspheming Islam by wearing a color reserved for descendants of the Prophet.[123] But dress came to represent a sort of legal garment because it translated in concrete form the jurisdictional place of an individual and the legal regime that he or she was under. Another designation used by beylical subjects, whether Muslim or Jewish, as well as by other communities, was inspired neither by religion nor by ethnicity but rather by legal protections; for example "Dimitri L'Inglizi" was a shorthand reference frequently employed by city folk to identify a Greek (or anyone else) who claimed English protégé status.

As was true in the Ottoman Empire, clothing was subject to state regulation modified by local custom and interpretation. The political messages driving "sartorial politics" was best illustrated by the apparel of religious minorities.[124] In the first decades of the nineteenth century, headgear assumed new meanings, since it communicated the status of those under foreign protection. By the 1820s, sumptuary laws for Jews were not always heeded; some had adopted European apparel. In response perhaps to the political humiliations of the 1816 Exmouth expedition, Mahmud Bey ordered all Jews, irrespective of nationality, to remove their European headgear; the "war of the hats" was in full swing. An English Jew from Gibraltar under British protection was arrested for refusing to conform to the dress code, unleashing a diplomatic crisis. The affair resulted in a compromise: European Jews could wear European hats; Leghorn Jews, an intermediate group and commercial aristocracy, were authorized to don white headgear; and Tunisian Jews had to return to their dark *calotte* (cap wrapped in a blue or black turban), setting them off from Muslims wearing the red shashiya.[125] But the clothing wars were not confined to Tunisia.

In his travels across the Maghrib and Mediterranean in the 1840s, Richardson observed sartorial shifts among Moroccan Jews in ports open to foreign trade that resonated with Tunis and elsewhere:

> When I was lately at Mogador, the European coat was an object of great distinction for a Barbary Jew to obtain and most surprisingly dazzled the eyes of the native Jewish ladies, and always had the effect of accelerating a matrimonial arrangement the delicate sensibilities of the Maroquine [Moroccan] Jewess being keenly alive to the distinction and protection which her husband acquired by putting on the dress of the Christians. I was told when at Tangier so many Barbary Jews had been over to Gibraltar and had adopted European dress that the [Moroccan] Emperor alarmed at such an innovation, which clothed and coated every one of his subjects with the protection of Europeans and put them almost beyond his power sent down an imperial order from Meknes to make them undress.[126]

After 1857, sumptuary laws for native Jews were abolished or slowly disappeared. However, as late as the 1920s, Tunisian Jews born before the Protectorate, including the grand rabbis, wore the shashiya and "traditional Arab" clothing; those born after 1881 tended to don European apparel.[127] But in the period that concerns us, city residents wore their "national costume." Maltese male laborers wore a distinctive garb as did Sicilian fishermen; Greeks were distinguished by the "distinctive shade of red" in their dress that identified them to passers-by. However, sartorial fashions in the precolonial era were far from stable and read in various ways: "dressed like a European" referred to social peers who had discarded "traditional" clothing for the somber costume of middle-class Europeans.[128]

Indigenous women's clothing signaled belonging to a religious community as well as to a specific village, region, or tribal group, although, when outside, urban women covered up under dark cloaks and veils. Tunisian Jewish women went about in the streets veiled in roughly the same manner as their Muslim counterparts, although they did not cover the entire face but only their mouths (true for urban Jewish women in Algiers at the time). Other nationalities, such as the Maltese women, donned long black cloaks when in public; their dark, unadorned bonnets, known as *faldettas,* were described as "immense," with long, attached veils reaching to the waist.[129] However, in the privacy of the home, or during social visits between households, sartorial codes were relaxed. When English ladies visited the bey's chief wife and her entourage at the palace in 1844, the Husaynid princesses initially appeared cross because their female guests wore drab, black garments inside the harim—the color and simplicity of their clothing was interpreted as a social affront. Once it was explained that these women had recently lost family members and were in mourning, the Tunisian princesses proved most welcoming. The clothing worn by bourgeois European women or their Tunisian hosts during ritualized palace visits functioned as a form of communication and amusement; the princesses found bonnets and corsets to be particularly curious.[130]

BABEL:
LANGUAGES AND COMMUNICATION IN THE CITY

Location in the central Mediterranean corridor means that Tunisia has always been a polyglot place, although languages constantly relocated and words moved about with dizzying speed at times.

> With regard to the prevalence of European languages in North Africa, the Spanish is spoken by Moors and Jews . . . in the south of Morocco, running up and along the coast as far as Oran, in Algeria; then from Algiers or Bona, begins the Italian, passing through all Tunis and Tripoli, and makes the tour of the whole of the Levant. Of course, these European languages are very imperfectly and corruptly spoken, and form the chief ingredients of the celebrated *Lingua Franca* now so universally known as to need no illustration: at the same time, in every part of the coast of North Africa are persons and a great many who speak the Spanish and Italian languages with purity, whilst in Tunis may be found professors of European languages, especially Italian and French.[131]

For our purposes, the critical question is how language, identity, and power were intermeshed. And heightened population displacements render the issue of communication central, although for the precolonial period it has hardly been studied. David Prochaska's work on popular street dialects of colonial Algiers has no counterpart for Tunis, and the languages of daily intercourse remain uncertain. The first systematic effort to commit the various patois to writing or later recording only began in the post–World War I era.[132] From the reign of Hammuda Bey, Arabic became the first language of the governing elite, although documents directed to the Porte continued to be written in Ottoman Turkish. The progressive decline of Turkish was largely due to the fact that the Husaynids no longer recruited troops from Anatolia after the 1811 janissary revolt. Kabyle forms of Berber (Amazigh) were spoken by the redoubtable Zuwawa (or Zouaves, in French) tribesmen from the mountains in eastern Algeria enlisted by the Tunisian state as military auxiliaries for their martial skills and inability to communicate with the local populace. Garrisoned around the country, and above all, in the capital city region, the Kabyles numbered between ten and twenty thousand in the early nineteenth century, but the formation of Ahmad Bey's modern army rendered them obsolete. The Zuwawa married local women, took up professions as artisans or cultivators, and gradually became more or less indistinguishable from local society, although names, dress, and language gave them away for a while.[133]

The slave trade was another major source of linguistic pluralism about which there is little evidence. Clearly a number of languages were spoken at the Bardo, in other palaces, and in the great households with large cohorts of domestic slaves and servants; the women's quarters housed people from Africa, the Mediterranean, Georgia, or Circassia, making for a linguistic stew. After the murder of 'Uthman Bey (r. 1813–1814) during a dynastic quarrel in 1814, his wife, Lalla Manana, then with child, was imprisoned. After she gave birth, the infant was placed in the care of an African woman, who raised him in isolation from the rest of the court for years. However, her language differed so from local Arabic that, when the hapless prince was finally released from prison, "he could barely make himself understood to fellow Tunisians."[134]

Until late in the nineteenth century, a kind of Italian, referred to as the "Italian of Barbary," constituted the regency's diplomatic language and lingua franca, although what it looked like in earlier periods remains uncertain. In *Voyage dans les Régences*, first published in the late eighteenth century, Jean-André Peyssonnel characterized the Italian employed at the Husaynid court thus: "The reigning bey speaks Italian or *petit moresque* a corrupted Italian mixed with French and Spanish." If the rulers spoke some form of Italian, they did not necessarily read it. "Bad Italian"—in the eyes of purists—was employed by the Husaynids for diplomatic and commercial exchanges with Europe until Italian was gradually, although not completely, replaced by French at the end of the nineteenth century. Christian Windler advances an important argument concerning Italian's wide currency, a fundamental difference marking Tunis off from Istanbul or Cairo: because *petit moresque* served for communication, it made Tunisia appear less foreign, strangely near, to Europeans.[135]

The mothers or wives of several Husaynid rulers were of Italian origins, from Genoa or micro-islands, such as San Pietro, off the southwest coast of Sardinia. And the practice of incorporating captives from the central Mediterranean corridor into the palace meant that some retainers and servants spoke various forms of Italian. Finally, the geographical shift in the recruitment of mamluks, away from Anatolia, the Balkans, or Circassia, to adjacent regions reinforced Sicilo-Italian linguistic and cultural sway. The significance of the "Italian of Barbary" for intercommunal communication may have meant that Corsicans—who spoke a form of ancient Tuscan and did not understand French until late in the nineteenth century—felt linguistically more at home, or at least less *depaysé*, than they might have elsewhere in diaspora.[136] In the *longue durée*, the prevalence of exchanges with Italianate regions should come as no surprise; from at least the Hafsid era (1229–1574), Tunis was peopled by traders and merchants from the Mediterranean to the Indian Ocean, but Catalonians and Italians always predominated.

In the multilingual street, hints of how people in Tunis communicated with each other on a daily basis, despite linguistic variability, are found in legal proceedings and travel accounts. When Joseph Greaves of the British Church Missionary Society arrived from Malta in October 1824, he brought five hundred copies of the Bible in Arabic, Italian, Greek, and Hebrew as well as antislavery tracts for distribution. During his tour of the Tunis slave market, Greaves was accompanied by a Maltese interpreter who spoke Italian to a "Moor," who in turn questioned the African female slaves in their own language about the conditions of enslavement.[137] The presence of large communities of North Africans from Algeria (the most numerous), Morocco, Tripolitania, and Egypt meant that many types of Arabic or Berber would have been heard in the streets, as well as Maltese and forms of Greek and Spanish to name only the most important. And as the "Italians" grew in numbers, a Sicilian dialect enriched with Neapolitan, Maltese, and Arabic expressions became the idiom of choice for denizens of the "quarter of the Franks."

During heated encounters in certain milieus, cursing and cussing drew upon Arabic, Maltese, and Sicilian, irrespective of the disputants' ethnic origins. The polyglot nature of invective in Mediterranean ports, such as La Goulette, is illustrated by an incident from 1837 in which a traveler arrived from Malta bearing a British passport identifying him as a Spaniard. A huge row broke out with the French vice-consul, Gaspary, who claimed that the Spaniard called "me a dog and a swine and insulted me in Arabic, Spanish, and Italian."[138] Finally, maritime dialects *(sabir)* were spoken on the North African littoral. Of varying mélanges of Arabic, Provençal, Italian, and Spanish, *sabir* was understood in ports or on the high seas but served only the most basic communication needs because of its restricted vocabulary.[139] While the Tunisian Arabic of the capital city was the most widely used medium of communication, as one approached Halq al-Wad or other ports, *sabir* became more prevalent.

Ability to navigate the linguistic pluralism of Tunis marked the individual as a player in the local culture—or the reverse, as not in tune with communicative complexities. Some were better armed to play the language game—the Maltese first and foremost, as they frequently commanded some form of Italian or English. Moreover, Maltese is a Semitic language with affinities to Tunisian Arabic; thus learning the local Arabic was relatively easy for the Maltese. Yet operating across linguistic fault lines was not always viewed positively; the Maltese were castigated by northern Europeans as "untrustworthy" precisely because they acted as communication brokers, as was true in other port cities. Polyglot intermediaries mobilizing local languages, however critical in a city of Babel, were suspect due to the presumed alignment of language with identity and political allegiance.[140]

But how and why had these "new" newcomers come in the first place? What choices or plans had gone awry and brought them to North Africa, and not somewhere else? What role did sheer chance play? And as importantly, why had they decided to leave home? What macrolevel forces lured—or forced—them from homes and villages across the water? At one level, elements such as class or social rank, profession, age, and gender predisposed certain groups to strike out for North Africa or elsewhere and others to stay put. At another level, cataclysmic events, such as the 1830 French invasion and the decision to make Algeria into a settler colony proved decisive in convincing people to search for work and fortune in Barbary. In the process, the older axis of mobilities in Mediterranean North Africa was reoriented; traditional currents of population movements that had long privileged exchanges with other Maghribi states, the Ottoman Empire, or sub-Saharan Africa shifted under the weight of people on the move. The next chapter assumes a hang-glider perspective of the central Mediterranean corridor as well as the rest of the sea to answer these questions, to the extent that sources permit.

2

Detours

Migrations in a Mobile World

Husayn Bey was clearly displeased and complained yet again in 1827 about paupers arriving from the Maltese islands to the British consul, who promised to "inform the governor of Malta of His Highness' observations . . . I have already written about this subject to the governor of Malta. If he has not found that the number of Maltese is rising in Tunis now, it is because usually there are as many who leave as who arrive. This fact can be verified easily by the number of passports which are always deposed at the British consulate [in Tunis]."[1]

But things scarcely improved in the next years. In 1829, a formal protest "was made by Hassuna [al-Murali], the Bey's interpreter, by reason of the increase in the number of Maltese settling at Tunis during the time of the country being in a state of distress, and which it has been for sometime past owing to the failure of the crops of oil and grain."[2] More grievous problems lay ahead. As gale-force winds gathered off the Gulf of Tunis, a ship arrived in the winter of 1836 bearing Maltese passengers of "different ages, sexes, and conditions." The initial refusal by Mustafa Bey to allow British protégés to land in La Goulette created an international "boat people crisis." While negotiations dragged on, the hapless passengers remained on the ship battered by high seas. In London's view, withholding permission to disembark when peace prevailed constituted a violation of treaties between the British Crown and the Ottoman Regency of Tunis. Threats of involving the Porte in the standoff and warships dispatched from Valletta eventually convinced the bey to change his position by April 1837.[3] Several years later, a ship from Istanbul sailed into La Goulette with a Circassian mamluk, Khayr al-Din, recently enlisted to serve the new Husaynid ruler, Ahmad Bey. The young man proved a loyal servant as well as enthusiastic reformer and brilliant statesman. Later appointed minister of the navy, Khayr al-Din grasped the implications of immigration into the regency and, through his own wide-ranging travels, realized that the world had become a smaller place.

Incessant squabbles over Maltese immigration and Khayr al-Din's arrival in 1839 from the Ottoman capital are emblematic of the changing dynamic of trans-Mediterranean mobilities that marked the century. From the 1820s until 1881, Tunisian officials, European consuls, and capital city inhabitants struggled to come to grips with the newcomers whose social class and sheer numbers gave alarm. That the pile of Maltese passports on Reade's desk remained more or less the same in 1827, no matter how many protégés departed, suggests that a pattern of "circular migration" was emerging—indeed a diaspora was in the making. Not mentioned is that the exact number of people coming and going could never be ascertained, since a lively trade in undocumented migrants was taking shape. Genuinely concerned, Reade had repeatedly contacted Malta's governor, apparently without much success, because British authorities were either indifferent to or openly welcomed the loss, however temporary, of "surplus" population. North Africa was on the cusp of becoming a social dump, a political landfill, for Europe's human castoffs. How might the historian think about the tangled problems raised by people on the move in the central Mediterranean corridor and beyond?

Over a decade ago, Leslie Moch underlined the importance of "mundane movements"—seemingly insignificant displacements from village to nearby town or from town to city. Somewhat in contrast, Mary W. Helms observed that "the morally (and politically) uncontrolled frontier need not be geographically very far away to be perceived as a 'distant' place."[4] Taken together, these reflections on distance and mobility suggest the ways in which migration transforms the far and near, the foreign and strange, and how danger and displacement can be either connected or uncoupled. The notion of spatially inconsequential, but critical, movement invites us to consider if the passage over the narrow waterway separating Tunisia from Malta or Sicily was mundane and how and why that might have altered after 1830, 1850, or 1881. Did the fact that the Maltese spoke a language distantly akin to Tunisian Arabic, or that Italo-Sicilian dialects constituted the regency's diplomatic lingua franca, render the voyage to North Africa less daunting? Since most subsistence migrants were Catholics, while Tunisia was a Muslim land, did religious difference make the journey seem perilous, at least in the years after abolition of the Christian slave trade? How did France's decision to make Algeria a settler colony transform migratory patterns in the central Mediterranean, notably the Tunis region? And why leave home in the first place? What forces encouraged or compelled island folk and others to depart for North Africa—and not another destination? Ultimately, one must ask whether the people in motion regarded themselves as migrants per se and, if not, how they experienced their own subjectivities in the places of self-exile.

This chapter provides a macrolevel charting of diverse population movements from the eve of France's invasion of Algeria to the Protectorate—as if the observer occupied a point somewhere above the sea—and an up-close ethnographic treatment of the people who left home temporarily or permanently, willingly or unwillingly, or somewhere in between. The primary coordinates are first and foremost North Africa, particularly Mediterranean Tunisia and Algeria. We observe people in motion mainly, but not exclusively, from the Gulf of Tunis, which offers front-row seats for viewing the full spectrum of migratory behaviors, their causes and consequences. One principal argument—that Algeria's conquest provoked not only substantial immigration to precolonial Tunisia but also displacements across the Mediterranean—takes the story farther afield. But first: what did older geographies of movement and travel look like before 1830?

GEOGRAPHIES: CAPTIVES, RENEGADES, AND OTHER BORDER CROSSERS

Mediterranean corsairs had raided each others' ships and villages for centuries, hauling off booty as well as captives, both Muslim and Christian, which rendered "the Other," an object of intense fear and loathing. Bin Diyaf's chronicle opens the account of Ahmad Bey's reign with the new ruler's parentage: "his mother, a slave girl taken in a raid upon the island of St. Pietro, came as a small child with her mother and her sister [to Tunis]."[5] One of the last attacks of this magnitude, the raid occurred in 1798 off the southwestern coast of Sardinia and netted treasures from the local church as well as 150 young girls for the Tunisian corsairs. But small-scale raiding persisted into the first decades of the next century. In 1815, the *kahiya*'s ship arrived in La Goulette with "five wretched Sardinians captured on land in Sardinia" and four Corsican sailors seized while fishing, although their fate seemed brighter since they were delivered to the Bardo palace where they "demanded assistance from the French consul."[6] Until 1816 hundreds of enslaved Christians were held in the Tunis bagnios, although under highly variable conditions; some were allowed to practice trades or crafts on the side, others were condemned to hard labor. Nevertheless, the systematic, legally sanctioned brutality suffered by the poor wretches banished to bagnios in penal colonies, such as French Guyana, was absent for the most part.[7]

During the heyday of Mediterranean corsair activity, ship captains, adventurers, or sailors serving Christian kings threw in their lot with the Muslim side, at times voluntarily, at others after capture at sea; some switched back and forth as the political winds demanded. Renegades settled in Tunis, Algiers, and other Ottoman port cities, at times marrying into local families; the most talented became *ra'is,* or captain, but risked imprisonment or death if they fell into Christian hands. This fact may have inhibited legitimate maritime trade between North Africa and Europe in earlier centuries because renegade ship masters were reluctant to put in to ports where they might be snatched up.[8] During the corsair centuries, countless North Africans were held as slaves in Europe, although their stories for the most part remain untold.[9] In 1816, just before Admiral Exmouth set out for North Africa, an English ship arrived in La Goulette from Leghorn with a Tuscan diplomatic envoy to conclude a peace treaty with the bey. Presumably negotiations entailed exchanges of captives, since onboard the ship "were forty-eight Tunisian slaves who had been found in Tuscany."[10]

Older historical treatments of the corsair epoch portrayed the Mediterranean as divided into warring and thus utterly distinct Muslim-Christian zones. This has been challenged on a number of fronts, not least because raiding of whatever sort facilitated transactions between the Maghrib and Europe. A type of maritime brigandage, raiding afforded a livelihood for Mediterranean islands and islanders and at times blurred the lines between privateering and corsair activity.[11] In this culture and political economy, captives furnished servile labor—mainly as galley slaves, domestic workers, or concubines—or handsome revenues from the ransom racket. Christian and Muslim maritime powers played the same game, although the elaborate system for ransoming Christian captives in North African ports, largely the work of Redemptionist orders, is better documented than the liberation of Muslims.[12] The series of treaties imposed upon North African states and naval expeditions in 1816 and 1819 ended, for the most part, this particular system of forced migration. What about other types of trans-Mediterranean movements taking place across a continuum running from voluntary to involuntary displacement?

GEOGRAPHIES:
THE CENTRAL MEDITERRANEAN CORRIDOR

The emphasis on Christian islanders or southern Europeans as migrants to the nineteenth-century Maghrib suggests that North Africans were disinclined to travel or try their luck away from home. Earlier scholars maintained that Muslims did not venture freely to Christian lands out of innate hostility, inspired by religious precepts. According to the older historiography, antipathy or indifference, together with lack of intellectual curiosity, conspired against first-hand contacts with, and knowledge of, Europe. Scholarship now argues that, while Muslims did not visit the Christian shores of the Mediterranean in great numbers until the nineteenth century, exchanges had always existed. Recent research has uncovered hitherto ignored Arabic travel accounts narrating sojourns in

European cities that contradict ideologically driven claims of Muslim aversion toward all things Christian and Western.[13]

North Africans from coastal cities, or even from desert entrepôts, took to the sea in search of adventure and fortune, as seen in the story of 'Ali bin 'Uthman al-Hammi, born sometime in the 1770s. Originally from the oases of southwestern Tunisia near the Algerian border, 'Ali made his way to Tunis, somehow joined the Napoleonic expedition to Egypt in 1798, fought against fellow Muslims, and served in Napoleon's Mamluk Imperial Guard for fourteen years before rejoining his home village on the Saharan fringe. He spent time in Marseilles before being rescued by Tunisian sailors aboard a vessel in port from a "race riot" against the Muslims and other easterners who had accompanied the French army back from Egypt.[14]

At roughly the same time that 'Ali journeyed to Egypt with the revolutionary army, a mamluk from the bey's court, Hassuna al-Murali (d. 1848), was captured by English corsairs and taken to England. Al-Murali spent nine years there, adding English to his command of Turkish, Arabic, and probably Italian. As his countryman 'Ali had fought with the French, so al-Murali acted as interpreter to the British army under Sir Ralph Abercromby in Egypt during campaigns to dislodge Napoleon's forces from the Nile Valley. Before his assignment to Tunis in 1825, Sir Thomas Reade traveled to Egypt where he encountered al-Murali in service to the British expedition. As the English consul later reflected: "I myself was acquainted with him [i.e., Murali] ... in Egypt where he was a general favorite. He is greatly attached to our [i.e., British] interests."[15] Apparently a quick study, al-Murali acquired a familiarity with British naval technology and, returning to Tunis, was named minister of the navy and afterward constantly praised Great Britain to anyone in the court who would listen—so much so that peers jokingly referred to al-Murali as *al-inglizi* (the Englishman).[16] Later travels took him to Marseilles in 1821, Algiers during the turbulent summer of 1830 to negotiate with French forces, Istanbul and Paris in 1833, Malta in 1838, and Paris in 1846, where he addressed the French king in English, a facility acquired in the British Isles.

Then there is the case of Mahmud, the *kahiya* of La Goulette and scion of a notable family. Soon after Husayn Bey came to the throne, King Louis XVIII died and the bey dispatched a personal envoy, loaded with rich gifts, to the coronation ceremonies for Charles X. Wisely, the choice fell upon Sidi Mahmud, described by a contemporary in this way: "He is about thirty years old, speaks Italian, has a pleasant, even shy, manner, is without fanaticism or prejudice, eats in European fashion, and is dignified enough to be admitted into the high society [of the Parisian court]."[17] For three months, Mahmud "feasted his eyes upon the marvels of France" and resided with his Tunisian entourage in a *hôtel* in the chic Faubourg Saint-Germain. During a grand reception at the Ministry of Foreign Affairs, complete with lavish banquet and a bevy of French ladies as dinner guests, Mahmud showed a marked preference for champagne, which, he took pains to make clear, was prescribed by his physician for health reasons.[18] Intrigued by the "Oriental" gentleman, the French press fell all over itself, singing his praises and regaling readers with detailed information on his clothing and skin color, which one newspaper reported was "similar to that of a very brown Frenchman." The *Journal des Bouches-du-Rhône* reported in March 1825 that "he is very imposing physically due to his height and his great strength. He wears a very rich costume indicating his high social rank which confers upon him much dignity. Moreover, he is very affable."[19] After a smashingly successful diplomatic mission, the envoy returned—perhaps reluctantly—to Tunis in August 1825 on a French frigate, a year before the Egyptian Rifa'a Rafi' al-Tahtawi (1801–1873) arrived in Paris with students from Cairo pursuing education in the French capital.

A few North Africans ventured west far beyond the pillars of Hercules—as in the case of Sidi Sulayman Mellimelni, who headed a delegation to Washington in 1805 to negotiate the release of Tunisian vessels seized by the American navy.[20] Troubles with the Kingdom of Naples erupted in 1832 after Husayn Bey accused its subjects of engaging in contraband in a Tunisian port. In the ensuing diplomatic uproar, another court favorite, General Salim, was dispatched in June 1833 to soothe the king of Naples with lavish offerings, thereby avoiding military hostilities.[21] Well-established traditions of diplomatic and commercial exchange with Europe explain why a Tunisian ruler became the first Muslim prince to make a state visit to a European court. In 1846, Ahmad Bey embarked on a tour of France accompanied by Khayr al-Din, Hassuna al-Murali, and Bin Diyaf. The visit ultimately exerted a tremendous impact upon the country's destiny, and Ahmad Bey took pride in being the first Husaynid ruler to sail across the sea.[22] Another kind of travel was occasioned by personal troubles at court. As the nineteenth century wore on, Malta offered haven to Husaynid officials fallen into disgrace. The Jalluli brothers, part of the ruling elite, fled Tunis for Valletta in 1840 after defrauding the central treasury; other state swindlers preferred Paris, as was the case with Mahmud bin 'Ayyad in the 1850s.

Although by no means as heavy as north–south traffic across the Mediterranean, displacements in the opposite direction brought city notables and even provincial types, such as 'Ali al-Hammi, to Europe driven by an array of motives, producing an equally wide array of outcomes. Muslim North Africans preferred Istanbul, Egypt, the Levant, and Hijaz as places of piety, pilgrimage, knowledge, trade, escape, or settlement more than other destinations. The same was true for North African Jews, who moved about from Morocco to the Red Sea to visit shrines, synagogues, or centers of learning or for family or commercial reasons. Transversal religious or economic orientations slowly gave way in the nineteenth century to vertical axes of movement, especially for North African notables drawn to Europe for medical care and, above all, modern education.[23]

Standard narratives of nineteenth-century encounters between North Africa and Europe dwell on diplomatic envoys, state visits, or official missions that brought students from Cairo or Istanbul to European capitals for studies. Less attention has been paid to journeys by people of ordinary means or to forced expatriations. Many North Africans who made the Mediterranean crossing after 1830 were involuntary exiles, the vast majority Algerians. Best known is the religious and political leader Amir 'Abd al-Qadir, who surrendered to General de Lamoricière in 1847, was imprisoned in France until 1852, and subsequently relocated to Bursa in Turkey; in 1855 he settled permanently with a large retinue from his home province, Oran, in Damascus on a pension from the French state and was later awarded the Légion d'Honneur.

In addition, hundreds of Algerian rebels were exiled to bagnios in Corsica or to penal colonies scattered across the French Empire; a few were transported to Nouvelle-Calédonie.[24] Some eventually made it back home; but their life stories as captives in imperial internment centers have yet to be fully narrated. Muslim children were forcibly dispatched overseas; during the terrible famine years of the 1870s, Catholic missionaries sent Algerian orphans to religious houses in Italy and in France. And those deemed mentally unhinged and dangerous by the colonial regime, including Algerian Muslims, suffered transportation to asylums in Marseilles, Aix-en-Provence, or Montpellier.[25]

As for North Africans seeking opportunity elsewhere, the journey of "la Belle Fatima," is particularly arresting. Rachel bint Eny, Belle Fatima's real name, was the daughter of an Algerian Jewish musician who had long resided in Tunisia. As a young girl, she accompanied her father from Tunis to Paris, where he performed in the Oriental orchestra at the 1878 Exposition Universelle on the Champs de Mars. After the exposition closed, Fatima's family settled in Paris, where she remained for the rest of her life. She became a well-known performer and opened her own *boîte,* or nightclub. Another force that fed south-to-north currents was Europe's insatiable demand for Islamic exotica cum religious performance. After the "discovery" by the French public of the 'Isawiya Sufi order, with its purportedly strange rituals, members of the order made regular theater appearances in Paris and London; some stayed on.[26]

As North African notables and ordinary folks began to travel to Europe under a wide range of circumstances, a reverse migratory current, numerically larger, gained momentum. Given that as late as the 1820s, when slave raiding had ended, the image of the Moors as "corsairs, pirates, and pitiless enemies of the Christians" persisted, how was North Africa transformed in the collective imagination from a site of captivity and apostasy into a migratory labor frontier?[27] What large-scale, middle-range, and local historical forces explain why Maltese or Sicilian peasants no longer saw Barbary as a land of "idolatrous oppression" but rather as a place of good fortune?

GEOGRAPHIES: WAR, PEACE, AND MOBILITIES

The Napoleonic Wars and French occupation of Egypt shook loose large cohorts of people from home; some ended up in Mediterranean Africa, blown there by chance or choice or both. For example, the famous circus strongman, Giovanni Battista Belzoni, born in Padua in 1778 to an impecunious barber, ended up in Egypt by serendipity in 1815, where he attempted to cajole Muhammad 'Ali Pasha into investing in a new irrigation system.[28] In addition to swarms of hucksters, like Belzoni, who went to Egypt freely, there were many others who were compelled to relocate to the Nile Valley. As part of the 1798 naval expedition to Alexandria, Napoleon rounded up laborers in Malta for transportation to Egypt as a coerced workforce. However disagreeable this experience may have been, some Maltese elected to remain there, despite long-standing apprehensions about Islamic lands. After seizing power in 1805, Muhammad 'Ali Pasha embarked on a Mediterranean-wide search for technicians to drive state modernization programs; among those recruited were the Maltese, because a small community already existed in Alexandria. Master carpenters and masons from the Maltese and other islands proved instrumental in reconstructing the port's defensive works and expanding docking facilities for the western harbor, which was opened to Christian shipping.[29]

Some of the people who ventured to Egypt during the Napoleonic interlude and settled permanently later sent family members to Tunisia, thereby creating new transversal currents of skilled labor exchanges between Mashriq and Maghrib. When, in imitation of Muhammad 'Ali Pasha, Ahmad Bey embarked on state reforms after 1837, his agents in Marseilles, Valletta, Leghorn, and Istanbul engaged military and scientific personnel from across the Mediterranean. Among Ahmad Bey's interpreters in the newly organized Ministry of Foreign Affairs, was Elias Mussalli, whose father had emigrated from the Levant to Egypt during the French occupation. Born in Alexandria in 1829, Mussalli exercised the profession of dragoman from an early age at Muhammad 'Ali's court. He was later recruited by a Tunisian diplomat stationed in Egypt, Muhammad Badr al-Din, who, like other agents, was scouting talent. An Orthodox Christian, Mussalli entered into Husaynid state service in 1847 and insinuated himself into local creole society by marrying the beautiful daughter of a resident Genoese merchant. Mussalli's counterpart, Antoine Conti (1836–1893), whose origins lay in Corsica rather than the Ottoman Empire, came from a family also established in Egypt during the Napoleonic years. Born in Alexandria as well, Conti arrived at some point in Tunis, where his linguistic abilities and deep understanding of Arab and

Islamic customs brought him to Ahmad Bey's attention; Conti's considerable talents won him a posting in the highest circles.[30] Individuals such as Conti and Mussalli acted as conduits of information, as bearers of ideas regarding political and social reform programs, between the Egyptian and Tunisian states. At the same time, the presence in Tunis of a relatively large expatriate community either directly employed by the Husaynid state or in trade and commerce functioned as a recruiting center for new labor migrants.

As for the flow of people in the other direction—from the Mediterranean's African shores to the north—after Napoleon's army was forced out of Egypt in 1801, French forces returned to Marseilles, bringing with them various and sundry Egyptians and Levantines compromised by their association with the occupiers. Upon arriving in France with an official Egyptian delegation, the Egyptian imam al-Tahtawi expressed utter dismay in 1826 at finding:

> In the city of Marseilles, are many Christians from Egypt and Syria, who left with the French army during its retreat. All dress in French clothes. There are few Muslims among those who left with the French; some have died and others converted to Christianity—God forbid—especially the Georgian and Circassian mamluks and women taken by the French [from Egypt] when they were very young, although I met an old woman who had retained her religion. Among those who converted to Christianity, there was a certain 'Abd al-'Al . . . who had been appointed by the French as agha of the janissaries during their time [in Egypt]. When they left, he followed them, remaining a Muslim for some fifteen years then he converted because of his marriage to a Christian woman.[31]

The precipitous increase in the number of Muslims or Eastern Christians residing in France's Mediterranean ports after 1801 might have made the sea's southern rim seem less menacing or foreign; yet tolerating "strangers in the city" during political tumult was quite another matter, as the peripatetic 'Ali discovered during the anti-Bonapartist "White Terror" of June 1815 that began with a popular campaign directed against the "Turks" in Marseilles.[32] Indeed, the rebirth of Marseilles after the Restoration was a direct consequence of the invasions of Egypt and Algeria, whose expeditions modified collective perceptions. If North Africa came to be viewed as a place where one could "make it," what role did artistic, literary, and propagandistic representations of those conquests play in these shifts?

The 1816 Exmouth expedition, with its widely commemorated bombardment of Algiers, reveals another crucible for changing attitudes, because the event was memorialized in an enormous panorama depicting the British navy pitted against the "Algerines." Painted by the English artist Henry Aston Barker (1774–1856) and exhibited in London in 1818 and later on the Continent, the panorama drew record crowds for years. Other painters of monumental landscapes immediately took up the challenge; in 1823, the Dutch artist Martinus Schouman, produced *Het Bombardement van Algiers,* a huge canvas full of fire and brimstone portraying the Algerian defeat. Another source in the demythologizing of North Africa as a place of danger and abjuration may have been the 1816 visit that Princess Caroline of Wales, unhappy wife of the prince regent (who later became King George IV in 1820), made to Tunis only days before the Anglo-Dutch fleet showed up. As touched upon in the introduction, Princess Caroline's presence in Tunisia, where she was chaperoned by a Husaynid prince on sight-seeing excursions and given a splendid palace for her retinue, complicated Exmouth's plans for attack. After returning to England, Caroline was accused by her unpopular husband of adultery with her Italian tutor, Bartholomeo Pergami, who accompanied her on the Mediterranean tour. The House of Lords debated the king's divorce action against his wife for weeks. The tumultuous proceedings were portrayed in a monumental painting, *The Trial of Queen Caroline 1820,* by Sir George Hayter, completed between 1820 and 1823. While the Lords "upheld her honour," and London's populace staunchly supported Caroline (which induced George IV to flee for fear of mob attacks upon Westminster), the by then queen died soon thereafter in 1821, a broken woman. Nevertheless, one can speculate regarding how the high-profile scandal surrounding Caroline's travels and the famous tableau of her trial and tribulations might have again influenced collective visions of the Barbary Coast. Certainly, her observations about Tunis were nothing but favorable:

> After I had visited Sicily for the sake of the antiquities I came here [to Tunis] and . . . I am quite in astonishment that all the wonderful curiosities of Carthage, Utica, Savonny, Udinna never have been taken much notice of. . . . I can assure you the soi-disant Barbarians are much more real kind and obliging to me than all the civil people of Europe for which reason I shall certainly remain with them as long as I can. . . . I have never been so happy in my life. . . . I am living a perfect enchantment. The dear Arabians and Turks are quite darlings. Their kindness I shall never forget.[33]

The smashing success of Barker's panorama inspired numerous painters, among them, Charles Langlois (1789–1870), to produce vast canvases depicting the 1830 invasion of Algiers. Langlois' "realistic" panorama of the French conquest was mounted in Paris and showed for eighteen months in 1833 and 1834 to sell-out audiences.[34] At least one artist, the Swiss painter Adolphe Otth (1803–1839), who worked in Algiers during the 1830s, decided to venture to North Africa to paint precisely because of the intriguing images of Algeria circulating throughout Europe. Leaving his native Berne in 1837, Otth journeyed to Lyon, the Rhône Valley, and Toulon, where he embarked for Mahon; from Minorca, the ship made a stop in Bône, where the Swiss traveler witnessed the small port's virtual destruction by the French army. By then Algiers, if not Algeria, had been under French military rule for seven years and had already attracted not only adventuresome artists and travelers but also uninvited laborers and settlers from the Mediterranean islands and southern Europe. Otth, whose truthfulness we have little reason to doubt, stated that he had made the somewhat perilous trip to North Africa to ascertain the veracity of the images seen in Europe.[35] Unlike many artists from the period, who were either French officers or employed by the army to document its exploits, Otth was purely motivated by artistic and intellectual concerns, which confers upon his work a certain authority, which is not to deny that his were value-laden images. One wonders if Otth himself had viewed the panoramas exhibited in Paris by Langlois, since the Swiss artist had studied drawing in the French capital for six months prior to setting off across the Mediterranean.

The impact that the wildly popular panoramas exerted upon viewers, who might have been tempted by the idea of travel to Barbary, remains a matter of conjecture. Nevertheless, Barker and his imitators had developed a new genre of aesthetic memorializing—a form of modern media extravaganza cum propaganda that promoted the idea of a subjugated North Africa, a place tamed enough for Europeans to settle and explore. It is indisputable that after 1830 the volume and velocity of textual and visual materials, however fanciful, circulating in Europe about North Africa and its indigenous peoples multiplied exponentially. Works such as Chateaubriand's *Voyage de Tunis,* part of a longer travel narrative appearing in 1811, had already exerted no small influence among the bourgeois classes, although both texts and images drew upon a much older fund of European artistic representations of the East, beginning with Nicolas de Nicolay's *Travels in Turkey* (1567).[36] But how did ordinary people become aware of new opportunities, however meager or ephemeral, in northern Africa?

WHY LEAVE HOME? INFORMATION AND MOBILITY

Contemporary scholarship on global migrations stresses that access to information circuits exerts a decisive impact upon migratory behaviors and flows.[37] From 1815 on, Malta operated as a huge informational intake or bellows, sucking in and spewing forth all manner of news about work to be had, higher wages, and free land or, conversely, about dangers "over there" in North Africa. With the introduction of steam navigation in the early 1840s—one of the first steamers arrived in Tunis from Valletta in March 1842—Malta evolved into the premier communications clearinghouse for the Mediterranean. Hearsay, tidings, and rumors from the Black Sea, Indian Ocean, and Atlantic world also went into the mix. Malta's supremacy in rumormongering resulted from the fact that British legal restraints on publishing were less restrictive than elsewhere. Orally transmitted news, tall tales, and plain falsehoods were committed to print with greater ease, legitimizing them; subsequently, greatly enriched information was folded back into oral circuits. A striking example was the utterly spurious report that a Catholic priest, Father Thomas, and his servant had been ritually murdered by Jewish rabbis in Damascus in 1840, a story that spread like wildfire throughout the Mediterranean, partially due to reporting in the *Maltese Times*.[38] Nevertheless, the year before, an accurate report from Tunis made La Valletta's papers with astonishing speed—a Maltese vessel loaded with smuggled gunpowder had exploded right outside Ahmad Bey's palace in La Goulette.[39]

Geographical location, the quantities of ships docking, and the number of people passing through—sailors, soldiers, travelers, diplomats, and traders—explain Valletta's brokerage position in collecting and disseminating news, however factual or fictitious. Let's take a typical shipping report from the period. In November 1839, merchant vessels arrived from Tunis, Newcastle, Sicily, Tripoli, Constantinople, Odessa, Wales, Greece, Trapani, Algiers, Glasgow, Gibraltar, and Jersey. Commercial ships departed for Smyrna, Messina, Odessa, Djerba, Oran, Bône, Alexandria, Trieste, Sicily, and Falmouth, although the destinations, crews, and cargoes of smaller vessels do not figure into this list nor does the hefty military traffic.[40] Thus, the central Mediterranean corridor, with its increasingly vibrant borderland culture, was constructed of lines of transmission conveying people, goods, and information in ever greater circulation densities. What push or pull forces, frequently acting in tandem, coaxed or thrust people from homes and villages?

WHY LEAVE HOME? THE ISLAND FORTRESS

People have always and everywhere left home for a whole gamut of reasons: to trade and traffic; to secure land or a living wage; for adventure, romance, or out of curiosity; to flee conscription, the law, arranged marriages, or murderous vendettas. If decades of warfare followed by peace convinced some to pack up and move, so did critical changes in state policies toward population movements. After 1815, older mercantilist opposition to emigration from the British Isles gave way to the imperative to relieve social adversity at home by populating the empire with "British stock."[41] Permanent white settlement in New Zealand, Australia, and Canada was encouraged, although many of those cast out to the imperial margins did not go freely. In contrast, Spain continued to—or attempted to—restrict emigration until the mid-1850s, with varying degrees of failure or success, which encouraged clandestine settlement, mainly in western Algeria. After 1830 France followed a slightly different path dictated by the urgent need to people Algeria, which primed the migratory pump in the central Mediterranean corridor and in turn influenced migratory flows to Tunisia. But first, what local conditions might have induced individuals or families to strike out? In some islands, ecological degradation, boom-and-bust capitalism, the persistence of latifundia, and overpopulation operated as "distress" or push factors in varying combinations. A relative concept, population overshoot is measured by a complex of elements—kinship organization, inheritance practices, legal regimes, and resource allocation in dynamic relationship with fertility, mortality, and environmental structures.[42] Sicily, the Mediterranean's biggest island, and, above all, Malta suffered relentless population pressures after 1815. "Malta for centuries has been one of the most densely populated parts of Europe . . . and social problems of great imperial significance have grown up around such an intense concentration of people."[43] In stark contrast, Tunisia counted fewer than one million inhabitants, averaging about three persons per square mile. Proximity to Sicily and Malta positioned it close astride a critical demographic frontier—more so than Algeria.[44]

Since Malta furnished the most immigrants to Tunisia and eastern Algeria for decades after 1830, and represented the largest expatriate community in Tunis until the massive Italian immigration of the 1860s, we begin with the archipelago of seven islands, only three inhabited, that lie virtually dead center in the Mediterranean, 58 miles south of Sicily and 179 north of Africa; Gibraltar is 1,118 miles to the west. In the seventeenth and eighteenth centuries, the island fortress functioned as a hub for privateering; indeed privateers' balance of payments depended upon plundering mainly Muslim ships and enslaving North Africans, although Christian vessels were not always spared. What do we know about the fairly large number of slaves from the Maghrib and Egypt? When Napoleon invaded Malta in June 1798, his forces discovered two thousand Muslim slaves from Algiers, Tunis, and Tripoli condemned to the galleys of the Order of Saint John of Malta.[45] At least one Tunisian qadi (judge) had resided on the islands along with free North Africans in the eighteenth century, about which, unfortunately, little is known. Enterprising Maltese acted as intermediaries for ransoming Muslim slaves held in the bagnios in Malta and traveled to Tunis and the interior, where they made considerable fortunes by locating slaves and delivering them to Tunisian families in return for money, horses, or grain.[46]

What about relations between North African slaves and the Maltese population? This is a critical question about which little is known, aside from recent research on earlier periods. The presence of numerous enslaved Muslims constituted a source of grave anxiety for Church authorities, who were especially alarmed about their impact upon Maltese women, "who eagerly sought out Muslim slaves to learn from them popular magical superstitions attributed to Islam."[47] One detects the myth of the "ignorant," lowly woman, always prone to religious error, at work here. Nevertheless, fears of heretical exchanges were nourished by the fact that many Muslims worked for households in the intimacy of the family; although, the vast majority labored in the galleys. If the Maltese corsair economy ended, for the most part, after 1815, the earlier defeat of the

FIGURE 6. Street in the Tunis madina, c. 1860–1900. The octagonal Hanafi mosque is in the background, with passersby whose dress indicates that most were North African. The image is unusual because the three people on the right edge—man, woman, and child— are dressed in a manner suggesting that they are Maltese or Sicilian of ordinary status. Professional photographers in the period rarely portrayed street scenes with indigent Europeans. (Library of Congress Prints and Photographs, LC-DIG-ppmsca-04985.)

Knights of Saint John by Napoleon's army dealt a mortal blow to island prosperity. While rapacious, the knights had financed most public works and infrastructure—charity, education, even the water supply—so their abrupt departure wreaked havoc, as did the French army's seizures of Church properties. In addition, Malta's textile industry had provided supplemental income for peasants in spinning and weaving during the second half of the eighteenth century. When the Spanish government prohibited foreign imports of cotton goods after 1800, Malta lost one of its biggest markets, although smuggling may have attenuated the blow somewhat.

It remains unclear how abolition influenced wage and labor structures in Malta, since some British officials argued that slavery's end created employment for "industrious inhabitants, whose interests are no longer, as they were then, opposed by the forced labor of slaves."[48] Yet, another dimension of Maltese slaving and corsair activity largely, but not exclusively, directed against North African ships existed that might explain changing economic conditions and in turn emigration. The lucrative traffic in humans—Muslim female slaves fetched the highest price—had permitted the islanders to purchase foodstuffs produced elsewhere, improving diet as well as standards of living. But after 1800, the knights were no longer; and the slavery-corsair economy, which had proved so gainful, was nearing its end. The Maltese were living far beyond their means.[49]

By the late eighteenth century, the population had risen to a point that the islands' peasants could only produce wheat and barley sufficient for four months' consumption; the rest was imported from Sicily, whose grain exports to Malta were regarded as a privilege to be granted or withheld, and from the Maghrib.[50] An official British inquiry from 1836 into misery and its impact upon emigration from the Maltese islands conceded:

> There is still much room for improvement in the condition of the lower classes here, and great distress prevailing among them is too evident; but whatever may now be the extent of the misery, it may be confidently affirmed to be less than it was in the time of the knights, if we merely consider the greater proportion of wheaten bread consumed within both islands. During the last years of the Order, the annual consumption of foreign wheat was about 43,000 *salms* or quarters by 100,000 inhabitants; at present, it averages about 57,000 for 115,000.[51]

By then, the islands imported two-thirds of their food supply; in addition to Sicily, Tunisia and to a lesser extent Tripoli supplied basic foodstuffs, particularly grain, livestock, and raw materials when agricultural conditions permitted, which explains why the Husaynid dynasty maintained commercial agents in Valletta.[52]

Offsetting negative changes in the islands' economy was the great natural harbor of Valletta, which served for a century and a half as home to Britain's

Mediterranean fleet. The presence of the navy, a war economy, and the relocation to the islands of English factories from Palermo, Naples, and Leghorn in 1806, as well as free port status between 1803 and 1813, provoked a financial—but also demographic—boom followed by a "bust." A series of epidemics after 1813 relieved population pressures, but the intermittent imposition of quarantines on ships from Malta until 1826 meant that other ports captured some of its trade.[53] Finally, the disorders attendant to the Ottoman-Greek Wars between 1821 and 1829, followed by the meteoric rise of Egyptian cotton, conspired to depress once more the islands' economy. This came as a massive French expeditionary force landed in Algiers. By then the Maltese "had surpassed the relatively huge figure of 100,000; or more than 800 persons per square mile."[54]

The census of 1828 revealed that the native Maltese numbered 115,000, while troops and foreigners brought the total to 120,000. British experts brandished the same menacing statistics: "the island of Malta for its size contains a denser population than any other part of the habitable globe . . . eight times or 800 % more densely inhabited than England at the time."[55] Between the late eighteenth century and the 1890s, the Maltese population nearly doubled, reaching at least 175,000 by 1891. While the second half of the nineteenth century brought a another economic boom as expanding naval dockyards provided employment for thousands of workers, Malta's men and women constituted its principal exports throughout the nineteenth century. British laissez-faire attitudes toward demographic woes did little to alleviate the problem and ironically peopled French Algeria and precolonial Tunisia with British subjects. While the Maltese do not appear to have settled in Algeria in appreciable numbers until 1830, as we have seen, they were sufficiently visible in Tunisia during the late 1820s to elicit protests from Husayn Bey regarding their inadequate means of livelihood.[56]

British officials were quick to point the finger at the Church's nefarious influence, and royal commissions on the causes of impoverishment always blamed the people for "multiplying their numbers beyond the demand for their labour." This 1838 account translates the full force of English Protestant prejudice vis-à-vis Catholic protégés:

> Nothing can be more true than this fact; when a lad arrives at state of puberty, he begins to think of marriage before he has made any provision for maintaining a family. The present system of endowing females is the cause of the most distressing consequences, as in numerous cases it is the only attraction which a young woman has for an individual who seeks her as his wife. However small the sum may be . . . when once in the hands of an idler, is soon spent in some hazardous project or speculation, if not in vice; and when he finds he can procure no more, either from his wife or from her relations, he leaves her to her fate, either to be again received under her parents' roof, or to seek a living for herself and family in the best way she can. This is not an exaggerated picture of very many cases in Malta; and besides

this, if the computation were made of the number of females at present on the island, whose husbands have left them for a foreign land [it] would . . . astonish.[57]

Catholicism, defective family structures, early marriage and the dowry, a dearth of educational institutions or even a credible apprentice system—all created poverty in the official British mind. Here we find classic bourgeois liberalism with its discourse of the "idle poor" as enunciated in Europe at the time; improvidence, coupled with a distressing lack of sexual restraint, characteristic of the "Mediterranean temperament," created lamentable social conditions in Malta. Of particular note is the statement about the astonishing number of females "whose husbands have left them for a foreign land." Across the narrow waterway separating the islands from North Africa, consular officials in Tunisia and French colonial authorities in Algeria voiced identical censorious sentiments.

Displaying increasing antipathy toward his imperial charges, Reade lamented that "immense masses of Maltese . . . literally swarm in [to] the Regency especially since the commencement of existing affairs in Tripoli . . . they are continually in litigation one with another [here in Tunis]."[58] The "swarming" of the Maltese into Tunisia, the direct result of the reimposition of formal Ottoman rule over Tripolitania in 1835, was a riposte to France's invasion of Algeria; the defeat of the local Qaramanli dynasty in Tripoli, which had boasted a small expatriate community of Maltese and Greeks, sent them en masse to Egypt or in greater numbers to Tunisia. Clearly good fortune did always not smile upon those forced to leave their island homes for North Africa. "The overplus population which finds an asylum in the Barbary States, in Egypt, Syria, and in Turkey, are chiefly of one class, consisting almost exclusively of labourers who have already more than satisfied the demand for their work, and are, consequently, many of them, even in a worse state than their poor countrymen, at home."[59] By 1847, the vice-consul Ferriere warned London yet again about the fact that "the population of Maltese-British subjects at Tunis has increased in the last twenty years from 500 to 4,000 at least. The greater number of them are of the worst class, disgorged from the gaols of Malta, expelled from the Island, and cast off destitute on the coast of Barbary." The consulate registered "257 fresh arrivals and only 73 departures" back to Malta, or perhaps some other destination.[60] It is, however, probably safe to say that, among the Muslim states ringing the southern Mediterranean's shores, Tunisia appeared the most familiar, the least foreign, for the Maltese.

WHY LEAVE HOME? THE BIG ISLANDS

Migratory pulses in the central Mediterranean corridor were deeply marked by urban densities on the Italian peninsula, where the largest city, Naples, counted nearly half a million inhabitants by the 1880s; not surprisingly Neapolitans were found in abundance in Tunisia, second only to Sicilians.[61] As on other islands, the Sicilian population began to climb rapidly; by 1890 it was estimated at 109 inhabitants per square mile.[62] Rural Sicily suffered from the persistence of feudal-like relations, absentee landowners, archaic methods of cultivation, small yields, usury and crippling peasant indebtedness, and declining markets for agricultural surplus. Roads linking one part of the island with another were lacking, ports had fallen into disrepair, if not ruin. One only has to read Giuseppe di Lampedusa's classic 1958 novel, *The Leopard,* to appreciate how these circumstances affected daily life. Semiautobiographical and historically accurate, the work opens in 1860 as the prince of Salina and his family laboriously make their way from Palermo to a nearby feudal estate in Santa Margherita; a short distance turned into a three-day trek by primitive transport.[63]

And Sicily was a place of hunger where the poor subsisted on prickly pear cactus and beans; potato cultivation, which could have provided cheap sustenance, was discouraged due to a popular belief that potatoes encouraged licentious behavior. The clandestine traffic in firewood and timber, often controlled by gangs, contributed to devastating deforestation, whose ravages meant that "by 1840 almost every hill-top was bare and eroded." In the lowlands, malaria reappeared due to disastrous forestry, agricultural, and river management. While the cost of labor was high relative to international labor markets, the absence of a skilled workforce acted as a brake upon development.[64] As was true for Malta, much of the island's food was imported, particularly wheat, which Tunisia sometimes furnished, in addition to livestock. Finally, a GPS reading reveals that Sicily's western coast—the ports of Trapani and Marsala—were "closer" to the Cap Bon by small craft than to eastern Sicily via road; in consequence, these ports sent the highest percentage of emigrants to Tunisia.

Seasonal labor movements are critical to intersecting push-pull factors because, after tending vines, picking grapes, or cutting cork, those returning home with money in their pockets may have induced others to try their luck across the sea. From the 1830s until the 1850s, some island workers engaged in temporary or seasonal migration linking Sardinia and Sicily with North Africa.[65] Each construction boom in Algeria or Tunisia attracted laborers, but downswings or disasters, such as the 1846 economic crisis, the 1848–1851 cholera epidemics, and the 1864 revolt in Tunisia, reduced numbers, if temporarily. Northern Italian workers were greatly appreciated due to their reputations as hard-working, frugal, and docile. Even the Sicilian cultivator was valued—when not denounced as a bandit or draft dodger—because it was believed that Sicily's harsh rural economy and rigid class structure predisposed the peasantry to unrelenting manual labor.[66] Freelance recruitment agents sprang up across Italy to entice laborers to North Africa, for a fee of course, with spurious promises about golden opportunities—in a manner reminiscent of today's *coyotes* operating along the American southwestern

FIGURE 7. Work and gossip in Taormina, Sicily, c. 1906. Peasants from a town in northwestern Sicily engaged in daily tasks that did not differ much from the way of life of Tunisian peasants at the time or that of fellow Sicilian farm laborers who had emigrated to North Africa. (Library of Congress Prints and Photographs, LC-USZ62–73731.)

borderlands. Indeed a major factor in labor relocation to North Africa was "the deceptions of Italian agents of emigration." Finally, collective notions about how best to succeed or, in the very least, escape misery played a role, above all, the "widely held belief that one must abandon one's homeland [i.e., Italy] to make one's fortune."[67] These elements and others conspired to make leaving home less daunting.

Fish and radical politics sent some Italians to the Maghrib for short-term stays that at times turned into permanent residence. Despite the dangers of captivity, island fishermen had long plied North African coastal waters unusually rich in tuna and coral. Beginning with the seventeenth-century concession granted to a Genoese family, the Lomellini, Sardinians exercised a virtual monopoly over coral fishing off the island of Tabarka; when the concession ended in the late eighteenth century, many Sardinians stayed on. After 1830, the numbers of fishermen shot up dramatically to the dismay of colonial officials in Algeria, Tunisian authorities, and locals for whom they represented fierce competition. Experiencing the annual arrival of foreign men of the sea as an "invasion," Tunisian villagers submitted a substantial corpus of complaint letters to the government.[68] But the important element is that the tradition of emigration from the islands to North Africa was already well entrenched. As population movements in the central Mediterranean corridor increased, another line of work opened up for the owners of small vessels—running ferry services between the islands and Algeria or Tunisia. Depending upon the season and winds, the trip took several days, or even more, but the crossing was less expensive than travel by regular ship and was available to those without papers. Thus fishermen and their small boats played an important transportation role in clandestine immigration to North African coastal towns as well as in smuggling.[69]

While the Maltese were the most numerous expatriate community in Tunisia until the 1860s, the Italians constituted the first to come as political refugees beginning immediately after the Restoration in 1815. Revolutionary upheavals erupted between 1817 and 1832 in the Italian north and south—Naples in 1820, Sardinia in 1821, and Modena and the Papal States in 1832. Each wave of state repression forced out rebels, Freemasons, and Carbonari; some went to North Africa, others to Egypt or the Americas.[70] The English missionary and abolitionist Joseph Greaves, who resided in Tunis, expressed astonishment in 1824 at the number of exiled Carbonari, including several priests politically involved in the movement, who lived there openly as a community.[71] After 1829, Tunis represented a political haven for the revolutionary followers of Mazzini and Garibaldi who met and conspired together at the Palazzo Gnecco in the madina.[72] Garibaldi, a participant in the 1834 Genoa uprising, was sentenced to death in absentia after escaping to France; he eventually sailed from Marseilles to Tunis in May 1835 on the corvette *Hélène,* commissioned by Mustafa Bey for the Tunisian navy. Numerous myths sprang up around Garibaldi's brief sojourn in Tunis in the popular European press, becoming more elaborate and baroque as the years passed. Included in the repertoire of legends and lore were the usual Orientalist fantasies à la Pierre Loti—that Garibaldi had fallen secretly in love with the bey's favorite wife, Layla, who eloped with him. In July 1835, Garibaldi left Tunis for Marseilles and from there sailed to Rio de Janeiro. He reappeared in North Africa in 1849, seeking asylum in Tangier where he wrote the first edition of his memoirs.[73]

Others politicos decided to stay on in Tunis, notably the Jewish republican, Gaetano Fedriani (1811–1881), who accompanied Garibaldi to Tunisia from Genoa, where both had been implicated in a Mazzini plot. Thanks to Count Raffo's patronage, which allowed him to pursue political activities as he cast about for work, Fedriani became the main propagandist for the "Young Italy movement" in Tunisia.[74] This same current of political expatriation brought Giulio Finzi to Tunis in 1829, where he established the first Italian printing press and dabbled in revolutionary politics. If figures like Finzi and Fedriani acted as intermediaries between the Italian expatriate community in the capital and the beylical government, creole patronage was absolutely critical to their careers.[75] Thus a sort of parallelism emerges between Italians seeking sanctuary in the regency and Tunisians finding haven in Malta or elsewhere in the Mediterranean's northern rim.

What about the migratory impulses in other islands? Compared with Sicily, life in rural Corsica was scarcely better, as the island had been ravaged by the local class conflict and economic turmoil attendant to the Revolution and Napoleonic years. Harvests were torched, ancient olive trees uprooted, and dwellings and estates perished in the flames.[76] Napoleon III's reign brought more travails, as Corsica's main agricultural commodities—wine, olive oil, and chestnuts—declined, in part the result of unfair trade practices imposed by the metropole. The eradication of malaria in low-lying areas brought an increase in population, and by the last third of the nineteenth century the older agropastoral system was headed for "ultimate collapse" due in large measure to demographic pressures building since the 1820s. Between 1780 and 1880, the population of the island doubled—from about 140,000 to 280,000. Corsicans emigrated in growing numbers to Marseilles, Algeria, and Tunisia after 1830 as well as Venezuela and the Caribbean. In colonial North Africa, the Corsicans encountered the same negative stereotypes as their Maltese and Sicilian counterparts.[77]

Other displacements to the east involved subjects of the sultan. The Greeks of Tunisia represented an important population—not due to numbers, which were comparatively insignificant—but rather because their ranks included Ottoman subjects, European protégés, and mamluks or renegades. A small Greek Orthodox community, resident in Tunis since 1645, was made up of mainly middle-class merchants numbering no more than several hundred individuals who enjoyed privileges denied European Christians because of their status as Ottomans. The Greeks mainly came from the Ionian and Aegean islands as well as Crete, Cyprus, Thessalonica, and Macedonia and controlled much of the trade between Tunis and the Greek Mediterranean, notably the lucrative commerce in spirits, silks, and vermillion (used for dying textiles) that had longed existed between Zante and Tunisia. By the nineteenth century, some occupied administrative

FIGURE 8. Disembarking from a ship, Algiers, c. 1899. The social diversity of the crowd on the dock indicates that ports and ships attracted a wide range of people—from native porters, French military, and ordinary folks to bourgeois travelers, whose class is apparent from their apparel. (Library of Congress Prints and Photographs, LC-DIG-ppmsc-05539.)

posts or served in the beylical army.[78] (The complicated processes that led some members of this community to abandon their status as ra'iya and membership in the Millet-i Rum in order to claim European diplomatic protection is discussed in a later chapter.)

However, political and economic circumstances akin to those in other islands may have encouraged Greek settlement in North Africa during the early nineteenth century. By the end of the eighteenth century, some of the seven principal Ionian Islands had converted, at least partially, from diversified agriculture to a monoculture in olive oil, used as an industrial lubricant in Europe, with the predictable consequence that the peasantry produced insufficient food for household subsistence. As was true in Malta, the Ionian Islands suffered greatly during the Napoleonic Wars. Invaded by the French army in 1797, they were occupied by Venetian, Russian, and finally British forces. By 1814, they fell into British hands, but nearly two decades of unremitting violence and upheaval made the notion of emigration more palatable. From 1815 until 1864, the Ionian Islands were under the protection of the British Crown; Sir Thomas Maitland, former governor-general of Malta, served as lord high commissioner. The Ottoman-Greek Wars (1821–1829), followed by the establishment of a small independent Greek state, reluctantly recognized in 1832 by Istanbul, may have also encouraged emigration and settlement in Tunisia and Algeria, although most diaspora Greeks preferred Alexandria. The Ionian Greeks established in Tunis were legally British protégés, although some sought protection from France, Italy, or Russia.[79]

The impact that these "mundane" migratory currents exerted upon collective thinking about the Maghrib as a place of temporary or permanent relocation demands further scrutiny, as does North Africa's role as a migratory stepping-stone in the trans-Mediterranean, and slightly later global, population movements then taking shape. But the most powerful stimulus for emigration from economically strapped islands or southern Europe came in the summer of 1830.

ALGERIA: PRIMING THE MIGRATORY PUMP

On July 20, 1830, the British consul in Tunis informed London of the momentous events then unfolding: "I have the honor to inform you that the intelligence of the capture of Algiers by the French forces arrived here on the 15th instant and although it was expected this circumstance would have created a deep impression in the Population of this Regency.... His Highness the Bey and His Government have taken such precautionary measures, as would effectually check any Disposition which might arise amongst the Turkish Population as well as amongst the evil disposed to disturb the tranquility of the Place."[80]

The assessment proved overly optimistic; the news of the fall of Algiers in the summer of 1830 provoked elation, terror, and anger in Tunisia.[81] Since Algeria had constituted the age-old military enemy, state elites initially celebrated their rival's defeat, not least because some French military leaders were favorably disposed to a Tunisian "protectorate" over the beyliks of Oran and Constantine, a project that quickly evaporated into thin air. The bey sent one of his closest advisors, Hassuna al-Murali, to Algeria as envoy and eyewitness to the invasion, which he observed from the safety of a French ship anchored off Algiers. During the month of April 1830, weeks prior to the attack, the massive French expeditionary force took on supplies in Tunis, a pattern prevailing for decades. Nevertheless, most received the bitter news of the fall of Algiers with sorrow mixed with trepidation; poets composed verses lamenting the Christian victory. After the long, brutal sieges of Constantine, a city with historically close ties to Tunis, the mood in the streets turned hostile, all the more so because the 1837 fall of Constantine sent waves of refugees into Tunisia.[82]

The Frenchman marched against [Algiers] and took her
It was not one hundred ships that he had, nor two hundred
He proudly has his flotilla defile before her,
Surging forth from the high seas, with powerful armies[83]

In the fourteen years separating Admiral Exmouth's 1816 expedition from France's invasion, the foreign community of Algiers, historically minuscule compared to Tunis, decreased dramatically. When the mighty French naval force sailed into sight in the summer of 1830, less than a hundred Europeans resided in Algiers, whose indigenous population is estimated at about 40,000. Many had departed after the 1827 altercation between the French consul in Algiers and Husayn Dey, followed by the three-year French naval blockade of Algerian ports. During the summer of 1830, the violence of the conquest and reports of military atrocities committed against Muslims and Jews caused ten thousand city inhabitants to flee to the countryside, to Tunisia, or to Morocco. Some refugees remained in permanent exile; others returned to find their homes, businesses, and streets occupied—another reason for relocation to adjacent Maghribi states or the Ottoman heartlands.[84] Made up of tens of thousands of soldiers and personnel, the expeditionary force nearly equaled in numbers the capital's total population; quartered in and around Algiers, this behemoth required vast quantities of food and supplies. The French fleet made the port of Mahon, on the island of Minorca, into a major supply center in 1830 and communication hub for the western Mediterranean, although it was never able to dislodge Malta from its commanding position.[85] The presence of the fleet was directly responsible for waves of emigration from Minorca to Algeria.

Heterogeneous in composition, the expedition's members, whether military or civilian, arrived with preconceived notions of, and prejudices about, not only Muslims but also other ethnic, religious, and cultural groups. One detects echoes of the earlier Napoleonic occupation of Egypt in evaluations of southern Mediterranean peoples flocking to Algiers. Indeed, some of those involved in the invasion of Algeria had connections with the Egyptian campaign; several descendants of soldiers or savants from Napoleon's invasion of the Nile Valley took part in the 1830 expedition to Algiers. One of the Arabic interpreters serving the French military in Algiers was a young man, Joanny Pharaon. Born in Cairo in 1803, Joanny was the son of Elias Pharaon, an interpreter of Syrian origins, who had worked for the French army during Bonaparte's expedition. After Napoleon's defeat in 1801 by the allied Ottoman-British forces, the Pharaon family settled in Paris, where Joanny later studied at the École des Langues Orientales, mastering Arabic and other Middle Eastern languages. This earned him a position with the 1830 invasion and the critical assignment of preparing a new legal system for Algeria based upon his 1835 study of French, Muslim, and Jewish law. Pharaon ultimately became a professor of Arabic at the Collège d'Alger and founding member of the Société Coloniale d'Alger. One important aspect of the Pharaons' trajectory is that the family undertook multiple and serial displacements—from Syria to Egypt to France and subsequently to Algeria. As Ahmad Bey and Muhammad 'Ali Pasha recruited families like the Pharaons, so did the French military eager to engage Mediterranean creoles, capable of acting as translators and cultural brokers.[86]

One of the first tasks confronting Algeria's new masters was to repopulate the capital as well as attract immigrants, hopefully from France, to people nearby villages. But herein lay the conundrum. Unlike many European regions at the time, such as the Italian or German states, or the Mediterranean islands, France was not overpopulated. And, aside from specific regions, such as the impoverished Auvergne that had traditionally exported surplus labor to Paris, the French, compared with other nations, were often reluctant to emigrate.[87] Many people arriving in Algiers just after 1830 were unsolicited workers from Sicily, Sardinia, Corsica, Malta, the Balearic Islands, and Greek islands. Unregulated immigration must have dramatically increased soon after the invasion, since in April 1831 a law was passed "establishing penalties for ship captains who disembarked passengers not in possession of passports."[88] Between 1830 and 1831, the Chambre de Commerce in Marseilles alone enjoyed the authority to deliver passports for emigrants to Algeria but, in view of the spontaneity and complexities of immigration, that right was subsequently assumed by the French state.[89] But neither Paris nor Marseilles was equipped to handle the influx of people.

The initial, disorderly settlement of Algiers was promoted by the dissemination of largely unfounded rumors around the Mediterranean. Several types of colonization programs were eventually organized principally for French nationals: military land grants to ex-army officers that failed miserably; private utopian experiments inspired by Saint-Simonian principles; and state-sponsored schemes for civilians. Yet in early years, many of the newly arrived enjoyed neither French nationality nor any connection to the military and therefore had little hope of legally acquiring agricultural property, with some exceptions, so they crowded into Algiers or surrounding villages. For these people, hearsay about free land and wages two to four times higher than in Malta or Sicily increased Algeria's attraction for peasants, unskilled laborers, tavern keepers, and artisans.[90] While fewer in numbers, some subjects of the Moroccan sultans and Tunisian beys were lured to Algeria to serve as translators or even fight under the French flag.

Here is one officer's view of the civilians from 1837: "A mob of social failures from every country, those freed from the bagnios and those who have escaped, grocers, sellers of liquor, café owners . . . involved in all manner of speculations, smugglers exploiting all imaginable branches of commerce."[91] Later on, state and private emigration societies were mobilized in the metropole to recruit "worthy settlers"—skilled, sober, virtuous—from targeted European populations, such as the Swiss and Germans, to offset nationalities regarded as morally objectionable. Gender and national stereotypes played a pivotal role since communities or nations known for their "respectable women" were preferred.[92] However, the chaos of the first decade made it easy for social "undesirables," women and men, to settle. Due to harsh, perilous conditions, middle-class wives of military officers or colonial administrators rarely joined their husbands at first; the majority of European women in Algiers were characterized in military sources as *cantinières* (camp followers). Population estimates for European civilians in 1839 revealed severe male-female imbalances, true of most immigrant societies in the earlier stages, although eyewitness accounts remarked upon the number of French and European women in the streets while noting the absence of "Moorish" women.[93] For women of modest means from islands, the promise of work proved irresistible, and soon an estimated 750 women in Algiers has been assigned to regiments as *blanchisseuses* (laundry workers) or *cuisinières* (cooks). Not all incoming females were welcomed with open arms—or rather, the fact that they were too warmly received by male laborers was viewed with trepidation. Soon after the invasion, a ship from Mahon filled with young women seeking farmwork was forbidden to disembark out of fear that they would prove both a financial burden and moral embarrassment. So many poor islanders entered the country that the "ardent colonizer, Maréchal Clauzel, was accused of turning the Algiers region into a dumping ground for Europe's dispossessed."[94]

For the French military command, sexually servicing the soldiers was most urgent to avoid even worse sexual dangers, homosexual relations; arrangements were made for "the importation of a substantial cohort of prostitutes, for whom every facility was taken to aid their arrival."[95] In Tlemcen, General La Moricière ordered the commanding general to "proceed with the recruitment and settlement of a female personnel who can cater to the pleasures, if not the health, of the men."[96] One of the army's first administrative orders entailed regulating prostitution: "On the 12th of June [1831], the municipality of Algiers was assigned responsibility for overseeing 'public women'; the measure complemented the decree issued on the 11th of August, 1830, establishing a medical dispensary. This measure so necessary for public health should have been taken earlier since the disorders [i.e., sexual] that this law aimed at ending had already made deplorable inroads."[97]

Recent studies have documented the French colonial state's enormous investment in organizing military prostitution, first in Algeria and subsequently in colonial Tunisia and Morocco.[98] Given Tunisia's location vis-à-vis Malta and Algeria, it is hardly surprising that Husaynid officials and European consuls became increasingly alarmed as women from the "lower orders" began to arrive in Tunis either directly from the islands or the colony. Viewing the simultaneous depopulation, peopling, and devastation of Algiers, Tocqueville, who had earlier toured another nation of immigrants in the New World, recorded this 1841 entry in his diary:

> First appearance of the town: I have never seen anything like it. A prodigious mix of races and costumes, Arab, Kabyle, Moor, Negro, Mahonais, French. Each of these races, tossed together in a space much too tight to contain them, speaks its language, wears its attire, displays different mores. This whole world moves about with an activity that seems feverish. The entire lower town seems in a state of destruction and reconstruction. On all sides, one sees nothing but recent ruins, buildings going up; one hears nothing but the noise of the hammer. It is Cincinnati [Ohio] transported onto the soil of Africa.[99]

As for the upper city, the Qasba, he stated that "Old Algiers seemed an immense fox burrow: narrow, dark, smoky. The population, at this hour, seems idle and dissolute. Indigenous cabarets where Moorish public girls sing and people drink wine. Mix the vices of both civilizations. Such is the external appearance."[100] In his voluminous writings on migration, Tocqueville, who participated in the 1846 official commission of inquiry into conditions in Algeria, observed with bitter irony that France had hunted down the Arab population to people the country with Sicilians, Maltese, and Spaniards.[101]

In 1847 the army inventoried the capital city's peoples. Of the slightly more than 100,000 inhabitants of Algiers and its suburbs, nearly one-quarter were consigned to a new administrative and eventually legal category—*indigène*—then understood to encompass Muslims, Jews, and "Négres." European nationals from over fourteen countries amounted to 68,734; less than half were French citizens, about 32,000. Finally, 10 percent of the city's populace was characterized as *flottante*—sailors who had jumped ship, indigents, those without fixed domicile, refugees, and criminals. In the lower city near the port, the ancient urban core—originally composed of graceful Ottoman structures, including mosques and palaces—was eviscerated to make way for a new sociospatial landscape populated largely by island folk, characterized as "nothing but unwanted Christians that the galleys and the prisons of Europe have vomited up upon this country since its conquest by the French."[102] In less than two decades, Algiers had become a city of minorities from every corner of the Mediterranean.

THE WORLD BEYOND ALGERIA

As noted above, potential migrants often made calculated decisions based upon a range of factors when faced with opportunities for "making it" in different parts of the world. Moreover, nineteenth-century migratory streams to North Africa must be situated within a global context, since distant labor markets influenced settlement patterns but so did unforeseen circumstances. The demand for labor in South America, combined with bad luck, brought some Europeans to Algeria. In 1846, hundreds of destitute German families set out for South America via Dunkerque. Unable to pay their passage to Brazil and stuck in port where they proved a financial burden, the Germans were forcibly dispatched to the province of Oran, where most eventually perished of malnutrition and disease.[103] The impact of false advertising extolling the glorious prospects awaiting workers in search of a better life, together with the terrible health situation in the Algerian countryside, is seen in this tragic incident reported by the British consul in Algiers in 1858:

> This day Thomas Avis a distressed British subject was forwarded to H M consul at Marseille on his way to England accompanied by his wife and five children. This man was engaged as a farm labourer by a Mr. Spreckley, the owner of a farm near Koleah in this province under an engagement to serve as such two years on completion of which term he came to this Office to request assistance and to be sent home as Mr. Spreckley having stopped his wages during frequent fever and sickness, and having made an unfair agreement with the man leading him to believe that this was a very cheap country. He had no opportunity of saving sufficient money to pay his passage home. The undersigned considers this a very hard case and has assisted the man and his family both in an official capacity and from his private charity.[104]

How many people in Thomas Avis's unenviable position, bereft of the kindness of strangers to assist with passage back home, ended up in Tunisia—or elsewhere?

Population movements were not only configured by rumors, false advertising, or serendipity. Improvements in maritime transportation—above all, steam navigation—and in interior communications, such as roads, and slightly later, the construction of rail lines, played a critical role in moving people around faster and in disseminating more widely information of varying degrees of accuracy about conditions in North Africa. By 1839, it was noted that "packets go from here [Marseilles] to Algiers on every Sunday and generally perform the voyage in less than three days." French warships transported passengers to Algeria divided into three classes: "the first class is for persons of worth who only make arrangements with the Captain for their stay on board and dined at his table," while second-class and third-class travelers paid 105 and 63 francs respectively. Although steamship transportation regularized trans-Mediterranean travel, the delivery of mails, and the movement of goods and peoples, contingencies constantly arose that slowed or changed the course of journeys—and perhaps life trajectories. For example, in 1839 the return from Algiers to Marseilles via Valletta demanded an extra seven days due to the quarantine in effect, while the trip to Malta took longer because a quarrel had erupted between France and Naples over port dues.[105] Unanticipated travel snafus such as this surely played a major role in who ended up where at any particular juncture.

European rail building influenced population shifts to North Africa in complex ways, as this case from Spain demonstrates. Although the vast majority of Spanish emigrants set out for South America, comparatively speaking, more Spanish settled Algeria, notably in the province of Oran, than any other national group, while relatively few relocated to Tunisia; nevertheless, emigration from Spain to Algeria indirectly affected migratory currents elsewhere. Consular correspondence from the port of Carthegena, in Murcia province, demonstrates that French consuls around the Mediterranean were tracking local and transnational conditions with an eye eternally attuned to Algerian demographic needs. In 1865 the French representative in Murcia speculated upon the consequences of rail transport from Madrid to Carthagena. In his view, the new line would not only alter how people and products moved between the Spanish coast and Marseilles but also between Algeria and Spain: "There are already nearly 100,000 Spanish in Algeria. . . . The civil war, excessive droughts, and very low wages for unskilled labor are the main reasons that the Spanish leave home for Algeria." In 1855, the rains completely failed and the French vice-consul in Alicante "delivered in a few months time, 10,000 passports to Spanish nationals going to Oran."[106] Whether they remained permanently in western Algeria or headed instead for the Americas is another matter.

The end of drought in Spain after 1855, together with the construction of a rail line from Madrid to Carthagena, pushed up the price of labor in the next decade; consequently, departures for Algeria fell to about two thousand annually. Boom-and-bust development projects, similar to those in Sicily at the same time, meant that after the line was completed, unemployment soared once again. The rail lines also introduced information from outside into the Spanish interior, which "brought Algeria as a place of settlement to the attention of Spaniards who previously would not have been aware of migration possibilities."[107]

Patterns of labor movement in one Mediterranean subregion furnished models for solving shortages elsewhere. Peasants from the Duchy of Lucqnes had traditionally followed the rail lines to Viarreggio and Leghorn from whence they sailed to Corsica, worked the harvest, and returned to their villages with supplemental income—until the annual cycle began all over again. French consular authorities in Spain sought to implement the Tuscan-Corsican model to resolve Algerian labor scarcity, but on a temporary basis, to avoid the problems already caused by the settlement of foreigners: "the people of Murcia could do this in Algeria." In addition, steamship service and rail lines with fixed schedules reduced the traffic in undocumented Spanish immigrants to Algeria. After 1862 the Messageries Impériales offered maritime transport linked to interior rail lines from Valencia directly to North Africa. "Spanish emigrants prefer the regular service since they are certain to be able to disembark in [their chosen] port in Algeria." This represented a marked improvement for Spaniards and others who had traditionally been lured to Algeria by unscrupulous captains who "worked for their own account" in the coastal trade, including smuggling, and transported settlers "on the side" for between six to eight francs. Not infrequently, hapless passengers were dumped willy-nilly along the shore against their will.[108]

Events at the other end of the Mediterranean Basin shaped North African migratory flows. Until late in the century, Maronite peasants were banned from leaving Mount Lebanon without permission from feudal lords. Predictably, the establishment of a French steamship service linking Beirut to Marseilles in 1835 undermined controls over the local movement of labor; the trip, previously as much as three months, now took several weeks. In 1841, the French parliament allocated funding for the construction of six steamboats specifically for the Marseilles-Alexandria line that included Beirut; by 1845, ships on regular schedules were in operation. After bloody confessional strife, aided by Great Power interventions, erupted in Mount Lebanon in 1840–1841, the French consul in Alexandria hatched a scheme to settle Lebanese Christians in Algeria in 1845, which was given serious consideration in Paris and Algiers, although it was not then implemented.[109] But the 1860 insurrections in the Lebanon and Syria, followed by the massacre and flight of Christians, made the Maronite peopling of Algeria more urgent and possible. In January 1861, the minister of war in Paris contacted Randon, governor-general of Algeria:

> A recent traveler through the Lebanese mountains proposes recruiting the Maronites. Maronite notables believe their people would consider emigration to Algeria and would welcome becoming French subjects since they are very attached to France, if they had the means to do so. Due to recent events in Syria, many Maronites have left their native soil in order to take refuge in Egypt, Greece, and Malta; it would be easy to direct this migratory flux toward Algeria. The Maronite Christians, who speak Arabic, are vigorous, sober, industrious, and already cultivate cotton, wheat, silk, and tobacco and would be eminently suited to cultivate these in Algeria.[110]

Documents from 1866 reveal that some Maronites did indeed settle in Algeria. In addition, permission to emigrate to Algeria was requested by five hundred families from Crete as well as Chinese, Maldive, South African, Swiss, Polish, and Irish nationals; clearly the famines that beset Ireland from 1845 to 1852 drove some to North Africa.[111] Some of these people found their way to Tunisia.

The eagerness of French officials to welcome Germans or Maronites contrasts with prevailing attitudes toward the Maltese. In 1832, several Maltese laborers arrived in Algiers on an English ship from Valletta. Initially the port police refused permission to disembark, ordering the men to return immediately to the islands on the same ship—unless the British consul in Algiers could vouch for their good behavior and adequate financial means. Refusing to provide such guarantees, the consul observed to French authorities that he hoped "the same advantage would be allowed to the Maltese as is granted to the great quantities of Germans and other people who have come here to work and that if they conduct themselves improperly, it will be just as easy to send them away then as now when they have done nothing to deserve it."[112] In this case, they were permitted to remain. However, many more were forcibly transported to Malta or dumped on vessels making the rounds of Mediterranean ports like nineteenth-century ships of fools, laden not with the insane but rather with unfortunate souls deemed undesirable.

After midcentury, British officials on Malta undertook more aggressive policies toward overpopulation, including publicizing colonization schemes in far-flung corners of the empire. A typical instance occurred in 1872 when the official gazette published an announcement from a colonial British entrepreneur in Jamaica recruiting Maltese laborers, both male and female, although naturally women's wages were greatly inferior. Immigrants were promised a house, garden, and medical services, the catch being that they would perform hard fieldwork and pay part of their passage to Jamaica. The appeal fell on deaf ears, because in Malta "these conditions are not seriously considered as appealing. First of all, it is too far way and the climate is different. In addition, the Maltese earn in Algeria 2 francs 50 per day [2 ½ times the salary offered in Jamaica] and the climate and the language are more or less the same [in North Africa]."[113]

"BECAUSE OF THEIR TURBULENCE AND VAGABONDAGE": DEVIANCE AND DISPLACEMENTS

In 1871, one observer commented that "Algeria has been looked upon by the Imperial Government, less as a colony than as a place for deportees and political offenders, whose misdeameanours were not sufficiently grave to entitle them to banishment to Cayenne but who still were dangerous to the peace of France."[114] Earlier theoretical literature on global migrations made a distinction between voluntary and involuntary movements, which has recently been questioned, particularly in light of the widespread practice of "shoveling out paupers."[115] In the course of the nineteenth century, North Africa was transformed into a human dump for the politically turbulent or socially unwanted—in addition to representing as a sort of "New World" for people suffering from the dislocations wrought by nation-state or empire building, warfare, and industrial capitalism. Shoveling out to Muslim lands represented a substantial shift in thinking regarding the mobility of subjects on the part of European states. Traditionally, the Chambre de Commerce in Marseilles dissuaded, or even proscribed, individuals from the "lower ranks" of society from seeking a living in Ottoman port cities, known as Echelles. While prohibitions on all French women were imposed from time to time, those from the artisan classes were targeted since they were, in the eyes of the chamber, likely to "foment disorder in the Echelles through their freedom to go about, [and] by the libertinage of their female servants."[116] The reference to women's "freedom to go about," presumably in the streets of Istanbul or other Ottoman cities, expresses a deep-seated anxiety about inadequate means for controlling expatriate females in their daily lives, public and private. And the alleged "libertinage" of female servants raises an intriguing question—were these European domestics in service to their countrywomen or to local women from Ottoman society? Entrenched attitudes toward female emigration changed in the course of the nineteenth century but mainly for middle-class Frenchwomen, who were encouraged to go to the colonies accompanied by husbands as part of a familial gendered civilizing mission.

With the abolition of African slavery and the trade in enslaved persons in Tunisia after 1840 and in Algeria in 1848, the involuntary movement of labor was principally through compulsory transportation for felonies or political crimes. (Clandestine slavery persisted of course.) Forced population transfers and the use of colonies as dumping grounds had been practiced for centuries and was part of France's (and other nations') ancien régime policies. In the eighteenth century, the Spanish government routinely banished convicts to presidios on the North African coast, particularly Oran, although the practice ceased in 1792 when the Algerians recaptured the city. This older use of colonies influenced nineteenth-century attitudes toward settlers universally regarded as misfits at best. As European governments increasingly viewed North Africa as a social landfill; criminals were discarded in Algeria or Tunisia upon release from incarceration in Europe. In June 1837, the French minister of the navy complained that the Tuscan state had previously delivered passports for Bastia or Marseilles to subjects or residents whom Italian authorities found "disorderly or given to vagabondage." However, measures were in place to assure that Corsica and Marseilles no longer served that purpose, and "currently the Tuscans are using Algeria and North Africa as a *poubelle* for casting away their social undesirables."[117] The difference between the nineteenth century and earlier centuries was the sheer quantity of people subjected to forced relocation, the fact that these were not enslaved persons, and the political backgrounds of the castaways.

After violent suppression of the popular uprisings in Europe between 1848 and 1851, a number of insurgents were exiled to Algeria. The rebels of June 1848 were considered dangerous enough to be "placed in a special disciplinary institution" near Batna, where they served long sentences at hard labor. Sent to Bône by ship, another 450 *expulsés* arrived in 1850, with many more to come after Napoleon III's coup d'état of December 1851, which sent 15,000 Parisians to Algeria to rid the capital of disruptive elements.[118] In June 1852, twelve women arrested for political activities were released from Saint-Lazare Prison in Paris for involuntary transportation, followed by hundreds more. Pauline Roland, an educated feminist, socialist, radical republican, and mother of three, was one of the women sent across the sea. Pardoned in 1859, most women elected to return to France, although two hundred remained.[119] The fate of some *transportés* reveals the challenge posed by the peopling of Algeria. One-third of the 1851 exiles promptly died of cholera; another third returned to France in a year's time, and others straggled off to the New World. The remainder stayed on, but most abandoned farming for casual or unskilled work in coastal cities. Nevertheless, many officials in Algeria and France opposed using the colony as a scrap heap for political rebels or as a huge incarceration facility for common criminals. As Louis Veuillot sarcastically remarked at the time, "our colony of Algeria is nothing but a hospital contained within a prison."[120] Not a few of the deported escaped to other parts of North Africa.

Ship desertions brought uncounted numbers of people to Maghribi ports; some lingered, others attempted to reach home—wherever that was. The poor devils condemned to the galleys frequently jumped ship in Tunisian ports: "the generality of the Maltese now here are persons of the most desperate character, many having been convicted of the worst crimes and sentenced at Malta to the Galleys."[121] In 1858, a novice seaman, Barthelemy Bergel, onboard the French ship *La Nanette,* deserted in Munastir, a smart move because the port's small size and location impeded policing. For two weeks, Bergel wandered about and eventually made his way north to Bizerte, where small boats constantly ferried people between Tunisia, Bône, and Collo. From his trajectory, it seems that the hapless Bergel was trying to reach Algeria. Unfortunately, he was discovered in Bizerte, arrested, and taken to Tunis, where the French consul general contacted officials in Marseilles about forcibly repatriating the sailor.[122] Soldiers in the French Algerian army routinely deserted or "got lost" or both. A Tunisian vessel from Tabarka reached La Goulette in 1839 with a soldier, Pierre Vaillé, claiming that he had been separated from his Foreign Legion unit by accident. Captured by Algerians in Bône's still unconquered hinterland, Vaillé was forced to work harvesting wheat, or so the story went. After his escape, Vaillé arrived in Tabarka where a Tunisian *ra'is* (ship captain) agreed to deliver him to the French vice-consul. Predictably, Mediterranean warfare brought increased military ship desertions; during the Crimean War, both British and French seamen jumped ship in North African ports.[123]

Soon after 1830, a maritime police force was created that, together with customs officials, closely surveyed each passenger debarking in the Algiers port, "carrying out inquisitorial searches throughout one's luggage" to prevent fraud and contraband.[124] This only encouraged those without papers, deserters, and others to head for Algerian and Tunisia ports under less vigilant control. Until 1881, military authorities in Algeria continually complained to the beys and European consuls in Tunis about lapses in regulating coastal ship traffic between the countries. Bône was a favored place for channeling people with or without papers into Tunisia. In Malta, the French consul delivered 383 passports for Algeria for the entire calendar year 1871; however, for the first six months of 1872 alone, 223 passports had already been furnished to people traveling to "all ports of Algeria but especially for Bône . . . in addition to those [Maltese or others] who go to Algeria via Tunis."[125]

Tunisian captains piloted small vessels linking Collo, Bône, Tabarka, and Porto Farina virtually free from surveillance. French consuls repeatedly protested that these ships failed to keep manifests of goods and people. By the 1870s, the governors-general regarded this maritime Greyhound service as hazardous to Algeria's security. A typical letter from 1876 stated that "Tunisian ships which frequent Collo are never in possession of their crew rolls or passenger lists indicating the number and names of passengers whom they transport. In addition, their patents of health are often incomplete and limited to stating the condition of the health of the ship when it left Tunisian ports."[126] In short, La Goulette or smaller port towns operated as gateways—or getaways—for deserters, escapees, and criminals headed to—or out of—Algeria. And if officials in both countries scrambled to stem the free flow of people, the constant *va et vient* between islands and the African littoral, combined with inadequate resources, made it an aleatory enterprise.[127]

France's determination to make Algeria a settler colony, and after 1848 an administrative part of France, transformed the central Mediterranean into an expressway scattering peoples across the Maghrib: the rural dispossessed and *sans travail*, adventurers and carpetbaggers, speculators and investors, missionaries and bourgeois travelers. And in a cruelly ironic way, the brutalities of military pacification sparked middle-class travel and tourism to Algeria as well as Tunisia. Bitter disillusion with Algérie Française intensified population exchanges and movements in the central Mediterranean corridor. Thousands of émigrés who had set out for Algeria only to see their dreams collapse continually petitioned Paris for repatriation permits with the result that even more people came and went.[128]

COUNTING THE PEOPLE WHO DON'T COUNT

Given these circumstances, attempts at quantifying human mobility are doomed to failure, in large measure because of the fluidity of categories used by those responsible for counting. On December 4, 1842, a French ship from Bône deposited in La Goulette a Monsieur Greff, three French nuns from a Catholic missionary order, the Sisters of Saint-Joseph, and "ten diverse Muslims" *("dix Musulmans divers")*.[129] The French vice-consul inventoried another ship in 1847 from Algiers that had onboard one French subject, one Tuscan national, and fourteen "Arab and Jewish passengers." Another ship arriving at the same time from Bône had twenty-two passengers, seventeen designated as *indigènes*.[130] The category *indigène* is of critical importance since it glossed not only "natives" but also acquired legal armature in Algeria. In this period, it could mean Muslim and Jewish North Africans, or only Muslims, or only Algerians, and so forth, and encapsulates the dilemma inherent in establishing the identities of people arriving in, or departing from, Tunisia. Even in colonial Algeria, subject to much more rigorous record keeping, "the statistics [for 1856] are not precise; they reflect arrivals in large ports by ships and steamships; but there is not a single inlet [along the coast] where Spanish boats have not discharged their load of [undocumented] immigrants."[131] Seasonal, circular, return, and/or clandestine population displacements, combined with floating taxonomies of race, religion, and nationality, rendered tracking and quantifying many groups virtually impossible.

A historical geography of displacements demonstrates how older circuits of travel and trade, new migratory pressures, processes, and politics as well as pure chance—some would call it rotten luck—brought Maronite peasants, Sicilian masons, Maltese carpenters, metropole insurgents, and transnational mountebanks of various stripes to North Africa. To these trans-Mediterranean axes of mobility was added a horizontal axis of movement, mainly Algerian refugees fleeing devastation by relocating to the Regency of Tunis. The land borders were porous, and individuals or families moved to and fro in response to conditions that promised opportunity or heralded imminent disaster. Some Mediterranean island clans, such as the Maltese Borgs, counted family in both countries, a form of insurance against an uncertain future. And uncertainties abounded, since Algeria suffered droughts, epidemics, and major revolts unleashed by the institutionalized violence inherent in settler colonialism. In Tunisia, the great revolt of 1864 discouraged fresh immigration for a while and even sent some émigrés back to island villages for a time. While the migratory torque of France's invasion of Algeria is indisputable, exoduses from the northern Mediterranean rim or the islands would have occurred anyway—as Alexandria's expansion and Maltese immigration to Tunisia during the late 1820s demonstrate.

We began the chapter by evoking Khayr al-Din's odyssey, on the one hand, and the diverse trajectories of entrepreneurs, middling folk, political militants, or subsistence immigrants, on the other, which represented two somewhat historically distinct, although overlapping, patterns of trans-Mediterranean movement. Khayr al-Din embodied the older Ottoman system of military slavery and palace service, by then in its twilight years, that had furnished capable—and sometimes rebellious—administrators and soldiers to North African provinces for centuries. The east–west axis of exchange, traditionally the most significant, ceded to—while never being eclipsed by—the imperialism of the vertical north-south axis. Migratory pulses along the latter transformed Tunisia and Algeria (and a bit later, Morocco and Tripolitania) into places of socioeconomic advancement for peoples who had previously not viewed Barbary in this way, in part because popular conceptions shifted relatively rapidly. Gradual as well as dramatic shifts in the relative importance of these axes of displacements reflected profound transformations in Mediterranean politics, economies, and social structures and the world beyond.

When Ahmad Bey took the throne, about eight thousand nonsubject "others" resided in Tunisia; by the eve of the Protectorate, the percentage of "strangers" had doubled from 7 or 8 percent to 15 percent or more of the capital city's population. These figures, however, furnish an incomplete picture of collective perceptions regarding the presence of newcomers. Actual numbers—which city inhabitants did not know—were less significant than visibility; foreignness was often calculated according to a sociomoral sliding scale. Where the immigrants lived, worked, and socialized in the capital, the foods they consumed, the sounds they made, clothing, and languages—all were components of visibility. By far the most significant element was the public behavior of each community's womenfolk, which was frequently translated into neighborhood whispers about private comportment. How did their diverse Tunisian hosts—state officials, religious leaders, fellow laborers, neighbors, creditors, or landlords—accommodate, ignore, or reject the newcomers?

In keeping with the frame of an ethnographic voyage, the next three chapters follow people around as they sought work of various kinds. As the crux of the migratory experience, making a living constituted a major incentive for leaving as well as deciding where to go. Most immigrants clustered in the Tunis region because it afforded more advantages. Individuals claiming military or technical skills peddled their knowledge to Husaynid officials and thus forged a range of relationships—patron-client, business partnerships, and so on—not only with the beys' courts but also with consuls, creoles, and regular folks. To flourish modestly or merely survive, people of ordinary means relied on their own labor, wits, kin, if a kinship network existed, the benevolence of neighbors or strangers, and, from the 1840s on, missionaries. Employment inserted newcomers, if only partially, into social networks and exchange circuits that eased integration, however imperfect. If fortune smiled, the immigrant may have urged family "back home" to contemplate a short journey across the Sicilian Channel or a longer one from more distant parts. Yet raw chance often disrupted the best-laid plans; a golden prospect on the other side of the water proved a siren's song. The webs of opportunities and choices that labor migration seemed to offer ran head on into the unexpected, contingent, and unforeseen.

3

Making a Living

*Domestic Service
and Other Forms of Employment*

During the early morning hours of Ramadan in 1833, sixty Neapolitan servants (*mustakhadimin*) in the Bardo palace's inner service slumbered soundly—too soundly—after a busy night of preparing food and serving their masters, the mamluks. Heedless of the *nawba* (military band) announcing the final meal before dawn, the hapless servants only awoke when the day's fast was announced.[1] Infuriated by their dereliction of duty (and perhaps hungry), the head mamluk ordered the Neapolitans punished by the *bastinado*. The fast-footed escaped, taking refuge at their consulate in Tunis; the rest received brutal beatings resulting in severe injuries. Incensed, the Neapolitan consul demanded justice from Husayn Bey. A diplomatic crisis was unfolding.

This episode offers a window, albeit a narrow one, into the culture of servants and household service, while raising larger questions about making a living. The Neapolitans had probably arrived in the Regency of Tunis as young captives who, after being freed in 1816, remained with their masters, perhaps for want of other options. Characterized in the Arabic sources as children (*al-mushashuwat*, from the Spanish *muchachos*), the Neapolitans may have been integrated into palace households as fictive kin, although admittedly at an inferior rank. At the time of the incident, they held the status of salaried workers but were also Neapolitan subjects under the diplomatic protection of the Kingdom of the Two Sicilies. After the ensuing uproar was resolved, many Neapolitans left the palace to seek their fortune elsewhere in the city. What possibilities awaited them?

The incident poses questions about the kinds of work available in a preindustrial *and* precolonial state on the cusp of a migratory surge and challenges us to think about where people found jobs and how recruitment operated. The move-

FIGURE 9. The Sea Gate and entrance to the Tunis madina, c. 1860–1890. Renamed Porte de France with the establishment of the Protectorate, the sea gate mediated between the new city, laid out in gridlike fashion on reclaimed land, and the old city, which remained relatively untouched during the colonial period. (Library of Congress Prints and Photographs, LC-DIG-ppmsca-04741.)

ment of labor among port cities like Tunis was influenced by myriad external factors and processes, including changes in legislation governing mobility across territorial boundaries, the end of legal slavery in various part of the globe, notably in the British domains, the availability of factory work on nearby islands or on the other side of the sea, and shifting labor demands worldwide. Work is never solely about wages or gaining one's daily bread but rather ensnares individuals and families in intricate networks, positioning them in the local order. And employment was shaped by gender, religious affiliation, legal protection, education, and class as well as by acquired skills or knowledge.[2]

Work can be approached from a number of perspectives. However, within the context of heightened immigration, informational and assistance networks became critical because certain social circuits offered the possibility of patron-client relations, among other advantages. Recent research defines networks as "phenomena that are similar to institutionalized social relations, such as tribal affiliations and political dynasties, but also distinct from them, because to be networked entails making a choice to be connected across recognized boundaries."[3] To the concept of some degree of choice can be added distinctions between homogeneous and heterogeneous networks, the latter more receptive to "new information and innovative behavior," particularly critical within the context of mobile populations. The notion that conversational networks undergirded specific types of social communication and conferred an "insider" advantage about opportunities is also significant.[4]

In probing the issues raised by making a living, this chapter examines activities implicating Tunis city dwellers and recent immigrants in a nested labor exchange system that often relied upon networks: domestic or household service, state or consular employment, and public works. Since these arenas remain largely unexplored, they receive more attention than other economic actors or sectors, notably the big-time import/export magnates, whose wheeling and dealing, already studied by historians, ultimately undermined Tunisian state finances.[5] Once again the focus is upon the capital city, as most labor migrants were concentrated there, but other regions are considered due to the intersections between the center and provinces. What were the major sectors of the economy, what did households look like, and how did the abolition of slavery affect labor markets?

PRODUCTION AND WORK IN TUNIS, CIRCA 1830

Even with Ahmed Bey's modernization projects, the economy did not afford abundant opportunities for large numbers of "outsiders" or even familiar strangers like the Maltese and Sicilians. Tunis counted at least seventy-five *sina'at* (corporations or guilds) that produced and distributed an array of goods and service—from water carriers, coffee vendors, and sweets confectioners to butchers, tanners, and weavers; the guilds remained fairly intact, although external pressures were building that eventually undermined them. Close-knit, guild members chose heads (*amins*) charged with ensuring quality by supervising producers and products. The manufacture of *shashiyas,* centered in Tunis and satellite villages, represented a protocapitalist industry generating considerable revenues and employment. A special market—the *suq al-shawwashiya*—sold finished caps to retailers for distribution in the rest of the country, the Maghrib, and the Ottoman Empire until cheaper, European imitations competed with the superior but pricier Tunisian headgear.[6] Silk weaving employed four thousand artisans, although raw silk was no longer produced locally but rather was imported from Italy and China. As with other *sina'at,* silk weavers were located in a specific quarter in the madina—near the dyers in today's Turbet al-Bey neighborhood. However, as with other such enterprises, the silk and *shashiya* industries offered little work for outsiders.

Many professions were dominated by religious and/or ethnic groups. Tunisian Jews monopolized tailoring and moneylending, while porters and stevedores were recruited from the southern oases; the *bakkals* (grocers) in Tunis came from the island of Djerba, which remained the case until well into the twentieth century. The barraniya, or outsiders—the Kabyles and oasis peoples in particular—banded together in specific city quarters and trades; Algerian artisans or laborers were overseen by an *amin* recognized by the beys. Public baths had long been monopolized by the Mzabites, an Islamic sect from the deep Sahara in Algeria; as late as 1890, thirty-five Mzabi *hammamjis* (bathhouse owners) still operated under an *amin*.[7] Nevertheless, the guilds were not impermeable to the kinds of changes introduced by labor migration, since a few immigrants were admitted into their ranks before 1881, although this is poorly documented. When the "new town" was constructed after 1863 on reclaimed land between the Sea Gate and the lake, the workers, mainly Sicilian or Maltese, were placed under the authority of the city's *amin*s and enrolled in one of the corporations, a move aimed at maintaining the traditional administrative order governing the relations of production.[8]

Women worked in a number of capacities, notably in textile manufacture, producing a wide array of items critical to household as well as village or pastoral economies; some female-produced goods were sold or bartered in markets and, as mentioned earlier, a special suq in Tunis provided a space for women of ordinary means to buy and sell wares. Women served female society as healers, midwives *(qabla)*, and beauticians, such as the *hannana* who specialized in applying henna to brides, singers, dancers, and prostitutes. Some of the numerous bathhouses in Tunis were reserved exclusively for women, offering work for female attendants often recruited from desert towns in the Mzab. Women regarded as exceptionally skilled in needlework or lace making held the respected status of *mu'allima* and taught household arts to girls within the domestic compound.[9] Yet the social organization of work offered meager opportunities for immigrant women in the urban economy.

The single-largest productive sector, increasingly subjected to the most abusive expropriation of "surplus," was the peasantry whose principal crops were olive oil and grains, followed by the diverse products of the oasis and pastoral economies.[10] Both the palace and the capital city acted as gigantic intakes that pumped labor, income, and produce from the Sahil, the northern wheat-growing regions, and from the interior, funneling them by means of various coercive mechanisms to Tunis. In times of scarcity or famine, the beys personally oversaw poor relief and tightly controlled food supplies for the capital city, always the first provisioned, to the detriment of the peasantry; this important distributive function extended to foreign city residents. Until the 1863 Anglo-Tunisian convention, followed by the 1868 Italian-Tunisian treaty, which together conferred property rights upon foreigners, Europeans theoretically could not acquire full title to land, farms, or businesses, although working land owned or held by Tunisian subjects offered a convenient cover. As was true in Izmir and Alexandria, locals and foreigners resorted to clever subterfuges to thwart restrictions on property holding, exploitation, or transfers. Some Europeans were able to actually purchases houses "under the cover of fictive deeds"; others "managed" olive groves whose revenues were collected through annual rents.[11]

THE BIGGEST GAME IN TOWN: THE BEYS' TABLE

Discussions of work must begin with the Husaynid household bureaucracy, which was not the "only game in town" but represented the "biggest game" because the dynasty sat at the confluence of commercial, financial, and economic relationships forged by revenue collection, tax farms, public works, trade monopolies, import/export controls, and international trade. Thus, the ruling family and court constituted the single-largest employer, followed by the guilds, which varied in size, output, and number of employees, and then local traders and merchants, whether indigenous, Ottoman Levantine, or European.

How did the great households generate employment and shape demands for labor? The Husyanids and their courts provided work to countless numbers through voracious consumption of foodstuffs, textiles, household goods, and luxury items as well as indirectly drawing upon the labor of many more. In addition to large cohorts of retainers, servants, guards, cooks, scribes, entertainers, healers, and court physicians, workers tended the extensive gardens and stables or engaged in manufacture. Swelling the permanent residents at the Bardo and other palaces were guests, visitors, and supplicants from around the country who lodged there sometimes for extended periods; other palaces, for example, the Muhammadiya outside the capital built by Ahmad Bey, required large infusions of labor, both local and imported. The Bardo complex constituted a "cosmopolitan" universe since it housed and gave work to people whose origins lay in Africa, Asia, and Europe. While most were Muslims, a small community of Christians and Jews served the palace; Europeans, particularly highly skilled craftsmen such as watchmakers and physicians, were on the payroll.[12]

Can we estimate numbers? Around 1829, the Sardinian consul, Count Filippi, stated that "the Bardo is occupied by the ruling family which owns a number of beautiful residential quarters, the rest of the area is occupied by the Mamluks and servants; the former number about 200, half of whom serve the princes by assuming different offices and responsibilities of the court, the remainder are divided into four companies and serve as the interior guards."[13] A reliable source, Filippi claimed that the palace complex contained about eight hundred people total, although he could not have known with any certainty about the number of temporary residents nor about the extensive women's quarters. Modeled upon the Ottomans, but on a less sumptuous scale, harims were guarded by eunuchs, many imported from Egypt. Depending upon personal inclination, some rulers took relatively few wives and concubines, while others, such as Muhammad Bey, were enthusiastically polygamous. The harims also relied upon small armies of personal attendants, nurses, cooks, and servants organized into the same carefully calibrated hierarchy as the beys' inner service and peopled by individuals of different religions and ethnoracial backgrounds, a veritable microcosm of Afro-Eurasia.[14]

The prince's table represented a critical space of patronage, performance, and largesse for a range of clients and audiences. Palace celebrations, whether religious, familial, or diplomatic in nature, mobilized sizeable numbers of servants or slaves and quantities of foodstuffs. In 1826, four of Husayn Bey's children—three sons and a daughter—were wed at the *bayt al-basha* (Bardo) in a collective ritual attended by religious, political, and tribal notables; the weeklong festivities, involving banquets and the distribution of presents to the populace, demanded large inputs of labor to orchestrate. As recent research demonstrates, the performance of hospitality fed the internal patronage system; the more sumptuous the banquets offered by households within the ruling circle, the more notables and clients could be dazzled and socially indebted.[15] In addition, pure drinking water for the Bardo's needs was inadequate; one of the slaves' chief occupations was filling barrels with springwater from the mountains outside Tunis, which were brought back by mules to the prince's table.[16]

Hospitality bestowed upon visiting dignitaries constituted one of the pillars of diplomacy as well as facilitating information gathering; the beys not only received delegations from Istanbul or military missions from Mediterranean powers in formal audiences but also entertained them. In July 1828, three Sardinian officials arrived to consult with their consul and then paid respects to Husayn Bey, who threw an elaborate dinner banquet in their honor at his country estate. From the 1830s on, the obligatory wining and dining increased precipitously to accommodate the stream of Europeans who came as envoys, job seekers, scam artists, and high-end travelers. Thus, its status as the epicenter of the state and economy rendered the palace a space of constant, at times feverish, comings and goings that consumed substantial revenues extracted from indigenous producers and required huge outlays of free or servile labor.

Tunis notables emulated the beys—indeed some were related to them—so the residences of high-ranking officials resembled those of the rulers in miniature. Typical in terms of organization and staffing was Dar 'Abd al-Wahhab, located in Bab al-Jazira, near the madina proper and adjacent to a major mosque, al-Mahriziya. Dar 'Abd al-Wahhab was comprised of a number of dwellings, shops, a stable, and bath and included wives, concubines, offspring, extended family, and clients. Due to the number of permanent or temporary residents and the myriad exterior social obligations, the household employed an array of domestics living at the complex who were under the master's supervision. Elite status necessitated the bestowing of alms and other forms of charity; each day the city's needy assembled before the *driba* (antechamber) of Dar 'Abd al-Wahhab, awaiting the distribution of food and clothing by servants. When the family patriarch, who held the important post of *bash hanba,* was absent at court, a Jewish steward assured household order by supervising servants and children alike.[17]

HOUSEHOLD SERVICE

The study of domestic service demands multiple disciplinary perspectives, notably labor, family, and migration history, inflected by questions of class, race, ethnicity, and gender. As with other types of transnational labor in today's global market, domestic workers secured positions through networks and, once employed, constructed new strands of networks. Gender tempers purely economic calculations because the factors influencing women's employment often differ from those governing men's work, above all, questions of morality.[18] But do these patterns hold true for a preindustrial North African state in the era before colonialism? How did the service sector offer both employment and social positioning for newly arrived Mediterranean folk of humble status or for those from more privileged social strata? Did employment as servants in elite households bring some measure of empowerment? And what does the service sector tell us about the workings of networks?

Sources for reconstructing the social world of servants are scanty at best; for this reason, research on nineteenth-century Tunis has largely ignored domestic service. Yet household employment constituted an intricate system of labor extraction juxtaposing individuals or families of dissimilar social ranks and sexes—and sometimes religions, races, legal statuses, and national origins—under the same roof, or at least in intense spatial proximity. Moreover as recent work shows, elite service was organized into status hierarchies so that distinctions must be made between, for example, personal attendants to the princes and simple maids.[19] As was true elsewhere, Tunisian marriage contracts often stipulated that brides from wealthy families be provided with servants. Some were recruited from impoverished families in the countryside, whose offspring were placed with socially superior households where they remained for years. Within extended kinship groups, families that had fallen on hard times might place young girls with wealthier relatives who, in exchange for household labor, would raise them, find suitable husbands, and eventually marry them off. Most of these arrangements were oral, although at times they assumed the form of written contracts registered with the qadi.[20] Other urban Muslim households engaged Jewish servants, while the mamluks and the palace employed Maltese, Sicilian, or Sardinian women in service, as we shall see.

The affair of the Neapolitans sheds some light upon the cultural norms of the time governing the treatment of servants or slaves as well as the existence of work contracts. In a heated conversation with Husayn Bey after the debacle, the Neapolitan consul reminded the ruler that when the servants "were freed from slavery, they elected to remain in the country where they had been raised as paid workers; and an employer does not have the right to beat his employees. . . . They could have been fired before the expiration of the contract *[nazila]*." To which Husayn Bey testily responded: "The custom in our country permits beating servants." A lively discussion ensued among the bey's closest advisors over the permissibility of inflicting corporal punishment; opinion was divided. The bey's secretary maintained that domestics, such as the Neapolitans, should not be ill-treated because they were *ahrar* (free).[21]

What did household service look like during the transitional period from enslaved service to free employment? The Englishman Godfrey Feise, who spent two years in Tunis just prior to Admiral Exmouth's expedition, provides an invaluable account of Christian captives serving the regency's ruling classes. In 1812 Feise calculated the number of European slaves in Tunis at around two thousand, a figure obtained from longtime residents: "Christian slaves are very few in number at present owing to the English having lately ransomed the Sicilians and Greeks of the Ionian islands. Those in the situation of slavery are now Neapolitans and Sardinians because the Tunisians are now only at war with Sardinia and Naples."[22] What tasks did they perform in this period? "Many Christian slaves fill places of trust and those who labor seldom have heavier duties than watering and attending to a garden. . . . Nor must we forget the poor obsequious Christian slave who stands with humble reverence behind his lordly master, holding his coffee cup and presenting him with Tobacco according as it may be required."[23] Outside the capital, captives were employed in a number of occupations: the secretary to the *kahiya* (governor) of La Goulette was a Christian slave, probably due to linguistic abilities, while the prime minister had a number of enslaved Christians in service on his country estate near Utique, twenty-two miles from Tunis.

Feise's manuscript sheds light upon those few captives fortunate enough to serve as social-status markers in elite Muslim households: "as Christian slaves constitute a great part of Moorish grandeur, those who can afford to purchase the greatest number and keep them the best clothed are considered as the first among the grandees of the Principality." According to Feise, Christian slaves in palace service were generally well treated since they were not only adequately nourished but also lavishly dressed in the Ottoman or "eastern style," minus, of course, the headgear reserved for Muslim men.[24] The clothing worn by Christian servants at the Bardo continued to draw sarcastic comments from Europeans. In the 1830s, a visitor declared that "the Christian domestics [in the bey's service] wear the most ridiculous costume that one could imagine"—which suggests that the servants retained their "eastern dress" and their significance as status indicators.[25] Perhaps some of the hapless Neapolitans who were punished so cruelly had sported this costume before their fall from grace in 1833.

Of course, until 1816 Christian slaves (and slaves from other regions) performed heavy manual labor under dreadful conditions, although those with skills enjoyed a better lot in an otherwise bleak existence. Together with free European nationals employed by the Tunisian state, slaves engaged in shipbuilding in Porto Farina until rapid silting up decreased labor demands as shipyards and trade languished. As for renegades, always a favorite topic for European writers, a report from 1845 maintained that "Renegade Christians were formally employed at the Court of Tunis, and in other parts of Barbary, and many Christian adventurers turned Turk [i.e., converted to Islam] in order to obtain these emoluments. But those times are passed . . . and now at Tunis [they are] but simple and conscientious Christians employed by the bey."[26]

Toward the end of his life, Mustafa Bey—Ahmad's father—attempted to organize a battalion of African soldiers by forced conscription. The idea probably came from Egypt's Muhammad 'Ali Pasha, who had created an army with captives seized from the northern Sudan, which failed abysmally, inflicting great suffering upon the slave soldiers.[27] In May 1836, the Tunisian minister Shakir proposed that Africans capable of bearing arms be pressed into military service to supplement the *nizami* (regular) troops always short of manpower. Soldiers were dispatched from barracks in Tunis with orders to round up anyone with "black skin" and forcibly conscript them. The press-gang seized slaves, ex-slaves, free Warglis (from the oases of Warqala, or Ouargla) from Algeria, Hamrunis from Morocco's Tafilalt, and Fazzanis from Tripolitania—even the *bawwab* (doormen) and grooms from the bey's stables were removed by force. "They took servants and gardeners and many stores in Tunis had to close [for lack of labor] and they even took individuals from Wargla who were employed in the French consulate . . . and the people of Tunis spent days talking about this."[28] The ill-advised experiment in building a "troop surge" came to naught as households and employers reclaimed lost laborers; Shakir, the butt of many a joke for hatching such a foolish scheme, soon thereafter lost his position and his life.

If the affair provides a narrow window into how race was conceptualized, identifying Africans solely by skin color would have been somewhat problematic given the degree of miscegenation in some sectors of Tunisian society; other indicators of African slave origins were the type of work performed, place of residence, dress, language, and names.[29] What is clear is that laborers from sub-Saharan regions were integral to the capital city's economy, workforce, and daily life in countless ways.

ABOLITION AND LABOR

Between 1816 and 1846, Christian and African slavery were abolished in Tunisia, although the shift from unfree to free labor was less linear, more gradual than treaties or abolition decrees would have us believe; the distinction between slave and servant was blurred in practice, if not in law. The immediate consequences of Admiral Exmouth's expedition upon the Tunis labor market remain unknown, although it must have had repercussions because the state and elite households lost large numbers of servile workers for their galleys, arsenals, shipyards, and domestic service.[30] But, as was true elsewhere, the end of "white" slavery did not mean that the currents that fed women into elite harims disappeared—far from it. Traditional marriage patterns among court mamluks and the prestige garnered from emulating Ottoman elite households meant that stamping out the trade in women proved daunting.[31] As familiar strangers, the mamluks were restricted in marriage partners to women from other mamluk families or, if very fortunate and highly placed, to Husaynid women; this significantly narrowed the range of available spouses, making Georgian, Circassian, or Greek women valuable. After the powerful Georgian mamluk Mustafa Sahib al-Tabi' (d. 1861) lost his first wife, Mahbuba, one of Mustafa Bey's daughters, he married a Circassian woman named Gülfinden (Rose Garden), although it is uncertain how or when Rose Garden arrived in Tunisia.[32]

However, following directives from London, English consular officials and sea captains interpreted the treaties abolishing Christian slavery to mean that Ottoman Christian subjects could no longer be traded. In October 1823, an English ship arrived in La Goulette from Smyrna transporting "women that the ship Captain supposes are Greek. When the [Tunisian] port authorities asked the English ship captain to disembark the two Greek women, he refused. When the Bey was informed of this refusal, he sent an order to La Goulette to have the ship captain land the women through the use of force and this is what just took place."[33] And a report from La Goulette in 1831 stated that

> an Austrian vessel arrived in this port on the 12th last [of September 1831] from Constantinople, having on board a Turkish Chouse [i.e., şavuş] charged to deliver to the Bey of Tunis the new military uniforms which the Sultan had directed should be worn in the future by the Bey and his Troops . . . I understand that this vessel has brought three Georgian women whom, it is suspected, are slaves, belonging to the suite of the Chouse, brought hither [to Tunis] for sale. Formerly great numbers of Georgian women were brought here. This however seldom happens now; but such as are sent are generally imported by Austrian vessels.[34]

Thus, the traffic in female slaves from Ottoman lands or the Black Sea intended for harim service persisted, although clandestinely and on a reduced scale, and women were often transported on European vessels. A curious episode with only fragmented evidence suggests the treaties signed by Tunis ending Christian slavery were not observed when it came to harim women. During the Greek rebellions against Ottoman rule on Chios in 1822, the widow and daughter of the Danish vice-consul to Chios, who had perished during the hostilities, were taken to Tunis and placed in the household of the *bash mamluk* who was married to one of the bey's daughters. Seven years later the French consul began negotiating their release.[35]

What about the trans-Saharan trade in enslaved persons? Credible figures are virtually impossible to come by, but it is estimated that about one thousand enslaved persons entered Tunisia annually just prior to abolition; the largest slave market was in Tunis, the *suq al-birka*.[36] Until 1846, most African slaves, male or female, were employed in domestic service performing a range of tasks that were not sharply gendered in nature. However, in the south they worked hard in the date palm plantations and gardens, where their labor was critically important to the oasis economy. The trans-Saharan traffic in humans not only shifted labor from one region to another but also introduced new musical and culinary forms—such as the dish known as *gnawiya* still prized today, which first appeared on the menu at the bey's palace kitchen in La Marsa sometime in the early nineteenth century—as well as different languages, beliefs, and ways of doing things. And not all Africans were, or had been, enslaved persons; for centuries, Saharan and West African Muslims had journeyed to Tunis on the pilgrimage, to study at the city's many religious institutions, and to conduct trade.[37] Nevertheless, most Africans came to Tunisia as enslaved persons.

Tunisian rulers and notables routinely manumitted household slaves in large numbers to celebrate Islamic festivals, family celebrations, such as marriages, or dynastic events. When the Baya Lalla Fatima, the ruler's wife, died in 1827, "her last moments on earth were marked by an act of goodness which will honor her memory forever, the freeing of five hundred black slaves."[38] At Husayn Bey's death in 1835, six hundred female and two hundred male slaves were liberated; when Mustafa Bey died in 1837, hundreds of his personal slaves were freed as well. Manumitted slaves were provided with notarized certificates from their former masters stating that they were free; female slaves, who did not always veil during servitude, were required to cover their faces once freed.[39] Employment in an elite household did not shield slaves from mistreatment, including sexual abuse, overwork, or ill health. Force-marched across the Sahara in dreadful conditions, those who made it adjusted with difficulty to the damp winter climate of the capital region. While there are few sources on African experiences or daily lives in service, the bey's chief physician, the French national Laurent Gay, noted in his medical treatise the sufferings of one of the Bardo's African slaves, a "young man of about twenty-five years who has been coughing for more than a year";

Gay also treated "a young African woman recently arrived from Bornou who is in service in one of the great houses of the Bardo."[40] But not all enslaved persons remained in Tunisia.

Great Britain's Mediterranean-wide abolition crusade launched in the 1820s meant that ships were subject to relentless scrutiny by British consular agents stationed in ports, notably Tunis, which dispatched enslaved Africans to other parts of the Ottoman Empire. Sir Thomas Reade aggressively interfered with the trade if it involved British or Maltese ships docking in La Goulette, submitting annual reports to London with statistics on ships transporting Africans. He also enlisted informants to provide data on the identity and status of passengers on vessels not flying the British flag. Between 1833 and 1835, ships from Austria, Tuscany, Greece, Russia, and the Ottoman Empire put in to port. Of the ships inventoried during a three-year period, Austrian vessels transporting enslaved persons were in the majority, a pattern seen elsewhere in the Mediterranean. This indicates that British abolition had created opportunities for other European nations to traffic in humans. In January 1836, Reade calculated that nine non-British vessels carried over three hundred Africans destined for Constantinople, Candia, and Izmir.[41] While Malta represented an important center for abolition efforts in the Mediterranean, the island functioned as an equally active hub for the contraband trade in enslaved persons (and prostitution) until late in the nineteenth century, which proved embarrassing to the Crown in view of British claims of moral superiority based on its leading role in global abolition.

Reade's alter ego was James Richardson, a member of the British and Foreign Anti-Slavery Society, sent in 1844 to Malta and Tunisia to direct abolition campaigns in Tripoli and the Kingdom of Morocco. His preoccupation with African slavery becomes clear from the marginalia inserted in his 1845 manuscript. One of Richardson's local female informants on the inner workings of the bey's household noted the presence of eunuchs guarding the entryway to the harim: "two ugly blackmen [sic], one of them, the most hideous fellow I think I ever saw." After this remark, Richardson appended an explanatory note, stating that "these men were probably eunuchs, notorious for their ugliness. From time to time the Barbary princes get a supply from the Levant. The Emperor of Morocco lately had a dozen sent him from Egypt when the author was in that former country [i.e., Morocco]."[42]

In the years leading up to Tunisian abolition, enslaved or recently manumitted Africans frequently showed up at the British consulate seeking refuge or work or both. In part this was due to the building's location near the Bab al-Bahr and adjacent to a main square and promenade that constituted a spatial and social mixing bowl. In 1830, an African female slave "took refuge in the consulate demanding her liberty from her Mistress who had sold her to a foreigner," as did "a slave boy who was accorded refuge" and remained in the consulate for several days. In 1829, a free woman and "Negress lately in the service of the consul general being oppressed by the chief of the Negroes," complained of mistreatment to Reade who allowed her to stay in the building until "a promise was made on the part of the Caid [qa'id] that she should no longer be persecuted."[43] Enslaved persons sought asylum at the Anglican cemetery, Saint George's, located outside of city walls in this period but near the Sea Gate and British consulate; indeed the cemetery was referred to locally as "the place of refuge."[44] Therefore, information about Britain's antislavery stance seems to have entered into neighborhood conversational circuits, which may explain the large number of asylum- seekers and petitioners at the consulate.

In August 1841, Ahmad Bey closed the principal Tunis slave market, and the next year the importation of enslaved persons was prohibited; by January 1846 the sale, purchase, and possession of slaves were outlawed.[45] Tunisia became a titular member of the London-based Anti-Slavery Society in 1842, another route to securing diplomatic recognition from leading European powers, especially Great Britain, as the letters exchanged between Ahmad Bey and the Anti-Slavery Society suggest.[46] Count Raffo and the Austrian undersecretary of foreign affairs to Ahmad Bey, Antonio Bogo (1794–1878), were credited with overseeing the abolition decrees: "he [Raffo] has been decorated by several foreign governments and gave great assistance to Sir Thomas Reade in the question of abolition of Tunisian slavery, and obtained from the British Government a distinguished mark of its favour"[47] But Ahmad Bey was sincerely dedicated to abolition, despite the considerable consequences at stake due to fierce opposition.[48] The end of slavery placed Tunisia in a legal situation comparable to American nonslave states before the Civil War, since slavery was only abolished in French Algeria in 1848. France insisted that fugitive slaves in Tunisia constituted the legitimate property of Algerian subjects and had to be returned to their owners. In the mid-1840s, an African slave from Algeria took refuge in the British consulate in Tunis. The English consul "was obliged to purchase the boy to get him freed . . . [because] all slaves are free on touching the Tunisian soil [in accordance with Ahmad Bey's decrees] with the exception of French Algerian slaves."[49]

GENDER, SLAVERY, AND DOMESTIC SERVICE

One strategy for viewing domestic service during the transition from servile to free labor is to enter the social universe of households, which, due to the sources, restricts us largely to the Husaynids or court notables.[50] European accounts contain almost the only ethnographic data that, despite inherent problems, offers evidence on the duties incumbent upon retainers and attendants. In 1833, 1835, and 1844, European women, some creoles, others short-term visitors, paid social calls to Husaynid women at the Bardo and the summer palace in La Marsa.[51] One of the earliest accounts is by Madame Berner, whose husband served as Danish consul for years. Significantly for the question of creoles, she elected to remain in Tunis after the consul's death. Her long residence makes her a credible source of insider information on household slaves as well as the key role played by an Italian woman in palace visits. "At the double gate of the harim, two Moors kept watch; and after one of them had retired, a few minutes to announce us, he returned with the interpreter, an Italian lady, who invited us to follow her . . . from the place where we were seated, we could see into several other rooms where on the ground sat a great number of black and white female slaves, some gossiping, others engaged in various occupations. The numbers which I saw, from time to time, certainly exceeded a thousand."[52]

In the same period, Sir Grenville Temple and Lady Temple sailed from Algeria to Tunis, where they lived for a number of months in a rented house in the lower madina. In late 1832 or early 1833, Lady Temple also visited the Bardo accompanied by her sisters. "We were received at the entrance of the palace by Giuseppino Raffo, the Bey's BashKasak, who, leading us up a short staircase, consigned us over to the charge of a Christian woman, who, addressing us in Italian, conducted us to a door, where stood her highness, the Lillah Kebirah, ready to receive us."[53] Since the bey's wife only spoke Arabic, the Tuscan woman served as interpreter. An African male slave stood by armed with a "large fan" in order to keep away the flies. Another account from circa 1844 documents the fact that entertainment was one of the duties incumbent upon women in service. "We must not omit the mention of the *indecent dance* prevalent in female society through all Barbary. Many hours are passed by the women witnessing this dance performed by their slaves in the solitude of the harim. Christian ladies are never pressed to witness it as the Mooresses know it would give them very, justly, great offence. It is performed openly at Jewish marriages, and such is the force of habits, however immoral, that European women of the lower sort [living in Tunis] sometimes perform this dance with great zest."[54]

During her tour of Tunisia in 1871, Lady Herbert (1822–1911) spent time in the La Marsa palace of one of the Muhammad al-Sadiq Bey's nieces then celebrating her marriage. After viewing the magnificent wedding trousseau, Lady Herbert and the other female visitors returned to the harim's main patio, where amusements had been organized. "A concert had been prepared for us of the usual Arab instruments, performed by twenty or thirty of the prettiest slaves in the establishment, all beautifully dressed. And then followed a dance, part of which consisted in wriggling the body in such a way that it appeared as if the stomach of the dancer was independent of the rest of her person, and to our intense astonishment it ended in a succession of somersaults, or turning head over heels several times in succession."[55] By this period, the trope of the "indecent dance" was integral to European expectations of Muslim society, but the documentation on dancers, instrumentalists, singers, and entertainers for harim women considerably expands our knowledge of the repertoire of tasks assigned to servants.[56] The claim that "European women of the lower sort" performed dances deemed erotic at weddings is equally intriguing and indicates that the informant had witnessed this spectacle herself, had heard about it from other upper-crust Europeans resident in Tunis, or had read about it in Orientalist literature.

In a long, detailed account from 1844, the English woman Miss Smith, who accompanied Mrs. Reade and her daughters on a visit to one of the summer palaces, provides more mundane evidence on daily life and domestic service. She observed servants at work: "several women apparently embroidering and making clothes for the family"; serving food: "the black and white attendants of whom there were many, placed napkins on our laps and handed us the refreshments"; and forms of etiquette observed in the circle of the bey's chief wife: "a black page entered and kissed the Lillah's hand, who then arose inviting us to go up stairs into her gallery." Clearly the English women had been enjoined to count the Africans, perhaps as part of Great Britain's antislavery campaign: "I have counted more than fifty of them [black female attendants] dressed in the gayest colours, attended with the *Kaed el-dar* [i.e., *qa'id al-dar*, a eunuch]."[57]

As for the 1835 account, the figure of "one thousand" white and black slaves seems high, although estimates may have been deliberately inflated for political reasons or perhaps the female visitors were simply overwhelmed by the sheer number of people in service. Another explanation is that foreign observers conflated servants with enslaved persons; even Europeans familiar with local society evinced uncertainty about the imprecise lines between servitude and free employment. While Bin Diyaf stated clearly that Ahmad Bey's mother had originally been a slave *(jariya)* captured during a raid, Richardson, not one to downplay slavery by any means, claimed instead that "the mother of Ahmad Bey was a native of the isle of St. Peter, off Sardinia, who being introduced very young at the Bardo as a servant, and not a slave, attracted the attention and won the favors of Sidi Mustapha, the father of Ahmad."[58] Nevertheless, if Lady Herbert was correct in characterizing the entertainers as slaves, this indicates that abolition had not reached into the women's quarters of the great households as late as 1871, which other evidence suggests as well.

Three decades after Ahmad Bey's bold act, Tunisia signed a convention with Great Britain in 1875 reaffirming commitment to abolition, which demonstrates that the trade in enslaved persons posed daunting problems of enforcement in Tunisia as elsewhere. As late as 1880, African women in Tunis remained in household service against their will but under the cover of marriage, a common strategy. In 1880, the British consul, Richard Reade (son of Thomas), lodged a complaint with the prime minister regarding three black female slaves, Anisa bint 'Abdallah al-Barnawy, Fatima Barnawy, and A'isha bint al-Barnawy, whose names indicate that they were from Bornu (or that this origin had been ascribed to them). The women had escaped from their late (i.e., former) masters "and at the instance of this agency and consulate general obtained letters of emancipation from the local authorities." Subsequently, an official in the bey's government had given the three women back to their former owners. Another woman, Maimuna, was in the same situation, although the official claimed that she had been married "in accordance with her own wishes." Repeated requests for Maimuna and her husband to present themselves at the consulate with papers for verification went unheeded. The British consul demanded that the women be immediately freed and that "the offending official be punished in such a way as to deter others from acting in like manner toward manumitted individuals."[59]

While manumitted slaves had been periodically fed into local labor markets, freedom on such a massive scale did not necessarily bring the liberty to choose a profession or seek new places of work. As in other parts of the globe, former slaves often remained with masters and households performing the same tasks in workshops, gardens, or homes. After 1846, freed African slaves swelled the ranks of the capital's least privileged strata and probably increased the pool of casual or unskilled labor; their numbers are estimated at several thousand.[60] Another issue specific to women is the possibility that former slaves were forced to earn their living as prostitutes, although fragmentary data on prostitution in Tunis during the 1860s suggests that only 8 percent of the women charged by police with this crime were of African slave origins.[61] In later notarial records, the category 'atiq (freed persons) was employed to designate domestics who were the children of emancipated slaves who had remained with the family.[62] By the eve of the Protectorate, a few fortunate Africans served as honor guards stationed in front of palaces in the madina's Qasba neighborhood. Dressed in "splendid costumes embroidered in gold," these retainers fulfilled concierge functions by announcing visitors or shielding their impecunious masters from the intrusions of persistent creditors.[63]

Once again, abolition raises questions about the labor required to run large, multigenerational households whose status was calibrated by the sheer number of servants and retainers. It leads us to ask whether competition existed between newly arrived subsistence migrants and recently manumitted slaves. And if free labor circulated widely between colonial Algeria and Tunisia, the movement of enslaved, or formerly enslaved, persons across borders must also be factored into the mix of motives for relocation.

PHYSICIANS AND COOKS

The duties performed by the "Italian woman" at the Bardo indicate that a regular parade of female visitors came to socialize, making the services of a female interpreter imperative. We have no knowledge of the harim guide's precise identity—perhaps she was related to the Raffo family or in service to them? By then many inner-service mamluks hailed from various regions of what would later become Italy. Most importantly, the Italian woman's position as a linguistic and cultural broker mirrors the functions of male personnel at the palace.

Throughout the nineteenth century, two types of professionals were in great demand in North Africa and the Ottoman Empire—the military expert schooled in the sciences of warfare and the physician trained in modern healing, although these were not necessarily distinct professions. Both acted as intermediaries between the northern and southern shores of the Mediterranean. From the late eighteenth century on, the beys' personal physicians were Europeans and the important post of *bash hakim* (chief savant) was frequently held by Italians. From Mustafa Bey's reign on (1835–1837), the number of European doctors at court increased precipitously; the rulers provided protection, employment, and *ijazas*, or certificates of competency in medicine. In 1842, Ahmad Bey selected as his personal physician the Leghornese Jew Dr. Abraham Lumbroso (1813–1887), born in Tunis, who wielded considerable influence at court—and not just in the realm of medicine. Lumbroso even accompanied Ahmad Bey on his 1846 state visit to France. (However, French doctors increasingly supplanted Italians, which reflected the shifting balance of power between Italy and France after the mid-nineteenth century.) As non-Muslims, physicians were "outside" the prevailing system of gender segregation in elite households, the other exception being eunuchs, whose status as nonsexed humans allowed them some access to the women's quarters. Laurent Gay, who arrived in 1788 as chief physician and ended his days in Tunis in 1823 after thirty-five years at court, composed an invaluable manuscript containing intimate details of his practice, which brought him into the very heart of the princely family. Gay cared for female as well as male members of the Bardo's households. He assisted at childbirths—or at least acquired exact information on birthing practices—and described the illnesses of, as well as the treatments for, his female patients: "a young widow from the house of Sidi [illegible] Bey has had a cough for a very long time and because of this suffered pains in her left side."[64] As a mark not only of favor but also perhaps of fictive kinship, Mahmud Bey had even invited Gay to dine at table with him in the palace "when the womenfolk were present." Frank, Gay, Lumbroso, and others contributed greatly to an improved public health infrastructure, notably measures to combat plague and cholera.[65]

Another plum job was an appointment as chief cook. The splendid dishes served during banquets represented a culinary microcosm of the Mediterranean world, as this 1835 harim visit account noted: "all sorts of sweetmeats and confectioneries which the country can produce, mingled with many delicacies from Europe were placed on tables and we helped ourselves at pleasure, using our hands not only for *bonbons* and warmcakes, but also for the *compotes*."[66] Therefore, individuals skilled in the cuisines of Europe were at a premium. Two French nationals who ultimately made it in the Tunis hotel business—Philippe Béranger and François Pascal—profited from Husaynid patronage as well as from the growing number of visitors and travelers in the capital; their success stories suggest the workings of assistance and informational networks.

Originally from the Var, Béranger arrived around 1840 and won an appointment as head chef to Ahmad Bey at the Bardo, an important post. Leaving the bey's service, perhaps after Ahmad's death in 1855, Béranger subsequently went into business for himself in 1858. In association with François Pascal, his brother-in-law, he ran the Hôtel de Provence located in Tunis. Pascal, a French subject who had also served as a chef to Ahmad Bey, worked as the *maître d'hôtel*. Pascal eventually left hotel work and with a Neapolitan subject invested in property near Sfax, where they cultivated olive and fruit trees. Things apparently did not go well for Pascal; in 1872 he was charged with outstanding debts by a British Maltese, Giuseppe Farrugia, who claimed that the former beylical cook owed him the considerable sum of 1,891 piasters. To avoid payment, Pascal fled to the Bardo, where he was afforded asylum. The British consul's position in the matter was that if the palace extended sanctuary to the delinquent cook then it should pay his debts.[67] The record is silent regarding how Béranger and Pascal had first come to the bey's attention; had they worked as cooks for local Europeans who then recommended them to the ruler? Clearly these men had made it in Tunis through their association with the palace and its patronage.

SERVANTS TO THE SERVANTS AND QUITTING SERVICE

A palace insider observed in 1835 that "the domestics and people in service [at the Bardo] are Neapolitans, Sardinians and Italians, most of them of modest social origins. They are all subordinate to the Bash-Kasak [i.e., master of the wardrobe] who is the Bey's favorite."[68] This refers to Count Joseph Marie Raffo, who was appointed to this important position in 1825 by Husayn Bey. In turn, Raffo employed his own servants and staff; for example, Louis Dalmas worked as the family gardener and the Genoese Gaetano Fedriani (1811–1881), who had arrived destitute in 1834 with Garibaldi, was hired as Raffo's secretary. Fedriani's close ties to the count explain his remarkable social mobility, for, after abandoning Italian politics, he prospered in international trade and subsequently became a high-ranking business associate in the Société Rubattino based in Genoa that operated a steamship line between Sardinia and Tunisia.[69] Among Raffo's servants was a Maltese couple who, while unnamed in the sources, became the object of intense political interest due to the wife's alleged sexual misbehavior.

In 1856, the English consul, Sir Richard Wood, wrote to Raffo requesting his direct intervention: "I feel that I can ask you to handle this affair since it appears that wife and husband were previously in your service."[70] Household service functioned as a social GPS, enabling elites, Tunisian and European, to keep track of social inferiors if need be.

Palace-centered patronage radiated out to subalterns who hired those "below them," thereby creating nested hierarchies of service, a sort of subcontracting operation. The apparent lack of solidarity among workers in this layered service sector is hardly surprising. In 1869, a wage conflict arose in the household of one of the most powerful palace officials, Mustafa Khaznadar (1817–1878). By then Anna Errera Vedova, an Italian national, had had it with her immediate employer, a French national, Madame Meunier, and went to the Italian consulate for assistance. Employed in the *khaznadar*'s La Manuba palace as a "giardiniera" (gardener), Mme. Meunier had hired Anna as a household servant, keeping her in a "miserable state" and forcing her to work without pay; madame, it was alleged, owed the abused Anna twenty piasters in back pay.[71] Since fights between, or over, servants in Tunis became progressively entwined with wider political antagonisms, one wonders if the 1869 quarrel was connected to heightened Franco-Italian struggles over Tunisia.

Despite the traditional Italian monopoly over certain positions, by the 1830s Maltese were increasingly employed by the palace or court officials. Ability to secure work may have been related to the persistence of the older practice of employing Christian slaves, to the fact that many Maltese spoke some Arabic and Italian, or to job references from the British consulate. In 1838, the English vice-consul intervened in favor of "Giorgio Battista Bartolo, an English [i.e., Maltese] subject living in Tunis; he and his wife have rendered a certain number of services for the Bardo palace for years; he is asking for remuneration from the bey [Ahmad]."[72] Since wage labor in Malta for females was restricted, domestic service represented the single-greatest source of employment on the islands, predisposing women to this type of work in diaspora.[73] Some Maltese women worked as wet nurses for court notables. In the best documented case, wet nursing entailed residing for months in the intimacy of one of the great households of Tunis. In 1829 the English consul reported that "a Maltese woman having suckled the child of a Mamluk according to agreement for 7 months, and the time being expired, but the Mamluk would not suffer her to quit the house, her husband applied at the Consulate."[74] The husband wanted the consul to arrange for his wife's release from employment so that she could rejoin her own family. After weeks of diplomatic exchanges, including appeals to the bey, the woman was allowed to return home; her back wages were paid to her husband. Another piece of evidence from the early Protectorate period demonstrates that some Tunisian notables still employed Maltese wet nurses. In 1886, the household of

Sidi Mustafa ibn Isma'il, who had served Muhammad al-Sadiq Bey, arrived back in La Goulette after an extended stay in France. One member of the entourage was the Maltese wet nurse, Grazia, who "breastfed the enfant, Sidi Mohammed, one of the sons of Sidi Mustafa."[75]

These incidents raise larger questions regarding interconfessional relationships, work, women, and gender. As is true in many societies, wet nursing in North African culture established ties of fictive kinship and thus wove complex bonds between families as well as imposing marriage taboos. The tradition had it that nursing five times with the same woman created kinship between the non-kin infant and the woman's own children. Joseph Raffo was regarded as Ahmad Bey's "milk brother" because Raffo's mother, Marie Terrasson, had nursed the young prince.[76] Did wet nursing create patron-client bonds between Mediterranean women of ordinary rank and Muslim dignitaries that might be negotiated to advantage when the need arose? On the other hand, that the Maltese woman and her reproductive labor were subject to three layers of male custodial oversight—the mamluk, the British consul, and her husband—indicates that migration and securing employment even in wealthy households did not necessarily enhance female agency—quite the contrary—and it entailed sexual dangers.[77]

Household employment provoked disputes over wages, conditions of work, and length of service that forced servants to leave palace employment, some through flight. Two Maltese women, Gracia Scotto and Anne Cuiccardi, were prevented from leaving a mamluk household in 1829 where they probably were employed as domestics. (The Scottos were an extended Maltese family residing permanently in Tunis; another family member, Guiseppi, was a wine dealer.) Apparently the women had assisted a fellow servant, a Neapolitan, escape from the Bardo and take refuge at his consulate. Due to Raffo's intercession, the two women were soon released to their families. Around the same time, a Jewish woman went to the English consulate in 1831 to seek redress from onerous working conditions: "being employed at the Bardo [she] complained of ill usage there and entreated the consul general's interference to obtain her liberation from her employ."[78] The "liberation" probably referred to the breaking of some sort of work agreement. However enlightened Bin Diyaf's position on the treatment of household labor might appear for the period, it surely did not reflect general practice.

DOMESTIC SERVICE BEYOND THE PALACE

Changing legal restrictions on emigration from European states, combined with the workings of transregional networks, shaped labor mobility in the central Mediterranean corridor. Creoles and resident foreigners had imported servants in earlier periods, although this was subject to national restrictions governing the movement of laborers outside of territorial boundaries.[79] Barnabé Fouques (1781–

1867), by profession a wool worker, was hired as a cook in 1829 for Mr. Ventre, a resident merchant in Tunis; however, Fouques' passport expressly stipulated that he return to France as soon as his employment ended. Whether he complied or not is unknown. After the regulations of the Chambre de Commerce in Marseilles were amended in 1835, French laborers were no longer required to obtain authorizations to seek their fortune abroad, nor were they obliged to deposit a *caution* (security deposit) to work outside the metropole.[80] In large measure, this was connected to France's efforts to construct a settler colony in Algeria.

From the 1830s on, growing numbers of middle-class Europeans in Tunis created new demands for labor beyond those normally supplied by kin, as did the establishment of hotels for travelers and tourists and increases in taverns, cafés, and restaurants. Ship manifests show a proliferation in the number of cooks and servants from Europe who came to work for consuls and creoles; some found their way into Tunisian households. In 1839 a cook hired by the creole French family, the Monges, sailed from Marseilles on the French brig, *L'Excellent,* arriving in Tunis in five days. Three years later, a Sardinian ship took four days to transport Alexis, the cook of the French consul, De Lagau, as well as "a woman who is going to Mr. Solal's household."[81] But the current also went in the reverse direction, as servants returned to Europe after the expiration or annulment of contracts or for other reasons.

Some never made it back. The Maltese man Angelo Saliba died in Tunis in 1850 after years at the British residence as personal valet to Sir Edward Baynes. The probate proceedings, completed in January, 1851, revealed that the Maltese steward possessed the following items: 436 piasters, one silver watch, one gold chain, a box of shirt studs, and other personal belongings. As valet to a master of high status, Saliba's position placed him at the top of the hierarchy, reflected in his worldly possessions. However, Saliba left behind debts; he owed 100 piasters to the Maltese priest, Father Stanilaus, and a Tunisian woman, Mabruka, came forward during the inquiry stating that she had lent him money that had not been reimbursed. Thus, servants engaged in various financial deals on the side, borrowing from and lending to social peers or neighbors, including women. The six-month period demanded for Saliba's probate proceedings indicates that putting a deceased retainer's affairs in order was a lengthy process because of the number of individuals under different jurisdictions who made claims upon the estate.[82]

Servants were frequently suspected of, or accused of, stealing. Monsieur Guemos, a French subject residing near the stone quarries of Jabal Caroub, claimed that he had been the victim of a string of thefts and violent acts. During the night of February 16, 1860, his home was broken into; the guilty party had entered through a window secured with a metal rod and stolen numerous possessions: a sack full of copper coins, hundreds of silver and gold piasters, towels, a silk cravat, a pair of gray pants, a kitchen knife, and ten pounds of mining powder. Guemos accused one of his Tunisian servants of the misdeed, an individual named Salah, who had been in his employ for five months but whom he had fired—after paying Salah his wages—several days prior to the break-in.[83] Unfortunately, we have no way of ascertaining whether the servant was wrongly blamed or not.

By the 1860s, domestic-help disputes had turned in international causes célèbres. French officials received a complaint in 1868 from the Italian consul regarding a French couple, the Messiers living in La Goulette, who refused to allow an unmarried Sicilian woman, Mlle. Passalaqua, to quit their service. Stated the French vice consul, "I ordered Messier and his wife to give back the Sicilian woman, who is a domestic in their household, based upon the explicit demand of the Italian consulate. The Messier couple has refused to allow Mlle. Passalaqua to go to see her consular officer. Just as my janissary was leaving the Messier house, after Mr. Messier had refused to hand her over without an order to take her away, Mme. Messier boarded a coach with Mlle. Passalaqua and left for Tunis."[84]

Months later, the affair of the Sicilian servant remained unresolved and in 1869 Mlle. Passalaqua's relatives, resident in the capital, demanded her belongings and nine months of outstanding wages, calculated at fifteen copper piasters per month of service. The list of Mlle. Passalaqua's personal effects in her previous employers' possession is somewhat surprising: four camisoles and an equal number of pantalets; a cap known as a "garibaldina" and a pair of gloves; two dresses; various clothing of wool, Indian cotton, and linen, and one dress of muslin; fives pairs of hosiery, and so on.[85] One wonders, given the quantity and nature of her personal finery, if she had indeed filled the role of a mere servant.

English governesses were increasingly in demand among expatriates. In 1869, Miss Peacopp worked for a French national, Monsieur de Serre, as a "tutress" for his daughter, but the child proved intractable because she "refused to learn anything but music," at least according to the governess. The manner in which de Serre hired the unhappy Miss Peacopp and the nature of her work contract are significant. De Serre had met the English governess while traveling through Italy and engaged her on the spot as a governess for his child in Tunis. Committed to writing, the work contract stipulated that Miss Peacopp be reimbursed for the cost of her travel to Tunis from Italy and receive fifty francs per month—which her employer reneged upon, giving rise to long drawn-out negotiations.[86]

By 1861 Richard Wood's summer residence housed a multitude of servants, including an English governess, and boasted a piano. As Wood's wife, Christina, observed in a letter to her husband, then on a mission in Syria: "The servants are getting on all right, with slips and fights now and then. If you could get hold of Zahran and bring him along as cook it would be a good dodge and thing. I believe Mohamed intends to leaving when his time is up. Don't forget to bring me some of the painted handkerchiefs of the gaudiest colors [as gifts for the servants]."[87] Not only was Mrs. Wood requesting that her husband locate their former cook, Zahran, who served the family in Syria before their relocation to Tunisia, but she noted that one servant had decided to give up his job. As interesting is the mention of "fights now and then" among the staff. Most revealing is that the wife of the English consul deemed it important to detail the activities of household help to her spouse absent in distant Bilad al-Sham.

As Mediterranean immigrants poured into Algeria after 1830, thousands of Algerians flooded Tunisia in search of social betterment. Most chose the Tunis region, where they sought work as servants. Hassan ibn Ahmad al-Jaza'iri, twenty-six years old, arrived in 1874 to work for a Tunisian family. Described by the French consul as "medium height, small moustache rather blond, squints slightly and speaks French," Hassan did not prove the ideal servant; after twenty days he was fired for reasons unknown. One evening, out of work and out of luck, the hapless Hassan, "being drunk on wine, entered without permission a European house near the Bab al-Bahr in order to ask for work. His state of drunkenness so scared the house's inhabitants that they ran to the Dabtiya [municipal police] who arrested him and brought him to the civil prison in Driba where he remained nearly 3½ months."[88]

Visited by the French consul at long last, and grilled about his papers verifying Algerian status, Hassan stated that "at the moment that he was arrested, he had his passport in his tarboush which was taken away from him by the agents of the police before he was imprisoned."[89] Hassan's story is plausible, since taverns dispensing wine blanketed the madina, Europeans of different social ranks resided in that neighborhood, and people frequently employed headgear as "pockets." Why had the Algerian languished in prison for so long before consular authorities were called in? The 1870s were marked by perceptible antagonisms toward Algerians—or toward any North African Muslims or Jews—claiming foreign protection. Perhaps Hassan's prison keepers viewed him as undeserving of special treatment, all the more so since he lacked the kind of patronage ties that would have brought speedy release. Sprung from jail, Hassan disappears from the record; he probably joined the ranks of the capital city's "floating population," which by then had grown substantially.

If middle-class Europeans or Tunisian notables engaged servants, so did the less fortunate who provided work to neighbors, family, friends, and business associates. The 1868 Giovanna Tellini criminal inquiry shows that individuals toward the bottom of the social pyramid hired others who were more destitute. The Tellini burglary and fencing operation are examined in a subsequent chapter, but the testimony of the Maltese lad, Gianmaria Hiberras, reveals a semi-concealed universe of casual help barely making it and thus driven into illicit activities to put bread (or couscous) on the table. Gianmaria identified himself as a *garzone (garçon)* in the employ of Annetta Barbera, a Spanish national born in Algeria but resident in Tunis, for whom he ran errands in the neighborhood and performed household tasks, such as drawing water; he slept in the kitchen of Annetta's rented rooms.[90] Unfortunately for Gianmaria, his employer was involved with a band of Maltese, Greek, and Italian thieves whose string of heists had netted large quantities of booty sold in contraband networks; as a servant, he was complicit. Gianmaria admitted to procuring skeleton keys from a supplier at Bab Cartagena, which landed him in the Italian consulate's office as an accomplice to the crime. Depositions from the criminal inquiry show that those of modest social backgrounds combined service with other forms of employment. Isaaco Sfez, a Tunisian Jew and a baker by profession, worked as a *garzone* at Giorgio's café near Bab Cartagena as well as in the neighborhood soap factory.[91]

Domestic service generated gossip and market hearsay. In September 1874, Prime Minister Khayr al-Din contacted the French consul general about a complaint lodged by the inhabitants of the Bab al-Jazira quarter. The rumor mill had it that Muslim girls worked as live-in servants for male French telegraph employees who resided in the neighborhood. Both the police and the consulate launched investigations. A minute inspection of the premises was carried out, witnesses were interviewed, and depositions taken—but nothing seemed amiss. In his report to Khayr al-Din, the consul noted that the police and the French janissary were in agreement regarding the facts:

> I received your letter dated 25 rajab 1291 in which you alerted me to the allegation that two Muslim girls were working as domestic servants for diverse French nationals in a caravanserail located near Bab al-Jazira. In the house named "Wakil Bab al-Jazir" which is rented by Monsieur Haeusser, an employee of the telegraph, there is no Muslim girl nor is there one at Monsieur Faussié's place, nor at any residence of the telegraph employees, as shown by the deposition made by Faussié as well as by the statement made by Sadiq, the Janissary, to whom an officer of the police showed the building in question.[92]

The incident was most likely fueled by collective resentment about the growing numbers of foreigners working in Tunis, but it probably specifically focused upon telegraph employees because the foreign-owned telegraph company had antagonized local society. The rumor that Muslim girls worked in households composed of foreign men gave voice to fears of sexual misconduct, and the apparently spurious accusations functioned as a lightening rod for deeper anxieties about moral disorder.

EMPLOYMENT BUREAUS:
CONSULATES AND THE TUNISIAN STATE

Outside of domestic service, what other sorts of work were available and how did networks operate in providing access to employment? As was true of the palace, consulates represented microcosms of the Mediterranean world due to the sociocultural diversity of their staff and the people conducting daily business. They also functioned as employment bureaus for local translators, dragomen, and servants and operated as job-placement agencies for protégés. It is quite possible that the wayward Neapolitan retainers were hired by a consulate, since years of serving the palace made them particularly valuable informants. A document from 1826 detailing the cost of reparations to the French funduq and consular residence shows that "Moorish servants worked at the establishment" as well as "janissaries" who lodged there in separate quarters.[93] By the 1830s, the recruitment of janissaries from the Ottoman heartlands for military service had ceased; the job description referenced guards, sentries, bouncers, and escorts. Some found employment with European consulates. "With their striking uniforms, their high fezzes and long mustaches, these aged Turks retained their dignified bearing but only served a modest role as bailiffs."[94]

If we were to enter one of the consulates near the Sea Gate, what or who would we find? Let's take the British consulate as example because spatial location rendered it within reach of many city inhabitants. Once inside, the visitor pushed through a crowd clustered around a table where mail was deposited "in order that each person may go and look for his letters and papers."[95] In addition to the throng of travelers, clients, or the aggrieved, various functionaries, or even the consul himself, might appear. In the 1830s, the British consulate employed an Arabic translator, several janissaries, and two "dragomen at the pay of 15 pounds per year." Ahmad and Muhammad, the dragomen, signed wage sheets in infelicitous Arabic, but aside from that their identities remain uncertain.[96] Contemporary observers conversant with the Mashriq noted that "the word dragoman implies a very different meaning in Tunis compared to Istanbul."[97] By custom, the consuls dealt directly with Husaynid beys in the course of formal audiences at the Bardo, which contrasts with the Levant, where consuls were forced to go through local dragomen when dealing with Ottoman authorities. "The worst disrespect that an aggrieved bey could show to a foreign representative [at court] was to order the consul to go through a Turkish dragomen" instead of addressing the ruler himself.[98]

In Tunis, the consular dragomen were called upon to defuse trouble-in-the-making in the streets, a function inserting them into the unstable jurisdictional space where beylical, consular, municipal, or Islamic authorities intersected. In April 1829, "a Maltese committed a violent assault upon a Moor who compromised the affair with the former by means of their respective friends, and the aid of the Dragoman, in order to prevent his [i.e., the Maltese assailant] being sent to prison."[99] In this case, the dragoman, probably a Tunisian, negotiated a harmonious settlement between a local subject and a Christian, which spared the Maltese from prison and preserved the peace. Another duty was to conduct consular officials through the teeming byways, performing crowd control. "It is usual for the consuls or other Europeans to be accompanied by a dragoman attached to their consulate, who, with a sword by his side, a magnificent swagger in his gait, and a big stick, clears the way with little ceremony."[100] This task was critical because it discouraged insults from passers-by; as discussed in a later chapter, earthy invectives in public spaces often led to serious trouble.

By midcentury, new positions were added to consulates in response to increased traffic, a direct consequence of immigration. A special officer was appointed at the British consulate to handle complaints from the Maltese population; but with thousands of protégés and "no salary attached to situation," one can imagine how the system worked.[101] By the time of Wood's appointment in 1855, a vice-chancellor, La Rosa, committed to writing the oral testimony from protégé-witnesses to disputes, since most Anglo-Maltese were illiterate. This raises significant questions concerning the archival record because the "facts" of a particular case or the evidence drawn up for consular proceedings were subject to multiple filters in the course of transcription and translation. A Maltese, Pisani, claimed three posts: chancellor or mediator, factotum, and first dragoman.[102]

Employment with consulates became more and more attractive for beylical subjects as the century wore on because it held forth the promise of various degrees of legal protection, in addition to other prerogatives, which explains why the British consulate received this request in 1856 from a Tunisian of good social standing: "Tayeb ben Mohamed El Medeni [sic], a native and resident of La Goulette ... seeks a position as an English janissary in the port."[103] What networks would have induced al-Madani to apply for this position? As the son of Muhammad al-Madani, one of the bey's naval lieutenants, the job seeker had grown up in La Goulette, then still a relatively small community, and his father surely knew the vice-consuls there. And because he served as an officer in the Tunisian navy, al-Madani the elder had access to diverse contacts at the port. In any case, al-Madani the son wanted the consul general in Tunis, Richard Wood, to provide him with the requisite decree from the bey's hand appointing him to the staff. Here the workings of networks created by residential patterns and professional links encouraged young al-Madani to petition Wood for a job.

In 1859, Wood requested permission from Muhammad Bey to hire a second dragoman for the Sfax vice-consul, as the number of Maltese there had shot up precipitously. The dragoman was to assist the consular agent in "preventing the quarrels that erupt among [protégés] during the night, especially because the consular residence is found in the Christian quarter." A second, Tunisian dragoman was needed because frequent nocturnal disorders required the round-the-clock presence of officials. "The consular agent can not demand that the same dragoman in his service at present spend every night in the consulate residence [away from his family]." Wood asked the bey for his *amra* (order) permitting the engagement of Muhammad ibn Hasana, "a man known for his integrity and good behaviour as the second dragoman."[104] Important is that the dragomen at times resided at the consulate and that the ruler's consent had to obtained in writing in order to engage a subject. The allusion to the Christian quarter as rife with nightly disorders refers to the exuberant tavern life then in full expansion, but could also reflect Wood's antipathy toward lower-class protégés, most Maltese. Who were the ideal candidates for the job? Officials formerly in beylical service, including ex-police agents after the 1860 organization of the Tunis *dabtiya*, were tapped for employment as dragomans to maintain social order among protégés or between protégés and beylical subjects. A job profile from 1863 required a person

> who is not only well known and respectably connected but who has likewise some experience in conducting affairs relating to the public service. It often occurs that many misunderstandings take place owing to the ignorance, want of experience and often times the culpable negligence of the subordinates; and it is therefore of importance to avoid these inconveniences that the persons who are entrusted with messages and with the transactions of the ordinary business of a chancery should be properly qualified to do so to the satisfaction both of the consulate and of the local authorities.[105]

In Wood's view, a former *hanba* (a sort of urban gendarme) named 'Uthman al-Scamari was the perfect candidate since he had served the bey's government for twenty-nine years. Critical to the job description was expertise in communication and translation in the wider social sense. Translators of various sorts had always greased the complex wheels of trans-Mediterranean exchanges, in addition to serving more dubious purposes.[106]

Finally, what about vice-consuls in ports other than La Goulette? Many "European" consular agents were Iberian, Italian, Greek, Levantines, and so forth—individuals of complex transnational backgrounds who had always made the Mediterranean world what it was. The English vice-consul in Sousse during the 1840s was a Jewish Tuscan subject named Ben Sasson.[107] The French employed an Algerian Muslim as vice-consul in the Chott Djerid oases and a Corsican served the British vice-consul in Bizerte during the 1830s. And then there is Judah ben Levy, the British agent and trader residing in Sousse who, when in Tunis, worked as a self-appointed informant for the British consulate, spying on his female neighbor's sexual comportment. Ben Levy, a devout Jew, was born in

Gibraltar, educated in London, acquired British citizenship, spent time in India, and carried on commerce between Lisbon, Marseilles, Malta, and the Maghrib.[108]

One duty incumbent upon consular authorities was to certify the competency of nationals seeking state employment, since carpetbaggers and scoundrels often showed up. The consuls vetted candidates, recommending some but nixing others. In 1860, Léon Roches contacted Mustafa Khaznadar concerning just such an applicant, Achille Varembey, a professor of history at the Lycée Impériale in Auch. Varembey came highly recommended by a member of Auch's city council, who wrote that he was "an educated, intelligent, and well-mannered young man . . . not a *rénégat* [emphasis in original] but rather had been strictly raised in Islam by his father, a man of the Ottoman race who had long traveled in the Orient." In his letter to the bey, Varembey claimed to have been born in France but was bereft of family and fortune. He sought work in the bey's chancellery since he had "long desired to reside and die in the Orient . . . the birthplace of (my) ancestors." In the same letter, Roches reminded the *khaznadar* about another candidate waiting in the wings for appointment as fencing master to the military school.[109] Whether Varembey ever surfaced is uncertain, but Roches' promotion of this particular job seeker was the product of grander currents of change.[110]

GETTING OUT OF FRENCH ALGERIA

The single greatest source of disturbance in the region was French Algeria, which boasted the largest standing army in North Africa; its presence swelled the ranks of job seekers in Tunisia. One preferred method for "getting out" was to procure a leave of absence and simply not return to Algeria. During the conquest of Constantine in 1837, Usman Bushnaq, an Algerian enrolled in the French spahi corps in Bône, arrived in Tunis, supposedly on temporary military leave. But Bushnaq showed little inclination to resume fighting under the French flag, despite the fact that his three-year engagement was not yet up. He petitioned the bey for employment in the ruler's service because "he [did] not wish to return to Bône."[111] And he was not alone. Indeed Tunisia came to represent as a sort of R & R station for officers and soldiers weary from battle in the beleaguered colony. Why did French consuls promote members of the African army for positions in Tunis, draining off badly needed expertise from the colony? Given Great Power wrangling over Tunisia, the appointment of French officers, instructors, and physicians blocked other nations from filling positions, a checkmate strategy. Moreover, nationals or clients appointed to posts in the bey's government represented yet another channel of insider information.

Somewhat under the radar is another category of mobile labor—unfortunate deserters, or *malfaiteurs,* of various stripes whose circumstances can be gleaned from the *Moniteur Algérien,* which from its inception dedicated pages to courts-martial and to those soldiers "condemned to suffer death, *travaux forcés,* imprisonment, and a variety of other punishments."[112] Small wonder that Tunisia attracted demobilized soldiers, deserters, or those condemned to forced labor in Algeria, who traversed the unpoliced frontiers looking for refuge. In 1842 a Greek ship captain deposited in Tunisia "five bad characters, most of whom are deserters from the Armée de l'Afrique, such as the *prétendu* physician, Dr. Courbeau, who is carrying false papers."[113] In addition, propaganda campaigns across Europe convinced soldiers serving in Polish, Prussian, and Austrian armies to join the Foreign Legion in Algeria in a manner reminiscent of Pentagon efforts in the early twenty-first century to engage youth for the killing fields in the Middle East. These recruitment drives created a steady stream of deserters because of false advertising. "Houses and gardens and vineyards, we were told we should have, even gold and silver, it was said, were lying in abundance in Africa and only required us, to cross the channell [sic] of the Mediterranean to pick it up"—this was the tale told by one hapless Prussian lured into the legion by spurious promises that duplicate those made to civilian labor migrants.[114]

Utterly demoralized by the lack of food, shelter, and even regular pay, the Prussian, who had fought in Bougie from 1834 on, fled to the eastern Algerian desert in 1841, where he encountered other deserters: a German from Aachen, an Italian from Rome, and another from Sardinia. After much suffering, chance smiled upon the Prussian solider. Crossing the border with great difficulty, he ran into the annual winter mahalla laboriously making its way across the oases under the command of Sidi Muhammad, Ahmad Bey's first cousin (who eventually succeeded him in 1855) and begged the prince "take me under his protection to Tunis."[115] Seventeen days later, the Prussian was presented to the ruler, who enrolled him in the cavalry. According to our Prussian informant, hordes of deserters roamed Saharan oases trying to find a way out. Finally, illicit passion played a part in cross-border military movements; the French officer and engineer, Joseph Desaulty, came to Tunis in 1832 because of a love affair in Algeria. In a double desertion, he not only abandoned his military post but arrived with his commanding officer's wife. It is not clear if Desaulty sought employment in the bey's army, although he surfaced later in Morocco where he converted to Islam and served the sultan as head of the Moroccan artillery.[116] Nevertheless, military job seekers continued to arrive from the east, although these were often European officers who had previously trained Ottoman or Egyptian armies. After a stint with the Turkish army, Luigi Calligaris (1808–1871), originally from the Italian Piedmont, accepted the directorship of Ahmad Bey's newly created military school. But Calligaris's later trajectory is even more intriguing. By 1850, he resigned his commission in the bey's army to devote himself to the study of Arabic, which eventually landed him a post as professor of dialectal Arabic in 1863 at the University of Turin.[117]

In addition to military cross-border movements, labor demands in Algeria shaped Tunisian labor markets, although research into this important issue is nonexistent. At first the colonial government in Algeria, ever short of workers, employed prisoners for public works projects, but this proved vexing because they often escaped to Tunisia or Morocco; so Italian and Spanish contract laborers were engaged. In Algeria, the Italians were critical to several key sectors: terracing, laying down stones for roads, and masonry. Labor exchanges, whether the product of aggressive PR campaigns in Europe, individual choice, or serendipity, not only increasingly linked Tunisia to Europe but also to Algeria, a pattern often overlooked in the secondary scholarship.

The contest over skilled talent, military or otherwise, may have convinced Ahmad Bey to loosen restrictions on European women coming into the country. In 1842, an English ship from Malta brought a number of women to Tunis, including a Madame Lecorbeiller, traveling alone, whose husband had been appointed to head the artillery squadron. When disembarking in port, Mme. Lecorbeiller was not subject to the kinds of restrictions earlier applied to unaccompanied foreign women.[118]

HIGH-END CONSUMER TASTES AND PUBLIC WORKS

What other forces lured wannabe job-seekers to North Africa, the qualified and the incompetent alike? Tunis notables began touring Europe, above all Paris, with growing frequency, which nurtured other exchanges related to immigration and work. Demands for hitherto unavailable services and products, novel tastes and consumption patterns, meant that high-end imported goods represented a mark of elite status. As the nineteenth century progressed, the beylical family and court sought expensive European manufactures for adorning palaces and gardens. This social behavior became so widespread that it acquired a name in Arabic: *tamaddun*—roughly, an increase in luxurious lifestyles. As indigenous elites vied with each other in acquiring expensive clothing and furnishings, their personal debts soared.[119] Visitors to the Husaynid palaces described interior apartments furnished with costly Parisian clocks or Venetian chandeliers as well as "sofas, chairs, tables, curtains, looking-glasses, pictures, oil-paintings, and prints in immense profusion" from France or Italy.[120] After Ahmad Bey's 1846 state visit to France, infatuation with foreign goods soared, as did the demand for skilled artisans to fashion Versailles-like residences. Mustafa Khaznadar's stay in the tony Hôtel de l'Orient in Marseilles inspired him to build an opulent Renaissance-style palace constructed by Italian architects in the Halfaouine district of Tunis in 1847. Some officials, notably Mustafa Khaznadar, opened accounts with French companies that filled orders for big-ticket items for select clients, such as the Société Pastré Frères in Marseilles.[121] Thus, as luxury merchandise poured in, court notables became saddled by ever more burdensome debts to export houses on the other side of the Mediterranean.

Each time that a new palace or residence was built, the demand for imported labor and goods rose, and this encouraged immigration because specific groups were recruited for certain kinds of work; Italians accomplished in elaborate masonry were at a premium. Imported building materials often came from Italy, although for furnishings "of the best kind," France was preferred. When Ahmad Bey initiated an enormous and costly palace complex outside of Tunis, the Muhammadiya, in 1844, it generated demand for skilled artisans, servants, and employees, many of them foreign.[122] These processes were inextricably linked to expanded state-financed building projects—improvements to the arsenal at Porto Farina or to the road system linking the capital with the provinces—and were inspired by Ahmad Bey's tour of Paris and Versailles, which had greatly impressed him and his entourage. They demanded engineering talent—for example, Benoit, Lambert, and Duchesne were hired as engineers for the Muhammadiya palace—as well as skilled masons, joiners, and carpenters. Urban renewal and other projects, such as the Zaghwan aqueduct construction, transformed the capital's physical configuration; the madina and its suburbs were brought within a single walled confine as newly constructed ramparts enclosed the entire area. The building frenzy, focused upon monumental edifices or the modernization of infrastructure, were processes at work elsewhere in the Ottoman Empire and eastern Europe. Tours in western Europe, above all exposure to the French capital and its wonders, drove rulers to embark on ambitious building programs—which provided work for some people for a time but emptied state coffers, tied fragile local economies to international bankers and pashas, and ultimately proved disastrous for the peasantry.[123]

By the eve of the Protectorate, the Husaynid family and allied elites were no longer the "biggest game in town," nor was the ruler's table the epicenter of patronage, power, and performance. Instead "getting the bey's ear" long enough to wring some expensive favor or ruinous concession from him or a courtier offered the best route to making it, indeed making it big, in a precolonial economy. Concession hunting by European companies or governments, beginning with the telegraph contract awarded to France in 1861, rendered the Tunisian state increasingly insolvent. In the 1870s, a light rail was built by a Genoese firm, Rubattino, causing Italian immigration to shoot up as formal and informal recruitment networks sent waves of workers across the Sicilian Channel. In addition to the building trade, Italians worked the mines and ancient marble quarries around Tunis; others hired on as ship pilots, mechanics in the arsenals, or as sailors—the last attracted by far the most Sicilians. Between 1834 and 1865, Italian immigration increased fourfold in response to labor needs in Tunisia as well as political upheavals in the Italian states. In 1856, the number of resident Italians was roughly calculated at 4,200, the majority of them Sicilians in the Tunis region. By 1881, 11,606 Italians were registered with the consulate, a figure seriously underestimating their numbers for reasons already discussed. The paradox of France's invasion of Tunisia was that the inflow of Italian labor jumped precipitously; ships were jammed with workers eager to be engaged to construct railbeds, roads, ports, and hydraulic works. In 1886, the port of Bizerte was modernized as were the ports of Tunis, Sousse, and Sfax in 1894, employing Italian labor. Only after 1885 did large numbers of immigrant families acquire plots of land, although as early as 1874 nearly five hundred Maltese families had secured small property of one sort or another, perhaps with capital earned in domestic service.[124]

The next chapter turns to look at petty trade and commerce, family-operated businesses, and the spaces of sociability—principally cafés, taverns, and hotels— which all afforded opportunities for advancement, although the poorest peddled wares in the streets to the indignation of established shop owners. If some new-comers became moderately prosperous and remained in Tunisia, others failed to achieve their dreams and moved on, although where they landed next in efforts to make a living is largely unknown due to the nature of the sources.

4

Making a Living

Petty Commerce, Places of Sociability,
and the Down-and-Out

Even in relatively tranquil times, foreign vagrants in the streets of the capital alarmed urban authorities and the palace, prompting Mustafa Bey to publicly declare that "the laws of the kingdom demand that individuals without means of subsistence are subject to expulsion from the country."[1] As discussed previously, "making it" required networks, patronage, risk taking, and serendipity, to name the most critical elements. How did immigrants lacking skills, family, capital, and connections generated by service to the rich and powerful survive in nineteenth-century Tunis? Petty commerce, cafés, taverns, and other spaces of sociability offered hope for a more or less secure living. While providing a way of subsisting, if only hand-to-mouth, some activities created disputes when they transpired in spaces deemed culturally inappropriate or when they competed with indigenous or creole proprietors. Moreover, the newcomers began to shove their way into occupations over which other groups had long enjoyed a socially sanctioned monopoly. High numbers of people involved in petty commerce or casual labor constitute an index of a bloated tertiary sector, indicating that other sources of work, however precarious, are hard to come by.[2]

What transpired when calamity befell families at the bottom of the social pecking order, when breadwinners fell ill, perished, or ran afoul of the law, or when employers downsized their workforce? One answer lies in the social responses to adversity unleashed by bad luck, the wrong decision, or by larger forces, such as epidemics or political upheavals, that brought ruin instead of riches. Failure to earn a livelihood—being "down-and-out"—accelerated the density of trans-Mediterranean labor movements and explains the ceaseless comings and goings of people from islands to North Africa and then back home again, or to another destination promising a better life.

CANDY AND PASTRY WARS

Small-business operations and peddling are not well documented; the evidence only allows for a partial reconstruction. Fortunately for the historian, candy and pastry wars periodically erupted in the streets. In 1830 the Tunisian proprietor of a funduq where poor male immigrants resided complained about a Maltese scrambling to survive as an itinerant sweets seller. The candies, concocted on a primitive stove in his miserable abode, not only covered the dwelling with black soot but also spread noxious smells and smoke into adjoining residences, greatly annoying the neighbors. Because housing was scarce, another way to make a few piasters was to surreptitiously sublet to newly arrived compatriots rooms rented from indigenous proprietors. Indeed the candymaker was subleasing his space from another Maltese with whom he had gone into the business in 1826. Offensive smells and unseemly sounds, often associated with newcomers and their struggles to survive or their forms of amusement, gave rise to endless complaints. Worse, the Maltese candy operation poached upon Tunis natives who enjoyed a monopoly over the sale of "various kinds of confectionary about the streets," and so British authorities were asked to prohibit the enterprise unless franchise rights had been paid.[3] But hawking wares in the markets did not just pit indigenous street vendors against immigrant peddlers. Shopkeepers paid rent as well as fees and could not compete with bargain-basement prices offered by unlicensed street retailers. The British consul was importuned in 1828 by "the principal Maltese and other traders" in the capital who demanded that itinerant vendors be prohibited from "selling their goods in the immediate vicinity of their shops to their alleged loss and injury."[4]

What kinds of goods beside illicit sweets were made and sold or bartered? By the 1850s, Italians, Spanish, and Maltese labored as carpenters, butchers, barbers, bricklayers, and shoemakers, selling products out of small shops or from their equally small homes. Nicola Sabuquillo, son of Pietro, was born in Cuenca in central Spain in about 1823. In 1860 he surfaced in Tunis, where he made a living as a bricklayer and rented a small room from an Italian woman. Some laborers did not even boast a roof over their heads; in winter's cold, many men slept outside, the Maltese in their carts, the Sicilians in small boats or on the work sites.[5] We have only scattered information about women and petty commerce. Vincenza, a Maltese woman, filed a complaint in 1829 with the consulate regarding a fellow Maltese, Guiseppi the carpenter, who had failed to deliver a bedstead for which she had paid half in advance; the consul sent for Guiseppi, who promised to produce the item forthwith. In addition, the impecunious carpenter owed

FIGURE 10. Outside a Moorish café in Tunis, c. 1900, one of the hundreds of cafés in the capital city. Of note is the individual dressed in European clothing, which suggests that these places of male sociability attracted a diverse clientele. (Library of Congress Prints and Photographs, LC-DIG-ppmsca-06041.)

money to a Tunisian subject who operated one of the shelters for poor Maltese males. The British janissary was dispatched to obtain the outstanding rent from Guiseppi, who appears to have been incapable of making a decent living in Tunis, or at least of managing his financial affairs.[6] Another form of petty trade was lending small sums of money at interest, which brought the same Vincenza some income—when her clients repaid the debt. Women also engaged in petty commerce, including brokerage. A Tuscan woman worked as a broker for a British subject from Gibraltar named Benedetti, retailing woolen garments produced in Spain. By the 1860s, the Dar Sabun (Soap Factory) offered casual employment to people from a wide- range of backgrounds and also apparently served as a hangout for thieves at night.[7]

Small-scale operations, resembling the peddling activities of Lebanese migrants in the New World, furnished income to *colporteurs,* many Maltese. What kinds of items were in demand? Tobacco, cloth, wool, fresh fish, and *polpi* (dried squid) were sold in the streets, to residences, or in coffeehouses by vendors acting as middlemen for wholesalers. In 1862, a Maltese arrived in Sfax with several cases of imported items: "trifling things of ladies wearing apparel, such as silk and cotton handkerchiefs, scraps, needles, etc., in small pasteboard boxes."[8] Obviously the customers for these items were women, but one wonders how indigenous retailers competed with door-to-door sales offering wares not locally available. The métier par excellence of the Maltese—in addition to contraband—came to be the carting and carriage business in which they predominated well before the Protectorate, although most drivers owned neither their horses nor coaches but rather leased them from the more prosperous. This eventually developed into a quasi monopoly in the grooming profession; wealthy Tunisian baldi families routinely hired Maltese to care for their mounts and carriages. Another trade was providing food to households; Albert Memmi's semiautobiographical novel opens with a Maltese goatherd making the rounds of Tunis neighborhoods selling fresh milk.[9]

By the time the pastry war erupted in the 1850s, Tunis had changed dramatically. Unregulated petty trade and carters congested the narrow streets: "The heterogeneous elements which form the bulk of the Christian population of Tunis, their utter disregard of the commonest form of decency and decorum, their recklessness and usurpation of the principal thoroughfares, which have become impassable and insecure from their having been turned into stables and workshops. . . . In one street alone, besides other animals, there are several hundred pigs which wallow in the public drains and impede progress of passengers."[10]

Given this state of affairs, it was hardly surprising that a public outcry arose in 1857 when a French protégé brashly set up a curbside enterprise to make pastries fried in olive oil and liberally doused with sugar. Worse, he had the temerity to conduct operations in a space adjacent to the Zaytuna mosque-university reserved for the most noble of occupations—where the suq of the shashiya makers intersected with the suq al-'attarin (perfume market). The affair went as high as Muhammad Bey and the French consul, unleashing the "battle of the pastries." The ruler ordered the entrepreneur to close down his venture in this quarter of the madina but allowed him to manufacture and sell his edible wares elsewhere. In the traditional order of things, the profession of pastry vendor (ftayri) was generally exercised by laborers from the villages of Matmata and Tatawin, known as the Jabaliya (people from the mountains) in the deep south; they also monopolized roasted chickpea vending and served as porters. That the head of state intervened to rid one street corner of a faux pastry chef to safeguard work for subjects who hailed from the extreme limits of the country was significant.[11]

Proper governance of urban space had always been the domain of the sovereign, the shaykh al-madina (city manager), and 'ulama'. Thus it was as much the place where the upstart chef had launched his business as his social identity that sparked the pastry war. By sending him off to another neighborhood, Muhammad Bey evinced solicitude for his subjects as well as an appreciation for public opinion, which had become increasingly vexed by intruders in the city's daily social and economic life. Other livelihoods linked to the markets were disrupted by the movement of labor from elsewhere in North Africa. In the past, people from the oases in southeastern Algeria, the Warglis, guarded shops and storage facilities at night, but an influx of Moroccans at midcentury challenged their positions as watchmen.[12] On a larger level, the allocation of jobs, however marginal, to specific groups from Tunisia's four corners—or from places beyond its political margins—incorporated the provinces into the center to maintain order, above all in the suqs and streets.

NEW TRADES AND INSTITUTIONS IN THE CITY

Some of the earliest immigrants boasted skills unavailable in Tunis at the time. One of the most critical technologies, the printing press, was introduced by an Italian Jewish political refugee, Giulio Finzi, who came to Tunis in 1829 as part of a wave of revolutionary young men fighting for the republic alongside Mazzini and Garibaldi; Tunis afforded them haven, whether temporary or permanent. Arriving as a young man aged twenty-five, with previous experience in Leghorn's printing trade, the founder of the Tunisian branch of the Finzis eventually set up a shop in the Palazzo Gnecco, in the lower madina where the current Rue de la Commission is located; several years later, Garibaldi sought refuge in the palazzo, spending several months there.[13] The business demanded highly skilled labor, especially since Finzi did not limit his operations to printing but branched out into bookbinding and book and newspaper distribution. However, machinery, as well as trained workers, had to be imported from Italy until printing and publishing came of age in Tunisia and, with it, expanded employment. Printing in-country was not allowed before the 1879 beylical decree authorized the installation of the lithography press; until then, Finzi sent work to Sardinia to be printed.[14] Giulio Finzi's trajectory of migration, politics, work, and social insertion is emblematic of many Italian political figures who belong in a special category; they were not directly recruited by the Tunisian state, nor did they necessarily arrive as subsistence immigrants "pushed out" of Mediterranean islands by misery or the laissez-faire position of local officials toward overpopulation. Similarly, at some point in the precolonial period, a Slovak tinker named Tomas Fasunek from upper Hungary arrived in Tunis, where he set up a series of small shops for mending pots and pans and producing metalwork, which indicates that labor recruitment networks were operating in eastern Europe as well, possibly via Trieste, Austria's Adriatic port.[15]

Other types of businesses were connected to the introduction of modern institutions, such as hospitals and clinics. In 1843, Abbé François Bourgade established the first hospital on Rue des Moniquettes in the madina, not far from the earlier

Spanish hospice, Saint Croix; a Maltese doctor as well as the Catholic Sisters of Saint-Joseph staffed the new institution. Soon thereafter a French national and watchmaker by trade, Auguste Payan, and an Englishman, Dupont, opened a pharmacy in Tunis and began importing medical supplies from France. Their establishment was located in Dupont's home which he sublet from Payan (who must have in turn rented it from a Tunisian owner). In any case, small middle-class businesses such as Payan's pharmacy offered few employment opportunities and competed with local healers and practitioners. By the 1860s, the Farmacia Il Maddaleno operated in the Hafsia quarter of Tunis, although its proprietor lost much of his inventory during a nighttime break-in while he was at the "Locanda Inglese having a drink and making love with the Spanish girl Annetta." Given the steady rise in physicians of various origins claiming medical degrees from European universities who were practicing in the capital, the demand and customers for pharmaceutical products must have grown. The 1891 inventory of officially recognized physicians in-country listed forty-two doctors holding diplomas.[16]

Unwonted urban problems introduced by the newcomers challenged city fathers to institute reforms in the capital. The municipal council, or *majlis,* was established by beylical decree of August 1858, one of the first administrative acts following the declaration of the Fundamental Pact ('Ahd al-Aman) that legally rearranged relations between the state and its subjects as well as between subjects and foreigners. A response to profound social malaise, the council represented a novel institution that encapsulated changes in definitions of space, law, and urban identities. In typical fashion, older ways for ordering the city were not totally dismantled but rather were subsumed under newer offices and functions associated with the shaykh al-madina. Much in contrast to Alexandria and Istanbul, then struggling with strangers in the city, municipal council members were not Europeans but were recruited from the ranks of the upper-crust baldis. Soon thereafter, the *dabtiya,* or urban police, patterned upon the Parisian force, was organized and deployed in both the madina and suburbs; agents were eventually stationed in other cities and towns, notably the Cap Bon and ports that were experiencing large-scale settlement and smuggling, although numbers were never sufficient to the task at hand. Agents could intervene in conflicts or crimes involving foreigners and Tunisians, and file brief reports, but could not arrest Europeans. As was true of the city's night guards, police agents were often recruited from the very social classes that authorities sought to control. And both groups were open to bribery; during a string of heists in the madina during 1868, the Greek thief Dimitri Caragias "gave the night guards two pairs of shoes" stolen from a shop to keep them quiet.[17] Forms of leisure and sociability offered certain opportunities to "make it," however modestly, although these spaces were rife with problems of order and disorder.

PLACES OF SOCIABILITY:
THEATERS, COFFEE, AND COFFEEHOUSES

At the start of the nineteenth century, visitors to Tunis lamented the absence of places of entertainment found in abundance in European cities. By day, the streets hummed with foot traffic, loaded pack animals, the noise of workshops, and the cries of vendors; but stores closed at sunset and inhabitants rarely ventured out of their homes or even neighborhoods after dark.[18] In the eighteenth century, public places of entertainment, such as theaters, had been proscribed. An attempt by resident traders to organize a small playhouse within the confines of the French funduq came to naught after a few nightly performances. When news of the theater reached Hammuda Bey (1782–1814), he insisted that it cease immediately. Under Husayn Bey, the theater would be reintroduced in 1826 by an Italian immigrant, Terzi, who organized Tunisia's first standing theater, named the Cartaginese, which conferred upon the capital city the perhaps exaggerated reputation as "the Paris of Barbary."[19] By 1833 Italian operas and comedies played at this theater on a weekly basis; from time to time a ballet was performed as was a *cirque olympique*. After 1847, Italian theater troops stopped in Tunis on a regular basis; a ship's passenger manifest listed "six actors, of which two are women" from Italy.[20] Relaxed regulation of the theater was perhaps a consequence of Ahmad Bey's 1846 trip to Paris, where the Tunisian delegation attended a number of performances. But the theater's growth was principally the result of immigration, especially from Italian lands, and was part of a much wider trend, seen in Cairo and Istanbul at the same time. Indeed, many Italian companies routinely performed in Tunis before going on to Alexandria for the season. Algiers acquired its first theater around 1832, Le Grand Théâtre et Cirque, whose performances tended toward military extravaganzas such as *La Bataille des Pyramides,* featuring live combat.[21]

As the nonsubject Mediterranean community grew, so did other spaces for amusement. The clientele for taverns and cafés, which did not require much start-up capital, increased. Catering largely but not exclusively to creoles or foreigners, these venues provided work for men and women, particularly widows, and the possibility of betterment, while generating intercommunal connections as well as contestations. Progressively, *tavernas* and *bottegas* invaded that older space of male sociability par excellence, the urban coffeehouse *(qahwa)*, first introduced in the late sixteenth century, although coffee consumption predated Tunisia's incorporation into the Ottoman Empire.[22] "Drinking coffee is universal in Arab households, the habit of getting together, smoking, playing cards, and sleeping in the places where coffee is served is as common as in the Orient. The cafés of Tunis are the most picturesque. They are found everywhere and vary widely in nature: tiny places in which no more than four clients can stretch out on mats as well as luxury coffeehouses that are as large as small mosques. The Tunisians love to chat and play cards."[23]

Well before the nineteenth century, coffee had become the premier beverage of hospitality and leisure. If public coffeehouses were deemed inappropriate for persons of high religious rank, the beverage was offered to guests in the privacy of the home as well as to visiting dignitaries at the palace: "as smoking and drinking coffee are among the Turks the two of their greatest enjoyment, the great number of coffeehouses is easily accounted for; the coffee is [also] served by traveling coffee peddlers."[24] By 1846 Tunis boasted over one hundred coffeehouses in the madina, with another eighty-three in Bab al-Suwayqa and sixty-five in Bab al-Jazira. Originally most coffeehouse proprietors in the madina proper were Turks, as their compatriots spent much leisure time in cafés not far from the Qasba. (One coffeehouse still operates in the *suq al-atrak,* or suq of the Turks, and provides exotic amusement to the busloads of tourists tramping through the madina.)

By the nineteenth century, the baldis had invested heavily in the lucrative coffee business, including female investor-owners.[25] Coffeehouses attracted clienteles whose diversity was reflected in architecture ranging from small "hole-in-the-wall" operations for simple consumers to spacious, luxurious venues for high rollers. In addition to socializing, male customers played cards, exchanged gossip, or listened to storytellers; it appears that some Maltese men frequented coffeehouses along with Tunisian or North African patrons from the late 1820s on. During Ramadan, cafés became spaces of nighttime amusement with makeshift shadow-puppet theaters—the *karakuz,* Turkish in origin, or the *pupazzi,* which were Italian—regaling audiences with ribald, frankly obscene stories. Musical bands with Jews, Maltese, and Sicilian musicians entertained passers-by in the streets. Cafés in popular quarters, such as Halfaouine, attracted not only native denizens but also newly arrived residents who reveled in the animated street life.[26]

As coffee prices fell in the nineteenth century thanks to expanded imports from the Americas, its consumption became so widespread that most could afford a cup from itinerant peddlers hawking wares in the markets. And the coffee craze provided work to more and more city inhabitants. By 1860 the city boasted 260 cafés, or about one café for every seventy-eight males, out of a total population of some 100,000.[27] The demand for the beverage meant that a brisk trade in contraband coffee, coffee-making implements, and sugar developed. During the 1868 criminal inquiry into smuggling and fencing, material evidence seized from Giovanna Tellini's rented shop included "sacks of coffee," quantities of "various kinds of sugar," and "eight cups as well as eight coffee-makers." Tellini herself had originally been in domestic service to a Jewish family and subsequently to an Italian pharmacist before she went into the café business herself, combining cups of coffee with breaking and entering.[28] Moreover, expanded coffee consumption, often accompanied by smoking, gave rise to a black-market tobacco trade, a commodity subject to state monopoly. Coffee ranked among the most distinguished guilds, and its *amin* (head) was a person of high status. But the physically grueling process of grinding the beans after roasting was largely done by African workers, perhaps manumitted slaves or their descendants.[29] Whether savored by grandees drinking from delicate porcelain ware or by ordinary folks sipping from simple cups, coffee, the symbol of leisure and hospitality, provided work for different strata of urban society.

But the business also attracted immigrants, particularly newly settled Algerians, who opened small coffee shops; some claimed French protection, which freed them from taxation and put indigenous proprietors at a disadvantage. Ultimately, the Tunisian state was forced to adjust the tax on local coffeehouses so that its subjects could successfully compete. After midcentury, Tunis artisans and guilds began to feel the effects of foreign competition; some workshops whose proprietors had made a living by selling local products, such as spun wool, converted their enterprises into coffeehouses.[30] In the previous chapter, we encountered the luckless Algerian servant, Hassan, whose search for employment while under the influence landed him in prison; Hassan's story is one example of many. Both cause and consequence of changes in older patterns of work and consumption was the growing popularity of taverns. Faced with the proliferation of establishments selling spirits, the state attempted to regulate "places of quarrels and disorders" and stamp out the contraband traffic in alcoholic drink. But prior to tracing the tavern boom, a brief excursion into the older wine trade is in order.

TAVERNS AND THE CULTURE OF PUBLIC DRINKING

That the capital counted few drinking establishments relative to Europe in the early nineteenth century was seen in a positive light:

> The riots and cabals so frequent in European cities are here very uncommon; this maybe attributed to the prohibition of wine and other strong liquors and although the Turks are in general very fond of the former; they seldom commit an excess. Various sorts of wines and spirits are sold in several national inns; at the English, Imperial and French. Of late, the bey has allowed the making of wine from the grapes grown in the plains of Carthage, and from thence called Carthage wine, thus sacrificing a few scruples of conscience to the general increase in revenues he finds thereby; logically pretending it is vinegar he is making and not wine.[31]

The state clearly recognized the hazards posed by popular places of urban sociability, particularly those combining nocturnal crowds with spirits. Scattered throughout the city were guardhouses with round-the-clock sentries whose duty was "to preserve peace and quietness in the streets and suppress any quarrel or disturbance that might accidently arise."[32] Thus the question arises: how did a society, whose principal space of male sociability was the café, adjust to the progressive introduction of a visible culture of alcohol and drinking houses, often combined with gaming—particularly in view of the fact that spirits (and gambling) violated Islam norms that the ruler was enjoined to uphold? Cloaking the production, taxation, distribution, or consumption of wine (*khmar;* or *shrab* in Tunisian) under the legitimate guise of *khall* (vinegar) represented an age-old subterfuge. Fernand Braudel's characterization of the place of wine in Muslim societies over the *longue durée* is worth recalling—the *"clandestin infatigable"* (hidden, yet enduring, transgression).[33]

Research on nineteenth-century Istanbul points to important distinctions in the social place of alcohol for the Ottoman capital compared to Tunis. Istanbul's considerable non-Muslim subject population meant that communities consuming wine and distilling and/or selling spirits lived side by side with neighbors for whom alcohol was forbidden.[34] Dragomen in service to European embassies in the imperial capital were granted special rights confirmed by *barat* (license) from Ottoman authorities to operate home distilleries.[35] But were state controls over alcohol at the heart of the empire similar to those in other Muslim lands? Tunisia had no indigenous Arab Christian community producing and consuming spirits in large quantities, although native Jews had long enjoyed the right to make wine for religious and communal use. In the eighteenth century, wine was subject to an *iltizam*—an exclusive monopoly over a specific product or productive activity granted by the ruler himself.[36]

Creole residents procured wine and spirits from all over the Mediterranean. At times, the consuls ordered shipments of alcohol; at others, ships docking in La Goulette sold whatever was available. In 1814, Pierre Gaspary and "people living in Tunis" arranged for the import of wines from Naples, Spain, and Bordeaux. Not surprisingly, merchants from Greece specialized in Greek wines. Elia Crassacupulo, a longtime Tunis resident, brought in wine from Samos, known as Kalva, on Greek ships under French protection; Sardinia was an important source as well.[37] In 1834, John Gibson, son of the former British vice-consul, importuned Sir Thomas Reade for wine from the consul's personal store because there was no "immediate prospect of a vessel from Leghorn from whence I expect a little port"; as was true of many drinkers, Gibson claimed that his doctor recommended wine for regaining his health.[38] Thus, merchants and consuls represented significant conduits for importing alcoholic drink into the country, although state authorization and payment of fees were required.

In 1816, Gaspary sought leave from La Goulette's governor to disembark eighteen bottles of rum and a case of wine, allegedly for domestic use, which entailed purchasing a permit from the governor, who procured permission directly from the bey.[39] A few years later, Mahmud Bey introduced new measures for the wine trade. In 1823, state agents at the port boarded vessels to ascertain the quantity and nature of shipments; manifests were scrutinized to prevent spirits from being unloaded clandestinely for distribution in contraband networks. Husayn Bey passed new taxes and regulations on alcohol imports in 1831: "wines, spirits, and rum could only be transported from ship to port storage facilities with a *teskere*" from the ruler; fees were calibrated by the type of alcohol in question. Transporting spirits from storage at the docks to Tunis via small barges, to sell, required a second permit "from the hand of the bey" and consumers paid another tax.[40] The increased use and sale of alcohol was reflected in the municipal council's operating budget in 1858, partially financed by a tax on wine and spirits sold or distributed by Europeans.[41] For the Tunisian state, the lucrative alcohol trade—however reprehensible in the eyes of pious Muslims—provided much-needed income. Nevertheless, if the wine trade filled state coffers, it provoked unending contention.

In 1862 "respectable British merchants" in the trade requested that the British consul, Sir Richard Wood, present a petition to Muhammad al-Sadiq Bey on their behalf. They alleged that boat crews charged with disembarking casks extracted "from the barrels a portion of the wine and have replaced it by water and in one case they have even been robbed a whole barrel." After an investigation, Wood ascertained that the charges were well-founded, as the unloading, storing, and levying of duties on wine imports were separate operations; because of this, customs house agents were not responsible for unexplained losses. To remedy the situation, the merchants requested permission to employ their own boatmen to transport cases and casks from ships to the customs office to prevent contents from being tampered with, or siphoned off.[42]

In addition to tightly monitoring imported wine and spirits, Tunisian officials regulated home production. Vineyards in the Carthage and Bizerte regions had long produced the grapes from which Jews and Christians made wine. In 1829, Reade contacted the bey "soliciting a *teskere* for 50 loads of grapes, which according to custom, is granted each year to the British vice-consul in Bizerte in order to make wine for his own use and that of his family" and claimed that traditional "rights of European subjects" were being undermined by local officials, thus his decision to go directly to the ruler.[43] Home brewing continued to create conflict; in 1874, Muhammad al-Sadiq Bey complained that European residents refused to pay the 10 percent tax levied upon pressed grape juice for domestic wine production.[44] Once again, regulations aimed to limit the use of a commodity proscribed by Islamic law and commonly viewed as a major cause of social disorder (*fitna*)—even behind the closed doors of households. And what about the public spaces of consumption and their origins in both the port and Tunis proper?

Some of La Goulette's first inn operators were Maltese who participated in the trans-Mediterranean system of ransoming captives. In the eighteenth century, Jean-Marie Mediona operated a tavern, about which little is known, near the port's bagnio where he offered shelter, food, and wine not only to travelers but also to those involved in redeeming slaves—either Tunisian Muslims held in Malta or Christian captives in Tunisia.[45] But by the 1830s, the port's taverns mainly served ships' crews, and Sicilians began getting into the business. In Tunis, Greek taverns and tavern keepers, many under French protection, operated from early on. A report from the 1830s stated that while European hotels were generally lacking, "one finds cabarets, called taverns, owned by Greeks where bread, wine, and meat is sold. In the taverns, the Moors, Turks, and Arabs are found mixed together. And since they leave the taverns completely drunk, the Franks and the Jews there are frequently exposed to their brutality."[46] By midcentury, taverns become the sites of quarrels, commotion, and knife fights involving patrons under different legal jurisdictions and thus unleashing interminable diplomatic uproar. During beylical or consular investigations into the causes of a barroom brawl, the narrative frame "explaining" violence inevitably evoked inebriated males in public drinking houses, a frame that nevertheless invites caution.

At the same time, small, unlicensed stores sprang up, selling wine to consumers *without* paying the requisite tax, which was "in formal contradiction with the conventions regulating the sale of spirits concluded between the Tunisian government and governments of England, Naples, and France." Suffering a price disadvantage, licensed Greek tavern keepers demanded in 1835 that the government sequester alcohol distributed by free-market vendors. To drive their complaint home, the Greeks petitioned the ruler, arguing that "the great number of places selling wine [without permission] is prejudicial to tranquility as well as to public safety which is daily undermined in Tunis because of the large number of strangers who arrive without means of support."[47] Noteworthy is that the Greeks viewed the Husaynid ruler as responsible for ending the prejudicial state of things and, characteristically, they blamed "strangers" in the city—most likely Maltese and Sicilians—as the culprits by linking precarious resources with illegal commerce. It is unclear whether the offenders were home brewing and then retailing spirits around Tunis, or if they had purloined imported wine and rum through contraband networks.

Two years later in 1837, the combined evils of gambling and taverns arose. While gaming in cafés had always been forbidden, the practice must have become widespread as evidenced by the bey, the shaykh al-madina, and the consuls collaborating on newly issued interdictions. At the same time, the bey ordered that taverns operated by foreign protégés be closed for Tunisian patrons one hour after the sunset, a decree probably aimed both at gaming and alcohol consumption.[48] Ahmad Bey reorganized the wine trade in 1852 by imposing stricter controls over establishments selling alcohol; the system of permits and taxes on the importation, storage, and distribution of wines and spirits was overhauled. Because of his critical mediating position between the palace and the creole or expatriate community, Count Raffo was charged with implementing the changes by imposing a uniform 3 percent ad valorem tax on imported spirits.[49] Ahmad Bey also insisted on taxing cafés selling retail spirits "drunk on the spot," which provoked an outcry by Europeans operating hotels and restaurants that served meals accompanied by wine.[50] Significant was the fact that some cafés also sold drink—in addition to coffee—and thus the older institution was increasingly conflated with taverns.

That same year, the ruler ordered a census of coffeehouses and wine shops in the capital city and port. In July 1852, the English consul inventoried establishments selling spirits whose proprietors were registered with the British chancellery. On the list were fifty-nine entries designating *taverna*, café, *bettola*, *bottega*, or, in one case, a *locanda*, or inn, although some establishments were characterized as both bettola and taverna. Not surprising, the popular Bab al-Bahr and Bab Cartagena quarters boasted a considerable number; one Maltese-run wine shop was located in the Jewish quarter. Women operated three establishments: Grazia Lammut, whose bottega was near Bab Sidi 'Abd al-Salam; Teresa Abdella's tavern in the vicinity of Funduq Ariscia; and Maria Muscat, who ran a bottega near Funduq al-Karma. Of the fifty-nine family names, all but one—Elia Angelacopulo, perhaps an Ionian Greek—appear to be Maltese.[51]

Of course, we have no way of knowing with any accuracy how much wine was sold surreptitiously out of stores or businesses ostensibly serving other purposes or introduced illegally, since as one source notes, "wine is contraband, but it is chiefly imported under the name of vinegar."[52] Finally, a key social figure emerges in this period—the tavern keeper. Since they often had relatively large sums of money at their disposal, tavern owners were beseeched by patrons, friends, and neighbors to advance loans, post bail, or otherwise assist those with cash-flow problems. Moreover, providing credit to customers involved tavern keepers, petty retailers, and others in complex urban networks that greased the wheels of a wide range of exchanges in the local microeconomy.[53]

WOMEN, WINE, AND OTHER MORAL AFFRONTS

The mention of women as wine-shop proprietors offers clues about employment in sectors other than domestic service, although these activities were not mutually exclusive. As family-run businesses, taverns provided a livelihood for women, although whether the household nature of the work offset the moral stigma of working in a quintessential male space is open to question. The critical element in safeguarding female virtue and family honor was the oversight of male kin. Since drinking houses constituted highly gendered social places, they imperiled collective honor if operated by "women without men." In the 1870s, an impoverished Maltese widow and her daughter, Hanna, earned their living by selling wine in the market district just behind the madina; at times their shop was open in the evening after normal business hours. This was brought to the attention of the police and British consulate. "And being without the protection of any man, they are exposed to be insulted by the common people who frequent their shop; and in reply I beg to state that I have directed the woman Hanna to shut up her wine shop at the time when the souk is shut up so as to prevent the common people from frequenting the shop at undue hours."[54]

Several important, yet implicit, aspects of the intersections between work, migration, and gender norms are illustrated by this incident. First, the "common people" probably referred to both European and Tunisian male patrons who "insulted" the two women even as they purchased drink from them. Hanna and her daughter sold spirits at night after normal hours, which violated urban codes, rendering them women of uncertain virtue, suspect in the eyes of neighbors. Most explicit is that the Maltese women were "women without men," deprived of male oversight; once again, the widow as a figure provoking moral anxiety arises. In this case, the English consul assumed a patriarchal role to ensure that his female protégés' behavior did not give public scandal and, therefore, threaten social disorder. A final element is that consular and Tunisian officials together claimed jurisdiction over the women because of their lack of male kin, occupation, and "lowly" social class.

In 1878, a local Tunisian official complained to Richard Wood about a "Christian woman," who served alcohol in a tavern owned by a Maltese proprietor, Giovanni Beyadah, in a town just outside of Tunis. Because of the unnamed Maltese woman's presence, "the persons who frequent it at night quarrel and fight among themselves, thereby creating great disorders and disturbing the public peace."[55] Once again, this incident demonstrates that women, especially of modest rank, were subject to interlocking disciplinary systems, consular and Tunisian. Moreover, the key role that gender played in defining "appropriate work" for women is unambiguous. If male tavern patrons squabbled, it was not because they had liberally indulged in alcohol and presumably were intoxicated; rather the woman's presence in a space coded as male was to blame. Since the tavern keeper was not a kinsman, the transgression was all the more serious. The consul instructed the Maltese tavern owner to fire his female worker and have her sent to Tunis, where presumably British officials would prevail upon her to mend her ways, find more suitable employment, or perhaps would send her back to Malta if all else failed. In any case, taverns sometimes offered more than just alcohol, since gambling, prostitution, the fencing of stolen goods, and contraband operations were often associated with them.

While the Tunis region boasted the largest number of drinking establishments, other coastal towns experienced similar problems. Mahdiya, not far from Sousse, counted a relatively large Maltese population overseen by an English vice-consul authorized to take measures ensuring social tranquility, although not without personal risk. Catholic festivals gave rise to public exuberance, since celebrations were always combined with drinking. In May 1846 just such a festival erupted in disorders among Mahdiya's foreign residents. To discourage excess, the vice-consul directed a Maltese who ran the town's café, which served as a billiard parlor, to close down, which he obligingly did. An hour later, a Corsican, Alexander Castellini, forced the tavern keeper to reopen his shop and serve alcohol to the male merrymakers. Things got out of hand and eventually a gang of Sicilians led by the Castellini brothers brutally attacked the vice-consul, sending him to the hospital.[56]

Several decades later, in Nabeul, also on the coast, another contention arose in 1862 over a wine shop run by a Maltese, Rosario, who committed a triple offense in the community's eyes. Not only was he selling wine and liquors out of his rented house without a license, but he also sold "articles of contraband." Worse, Rosario habitually climbed the terrace, which overlooked the courtyards of adjoining Tunisian homes and gave him a bird's-eye view of womenfolk in the intimacy of the domestic unit.[57] A greater affront to Muslim sensibilities occurred in 1874 when a Maltese opened a tavern opposite the great mosque in Nabeul, provoking communal outrage. Initially refusing to cease operation, the Maltese finally closed shop after repeated admonitions from Richard Wood, who emphasized the necessity of respecting "the sanctity of the place."[58] Transgressions such as these were widespread; another incident occurred in 1878 in Manzil al-Tamim, outside of Tunis, where Ben Giuseppe leased a shop adjacent to the congregational mosque. While the shopkeeper had at first sold articles that were "unobjectionable," Giuseppe subsequently turned his enterprise into a tavern, which prompted the town's inhabitants to petition the government.[59] Finally, a report from 1882 provides rare information about the manufacture and sale of spirits by minorities: "the natives do not drink wine but they like strong liqueurs and *eaux de vie* which not being fermented are not forbidden by Islam, boukha, raki, etc. The Italians and the Jews sell and distribute these liqueurs at very cheap prices."[60]

New places of sociability continued to pose problems of policing and public tranquility well into the Protectorate; contemporary observers claimed—perhaps with exaggeration—that the ratio of taverns to residents in Tunis was equal to France.[61] In 1878, Tunisian authorities again lamented that the regulations dictating tavern closures at 10:00 P.M. to avert "violent clashes and disorders" remained ineffective. Even when they shut down at the required hour, their customers lingered inside; some went out in the dead of night to "commit robberies and other disorders" and violent acts, such as a shooting in which "a man fired a pistol at another wounding him severely."[62] Consuls and city officials issued antiloitering regulations forbidding patrons from dallying about in places of male sociability after closing time but, without adequate means of enforcement, such measures remained dead letters.

The culture of alcohol consumption not only fostered boisterous gatherings but also introduced unaccustomed forms of nighttime deportment—"drunken brawling, random gunshots, and loud singing." A municipal ordinance proscribed musicians from performing in the streets after 10:00 P.M. This was directly tied to an incident from Christmas of 1860 when Catholic Sardinians engaged in a riotous, noisy celebration, surely aided by liberal doses of alcohol, which dismayed their Muslim neighbors.[63] Regulations and prohibitions, whether for gaming or consuming wine, were systematically flouted, which is clear because they were reissued repeatedly until the eve of the Protectorate. Thus, the Mediterranean migrants had invaded all manner of urban spaces— not only places of work, residence, and sociability but also the spaces of smell, sound, and noise, which always have a culturally determined moral content. Tunis, previously a sleepy, serene city without much nightlife—or so old-timers claimed—had been utterly transformed by the combined forces of migration, the search for work, and the introduction of public drinking as both a form of leisure and livelihood. But most critically, new popular urban places had destabilized traditional patterns of street making and spatial gendering.

FROM FUNDUQ TO TOURIST HOTEL

As the coffeehouse suffered competition from the tavern—or in some cases merged with it—various kinds of traditional lodgings for temporary visitors or workers were in the throes of change. In the nineteenth century, the term *funduq* had two meanings. Originally it designated a caravansary, inn, or hostelry sensibly located on the edge of Tunis near city gates so that merchants with pack animals and bulky goods could be conveniently accommodated. In addition, because the older European consulates formed a complex of buildings that served as residences, prisons, lodgings, storage places, and at times, hotels, these compounds were referred to as funduqs.[64] Other smaller funduqs were scattered around, particularly in the two *ribats,* where they served a largely Tunisian or North African clientele composed mainly of single males from other parts of the country or foreign traders residing there momentarily while conducting business. Numerous *wakala* provided lodgings for transient, down-at-the-heel males, much like a hostel or YMCA. The consular funduqs aside, neither the popular funduq nor *wakala* were intended as permanent family residences, although at times very poor people ended their days there for lack of alternatives.

After midcentury, some of these shelters became homes away from home for impoverished Maltese or Sicilian bachelors or entire families. Other short-term residential establishments, especially in the two suburbs, turned into "veritable taverns and gathering places by night that were frequented by prostitutes."[65] While the entire capital city was transformed by the convergence of immigration, housing shortages, and the scramble to find work, the more popular quarters experienced a growing confusion in the use of spaces—whether for leisure, work, or residence—that had previously been distinct or subject to specific spatial norms and temporalities. Remember the Maltese sweets peddler who churned out sticky wares in his rented room in one of the city's funduqs? At the same time, the hotel business aimed at a transnational middle-class clientele took off in the capital, offering some work and social mobility to migrants until landownership and agricultural exploitation later opened up. What forces, local, regional, and transnational, conspired to put Tunisia on the tourist map?

One element was that the Tunisian political class sought, if not full admission into the charmed circle of European nations, at least recognition as a minor Mediterranean player. Participation in international exhibitions offered one avenue: products and handicrafts were sent to the universal expositions of 1855, 1867, and 1878 held in Paris; in 1879, the Tunisian government participated in the Exposition Industrielle et Agricole held in Constantine and Bône. In the 1855 Paris exposition, the workshops of Tunis were represented by ornate, handcrafted arms and fine handicrafts as well as "authentic native" artisans.[66] International forums exposed Europeans to Tunisia, promoted the country, and probably increased the pool of labor migrants, although the endless succession of world's fairs, colonial expositions, and other such extravaganzas exerted the most profound impact in the domain of trans-Mediterranean tourism and travel.

The creation of regular steamship lines linking Tunis to Algiers, or to Alexandria and other Ottoman ports as well as Europe, encouraged mobility on a hitherto unimaginable scale. In 1847 a steamship sailed directly from Toulon to Tunis in only sixty-three hours, a record crossing. Seven years later, in September 1854, an English steamer arrived in Tunis from Alexandria in seven days after first putting in at Valletta; the trip from Malta had only taken twenty-four hours. Of the 1,092 passengers, 432 debarked in La Goulette; 610 went on to Algiers, and 50 set out for Gibraltar. Many were Muslim pilgrims returning home from the Hijaz and Egypt, but others were newly arrived investors, job-seekers, travelers, and tourists. By the 1870s, steamers made the crossing from Tunis to Palermo in forty-five hours, which compares favorably with today.[67] Regular steamship lines and postal services grew in importance during the 1860s, thus making travel more predictable.

In the 1860s, the Tunisian government's official organ, al-Ra'id al-Rasmi, began publishing the timetables of shipping companies carrying passengers and freight between Tunis and provincial ports, such as Sousse or Sfax, and the rest of the Mediterranean world. Some of the earliest issues from 1860 contained the following announcements: "the owner of a company in Marseille has steamboats going from Tunis to Malta and from Tunis to Algeria, to Annaba, to Oran to Alexandria, and to Marseille"; "the Sardinian steamship company, Rubattino, announces that a mailboat going between Tunis and Cagliari will also take passengers"; and "the French company, 'Les Messageries,' announces that the steamship, 'the Marabout,' is expected in Tunis on Thursday."[68] The fact that these notices, including advertisements, were published in Arabic indicates that a local clientele for shipping information existed.

By the fin de siècle, wealthy travelers purchased first-class tickets from the Parisian company Pacquebots Tonache, boarded the rapid night train from the Gare de Lyon to Marseilles, and registered bags all the way to Tunis; the duration of the crossing was between thirty-one and forty hours. A bit farther to the east, the opening of the Suez Canal in 1869, together with other factors, unleashed a veritable flood of English tourists upon the Mediterranean world; many stopped off in North African ports—particularly Algiers, where certain hotels catered specifically to them—as they made their way to or from India.[69] But increasingly, English visitors made the crossing to the Maghrib to escape the rigors of winter, travel that represented the incipient stages of transnational seasonal or medical tourism.

Fueled by the imperialism of modern movement, Algeria's booming hotel and tourism business exerted considerable torque upon Tunisia for tourists, labor migrations, and urban infrastructural development. If Sir Grenville Temple characterized the four grand hotels in Algiers in 1832 as "execrable," by the 1840s Algiers boasted better establishments, such as M. Latour-Dupin's hotel located on the Place du Gouvernement, described as "very beautiful and built in French, or rather Parisian style, with large windows and arcades made to resemble those on the Rue du Rivoli."[70] Another favored destination was the Hôtel de l'Orient, which boasted "every luxury, moderate charges, and an excellent *table d'hôte*"; some of its clients traveled on to visit Tunisia, including Lady Herbert and her daughter.[71] As travel rapidly expanded by the 1870s, increasing numbers of tourists combined excursions to Roman sites with extended stays to recover from tuberculosis or other ailments.[72] As importantly, Tunisia had became a place of repose and leisure for weary officers from France's enormous African army. By the century's close, Tunisian hydrotherapy stations were reimagined by French promoters as curative way stations for reacclimatizing colonials leaving the tropics for the metropole in the same way that Egypt, particularly Alexandria, served as decompression chambers for British Raj officials returning to the heart of the empire.[73]

It is uncertain when the first modern hotels were established in Tunis or the port, in part because the meaning of "modern" remains contested. The Eymon establishment was one of the earliest; from the late eighteenth century on, the family opened a small *auberge,* or inn, with four or five rooms on *nahj Sidi al-Murjani* that also offered meals and food for home consumption at reasonable rates.[74] In 1824, the Imperial Inn, in operation for two decades, was run by a Genoese and had a clientele that was mainly masters of merchant ships. Its "daily expense, including breakfast, dinner, supper, and sleeping room, is about a dollar; for another separate apartment, which cannot always be had, a small additional charge is made"; in contrast, the nearby English Inn was "kept also by an Italian; but the accommodations, it is said, are far inferior."[75] A traveler reported in 1835 that "since the natives never stay in hotels or inns, [indigenous] establishments do not exist in Tunis. The Europeans have three hotels in Tunis, the Hotel of Naples, for Italians, the Hotel of England, and the Hotel of France which is the largest and the most frequented and here travelers finds good food and all desired commodities. . . . Tunis has numerous markets [but] there are only six public squares for walking. The only public square which merits the name is the Bab al-Bahr which serves as a place for closing business deals."[76] Not surprisingly, hotels were located in areas most likely to attract visitors and merchants—the Sea Gate and the adjacent promenade—which already represented an important collective space for conducting business as well as for strolling. Also intriguing is the fact that each hotel catered to their own nationals due to language, social expectations, and cultural considerations.

As with wine shops and cafés, hotels provided work for women, particularly widows, and operated as mechanisms for social betterment for people who left domestic service to go into business on their own. The Hôtel de France near the consulates and Sea Gate was a small establishment run by Madame Cécile, who had earlier been a chambermaid to Madame de Lesseps; it won rave reviews for its lodgings and meals.[77] Joseph Tournier, who died in Tunis in 1870, took over this hotel first as manager and later as owner. He represents a paradigmatic case of social mobility, since he arrived from France around 1844 as a *valet de chambre,* subsequently becoming an innkeeper. The same held true for his common-law wife, Lazarine, who came in 1848 as a chambermaid. In 1867 a European guest described their establishment as a "Moorish house converted into a hotel which is one of the most comfortable in Tunis."[78] If the growth of tourism and the hotel business furnished work for newcomers and amenities for creole residents, it only exacerbated the already critical housing crunch in the capital. The same source states that the hotel had once been a "Moorish" home where presumably local families had resided before renting the structure to French hoteliers. Profiting from palace patronage, Eugène Bertrand, who had served the bey as a civil engineer, took over the management of yet another establishment, the Hôtel de Paris in 1864, which he later acquired as property. In this same neighborhood, European bakeries and Italian ice-cream makers also set up shop.[79]

Due to immigration and Tunisia's critical importance for the French navy,

La Goulette's facilities grew. Madame Barrillet, a widow, ran a hotel in the 1870s that catered to Europeans; and in 1863, Pierre Bariette, formally a stonemason in Algeria, opened an inn at the port, which by then also boasted its own Hôtel de France. Following a path similar to Bariette's, Philippe Michel, born in Marseilles in 1818, arrived in Tunis in 1850 after serving in the Armée d'Afrique. Michel first taught mathematics at the newly constructed Muhammadiya palace, where he established ties with the Husaynid family. Five years later, he set himself up as an innkeeper, drawing upon the labor of his wife and daughter. As might be expected, hotels were scenes of conflict between guests and proprietors. In 1873 a wealthy couple from Belgium checked into Michel's hotel. Madame Cerenhe brought along with her "trucks of belongings" and a maid; at some point during their extended stay, a huge altercation erupted, apparently over unpaid hotel expenses that demanded consular mediation.[80]

Hotels became places of political intrigue, frequented allegedly by spies and *malfaiteurs* who were monitored by consulates. The arrival in 1865 of "suspicious individuals" from Malta provoked a flurry of anxious correspondence between Paris, Algeria, and Tunis:

> The French consul in Tunis just sent to [Paris] details on the presence of a soi-disant Turkish officer who attempts to surround himself with the greatest mystery. Ibrahim Effendi Bey [the name he has given himself] came to Tunis from Malta on the *Arno*. He was accompanied by an individual from Moravia by birth who came from Alexandria, joining Ibrahim Effendi Bey in Malta; he had himself registered on the pacquebot's passenger list under the name of Kustchera, Adolphe. Both men also in the same register claimed to be merchants but as soon as they had arrived in Tunis, they unwittingly let it be known, through indiscretions, that they were not in fact merchants. Ibrahim claimed to be a major in the Sultan's army.[81]

The consul, Duchesne de Bellecourt, had them tailed to learn more of their suspected machinations. At first the travelers took rooms at a bourgeois hotel run by a Frenchman but, perceiving themselves under surveillance there, they decamped to a nearby "native" funduq less amenable to outside scrutiny. The influx of tourists generated more work for resident consuls because the opportunities for diplomatic wrangling—whether over unpaid hotel bills, maids, or stolen belongings—rose steadily with the swell of passengers debarking in La Goulette. If the growing demand for spies and informants offered some job opportunities, the need for translators and guides provided work as well, notably for the Maltese, and from very early on. Typical was the German traveler Christian Ferdinand Ewald, on a mission in 1835 to convert the Tunisian Jews. Ewald journeyed from Tunis to Gabes along the coast, a considerable distance and a trip full of perils in this period, accompanied by freelancing Maltese travel guides.[82]

As royal visitors like Caroline, Princess of Wales, drawn by Tunisia's spectacular antiquities, gave way to bourgeois tourists seeking better health, the city's service sector grew, providing more work. At the same time, people who chose to linger in Tunis indefinitely reveals another pattern: that traveler, tourist, and job candidate became commingled.[83] Hotel clients reflected, while enhancing, the capital city's cosmopolitanism after midcentury, as well-heeled tourists, bankers and pashas of international finance, and shrewd entrepreneurs from around the Mediterranean arrived in greater numbers thanks to improved, cheaper transportation, the lure of the exotic, personal or political difficulties, or dreams of striking it rich. Taverns, hotels, theaters, restaurants, and other urban amenities sprang up, attracting more people whose motivations for relocating are reflected in ship manifests. In earlier decades, most middle-class passengers tended to be military or scientific personnel seeking employment with the Tunisian state, and notably the new army. At midcentury, a typical ship arriving in port carried passengers exercising these occupations: traders in import/export; French colonial military officers; a blacksmith; women traveling with family members; a French sculptor named Beaugrand; and a Mexican engineer.[84] By the 1870s, a typical ship's manifest listed the following: Salvatore Aylon, an Italian wig maker; Giacomo, an Italian hydraulic engineer hired to bring water from Zaghouan to Tunis; a hotel keeper; two master bakers; a hatmaker; a dentist; a watchmaker; a wine merchant; several carriage makers; and a manufacturer of fizzy lemonade drink, the cola of the day.[85]

But ships coming from Bône or Algiers introduced less savory characters, even as Algeria's hotel business influenced Tunisia's attraction for tourists. By the eve of the Protectorate, interior towns had hotels of dubious respectability; many were owned or run by "expatriate" colonials from Algeria. The holy city of al-Qayrawan (Kairouan) boasted a Hôtel de France, although it surely did not win glowing notices in tourist guides then making their appearance. As the social center for a handful of resident colonial officials and settlers, mainly Italians or Greeks, the Hôtel de France assembled a clientele "of the worst type, having come here from so far away undoubtedly to escape a past replete with nefarious deeds." If the patrons left much to be desired, the place itself was not five-star: "it is a frightful den of iniquity, run by a shameless [devergondée] Spanish woman" who had come from the Constantine, where she had earlier worked in the business. Late into the evenings, Sicilians and Greeks, "who represent civilization here, gather together at this shady hotel run by the Spanish woman. . . . They drink, sing noisy songs, get into fights, and give themselves over to alcohol till dead drunk."[86]

However, the belle époque for Tunisian tourism had to wait until the first years of the twentieth century, when policies specifically aimed at developing the country's infrastructure and encouraging European, particularly French, tourism were worked out by a newly created Tourism Committee founded in 1903. The year before, the Tunisia Palace Hotel had opened its doors with great fanfare, claiming the status of the "most beautiful hotel on the African coastline." In addition to its 150 rooms and furnished apartments, French cuisine, fine wine cellars, electricity, gardens, and telephone, the Palace Hotel offered hydrotherapy and advertised the fact that "all of its rooms were exposed to the sunlight," which voiced the principal promotional message—that Tunis was the perfect spot for winter medical tourism. Not surprisingly, the role of physicians and the medical establishment was paramount in the elaboration of this kind of transnational capitalist enterprise; although, as discussed at length in chapter 8, the confluence between medicine and tourism lay decades earlier in the mid-nineteenth century.[87]

HARD TIMES:
POVERTY, CHARITY, AND RETURN MIGRATION

Poverty is a relational concept whose economic definition, sociocultural meaning, and manifestation changed in the course of the nineteenth century.[88] Nevertheless, a good working definition is "the shortage of pecuniary and non-pecuniary resources that threaten the survival of the individual and the family," which raises the issue of how different groups measured survival and evaluated the resources, including social capital, needed to maintain subsistence.[89] Poverty among European or Mediterranean residents in precolonial Tunisia has not yet been studied in depth, mainly because of the false notion that—as "Europeans"—they naturally occupied high, or at least secure, places in the social hierarchy.[90] But not everyone realized their dreams and misfortune was never far away; when jobs evaporated, fragile mutual aid unraveled, or collective welfare mechanisms failed, then impoverishment ensued. At times, unfortunate individuals or entire families were forcibly repatriated or dumped on ships heading for other ports. And the world of immigrant indigents not only resembled the social universe of the indigenous poor but intersected with it.

The country suffered recurrent epidemics from 1817, when plague, absent for decades, reappeared and was followed by a new disease, cholera morbus, that endured until late in the century. Insufficient or failed harvests linked to drought, pestilence, and political turmoil, especially the 1864 rebellion, plunged the peasantry into extreme distress. From 1866 on, beggars and vagabonds from city and countryside overwhelmed municipal authorities, their presence provoked by the revolt's brutal suppression by armed forces under General Zarruq's command. Bin Diyaf provided a horrifying account of the famished as they swarmed into Tunis from village and tribe, often expiring in the streets. Food became so scarce that storekeepers no longer dared display wares in front of shops; hordes of starving people even threw themselves upon trays of ceremonial bread, traditionally carried in the streets, during funeral processions.[91]

As part of its religious functions, the palace provided some poor relief in the form of grain distribution to the urban needy, particularly during acute crises in the agricultural sector, although Islamic welfare institutions supported by *awqaf* (or *ahbas*) furnished most public assistance. Destitute men found shelter in the *maristan,* women in the *takiyas* (shrines), but these proved inadequate as the century wore on.[92] One of the largest, best endowed, and most sacred shrines was set apart for women—the tomb of the thirteenth-century holy woman, Lalla Manubiya (d. 1267). Venerated as the patron saint of Tunis for her miraculous powers, Lalla Manubiya's tomb-shrine was the object of weekly pilgrimages. Muslim women sought refuge there from abusive husbands, uncaring families, poverty, or distress; some resided for years within the confines of the large sanctuary, even dying there.[93] City notables were not necessarily immune from disaster, since political intrigues resulting in the loss of fortune sent vulnerable family members into shelters. When Mustafa Khaznadar seized Hamida Chebah's properties, his daughters were left "in total misery and without adequate nourishment, forcing them to reside in one of the tombs of the Muradid princes."[94] Whether non-Muslims sought haven in Islamic shrines is a question worth pursuing; but the Husaynid state did offer assistance to nonsubjects, to the extent possible, distributing grain to the urban foreign poor during shortages.[95]

But the fact that some immigrants begged in city streets from the late 1820s on was quite another matter. Collecting alms in public spaces was not, in and of itself, at issue—indigenous women and men importuned the fortunate for donations, especially in the vicinity of religious buildings or in the entryways to wealthy households. But these newcomers were outside the purview of Muslim charitable organizations and the state enjoyed only tenuous, and increasingly contested, jurisdictional authority over their daily lives and comportment. Until the first Catholic female order arrived in the 1840s to organize health, education, social welfare, and, above all, to shield female morality from ever-present sexual dangers, the consulates assumed principal responsibility, however reluctantly, for down-and-out nationals or protégés.[96]

While their poignant saga occurred a bit earlier than the period that concerns us, the Fassy family's trajectory represents one of the best documented cases of Europeans falling into misery. Their sad tale also brings together both sides of the Mediterranean in terms of the search for work and social assistance as well as laying bare collective attitudes toward indigents in small expatriate communities. Dominique Fassy (1754–1818), a master sailmaker from Marseilles, had been recruited from Tripoli in 1815 by the French vice-consul in La Goulette, Pierre Gaspary, who was a relative.[97] Employed in the bey's naval yards, Fassy eked out a living made precarious by his steadily increasing offspring. Regarded with opprobrium by European neighbors, the Fassys and their six children lived one step away from poverty and borrowed to purchase food. "Mr. Fassy . . . does not have a cent to his name and owes money to everyone in La Goulette because of which the family is often tormented."[98] During Mahmud Bey's reign (1814–1824), a plague erupted in 1817 and persisted until 1820, carrying off a good proportion of Tunisia's population. By November 1818, three members of the Fassy family— father, mother, and one child—had succumbed, leaving five orphans ranging in age from three to sixteen years as well as enormous debts.[99]

For the next months, the children were kept alive thanks to the daily generosity of neighbors in the port, including several "Turks" who furnished basic provisions. The French vice-consul sent servants with bread, meat, and oil, but the plague had compromised agricultural production so food was scarce. Because of their penury, finding a captain who was willing to transport the orphans to Marseilles proved daunting. Finally in April 1819, a Swedish vessel carried the children to France, much to the relief of consular and Tunisian officials and the European community. They left behind a string of debts that took years to settle. One of the intriguing dimensions of this tale of woe is that Muslims (either designated as "Moors" or "Turks" in the sources) provided assistance to the orphans in La Goulette, indicating that religious differences did not deter charitable acts by neighbors or local do-gooders.[100]

Unlike so many "down-and-out" tales without closure because of inadequate sources, the story's sequel is found in the archives of the Chambre de Commerce in Marseilles. Application had been made by the French consul in Tunis for the care of the Fassy orphans to the Hôpital de la Charité and the Société de Bienfaisance in that city. Upon arrival, the youngest girl was placed in an *"école d'industrie"* supervised by Catholic sisters; the two older girls were taken in by the *société* until they could be placed as boarders with another Catholic order. But there is a final, curious element to the Fassy affair that brings us back to the problem of labor, migration, and worker recruitment within the matrix of intersecting networks spanning the sea. In June 1819, soon after the orphans had returned to France, their deceased father's nephew, Pierre Fassy, also a master sailmaker in Marseilles, contacted the French consul in Tunis. Pierre desired to replace his deceased uncle and requested the consul's intercession with the bey for employment.[101]

The Catholic registry archives in the Tunis Cathedral also reveal important dimensions of mobility and poverty. Families frequently moved back and forth from Tunisia, Algeria, Sicily, and Malta, evidence of a culture of social instability caused by the struggle to find adequate work and housing. That families were forced to move around compromised the domestic unit's ability to provide for members when things got tough—or even in the best of times: "the configuration of the European population of Tunis around 1850 [shows] an unstable population of immigrants, prolific as much as they were miserable."[102] As was the case elsewhere, compassion, mixed with a desire to guarantee the collective honor of a particular national group, underlay poor relief. Poverty-stricken families, like the Fassys, constituted a communal embarrassment and thus the consulates organized *caisse de secours,* or assistance funds, for cases of dire need. In 1825, the French consulate in Tunis boasted an account of two thousand francs "for any Europeans and for indigent French families."[103] Widows often applied to the consulates and even to the beys for succor, although they were viewed with unease by the authorities, even if personal resources proved adequate for leading respectable lives.

Emanuelle Skiano, a Maltese widow, sought help in 1830 from the English consul some two years after her husband's death, which had left her alone with a child to support. At first she had found work at the bey's palace, probably as a servant, but "her employer had no further occasion for her services, and [she] could not obtain other employ."[104] Skiano begged for financial assistance for her passage back to Malta, which was eventually arranged through the consul's intervention. When violence claimed the life of the breadwinner, families fell into misery. Sometime in the 1860s, Paolo Vassallo, a "quiet and honest" Maltese worker living in Tunis, made the mistake one evening of urinating against buildings lining the street. As he was relieving himself, an unknown assailant stabbed him in the back—street rumors blamed it on a deranged Tunisian. While he survived the attack, Vassallo led "a lingering and painful life which prevented him from work." His large family survived only through public generosity, and after Vassallo's death the British consulate made a charitable offering of thirty shillings "to free itself from the continual and importune prayers of his poor widow."[105] During the cholera epidemic that followed in the wake of the 1864 revolt, consulates organized benevolent subscriptions to collect funds from the more fortunate to aid families in economic straits.

Not infrequently, consuls had to repatriate individuals or rescue entire families in distress at the port. In 1816 a "miserable" young man from Naples, "a shoemaker without a dime," who had come on a fruitless search for family members, found himself stranded and without funds to return home.[106] In the 1830s, the Fiorintinis were supported by the French vice-consul, Gaspary, and another unfortunate family, the Romanis, resided with him because mother and child had taken ill as they were about to board a ship. In 1847 Captain Bitirac, commander of a French vessel, was paid fifty francs for the passage and sustenance "from Tunis to Marseille of the Widow Tarbourich and her three small children."[107] In a busy Mediterranean port, ships of all nations put in and crew members frequently found themselves in adverse situations. In 1828 the head of the French traders contacted the Chambre de Commerce in Marseilles regarding the plight of sailors: "it often happens that the sailors of a sunken ship, for lack of anywhere else to stay, if the only inn in the city is full, are forced to camp out in the courtyard of the consular building or in its upstairs galleries where they are exposed to the elements; often the sick are refused shelter at the inn or only admitted into the inn with great reluctance; the inn serves as a shelter for all the captains, sailors, and voyagers of all nations."[108]

Thus far we have seen how ties of one sort or another with the Husaynid palace, consulates, or creole bourgeoisie led to job opportunities as well as charity and assistance. But if some skilled laborers benefited from state-sponsored building projects, such as palace construction or urban renewal, others lost their livelihoods. Sometime before 1846, a French baker, Astoin, rented part of a building on the edge of the madina where he baked, sold bread, and resided with his large family. Being adjacent to the Sea Gate, the bakery attracted a good clientele and business flourished, for a while. But in October 1846, city authorities gave Astoin twenty-four hours to quit the locale owned by the municipality, since a guard post was to be built there. In his haste to comply, Astoin left behind personal effects, furnishings, and baking equipment worth 125 piasters, a considerable sum.

Burdened with too many children, Astoin next took refuge in a building occupied, but not owned, by Ghiggino, a Sardinian subject who put at the baker's disposition an oven and lodgings. But adversity dogged Astoin no matter what. Restoration of the Bab al-Bahr quarter was initiated in 1847 when Ahmad Bey ordered the demolition of houses, shops, and a portion of the ramparts near the Sea Gate, which abutted onto Astoin's new shop-residence, as these were state properties. Construction dragged on, blocking the bakery from its customers, so the hapless Astoin ceased baking bread.[109] Worse still, he and his family were forced to reside for an entire year next to open sewage drains in a partially demolished structure. After these unappealing lodgings were destroyed during the next phase of urban renewal, Astoin and his family were out in the streets again.

Astoin's successive miseries raise a number of questions. One pertains to food production and consumption. Most Tunisians ate brown bread, khubz asmara, formed into round, flat loaves baked in communal neighborhood ovens; provincials from the southeast specialized in baking bread and making fried sweets.[110] Was Astoin's failure to "make it" in the bakery business only due to the vagaries of urban reconstruction? Or was he regarded as a competitor in the eyes of established neighborhood bakers? Given that his operations were situated where many European residents worked and lived, were most of his customers from that group? The baker's relationship with his Sardinian friend demonstrates the workings of informal assistance networks—irrespective of nationality—among members of the down-and-out struggling to secure a living wage and a put a roof over their heads.

As discussed earlier, the service sector, particularly domestic service with the "right" patrons, partially integrated outsiders into the local economy in the way that property holding later on "tied people to communities."[111] In contrast to the lucky few, such as the beys' former cooks, retainers, and military personnel who made good for themselves in the café or hotel business, Astoin claimed no great patrons, although the French consul intervened repeatedly on his behalf, to little avail. The heart of the matter was that foreigners did not yet enjoy property rights; the baker's nomadic existence in the heart of densely populated Tunis sprang from this. Deprived of the networks necessary for social insertion and modest success, Astoin—and countless others—discovered that leaving home in pursuit of fortune entailed nothing but misfortune. Did he and his family remain in Tunis, relocate somewhere else, perhaps Algeria, or return to France on a ship with the consul's assistance? We will never know given the record, but there were many like the baker who arrived with high hopes, met only adversity, and moved on. Nevertheless, as suggested at the outset of this chapter, the hard times fueled population displacements in the central Mediterranean corridor and beyond. Many people who did not make it were reluctant to return home and admit failure to family members or fellow villagers, so they went elsewhere, creating new diaspora communities or swelling the ranks of already extant diasporas around the Mediterranean's southern or eastern rim.

There were, however, other ways to survive, even to amass a bit of money. But one needed to take risks, have few scruples, or simply be desperate enough as well as enjoy access to networks conjoining international maritime trade and transport with the back alleys of the madina or the docks of La Goulette. The flourishing international contraband trade offered possibilities for making it; in many cases, it was difficult to discern where "legal" trade and illicit exchanges began and ended. Local, regional, or trans-Mediterranean smuggling operations were covertly combined with other occupations—carting, tavern keeping, and fishing. Thus, the social universe of contraband was composed of men, women, and households making an honest living in forbidden items—alcohol, kif, tobacco, and so forth—whose circulation and distribution linked city, hinterland, and port with the wider Mediterranean, the Caucasus, and even the Atlantic world.

Making a Living

The Sea, Contraband,
and Other Illicit Activities

Demands for rides in seaside villages were brisk in summer and the evening of July 5, 1874, was no exception. Alexander Buhagiar, a Maltese coachman operating a leased carriage, was ferrying passengers around La Marsa. Buhagiar, who was drunk, already had several people in his coach when two Italian ladies, Margherita Cariglio Livolsi and her sister, signaled for him to stop and began bargaining over the fare. Intoxicated, but still able to navigate, Buhagiar "persuaded, if not forced," the women to enter the vehicle. After he deposited one passenger at the home of a Sicilian family, the women realized the driver's condition. They attempted to alight but Buhagiar "prevented them by forcibly shutting the door and turning the horses head once more towards the Marsa station." Alarmed by the driver's inebriation, the second passenger, a Tunisian Jew named Hai Seneja, leapt from the moving carriage. As he jumped, Hai Seneja told the women that "the coachman intended to take them for a 'kif' to Goletta." Frightened, the hapless Margherita hurled herself from the vehicle, fracturing her arm. In the consular inquiry that followed, she sought compensation to the tune of one thousand piasters from the Maltese. While the court admitted her claims against the coachman, it also determined that, since "the driver Buhagiar appears to be a man wholly destitute of means, recourse should also be had against the owner of the carriage, his employer."[1]

The 1874 incident illustrates many things: the workings of the carriage trade; how people of diverse backgrounds moved around; that men and women shared the same space in vehicles; and how a Maltese driver's imprudence spiraled out of control into consular proceedings involving a number of European powers and Tunisian justice. All of this may have cost him his livelihood and put him out on the street—or got him repatriated to Malta. However, Hai Seneja's warning about Buhagiar's evil intentions toward the women—that he intended to "take them for a kif"—made me pause. While Hai Seneja may have been a prankster, still the mention of kif in La Goulette terrified Margherita to the point that she too bailed out of the carriage, leading to physical injury. For respectable city dwellers, the port signified a place of ill repute where transients and low life dabbled in illicit pleasures—alcohol, prostitution, and drugs. In the nineteenth century, "kif" meant smoking hash and also referred to immoral nocturnal gatherings with singing, dancing, and erotic indulgences involving courtesans and male clients.[2] The trade that brought the forbidden intoxicant to drug users in La Goulette or Tunis was enmeshed in much wider, intricate networks characterized in Arabic sources as *kuntra*, from the Italian *contrabbando*, that crisscrossed the sea. In nineteenth-century Tunisia, certain professions—tavern keeping, carting, fishing, stevedoring, and seafaring—were rife with potential for fraud that slid seamlessly into enterprises labeled as illegal and/or criminal.

This chapter extends our ethnography of making a living by investigating occupations linked to the sea, such as fishing or small-craft coastal trading, and their association with "licit" and "illicit" exchanges integrating North Africa into trans-Mediterranean systems. Since my earlier work has reconstructed the interior overland sections of the contraband traffic along the Tunisian-Algerian borders, the chapter focuses upon its maritime circuits.[3] It argues that subsistence migration increased the volume of "extralegal" transactions and clandestine bargains, one of whose nodal points was the Tunis region and the Cap Bon (or Ra's al-Dar). Guesstimates of the volume or value of trade, impossible to determine given the sources, are less important than mapping the dense flows of labor, goods, services, and capital undergirding the political economy of contraband in relationship to labor migration. That the actors involved hailed from different religions, nationalities, ethnic groups, and classes renders this a perfect vantage point for probing intercommunal relationships.

Needless to say, contraband was nothing new for the Mediterranean world, but it did play a part in the sequence of events culminating in the 1830 French occupation of Algeria. Among the Algerian ruler's (Husayn Dey, r. 1818–1830) major grievances against France—in addition to outstanding debts—were the machinations of the French consul in Algiers, Deval, and his nephew, the vice-consul in Bône. In flagrant violation of treaties, the vice-consul armed French factories in the small port with cannons and openly engaged in contraband. In 1824 the dey accused the Frenchmen of illegal trade, ordered a search of the vice-consular residence in Bône, and imposed a 10 percent tax on merchandise imported from France. The 1827 fly-whisk incident in Algiers, during which the dey allegedly struck the French consul, was used as a pretext by France to invade

Algeria three years later.[4] In 1832, contraband threatened to trigger warfare between Tunisia and Sardinia after the bey accused a ship captain flying the Sardinian flag of smuggling.

Scholars of contemporary global labor migrations have long noted the complex links between the growth of so-called informal sector economies, including smuggling, and the expansion of immigrant populations. Unauthorized or unregulated commerce arises from the fact that labor migrants frequently dominate small entrepreneurial activities, which represent a "survival mechanism," a "vehicle for rapid economic ascent," or a strategy for "reconciling economic needs with culturally defined obligations."[5] However, defining income earning as "illegal" adopts the state's viewpoint in the same way that characterizing economic niches as "informal" suggests that recognized procedures were lacking, which was not the case. Moreover, rigid distinctions between criminal and noncriminal should be made with caution, since the criminalization of specific forms of exchange and the social groups associated with them stems from the observer's positioning. Recent work warns against conceptualizing the informal sector as an autonomous, parallel system of exchange, arguing instead for a model that interprets activities labeled "contraband" or "unregulated" as special economic niches within a single but structurally diverse economic system, which seems to fit the Tunisian case.[6]

Finally, the nineteenth-century contraband economy reveals flaws in earlier scholarship that relied without question upon the texts of treaties to chart economic transformations in the relationships between Europe and the Ottoman Empire—notably the much touted 1838 Anglo-Ottoman Commercial Convention prohibiting state monopolies and imposing import and export duties on trade between Great Britain and Ottoman provinces, including Tunisia. Nevertheless, if states have always attempted to control flows of people, goods, and ideas, the nineteenth century witnessed a dramatic expansion in the modern state's drive for "legibility" and thus the social fixity of populations and resources.[7]

This chapter first explores occupations linked to the sea, which formed the infrastructure of contraband because most commodities were transported by seamen who forged or tapped into circuits distributing the proscribed as well as the permissible. Next we turn to state and religious prohibitions governing the possession, use, or sale of certain commodities, together with efforts to stamp out exchanges deemed illegal and/or immoral, principally prostitution, which represented another clandestine way of making a living. Why specific regions, such as the Cap Bon, became pivotal to the flowering underground economy is analyzed, as is the criminalization of specific social groups viewed as inveterate smugglers. The discussion concludes with the Tellini case of 1868, the best documented of the contraband dramas, which takes us into the quotidian local universe of the thief and fencer in the Tunis madina.

THE SEA AS OCCUPATION

Ports functioned as the interface between North African producers of grains, livestock, and oil and Mediterranean distribution networks and presented the first or last chance for the state to tax, limit, or proscribe seaborne commerce and population movements. The modern world is incomprehensible without a social history of the sea that takes into account the existence of "oppositional cultures" among seaman on ships or among port laborers whose toil underwrote the global maritime economy. Sailors, captains, and fishermen are almost completely absent from the Tunisia's historical narrative, which is curious in light of the country's long, intense involvement in the Mediterranean. And the history of maritime communications between the Maghrib and Europe from 1830 on, or among different North African states, remains unexplored; what little scholarship exists rarely finds its way into conventional accounts.[8] Nevertheless, it is important to assemble what is known.

Ports were places of violence provoked by international antagonisms that resonated locally, by labor competition, or by quarrels among dockworkers, sailors, and free traders engaging in deals "on the side."[9] Just as immigrant workers or Algerian exiles poached on the Tunis café business, so laborers who had long worked the sea, ships, ports, and wharves were marginalized by newcomers. Violent clashes erupted not only between Tunisian and foreign laborers but also among different national or protected groups. An especially bloody altercation broke out in 1836, bringing chaos to La Goulette:

> If the Maltese had truly been the provocateurs in the fight, the fact that they made use of this kind of weapon proves to the contrary that this was a case of legitimate defense. It is improbable that these two Maltese, men of low standing, porte-faix by profession, impelled by the need to earn a living far from their country would be foolish enough and violate their own best interests by committing in cold blood, and without a motivation, an act of violence toward those who wanted to offer them an employ—unless some violent incident took place.[10]

By the eve of the Protectorate, travelers noted that the Maltese had taken over the profession of boatman: "a crowd of Maltese *bateliers* swarmed over the steamship as it arrived in port offering their services as ferrymen."[11]

If ports furnished employment on the docks or in customs houses, flourishing cabotage linked North African ports with each other and the islands. Because roads were poorly maintained, if at all, and bandits posed an ever-present threat, communications between the capital-city region and its provinces were assured by small boats, many under Tunisian captains. Water-shuttle services—not unlike today's *louages,* or intercity taxis—sailed from La Goulette to Djerba, Tripoli, or Alexandria, or north to Bizerte, Tabarka, and on to Bône and Dellys.

FIGURE 11. Transporting barrels of olive oil, c. 1890. Tunisian boatmen, judging by their dress, rowing barrels of olive oil, one of Tunisia's prime exports, out to waiting steamships. (Charles Lallemand, *Tunis au XIXe siècle* [Paris: La Maison Quantin, 1890].)

Seaborne transportation swelled during the annual pilgrimage to the Hijaz. During the hajj season, Tunisian vessels ferried Muslims to Alexandria, a collecting point for the Cairo pilgrimage caravans to the holy cities. Weeks or months later, North or West African pilgrims were picked up in Alexandria and deposited in home ports along the coast. In October 1831, a ship arrived in Sfax from Alexandria with ninety passengers, many returning pilgrims.[12] A Tunisian *shabbak* arrived in three days from Bône in September 1840 with forty-eight Muslim passengers, most bound for Mecca, and another ship, the *Zaytun,* came from Algiers under the command of Ahmad Sfaxsi with fifty-three Muslim passengers. Sfaxsi was obviously operating a hajj travel agency between Algeria, Tunisia, and Alexandria, since he showed up several months later with returning pilgrims. The hajjis' origins are difficult to determine because caravans brought peoples and goods from across northern Africa to Maghribi ports, and ship manifests invariably listed the passengers as "Muslims," "indigenous," or "pilgrims."[13]

    In addition to the Hijazi traffic, consular port records reveal other patterns typical of coastal transport, which involved a heterogeneous social world composed of island immigrants without papers, sailors who had jumped ship, army deserters, prostitutes, criminals, and debtors fleeing creditors. In June 1839, the ship *Mabruk* arrived from Bône in five days with fifty passengers, as did a Tunisian boat from Tabarka with a French military deserter onboard whom the Tunisian *ra'is* had under his supervision with orders to deliver the person to the French consulate, probably for forced transportation to Algiers or France. Several months later, in August 1839, the *Mabruk* returned under Captain 'Ali al-Binzarti ('Ali from Bizerte), this time with fifteen passengers; the trip to La Goulette took seven days from Bône, two from Tabarka, because ships stopped off here and there picking up or unloading people and goods—which rendered surveillance unfeasible.[14] In this way, travelers of different nationalities, religions, and social station were moved around the central Mediterranean corridor, together with highly diverse commodities, some of which were contraband—"armpit smuggling." (One wonders what impact the establishment of regular steam connections exerted upon this older form of transport.)

Not all ships flying the Tunisian flag were what they seemed. When James Richardson sailed from Sfax to Djerba in May 1845, he boarded a small "lugger" named *Mystico,* which belonged to a Maltese captain and was entirely manned by Maltese sailors. Nevertheless, the ship sailed under Tunisian colors "for the advantage of having no port-dues to pay on any part of the coast. Any captain can assume the Tunisian colours . . . but then there must be a nominal Moorish captain."[15] Sir Richard Wood alerted Muhammad al-Sadiq Bey in 1862 to a serious breach of maritime law—Maltese ships navigating under the Tunisian flag as a subterfuge: "but as these vessels are mostly engaged in the contraband coasting-trade, they find it easier by these means to evade the control of Her Majesty's Consulate General in the exercise of their nefarious vocation, which circumstance however is a matter for the sole consideration of the fiscal officers of the [Tunisian] government."[16] An age-old ruse on the high seas, flying the flag of another nation in order to thwart detection was common practice in the nineteenth century as it had been in the past.

Seamen—sailors, captains, and fishing crews—had always engaged in unfettered trade, deploying a range of creative ploys to traffic in forbidden commodities, as profits were high and sanctions mild. Weaponry and firearms of any kind were first on the list of prohibited—and desired—objects. However, tobacco came to be the number one item smuggled, judging by the frequency of seizures in the Tunis and Cap Bon regions. The capital city boasted hundreds of coffeehouses— the site par excellence for consuming the divine herb—and the café represented the favored male haunt for the rapidly expanding immigrant population. In addition, soldiers from the Algerian army flooded Tunisia; many frequented cafés, combining socializing with selling smuggled tobacco or kif.

Certain types of vessels lent themselves to the contraband trade, or at least to one phase in the movement of goods and people. The *shabbak,* a light, shallow-draft vessel, could put in to small ports or coves with minimal muscle power. Others were the *sandal* or *sandali,* a flat-bottomed boat, pointed at its two ends, specifically constructed to shuttle merchandise between moored ships and land, or larger craft with one or two lateen sails employed as lighters for unloading or loading vessels. (Brightly painted talismanic symbols to ward off the evil eye, such as the hand of Fatima or the ubiquitous fish motif to assure a bountiful sea harvest, still adorn some of these boats today.)[17] One question demanding more research is that of ship construction. During the 1840s in Sfax, a resident Maltese hired local Tunisians to build a small schooner under his supervision made of olive wood instead of oak, which was scarce and expensive. An early example of outsourcing, the cagey Maltese had his vessel built far more cheaply than in Malta because the Sfaxian laborers worked "for a quarter of a dollar per day, instead of a dollar, as in Malta. The schooner looks pretty well, and honours this combination of Maltese and Moorish genius."[18]

FISH AND FISHERMEN

The configuration of Tunisia's continental shelf makes it one of the few places in the Mediterranean with substantial daily tides—as much as three feet—which produce unusually plentiful banks of coral and sponge and an abundance of fish and shellfish; these banks have attracted fishermen since antiquity.[19] The Tunisian state traditionally granted concessions to foreign companies or court favorites to exploit these riches in exchange for annual tribute or rent; Hassuna al-Murali obtained the right to establish a fishery in the noxious lake protecting Tunis in 1862. A major source of prime quality tuna, the Cap Bon boasted one of the first modern canning facilities, established at Sidi Dawad situated near the tip of the peninsula. Husayn Bey bestowed this concession upon his minister of foreign affairs, Joseph Raffo, in 1826; renewed by later rulers, the operation made Count Raffo a wealthy man, and the facility was owned by his descendants until 1905. (Tunisian shops still sell cans of tuna under the trademark "Sidi Dawad"; regarded as exceptionally high-grade, most is now exported to Japan.)[20] Sixty-two miles separate the Cap Bon from Sicily, whose lights can be dimly perceived on very clear nights. As ports on the island's western edge, where the channel is narrowest, Trapani and Marsala sent by far the largest numbers to Tunisia, first mainly as fishermen or smugglers and later as farmers.

Richard Wood's daughter, Mary, provided an arresting eyewitness account of the fishery in her unpublished notebook dated 1879, although she had observed its workings somewhat earlier. The Woods were great friends with the Raffo family, and Mary had obviously spent considerable time at Sidi Dawad. The cannery provided work for two hundred persons for catching and salt-curing fish; the permanent staff included a manager, secretary, doctor, and chaplain, but most were seasonal fishermen there from early May until late June. Mary Wood tells us that "generally the same men return year after year; some are old men who first came when boys and have never missed a season." At the start of the day, the *capo ra'is* (master captain) climbed into a small dinghy before the crowd of fishermen assembled onshore, prayed for Saint Peter's blessing and called out "ajutaci Jesus" ("help us Jesus"). As the Sicilians, dressed in bright clothing, began laboriously hauling in the nets, "one of the men begins a weird chant composed of short verses and after each the whole crew takes up a kind of plaintive wail. . . . The singer usually improvises as he goes along and when strangers are present some complimentary verses addressed to them are introduced."[21] Whether local Tunisians were employed at the Sidi Dawad fishery is unknown.

Proximity and the lure of fine catches brought a veritable tsunami of fishermen to Tunisian shores annually, but the industry cannot be understood without reference to colonial Algeria. The first male laborers to settle Algiers after 1830 were adventurers, construction workers, and fishermen. For the most part, the fishermen were seasonal, harvesting the sea in ways that had existed for centuries; they lived on beaches, bringing along food and supplies from island villages. Realizing that the French presence had become permanent, they settled in small ports, such as La Calle, or in Algiers whose marine quarter was predominantly peopled by Sicilians and Neapolitans who operated cafés, taverns, and small shops. But others remained seasonal fishermen and their numbers steadily increased; travelers reported several hundred Italian coral boats off La Calle alone in the 1870s. From 1843 on, French colonial officials passed legislation limiting access to Algerian waters. While enforcement was problematic, to say the least, the passage in 1888 of yet another law in Algeria banning Italians from exploiting coastal waters sent them elsewhere.[22]

By the 1870s, the Italian consul in Tunis, Machiavelli, estimated that two thousand fishermen harvested coral, sponge, and tuna from Tunisian waters. While there is no way to calculate numbers, the Italian-Tunisian treaty of 1868, guaranteeing fishing as well as property rights, must have heightened the exploitation; small towns, notably Mahdiya, immediately felt the treaty's noxious effects. To make matters worse, fishermen from Bari and Naples introduced new methods for harvesting fish that put local competitors at a decided disadvantage.[23] Documentation on labor relations in the precolonial fishing industry is scarce but hints of conflict exist. In the Sfax region, home to bounteous sponge banks, Maltese, Italian, and Greek fishermen increasingly monopolized the lucrative catch, denying Tunisian fishermen their fair share. While the Tunisian government filed endless complaints with various consuls, things came to a head in the 1870s. But it was not only struggles over resources that angered the inhabitants of coastal towns; the behavior of the foreigners also provoked controversy. In 1879, the prime minister informed the British consul general of the "misconduct of the Greek sailors engaged in the sponge fishing trade in these waters when on shore or in this town [i.e., Sfax]." The Greeks in Sfax had increased in number to about six hundred, and the fact that some were French protégés and others were under British protection created jurisdictional headaches. During sojourns onshore, the fishermen "created disturbances when under the influence of drink."[24]

Consuls attempted to restore peace by arresting the offending parties or forcing ship captains to assume responsibility for fights among crews onshore. But when locals and foreign seamen came to blows, the likelihood for generalized social discord in coastal villages or towns increased. In typical fashion, European consuls blamed the Tunisian state because, as they put it, "unfortunately the force which the local authorities can put at our disposal is but very slight indeed."[25] Grievance letters to the government from residents of towns such as Mahdiya or Munastir denounced the fishermen as morally suspect because of their nomadic life on the sea and conduct on land, characterizing them as "marauders and drunks."[26] In addition, the frequency of ship desertions meant that unknown individuals were roaming about at large, causing social anxieties. The case of a Greek boy found wandering the streets of Sfax in 1879 was emblematic of a problem that had existed for decades. The lad had jumped ship from a Greek boat docked in Gabes "owing, he said, to ill treatment, and was found about 35 miles from this town [Sfax] and safely accompanied here [to Tunis] by two Arabs."[27] Even the Protectorate, with far greater coercive force at its disposal, could neither discipline the fishermen nor prevent ship desertions. During the early decades of French rule, thousands of fishermen from across the Mediterranean worked the coastline largely free from police, customs, or consular surveillance. And the 1886 Franco-Italian treaty granting Italians the right to exploit Tunisian waters only fixed in law practices dating back decades.[28]

The temptation to engage in smuggling—indeed those involved may not even have regarded these exchanges as illicit—was irresistible, and many fishermen employed their small vessels to smuggle goods and people back and forth.[29] As early as 1837, the British consul alerted the bey regarding the fact that the men of the sea did not only harvest fish or coral: "I have no reason whatever to suspect that the Maltese are very deeply engaged in smuggling ammunition ... but on the contrary, I have every reason to believe that it is carried on principally by the Sardinians, Tuscans, and Neapolitans, particularly in the boats of these three nations which are employed in the coral fisheries near Tabarca [sic]; and even some of the French subjects themselves have been know to have been engaged in it."[30]

Questions regarding the intersections between the fishing industry, sea transport, and the contraband economy should be raised, although, given the paucity of the data, definitive answers remain elusive. First, it may be that the seasonality of fishing, determined by availability of catches, winds, and currents, shaped the periodicity of smuggling. And the contrary winds and dangerous seas of winter may have rendered contraband a primarily summertime system of exchanges, at least for commodities moved about by small craft. Finally, the national finger-pointing—Sir Thomas Reade maintained that other nations' protégés were to blame—became characteristic of the nineteenth century's "contraband wars."

GUNS AND GUNPOWDER

"At midnight on the 29th of dhu al-qa'da 1268/1852, a fire broke out inadvertently and reached the gunpowder magazine at the Burj Kabir known as Burj Zuwara in the Jabal al-Akhdar near the capital city and it blew up the magazine and destroyed the side of the tower and this occurred during the bey's illness [i.e., stroke] when he was in Halq al-Wad and the people were shaken by this incident and regarded it as an evil omen."[31] Gunpowder and firearms represented special commodities, more so than tobacco, hash, rum, or counterfeit currency. Powder and ammunition posed considerable risks not only to smugglers but also to those residing near stockpiles or hidden caches. Sacks of combustible materials concealed in homes or shops in the Tunis madina or other densely populated towns frequently exploded, demolishing buildings and causing loss of life. Firearms and powder in the "wrong hands" threatened state control over the periphery and tribal areas always loath to render tribute or to hand over local wrongdoers without the threat of, or recourse to, armed force. Thus arms and powder, like contraband in general, indexed the state's health as robust, ailing, or somewhere in between. On the other hand, the purveyors of gunpowder often gave themselves away when they imprudently lit cooking fires in proximity to their stashes.

The Husaynid government interdicted the importation, production, or sale of gunpowder by nonstate actors, as most states did. But periodic renewals of the ban on firepower indicate that it was systematically violated. A monopoly, gunpowder was produced in the capital, mainly in the Qasba where Husayn Bey had a new factory established in the former garrison of the disbanded janissaries. The state stored gunpowder in magazines around the country, guarded by garrisons; one location was Bizerte, another smuggling center located a full day's journey from Tunis. In the nineteenth century, the town counted twelve thousand inhabitants and six hundred soldiers. As the north's largest port adjacent to the border, Bizerte was covertly monitored by French naval officers because of its pivotal role in the exportation of gunpowder to Algeria.[32]

In November 1833, state agents arrested an Algerian from Constantine as he was conveying "three hundred weight of gun powder from this Regency to Constantine." The culprit confessed that he had purchased the powder from Nicola Mannuci, the son of the British consular agent in Bizerte, a Corsican named Giuseppe Mannuci. According to informants, Nicola had stored "a very consider-

Tunis. Mauresques en costume de ville.

السلام عليكم

FIGURE 12. "Moorish" women in street clothes, c. 1900. This postcard produced in Tunis but sent from Bizerte purports to show two Tunisian women posing for the camera, although their true identity cannot be known with any certainty. The Arabic inscription over the door in the background reads "Peace be with you." (Postcard, 1900; author's private collection.)

able quantity of gunpowder in his house [in Bizerte] which he was in the habit of selling to the Constantine Moors." Once this information reached the Bardo, Husayn Bey directed the British consul to send his agent to Bizerte to examine Nicola Mannuci's premises. What was discovered? Sacks of the stuff were found "in a very insecure and almost open room and if any fire had accidentally got to it, it would have destroyed all the houses in its immediate neighborhood."[33] The origins of the powder were uncertain—had it been pilfered from a local beylical storage facility? Or had it been ferried in by small boats in the dead of night, perhaps from Malta? The fact that British subjects had been apprehended funneling war materials to Algerian rebels caused the French consul to pressure the Tunisian government to end the traffic. Finally, Reade proposed retracting British protection from the wrongdoer:

> Mr. Nicola Manucci is of Corsican origin but enjoys the British protection here, in consequence of his being a son of the British Consular Agent at Biserta [sic]. Independent of the contraband transaction above mentioned, he bears a very indifferent character and I propose to take the protection from him, provided you see no difficulty in my so doing. I have heard several times of reports having been spread in Tunis that the Arabs of Constantine were supplied with arms and ammunition by British Subjects, and I have also seen paragraphs in French newspapers to the same effect, which induced me the more readily to comply with the Bey's request.[34]

The Manucci brothers could not stay out of trouble, since another family member, Antonio, was later accused in 1855 of stealing barley from a state-owned grain storage facility in Bizerte. However, when Muhammad Bey demanded justice, the British consul cagily replied that Antonio Manucci was neither a British subject nor a protégé and therefore nothing was to be done.[35] It was not only British subjects who made big bucks in this traffic. A French Algerian protégé, Muhammad Darregi, resident in Tunisia, clandestinely sold gunpowder in Bizerte until 1851, when he accidentally set himself on fire, bringing to public attention his involvement in shady enterprises. Oddly enough, after Bottary, the French vice-consul in Bizerte, sent Darregi to Tunis for interrogation, the Algerian was freed because the consulate "did not find anything that made him suspect."[36]

Rivaling Bizerte was Porto Farina, some five hours' ride from Tunis, by then suffering grievously from rapid silting up as the Majarda River changed course; only small, flat-bottomed *sandals* could navigate the lake. The chief licit occupations of its few thousand inhabitants were fishing and olive oil production; after the French conquest of Algeria, contraband became Porto Farina's prime source of revenue due to location. In 1832 the diplomatic crisis between Sardinia and the Tunisian state mentioned early in this chapter erupted.

> In 1248/1832 an estrangement occurred between the bey and Sardinia because the [Sardinian] ship captain loaded his small vessel with forbidden items that could

only be exported with special permission and the payment of the *sarah;* this trans-pired on the shoreline near Ghar al-Milh. When news of this came to the attention of the kahiya of the port, he . . . placed the ship under guard and when the captain tried to throw the [contraband] merchandise overboard, the governor had the ship taken by force; the forbidden items were discovered on board. It was the practice at the time to seize the ship and all of its contents if it contained forbidden items.[37]

Significant is the reference to the "practice of the time," which made proscribed items and the ship bearing those goods subject to seizure for the Tunisian government, a principle hotly contested by the Sardinian state.

The sources do not state the nature of the merchandise that the captain franti-cally attempted to conceal from port authorities but from this period forward Porto Farina's reputation as a contraband firearms and gunpowder paradise soared.[38] Introducing arms and gunpowder in the dead of night by small boats and then smuggling the goods overland to Algeria became the town's principal source of prosperity, a trade monopolized by the Maltese. But this may not have been all that new, since the port had played a major role in the earlier corsair economy and in its heyday came in third after La Goulette and Bizerte. Thus successful conver-sion from maritime raiding to seaborne contraband suggests the persistence of a regional political economy and culture based upon specific kinds of exchanges. Two years later, in 1834, the small port was the scene of a dreadful accident after an enormous gunpowder cache—a veritable arsenal—stored in the basement of a Maltese home caught fire; many adjacent homes and their inhabitants were blown to pieces. After this, the government attempted to clamp down on the trade but failed singularly, not only because many involved were foreign protégés, but also because expatriates worked hand in glove with local North African accomplices, who knew best the soft spots in state surveillance and control. The 1834 explosion was neither the first nor the last time that such an incident occurred; throughout the nineteenth century, many an unlawful trader literally blew his cover after light-ing up a pipe of contraband tobacco *chez lui.*[39]

Even the beys in their palaces were not immune from the disturbances occa-sioned by the trans-Mediterranean contraband trade. During the summer months, the rulers and their courts moved from the capital city to palaces near La Marsa or the port. Unfortunately, small Maltese vessels anchored in the La Goulette canal adjacent to the bey's palatial windows. In 1839, things came to a dramatic head:

> Regarding the smuggling of gunpowder into this Regency by Maltese *speronares,*
> a dreadful accident happened to one of these vessels which claimed to be bringing
> dried fruit and biscuit from Malta to Tunis. All the cargo had been unloaded in La
> Goulette, except nine bags of biscuit. The vessel blew up with a tremendous explo-
> sion, destroying every window in the houses of La Goulette near where the boat
> anchored and shaking the houses to their very foundations. One adjacent Tunisian

boat was sunk by the explosion. Eleven crew members perished and the [Maltese] vessel was literally blown to atoms. It had on board 117 barrels of gunpowder. The smuggling of gunpowder by the Maltese has lately reached an enormous pitch. I attribute this to Mr. Ancrom, the acting [British] consul, encouraging the Maltese during my absence [Reade was in England at the time]. The Bey complains to the British consul and to the European population about this; particularly since the Maltese live in the European fonduqs in the city and store gunpowder in great quantities in their dwellings, where they smoke and cook in the same rooms where the gunpowder is stored. In bad weather, the Maltese vessels anchor in the canal right near the Bey's palace. [The contraband trade] is difficult to repress for the Bey since European powers will not permit Tunisian authorities to board European ships to see if the cargo matches the customs declarations. In addition to contraband powder, for the last five years, the introduction of false [counterfeit] piasters from Marseille and Italy has ruined Tunisia's commerce.[40]

This same incident was reported on November 16, 1839 in the *Harlequin or Broadsheet of the Mediterranean,* a bilingual, English-Italian newspaper published in Valletta and sold at Sa'id's coffeehouse on the Strada Reale. Entitled "Accident at Tunis," the article noted that the *speronara* "*SSMO Cristo* having still on board a portion of her cargo, consisting of sundry wines, bread, and some barrels of gunpowder, was on Sunday, the 10th [i.e., November 1839] at half past seven, p.m., blown up, eight of the crew and three persons from the shore suffering the loss of life. Many are the reports as to the origin of the accident. . . . A Maltese lad, one of the Speronara's crew, had been punished for some misdeed—when on remarking that he would have his satisfaction was repunished—and almost immediately lighting his lamp he went below and set fire to the powder."[41]

Needless to say, accounts of illicit trade and clandestine commerce demand careful scrutiny; their very existence poses fundamental problems for the historian. How was it known that 117 barrels of gunpowder were aboard the Maltese *speronara,* if the vessel was "literally blown to atoms"? Why was Ancrom encouraging the contraband activities of his Maltese protégés, who scarcely needed additional goading? Was the cabin boy being made into a scapegoat? And who carried the news of the La Goulette explosion so rapidly to Malta for immediate publication in the Valletta newspapers?

One of the best documented family contraband operations was run by the Maltese Francesco Bartalo and his wife, who lived in the small European quarter of Gabes. The port's location near east–west routes linking the oases of southern Tunisia with the largely unpoliced border regions made the small oasis perfectly situated to channel gunpowder and firearms via chains of intermediaries to the tribes and Algerian rebels. The Bartalos acted as brokers in the gunpowder traffic linking Malta with Gabes and the Sahara during the early 1850s. Shipments of powder were unloaded from small vessels in the dead of night on the beaches. Francesco and his wife then bought and stored the sacks of contraband in their home—of special note is the role of women in the household economy of smuggling. Tunisian tribal purchasers paid in currency or kind for arms and gunpowder, which was transported by caravans to turbulent frontier towns where other dealers took them into the Algerian interior. And profits could be quite high, particularly during the frequent uprisings that shook Algeria as France attempted to pacify desert peoples from 1844 until the 1880s.[42] However, the 1864 revolt in Tunisia momentarily reoriented the transnational armaments trade, linking Mediterranean suppliers and local entrepreneurs with distributors and markets in Algeria. As the largest rebellion in modern Tunisian history gathered force, the need to supply shock troops with the tools of resistance turned the munitions traffic into a national affair, for a while at least, demonstrating the recurrent interplay between local upheavals, supply and demand, and transnational extralegal marketing systems.[43] However, after the revolt was put down with great violence, it was business as usual and caravans bearing munitions headed once again for the Algerian borders.

A critical dimension in the flexibility of commodity chains was the very fact that licit and illicit behavior were seamlessly combined—as is true in the contemporary global economy—which made stamping out the illegal component a daunting task. In an urban household case, the Maltese Nicola was summoned before the British consul in the capital in 1874 and ordered to refrain from retailing contraband. In addition to selling legal items, Nicola surreptitiously dispensed gunpowder from his two stores in the Tunis madina; he was apprehended after another fire broke out in one of the shops.[44] Whether Nicola did in fact abstain from this lucrative business after being caught red-handed is unknown. Ample evidence shows that repeat offenders evaded justice and returned to their illegal pursuits, frequently due to jurisdictional snafus in the realm of justice. In November 1869, Muhammad al-Sadiq Bey demanded "the expulsion of Lorenzo Mifsud from the Regency on the ground that he *will not desist* [emphasis added] from acts of contraband and from injuring olive plantations"—the Maltese had been caught in the act before. Wood replied that he lacked the authority to expel Mifsud because the consul could not "condemn a British subject previous to the allegations preferred against him being proved before her Majesty's consular court."[45]

While Mifsud's smuggling recidivism reveals broader patterns in the contraband economy and the growing contradictions in consular protection, his attacks on olive groves is somewhat baffling. The deliberate destruction of valuable trees, above all olives, was a well-entrenched form of revenge in many Mediterranean islands, for example in both Corsica and Sicily, during this period.[46] Because olive

trees represented considerable capital and were principally owned by beylical subjects, were Mifsud's actions fueled by vengeance against his Tunisian neighbors? Had they turned him in to local authorities?

PROHIBITED PLEASURES: HASH AND TOBACCO

In addition to firepower, tobacco was prized in the clandestine trade between Algeria and Tunisia, within Tunisia itself, or between North Africa and the islands—thanks to the complicity of local officials. Proscribed when first introduced into North Africa, coffee and tobacco were regarded with a malevolent eye by religious authorities until the eighteenth century, when the Maliki 'ulama' no longer condemned the use of these substances, in large measure due to social pressure from below. Tobacco was widely indulged in by all social strata, including women; it was chewed, smoked, and used as snuff, but even the rulers were careful not to indulge in front of members of the shari'a council.[47] Tobacco was grown in the oases of southern Algeria and Tunisia in small quantities, but by the nineteenth century most was imported from Turkey or the Americas via Malta, although the trade had always been a state monopoly, subject to the *lazma*. As the number of coffeehouses expanded, so did tobacco consumption.

As was true of alcohol, narcotics were quite another matter for both the state and the 'ulama'. The most common stimulant was known in North African Arabic as *takruri* (hash, Indian hemp) or *kif*, a hallucinogenic drug derived from the resin secreted by the flowers of female hemp plants (cannabis sativa). Takruri had grown wild in the Rif mountains for centuries before local entrepreneurs began cultivating it largely for export. Whether Morocco supplied Tunisia with kif in the nineteenth century is unknown given the lack of scholarship concerning the question.[48] In 1814, 'Uthman Bey ordered that all the "green tobacco known in our country as takruri be burnt down on the shores of the *buhaira*," which indicates that it was cultivated in Tunisia.[49] Measures like this probably placed the takruri trade more firmly into the hands of smugglers. But its use, however discreet, appears to have become generalized with the expansion of cafés and other places of popular amusement where tobacco was consumed; takruri was tolerated under the Protectorat but proscribed after 1956.

One dimension of the growing contraband traffic in kif and tobacco was its connection once again to social dislocation in colonial Algeria, where immigration and the spread of popular cafés encouraged the drug trade. French officials noted with alarm the increasing use of hashish among Europeans and Algerians, although hard evidence from the precolonial era is scarce and therefore quantifying expanded usage after 1830 perilous. In the years just after the 1837 French occupation of the city of Constantine, "the use of this substance had been limited, reportedly to a 'few bad subjects.'"[50] But the steady growth of coffeehouses and taverns during the next two decades meant that by 1851 the city boasted several dozen cafés or shops that openly sold the drug, which was used in public. Enter the medical establishment in this story. In the prevailing wisdom of the time, the drug produced "frequent cases of 'aliénation mentale'"—more so among Muslims believed prone to insanity and "fanatic" behavior, at least according to colonial officials.[51] Advocates of antidrug campaigns faced an insurmountable obstacle—European nationals were deeply implicated in the lucrative commerce. Figures from 1851 alone are startling: in an eight-month period, 9,083 pounds of hashish were legally introduced into Constantine, with taxes paid on the product, but much more was available through smuggling networks. Some of the biggest users were in the military; allegedly, the *tirailleurs indigènes* (native troops) were especially fond of hashish and they not only frequented coffeehouses in large numbers but also constituted "a common source of public disturbance."[52] Although, once more, it may be that native troops offered a convenient target for social opprobrium.

Here is how the traffic between Algeria and Tunisia operated in one case. A report from an informant in Bougie (or Bijaya, on the coast between Algiers and Bône) in 1856 stated that "contraband has been occurring on a large scale and for a long time in the *cercle* of Bougie or rather in the *cercle* of Jijalli. Each time that an unloading of contraband takes place, one or two fires appear on the coast. The most active individual in this illegal commerce is Juan Onoffre, a [Spanish] tobacco merchant in Bougie; he is associated with the qa'id of Mansouriah."[53] This account is particularly valuable because it shows that the local qa'id, appointed by the French, worked hand in hand with a European associate. And it reveals how smugglers communicated with one another—fires along the coast in the dead of night. It also adds to the store of knowledge about temporalities in the contraband trade—the bulk of large-scale exchanges probably occurred at night, and most likely during the summer sailing season. If Sicilians and Maltese dominated the trade in the central Mediterranean corridor, they were not alone; entrepreneurs from Sardinia, Corsica, Naples, and Leghorn participated actively in exchanges linking Europe and the islands with Tunisia and Algeria. From Gibraltar, a smugglers' haven from the 1840s on, Spaniards and British nationals of various sorts organized the Moroccan and western Algerian branches of the trade, although merchant-smugglers, like Juan Onoffre, were found up and down the North African coast.[54]

Evidence suggests a link between the growing presence of French or Algerian soldiers seeking refuge or employment in Tunisia and the traffic in takruri and tobacco; the *tirailleurs* and Zouaves appear to have been the most heavily involved, or at least the most frequently apprehended. In April 1868 an Anglo-Maltese, Giovanni Attard, was driving a carriage to La Goulette with twenty-four thousand piasters on his person, an unwise move, when he was accosted and relieved of his money in full daylight. Later, two Algerian Zouaves, Bil Qasim al-Tawil and Muhammad ibn Isma'il, were accused of robbing Attard.[55] The subsequent inquiry produced depositions supplied by an Italian subject, Domenico Planeta, the accuser, and the Algerian soldiers. In his testimony, Muhammad stated that he was originally from Milianah (southwest of Algiers), was forty-two years old, and resided in Tunis where he sold tobacco for a living. Confronted with Planeta's accusations, the soldier riposted that

> Paolo Valenza and Domenico Planeta have on several occasions provided me with contraband goods. They stole a pair of pants from me and seven sacks of takruri from one of my friends which they then sold to me. I bought 21 sacks [of takruri] from them for 1,310 piasters. . . . Last Saturday, I went to La Goulette for business when I was accosted by Domenico who demanded that I pay him 45 piasters for storing the [contraband] tobacco. I invited him into a café where I was sitting with two other individuals, but he refused, and after I left the café, he began to insult me. Two of his co-patriots joined him in ganging up on me. I went immediately to complain to Cubisol [the French vice-consul] when Domenico caught up with me and continued to insult me even in front of Cubisol. I pursued this matter with the vice-consulate of Italy in La Goulette. Witnesses were called and Domenico was put in prison. That is surely why Domenico made this deposition against me. As for me, I had nothing to do with the theft on the road to La Goulette, nor do I know the identity of the thieves.[56]

Questioned about his knowledge of the theft, Muhammad responded that "the affair was the topic of discussion in the entire city" but claimed to have been in Tunis that day and not in La Goulette.[57] His alleged accomplice, al-Tawil, produced a notarized certificate proving his alibi at the time of the robbery, which got him sprung from preventative detention.

What is significant about the soldier's testimony is that he sought to discredit his accuser's allegations by squealing on Planeta's smuggling operations, which rendered the Italian's deposition suspect. The story of sacks of takruri and tobacco must have constituted a credible narrative in that milieu—otherwise why use it for a defense? On the other hand, Algerian soldiers in Tunisia may have occupied the same unenviable social position as the Maltese—convenient targets for reproach. Of note is that the inhabitants of Tunis were abuzz over the daring robbery, which suggests the existence of a common fund of talked-about events running through communication circuits, especially when it came to police-blotter news. But where might the unlawful items have come from?

Thus far we have plotted out some of the coordinates in this system—or interlocking systems—of exchange, principally for Tunis, Bizerte, and the south where the firearms business was booming. By centering a social geography of smuggling in one of the Mediterranean's strategic choke points, the workings of tobacco and hash ventures emerge.

THE SICILIAN TRIANGLE:
THE CAP BON, MALTA, AND SICILY

In the course of the nineteenth century, the Cap Bon emerged as the contraband capital of the central Mediterranean corridor, judging by records of seizures in the beylical archives, particularly the *dabtiya* (police) records, and correspondence between the Tunisian government and European consulates. Of the various factors explaining the peninsula's pivotal role, location vis-à-vis the two adjacent islands is the most critical; the stretch of sea in between Sicily, Malta, and Tunisia's northernmost tip represented a "Burmese Triangle" for extralegal marketing and marketers. While the distance between Tunis and the Cap Bon was not great, the absence of good roads and the fact that only the villagers knew how to negotiate the maze of trails meant that the state agents from the capital were often ineffective in combating unlawful import or export—when those same agents, chronically underpaid throughout the period, were not directly involved themselves.

Historically, the Cap Bon was among the most agriculturally prosperous regions of Ifriqiya; its olives, cereals, hides, livestock, and fruits were chronically in short supply in nearby islands. Tobacco in any form had always been a state monopoly—*lizmat al-dukhkhan*—and in 1840, Ahmad Bey, eternally in need of more revenues for his modern army, issued new regulations on the sale of tobacco. These measures, together with rising demand, made the clandestine cultivation and processing of tobacco and takruri into one of the Cap Bon's specialties; indeed, in some places, the cultivation of food crops was neglected in favor of the much more remunerative tobacco or Indian hemp plants. Moreover, the peninsula's small harbors were well sheltered from the often savage winds; Kelibia became a favored place for ships coming from the islands or from southern Tunisia and Tripoli. Indeed many Maltese and Sicilian labor migrants arrived in the country for the first time via the Cap Bon's ports.[58] What conditions on the nearby islands worked to make the triangle one of the busiest maritime markets for contraband goods?

Let's begin with Malta, which as already noted had earlier functioned as a hub for piracy, privateering, and even after abolition for the trans-Mediterranean slave trade, in short, as the "command center for the principal smugglers from all the countries of the Mediterranean world."[59] In addition to tobacco and gunpowder, a perennially hot item was spirits, which Malta did not produce. To meet high demand, shipments from Spain and Portugal were smuggled in. The annual statistic survey of British Malta for 1836 noted under "Municipal Services and Expenses" that because the charges were "heavy for the prevention of contraband," the cost of suppressing it was scarcely worth the outlay of funds.[60] British officials advocated decreasing import duties on the most desirable products, such as wine or tobacco, since onerous duties would be "defeated by contraband" or neutralized by the expenses incurred by preventing illicit traffic. "If a heavy duty were imposed on articles of small bulk compared with value, there would be no other way of preventing contraband than by subjecting individuals coming on shore to a personal search."[61] In short, given the massive ship traffic through Valletta, the need to balance the imperial budget, and the ceaseless comings and goings of island inhabitants, British officials clung to their laissez-faire stance, for the most part, toward the political economy of contraband—not unlike their position on overpopulation and emigration.

As was true of sea-girded Malta, Sicily had long represented another smugglers' paradise. Yet Great Britain's occupation between 1806 and 1815 expanded operations because the island's merchant marine was enlarged and encouraged to engage in contraband activities during the Napoleonic Wars. After 1815, the merchant marine carried on with smuggling, in part due to high export and import duties on legal trade and equally high returns, but also because Sicily produced little in the way of marketable exports in this period. Lacking iron, good coal, timber, and a decent internal communication system, Sicily's silk, glass, and sugar-refining industries had collapsed. In 1839, the island expended large sums of money on imported coffee and sugar, whose figures are suspect because of a rampant smuggling economy, mainly in imports. Commercial data are unreliable, but the French consul estimated that for the 1830s "six to eight times more coffee and tobacco" were brought to the island than recorded in official statistics because, as was true elsewhere, underpaid customs officers brazenly aided and abetted contraband; in other words, "there was no country where the laws were more openly evaded."[62] In addition, a substantial out-the-back-door trade in cigarettes manufactured in Valletta and sold in Sicily and Tunisia linked the islands and African shore in triangular black market exchanges. But as importantly, by midcentury countless numbers of Sicilians moved between the island, La Goulette, or the Cap Bon in search of work.[63]

From 1861 to 1881, state seizures of tobacco and takruri for the Cap Bon— 89 out of a total 129 cases—far outweighed other illicit commodities, such as gunpowder, counterfeit money, or agricultural products; of course, this was only a small portion of the actual amounts in circulation. Moreover, if leading actors were Maltese and Sicilians, they closely collaborated with members of the local underworld, for example, the notorious smuggler-soldier from Nabeul, Muhammad ibn 'Umar, apprehended with huge quantities of tobacco and takruri in 1861. Italian and Maltese ships, often with heavily armed crews, took part in the remunerative trade.[64] Rapid advances in maritime communication also fueled the contraband economy. In 1853, the British consul informed Ahmad Bey that regular steam communication between Malta, Sardinia, and Tunisia would be established; ships would call in Tunis, Sousse, Munastir, Mahdiya, Sfax, and

Djerba, places marked by high immigration and flourishing contraband sectors. This news only increased the bey's apprehensions about two interrelated dangers. One was contraband; the other was the public health menace posed by "the continual and rapid arrival [in Malta] of steam and sailing ships from ports in England where the Asiatic cholera has unhappily made its appearance," since the 1851 cholera epidemic remained a fresh, bitter memory.[65] But improved transportation provided further impetus for illegal commerce already undermining the state treasury and with it Ahmad Bey's attempts to modernize his realm. As ominously, smugglers and their illicit traffic provoked intercommunal dissension, leading to the internationalization of local crises.

STAMPING IT OUT:
MAYHEM, MURDER, AND STATE REGULATIONS

The 1843 Paolo Xuereb affair brought a sea change in public awareness regarding the twin problems posed by unregulated trade and population movements. Among the most lurid, sensationalized homicides of the precolonial era, it involved a recent immigrant from Malta, Xuereb, who murdered a Tunisian dragoman in service to the British consulate as well as another Maltese, Savirio Galia, servant to Thomas Reade. Galia's salary proved inadequate for his large family, so he farmed a piece of property outside Tunis leased from a Tunisian proprietor named Bin 'Ali. Since the farm and mill proved too much to work alone, Galia hired a fellow Maltese as overseer. Unhappily, he chose Xuereb, about whom little was known at first; soon, other Maltese who had just arrived made it known that his new farm steward "bore an infamous character; that he had killed, or attempted to kill, a man in that island, and had been banished therefrom." Moreover, when Galia visited the property, he realized with dismay that Xuereb had turned it into "a receptacle for every kind of contraband."[66] Apparently someone had informed the palace of Xuereb's activities, since Ahmad Bey ordered that he quit the premises. The tragedy commenced when Galia, accompanied by the Tunisian dragoman Yusuf ibn 'Abdallah, journeyed to the farm in December 1843 to expel the overseer. Unfortunately, Xuereb possessed a firearm—perhaps from smuggling networks?—and appeared dressed "in a burnus [cloak] from which he drew out a double-barreled blunderbuss and fired upon both men, mortally wounding them."[67] Here once again, we see North Africa as a social dump— British officials had banished Xuereb to rid Malta of a criminal.

Things were scarcely better outside the capital city region, as numerous incidents attest. The palace protested to the British and French consuls in 1858 that "the public peace is disturbed by several subjects together with some of the Europeans living in Mahdiya where the principal cause of agitation comes from the traffic in contraband which a large number of Maltese residents carry on openly there." At the same time, a Catholic cleric in Mahdiya sent a petition to Tunis that was signed by most of its European inhabitants; the petition complained about the hostile spirit of the native townspeople toward resident foreigners, evidenced by the steady escalation in violence and mayhem. In October that same year, things came to a head with the attempted murder of the French consular agent in Mahdiya, Arnaud, by Muhammad al-Kassarawi, a well-known professional assassin.[68] What was the Tunisian state's response to declining security?

From Ahmad Bey's reign until the Protectorate, the government evolved new measures for controlling illicit trafficking. For example, the governor of La Goulette, Sidi Mahmud, was ordered in 1839 to prohibit nocturnal ship movements. No ships were to enter or leave La Goulette after sundown and the keys to the port's doors, formerly held by the governor, were now entrusted to the commandant of the military garrison; the enormous chain barring entrance to the port's canal was secured from one hour after sunset until sunrise to prevent undetected arrivals or departures. Predictably, European consuls, merchants, and ship captains balked. Characterizing them as "irregular and a nuisance," the French consul protested that the new regulations hampered legitimate commerce since during bad weather many vessels put in to port late at night and their merchandise would be spoiled by any delays; "foreign ships should be allowed to lift up the chain closing the port [in order to set sail] at night."[69] These objections reveal a major contradiction in French policy. On the one hand, it was imperative to supply the huge colonial army with Tunisian products, which also promoted France's commercial hegemony in the country, through "free-trade policies"; on the other hand, the armaments traffic had to be halted by stricter controls on commercial movements.

In response to endless protestations, the consuls issued and reissued instructions to agents stationed along the coast from Bizerte in the north to Djerba in the south. In 1858, measures to stop trafficking in counterfeit currency, so ruinous to the state treasury, were announced. Beylical officials were accorded the right to determine when and where boats could land; disembarkation during the night was prohibited. If vessels were suspected of smuggling, Tunisian authorities were to immediately inform the nearest consular agent, who alone had the right to arrest or detain suspects under foreign protection by treaty.[70] At the same time, regulations enjoining observance of quarantine were promulgated. As the Sanitary Board expanded operations to deal with the scourge of cholera morbus and other epidemics, the increasingly strict application of quarantine may have promoted smuggling; thus contraband, quarantine, and cholera worked together.[71]

As gateways for goods and people, and points of interdiction and interception, customs houses became zones of friction, dispute, and vengeance. While the fragmented record does not allow for tracing operations in detail, episodic evidence suggests the antagonistic nature of social dynamics at these critical mediating junctures where international and domestic trade meshed and where port authorities negotiated with foreign importers, merchants, and local consular agents. Joseph Levy, a British protégé, imported coffee from the Americas via Gibraltar and Malta into Sousse; he also served as vice-consul in the port. As he vainly attempted to claim his recently arrived shipment from Valletta in January 1851, customs officials subjected him to endless vexations, which prompted an enraged letter to Tunis.[72] The same dynamic held in Sfax, a hub of smuggling throughout the nineteenth century, when in 1862 a Maltese petty trader went to the port to take possession of his imported goods: "The Custom house officer's son for spite's sake, because the Maltese had sold to him on a previous occasion some cheap things, ordered the Maltese to take out from the case all the boxes to be examined at the Marina. The Maltese observed to one of the officials then present, that his small parcel of things would be spoiled by so doing and begged and implored that they might allow him to retire his cases to his store as customary where they might open and examine all his goods as had been formerly done."[73] It is uncertain whether the customs official suspected the Maltese of contraband, was merely doing his job thoroughly, did not receive an expected bribe, or was truly acting "out of spite" in revenge for an earlier transaction that soured.

SCAPEGOATS AND SCAPEGOATING

Frequent, at times quite violent, attacks upon individual Maltese are recorded but the motives are rarely provided. In 1836, a Maltese residing in a miserable garret in the madina was found hung by the neck, although the street rumor had it that he had not committed suicide but rather had been strangled; another Maltese disappeared from a popular quarter in one of the Tunis suburbs and was never seen again. The number of assaults on Maltese by soldiers garrisoned in ports around the country is striking—beatings with sticks, "several to the point of death," or thefts of money.[74] How can these incidents be explained? Were the Maltese too numerous, or rather too visible? Were they perceived as without effective protection from the British consulate? Were some attacks due to contraband or other kinds of deals gone bad? Or were they seen as labor competitors? Were international forces at play, perhaps competition between France and Great Britain over spheres of influence in Tunisia?

Criminalized by other communities, by the Tunisian government and its subjects, and by their own diplomatic representatives, the Maltese represented the scapegoats of the Mediterranean expatriate underworld. Of the groups mentioned in Bin Diyaf's multivolume work, the Maltese are cited in negative fashion most frequently, followed by Sicilians. This characterization began quite early during the initial migratory influx of the 1830s, if not before. For example, when in 1835 the French agent in Sfax, Guerola, was accused of smuggling gunpowder, he shifted the blame to the city's Maltese population despite the fact that state port agents had not reported their involvement. Reade, hardly partial toward his island protégés, retorted that "many of [the Maltese] are equally if not more respectable than Mr. Guerola himself. . . . Guerola's statement if not altogether mistated [sic] is at least greatly exaggerated."[75] The battle continued into subsequent years when the French consul, Deval, in May 1836 sent letters to Mustafa Bey from the vice-consul in Sfax containing evidence that recent disorders in the port "were committed in this city by diverse Maltese who reside there. . . . I would hope that your Majesty would take measures to guarantee the security and the property of the Europeans established in the city of Sfax and also to put an end to the contraband in war munitions that continues to be carried out with impunity and in a scandalous manner."[76]

The contraband wars represented imperial maneuvers in another register. A diplomatic mission from Algeria led by General Damermont in 1837 aimed to persuade Ahmad Bey to "invite" the French navy to station ships in Tunisian waters to "examine all vessels approaching under whatever flag, in order to check the importation of arms and ammunition."[77] Once again, the French played the Maltese card, arguing that Maltese vessels alone transported contraband arms between Tripoli, Tunisia, and Algeria. Wisely, the ruler declined the general's offer, observing that this would place the entire coast in a state of permanent blockade, seriously undermining the legitimate trade that was a principal source of revenue. The battle over smuggling, which increasingly conflated ethnicity, migration, and criminality, translated fierce European struggles over the Husaynid state with protégés serving as proxies. Accusations of wrongdoing aimed at a specific community represented the nineteenth century's version of immigration and border-security hysteria—a way of scapegoating targeted minorities with fears about "strangers in our midst." As the largest Christian minority in the country, a community living cheek by jowl with indigenous Tunisians or North Africans, often in the poorest urban quarters, the Maltese were the most conspicuous in earlier decades. As Sicilians and others began to settle in large numbers, the Maltese became less socially visible, although they maintained their investment in the contraband trade that frequently resulted in acts of violence, even murder, as the 1843 Xuereb case demonstrated.[78]

CONTRABAND DESIRE: PLEASURE INDUSTRY OR LOVE WITH THE WRONG PERSON?

This chapter opened with the tale of a carriage ride gone awry after Alexander Buhagiar, the Maltese driver, threatened to take his passenger, Margherita, to La Goulette for a "kif," which she interpreted as some sort of illicit amorous adventure involving drug use. Since the sex industry is not well documented for the port, our journey into the social universe of unlawful sexual transactions begins with a tour of the present-day madina.

Anyone who wanders through the narrow, densely packed streets of the suqs immediately realizes the difference between the two main commercial arteries, Shari' al-Qasba and Shari' Jama' al-Zaytuna. The latter is mainly, though not exclusively, bordered by shops, boutiques, banks, and cafés catering to tourists; stores are licensed by the state and accept credit cards. One of the few exceptions is located at the entryway to the square adjacent to Bab al-Bahr—a humble stall selling brightly colored, embroidered leather slippers worn by Tunisian women in the past. This business is more characteristic of the madina's second thoroughfare, Shari' al-Qasba, which parallels the first artery. Here shopkeepers offer wares appealing to local families of modest means; shoppers rub shoulders with street vendors with pushcarts, itinerant peddlers, and hawkers of every conceivable commodity produced by the global economy—from pirated rock music CDs, to counterfeit designer jeans, to luxury "Swiss" watches. In this lively commercial sector, sellers and buyers, men and women, are Tunisian for the most part. Casual laborers looking for work hang about, and a discreet inquiry to the right person procures morally questionable items—a contraband bottle of Johnny Walker or sexual favors. Not far away is the red-light district home to (now) legal female prostitution controlled by the state, which mandates periodic medical examinations. In the precolonial and colonial eras, the flesh trade was confined to specific quarters, often located on city peripheries where people and economic activities associated with the countryside or with outsiders came into contact with the city. One quarter reputed for its flourishing sex industry is, and was in the nineteenth century, the area around "Sidi 'Abdallah Guèche" in the southeastern end of the madina on a dead-end alley near Rue Zarkoun—precisely the neighborhood where many newly arrived immigrants resided after 1830. This quarter remains the heart of black market exchanges and its name is coterminous in meaning with *bordel* (brothel) for contemporary city dwellers.[79]

Documentation for the study of prostitution in nineteenth-century Tunis is surprisingly scarce, as is data on sexual commerce between different religious communities, with the exception of a few spectacular cases of interconfessional sex, often ending in tragedy. With the 1830 invasion of Algeria, an international trade in women to service the army was organized, but its consequences for Tunisia do not show up much in the sources. As for the Arabic documents, while the *'ahira* (prostitute; also courtesan) figures in judicial opinions, medical treatises, and state fiscal records, prostitution overall constitutes a "history consigned to collective forgetfulness."[80] After the creation of the municipal council, followed by the Tunis police force, arrest records for prostitutes (and smugglers) become more ample. Scholarship on prostitution normally distinguishes commercial sex from love with the wrong person, but in the records from the time they were sometimes confused. Forbidden love fell into the category of the clandestine because contraband desire transgressed religiocommunal boundaries. In the armature of those policing boundaries, charges of prostitution, however untrue, offered a particularly potent sexual weapon to wield against a rival community.

The study of the sex trade as well as star-crossed lovers raises problems similar to, but different from, extralegal exchanges of tobacco, wine, or kif. Women's voices are rarely heard, and when they are, the circumstances surrounding the record's production were generally inimical to female agency. In addition, it is essential to consider how different societies control and punish women deemed sexually deviant. Some states forcibly exiled women regarded as dangerous—the dumping of English women branded morally undesirable in colonies like Australia comes to mind. In others, women were confined to asylums, convents, state-run brothels, prisons, or guarded houses. Until Ahmad Bey's reign, the conventional punishment for Muslim women accused of *zina'* (unlawful sexual relations), particularly with non-Muslim men, was death by drowning in Tunis's lake. Later on, women judged guilty of sexual misconduct were expelled to bleak, uninhabited islets near Sfax, which served as a female open-air prison. "There are no ports in these islands. The Bey exiles or transports all the women of abandoned morals to the Kerkennas, whilst the island of Jarbah [Djerba] . . . is made in part a convict settlement for men."[81] What institutions traditionally managed the sex industry for Muslim men and women—a critical distinction since even prostitutes were expected to observe religious communal boundaries?

Until Mustafa Bey abolished the office in June 1836, the *mizwar,* dating back to early Ottoman rule, constituted a sort of state pimping operation. By the Husaynid era, the mizwar policed urban morals, notably prostitutes and courtesans; the holder purchased the office from the ruler in return for a fixed annual rate—a kind of sex tax farm. The financial mechanism was analogous to other tax farms *(lizma)* organized for activities such as the production and distribution of wine and alcohol. The mizwar kept a "list of the most beautiful girls who were forced to pay a certain percentage of their earnings to him varying with age and beauty and exercised the right to punish women practicing their trade without permission or without being registered in his rolls."[82] Eventually he gave permission to the women to marry and leave the business, presumably after income dropped below certain levels due to advancing age and declining allure. Once again, the sources are silent on many dimensions of this office, although a European traveler claimed in 1835 that a Turkish madam oversaw Muslim prostitutes in the capital. Some scholars argue that the women involved in this particular sex industry were not prostitutes in the European sense of the term but rather were courtesans.[83]

But we should question whether the practice truly ceased after the ruler abolished the institution—did other social actors assume some of the mizwar's functions? Between 1836 and the advent of French rule over four decades later, prostitutes tended to cluster in specific city quarters in a trade that was largely nocturnal and private, as opposed to semipublic and state managed. With the abolition of slavery and the slave trade, some manumitted African women entered into prostitution in the quarters of the city peopled mainly by freed Africans, for example, the dead-end section of Bab al-Jadid.[84]

Sexual relations between Muslim women and non-Muslim men were not taken lightly. The punishment was death for both parties in the early years of the century—which explains the culture of secrecy around reporting transgressive desire or commercial sex. In 1823, a Christian man resident in the capital was beheaded for sexual indiscretions with a Muslim woman, who herself suffered death by drowning.[85] A notorious affair from 1831 proved the impetus for changes in the punishment meted out to interconfessional sex. That year, a Greek living in Tunis established a *liaison amoureuse* with a "Moorish" woman who visited her lover—or paying customer?—in his residence, which caught the attention of neighborhood busybodies. One day as she left the Greek's home, she was apprehended and dragged off to the Bardo to meet her fate—death by drowning for fornication. "We have been perfectly tranquil since I last wrote you except in one instance, which happened lately and which instance I must say was disgusting and disgraceful to humanity. An unfortunate Moorish woman who had been suspected of having intercourse with a Christian, a Greek, was seized by the Police, taken before the Bey and condemned to be paraded naked publicly through the streets of Tunis and afterwards thrown into the Sea."[86]

While the pursuers turned the city upside down searching for her lover, their efforts were in vain; he had fled aboard a ship bound for Malta.[87] Were the accusations of sexual misconduct true, or the result of a smear campaign, a vendetta, or some personal grudge? And was it a question of mutual love and desire or a simple business transaction? Even after 1856, when the death penalty for a Christian or Jewish male surprised in flagrante delicto with a Muslim woman was lifted, it was prudent for compromised men to leave on the next boat, something that was difficult or impossible for women accused of sexual misconduct.[88] Controlling desire introduced transformations in city space. In a letter addressed to Khayr al-Din in May 1873, the municipal council's president filed a report on a neighborhood in the madina near the Jewish quarter where prostitutes had taken up residence; the quarter's families lodged endless streams of complaints. The council worked out a compromise by constructing a door separating the contested neighborhood space into two zones, thus creating a sort of ghetto for both Muslim and Jewish prostitutes. Mapping the area reveals that the density of taverns, functioning as places for solicitation among other things, correlates with high numbers of arrests. Indeed, the household where Giovanna Tellini lived and participated in the thieving and fencing ring was close to the quarter known as al-Kram, which had a large Christian population and an equally large number of taverns by the 1860s. In June 1861, a Muslim woman, A'isha bint Muhammad al-Sfaxi, was arrested near a tavern door not far from the Jewish quarter; charged with prostitution, she was sentenced to two weeks in prison. As was true for drinking establishments, certain markets or places of temporary residence, such as bachelor funduqs or *wakala* attracted women making a living in the sex industry.[89]

Clearly, waves of settlement in Tunis rendered more difficult the policing of religious boundaries that traditionally constituted sexual boundaries as well. But street justice for non-Muslim men involved with Muslim women could be just as lethal and effective. In March 1877, Europeans contacted the French consul regarding a fellow employee who had abruptly disappeared. Of French nationality but "speaking Arabic perfectly with an Algerian accent," and described as "of military bearing," Auguste Chauvel had worked in Tunis from September 1876 until February 22, 1877, when he requested the day off.[90] After eight days passed and he failed to reappear, his associates, fearing the worst, organized a search party. Either imprudent passion or love for hire explained Chauvel's strange absence, since he "had established relations with a Moorish woman whose residence and name are unknown and these relations leads us to think that he could have been the victim of his temerity," or perhaps, of his libido, as the letter coyly suggests.[91] In response, the consul contacted the prime minister demanding that the Tunisian government discover his whereabouts. Once again, it is uncertain whether the "Moorish" woman was a prostitute, Chauvel's lover, or even if the *liaison dangereuse* was the true cause of his hasty departure.

The role of the consuls as moral guardians included the sexual policing of women and men under their jurisdiction. Sexual "border patrols" in turn depended upon a network of informants who gathered intelligence and snitched on others, bringing misconduct to the consuls' attention—probably the same folks who squealed on neighbors or associates involved in smuggling. Judah ben Levy, a British protégé, wrote a long letter to his consul in 1852 replete with salacious details about a Jewish woman living across from him who entertained nighttime visits from Muslim males while her husband was away. According to ben Levy, Abraham Temim, a fellow Jew, allowed his wife to consort with a Muslim neighbor: "I have seen the man [Muhammad] enter the room of Abraham Temim whilst he is absent and remain with his wife."[92] A "peeping tom," ben Levy urged the consul do something about his female neighbor's misdeeds, but the consul declined to get involved. As is true today, neighbors policed morals more closely than any urban institution and therefore the question of why the quarter rendered up its secrets arises. By the very nature of their social positioning, minorities tended to be gravely concerned with moral blame occasioned by female behavior and, in consequence, closely guarded sexual and other secrets to limit intervention by outside authorities. Internal problem resolution was the preferred course of action, which often entailed discreet banishment of the parties involved in a scandal.[93]

As for women under European protection, the intriguing silences in beylical and consul documentation stem in part from the practice of relying upon conversation, rather than written correspondence, when the shameful matter of sexual behavior had to be addressed. If carnal relations were committed to writing in letters exchanged between consuls and members of the beys' government, less formal note paper was used in place of official stationary. And writers employed coded language or circumlocutions, such as the expression, "the woman in question." In these somewhat rare documents, reference is made to earlier conversations about "women of easy virtue," as seen in the letter marked "private" that was exchanged between Richard Wood and the prime minister's office in 1876:

> I have had the pleasure to receive your private letter of the 11th of October conveying to me the request of his Excellency the Prime Minister in the name of His Majesty the Bey to embark by the first conveyance the woman in question with injuction never to return to this country again. I will do my utmost to carry out the wishes of His Highness which are founded on considerations, the importance of which have not escaped my attention. In anticipation that His Highness would decide that she should be sent out of the country, I wrote yesterday to a friend at Malta to persuade some family to receive her. It is not every family that will receive a stranger in their house.[94]

Once again, missing are details regarding whether the alleged sexual misconduct involved sex for money—freelance or organized prostitution—or love and desire between partners from different religious communities. Of course, malicious rumors about women from another social group whose collective honor was at stake represented the best way of seeking revenge upon "the others," by besmirching female reputation. In any case, every year European consuls had to rescue and forcibly repatriate young women charged with prostitution.[95]

The sources hint that false charges of sexual immorality were manipulated in local communal quarrels, although determining their veracity is not easy. A year after Chauvel disappeared from Tunis, Munastir's governor protested to Muhammad al-Sadiq Bey in 1878 on behalf of the Muslim population about a Maltese woman, Consolata Scinga, who "kept a disorderly house" in the European quarter, which by then had several hundred foreign residents. Richard Wood was asked to investigate the allegations. While Consolata's untoward behavior was never explicitly defined, the accusation—"keeping a disorderly house"— implied sexual impropriety. Her accuser, a native of Munastir, had lodged a formal complaint with the governor because she "received visitors in her house until late at night" and neighbors reported "noise, scandals, and tumult" in her household, which operated as a freelance "bottega" or tavern.[96] (The word "scandal" invariably denoted sex for sale.) In this case, the consul interpreted the grievance as spurious; it had been provoked by a local quarrel between the Europeans and their Tunisian neighbors, perhaps over a rented house. And bitter disputes over rents or rental properties escalated sharply in this period as more immigrants poured into a country increasingly short of residential dwellings and as the peaceful and law-abiding strove to keep neighborhoods tranquil.

Because of the large numbers of transient males, particular neighborhoods in provincial ports acquired reputations as places of clandestine pleasures. Proximity to Algeria meant that Bizerte hosted not only fishermen but also French military or commercial ships and crews. In 1862, a protracted uproar erupted over the presence of prostitutes; the city's majority Muslim inhabitants refused to allow the women to remain in or even near their neighborhoods. In response, local authorities installed the undesirable females in a quarter where most Europeans resided.[97] This move did not sit well with anyone, including Wood in Tunis:

> I avail myself of the occasion to enclose for your perusal a letter from my [British] agent in Bizerta [sic] who appears very anxious that some common prostitutes who occupy a house in the vicinity of his own residence should be forced to remove to the locality where such persons usually locate themselves. Mr. Spizzichino whose morality appears greatly shocked has written to me twice on the subject. I do not know what the laws are regarding such a nuisance but I feel confident you will kindly do your best to free Mr. Spizzichino's neighborhood from the presence of females who must attract all kinds of bad characters to it.[98]

Several things are of note. Wood here referred to specific quarters in Bizerte known for their "infamous character" and argued that women of easy morals should not be allowed to operate outside of designated spaces. Second, prostitutes not only violated codes of moral conduct but also attracted other kinds of criminal behavior. Finally, the women involved appear to have been Muslims and therefore subject to beylical authorities, who by this time seemed less concerned with proscribing sexual contraband between non-Muslim males and Muslim females than with spatially enclosing "debauched women."

It was not until 1882, one year after France's invasion, that a brothel (maison close) was created in Tunis near the European quarter on Rue al-Maktar. The city's Muslim inhabitants fought bitterly for four years to prevent the establishment of state-sanctioned bordellos but lost their battle when Protectorate officials decreed on March 16, 1889, that "public women were required to register with the morals bureau on a special list."[99] In a curious twist to the pleasure industry, the colonial regime resurrected in part the older Ottoman institution of the mizwar, minus of course the sale of that office, and relied upon modern medical hygienist arguments to defend state-sanctioned pimping.

THE TRIAL OF GIOVANNA TELLINI, 1868

This final section dissects a household and city quarter in the Tunis madina to peer into the spaces where the local and transnational worlds of the thief, smuggler, fencer—and perhaps prostitute—converged and then sent out runners far and wide across Tunisia, Algeria, and the Mediterranean. This in turn allows us to chart commodity flows as part of globalization from the bottom up.

The madina and its two suburbs hosted clandestine exchange economies that drew a wide swath of urban society into partnerships reminiscent of the classic 1937 film set in the Algiers Qasba, *Pépé le Moko*. If one listened carefully at night, bizarre sounds resonated through the dim, deserted streets—the whistle of robber bands—as they communicated before breaking into dwellings or shops. Each had its own peculiar signal, which served the same function as nighttime fires along the coast. Given the number of reported break-ins during the period, a veritable symphony of night whistles must have characterized Tunis after dark. As Gianmaria Hiberras, a Maltese servant in the Tellini household, related during his testimony in February 1868: "Yesterday evening, I was lying in bed when I saw Giovanna get up and open the door. I did not hear any sound like whistling because you know how when they steal they whistle."[100]

In 1868, the Italian consulate instituted criminal proceedings for grand larceny against an Italian woman, Giovanna Tellini, and her alleged accomplice, Biagio Veglione, although a huge cast of characters from across the Mediterranean as well as beylical subjects, including the police, were implicated or called to testify. The trial record, written in the Italian employed in Tunisia—infused with spoken Arabic and other languages—represents one of the few extensive records devoted to immigrant women and men of ordinary means and their social universe.[101] Containing oral testimony as well as detailed documents generated by on-site investigations, the proceedings help to "open up" the local world of recent immigrants as well as the indigenous down-and-out. Our principal concern, however, revolves around what this docudrama tells us about the way in which theft, fencing, contraband, crime, daily life, and making a living coalesced.

In Giovanna Tellini's initial testimony to the consular court held at the Italian consulate located near the Sea Gate in February 1868, we hear the following: "I am Giovanna Tellini, daughter of Antonio; I am forty years old, born in Cala [Pisa] and residing in Tunis for the past ten years. I am single, an Italian citizen, Catholic, and illiterate. I rent the shop [in Tunis] from the Greek, Dimitri Papadopolo, but I am partners in business with Annetta, a Spanish citizen, single, as well as with Dimitri L'Inglisi [Dimitri the Englishman] who is imprisoned at this moment." Giovanna added that she shared the house with her *sedicente marito* [common-law husband], a Spaniard named Nicola Sabuquillo.[102] Her friend, Annetta Barbera, who had relocated to Tunis from Algeria, also resided there with her lover. When in February 1868 the authorities burst into their house in the lower madina not far from Bab Cartegena, all its inhabitants, with the exception of Giovanna, had been bed-ridden for weeks with the typhoid fever then raging in Tunisia, one of the many deleterious aftershocks of the 1864 rebellion.

What was stolen, fenced, and traded through both licit and illicit networks? Inventories of the various rooms in Annetta and Giovanna's residence yielded up considerable quantities of stolen and/or contraband items—tobacco, coffee, white and brown sugar believed to be from the Americas, a keg of gunpowder concealed under the floorboards, a recently fired pistol, and a large cache of silver and gold coins from around the Mediterranean; the coinage was stored in a sock that served as a bank. Socks or shoes appear to have been favored hiding places for small precious items, money or jewels, since this form of "bank safety deposit" reappears in other sources. Scales for weighing commodities like tobacco, gunpowder, or coffee were present, as were cigarette papers and the accoutrements for making and selling cups of coffee to café customers. More to the point, instruments for breaking and entering were discovered in abundance: twelve skeleton keys, picklocks, files, crowbars, lengths of rope, and a diverse assortment of keys to homes and shops in the neighborhood, including some keys to the nearby English Inn.

Making matters worse for the accused, a large cache of personal belongings, already reported stolen by families or businesses in the quarter, was uncovered: pieces of red silk, wool cloth, a skirt of cambric, pairs of women's trousers, new and old shoes, old black hats, a hammam bath towel *(futa)*, lots of eyeglasses, and so forth. What is striking about many of the inventoried items is the way in which they were sorted; some were listed as *"a uso Israelita"* or *"a uso arabo,"* which indicates the thieves had broken into households or shops belonging to Jews and Muslims as well as Europeans. Moreover, witnesses in the proceedings identified objects as "used by Jews" or "worn by Arabs"—so we are back to clothing as a fundamental signifier of belonging or difference.[103] But other commodities—soap, matches, playing cards, and candles, in addition to what Giovanna claimed were innocent jars of face cream and mustache wax—reveal the kinds of goods found in households from this social stratum. We learn something about daily diet: rice, potatoes, chestnuts, nuts, and raisins, although more prosperous classes had far richer tables. Yet, looking at the important issue of diet from the perspective of consumption and social class, by this period sugar and coffee—neither produced in North Africa—were no longer in the luxury-item category since ordinary people indulged in them, if only sparingly.

Even when confronted with the mountain of physical evidence seized from her shared dwelling cum shop, Giovanna denied everything in her first testimony, given on February 27, 1868. Fortunately we have the Maltese servant Gianmaria as another witness. Responding to the conventional menu of questions asked in the trial proceedings, Gianmaria identified himself as "almost fifteen years old, native resident of Tunis, English citizen, single, Catholic, and illiterate," although he might not have self-identified in this manner in another context.[104] In a burst of solidarity with the servant, Giovanna betrayed Gianmaria by claiming that he had placed the stolen items in her room and was therefore the guilty party. Gianmaria returned the favor by changing his testimony in midstream and spilling the beans.

From the *garzone,* intimate details of burglary and fencing emerge. This is how the thieves went about their nightly business. Before going out on a job, Dimitri put a "pair of yellow shoes" (probably soft leather slippers) on his feet since they did not make noise. Then the robbers climbed to rooftop terraces where they were lowered down by rope into courtyards or blind alleys. The shop of "the Jerbi *bakkal"* (a grocer from the island of Djerba), for example, was hit twice by the band, which hauled off rice, soap, sugar, coffee, nuts, and a large weighing scale. To avoid making a commotion during a heists, skeleton keys were used. Shown one of the keys, the servant Gianmaria stated that he recognized the new one with yellow wax on it because he had "taken measurements of the keys with paper and then Sebastiano's brother-in-law had a key made at Bab Cartagena."[105] Giovanna's role was to store, conceal, and fence what her male acquaintances—the Greeks Dimitri and Atanasio, the Italian Veglione, and others—stole from houses, shops, or other neighborhood establishments, such as the inn. When they returned with the purloined goods, the burglars hid them in the house and waited a few days before dividing up the loot. The sacks of sugar discovered in Giovanna's room were a gift for serving as an accomplice, which she then recycled into her legitimate café operation. Whatever was not retained for personal or household use was marketed in Tunis, La Goulette, Matar, and as far away as Algeria. However, things changed dramatically after consular and beylical authorities rounded up some of the members of the robber band and incarcerated them.

In her second testimony on March 12, 1868, Giovanna recanted but appealed to the implicit gender norms of the time, social milieu, and place to gain a more sympathetic hearing. She stated the following: "I want to correct what I said the other time. I was fearful *[compresa dalla paura]* that if I failed to narrate the events the way they want me to, they would carry out threats against me. I am a weak woman *[debole donna]* who gave in but now that I have heard that the great part of them [the thieves] are under arrest at the Driba [Tunisian prison] I want to tell the truth."[106] In addition, Giovanna said that the "Locanda Inglese," the nearby English Inn, served as a place of illicit amorous encounters. What is truly unique about this record is that it let slip, in an aside, a fact about consular investigations that was hitherto unknown. The authorities searched Giovanna's person *(sulla persona)* looking for stolen goods concealed on her body, which leads one to ask how social class entered into this procedure? Would middle-class women have been subjected to the same treatment, to a physical search? Although no incriminating possessions were found on her person, Giovanna's shoes appeared to have been stained with a substance implicated in the burglaries, so these were confiscated.[107] As with most of these accounts, the next chapters are, *hélas,* a mystery. Did the incarcerated thieves eventually get sprung from Tunisian prison? Were they deported to Sicily, Spain, or Greece? Did Annetta and Giovanna remain in Tunis after 1868? Or did they move elsewhere—perhaps to Algeria? Who ratted on the operation in the first place and why? And how representative was the Tellini drama?

The numerous testimonies given over months of proceedings confirm fragments of evidence from other stories. One is that Giovanna's household was composed of people not related by kinship—or even nationality—but rather linked by socioeconomic status, the experience of immigration, "criminal" activities, and perhaps by love and affection. The second dimension of the household is that it confirms the practice of concubinage, which missionary records from the period obliquely characterized as a serious moral problem among the migrant Catholic population in Tunis. Moreover, the rented building served as a front—as an apparently legitimate shop for selling clothing, shoes, and so forth, as well as a café, the Caffe della Genina—which shows that criminal things, illicit flows, and honest work bled into one another. Also seen is that intermarriage between Sicilian, Greek, and Maltese expatriates occurred by this time, although the fact that such marriages were mentioned is significant.[108]

In addition, the story divulges how transnational networks of labor migration, commerce, and smuggling nourished the circulation of products and commodities from the Mediterranean and elsewhere. Tiny details allow us to reassemble the social networks that Giovanna and her collaborators tapped into to make a living in association with a range of other folks—Jewish musicians, Maltese servants, Spanish laborers, Tunisian bakers, and so forth. At another level, the story shows how ordinary people thwarted the state, police, and European consular authorities—for awhile at least—but also victimized neighbors by breaking, entering, and making off with their few, cherished possessions.[109] And the case demonstrates once again that international smuggling was fed by a local organized criminal ring based in a household economy partially controlled by women. (Finally, we might ask how the economic dislocations increasingly plaguing the Tunis guilds influenced theft, fencing, and smuggling rings, because guild members experienced mounting difficulty in making an honest living.)

Thus, the document itself, the proceedings, can be interpreted from several different angles: as a genre of diplomatic inquiry that shaped oral testimony by imposing a menu of predetermined questions, deeply marking responses; as an ethnographic document providing key evidence about material conditions and daily life; as an artifact translating the cultural intimacies of city people who occupied more or less the same social rank; as a tale whose plot, cast of characters, and denouement—or lack of—reoccur interminably in precolonial, and to an extent, in colonial Tunisia; and as a libretto showing how legal pluralism worked in the decades before colonialism.

The last story we will look at here, which admittedly occurred in an unusual year, concludes our consideration of contraband while forming a bridge to the next chapter on legal pluralism. In 1881 the holder of the tobacco monopoly in Tunis reported the following:

> The *fermier de tabac* learned that there were 26 sacks of tobacco hidden in the basement of a dwelling inhabited by Anna Borg, a British-Maltese protegée. The *fermier* obtained permission to inspect her premises but upon arriving there and asking to search the room, Anna refused them entry and said that she could only allow the British janissary, a Tunisian named Hamda, to enter. The janissary arrived and went into the room, he later emerged and claimed to have found nothing. But the delegation from the French monopoly saw leaves of tobacco scattered around the dwelling and insisted on going together into Anna Borg's room to search. The British janissary refused, saying he did not have an order to do this. The British consulate and the English janissaries know perfectly well that Anna Borg is habitually involved in contraband and that already four or five searches have been done at her house recently.[110]

The account raises several questions. First, who was Anna Borg? Unlike Giovanna Tellini, who had only recently immigrated to North Africa, Borg was part of a large Maltese clan long resident in Algeria and in Tunisia, since the family name appears on ships' manifests and consular correspondence from early on. Second, while she might be dismissed as a small-scale retailer in black market tobacco, situating Borg's enterprise within a global perspective lays bare international commodity flows because the tobacco purveyed came from diverse sources—Algeria, Turkey, the Levant, and the Americas. Third, Borg was obviously a repeat offender, suggesting that if "a get tough on crime" policy was in place then inspecting her premises constituted a "pick up the usual suspects" strategy. On the other hand, Borg's house had been searched four or five times, so she must have figured out a surefire strategy for rapidly disposing of incriminating evidence. Nevertheless, twenty-six sacks is a lot of tobacco to move out quickly—if indeed the informant was correct—so perhaps she had accomplices?

Anna Borg knew well the rules of the game because she was cognizant of the fact that only the English janissary had the right to enter her premises lawfully. Allegedly a repeat offender, Borg felt relatively free to flout local regulations regarding the sale of products theoretically subject to state monopolies, which shows that people manipulated the system of protection to advantage or relative disadvantage. Thus the outlines of a confluence of elements can be dimly perceived here—that consular protection had evolved into a racket empowering individuals or groups wily or bold enough to massage protégé status for their own purposes. The "English janissary," a Tunisian named Hamda, may have been complicit in Anna's recidivism, since he made certain that he alone inspected her premises in strict accordance with established rules and customs—which may have gotten her off the hook yet again. Was Hamda in league with Borg in the tobacco trade? Had she paid bought his silence and collaboration or had she failed to pay off others in the madina?

But there is another dimension to the Borg affair—constructed gender norms inflected by class and protégé status. Borg made a living trading in contraband tobacco, perhaps with greater impunity than male counterparts, as consular officials were reluctant to arrest women, particularly European women, unless sexual misconduct was alleged. A gendered division of labor marked the contraband trade in which European women of modest substance profited from concealing and selling forbidden or stolen items; men tended to monopolize the sea transport, unloading, and distribution of forbidden goods from port of entry to the place of sale. But someone had ratted on Anna Borg—as someone had informed on Giovanna and her associates. Various state and nonstate actors maintained networks of spies, informants, and tattlers scattered across the city. Was there some sort of layered protection racket whereby the dealers in forbidden items paid off local big men in the madina or port to keep quiet? And did crime rings, like the Tellini group, feed into local mafia-like associations?[111]

The case of the thief Salvo that transpired only three years prior to the Protectorate illustrates in cameo the major issues posed by law, justice, and social order. Salvo, son of Vincenzo, the Maltese, thought that he had finally struck it rich in October 1878 but a few hours later, the night guards on patrol in the madina noted with alarm that some shop windows had been forcibly removed and property stolen. A search ensued for the purloined goods that were discovered in the adjoining shop leased the day before the burglary by the same Salvo, who had tools in his possession for removing walls and windows. As he endeavored to escape, he was seized, tried for the crime of breaking and entering, and found guilty by the British consular court. His sentence was harsh—one year's imprisonment with hard labor—but noteworthy about Salvo's case was that he was sent to Malta's prisons to "undergo his punishment."[112] In earlier decades, he might have been locked up in a Tunisian prison, escaped punishment by fleeing on a passing ship, been banished but not repatriated; or he might have languished in legal uncertainty, since punishments for certain crimes committed by Maltese protégés in diaspora were subject to negotiation on a case-by-case basis, including the critical question of what kinds of evidence could be admitted to court in Malta—if indeed those courts would even agree to hear such cases. If Salvo had chosen an inauspicious moment for his break-in, he seemed unaware of how to manipulate the system of legal pluralism in the way that Anna Borg or countless others before her did.

MAKING A LIVING IN THREE ACTS

As a trilogy devoted to making a living, the last three chapters unravel a few of the social skeins generated by migration, settlement, and work from the inside out, in ever expanding circles—starting with the Husaynid court and house-hold bureaucracy, domestic service, petty trade, the coffee and hotel businesses, and occupations tied to the sea. Plotting out these ways of earning a livelihood exposes the workings of extralegal, unregulated, or illicit niches, which were structurally dependent upon the precolonial economy but ultimately hollowed it out, integrating Tunisia more firmly into the central Mediterranean corridor and the world beyond. If elite households represented social microcosms of the Mediterranean, so did the humble residences of city residents such as Giovanna Tellini and Annetta Barbera. While forced concessions to European companies, military modernization programs, usurious financial operations, and indigenous elite preferences for imported luxuries ensnared the state and economy in trans-national networks, so did the out-the-back-door enterprises of cunning entre-preneurs like Anna Borg and the social actors associated with the 1868 madina crime cartel.

What precolonial beylical or consular authorities branded as "contraband" looked vastly different to the people who trafficked in goods, services, and infor-mation through age-old, or newly forged, exchange circuits. Those who oper-ated in this arena did so despite—or because of—the fact that states around the Mediterranean increasingly sought to suppress these activities, or in some cases to encourage them to best international rivals. The heart of the matter consisted of networks. Some were quite local, confined to a city quarter (*hawma*) or street whose inhabitants lived in close proximity, sharing in the neighbor-hood's accumulated lore. Other social filaments generated by family ties, debt, work, or village origins reached across the short span of water separating western Sicily and Malta from the Cap Bon and Tunis. Some networks were governed by older cartographies of movement. The cabotage sailing routes connecting Bizerte, Tabarka, and Ghar al-Milh with Bône or Algiers ran along well-worn itineraries but transported new kinds of passengers and commodities after 1830. Other networks implicated ruling elites, European consuls, and big-time mer-chants in international operations linking Tunis with Valletta, Leghorn, Algiers, Marseilles, or Paris.

People were contraband then as they are today—ship captains frequently transported undocumented travelers from Europe to North Africa as well as slaves, even after British and then Tunisian abolition. The end of slavery rendered the trade in enslaved persons illegal in Tunisia but more lucrative (and risky), so that traffic persisted, although on a reduced scale, particularly in Saharan regions and at sea. At least until 1890, although in a reduced numbers, contraband slaves were brought in from the western Sudan, among them freeborn Muslim women.[113] As for information cum contraband, the dissemination of vitriolic political tracts, printed in Sardinia or Malta and attacking unpopular state policies in Tunisia, were smuggled into the capital city in the same way that Masonic leaflets or radical political publications circulated clandestinely among Italian and North African ports. The processes whereby ideas and ideologies were smuggled into Tunisia duplicated the Ottoman heartlands during the 1860s, when radical Turkish émigrés cum political refugees in European cities printed newspapers deemed subversive by the Porte, arranging for Arabic and Turkish journals published in London, Paris, or Vienna to be introduced clandestinely into Istanbul.[114]

What I have characterized as "contraband" raises significant issues for the Maghrib's modern history in several interrelated realms. First, it reveals the nature of, and complex processes leading to, greater commercial and financial entanglement with Europe and a concomitant reduction of economic ties with the Ottoman Empire. Second, the social identities and activities of free trading agents suggests that the nineteenth-century Mediterranean's peculiar brand of "informal economy" could be interpreted as a form of resistance to the intrusions of centralizing states or imperial formations or simply business as usual. One way of conceptualizing black-market operations and smuggling in the aggregate is as "globalization from below," since much of the coffee and tobacco imported illegally into Tunisia from Malta no longer came from Anatolia or the Red Sea but from the Americas.[115]

While Maltese involvement in smuggling is well documented for the nineteenth century, a number of other groups played lead roles. But the Maltese in North Africa had made the contraband traffic into a specialty—so much so that the words "Maltese" and *contrebandier* had nearly coterminous meanings in local parlance by the end of the century. Honor, masculinity, and contraband coalesced to create a new picaresque social figure—the smuggler as neighborhood hero, or thug, depending upon one's view—who resembled the older Ottoman *qabaday*, the tough, street-smart guy who ruled his turf in the city quarter.[116] Nevertheless, the general social dynamic that criminalized visible and vulnerable minorities during periods of intense social reordering should make us wary. And it may be that participation in exchanges and activities branded as extralegal or morally illicit by the state both eased social insertion and marginalized members of fast-growing expatriate communities.

Third, unsuccessful efforts to rein in or stamp out contraband serve as a gauge for the state's declining fortunes and the role of shrewd, freewheeling entrepreneurs as well as local or transregional big men in that decline. For the Tunisian dynasty, extralegal exchanges constituted an index measuring the state's power to tax the productive activities of subjects as well as nonsubjects residing within its borders. Ironically, the more beylical officials attempted to come to grips with the financial losses incurred by the increasingly flagrant traffic in goods normally subject to taxation, to customs duties, or state monopoly, the more smuggling became a free-trade zone where subjects and foreigners supplied the wants and needs of daily life—including the prime instruments for resistance, firearms and powder. In a sense, the contraband economy became the prevailing way of doing business because the state had failed in its obligations to its own subjects. The increasingly promiscuous sex industry constituted smuggling in another register, since "contraband desire" represented one way of making a living. However, the moral implications of prostitution, or merely love with the wrong person, and its significance to the construction of religiosexual communal borders meant that, when the Husaynid state failed to police those borders, it forfeited considerable moral—and by extension, political—capital by the eve of the French Protectorate.

Related to this, as productive activities and resources were increasingly removed from the state's fiscal reach, its political clout vis-à-vis more powerful nations steadily eroded. The Tunisian state's attempts to stamp out unregulated commerce were opposed by some foreign merchants and consuls who argued that "the new rules will interfere with trade and will bring no good to the country."[117] If the second phase of modern state reforms initiated by Khayr al-Din had been allowed to mature, outcomes might have differed—somewhat—but by then it was too late. From the 1870s on, the practice of illegitimate commerce had evolved into something else—corporate contraband in the style of today's unfettered, offshore Halliburton or Carlyle groups. By the mid-1870s, the navigation company Valery transported more than just passengers or goods; the company's agent in Tunis, a Roman citizen, Domenico Mangano, used the cover of shipping to clandestinely introduce counterfeit Tunisian piasters, carefully crafted knock-offs made in Switzerland, into the country, wreaking further ruin on an already bankrupt fiscal system.[118] And it is quite possible that behind-the-scenes big men managed some of the earlier, more apparently populist forms of smuggling. The consul general of Germany, Julius von Eckardt, who assumed his post in 1885 and remained for four years, expressed shock over the behavior of fellow diplomats in Tunis. Consuls who had served under the ancien régime longed for the good old days, before French rule, when they had participated with impunity in the illicit traffic in takruri and tobacco, organized by their compatriots, from which they too had benefited handsomely.[119]

Thus contraband evolved into a sizeable exchange economy flowing across

North Africa and the central Mediterranean corridor where it fed into other systems. Its robust nature can in part be explained by jurisdictional snarls in the realm of justice so characteristic of the precolonial (and early colonial) state.

The next chapter addresses the increasingly intractable issues of law, justice, and social order in relationship to high levels of immigration. By the nineteenth century, Tunis was among a string of port cities stretching from Tangier to Alexandria to Izmir where largely unregulated foreign settlement, European meddling in trade, commerce, and law, state building by local rulers, and efforts to superintend strangers in the city had generated incessant legal wrangling and jurisdictional sparring. Confusion in the realm of justice was further complicated by the Ottoman Empire's steady, if partial, dismantlement at the hands of European states. As former provinces were gobbled up, becoming colonies, spheres of influence, or client states under Great Power guardianship—as did the Kingdom of Greece declared in 1829—legal uncertainty increased. Paralleling Ottoman dismemberment was Italian unification, which produced similar jurisdictional tangles, although the literature rarely juxtaposes Italy's turbulent making with the Ottoman Empire's equally tumultuous unmaking. However, these twin processes came together in particularly intense combinations throughout the central Mediterranean corridor.

6

From Protection to Protectorate

Justice, Order, and Legal Pluralism

The taverns and cafés that sprang up in Tunis and La Goulette were the scenes of interminable altercations fueled by alcohol and affronts to male honor. One Saturday evening in 1870, Nicola Malinghoussy, a soldier in the pope's army, got drunk and insulted several persons in a tavern at the port. Assuming he was a protégé of France, the outraged patrons stormed to the nearby French vice-consul to lodge a complaint. Yet Nicola could produce no valid document establishing French protection. Soon thereafter, he declared himself a Venetian subject, so the Italian vice-consul had Nicola arrested and thrown in prison. Apparently Nicola sobered up enough to locate his passport delivered earlier that same year in Alexandria, Egypt, by the consul general of the "King of the Hellenes." Sprung by the Italian consul, he was then handed over to the Russian agent responsible for some diaspora Greeks. The Russian had Nicola incarcerated until the next Sunday; since prison facilities were scarce, the disorderly soldier was confined onboard a Tunisian *aviso* (ship) in dry dock near Muhammad al-Sadiq Bey's military arsenal.[1] Nicola's apparent remorse convinced the Russian consul to release him temporarily so he could fetch his belongings and carry them back to the ship-prison. Instead, the wily soldier went on the lam and, while the janissaries searched all over La Goulette for him, he slipped onto a small boat crossing the lake to Tunis. Informed of this betrayal, the Russian had Nicola arrested yet again and locked up in a Tunisian military prison. At this point, additional evidence of Nicola's moral turpitude was scarcely required. But soon the Mother Superior of the Sisters of Saint-Joseph convent came forward with a deposition detailing the soldier's foiled assassination attempt on two priests to avenge an unspecified offense.[2]

Eventually, Nicola was hustled onboard a French ship heading for Bône and expelled. Here the jurisdictional map becomes even fuzzier—why was Nicola dumped on colonial authorities?[3] Was it because of his alleged status as a Zouave in the papal army, a conjecture that, if true, might make him subject to French military law? Would he be condemned to forced labor in Algeria, the fate of many individuals accused of crimes whose status was uncertain? Or would he be banished on yet another ship bound for somewhere else in the Mediterranean? Could he be sent to France and perhaps eventually deported to French Guyana?[4] And did Nicola himself really know (or care) about which jurisdiction he was under? Once expelled from Tunisia, Nicola's destiny would be decided by the very category then in a state of flux and subject to varying interpretations and widely differing outcomes—politicolegal belonging.

As elsewhere in the Ottoman Empire, justice in Tunisia traditionally rested upon the fundamental principle that religious affiliation determined personal status under the law. Resident non-Muslims, who were mainly European Christians or Jews, had safely engaged in trade and commerce for centuries under the protections guaranteed by the Capitulations, conceded by the Porte to European states, as well as bilateral treaties concluded between the rulers of Tunis and various Mediterranean powers. The aftermath of the Napoleonic Wars, however, brought rude shocks to the system; thrown into disarray was the ideal template for maintaining order and securing justice for religiously heterogeneous populations sharing the same space. More people moving about in ways different from previous centuries constituted a prime motor for change. Human mobility on an unprecedented scale incubated new forms of imperial interventions into the Muslim states on the Mediterranean's southern and eastern rims.

This is a story narrated by older scholarship on the nineteenth-century Ottoman Empire in which mixed or consular courts proved the Trojan horse for foreign meddling.[5] The seemingly endless disputes over jurisdictions were interpreted, however, according to narrowly construed notions of imperialism—and not as significant in and of themselves for understanding local social worlds. In that earlier scholarship, the legal quagmire created by conflicts involving the subjects of local rulers, recognized protégés, resident expatriates, recent immigrants, or familiar strangers under shifting or uncertain jurisdictions was presented as an episode in modern Middle Eastern history, not as one chapter in larger struggles unfolding across the world in much the same manner and period. Conflicting jurisdictions are universal phenomena, which haunt our world ever more today due to high-intensity "globalization." The Iranian exile Mehran Karemi Nasseri, who resided at Charles de Gaulle Airport for years awaiting an exit visa to quit French territory, immediately comes to mind.

In older imperial formations, such as the Mughul or Ottoman empires, claims of legal authority over religiously and culturally diverse subject populations led to communal or religious tensions, and at times outright conflict, yet in practice evinced a high degree of flexibility. As large numbers of Europeans became parties to conflicts in multicentric legal orders in South Asia or the Middle East, protracted jockeying over local jurisdictions carved out sizeable zones of legal uncertainty long before the imposition of colonial rule. From roughly 1800 on, small, seemingly trivial disputes intersected with larger political, legal, economic, and demographic transformations that expanded the reach of European empires from below or from the margins. Scholars now argue that older, precolonial legal practices and arrangements not only determined the nature of colonial regimes globally but ultimately the contemporary international legal order. For our purposes, legal pluralism is understood as "the coexistence within a given area of multiple state and non-state bodies that propose norms, settle disputes, create authoritative categories of knowledge, distribute resources, and impose sanctions."[6]

This chapter studies legal pluralism in precolonial Tunisia, notably in the capital-city region, as a unified field of social action that was a single, albeit moving, canvas. It mobilizes evidence from small-scale disputes to trace the ways in which women and men quarreled, schemed, cooperated, or merely went about their daily business and in so doing transgressed, manipulated, pushed out, or simply bumped up against jurisdictional boundaries. Such an approach duplicates the actual practices of beylical or Ottoman subjects, long-term European residents, and Mediterranean immigrants of indeterminate status as they sought redress of grievance, recovered outstanding debts, disproved accusations of wrongdoing, or wreaked vengeance upon neighbors, creditors, or ex-lovers. But cases and contests from elsewhere are examined because events in a provincial seaport, such as Mahdiya, inevitably had repercussions in Tunis and vice versa. Moreover, as was true of contraband, our story does not stop at the border between Tunisia and Algeria.

We begin with an examination of beylical and consular justice and the ways in which they overlapped. The task of maintaining sociolegal order meant that consuls entertained constant, often daily, communication with the Tunisian ruling class, which forged a commonality of interests and shared worldviews, especially in earlier decades. This became particularly evident when female comportment was at stake, and thus it is argued that consular politicolegal protection implied the sexual policing of women in ways that directly implicated beylical officials. It is also necessary to reconstruct local disciplinary regimes that incorporated newcomers into the existing system, tolerated the less than desirable, imprisoned wrongdoers, or expelled the troublesome. Variant legal remedies and strategies went into the mix of agreed-upon "ways of doing things" recognized by Tunisian and consular authorities alike—at least for part of the precolonial era. A constitutive element of multicentric orders is "forum shopping," through which individuals appeal to competing legal authorities to secure a more sympathetic hearing and hopefully successful outcome. Women often employed forum shopping as a strategy given that gender codes limited, or even barred them, from seeking out other legal venues.[7]

Gender constituted a central element in legal pluralism and, because women were relegated to special jurisdictional spheres, a section of the chapter deals specifically with female conversion as a form of protection switching. Algerians in Tunisia presented uniquely complex legal issues for French and Tunisian authorities, and therefore the status of expatriate Algerians receives separate treatment as well. People sorted themselves out according to blueprints or scripts informed largely, but not exclusively, by their understanding of what justice and jurisdiction meant at any given moment. At the same time, "protection" shifted in response to internal and external forces; the meanings attached to "protégé" proved transient, elusive, at certain junctures. This sorting out drew upon implicit rules of the game, rules often fully understood only the by insiders. That inside is what we are after.

THE PRINCE AND THE PROTECTED

"It will be seen that the characters of the later Beys of Tunis are not those of monsters of caprice and crime . . . on the contrary, they might be advantageously matched with many of the sovereigns of Europe."[8] The logic of the Husaynid dynasty's acknowledged authority and legitimacy demanded well-orchestrated displays of benevolence, munificence, and pageantry. However, the lynchpin was the ruler's chief duty—protecting Muslims and Islam—and dispensing justice in accordance with religious dictates, customary law, and cultural practices. Even without a growing resident community of non-Muslim, non-subject people, pre-colonial Tunisia displayed the characteristics of a complex legal order because of the presence of two Islamic *madhhab,* Hanafi and Maliki, as well as the evolution of state law as distinct from religious law and the importance of customary law—*'urf*—in the countryside, particularly among pastoral-nomadic groups. The rabbinical courts for indigenous (as opposed to European) Jews represented another dimension of legal pluralism, since at times Jews appealed to Muslim authorities for redress. And, in theory at least, Ottoman law applied to Tunisia as a province of the empire.[9]

By the nineteenth century, the beys had usurped some of the functions that were theoretically the purview of Muslim jurists. Since classical Islamic political theory did not recognize separation of powers, the head of state was considered the highest Muslim judicial authority; thus the beys enjoyed the title of *qadi al-qudah* (chief qadi). For most questions relating to personal status and property, the qadis, as arbiters and interpreters of the law, and shari'a courts retained

FIGURE 13. The Bardo palace throne room, c. 1899. The Husaynid rulers formally received foreign diplomats and Tunisian government officials in this audience chamber, whose eclectic ornamentation reveals aesthetic and artistic elements from North Africa, the Ottoman Empire, and Europe. (Library of Congress Prints andPhotographs, LC-DIG-ppmsca-06034.)

competence. However, the rulers usually claimed jurisdiction for capital cases but delegated authority in other matters to local officials or to corporate groups, like guild masters, to define and punish minor infractions. In legal quarrels over land ownership or use, the qadis' opinions were paramount; because of this, the system they administered became the prime object of attack by Europeans seeking to establish private property rights. In any case, "a rudimentary distinction between religious and civil law" had emerged by the nineteenth century, if not before, although most litigation was overseen by the qadis "as the normal representatives of the judicial process."[10]

In the palace complex just outside Tunis proper, state and Islamic law converged at the Bardo's "hall of justice," which among other things functioned as an appellate court. In the *sahn al-burj* (tower courtyard), the beys entertained all manner of supplicants, paying keen attention to charges leveled against corrupt provincial officials. Europeans observing the daily audiences expressed astonishment at the fact that tribal peoples, women, and those of humble rank were received to lay forth their grievances. One witness to the proceedings at Ahmad Bey's palace in 1845 noted that "At the Bardo the bey holds a Court of Justice—a supreme tribunal—in the presence of his grand functionaries, where, however, the meanest of his subjects may prefer the smallest complaint and is sure to have hearing. At this palace-village, the Bey usually receives the Consuls and various representatives of European Powers, and any extraordinary embassies from the Porte and Christian Princes."[11] Not all rulers were as attentive to, or enthusiastic about, dispensing justice to all comers. Ahmad Bey was chastised for infrequent attendance and therefore neglecting his paramount duty as a Muslim sovereign. Finally, the intersections between beylical and Islamic law were embodied by the Bardo's *majlis al-shari'a* with which the ruler was to consult on a regular basis, although this too varied.[12] On a day-to-day basis, the administration of justice came to be patterned by what might be called the rhythms of seasonality. As the nineteenth century wore on, the beys, their courts, and the consuls spent extended periods of time in summer villas or palaces by the sea instead of the Bardo, which slowed matters considerably. As parties to a squabble increasingly came from different religious communities, the observance of three consecutive holy days rendered justice positively sluggish, since business could only be conducted during the four remaining weekdays.

CAPITULATIONS: FROM CONCESSION TO PRIVILEGE

For international diplomacy, the Bardo's hall of justice represented a critical space that provided access to the throne in the same way that entrée to the bey's table confirmed or conferred favor. Yet from 1830 on, established ways of conducting diplomacy were under attack due to the occupation of Algeria and the expansion of European military clout around the Mediterranean. Would-be powers, such as the Kingdom of the Two Sicilies in Turin, sought greater recognition among the concert of nations at the expense of weak states like Tunisia by refusing to observe older court etiquette. In 1830, the Sardinian government presented a list of diplomatic grievances, including demands that consuls not be kept waiting at the palace for hours to confer with the bey. Another bitter controversy arose over the older ceremony requiring the consuls to kiss the ruler's hand during audiences. Contested by the revolutionary French government in 1796, and the British and Americans after 1816, as an unacceptable symbol of autocracy, the practice was abolished in 1836 after the French consul refused to make the ritual gesture, since it was no longer employed in Christian courts or even in Istanbul. In 1830 France imposed new treaties upon Tunisia (and Tripolitania) under the pretext that corsair activity—which had largely ceased years before—had to be eradicated, an excuse that figured in French justifications for invading Algeria. The treaty also ended, among other things, compulsory gifts to the beys.[13]

In the course of the nineteenth century, two ideal grids or templates for order-ing sociolegal relations in Ottoman lands collided—the much older Capitulations and the Tanzimat decrees proclaimed from 1839 on. The older system, the Capi-tulations, dated back to the sixteenth century when clauses were inserted in the 1569 treaty between France and the Porte granting special legal, religious, fiscal, and commercial rights and privileges to resident foreign merchants and repre-sentatives. In a quid pro quo arrangement that was mutually beneficial to both parties in that period, Europeans conducting trade and diplomacy in a Muslim empire were first of all guaranteed security of person and property. From this concession came the freedom to maintain religious buildings and worship freely, exemption from local taxes and sumptuary codes, and the enjoyment of testa-mentary rights. The second principle, extraterritoriality, established consular jurisdiction, which meant that Europeans in Ottoman lands had recourse to their own consular courts for most legal matters. In return, the Ottomans were spared the bother of providing justice to nonsubjects and in return enjoyed access to a range of Europe goods, notably military ware. These rights were eventually extended to other European states and in theory applied to all Ottoman prov-inces, but by the nineteenth century local practices varied widely and wildly.[14]

Nevertheless, the Capitulations did not necessarily shape the actual legal ter-rain in Tunisia because the Husaynid princes (and their predecessors) had long concluded bilateral treaties independently of their Ottoman overlords. Observers invariably noted "the virtual independence of these Beys, they are permitted to make separate treaties and contract alliances with all the powers of Europe; to make peace or declare war against them, without any advice or consultation with the Porte, and any other Mussulman authorities."[15] Between 1270 and 1881, Tunis concluded 114 treaties with various and sundry powers; a separate treaty was signed with France in 1605 and another in 1662 with England, although the earliest recorded document was the thirteenth-century treaty with Aragon. With the advent of new rulers to the throne, these treaties were often renewed, but not always. Trade had long been the principal crucible for diplomatic relations, and treaties guaranteed the crucial *droit de résidence* (right of residence) that protected merchants as well as their goods when they were engaged in commerce and residing in Muslim lands. As was true generally throughout the Ottoman Empire from the 1660s on, the Tunisian state increasingly enclosed nonsubject communities within specifically designated spaces in the capital city. The right of residence constituted the pivot of concessions (in Tunisia, sometimes referred to as *shurut*) to resident non-Muslim nonsubjects The social fact of enclosure exerted a tremendous influence upon the spatial configuration of pre-nineteenth-century Tunis but was progressively undermined by immigration, the housing crisis, and the more or less spontaneous physical expansion of the city extra muros long before colonialism.[16]

Before plunging into the progressively tangled thicket of competing jurisdictions and alternative legal remedies, we need to recreate the social world of the consulates, which dealt with a spectrum of individuals on a daily basis—their own nationals, beylical subjects, runaway slaves, travelers, and other city inhabitants of divergent backgrounds. In part, the recognized right of consular jurisdiction accounted for many—but not all—of the judicial and social responsibilities assumed by consuls and consulates, although the lines of demarcation among competent authorities had always been elastic and therefore large areas were subject to daily, at times interminable, negotiation and compromise.

THE CONSULATE AS SOCIOLEGAL UNIVERSE

By the 1830s there were some fourteen consulates in Tunisia, representing an assortment of nations and empires as well as emerging states and nationalities. The legal situation of Italians in Tunisia prior to unification was especially knotty, with five consulates exercising jurisdiction.[17] Even consular officials evinced uncertainty about who belonged where in the moving legal checkerboard. With more and more people showing up in Tunisia (and Algeria), the bean counters in the British and French consulates, which kept the best records, became overwhelmed; however, many newly settled folks avoided contact with authorities. As was the case with the characters involved in the 1868 contraband and fencing operation—Giovanna, Gianmaria, and Annetta—they probably steered clear of consulates for obvious reasons, until misfortune fell from the sky.

Until the Protectorate, the consulates represented the principal mechanism of social insertion—or exclusion—and therefore created opportunities for, as well as limitations upon, protégés or nationals. Theoretically, the consuls were accorded generous power since they assured law and justice: investigating crimes; imposing fines or punishments, including imprisonment or expulsion; conducting probate proceedings; resolving debt or inheritance disputes; and so forth. They assumed the duties of policemen, judges, notaries, and FBI agents by interviewing parties to disputes, taking depositions, and gathering evidence at crime scenes. Consulates oversaw the drawing up of affidavits—written statements made under oath before a competent authority, notary or otherwise; and depositions, the written testimony of witnesses under oath. These legal acts were conveyed by signature and seals. In 1852, Lombard, a French citizen complained about the behavior of Angelo Pittalugo, a Sardinian, accused of *"un attentat à la pudeur,"* or sexual assault upon Lombard's son, age unknown. To launch an investigation, the French consul brought the Lombard couple to the consulate to draw up a deposition, which was submitted to Sardinian authorities for investigation.[18] At times, consulates functioned as pawnshops, primitive banks, and secure depositories for valuables. A consul acted as a public health agent by granting bills of clean health and clearance to ships under his nation's flag; decisions regarding quarantine either facilitated or hampered trade. Until Catholic missionaries arrived in the 1840s to establish educational, health, and charitable organizations, the consulates filled critical social welfare roles: as places of refuge, administering poor relief and charity, as marriage minders or menders, as moral guardians, and as mediation bureaus.[19]

When contention erupted among business partners, neighbors, families, or individuals from different diaspora communities, some looked to consulates for conflict management, although they might appeal to Tunisian officials, church authorities, friends, or kin for mediation as well. Of course, the nature of the documentation predisposes the record to social conflict and thus should inspire cautious interpretation. Prior to massive Italian settlement, the Maltese were the most likely to seek consular mediation. This was particularly true in earlier decades because Church or familial peacekeepers were absent, and the Maltese were the single-largest expatriate community. Moreover, many Maltese acquired some facility in Tunisian Arabic, English, and Italian, which meant that they entertained intense interactions with a greater cross-section of Tunis than most, thereby increasing the likelihood for disagreement. The examples discussed in the next paragraphs are taken mainly from the period just prior to 1830 in order to demonstrate that, while the French invasion of Algeria worked as a "migratory pump" across the central Mediterranean corridor, some, perhaps many, of the sociolegal patterns introduced by large-scale, spontaneous immigration were already in place.

Detailed logbooks kept by the British consulate from the late 1820s until the 1830s recorded the daily, at times hourly, appearance of people looking for conflict resolution; it provides a porthole view of how things worked. Here is the entry for August 2, 1828: "a trivial dispute occurred between two Maltese which was speedily adjusted." This laconic sentence is a leitmotif that reoccurs throughout the logbooks until this type of documentation disappears from the archive. The fact that individuals were often not named but merely identified as "two Maltese" raises questions. Could it be that consular officials did not deem naming important? Was it a sign of disparagement and/or an acknowledgement that since the Maltese moved in and out of Tunisia so rapidly, and in such great numbers, that it was not worth the bother to provide family names? But others were identified and thus named, perhaps because they were longtime residents or habitués of the consulate.[20]

Squabbles over financial arrangements provide fragmentary clues regarding women's relationships with those from different religious communities. In December 1829, a Tunisian Muslim woman sought redress from the British consulate; she "laid a complaint against Fsadney, the Maltese, for having about 8 months back obtained 800 piasters from her, assisted by one Baba Mustafa, a Turk."[21] This incident, and others like it, demonstrates that Muslim women entered into business partnerships with Maltese men, or at least loaned them money. When her creditor proved insolvent, the "Moorish" woman (as she is identified in the record) felt no hesitation about personally lodging a protest with consular authorities. Was Fsadney her neighbor? And what about the Turk, Baba Mustafa? We will probably never know, but the Moorish woman did appear to be conversant with the system of protection—otherwise why would she have bothered going to the British?

As housing became a scarce commodity, rental disagreements escalated, mainly but not exclusively between foreign protégés and Tunisian subjects, who held city properties in one form or another. The same room or apartment might be rented to three different parties; subletting rooms without the owner's knowledge was apparently quite common, and because arrangements were oral in nature, the potential for bickering over a particular residence was virtually limitless. As illustrated by the two-year ordeal of the French baker, Astoin, discussed in chapter 4, agreements were broken at will. Astoin's endless search for rented rooms for his bakery and domicile in 1848 led the French consulate to organize a formal inquiry, gather testimony from witnesses, and examine physical evidence.[22] These cases are significant because they signal a growing willingness by diplomatic representatives to become more deeply involved in the intimate domestic affairs of protégés of modest social rank. The careful attention paid to seemingly inconsequential matters arose from the desire to avert potential conflict before it engulfed a family or neighborhood, or worse, seeped into intercommunal relations, which in turn could provoke the kind of violence that activated legal wrangling.

While the consulates attempted to assure the safety of nationals, some under their protection resided far from Tunis. During a robbery at their home in 1838, a French national, Auberger, and his wife were murdered in a remote part of the countryside. The double slaying scandalized local French merchants, who submitted a formal complaint to the Chambre de Commerce in Marseilles that laid the blame for the double murder on the incompetent "French consul who fails to care for nationals and protégés."[23] This and other incidents demonstrate that if the consuls were the prime peacekeepers and protectors, they themselves were supervised by their own communities. In reality, protection proved an ideal—not real—political and legal template because the consuls frequently lacked the means and/or the will to fully supervise the mobile populations under their administration. Sir Thomas Reade's 1833 lament about British protégés sums it up: "They complain of my not rendering them justice. How can I? I have no authority."[24]

"AS IS THE CUSTOM IN THIS COUNTRY"

Legal treatises devoted to law in nineteenth-century North Africa composed by French jurists came mainly from the pens of colonial officials in Algeria, who emphasized inalienable difference in law, procedure, and custom when comparing European and Islamic jurisprudence.[25] Local, often orally transmitted remedies for conflict resolution were subsumed under the rubric of "customary law," which called forth its binary (and superior) opposite—rational, codified European justice. In this landscape of assumed incommensurability, Islamic laws or practices were portrayed as unambiguously distinct. However, in precolonial Tunisia, there existed considerable (although not always acknowledged) overlap in consular and beylical justice in terms of customary norms and procedures. Moreover, intersections operated not only in the realm of mutually agreed-upon ways of doing things but also in formal procedures governing, most importantly, admissible evidence. Depositions drawn up by Islamic authorities—*shahadat amama al-mahkama*—were admitted as evidence in some cases, above all, in murder cases involving victims from different religious or national communities, as seen below in a Maltese murder case from 1843, and in the alleged murder in 1874 of a Tunisian woman, Zaynab, by her Algerian husband, an expatriate under French protection.[26]

As recognized instruments, bilateral treaties concluded between Tunis and European states assumed the existence of a mutually shared and recognized legal universe but, I argue, so did the customary practices observed by beylical authorities and consuls, at least for part of the century.[27] A constant refrain in documents penned by both Tunisian and consular officials translates the signal importance of locally defined legal praxis: "as is the custom in this country" or according to "the invariable custom of the place." In his December 1843 letter to the Earl of Aberdeen regarding the Maltese murder imbroglio, Thomas Reade reminded his superior of the way things were done with this phrase: "according to what is customary in this country."[28] Tunisian authorities employed the same formula in Arabic: *"kayfa al-'ada bi biladna"* appeared in similar exchanges with European counterparts.[29] But customary ways of doing things were not always observed. When in October 1836 the bey had four Maltese arrested on suspicion of robbery and refused to observe "invariable custom" by releasing them to the British consul for punishment, a man-of-war under the command of Rear Admiral Sir Thomas Briggs arrived from Malta. Mustafa Bey relented and handed the four Maltese over to the consul. To exert moral and political pressure upon both the Maltese and the Tunisian government, Reade proposed that the British navy dock in La Goulette on a regular basis: "It is much to be lamented that our vessels of war do not shew [sic] themselves more frequently . . . it is now near 12 months since one was here . . . scarcely a week passes without French

[war] vessels coming."[30] Progressively from this period on, these older, often implicit mechanisms for managing conflict in a multicentric legal order were eroded.

If customary procedures were a product of the accumulated weight of the past, they were also a consequence of indifferent record keeping, which meant that many a consul "made it up as he went along." Until at least 1847, the British consulate lacked copies of treaties concluded between London and Tunis determining jurisdictions and procedures, in this case the 1757 treaty. In 1847, Louis Ferriere, Reade's successor as consul, had to beseech his own government to supply him with a copy of the most recent treaty: "It would be highly desirable that a Copy of the early treaties between the British Government and that of Tunis should be kept for general reference in the Consulate; where they do not appear to exist, for the present Vice Consul has never been able to get a sight of those important documents during the six year he has been at his post."[31]

A similar situation obtained among French nationals residing in the beylik, many of whom were completely ignorant of the texts of treaties theoretically governing their lives and livelihoods. "The result is that they do not know their rights and a great uncertainty governs their relationships with the *indigènes*, or their relationships with or participation in local activities."[32] At times European consuls temporarily ceded recognized rights of protection over nationals or protégés to the Tunisian state. As an interim measure in 1862, Sir Richard Wood requested that Muhammad al-Sadiq Bey place British subjects in Porto Farina under his protection because the British agent's recent departure had left the town's mainly Maltese population

> without authority to whom they can apply for assistance in their affairs and protection of their persons. Would your Highness permit the [Tunisian] Governor of Porto Farina to temporarily take under his protection the British subjects residing within his district . . . in order to aid them in the adjustment of their affairs and keep the British general consul in Tunis informed of any occurrences. In the event that your Highness should be pleased to accede to my request, I further hope that your Highness will give a similar permission to the Governor of Tabarca [sic] in favour of the few British subjects who dwell in that distant locality and who are without protection.[33]

Precedents for such arrangements are found in earlier centuries; for example, the Spanish Catholic missionaries, the Trinitarians, were placed in 1791 under the "immediate protection of the bey," a consequence of the French Revolution.[34] It is noteworthy that Wood's 1862 request employed the term *al-raʿiya*, meaning "protected flock," to refer to the British subjects for whom he sought Husaynid protection (the Arabic equivalent is *himaya*). This suggests that in day-to-day negotiations protection was understood not as a legal absolute but as representing a spectrum of rights and privileges with inherent plasticity in interpretation. If the texts of treaties or other legally binding instruments were essential for the rules of the game, the situational parsing of clauses or provisions—not to mention problems of actual translation—were always subject to a range of local meanings, understandings, and applications. Finally, the more energetic consuls not only acted on behalf of their nationals or protégés but also at times intervened to defuse tensions *between* subjects of the bey to preserve social order in the capital—which again suggests mutually observed norms.

The consulates attracted a wide array of people on a daily basis and employed heterogeneous staffs—Tunisians and other North Africans, Europeans, creoles, Muslims, Christians, Jews, and transimperial people on the move. Thus, they represented the Mediterranean world in miniature and, as such, were akin to the beys' courts and households by virtue of their religious, racial, ethnic, or social diversity. Another shared "way of doing things" was the local culture of sanctuary.

ALTERNATIVE REMEDIES: SANCTUARY AS FORUM SHOPPING

Consular courts represented one significant legal resource for resident nationals or protégés as well as for beylical subjects and others. But the word "court" demands spatial analysis because the actual places dedicated to legal proceedings served multiple purposes—mediation, brokerage, poor relief, prison facilities, and finally sanctuary, which represented one expression of forum shopping. "There is not any House in Tunis, in the least calculated for a Consulate, unoccupied, but indeed was it otherwise, it would not be desirable to relinquish the present one; for its situation is much preferable to any other in the City. [The British consulate] adjoins the entrance by the Sea Gate, which renders the access to it much easier than to any other Consulate, except the Swedish one, which is affronted to it."[35]

Location was everything. The British consulate's placement made it especially busy on any given day. In the political culture of nineteenth-century Tunisia, specific spaces and the social practices associated with them translated into a type of forum shopping. Some city inhabitants of whatever religion or status attempted to mobilize all of these spaces—saints' shrines, the bey's *saqifa* (antechamber, i.e., "roofed gallery or passage"), consulates, church cemeteries, and ships—at one time or another in the hopes of securing a more favorable hearing, to momentarily suspend violent conflict, evade pursuers (especially creditors), or to dramatize their plight. Since the performative possibilities that different spaces offered were critical to calculations, forum switching is best understood through an ethnography of the actual sites of redress.

The bey's saqifa and the consulates shared features relating directly or indirectly to the realm of justice, but the Bardo was some distance outside city walls and less accessible than consular buildings whose right of asylum was respected by local authorities. Indeed, consular correspondence employed a variant of the Arabic term *saqifa* to denote a space of sanctuary: "a Moor having stabbed one of the Dragomen of the French Consulate, took refuge in the Skeif [i.e., saqifa] of the British Consulate, and a Hamba . . . endeavored to apprehend and remove him thence by force, but was prevented and the French Vice Consul and the Eleve Vice Consul applied to have the Moor surrendered to them but the Skeif being a place of Refuge and security, the application was refused."[36] Before abolition, African slaves sought haven among the tombstones of Saint George Church, as extraterritoriality extended to cemeteries whose location extra muros in this period made them all the more attractive.[37] Ships moored in port were sometimes employed as sanctuaries, although La Goulette was a fair distance from Tunis and not easily reached by most.

The following snapshot from a day's drama during the summer of 1828 clearly shows that consular buildings were collectively viewed as neutral spaces, even by subjects of the bey. "A Moor, being pursued by another Moor for debt, seized the column of the British consulate door to seek protection, the creditor attempted to hinder him, but he escaped from his hand and took refuge in the consulate, on which the Dragoman of the consulate brought a Hambi [sic, a *hanba*] and conducted the creditor to prison for attempting to hinder the debtor from seeking refuge in the consulate."[38] Here the "wronged party," the creditor in hot pursuit of someone owing him money, was conducted to prison by a local official for not observing customary norms. The British consul's acquiescence to the outcome indicates awareness of, and agreement with, how the system worked.

In another example, indigenous Jews sometimes sought asylum at the consulate during street altercations. On one occasion in August 1828, a Jew took refuge in the consulate because he was "pursued by a Moor a little inebriated and riotous." The dragoman hailed a member of the urban gendarmerie and the drunken "Moor" was carted off to Tunisian prison.[39] The intervention of Tunisian authorities demonstrates that consular and beylical policing worked together to keep the peace. One is struck by the humble social origins of many seeking sanctuary, which at times shaded off into forum shopping. But when court notables took refuge in consulates, the ante was upped to dangerous levels.

In 1837 the French consul contacted Hassuna al-Murali, the bey's first secretary and interpreter, with news of an unfolding drama at the consulate where Hammada b. al-Hajj had taken refuge for several months to escape the alleged persecutions of his brothers in a battle over family inheritance. Significantly, the brothers had enlisted the bey's support. In the French consul's words: "In vain, I have told Si Hammada Belhadj [sic] that I have been assured by the Bardo that he has nothing to fear from the bey. However, Si Hammada persists in refusing to leave the asylum of the French flag; he wishes the bey to order that these differences be submitted for adjudication either to the Chara [Islamic court] or to the tribunal for commerce."[40] By using the French consulate as a residential hotel, Hammada's strategy was in large measure performative—to dramatize his predicament which then became a public, citywide drama. From this period on, a whole host of Husaynid subjects—palace mamluks, the notable Jalluli and his family, and even a high-ranking Tunisian military officer—sought temporary asylum at European consulates, although affording sanctuary was often viewed with opprobrium by ministers in Paris or London.[41]

In the next decades, commonly agreed-upon rules were worked out. In 1864, after Pietri Bogo, a Tunisian subject of Italian origins, got into an altercation with Joseph Gandolphe, a French protégé, Bogo fled to the Swedish and Norwegian consulate. Tulin, the consul, stated that, "according to *local* [emphasis added] custom, a foreign national can only take refuge in the consulate of any power for a total of three days only after which time the consul is required to render the refugee over to whomever is responsible for him."[42] After three days, Bogo would be handed over to the appropriate authorities. Consulates constituted spaces off-limits to political authorities and theoretically open to most, whether protégé or not, but there were temporal limitations. Maneuvers such as these posed grave dangers because they not only lent themselves to outside meddling but eventually carved out jurisdictional zones outside of beylical or Islamic justice. However, this strategy was gendered; residence at a foreign consulate was normally not an option for Muslim city women, unless they were slaves or ex-slaves, since to harbor these women would dishonor their kin. In some cases, women who had taken asylum in consulates were delivered over to a shrine *(zawiya)* in Tunis for safe haven until matters could be sorted out. This is what occurred in 1879 when a "negress by the name of Halima bint Aly el Bernaouy [sic] belonging to Sidi Haydar has fled to the consulate. I have sent her to the zawia [sic] until you kindly procure for me her manumission papers."[43]

The most popular places of sanctuary were shrines, which had an ancient pedigree in North Africa; Tunis was densely peopled by saints and their tombs, with countless others scattered around the country. The tomb-shrines of holy persons, male and female, were universally regarded as spaces of *hurma* (holiness) where the sacred powers of the deceased or living saint trumped the state. In a sense, the saint's shrine constituted a jurisdictional blank space that did not so much resolve conflict as suspend it; when refuge seekers left its confines, they were fair game for pursuers. Muslim shrines afforded haven to subjects hounded by state authorities for taxes, by irate creditors seeking outstanding debts, by parties to a vendetta, or even to murderers pursued by the victim's family; as such, they were more or less democratic.[44]

However, some wily individuals set up house and even businesses within a shrine's sacred precinct, remaining there for weeks, even months at a time. In this way, long-term haven seekers dramatized their plight, turning it into a multi-act performance that ultimately threw the affair into the court of public moral opinion—or caused the aggrieved party to abandon hopes for justice. However, the extended-residence strategy generally favored natives, since a kin network was needed to supply provisions on a regular basis and bribe the guards posted outside the shrine. It is no small wonder that European consular authorities increasingly demanded an end to saintly neutrality, sacred extraterritoriality, for wrongdoers.[45] Seeking asylum in a shrine or sanctuary, assisting in person at the Bardo's hall of justice sessions, or designating an agent *(wakil)* to represent one's case were options open to some, but not all—what other avenues were available for redress?

A discursive expression of forum shopping was the petition soliciting assistance from the bey or powerful court figures; at times this was used by non-subjects to do end runs around their own consuls. Subjects and nonsubjects made good use of the pen to file *shikayat* (complaints) but, needless to say, those who were literate or could afford the services of a *katib* (professional letter writer) benefited most. Foreign nationals petitioned the Tunisian ruler or members of the court to get a better deal than that offered by their representatives. The beyli-cal archives contain abundant complaint literature claiming that justice had not been served in other legal forums and/or seeking favors. Resident Europeans petitioned the Tunisian state for resolution of conflicts, employment, donations to charities, or assistance with housing or rental disputes. In parallel fashion, beylical subjects increasingly turned to European consuls for momentary succor or degrees of informal, and increasingly, formal legal protection.

Letters from European residents contained in these records, titled *"shakayat mukhtalifa min al-ra'iya al-ifranjiya"* (diverse complaints from foreign Christian subjects), were at times directed to the ruler or his entourage without initially going through a diplomatic or other kind of intermediary; at others, a petitioner sought to counter a previous consular decision at variance with the hoped-for outcome.[46] Not all petitions addressed directly to the Husaynid political elite constituted forum shopping. Because the palace controlled scarce resources, peti-tioners also appealed to the beys for favors that only they could dispense.

Since trade has historically constituted one of the principal vectors of legal pluralism, commerce, business partnerships, and especially credit operations ensnared city inhabitants in financial relationships that often turned sour or worse. A major source of social strife was debt, which often demanded both beylical and consular intervention. Creditors worried that debtors would slip away to other ports, a frequent occurrence. One preventative measure was to confiscate travel papers until the debt was repaid or until a third party guaranteed the outstanding obligation.[47] However, the single most critical consular function was determining the legitimacy of claims for protection, which also necessitated counting people and keeping tabs on their whereabouts; heightened immigration, together with other factors, rendered this a daunting enterprise from midcentury on.

PASSPORTS, PAPERS, AND IDENTITIES
IN AN INCREASINGLY MOBILE WORLD

What mechanisms were deployed to calculate the numbers of protégés as well as certify identity and therefore the right of protection? First, counting: In July 1844, London demanded that the consulate in Tunis provide statistics; significantly, it took a year and a half to comply. The 1847 "Return of the Number of Maltese and other Subjects under British Protection in the Regency of Tunis" stated that "the number of persons who *appear* [emphasis added] enrolled as British protected subjects . . . amount to 5,800. I beg to observe to your Lordship that the number of these Subjects continues annually to increase, there having been 257 fresh arrivals, and only 73 departures registered during the year."[48] In the appended table were listed 3,020 Maltese, including women and children in Tunis and La Goulette; 160 Ionian Greeks; 38 natives of Great Britain, Gibraltar, and elsewhere; to which were added 1,082 Maltese and others outside of the capital, for a grand total of 4,300. But here a caveat was issued: "Add probable number unregistered about one third" more, bringing the total to somewhere around 5,800. Next year's report in 1848 showed an estimated total of 6,100 but, for the first time, the consul broke down the Maltese subjects of Tunis into categories: 2,139 men; 745 women; and 1,046 children.[49]

These figures, however inexact, demonstrate that registered males outnumbered females at a ratio of nearly 3 to 1, a demographic pattern characterizing initial stages in migratory movements and settlement worldwide. Nevertheless, moving about was increasingly becoming a family affair, and the floating populations of Tunis—whether Maltese or not—counted domestic units in addition to bachelors. Providing home governments with statistics of certain imprecision and uncertain value was directly related to another task that demanded considerable time, "indorsing [sic] and filling up passports."[50]

A duty of increasing import was certifying legal personhood by verifying the identity of presumed nationals or protégés. This act, at least theoretically, established the legitimacy of other functions: collecting fines or outstanding debts, incarcerating unruly or criminal protégés in a local prison, issuing expulsion decrees or repatriation orders, and so forth. The nineteenth century witnessed a dramatic expansion in the state's repertoire of coercive methods for ensuring governance over populations and resources—both within, and outside of, national or imperial frontiers. Enter the passport or something like it. As an instrument of identification, the passport underwent rapid change as political elités around the Mediterranean, indeed around the globe, sought to firmly attach some people to stable, decipherable spaces for a wide range of purposes—surveillance, military conscription, punishment, and labor extraction—while relegating others to a legal wilderness. One need only think of the 1915 Native Registration Ordinance in British-ruled East Africa mandating that all native males over sixteen years old carry passports or suffer the legal consequences.

One objective was to rein in the border crossers or, more to the point, the border straddlers, those whose legal identity could not be pinned down with accuracy. In 1830, when warfare between Tunisia and Sardinia appeared imminent, the Sardinian consul, Filippi, presented twenty-one grievances to the ruler, principally economic in nature. However, several jurisdictional matters were at stake—particularly the status of the "brothers Gianni" resident in Tunis because "it was not clearly and explicitly understood whether the brothers were Sardinians or Tuniseen subjects."[51] The Gianni brothers' questionable status represented a common feature of the older Mediterranean system, particularly during the corsair centuries when renegades and others had switched political allegiance and religious affiliation to improve their lot in life or in response to situational contingencies. However, after 1830, governments sought to fix national and thus jurisdictional lines more firmly.

Responding to London's request for information on how papers were issued to subjects residing in Tunis, Reade offered a frank assessment in 1831 of the tribulations posed by delivering passports to the largest community of British protégés, the Maltese. Significantly, he stated that he followed the system already in place, which required an application process, although passports were virtually gratis because "nearly the whole which are applied for [are] by the poor Maltese, who are unable to pay anything for them. They usually come to this Place quite destitute, and the little they are enabled to gain is but calculated to meet their customary expenses, added to which they are so much addicted to moving about that they seldom or ever remain here more than a few months so that when they leave it [Tunis], they possess but little money." However, ships and ships' masters were another matter, since "the masters of the merchant vessels are the only persons from Malta who could afford to pay for them [passports] but they do not require any, having always the customary ships' papers issued upon their departure, for which they are charged and for which I give audit in my contingent account."[52]

Reade's successor, Louis Ferriere, pressed the home government in 1847 for permission to levy passport fees upon the Maltese who "after a few years residence in Tunis frequently return to their country with little fortunes"; all other consulates demanded fees by this time, even the British consulate in Algiers.[53] Ferriere followed the consular crowd by imitating procedures in force among other nations, although British regulations varied significantly from port to port, something of which London seemed blissfully unaware. And if some protégés did return home to Malta with "little fortunes," what were the consequences of imposing fees upon those lacking the means to pay, the case for the vast majority of Maltese? Such a policy may have encouraged emigration to other Mediterranean ports where fees were not charged or may have discouraged the Maltese in Tunis from even going to the consulate, undermining consular control over its protégés. Ferriere's disparaging assessment of his most numerous protégés echoed the sentiments held by most European consular officials vis-à-vis nonnationals under their protection, especially those from Mediterranean islands, illuminating the fraught relationships between protected and protector.

In Tunis, the consulate rarely granted passports to "any other but British subjects," although, according to Reade, on occasion "Moors" had applied. In these cases, passports were arranged for North Africans who had "been of service to the British interests, such as giving me [i.e., Reade] *information* [emphasis added] at times when I could not obtain it from any but Moors."[54] In the prior six years, only "three or four Moors" had been thus rewarded, according to the consul. As always, the imprecise term "Moor" could mean many things, but a close reading of the documents implies that Tunisians in the capital were probably the beneficiaries of the consul's calculated diplomatic largesse. Here is a key aside about the recruitment of native informants that constitutes an unusually frank admission of consulate spying operations as well as of protection extended to Muslim Tunisians (or North Africans) for covert activities. Unclear are the terms of the protection thus extended as a reward for information gathering. Was it temporary? What did the passports granted to the Moors mean in practice? And what kinds of jurisdictional tangles might later emerge from this concession? How did this practice relate to the older tradition of furnishing letters of introduction for "respectable travelers" bound for other Mediterranean ports (which, however, distinguished them from bone fide protégés)?

Europeans without permanent representation were at times furnished with British passports, although infrequently, since most middle-class travelers arrived with some sort of papers in hand. In those few instances when a British passport was accorded to a European nonnational, Reade recorded "the nation to which the bearer belonged" in the document; the bearer was informed that "the passport itself gives them no advantages, except probably in some measure it causes more respect to be shown to them than would otherwise be the case."[55] The mention of "respect" is critical because it shows that these letters guaranteed to a third party the bearer's social-moral qualities. Other consulates in Tunis granted passports and/or letters according to the same principle—as far as can be ascertained. And the Tunisian state issued passports to its subjects traveling to other parts of the Mediterranean. Ahmad Bey's consular agent in Malta, Antonio Farrugia, furnished a Tunisian Jew, Haim, with a passport in 1844 so that he could conduct business in Messina, Sicily. And the beys routinely furnished Tunisian ships and captains with letters of protection.[56] In the older Mediterranean culture of trade and travel, letters certifying protection, personal recommendations, or attestations of the bearer's worthiness overlapped to a degree. These documentary attestations were not always appreciated; a Swiss officer who had served the king of the Two Sicilies sarcastically observed that in Tunis they were akin to the letters of good conduct furnished to domestics leaving service to search for work elsewhere.[57] Ways of monitoring people in motion, however, were on the cusp of change as mechanisms for fixing identity merged, if unevenly, with newer instruments that authenticated protégé status and conveyed jurisdiction. Yet the correspondence between London and Tunis demonstrates how little imperial centers apparently knew, understood, or cared about consular procedures, at least in some places.

In contrast to the birth of the modern census, whose genealogy is fairly linear, the passport had hybrid origins. Slave systems historically employed physical markings to designate as property enslaved persons, whose bodies served as a kind of corporeal identity card. Related to this, the forced transfer of "free" labor from one end of Britain's vast empire to another distant corner played a role in the passport's emerging configuration. At the request of the East India Company in 1838, the British parliament passed the first passport legislation to organize the mass displacement of indentured South Asian laborers to areas suffering from worker shortages because of slavery's abolition. Written descriptions of physical "features" informed by racial thinking increasingly served as tracking devices for populations scattered across the globe by modern imperialism. If the British public had been adverse to the notion of a passport until the mid-nineteenth century, on the continent a passport system had been in place well before the French Revolution, mainly for policing internal displacements, in which physical traits played an important role.[58] Once again, as people moved about more widely, and particularly with the spectacular growth in travel by those from the popular classes, the urgency for a state-sanctioned system of uniform identity papers grew.

From the late 1840s on, states ringing the Mediterranean began to inventory unfortunates exiled to the sea on ships circulating from port to port. In the bureaucratic mind, physical description became more salient. The British government began keeping records of individuals who had fallen afoul of Ottoman law, consular justice, or both and thus were subject to expulsion in accordance with provisions of the order-in-council of June 19, 1844. Circulars were dispatched to British posts in port cities such as Tunis and Tripoli, or to islands like Rhodes, listing the names and crimes of "the following individuals [who] have been expelled from the Ottoman Dominions."[59] These circulars were intended

FROM PROTECTION TO PROTECTORATE 219

to identify unsavory characters who might seek to disembark in ports and claim protection.

The 1848 "List of British Maltese and Ionian Criminals Expelled from the Turkish Dominions" included columns listing name, nationality, age, height, hair description, particular marks, statement of crime, and observations. All on the list were males between the ages of twenty and thirty-three; twelve were from Malta, the rest from the Ionian Islands. Three categories for identifying *malfaiteurs*—height, hair, and eye color—do not appear particularly valuable: "rather small, tall, middle" described height, while hair and eyes were invariably characterized as "black." As for the men's crimes, these ranged from murder, stabbing, robbery, and breaking and entering to extortion, breach of the public peace, resisting arrest, and escape from prison. One offense arose from a domestic dispute; Carmelo Ventura, from Malta, was charged with "cutting and maiming his wife." Most intriguing are the descriptors contained under the heading "particular marks." Here physical, behavioral, and moral attributes were conflated: "loud voice," "gesticulates," "habit of biting upper lip," "dark color," "stout," "swarthy," "sallow complexion," and "sneaking appearance." Predictably, morally resonant hues—dark colors—were associated with individual depravity. Therefore, body markings, racial features, and reprehensible forms of behavior committed to writing marked protégés as criminals.[60]

WHO ARE YOU AND WHERE DO YOU BELONG?

Problems of disputed, shifting, or uncertain jurisdictions increasingly bedeviled the Husaynid state, European nations, and foreign representatives. This was also true for travelers or migrants uncertain about—or indifferent to—their "national" and thus legal status. A French officer in the 1850s portrayed one border crosser thus: "Allegro is somewhat French. This status appears to bother him slightly and I am uncertain whether he would, if it were possible, seek to become Tunisian once again."[61]

While never very numerous in Tunis, the Greeks were another growing community; their settlement was partially a result of the Ottoman-Greek Wars of the 1820s that sent waves of expatriates to North African port cities and the fact that from 1815 until 1864 the Ionian Islands were under the British Crown. Some Ionians claimed British protégé status; others placed themselves under the protection of France or Italy, while others sought Russian jurisdiction.[62] Because the new Greek state had not yet appointed a consul to Tunis, Reade stepped into the breach to extend protection to Greeks in 1835, informing London that they were "equally litigious and ungovernable as the Maltese and consequently cause an infinity of trouble to the consul general." The consul had failed to fully grasp jurisdictional complexities, since the foreign secretary demanded an explanation for extending protection to Greeks not under formal British rule: "Why so unless they be Ionians?"[63]

Churches, including the Greek Orthodox, must also be added to the mix of conflicting jurisdictions. Lines of jurisdiction between consular and ecclesiastical authorities remained unclear throughout the nineteenth century. In 1828, Astagio Casveriti, an Ionian subject, lodged a protest with the British consulate against the Greek priest in Tunis. The complaint alleged that the priest had drawn up a will for Casveriti's deceased brother that later proved invalid; Astagio was outraged and sought redress. The consul decided that the matter fell outside his purview because the will had been drawn up by church officials and therefore he referred it to the "proper [church] Tribunal at Zante" on the island of Zakinthos, which at that time might have been as much as nineteen sailing days from Tunis.[64] By turning to the British consul, Astagio had hoped for a more sympathetic forum and alternative legal remedy, one that was much closer to home.

What about travelers whose status was in doubt? In 1837 an intriguing ménage à trois arrived in La Goulette—a mysterious male named Miranda, accompanied by two unnamed women. Coming from Malta with English papers that identified him as Spanish, Miranda planned to settle in Tunisia but soon encountered intractable jurisdictional problems because neither the Spanish nor any other consul would certify him as a protégé. Malicious tongues in Tunis hinted that the women were not really his wife and sister-in-law, as Miranda claimed, but rather his two wives. "He appears to be an adventurer, it is said a Moroccan Jew. He and his wives are without any means of existence and have subsisted until now through handouts and charity . . . which are no longer provided them due to their bad behaviour."[65] When Pierre Gaspary, the French vice-consul in La Goulette, told them to get off the dole and find work, Miranda insulted Gaspary in a medley of languages and threatened to shoot him, which got all three newcomers incarcerated in a Tunisian facility until a consensus could be reached about their fate.

Expulsion offered the cleanest solution but a jurisdictional imbroglio arose. Since the threesome were not recognized protégés of any state, repatriation was not an option; and expulsion to Malta, where they had last been, often failed because simply returning to La Goulette on another ship was easy. After much deliberation, the Tunisian government and the consulates resolved the matter by dispatching Miranda and his women to Alexandria on a Tunisian vessel. Perhaps they would be welcome in Muhammad 'Ali's Egypt and would remain there. What is significant is that Tunisian authorities were obliged to put them in prison until their fate could be determined. Of course, given the nature of the sources, Miranda's voice is completely absent. He may have been a man without a country, but Miranda was by no means alone in the period.

Ship captains, crews, cargo, and passengers presented knotty jurisdictional issues. In March 1834, a Greek brig schooner, the *Sparta,* whose master was

Anastasio Ghirza, arrived in Tunis from Greece under British protection. Passengers and goods were disembarked without incident, but when Ghirza loaded up a human commodity—African slaves—for a run to Constantinople, the British consul intervened, informing the captain that the transport of slaves was prohibited. "He then was desirous of changing his protection from the British consulate to that of Russia, which I [i.e., Reade] likewise objected to, observing to him, that as he had originally taken the British Protection in Greece, he was bound to remain under that protection until his return home."[66] As noted earlier, Reade was a fervent abolitionist and, upon his arrival in Tunisia in 1825, had established regulations for the validation of ships' papers for vessels conveying Africans; only captains able to produce official documents certifying that the Africans had been emancipated were cleared. Of course, such actions were legally restricted to captains under British protection, who could, upon return to port of origin, switch to the protection of another nation less committed to abolition, such as Austria, something that Captain Ghirza may have subsequently done.

As is true today, protection was withdrawn for various reasons, normally after the commission of some illegal act. The previous chapter discussed the Corsican Nicola Manucci, who benefited from British protection because his father served as consular agent in Bizerte but whose penchant for gunpowder smuggling resulted in the revocation of his protégé status. An 1851 money scheme demonstrates similar jurisdictional messiness followed by revocation. The brazen counterfeiting of Tunisian state bank notes or coinage created enormous insolvency problems for the Husaynid treasury; however this faux money scheme involved unusual actors. Ahmad Bey himself accused two Europeans with counterfeiting piasters and lodged a complaint with the French consul. The first alleged culprit, Kratky, a Prussian lithographer, was employed by Abbé François Bourgade, founder of the first missionary schools, to publish teaching tracts. Kratky was under the jurisdiction of Sweden, which represented Prussians in Tunis. "The second individual is a tailor named Feder who while he benefitted [sic] of French protection is none the less a Prussian and therefore under the same jurisdiction as the lithographer."[67] Although Feder had been granted protection at one time or another, when push came to shove the French consul punted by maintaining that the tailor was a Prussian subject under Swedish jurisdiction, and thus was not his problem.

Aside from the Fassy children discussed in chapter 4, expatriate children receive only occasional mention in archival documents. Children's cases reveal the range of consular duties and the complexities posed by rendering justice in a port city that now included families as well as minors without kin. In 1853 Dr. Mansfield and his wife, both British subjects, adopted a child, Émile, abandoned by his French parents, and an orphan girl, Marie Dugue, about whom little else is known apart from the fact that Mrs. Mansfield claimed to be the girl's *tutriçe*, or legal guardian. Apparently, Émile's life with his adopted family did not go well. Mansfield later accused him of stealing two thousand piasters and demanded that the French consulate bring the young man to justice. But herein lay the conundrum. The adoption had been certified by a notarized act *(acte notorié)* as a private adoption, which did not meet the conditions of legal adoption under French law at the time.[68]

Which legal authorities should or could pursue the matter? In 1864, the status of the orphan girl, Marie, arose because the Mansfield couple could not produce authentic documents for her adoption. As for the wayward Émile, the French consul deferred a decision about his fate until the "Procureur Imperiale" in Tours could render an opinion. Until that time, "the young man can not leave Tunisia" and, should he be found guilty by the correctional tribunal, "he will be punished."[69] The practice of referring especially tortuous cases to tribunals or legal authorities outside of Tunisia—in Europe, Malta, or French Algeria—became increasingly common as the century wore on. (The case involving Marie and Émile raises another issue worthy of scholarly study—the fate of orphaned or abandoned children.)

Due to the emerging ethnic division of labor, employment disputes became routine because work sites frequently involved individuals under several jurisdictions. Typically, skilled laborers were Italians or Maltese hired for building grand structures—whether a new beylical palace or the British consul's villa in La Marsa. The construction of the Chapel of Saint Louis in Carthage was initiated in August 1840 under the auspices of the French consul but with generous support from Ahmad Bey. Cristofaro Falzon and Salvatore Borg, master Maltese masons, had been engaged to build an enclosure around the chapel, but relations with the French architect, Jourdain, deteriorated and a squabble broke out. After much wrangling, differences of opinion regarding employment contracts could not be solved locally and the matter was sent in 1842 to a court in Malta, for lack of alternatives.[70] By the 1860s, the courts in Malta handled some criminal matters originating outside the islands involving members of the Maltese diaspora, particularly homicide cases. After Vincenzo Azzopardi murdered Caterina Vella in 1867 on the island of Djerba, he was speedily dispatched to Malta, where he was tried and executed. While we do not know the outcome of the Mansfields' adoption woes or the quarrel at the chapel, the fact that cases were increasingly referred to tribunals outside of Tunisia because local justice was unable to resolve matters is significant. An already convoluted system of legal pluralism was becoming entangled in transnational jurisdictions.[71]

As the illustrations above suggest, protégé status was in practice quite murky. In conceptualizing how the system worked on the ground in daily life, it is more accurate to see consular protection as a continuum or range of options shot through at key intersections with holes, gaps, collisions, and dead ends rather than clearly delimited lines of legal authority. What kinds of coercive instruments did consular authorities have at their disposal for dealing with unruly or criminal protégés?

PUNISHMENTS, PRISONS, AND PRISONERS

Punishments ranged from fines and/or imprisonment, to expulsion, banishment, or deportation, although the porous nature of Tunisia's water frontiers, and the number of small boats moving between the islands and African coast, meant that physical exile was not an effective measure. The issue of prisons raises the important question of incarceration for expatriate nonsubjects, which has attracted no scholarly attention. In the early nineteenth century, few if any of the consulates had prisons as such, although consulates held persons accused of nonviolent crimes—petty thievery or nonpayment of debts—in short-term confinement. Some foreign consulates eventually established detention facilities, although this did not preclude looking to Tunisian penal authorities for assistance. And as seen in the case of Nicola, the drunken solider, ships served as temporary places of incarceration for those awaiting transportation elsewhere.

Tunisian facilities had existed for centuries, although the state penal reform of 1860 and Khayr al-Din's prison reforms of the 1870s modernized the system in accordance with European norms.[72] The main centers of incarceration before the 1870s were the *zandala* (or *zindala*) at the Bardo; the *karraka* in La Goulette; and a prison in the madina's Qasba district; later the police prison, the Dabtiya, was added. Originally a bagnio, the *karraka* had been transformed into a penitentiary for common-law prisoners condemned to forced labor. Chained in pairs with leg irons, inmates cleaned the streets of La Goulette or worked in the port. While the tasks were not terribly demanding, prison conditions—food, housing, and so forth—were deplorable. At times, a hundred men shared a single, large room; daily rations consisted of a bit of olive oil and several pieces of bread.[73]

When the need arose, the British consulate rented incarceration space in La Goulette from the Tunisian government, paying per head for each prisoner, the vast majority Maltese. There is mention of this practice in the sources from the late 1820s on; for example, in 1828 "two Maltese inebriated had a dispute in the streets with a Moor." This conduct landed them in a Tunisian prison where they "remained confined until the disturbance passed away."[74] In 1850, a fairly typical year, there were nine Maltese males incarcerated in the *karraka* for which the consul paid "143 piasters or 5 pounds sterling, 12 shillings and six pence" for the entire year.[75] Over a decade later, during the 1860s, another prison housed British prisoners in miserable conditions alongside convicted Tunisians, until pressure was brought to bear to separate the inmates according to nationality.[76] Incarceration served not only punitive functions but also social and political goals—to allow tempers to cool as memory of some egregious incident subsided, to get troublemakers off the streets, or to demonstrate to other consuls or the Tunisian government that a crime, infraction, misdeed, or moral breach was taken seriously. For certain offenses, bail could be posted if family or friends could come up with the money needed. Tavern keepers, who had ready cash on hand, frequently offered security for the accused so that they could be freed until trial, although this would clearly favor the better off.[77] But prisons served other purposes.

Harmful speech, slander, and malediction were considered perilous crimes because they provoked street fighting, which could quickly escalate, getting out of hand. A special category of injurious speech—blasphemy of Islam—carried the ultimate penalty, death, although the status of an alleged offender often determined the outcome. One fall evening in 1851, Vassali, a Maltese, and Lieutenant Romain, a former French officer who had probably fled Algerian battlefields for Tunisia, were returning from the port to town when they got into a verbal brawl with beylical guards at the state tobacco warehouse. Since it was dark, the guards probably suspected that the men intended to make off with some tobacco, much favored by smugglers, so they ordered Vassali and Romain to quit the premises. The Maltese excelled in the art of polyglot invective and so Vassali "made some observations in Arabic to the bey's officials [and] one of them fired with a gun upon the two and they were obliged to flee the scene and take a long detour in order to regain Tunis."[78] This is a fairly typical story found throughout the periods studied here, although its ending was happier than most such incidents, which frequently erupted in collective violence and physical harm. Curses landed people in jail where prison time defused—or so it was hoped—the social antagonisms created by public insults, usually to male honor.

Maledicta and vendetta were intimately intertwined; the fact that vendettas endured for years among the population of Tunis indicates the stability of an unstable population—much given to coming and going—since the memory of an offense experienced by a single community was transmitted over generations. For this reason, women accused of slanderous speech were rebuked by the British consul and instructed to hold their tongues because malicious gossip had a way of spiraling out of control, although it should be remembered that gossip was often defined as a female transgression. The daily logbook noted that "a dispute took place between a Maltese woman and the son of Busatilli, the Maltese, in consequence of some slanderous expressions used by the latter, the parties were reprimanded and recommended to live quietly." Again in 1830, it was tersely observed that "a dispute arose between two Maltese women when they were recommended to live more peacefully and as good neighbors."[79] Insults, no matter how petty, were experienced collectively and the keepers of the peace feared vendetta—which explains the rapidity with which consuls or beylical authorities intervened in seemingly petty personal matters. If moral persuasion or a short prison sentence failed to produce the desired result—the calming of clan or communal passions—expulsion was employed as a measure to avoid decades of urban violence triggered by vendetta. Indeed, a key component in the decision-making process regarding both imprisonment and transportation was the potential for a vendetta that, like family property, was inherited.

On All Saints' Day 1853, Joseph Balloti, a Roman subject and French protégé, was implicated in a murder committed by a Sardinian, Mugnaini, who killed a fellow subject, Agostino Livolsi. Depositions from three Sardinian witnesses, together with Balloti's interrogation, proved his innocence. Balloti had been incarcerated for twenty days until this finding, and at first the French consul deemed this adequate punishment for his role in the unfolding of events, which began as violent verbal sparring and ended in tragedy. Yet serving time brought neither liberty nor a wrong expunged because French law admitted *double punition,* so the consul decided that, "desiring all the same to avoid any new conflict between this individual [Balloti] and the family of the murdered victim, by prudence I sent him off on a ship."[80] Expulsion not only functioned as a substitute for imprisonment or as another kind of punishment but was the preferred solution because it was cheaper, faster, and forestalled—or merely delayed—future difficulties. One wonders if the hapless Balloti simply reappeared later on another ship.

Nevertheless, the fear of vendettas was surely manipulated by consular or imperial authorities for political purposes, revealing social prejudices. The British government justified its rule over the Ionian Islands in part due to the high level of "male interpersonal violence, exemplified by the ritualized knife duel so favored by Ionian plebians."[81]

FLOATING POPULATIONS, FLOATING PRISONS: EXPULSION AND DEPORTATION

In 1835, Thomas Reade noted, "The conduct of the Maltese I am sorry to say continues to be very bad . . . whenever [it] has been fully and fairly proved to me, that Maltese have committed depredations, I have always sent them away, so that the Bey can not say that their conduct has been entirely overlooked. At this moment, I am under the necessity of sending back eight who have been convicted of having broken open a British merchant's store and robbed property to a considerable amount, some of which however has been recovered."[82] For centuries, states looked to the Mediterranean as a maritime dumping ground and/or a vast makeshift prison for their unwelcome "foreigners," however defined by law or practice, or for punishing subjects by physical removal. Banishment, expulsion, deportation, and repatriation represented variant expressions of seaborne internment, and hopefully permanent exclusion, from a particular territory. But expulsion and repatriation were not equivalent, since expelling an undesirable did not necessarily result in forced return to the country of origin. The Husaynids routinely issued expulsion orders to purge the realm of undesirable subjects, above all, rebellious retainers. In 1837, Mustafa Bey decreed the exile of the disgraced courtier Qara Muhammad, who was imprisoned until a ship could carry him away to Egypt. Others were sent off to Istanbul.[83]

This appears to have been common practice; moreover, the traffic in exiles between Tunis and other Ottoman territories was two-way. A Tunisian delegation returned from the Porte in 1835 with a lavish decoration *(nishan)* for the new enthroned ruler, Mustafa Bey. But that was not all that delegation brought back from the heart of the empire; the sultan demanded that the Husaynids welcome one hundred individuals whose crimes warranted banishment from Istanbul. With an Ottoman warship in La Goulette, the ruler could scarcely refuse. However, after a few days, the exiled men pleaded for release, which the bey obliged by boarding them on ships willing to take them anywhere—so long as it was out of Tunisia.[84]

If one of the political services that the Porte expected from Tunis was to relieve the eastern reaches of the empire of unwanted persons, the beys used Egypt and Tripolitania in the same way that European states looked to North Africa as a social *poubelle*. The British consul contacted the Bardo in 1829 about an "Algerine Turk," who after an assassination attempt upon a Maltese protégé named Sorio had been sent to a Tunisian prison. Subsequently, Reade spied the Turk "at liberty in the market place" and demanded that the ruler either incarcerate him once more or hand him over to the local representative of the dey of Algiers. Instead, Husayn Bey took the easy way out—he ordered the Turk transported on a vessel bound for Alexandria.[85]

What about expulsions of foreign nationals that violated treaties and/or customary practices? In 1836, Mustafa Bey touched off an international incident when he expelled an entire community from his realm in December 1836, precipitating the boat-people crisis: "I am under the painful necessity to reporting to your lordship that HH [His Highness] the Bey has ordered from this Regency the whole of the Maltese population."[86] Genial by nature, Mustafa Bey's patience had been severely tried by years of mounting turmoil and violent crimes that street rumors blamed on the Maltese. Christmas of 1836 proved an especially tumultuous season. During the evening of December 27, a gang of Maltese broke into a Sicilian household and killed the master's son in revenge for a homicide the previous day:

[The Sicilian had] murdered a Maltese, and wounded another in a most dangerous manner, so much so that his life is despaired on, in one of the public streets without any reason whatever; and seeing that he was not arrested, but allowed to be concealed in his father's house [which] raised the lower class of Maltese to such a pitch of excitement, that they thus took the law into their own hands. They did not molest any other person, not even any of the Family [of the murdered Sicilian] but were determined to have revenge for the murder of their fellow countrymen, who was a universal favorite and greatly beloved of them.[87]

Had the Neapolitan consul arrested his protégé more quickly, the uproar would not have occurred, or so the British consul reasoned. This was too much. On December 28, 1836, the ruler gave the entire Maltese community three days to pack up and leave for good. As the aggrieved bey explained: "You must be aware of the insurrection of the Maltese in Tunis and how they have committed disorders and assassinations as if on a field of battle . . . to the point of creating turmoil in the city and these disorders have so shaken the inhabitants that they despair for the security of their persons and property . . . the Maltese arrive [in Tunis] without work or profession."[88]

For months that winter, the affair dragged on. Ships bearing Maltese passengers were not allowed to disembark them in La Goulette during January 1837, but later warships from Malta arrived to reinforce British insistence that expulsion violated the Anglo-Tunisian Treaty of 1751. Gunboat diplomacy forced the bey to partially relent by decreeing that only those Maltese without proven occupation or accused of crimes should be forcibly removed.[89] Finally, under immense pressure, Mustafa Bey rescinded the expulsion order after the British ambassador to the Porte complained to the grand vizier in Istanbul, who sent a letter to Tunis warning that "English merchants and subjects who are residing in Tunis must be protected and well treated."[90] As the sultan pointedly reminded the Husaynid prince, Istanbul regarded him as a subordinate, and the Capitulations trumped local justice. If street violence and vengeance had led to the expulsion order, international badgering blocked the removal of a population, many of whom were recent immigrants. This spared British officials the expense and bother of repatriating thousands to the already demographically saturated Maltese islands; more importantly, Mustafa Bey's humiliating treatment constituted a public pronouncement that no Muslim state could unilaterally expel European protected subjects or violate treaties. And the affair produced a rare show of amity between the French and British consuls, since the same fate might befall the increasingly numerous French Algerian subjects in the country.

Thus far we have mainly considered cases in which the sultans and beys banished their own subjects or fellow Muslims—in addition to the rare instance of a ruler attempting to rid the state of unwanted British protégés. What about the European consulates? Since at least the seventeenth century, expulsion figured in legal acts governing French nationals residing in Tunisia. Normally, the process took place in stages: attempts at moral persuasion, consultation, and, if all else failed, an administrative order by the country's elected head decreeing expulsion. Prior to the nineteenth century, the largely bourgeois members of the French nation were threatened with expulsion for three violations of ancien régime mercantilist legislation: contracting marriages without authorization, trading freely, and overstaying visas or continuing to reside in Tunisia beyond the time allotted. Those who flouted the rules were most often merchants "who had contracted close relations with indigenous notables" after spending many years in the country; they invariably pleaded that they could not leave Tunis until outstanding debts had been recovered or obligations paid off.[91] To avoid expulsion, which theoretically required immediate return to France, some acquired Husaynid protection, while others placed themselves under the jurisdiction of other European nations. These were precisely the kind of maneuvers that blurred lines of jurisdiction and belonging, thereby increasing the tangle of legal pluralism. Since the Maltese were the most numerous community during the early decades of the nineteenth century, not surprisingly they were subjected to expulsion most frequently.

In 1833, Reade noted that "a Maltese killed a Moor, and was immediately arrested by the Bey's authorities and carried to the prison at the Bardo. This circumstance created an amazing sensation in the Place and I have experienced an infinite deal of trouble and anxiety to get him [the Maltese] delivered to me. I embarked him immediately for Malta."[92] In the same period, two "Moors" were murdered on the highway by Neapolitans, who were arrested, delivered up to their consul, and expelled—to where is unknown. And the practice continued until the Protectorate, as correspondence exchanged between the Tunisian government and various consuls demonstrates. However, deportation and repatriation to country of origin encountered obstacles if national status was contested; even if a miscreant's jurisdiction was unambiguous, funds to pay for ship transportation were frequently lacking. Women's expulsion and repatriation was particularly delicate because consuls took it upon themselves to arrange for supervisory bodies or institutions—convents, families, and so on—to guarantee morality once the woman had reached her country of origin. This appears to have been standard practice, since it transpired in other North African port cities. In 1858 the British consul in Algiers reported that "Mary Gatt, the wife of a Maltese, was this day forwarded to the care of Her M consul at Marseilles to be forwarded to Malta."[93] However, the physical removal of delinquent protégés or nationals was not only limited by available resources but also by the local play of politics at any given moment. For women accused of sexual misconduct whose presence proved an embarrassment or worse, moral persuasion was the preferred course of action for both the consuls and the Husaynid state, since it allowed officials to quietly send off females who had defied patriarchal authority.[94] The same situation obtained across the border.

Colonial officials in Algeria became increasingly intolerant of vagrants, indigents, or others who might burden the country's inadequate social welfare and penal systems; some Tunisian subjects ended up in colonial institutions. In 1846 Mahmud ibn Shaqru was forcibly expelled from Bône because he was judged insane. In the words of the officer issuing the order: "I inform you that by the boat that is carrying this missive I have deported Mahmoud ben Chaqru [sic], a Tunisian subject, whose state of *fou furieux* [violent insanity] forced me to shut him up in the prisons of Bône. I ask that this poor unfortunate man be treated with the kind of consideration that his unhappy state warrants."[95] What is interesting here is that Mahmud was able to establish that he was a subject of the bey—despite his state of madness. Finally, French colonial authorities routinely expelled, or refused to allow back into Algeria, a wide range of Europeans, many of whom later turned up in Tunisia.

Various types of shoveling out were universal methods of internal moral cleansing as well as border controls that increased during the century under the weight of heightened population displacements. Yet expulsion varied considerably in time, place, and with social class; those without adequate fortune or "vagabonds" were the most likely to be sent packing. Since poverty was criminalized in this period, whole families resident in Tunisia lived under the threat of forcible removal if they proved without the means to lead decent lives. But there were other reasons for being forced out.

CRIMES OF THE HEART: CONVERSION

While women appealed to their own religious or consular courts, and Husaynid subjects sought redress from the beys, they did so less frequently than men, which made alternative mechanisms more important.[96] Consular justice varied according to age, social class, nationality, and above all, gender; in consequence, opportunities for manipulating the system of protections as well as sanctions or punishment varied considerably. As legal minors, women were presumed under the same national or imperial protection as husbands or male heads of household, although divorce, abandonment, and widowhood complicated matters. Indeed, the single most contentious issue for European expatriates in Ottoman lands was the issue of female residence. Widows who elected to remain in port cities after their husbands' death had long been singled out as especially problematic, although this changed as the immigrant population of Tunis grew.[97] Among the most commonly employed strategies for getting a better deal, avoiding retribution, or merely improving one's situation was switching protection, an option available principally to men.

Although it held enormous repercussions potentially reaching far beyond the borders of Tunisia, one avenue for changing status was open to expatriate women—conversion from Christianity to Islam, which represented "a ritualized form of border crossing."[98] Yet it was much more. Conversion was tantamount to migration, a sort of physical displacement—leaving home in the legal and sociocultural sense. Converts also normally abandoned their birth communities. Conversion triggered the play of jurisdictional forces among Islamic, beylical, and consular authorities. It brought in the shari'a court since, according to Islamic law, the qadi had to provide written documentation that the conversion was entered into freely; the term employed was 'itinaq (from 'anaqa, "to embrace") or dakhala, "to enter" into Islam. In some cases, a convert to Islam changed his or her mind, despite the severe penalty for abandoning Islam—death—at least theoretically; however, in these cases, the beys and consuls often worked out covert arrangements for sending the convert-apostate outside of the county.[99] A highly complex issue, conversion must be thoroughly contextualized and historicized and cannot be fully explored here; rather it is analyzed as a form of border crossing open to some women for changing status and perhaps improving their life options.[100]

The scanty record on conversion assumes without question that embracing Islam did not entail an interior, spiritual transformation or commitment; there are resonances with earlier captivity narratives fixated on renegades "turning Turk" as well as with the nineteenth-century Orientalist discourse on harims. And conversion was gendered. For European men, for example, deserters from the French African army who fled to Tunisian court, embracing Islam was interpreted as a situational response to unfavorable circumstances or as a bid for promotion or both, although by then conversion was not a requisite for holding military or political office.[101]

In the case of female converts, it is presumed that the women were young, ignorant, orphans, or from socially dispossessed groups seeking advancement (or all of the above) or were members of elite harims—concubines, servants, or slaves whose masters had "pressured them to convert," although under Islamic law Muslim men may contract valid marriages with non-Muslim women.[102] This may well have been the case, but the documents are silent about other motivations. Scrutiny of the record shows that conversion sometimes began with a "crime of the heart," love with the wrong person, someone from "the other side" of the religious divide, which was universally seen as a serious moral lapse. Since the poorer communities of Tunis were not necessarily segregated but occupied the same city space, often the same housing units, the temptation to "fall for" a neighbor or a tradesman in the quarter's market who professed another religion was ever present. As importantly, conversion offered escape from an unhappy marriage, since divorce was impossible for Catholics and extremely difficult for other Christian women. Thus, it is hardly surprising that "the fear of conversion to Islam haunted the Catholic hierarchy in Tunis."[103]

For women in particular, "becoming Muslim" cast a family crisis or troubled union into the public arena, unleashing communal opprobrium that could spark sectarianism and violence. Abandoning the "faith of one's fathers" had a dangerously elevated performative value, not unlike a sensational homicide involving parties under different jurisdictions. And if, or when, a conversion developed into a citywide drama (which not all did), other forces—local political struggles or international diplomacy—could well determine the outcome. If violations of sexual norms tend to be occluded in the sources, women whose rebellions assumed the form of conversion were doubly excised from the record. While most documentation comes from the late nineteenth century, there is fragmentary evidence for earlier decades.

Some Christian women converted to Islam to escape cruel spouses or loveless marriages. In July 1830 a ship arrived from Smyrna with the wife of an Ionian Greek merchant, Demetri Apostolate, who resided in Tunis under British protection. When Apostolate went down to the port to claim his wife by producing the required disembarkation permit, he was informed by port authorities that she had been "sold as a Musulwoman," apparently to the local Algerian *wakil*. Apostolate immediately stormed off to the British consulate, demanding that officials intercede with the bey so that he could "regain possession of her." After much diplomatic negotiation, consular officials went to the Bardo to procure the Greek woman and restore her to the husband. However, an unpleasant surprise awaited them. "The Woman was at length forthcoming, and the Bey afforded every satisfaction, still the woman declared it was of her own free will she turned a Musulwoman and that she would know no other religion, and from her husband having deserted and ill-treated her, she would remain where she was [in Tunis] and would not return either to him or to her parents [back in Greece]."[104]

There was little the consul could (or wanted to) do and so, "as was the custom, he legalized the certificate of the Ionian Greek [Apostolate] stating the fact that his wife having voluntarily abandoned him, and turned Musulman."[105] For the Greek woman, conversion had terminated a marriage marred by maltreatment and, as importantly, enabled her to avoid forcible repatriation to her homeland where she would have been placed under the supervision of her birth family or in-laws. Moreover, her status as the spouse of the Algerian representative to Tunis spared her any further harassment by her ex-husband or his community. British willingness to accede to the Greek woman's wishes without prolonged diplomatic wrangling beckons us to consider the play of transnational forces at work in the summer of 1830. At that moment, the French invasion of Algiers was underway, unleashing a political firestorm around the Mediterranean. Since British officials in Tunis sought to wring maximum diplomatic benefit from the Husaynid government in this climate, they apparently decided not to intervene further.

Another conversion eight years later posed more complex problems. In 1838, a fifteen-year-old Maltese girl, Grazia Abela, abandoned her husband for a Tunisian Muslim and publicly made known that she had converted to Islam. Whether she did so out of passion for her new love or to escape an unhappy marriage or both is uncertain. The Maltese community reacted violently to Grazia's "betrayal" and pressured the British consulate to make formal demands to Ahmad Bey to hand her over to her husband. The next year, however, she upped the ante by claiming that conversion to Islam made her a subject of the bey; she was no longer under British protection. Grazia's motives for this strategic move are unstated in the record, which is entirely from the hand of consular officials. Clearly, she desired a total break from her husband and community. But significantly, she seems to have grasped how the jurisdictional game was played. At first, the bey demurred to intervene and force Grazia to abandon her Tunisian lover, but the ruler eventually caved in because Great Britain represented a valued ally against French and Ottoman encroachments in this critical moment in trans-Mediterranean politics. Grazia later had a change of heart—how or why is unknown—and sought to undo the damage, but it was too late. Explanations simply claimed that the young woman "regretted her conversion." Yet consular authorities did not reunite her with her Maltese husband still in Tunis—to whom they maintained she was "attached through the in-dissolvable bonds of marriage"—but rather forcibly removed her to Malta.[106]

These incidents, and others, triggered a flurry of correspondence between British officials in Tunis and London from 1839 until well into the 1860s. Crown lawyers submitted lengthy briefs on how conversion altered protection, legal status, and political allegiance as similar cases arose. It was determined that "a married woman whose husband still adheres to his allegiance to the British Crown, and continues to be a Christian, cannot by the change of her own religion, put off her allegiance, or exempt herself from the same liability to the jurisdiction of the British Consul to which her husband remains subject." Yet it was also decided that "Her Majesty's Consul at Tunis is not armed with any authority to prevent British subjects, whether male or female, from embracing the Mahometan or any other religion they may think proper to adopt."[107]

A conversion in 1865 by a Maltese widow, Maria Callus, was another "crime of the heart"—she had fallen in love with, and apparently wed, a Tunisian subject; and she converted to Islam, which once again was not a prerequisite for valid marriage, despite what the British consul claimed. Here the record is a bit meatier because new legal uncertainties arose over guardianship of minors. In November 1865, Richard Wood wrote directly to the bey to inform him that "a certain woman by the name of Maria Callus, a British subject, and widow of Paolo Sapian, also a British subject, has become a Mohammedan in order to marry a Tunisian subject. Being of age and consequently free to dispose of her person, her Majesty's consulate general does not pretend to interfere in her affairs. She has however four children, three girls and one boy by her deceased husband Paolo Sapian, who being minors are under the tutorship of their Uncle."[108]

Despite claims to the contrary, the British consulate brazenly interfered in family life by claiming legal tutorship over Maria's minor children—three girls and a boy—who, after her marriage to the unnamed Tunisian, resided together with their mother and stepfather in the newly formed conjugal unit. One justification offered was that the uncle-tutor lived in Malta—not terribly distant by this time—and not Tunisia. But the fundamental pretext marshaled was that "in consequence of the immorality of her conduct previous to her second marriage" she had forfeited her maternal rights; Maria's children became wards of British officials in Tunis. From the record, we can only speculate regarding what "immorality" entailed—cohabitation with her Muslim lover-then-husband prior to marriage? Or was this merely a slur to punish Maria for "going over to the other side"?

What is telling in the 1865 case is that Wood directly implicated Muhammad al-Sadiq Bey from the start by insisting that the ruler send the superintendent of police to seize the children. Moreover, the consul assumed legal guardianship of the children because they were the offspring of a woman judged immoral. Was the decision to remove the children taken to forestall the social, moral, and political embarrassment posed by a "mixed" family? We can only imagine the tearful scene at Maria's new household when the police and British dragoman came to take away her children. The story of Maria Callus encapsulates the dilemma of women, particularly of widows, who as "women without men" were deemed the most disruptive when they resided away from "home," where the social controls of extended kin, church, and state were attenuated. As Laura Tabili so aptly put it, "empire is the enemy of love."[109]

Thus far we have focused mainly upon Christian Mediterranean groups whose passage through, or settlement in, Tunisia generated policing and jurisdictional dilemmas. But movements out of Algeria—Muslims and Jews as well as European criminals, forced laborers, soldiers, and law-abiding folks—created enormous contention and long drawn-out negotiations over politicolegal identity. Algerian Muslim border crossers who claimed France's protection came to be regarded as deserters, if not apostates, from their own religious and cultural community.[110] This state of affairs persisted well into the Protectorate.

MORE BORDER CROSSERS: ALGERIANS IN TUNISIA

Léon Roches, the French consul recently stationed in Tunis, received a letter in 1858 from the vice-consul in Sousse requesting instructions regarding a certain Ahmad ibn Ahmad, whose situation appeared more complicated than most. Allegedly a former soldier in the eighth regiment of the *tirailleurs indigènes*,

Ahmad had settled near Sousse sometime prior to 1858. Local authorities had decided that, as a Muslim, he was a subject and they levied a hefty tax of thirty-six piasters on him. Hoping to avoid taxation by claiming French protection, Ahmad contacted the vice-consul, who proved decidedly less than helpful: "Since I have no information on this *indigène* who could be Algerian but who also could be Tunisian, and even from the village in which he lives now . . . [but] even if he had served in the [African] army, I can not say whether he is a French subject." Instead of a tax break, Ahmad, much to his chagrin, was ordered immediately to Tunis to regularize his situation by furnishing "all necessary papers to justify his protégé status."[111]

Some years later, Hajj 'Ali ibn Sharuf, originally from the Suf oases in southeastern Algeria, died in Tunis. In accordance with Islamic law, the administrator of the *bayt al-mal,* assuming the deceased was a Tunisian subject without heirs, went to his household in 1873 to inventory the property. Up stepped a fellow countryman, Shaykh al-Qasim, the Algerian *wakil* (overseer), who declared to the French consul that the deceased came from Algeria.[112] In this case, a Muslim whose honorific indicated that he had performed the hajj had settled in Tunisia, where he ended his days, and this provoked a property dispute. In the earlier affair, Ahmad claimed to have served under France's flag but only sought protection after vexations arose—which surely invited opprobrium from other Muslims. Ahmad, the soldier, and Hajj 'Ali epitomized the complex trajectories of those Algerians who left home for a new life.

There had always been a large Algerian community in Tunisia, many of them laborers from the oases. And Tunisians had ventured west, especially to Constantine, for trade, opportunity, marriage, or tax evasion; after 1830, some beylical subjects even enrolled in the French colonial army. Generally, French protection came into play with conflicts over debts, taxes, property, or inheritance or during criminal proceedings. Theoretically, the French consulate in Tunis was charged with protecting Algerian interests, providing justice, and overseeing matters related to civil status, which could mean ensuring that Islamic law was enforced. As in Algeria, cases governing marriage, divorce, and child custody or support were under local Maliki courts. For the Husaynid state, the Algerians engendered intractable political and moral dilemmas, tied to religion, and the imperative to protect fellow Muslims from persecution. The government became increasingly exasperated by their presence, which offered limitless opportunities for French interventions, often after a minor row got out of hand. Algerians in post-1830 Tunisia (or Morocco) faced choices that amounted to a Faustian bargain. Many Muslims seeking refuge in Tunisia did not claim French protégé status because it was interpreted negatively. Yet by refusing, or simply not claiming, France's protection, they became beylical subjects by default, subject to taxation and local justice, an unappealing prospect. Similar patterns can be observed in nineteenth-century Morocco, which welcomed numerous exiles, dissidents, or refugees, as did the eastern Ottoman Empire, most notably Greater Syria.[113]

In his 1847 report, Lieutenant Prax, a naval officer, amateur ethnographer of Saint-Simonian persuasions, and probably a spy, completed a detailed study of Algerians in Tunisia during an extended stay in the capital. He found that merchants, for the most part, considered themselves beylical subjects by virtue of religion. However, artisans and laborers fell under two jurisdictions, beylical and French. Prax's account contains valuable information regarding the older office of the *amin* in the post-1830 order: "Those Algerians under beylical protection are administered by an *amin*, al-Hajj Muhammad of Algiers [who] left Algiers for Tunis in 1840 after waiting 10 years for the French government in Algiers to indemnify him for buildings [belonging to him] destroyed to make way for public works . . . an Algerian who is a subject of the bey can only return to Algeria with the permission of the *amin* who procures a *teskéré* [permit] from the bey allowing the Algerian to return home."[114]

The Husaynid state had long controlled movements into and out of Tunisia, particularly by sea, requiring departing subjects and nonsubjects to obtain certificates attesting to freedom from debt. However, the practice of delivering permits to Algerians returning to their homeland appears to have been an innovation directly linked to increasing settlement. (Although, it may have been that French officials insisted at some point that the beys impose this regulation.) While many Algerians claimed beylical jurisdiction, "the most numerous were under French protection," at least according to Prax. "The Algerian who has a *teskéré*," wrote Prax, "presents himself to the French consulate in Tunis and the chancellery delivers to him a passport which costs 8 francs."[115]

FROM *TESKÉRÉ* TO *CARTE DE SÛRETÉ*

After escaping colonial rule through emigration, some Muslims and Jews in Tunis placed themselves more or less willingly under French protection, although the rules governing protégé status changed constantly in response to fresh arrivals and changes in the legal status of Algeria and Algerians, particularly the 1848 legislation making the colony an administrative part of France, the 1859 decree, the 1863 *sénatus-consulte,* and the 1870 Crémieux law conferring citizenship upon Algerian Jews, which raised new jurisdictional issues. As more and more people poured over the Tunisia-Algeria border, the task of French consular officials became complicated, for it was not easy to determine who could legitimately claim protection. Two main periods of experimentation can be detected: trial and error in both Tunisia and Algeria between 1830 and about 1850; and subsequent efforts to stabilize Algerian expatriate status by regularizing available instruments for determining identity in an era when migratory populations and processes were increasingly heterogeneous and thus resistant to uniformity.

One of the first mentions of a *carte de sûreté* for Algerians residing in Tunisia came in 1838 when French merchants in Tunis complained to the Chambre de Commerce in Marseilles about the fact that "200 blows of the *bastinado* were inflicted upon an Algerian by Tunisian authorities, despite the fact that the Algerian had been issued a *carte de sûreté* by the French consulate."[116] While the reasons for the beating were unspecified, they were most likely tied to tax evasion. By directly contacting Marseilles, the merchants went around the local French consul, suggesting to authorities in France that he was incompetent. And bringing the incident to the attention of the Chambre de Commerce internationalized the plight of Algerian expatriates. Most intriguing is the *carte de sûreté* itself: Was this more or less the same instrument that had evolved into an internal passport in France by this period? Or was it a French adaptation of the beylical *teskéré*, which had long existed and had been used for multiple purposes, including controlling the entry of foreign women into the country? Or was it a hybrid instrument—a combination of local Tunisian and consular procedures?

Algerians employed by the French consulate encountered hostile treatment as well. By 1855, Muhammad ibn Rabih, originally from Constantine, had resided in the Djerid oases for years as French vice-consul. Prior to leaving his country, he had obtained a French passport in Bône delivered on July 7, 1845; upon arrival in Tunis he deposited his passport with the consulate in 1846 in exchange for a *carte de sûreté*. For years, Rabih was harassed by local officials, perhaps because of rumors that he operated as a French spy; he even made the long journey to Tunis at some point to lodge a formal complaint. By 1855, his situation had become untenable; the qa'id had arrested him, seized his property, and dispatched him to the capital for imprisonment. Despite the consul's insistence that Rabih was a protégé, as confirmed by a passport and other papers, the bey maintained that he was a "Tunisian from the Jarid [Djerid]" and thus his subject.[117] This was not a propitious moment to argue the case of an (alleged) protégé, even one who had long worked for France. Ahmad Bey had just died in May 1855, and the war in the Crimea had not gone well for the Tunisian military contingent sent to aid the sultan.

Léon Roches, who had served in Algeria for years, arrived in July 1855 to assume the office of French consul general in Tunis. It was no coincidence that Roches immediately introduced modifications. The year 1854 marked the first time that French authorities in Algeria intervened directly and massively in Islamic law by attempting to establish a unified legal system; in 1859 colonial courts assumed appellate jurisdiction for decisions rendered by Islamic tribunals.[118] Roches sought to systematize the rules of the game by initiating a census of Algerians in Tunisia. All current as well as future protégés were to carry a *carte de sûrté* in Arabic, with the bearer's name, place of birth, and the date of inscription in the registers of the consulate. Physical characteristics were also part of the identification process. Moreover, "any Algerians who remain more than three years absent from Algeria or from another piece of French territory will no longer be considered a French subject," a rule that did not apply to those who had settled in Tunisia before 1855.[119] The matter of enforcement must be raised, since neither the Husaynid state nor colonial state commanded the resources necessary to police maritime and land borders or mobile tribal populations.

Algerian Jews under French protection faced reprisals from local religious and/or beylical officials, particularly when political tensions between France and Tunisia erupted. In 1851 the vice-consul in Sfax alerted the consulate about "the violent and arbitrary arrest of an Algerian Jew living in Sfax named Chaloum Botbal; the Qadi of Sfax . . . arrested Botbal and subjected him to corporal punishment as well as detention."[120] Since Botbal was a recognized protégé, this gross violation called for intervention by the bey himself to make amends. The status of indigenous (i.e., Arab) Jews, whether residing in Algeria or elsewhere, was later resolved at least legally by the 1870 Crémieux decree, although Algerian Jews in Tunisia endured endless ambiguities, conflicts, and heartbreak well into the Protectorate. Marriages between Algerian and Tunisian Jews residing in Tunisia under different jurisdictions presented some of the most intractable of the post-1881 legal questions.[121] (Not all Algerian Jews were mistreated; many emigrated to Tunisia to escape the viciously anti-Semitic European colons and colonial officials who initiated anti-Jewish riots in Algiers and elsewhere in 1897.)

Some cases involving Muslim protégés increasingly entangled French consular justice in Islamic jurisprudence governing personal status. "Deadbeat dads" behind on alimony and child support triggered proceedings in 1866 when a divorce dispute involving a Muslim, Hajj Sasi, born in Algeria but resident for sixteen years in Mahdiya, broke out. Hajj Sasi repudiated his Tunisian wife, who then brought a formal complaint against him with the qadi in Mahdiya "to obtain from her ex-husband money for her upkeep and her children. The public proceedings were quite stormy. "After a heated argument between the two ex-spouses, it was decided by the Qadi and agreed upon by the two parties to the conflict in the presence of our [i.e., French] janissary and witnesses—that our protégé, Sasi, was to pay 25 piasters per month to his abandoned family; he also rendered a 10 piaster advance. This affair took place publicly and above all, established the nationality [*nationalité*] of our subject [*administré*] who, satisfied, returned to his village, being advised to keep his engagement."[122] We do not know if Hajj Sasi adhered to his obligations or not. In many cases like this, the Algerians hailed from oases whose populations had a long tradition of seeking work or pursuing religious studies in Tunisia. Of paramount significance is the use of the term *nationalité*, then the object of intense legal and legislative debate in France.[123]

One morning in the spring of 1874, Zaynab, a female singer and head of a musical troupe with six other women that performed for wedding parties lasting well into the night, failed to return to her home in Munastir. Suspicion at once fell upon her ex-spouse, Hajj Muhammad ibn ʿAli Sca, who claimed French protection by virtue of a passport delivered in Bône in 1868 and stamped by the consulate in Tunis in 1869. According to Hajj Muhammad, he had been a sailor but subsequently settled in Munastir to work as an olive oil merchant. At some point between 1869 and 1874, he married and divorced Zaynab, who had a daughter, Amina, by a previous marriage. Zaynab's mysterious disappearance and the resulting investigation raised doubts about his story. Amina initiated proceedings against her ex-stepfather with the qadi of Munastir; her long deposition was recorded (in Arabic) by two notaries and included the names of the female musicians who performed with the missing Zaynab.

In the document, admitted as evidence in the consular inquiry, Amina accused Hajj Muhammad of seizing her mother's possessions prior to the divorce, murdering her as she returned home late that night, and concealing the body. Amina also implicated Hajj Muhammad's younger brother, al-Qasim, who was considered by local society a Tunisian subject native to Munastir. Both men were imprisoned while the investigation was pursued. While Hajj Muhammad maintained that he was innocent and the target of a "smear campaign," the town's inhabitants declared that he was "capable of doing what he had been accused of," and, like his brother, was originally from Munastir, not Algeria.[124]

Here our documentary trail runs dry; the outcome remains a matter of speculation. Nevertheless, the questions raised are important. Clearly Amina's mother abruptly went missing one night. As a wedding performer, Zaynab must have been well known and probably well loved, although female musicians often bore the social stigma of their trade. Yet public opinion made no mention of this but rather insisted that Hajj Muhammad's character was infamous enough for him to have committed a violent deed. Foreign protection held huge fiscal advantages for those in the olive oil trade, yet openly claiming it thoroughly antagonized fellow Muslims—until accusations of murder made such a move expedient. Was Zaynab's ex-husband indeed a murderer or was he the victim of character assassination as he claimed? Was Hajj Muhammad really a French subject, and what about his brother? If Muhammad's papers were forged, what does this tell us about the social response to bureaucratic efforts to fix identity, determine jurisdictions, and bring justice to mobile populations?

With each regulation, enterprising individuals found ways to contravene or manipulate the rapidly shifting rules of the game to advantage, at least momentarily, which prompted additional measures to count, catalogue, and stabilize people in motion. If these steps appeared to clarify the legal situation, at least in the administrative mind, false passports and papers circulated widely as immigration to Tunisia expanded, as shown by this 1860 missive from the French consul: "I received your letter in which you asked to know if Raphael Cato, born in Tunis, but carrying an Algerian passport, was considered a French subject. While this merchant is carrying an Algerian passport, he has never been considered such by the French consulate [in Tunis]."[125] A mere five years before the Protectorate, yet another attempt was made in 1876 to regularize the legal status of Algerian immigrants. Entitled "Proposed Convention to Grant Tunisian Naturalization to Algerian Immigrants," the plan came to naught. It was too complicated and perhaps too late.[126]

By the eve of colonialism, Algerian expatriates had become the target of collective social resentment, as is true of refugee populations worldwide today. Antipathy was expressed in multiple venues and ways. The European hospital established in 1868 admitted Europeans, Tunisians, and Algerians, although for the last two categories it is difficult at times to distinguish patients' origins solely by names. But the Muslim hospital, al-Sadiqi (later renamed the Maristan 'Aziza 'Uthmana), near the Dar al-Bey, was quite another matter. Its statutes specifically excluded Algerians because they "were considered as traitors to their religion and the exclusionary clause barred them indirectly" by explicitly stating that admission was limited to "only poor sick people originally from Tunisia."[127] In view of the constant to and fro between the two countries both before and after 1830, what did "originally from Tunisia" mean? Nevertheless, a new definition of what it meant to be Tunisian was emerging out of the legal chaos created by mobilities.

Some things, however, could not be resolved by forum shopping, alternative legal remedies, novel forms of governance, or compromise and in the long-term proved to be turning points. The older legal culture with its tradition of shared, if disputed, procedures and habits, was progressively undermined by the waning political fortunes of the Husaynids and Ottoman Empire, more muscular treaty making by European powers, the standardization of diplomacy, and intensified immigration.

FROM MURDER AND MAYHEM TO THE TANZIMAT, CONSTITUTION, AND REVOLT

Run-of-the-mill disputes laid bare jurisdictional gaps or contradictions, offering golden opportunities to manipulate legal boundaries to personal advantage. Criminal cases, theoretically subject to the clearest or the least disputable treaty provisions, provoked the greatest controversies, since interconfessional murders or homicides unleashed passions that turned into high-profile struggles that mobilized communities and at times European states and the Porte. Several cases jolted traditional arrangements: the 1843 Paolo Xuereb double murder, and the 1857 Batto Sfez execution that ultimately led to the Tunisian version of the

Tanzimat, the 'Ahd al-Aman (Fundamental Pact), followed by the 1861 constitution and the largest revolt in Tunisia's modern history.

For months, Tunis was spellbound by two brutal murders in December 1843; public sentiment became so frenzied that the ruler stationed his newly organized *nizami* army around the city. Most of the characters made an earlier appearance in chapter 5, on contraband, but this is how it all began. Together with two accomplices, Paolo Xuereb, recently arrived from Malta, killed a Tunisian, Yusuf ibn 'Abdallah, serving as British dragoman, and a fellow Maltese, Savirio Galia, during a heated dispute over Xuereb's smuggling activities. Ahmad Bey insisted on trying Xuereb for his subject's murder under Tunisian law, which was permitted by treaty. The British consul was in agreement because he believed that justice for the victims could only be assured in a local court, not in Malta. Even if judges in Valletta would consider the case, uncertainties over admissible evidence impeded justice because the courts were not always "empowered to take cognizance [sic] of crime committed in this Regency by the admission of written evidence taken upon affidavit before the consul."[128] And London supported Thomas Reade's position.

At first, the three men were held in the British consulate in Tunis, but by March 1844 they were delivered to beylical authorities for incarceration in the La Goulette prison, since street unrest had broken out in Tunis. The collective fury of the Maltese and other Europeans over the change in jurisdiction introduced a novelty into the city's political culture. Pamphlets, broadsheets, and placards, mainly written in Italian, were circulated and pasted on walls, vilifying the British consul for placing the accused under local law. A virulent anti-Reade campaign was organized in Malta; the controversy soon involved all foreign consulates, particularly once arrangements for trial got underway in March 1844. The French consul played the religious card by claiming that, since the three men were Catholic and France represented the Holy See to Tunisia, they were under his protection; Pierre Gaspary noted that "two Maltese came to see me asking me to intercede on behalf of three Maltese who are in jail here in La Goulette prison and have been abandoned by the English consul to the justice of the bey; they have been condemned to death . . . they seek French justice by the fact that the three condemned men are Catholic."[129]

By all standards, Tunisian legal authorities conducted the trial in a thorough and judicious manner. After months of consular infighting, protests, and shiploads of dispatches between London, Paris, Tunis, and Malta, on June 5, 1844, Paolo Xuereb was executed by strangulation, the customary sentence for murder. Nevertheless, Ahmad Bey granted a six-week stay of execution after the guilty verdict was rendered in a vain attempt to arrange for blood money as compensation instead of the death penalty, an offer rejected by the family. The murder, trial, and execution that roiled expatriate communities bring together the many facets of legal pluralism examined in this chapter: attempts to switch jurisdiction based upon religious affiliation; how beylical and European justice operated in tandem—if circumstances permitted; the potency of consular politics; and the weight of public opinion not only within Tunisia but also in the central Mediterranean corridor, which increasingly intersected with imperial projects in Europe. But most significantly, the pandemonium created by the Xuereb affair caused Husaynid rulers to resist pressures from Istanbul and the Great Powers to implement Tanzimat reforms, as they had the 1838 Anglo-Ottoman Commercial Convention, for a while.

From 1839 on, the Ottoman Empire embarked on a series of administrative, political, and legal reforms. The first Tanzimat decree of 1839—the imperial rescript, Hatt-i Sharif of Gülhane, which inaugurated the Tanzimat era (1839–1876)—reordered legal relations between the sultan's diverse subjects, but Ahmad Bey politely but firmly refused to comply; a second set of decrees in 1856 expanded upon the earlier reforms. His successor finally acquiesced after France and Great Britain relentlessly badgered Muhammad Bey because of an unfortunate case of negligent homicide in 1857. This time the uproar was over a Tunisian Jewish subject, Batto Sfez, who had accidentally killed a Muslim child while driving his cart through the crowded streets of Tunis. In the quarrel that ensued, Sfez was charged with publicly blaspheming Islam, an act punishable by death. Condemned and executed, Sfez became a cause célèbre for Léon Roches and his British counterpart, Richard Wood, both of whom presented the ruler with directives for far-reaching judicial and economic changes. When Muhammad Bey agreed to only part of the demands, a squadron of French warships put in to La Goulette in August 1857.[130]

The 1857 Fundamental Pact proclaimed the civil and religious equality of all subjects, made a commitment in the future to institute criminal and commercial legal codes consonant with European codes, abolished state monopolies, and established mixed courts for cases involving Europeans and beylical subjects. However, Muhammad Bey died in 1859 before these provisions could be implemented. With a good deal of prodding from Roches, Muhammad al-Sadiq Bey promulgated a constitution, drawn up by Khayr al-Din and his circle in 1861; one of its most important provisions was the right of foreign property ownership. As in the Ottoman heartlands, the declaration of legal equality between resident Europeans and indigenous subjects was greeted with dismay by many expatriates, who saw local consular jurisdiction as a "better deal," since it was more easily manipulated. In effect, European protégés desired that the older Capitulations be conjoined with some Tanzimat decrees to provide an even wider menu of legal remedies, options, and subterfuges. In the eyes of Muslim subjects, the proclamation of a constitution contradicted the cherished belief in the Quran as the sole source of law.[131]

As the Husaynid state's political and financial fortunes plummeted during the early 1860s, the government made rapacious fiscal demands upon its subjects and contracted a disastrous usurious loan in 1863 from Parisian bankers. Increasingly, indigenous dragomen, vice-consuls, and other "native" staff sought consular protection, which varied in degree and meaning but contributed to the tangle of jurisdictions, a phenomenon present throughout the Ottoman Empire and also in the Moroccan state.[132] In the spring of 1864, disquieting news reached Tunis about a tribal revolt in the border regions near Le Kef, led by a local figure, 'Ali ibn Ghadaham, who assumed the title of "bey of the umma" and demanded an end to the 1861 constitution. The long revolt and its ferocious suppression by the beylical army created the perfect financial storm that culminated in state bankruptcy to various European lenders in 1868–1869 and the establishment of the International Finance Commission. It was only a matter of time. In April 1881, as warships shelled Bizerte and Tabarka, a French army invaded from Algeria on the flimsiest of pretexts and arrived before the Husaynid palace in the Bardo by May 1881.[133] The constitution remained a dead letter.

While 'Ali Bey (r. 1882–1901) and Paul Cambon, France's first resident general, negotiated the terms of the La Marsa Convention that created the French Protectorate machinery during the spring of 1883, another international drama erupted in the same neighborhood. On the evening of March 11, a telegram was dispatched to the Ministry of War in Paris by a French officer stationed in the port: "This evening in La Goulette around 5:00, a drunken Italian came and urinated close to the guard house in front of the gate to the [French military] barracks. In accordance with rules, the guard ordered the man to retreat but instead, without any motive, he fell upon [the sentinel] beating him with his fists." After arresting the Italian, the sentinel sought to imprison him but, at that very moment, the Italian vice-consul magically appeared. Snatching the prisoner, he cried out, "I am the Italian consul. This is my man; he doesn't belong to you," and conducted him to the consulate.[134] The officer dutifully telegraphed Paris to inquire as to whether the Italian consul could legally be compelled to release the incontinent, drunken individual for imprisonment in La Goulette's French gendarmerie; the Franco-Italian struggle over Tunisia was being transformed into a cold war lasting well into the twentieth century.

FINAL VERDICTS

What long-term pattern can be teased out of our journey into order and disorder, justice and injustice, law and the lawless? In making sense of legal predicaments, such as those faced by Nicola Malinghoussy, the pope's soldier, several things emerge. First, in that specific case, the café patrons knew who was under the protection of which Great Power—or should have been—since they first appealed to the French vice-consul. This was a reasonable course of action; until Italian unification, France claimed Romans as protégés, although this had changed by 1871. But the La Goulette folks seem to have been unaware and followed an older script. In effect, protégé status operated in parallel fashion to class or religion by providing a map for locating individuals and rights within the context of multiple, layered displacements—sociodemographic, political, and legal. As understood by actors on the ground at a particular moment, protection at times trumped conventional categories of difference, while being shaped by them. Never static, protection functioned as a common language—in a city of Babel—for sorting, identifying, facing unfamiliar demands, and making one's way. For the vast majority of people, staking claims to one legal status or another demonstrates the instrumental nature of protection seeking as a means to an end. Interpreted from this vantage point, precolonial Tunisia underscores the need for more finely grained scholarly scrutiny of the floating and therefore contingent meanings for, and uses of, protection and protégé status over time and space.

The Tunisian case buttresses current scholarship that argues that the (alleged) inherent antagonisms dividing the Ottoman Empire and Muslim world from Europe are the product of selective memory—a denial of deep, abiding exchanges in many realms, including law.[135] Here the notion of a local legal culture is fundamental because that culture was constructed by the accumulation of *choices* about justice rather than only *rules* about justice, a critical distinction.[136] Local legal bodies and forums, together with the surrounding community, defined the permissible and impermissible and determined when and how to punish wrongdoers, whenever feasible. The growing cosmopolitanism of Tunis (and Alexandria, Beirut, and Istanbul, to name only a few) was both cause and consequence of the legal-political imbroglios unleashed by people on the move, who crossed borders as they called into existence new kinds of borders. The interconnections between legal pluralism and cosmopolitanism demand serious study because the latter represented something more than mere cultural and linguistic diversity, or the collective expressions of social difference that nevertheless allowed for living side by side, in a particular place. Whether some of these local ways of doing things were restricted to this particular African Mediterranean state and port city during the precolonial period is a comparative historical question worth posing.

Second, the endless stories of brawls—in streets, taverns, or cafés—begin to sound alike. The facts of a particular case, assembled by beylical and consular authorities, were inserted into a specific narrative envelope—in a manner reminiscent of "pardon tales"—and constitute a genre in terms of structure, sequence of events, and denouement. Local Tunisian and consular officials explained disorder by appeals to class—those guilty of disturbing the peace hailed from "the lower ranks," and they triggered outbreaks of *fitna* (social discord). Religious differences, while invoked as explanatory devices, did not always play a major role. When foul-mouthed invective or aggression transformed a minor fracas into urban unrest or even international causes célèbres, other causative elements must be considered. Daily struggles for increasingly scarce resources like work and housing, and meta-events such as famine, disease, and rebellion, all strained communal relations.

Many accounts appear curiously apolitical, although settlement in Tunis made it a highly politicized environment. As early as 1824, it was noted that "there are a good many Carbonari in Tunis who have been exiled from Naples, in consequence of their political opinions."[137] Immigrants were not only subsistence migrants but also members of Masonic lodges and/or of political groups of various stripes, including anarchists. Later on, a branch of the Mafia set up shop in Tunis, which the spectacular 1894 murder case involving three Sicilian mafiosi brought to public attention.[138] Nevertheless, investigations of a multinational fracas tend to ignore the possibility that ideologies embraced by parties to a conflict were at work.

This chapter also argues that consular jurisdiction entailed the policing of women and that "protection" and sexual supervision displayed a remarkable parallelism. While the consuls sometimes resisted demands by the Tunisian government to repatriate unruly male protégés, they responded with alacrity to charges of female sexual disorder. Men found guilty of violent crimes were most likely to be forcibly deported but so too were women accused of sexual transgressions, although persuasion was employed to convince "dangerous females" to leave voluntarily. Fearing charges of immoral conduct invariably leveled at their women, minority communities normally avoided actions that would call in outside authorities, which in turn poses the critical question of why communities delivered up their secrets at some times while jealously guarding them at others.

The legal armature of the modern nation-state was assembled by virtue of transnational, if piecemeal, processes, some of which occurred on the outermost margins of imperial formations. But cases from the present chapter (and others) show that issues of civil status, protection, and jurisdiction were debated far beyond the actual limits of empire—in an autonomous Muslim state. However much British consuls railed against their island protégés, Maltese males rarely presented jurisdictional uncertainty, unlike other expatriate groups such as the Greeks and Italians. When Maltese women converted to Islam, grave legal questions arose. If women and gender continue to be treated as somewhat inconsequential to constructions of modern global legal orders, the "crimes of the heart" committed by women like Grazia and Maria nudged at legal understandings of how civil status and religious affiliation figured into "national" belonging. That women of quite ordinary status, some unnamed in the sources, provoked legal controversies addressed by government lawyers at the heart of European empires should give us pause. Algerians settling in Tunisia after 1830 created another formidable gray zone where national and international law was made and unmade.

In *The French Melting Pot,* Gérard Noiriel argued that by the late nineteenth century "the identity paradigm was undergoing fundamental changes" as novel practices and procedures for marking foreign and foreigner, for legal inclusion or exclusion, crystallized in France.[139] How did French imperialism, settler colonialism, and population displacements in North Africa and the central Mediterranean corridor push at the emerging identity paradigm? First, the presence of one of the largest standing armies in Africa at the time, positioned just over the border, constituted the elephant in the room—a vector for wide-ranging upheavals within Tunisia. From the 1830s on, a steady stream of deserters from the African army introduced French military law into the mix of knotty legal quandaries facing beylical and consular authorities. But religion constituted the most vexing of all. The growing Algerian presence caused the beys and 'ulama' to see their right—indeed duty—to protect fellow Muslims in light of the unpleasant reality that thousands of resident protected colonial subjects invited outside intrusion.

Legal and political authorities in Algiers and Tunis devised classificatory schemes for expatriate Algerian subjects, even those not deemed criminal. Critical to incipient methods of identification were diverse kinds of passports as well as the beylical *teskéré* and *carte de sûrté.* Regulations, such as Léon Roches' 1855 administrative order on identity papers, did not prevent myriad cases of disputed Algerian origins, and thus of uncertain jurisdiction, which reoccurred before and long after 1881. The development of legal instruments for Algerians in diaspora suggests that a mix of laws were applied to, perhaps even fashioned in, refugee-receiving states, such as Tunisia and Morocco after 1830. Clearly, French law marking specific individuals and groups as subject to novel types of legal inclusion or exclusion occurred both within the metropole as well as outside it. For France, Algerian expatriates posed issues analogous in many ways to those confronting Great Britain and other imperial powers. In roughly the same period, physical attributes began to assume importance for European consuls in Mediterranean port cities as they sought to track nationals, protégés, and subjects, notably those accused of/or exiled for crimes. Did the category "Algerian" acquire a new legal armature and cultural meaning in precolonial Tunisia?

But wringing benefit from competing jurisdictions was by no means limited to Europeans; it became a game that two could play, even the colonized. The Tunisian writer and political activist Mahmud Bayram al-Tunisi (1893–1961) was born in Alexandria under British rule imposed in 1882. Al-Tunisi wielded a wickedly mordent pen and composed satirical tracts criticizing the Egyptian royal family for complicity with the colonizers. Because al-Tunisi was an expatriate colonial subject, he was under France's protection and the French consulate worked tirelessly to block efforts by Egyptian and British authorities to arrest the writer for his inflammatory prose.[140]

The flow of traffic out of Algeria was not only made up of Muslim or Jewish refugees, riff-raff, or the down-and-out—far from it. In the next chapter, we encounter the men of the cloth and virtuous women from new female Catholic missionary orders who showed up as well. The Sisters of Saint-Joseph de l'Apparition might be considered Catholic dissidents who chose to leave—or more precisely were expelled from—colonial Algeria by 1840. The impact of expulsion upon the order's growth in eastern Ottoman lands was a social fact whose importance cannot be overemphasized. Yet their missionary work in North Africa raises larger questions about the multiple and complex, as well as contradictory, relationships between religion and empire. What kinds of strategies, networks, and patronage allowed the Sisters of Saint-Joseph, founded by Emilie de Vialar, to flourish in a precolonial Muslim state? Why did Muslim princes receive into their realm foreign missionaries, educators, and do-gooders in an era of growing European interventions? And what does this tell us about relations between Islam and Christianity? How the founder and her small band of sisters even ventured to North Africa in the first place leads us to southwestern France just prior to 1830.

7

Muslim Princes and Trans-Mediterranean Missionaries

In 1850 an unusual event occurred in a city traumatized by the onset of a much-feared disease, cholera morbus. Ahmad Bey awarded the dynasty's highest decoration to Fidèle Sutter (1796–1881), the Holy See's *vicaire apostolique de Tunisie*, for invaluable medical assistance provided by female missionaries during the pandemic that reached the capital in December 1849 and wreaked havoc for years.[1] This outbreak carried off a good percentage of the population, notably the poor, as well as several nuns from the Sisters of Saint-Joseph de l'Apparition (hereafter SSJ).[2] A sort of Légion d'Honneur, the medal, called Nishan al-Iftikhar (the medal of glorious achievement), worth thousands of piasters, had only been bestowed upon one other missionary–Abbé François Bourgade in 1845—as it was normally reserved for court notables or visiting dignitaries. Indeed, the first foreigner to receive the *nishan* was King Louis Philippe's son, the Duc de Montpensier, during his tour of Tunisia.[3]

Again in 1856, Muhammad Bey accorded the same honor to the Capuchin vicar Anselme des Arcs for medical care during another cholera episode that claimed several more SSJ sisters, as they tended the sick irrespective of religion.[4] In the early years of the Protectorate, the *nishan* was directly conferred upon a female religious instead of through clerical intermediaries; it went to Sister Céleste Peyré for her years of teaching at the Sidi Saber School, the first girls' school in Tunis. But the most spectacular ceremony was the double award for Joséphine Daffis (1812–1894). In 1890 the seventy-eight-year old Daffis received the Légion d'Honneur from the hands of the *contrôleur civil* of Sousse and also the *nishan* for her work as teacher, doctor, and pharmacist.[5] This litany of awards to Catholic missionaries, some granted by a Muslim state, others by French

FIGURE 14. Catholic missionary school for Tunisian children, c. 1900. This postcard
shows a member of the order founded by Cardinal Lavigerie, the Soeurs Missionnaires
de Notre-Dame d'Afrique, or White Sisters, with female pupils from a handicrafts
school in Carthage. (Postcard, 1900; author's private collection.)

consuls or colonial officials, invites reflection concerning why and how different kinds of states, societies, and local communities concluded pacts with missionaries, particularly with women in transnational orders.

Founded by Emilie de Vialar (1797–1856), the SSJ initially worked in Algeria but subsequently was forced to relocate to Tunis, where a Muslim prince welcomed them. This chapter looks at the order in both Algeria and Tunisia to address two sets of interrelated issues: first, to understand missionaries as migrants in larger currents of trans-Mediterranean population movements during the long nineteenth century; and second, to explore relations between missionaries and a Muslim society in the precolonial and early colonial periods. Indigenous Christian minorities did not exist in Tunisia, as was true in Egypt or in eastern Ottoman lands, and thus the appearance of religious women in public and private had no local cultural counterpart. By viewing members of the SSJ as simultaneously migrants or travelers *and* missionaries, we can better grasp how they were transformed by multiple displacements across political or cultural boundaries. For nearly forty years, the SSJ was the only female congregation in Tunisia; it eased the path for later Catholic missions by providing models for organizing social work and daily life, for seeking patronage and recruiting students. In addition, Protestant and Jewish missionaries are considered here, including the "secular" Alliance Israélite Universelle, since different missions fed into one another. But this story must be inserted into a grander narrative of migrations across the Mediterranean as well as population exchanges between colonial Algeria and precolonial Tunisia. The chapter concludes with a brief consideration of how the decades-old relationship between the Husaynids and the Catholic teaching orders complicated the French Protectorate's application of the laws of separation, beginning in 1903.

How did banishment by clerical and French officialdom in Algeria, combined with acculturation to a largely Arab Muslim society *before colonialism,* shape the SSJ's work? Along these lines, how did missionary activity—Catholic, Protestant, or Jewish—influence migratory flows in the Mediterranean? On a broader level, how might an analysis of the local education that missionaries received in nineteenth-century Tunisia recast those missions as a decisive moment in North African history, not as yet another episode in European empire?

MISSIONARIES AND EMPIRES

Modern empires and missions have long been close, if acrimonious, traveling companions. In consequence, scholarly literature on the interplay between imperialism and missionary societies has seen a number of phases. In its first stage, the official transcript on missionaries depicted them as heroic bearers of Western civilization and Christianity. Yet the unofficial transcript generated by colonial officers, settlers, speculators, and merchant-barons frequently disparaged, or even attacked, those "doing God's work" as unwelcome troublemakers.[6] As empires were dismantled, revisionist scholarship for the most part demonized Christian missionaries of various stripes for complicity in imperial conquests and the exploitation of colonized peoples. The third wave of research emphasized the agency of the colonized vis-à-vis those peddling the Gospel, salvation, and European middle-class values.[7] The most recent work, often grounded in gender theory, argues that foreign missionaries were assimilated in varying degrees over time to the very cultures and societies targeted for sociocultural and spiritual transformation. And research on world regions where large-scale conversions occurred maintains that native converts suffered from a "false consciousness" when they embraced Western social norms, such as individualism or bourgeois family structures, yet remained racially inferior in new faith communities. Orwell's 1934 novel, *Burmese Days,* with its devastating portrait of how the Anglo-Anglicans treated local converts, revealed the ways in which conversion complicated not only hybrid colonial societies but also the conduct of empire.[8] Therefore, reading the vast archive generated by missions against the grain lays bare deep antagonisms between colonial powers and missions as well as fierce competition among missionary societies for followers, resources, and underwriters back in the metropoles.[9]

However, a distinction should be made between places like South Africa, with high conversion rates, and North Africa, where, with the exception of the Kabylia in eastern Algeria, conversions were relatively rare. Many missionaries operating in the nineteenth-century Maghrib did so with the knowledge that "saving" Muslims would not be easy, which determined how they went about their work and garnered support locally or back home. Another difference arises from the presence of Christian minorities in Muslim lands. In nineteenth-century Egypt, the ruler Muhammad 'Ali Pasha received petitions from the Coptic Church hierarchy demanding that Anglo-Protestant missionaries be proscribed from proselytizing because the Coptics feared losing members—an apprehension shared by Eastern churches in the Levant for good reasons. Therefore, comparative studies of transnational missionary activity in the nineteenth-century Ottoman Empire must take into account regions with indigenous Christian communities.[10]

Because of the historically tortured relationship between church and state in postrevolutionary France, scholarship on missionaries in the French Empire lags behind work on British colonies. Currently, women's history and gender theory have reinvigorated research into France's empire and awakened interest in Catholicism *d'outre-mer.* One fact that has not received due attention in migration or missionary studies is a somewhat astonishing statistic. In the nineteenth century, thousands of women in French Catholic orders numbering over forty congregations fanned out across the continents; some, perhaps many, of these female religious were not French nationals, an important point.[11] The relative weight of these female missions beckons us to think about the fact of women in motion, on journeys far from home frequently undertaken without male kin, guardians, or morality minders. Indeed, the substantial hagiographic literature reconstructing Vialar's life reads like a logbook of trans-Mediterranean travels. Because of this, her detractors, of which there were many, portrayed her as a woman overly fond of traveling.[12] But do the sources allow us to shift the perspective in order to view missions from the vantage point of Muslim North African societies?

THE PROBLEM OF SOURCES

Despite its potential contribution to the modern Maghrib's history, research on missionaries is not abundant. Even the canonical narrative of British-French-Italian rivalry over precolonial Tunisia fails to see missionaries and their schools as significant political actors—aside from references to figures such as Charles-Martial Lavigerie (1825–1892), archbishop of Algiers in 1866, founder of the Missionaries of Our Lady of Africa (Missionnaires de Notre-Dame d'Afrique; colloquially known as Pères Blancs, or White Fathers, because of their dress) and the Missionary Sisters of Our Lady of Africa (Soeurs Missionnaires de Notre-Dame d'Afrique; Soeurs Blanches, or White Sisters), and later cardinal of Carthage. As was true for the Mediterranean subsistence migrants who came, settled for generations, and departed with independence, Christian missions appealed to few historians until recently, aside from several scholars who were granted unusual access to local records still in Tunisia. The copious primary sources are not easily available to researchers in Tunis (which was my experience with the SSJ archives) or are difficult to locate, since some records were repatriated helter-skelter to France or Rome; others remain in situ but uncatalogued.[13] Predictably, mission accounts fall into the genre of highly stylized narratives of unparalleled virtue and spiritual heroism that elicited heartfelt appreciation for the orders' selfless work among North Africans. Ordinary people would have encountered missionaries in medical, charitable, or educational institutions, or in the streets, but there is little archival material extant (or *available*) on the nature of these encounters, on what they meant. However, the Tunisian state maintained correspondence with churches, missionaries, and, in some cases, with ecclesiastical authorities in Europe, the Holy See being a case in point. Another paper trail exists because the impecunious sisters ceaselessly petitioned the beys, court officials, creole notables, and European consuls for assistance. Nevertheless, the sources remain silent on a number of critical issues. But material culture, including clothing, offers some clues, however elusive. The personalities and social origins of the founders of female orders were crucial to their historical evolution.

FRENCH COLONIALISM AND FEMALE MISSIONARIES

Emilie de Vialar was educated and of independent means, and her class and upbringing had much to do with the SSJ's trajectory, although contingency played a not inconsiderable part. Born in Gaillac near Toulouse in 1797, Vialar descended from minor, somewhat suspect, provincial nobility; her maternal grandfather, Le Baron de Portal, had served as King Louis XVI's personal physician and, when he died in 1832, he left her a small fortune, 300,000 gold francs. By then Vialar, educated in Paris by the Sacré Coeur (Society of the Sacred Heart), was in her midthirties, showed no inclination to marry, and lived in her father's house in Gaillac. Extremely devout, and inspired by Catholic reform movements in Restoration France, Vialar had not intended to found an order of religious—and even less, a society of missionaries. Rather, she employed her inheritance to create a lay social welfare establishment (an "institute") in her hometown in 1833, which attracted young women yearning to devote their lives to the poor and imprisoned. The next year, she sought official recognition from the archbishop of Albi for what was rapidly becoming a novel type of female congregation—one without walls or cloisters but with vows, habits, and a rule comprised of fourteen articles, composed by the founder herself.[14]

Saving "infidel souls" in foreign lands was not Vialar's initial preoccupation; the turning point came when her younger brother, Augustin, sought adventure in Algeria soon after the conquest. In 1832 he organized an ambulance corps in Algiers, although whether he had previous medical training remains uncertain. After the July Monarchy resolved to retain Algeria in 1834, Augustin contacted his sister, imploring her to relocate temporarily to establish schools and hospitals in the capital, where a cholera epidemic raged as it did in some French ports. Vialar and three sisters—Heurette, Justine, and Julie—prepared to leave for Algiers via Marseilles in July 1835, but the disease had paralyzed the French city so they embarked from another port on the same ship as General Clauzel, which fortuitously provided an entrée to the highest military circles. Between 1835 and 1839, the SSJ created schools, hospitals, and orphanages in Algiers, Bône, and Constantine, largely financed by Vialar's personal fortune. In a sense, the women followed in the wake of the French army as it conquered eastern Algeria, devastating the land and people. The sisters dispensed social services to Muslim and Jewish communities as well as to the increasingly numerous and largely impoverished European civilians for whom the French military was unable or unwilling to provide.[15]

In the capital, colonial authorities begged the SSJ to assume responsibility for the civil hospital that was overwhelmed by cholera victims; the sisters created clinics outside of Algiers, including one specifically for Jews. Until 1836, the congregation had resided with Augustin, but Vialar began searching for a building to purchase. A temporary mission had become permanent. Since the French army had seized numerous homes and structures, Vialar acquired an immense house in the Qasba district perched above the capital. This greatly aided the congregation's expansion as more women came from France to work in the colony. The next year, the municipality turned the civil hospital over to the sisters, who numbered fourteen, and asked that they tend to the burgeoning prison population. In addition, home visits were organized for Muslim and Jewish families; before long, word of their activities spread to the ravaged countryside. From the Kabylia, a delegation of villagers arrived requesting medical assistance.[16] By 1840 the SSJ numbered about forty women; that year Vialar and several sisters made a first exploratory visit to Tunisia. She had only been in Tunis for three weeks when alarming letters from Algiers implored her to return immediately.[17]

EXPULSION, EXPANSION, AND IDENTITY

The SSJ's work had not met with universal approval—far from it. Soon after 1830, Masonic lodges in Algiers spread rumors that the sisters were proselytizing among the Jews and Muslims. Yet reproach came from an unexpected quarter. In 1837, the new bishop of Algiers, Antoine-Adolphe Dupuch, took up his office. That spring Vialar, several sisters, and Dupuch traveled through the Constantine region, where Vialar cured a powerful tribal chieftain from Biskra, "the serpent of the desert," who received daily medical treatments.[18] Threatened by Vialar's independent spirit and social class—not to mention her gender—Dupuch embarked on a campaign to undermine the SSJ's founder as well as the order itself in Algeria, France, and Rome. A principal grievance was Vialar's refusal to place her congregation directly under the bishop's authority. Moreover, Dupuch suspected that the SSJ's spiritual director, Abbé François Bourgade—on which more below—was advising Vialar to stand firm.[19] After a series of public disagreements between Vialar and Dupuch, the sisters were expelled from Algeria—one of the most extreme examples of antagonisms between male and female religious. In 1842 all SSJ educational and charitable houses were closed and Dupuch recruited the more compliant Filles de la Charité (Daughters of Charity) to replace them. In January 1843, Vialar was back in Algiers in a vain attempt to recover some of the personal funds expended during eight years of work; most of the sisters had returned to Gaillac—for a while. In 1845 Dupuch lost the bishopric due to his untoward behavior.[20]

This event—a double expulsion by a Catholic cleric and complicit colonial officials—constitutes an irony in the annals of the French Empire; the order retained a long-term memory of being forced out by "Christian" authorities. As late as 1938, a biography of Emilie de Vialar evoked once again expulsion; in his preface, Cardinal Pignatelli de Belmonte bitterly noted that "Algeria had banished her."[21]

The grievous experience of forced exile, and the traditions surrounding this defining moment in the order's early history, played a significant part, I would argue, in its sense of identity once in Tunisia. Indeed the collective memory of banishment persisted for over a century, if not longer. In an interview conducted in 2006 with two SSJ members at the mother house in Tunis, the sisters remarked on several occasions that the Muslims had always shown more appreciation than the French state or colonial officials.[22] Vialar's forced expatriation forms a leitmotif in her life story narrated as a tale of divinely inspired resolution and triumph in the face of great adversity, qualities that bore witness to spiritual worthiness for elevation to sainthood in 1951. Nevertheless, the role of contingency arises. Had the SSJ remained in Algeria, with its insatiable demand for nurses, teachers, and social welfare institutions, would the order have expanded as rapidly as it did across North Africa, the Mediterranean, and the Ottoman Empire? And if the founder's ship from Tunis to Rome had not been blown off course in 1845, forcing Vialar to spend weeks in Valletta, would Malta have figured so prominently in the congregation's movement eastward? Finally, that her personal finances were depleted by the time that she left Algeria proved critical to the order's subsequent trajectory and assimilation into Tunisia.

While Vialar's initial involvement in Algeria was serendipitous, deteriorating relations with Dupuch and the opening of a religious house in Tunis in 1840 were connected in her thinking; expansion across the border would intimidate her clerical adversary and serve as a backup for the precarious Algerian houses. Vialar characterized Tunisia as an "infidel land"—not least due to the alleged "irreligion" and moral laxity of its Mediterranean Catholic immigrants. But she also realized that its location was "as significant as Marseilles"—a port of entry to the eastern Mediterranean Basin.[23] Expulsion and relocation strategically positioned the order within easy reach of Malta, the next site for SSJ establishments. Mapping out Vialar's displacements, we find that she traveled extensively between Tunis and Malta, visited Rome in 1841, and journeyed as far east as Athens and Siros. While she never went to Jerusalem herself, a house was opened there in 1848.[24] In 1852 the order opened a second house in Marseilles, placing the SSJ squarely in one of the Mediterranean's busiest ports and the maritime center of the new French empire, which facilitated expansion east as well as to West Africa and the Americas.

Evolving into a primarily teaching and nursing congregation, the SSJ attracted numerous sisters, eventually ranking third in importance among French female orders. But this spiritual success story was part of larger processes at work in Europe and elsewhere. In the same period, lay Catholic organizations focused their energies upon the Ottoman Empire, particularly during the Crimean War, when a coterie of Parisian intellectuals founded in 1854 a society, Oeuvre des Écoles d'Orient, to promote schools and solicit funds to support French religious communities in the Near East. One of its ultimate objectives was to persuade Eastern Christians to return to Rome. By a singular happenstance, Lavigerie became involved with this movement while still in France, which aroused his interest in North Africa and induced him to accept the post of archbishop of Algiers in 1866.[25] However, his work differed markedly from the Oeuvre's mission in the Levant; in Algeria, the Church struggled to keep Catholics in the fold as well as to neutralize the ferocious anticlericalism of many colonial officials and European settlers.

THE CHURCH IN A MUSLIM LAND

The reception afforded the SSJ by Ahmad Bey was partially shaped by the Church's historical status in Tunisia. One major reason for its presence was the Mediterranean-wide traffic in human beings that marked the sixteenth to early nineteenth centuries. During the heyday of corsairing, the thirteen bagnios in the Tunis region held as many as eleven thousand captives; some had chapels overseen by Redemptionist orders, such as the Spanish Trinitarians. These orders were less concerned with social welfare or reform than with ransoming and redemption, interrelated tasks, since purchasing Christian slaves in a timely fashion decreased the temptation to convert to Islam. If ransom and return to Europe could not be arranged, the presence of clergy in the bagnios might dissuade enslaved Christians not "to turn Turk," or so it was reasoned. However, tensions colored relations among the principal orders in Tunis—Capuchins, Trinitarians, and Lazarists. The 1816 Exmouth expedition, France's 1830 occupation of Algeria, and the growing Italian expatriate community in Tunisia rendered relationships among the leading Catholic powers increasingly rancorous.[26]

As seen in chapter 3, substantial numbers of European slaves were attached to the palace as military personnel, retainers, or servants. Christian slaves in service to the Husyanids enjoyed access to a chapel in the Bardo palace complex, where priests ministered to the faithful and baptized children on Sundays. The chapel remained open until 1845 when presumably the organization of a new parish in the capital city rendered it obsolete. While a number of small chapels, some very ancient, were scattered around the country, two churches dated from the seventeenth century. The oldest was the Greek Orthodox, established in 1645 when the Patriarch of Alexandria recognized the community in Tunis. As Ottoman subjects, they were protected by the Husaynid rulers and were the beneficiaries of state largesse, including the donations of buildings for religious worship. Clergy named by Alexandria ministered to the faithful, whose numbers never reached more than several hundred in the period before the new orthodox church was erected in 1847 in the European quarter of the madina (the present-day edifice is located on Rue de Rome in what was once the colonial city).[27] In 1662, a Roman

Catholic church, the Church of Sainte-Croix, was established in the *"quartier franc."* Under France's protection, it was administered by monks, who registered births, marriages, and deaths as well as caring for the Saint Antoine graveyard dating to the seventeenth century. In 1833, Husayn Bey authorized the new Parish of Sainte-Croix, perhaps in gratitude for assistance rendered during an attempted coup in 1829 that endeared local clergy to the dynasty.[28] That year, Husayn Bey was taking the waters at his palace in Hammam Lif, serenely unaware of a seditious cabal hatched by some of his own soldiers. Unfortunately (or fortunately), the scheming soldiers frequented a tavern in the Qasba run by Luigi Sabetta, who overheard their plans to dethrone the bey by force. Sabetta immediately informed Père Alexandre di Massignano, who lived nearby, of the plot; the priest alerted the French consul, who in turn hurried to warn the ruler. After the rebels were executed or exiled, the bey not only handsomely rewarded Sabetta but also assumed a position of "great tolerance toward the Christian community."[29] In addition, saint veneration and miraculous cures accommodated spiritual traffic between Muslims and Christians—as for Muslims and Jews. When a statue of Saint Lucie in a chapel in Tunis cured a Husaynid family member of blindness sometime before 1816, the ruler ordered that oil lamps be kept burning night and day in front of the statue.[30]

At some point in the precolonial era, the pilgrimage of Notre Dame de Trapani became an annual event in La Goulette, attracting throngs of Sicilians and Maltese as well as Muslims, who sometimes participated out of reverence for the mother of Jesus. (Many Muslim women called upon Mary for succor and blessings during childbirth.)[31] Among the cultural phenomena that scandalized northern Europeans was the spiritual promiscuity of the Maghrib's religious communities—the fact that Jews and Muslims sought the blessings of powerful holy persons at shrines "belonging to" the other faith. That the baroque religiosity of Mediterranean Catholics offered a space for Muslims in popular street processions in the Virgin's honor proved once more that Maltese or Sicilians were *"de race Africaine."*

In 1833, the French consul, Deval, wrote to Husayn Bey regarding "daily increase in the Europeans who have come here to settle and whose numbers have for a long time now demonstrated the inadequacy of the building used for Catholic services which is in great need of enlargement."[32] The consul requested permission to build a new church either where the present establishment stood or within easy reach for the faithful. Given the number of petitions to repair or build Catholic buildings in Tunis or other towns, it seems that the civilizing mission was about keeping immigrants in the Church and ensuring that families acquired the rudiments of middle-class sobriety—all the more so because the temptation to embrace Islam was ever present. By 1850 six parishes were found throughout the country.[33]

The older orders had been exclusively male; the SSJ was the first female congregation active in North Africa. As was true of their predecessors, the sisters took a vow of poverty and, since Vialar's personal fortune was largely exhausted, soliciting donations for charitable work became essential for survival and demanded extensive networking with local notables or benefactors. Finally, the sisters' well-established practice of home visits, first developed in Algeria, was continued and thus they freely moved about the capital or in provincial cities and towns.

MUSLIM PRINCES AND CATHOLIC MISSIONS

Of the nineteenth-century rulers, Ahmad Bey proved the most solicitous toward the Church, perhaps because of his mother's influence. Catholic by birth, Francesca Rosso was captured as a young child, raised in the Husaynid inner circle, and married to Mustafa Bey, Ahmad's father, to whom she gave a number of children. As the prince's mother, Francesca was the most powerful woman in the realm. Referred to as the Sardinian by some members at court, Ahmad Bey frequently consulted his mother about affairs of state, sometimes before seeking the counsel of favorites. He even requested that she not veil when his ministers were present, since "she is my mother and yours."[34] On the eve of his departure for France in 1846, Ahmad sought his mother's blessing. During his state trip, the Tunisian ruler specifically asked to visit several churches and posed questions about the religious iconography and statuary. He maintained correspondence with Pope Pius IX regarding the protection accorded to churches and missionaries.[35] Nevertheless, Ahmad Bey's benevolent attitude was probably motivated as much by the redoubtable French army and navy in Algeria as it was by his mother's predilections—or those of favored courtiers, such as Count Raffo, a Catholic.

Yet the local clergy in Tunis did not hesitate to appeal to the bey for assistance. In January 1845, the "Christians of Tunis" petitioned the ruler through the intermediation of two priests about the shortage of city space to conduct Sunday services; and he received "two delegations of tujjar [merchants]" with a request for a more commodious building, which was granted.[36] During the cholera epidemic and resulting famine of 1851, the bey ordered the wakil al-rabita (official responsible for the city's food stores) to grant five-fifty qafiz of grain to the Catholic bishop for "disbursal among the [Christian] poor in Tunis" under his spiritual care.[37] And in July 1849, a Catholic burial procession wound through the streets. Laid to rest was Jean Matteo, born in 1759, who for forty-six years had served as a priest-slave in the bagnios; manumitted in 1816, he had remained in Tunis to tend to the flock. While funeral processions from the European quarter to the burial grounds had always been permitted, this one departed from past custom because the cross was prominently displayed in front of the cortege, which had not been allowed previously.

Yet currents of reform in the heart of the Ottoman Empire were also at work. The Husaynid political class followed events in Istanbul closely, particularly after the 1839 imperial rescript, Hatt-i Sharif of Gülhane, expanded the rights of subject religious minorities, followed by the 1856 decree. What is striking from a comparative historical perspective is that the streets of Ottoman-Mediterranean ports increasingly served as stages for Christian pageantry. In 1842, one of the first celebrations of Corpus Christi took place in Izmir, with Ottoman dignitaries in attendance and the display of a large cross. Scholars attribute these increasingly public performances to the Tanzimat, but the growing clout of European nations was decisive as well.[38] In contrast, after anticlerical officials seized control of the Algiers municipal council in the early 1870s, they banned Corpus Christi processions in the streets of the capital.[39]

THE CHAPEL OF SAINT LOUIS

The construction of the Chapel of Saint Louis signaled a departure from customary practice because the Husaynids conventionally granted already standing buildings for a modest rent or even gratis to churches or missionary orders for purposes of worship, education, or medical services.[40] On the eve of France's invasion of Algeria, Husayn Bey had bequeathed to the French monarch a piece of land in Carthage, where tradition held the crusader-king Saint Louis had died in 1270, to construct a memorial. Only in 1840 did the French consul, de Largau, reach agreement with the Bardo that the chapel would be built in La Malga, near Byrsa hill, with a commanding view of the ancient Punic ports and the sea. At the time, the area was almost deserted except for a few mud huts, tents belonging to bedouins, and a Muslim cemetery with the *qubba,* or shrine, of Sidi 'Abd al-'Aziz, a widely venerated holy man. With great fanfare, the chapel's first stone was laid in August 1840 as a Maltese priest, Father Emmanuel, celebrated Mass outdoors on a makeshift altar.[41]

The ceremony's military dimensions should have given pause, although it is not clear if any Tunisians were in attendance. Sailors in combat dress from France's fleet docked in La Goulette formed an honor guard as the French flag was conspicuously planted near the altar and warships blasted out a twenty-one-gun salute. If the edifice was designed to resemble the royal chapel at Évreux, its building materials evoked several millennia of Ifriqiya's history, the pagan and Christian: stones from Roman and Byzantine sites; marble from the quarries near Soliman; and brick vaults imported from Genoa. A year later, the chapel's completion furnished the occasion for more militaristic rituals. It soon became a space of sociability for French residents, a shrine for sailors in port, and until abolition, a place of refuge for African slaves. However, without Ahmad Bey's generous assistance, the chapel would have taken much longer to construct; since the nearest towns, La Marsa and La Goulette, were several miles distant, the ruler furnished much-needed workers, water, and supplies.[42] This contrasts with the politics of sacred buildings in colonial Algeria, where the French army seized mosques and other Islamic structures, converting them into churches, military barracks, municipal centers, and even stables.[43]

Finally, the chapel was strategically located within reach of coastal watering spots, where the consuls spent the summer months so as to be in close proximity to the beys and their courts when they relocated to seaside palaces during the season. By a coincidence, Emilie de Vialar and several SSJ members participated in the chapel's consecration in 1840 during their exploratory visit to Tunisia; it was no accident that Vialar's confessor from Algeria, Abbé Bourgade, was named chaplain for the chapel in 1842.[44] Finally, due to the chapel's location among vast, although largely untouched, ruins of classical civilizations, it eventually served as the nucleus for archaeological excavations as well as for international conflicts over the site and its meanings.

THE BEY AND THE SISTERS

Let's turn to the question of Ahmad Bey's relationship with the sisters. Diplomatic agreements between the Holy See and the Husaynid state stipulated that new Catholic establishments obtain the ruler's explicit authorization, which explains why Vialar personally contacted the bey in 1840 about opening schools and clinics.[45] The principal reason for the SSJ's warm reception was immigration and the social origins of the newcomers, who included a large proportion of men without families. Given to public drunkenness, street violence, and vendettas— or so their detractors claimed—they had provoked diplomatic crises on a number of occasions. Moreover, by this period, a number of Spanish Catholics had settled in Tunisia; characterized as "spiritually and socially deprived," the community counted "traders, unemployed soldiers, political refuges, and dishonest persons" in the eyes of their social betters.[46] Therefore, the palace looked to the SSJ to minister to an unruly population over whom the beylical state enjoyed little formal legal jurisdiction, a situation made worse because the consulates lacked the personnel, the resources, or the will to deal with the growing problem. In short, the Husaynid prince and consuls viewed the SSJ as had the French military in Algeria—as unpaid social workers and guardians of moral order.[47]

Bourgeois residents also regarded the female missionaries favorably; private communications between the consuls and the palace voiced identical apprehensions about social disorder, which eased the way for the sisters. In his 1854 letter to Ahmad Bey, the French consul Béclard extolled the Sisters of Saint-Joseph "who have come to the Regency of Tunis in order to console the miserable and to heal the sick. In addition, the sisters teach young Christian girls the fear of God and work to instill morality in those girls seduced by the lure of vice."[48] The delicate references to vice and virtue betrayed widely shared concerns about female immigrants and sexual misconduct. What better moral beacon for vulnerable women than the chaste Catholic sisters?

Given these anxieties, it is not surprising that Ahmad Bey gave permission to Vialar and five sisters to set up schools for European children and to dispense public health care. The ruler provided state-owned buildings, loaned or rented, that over time turned into long-term leases or gifts, which proved instrumental in permanent settlement. This was the case of the first school located at Sidi Saber in the madina adjacent to the European quarter that was rented to the SSJ for a modest sum. (It is now the Catholic Diocesan Library in Tunis.) The establishment opened its doors to its first class in September 1842 with twenty-five students—ten Maltese and fifteen Italians; Vialar served as its first director. Four years later, 120 girls were enrolled, and most paid no tuition. Several Jewish and Muslim families native to Tunis inquired about sending their daughters to the school—if separate classes could be arranged, since the curriculum was grounded upon a thoroughly Catholic education. It is uncertain whether this request was acted upon at the time; only later in the century do a few Muslim and Jewish girls show up on enrollment lists. The significance of this school cannot be overemphasized, since it represented a landmark in terms of girls' education outside of the household.[49]

In 1844, a small outpatient clinic with ten beds and a pharmacy was opened adjacent to the Sidi Saber school on today's *impasse des Moniquettes,* a corruption of the original Italian *monachetta,* or "little sister"; the SSJ supported the clinic through constant appeals for donations. In La Marsa a novitiate was established whose earliest novices were largely drawn from Italian or Maltese families, which was significant. The novitiate signaled two trends: first, that the SSJ was localizing its mission by recruiting members either born in-country or recently arrived, instead of relying upon Europe for fresh recruits; and second, that the order intended to expand the scope of its activities through on-site religious vocations. The social backgrounds of the first novices also brought a range of benefactors, including the influential Count Raffo. Between 1842 and 1880, houses and educational, medical, and charitable establishments were created from Bizerte to Sousse, Munastir, Mahdiya, and Sfax. Once again in contrast to Algeria, where missionaries moved into the countryside in the wake of savage military expeditions, the SSJ in Tunisia followed the line of mainly Catholic immigrant settlement along the coast.[50]

As was true for schooling in Europe at the time, considerations of class deeply informed SSJ educational policies. In 1855 five SSJ members opened a girls' school in La Goulette with "very meager resources and a small building," which reflected the social origins of the pupils whose families were probably working class and employed in menial trades in the port.[51] Bourgeois girls attended better-appointed institutions, such as the La Marsa school housed in a palace for the daughters of the Euro-Tunisian notability; for a while the French government supported it with an annual allocation of six thousand francs. It was expensive and thus rare for creole notables to send daughters to Europe for education; thus, this school and others like it filled a hitherto unmet demand, while paradoxically fixing these families more firmly in local society. Little is known about the tuition-free schools for girls of modest means, but here the SSJ may have combined elements from an older, indigenous urban institution, the dar mu'allima (learning circles), which the sisters may have encountered during home visits to Muslim families, with French curriculum.

Many neighborhoods in Tunis or other North African cities boasted home-based learning circles where girls between five and twelve years old were taught by mu'allimat (teachers), women recognized for skills in domestic arts, above all, needlework; pupils were instructed within the confines of the household for a modest fee. The SSJ adopted a two-track system that provided an academic curriculum, plus needlework, for middle-class girls and instruction in handicrafts, mainly needlework, for those from poorer families, although Catholic teaching formed the core of both tracks. The prominent place accorded to needlework in Tunisia reflected pedagogy in teaching congregations in France at the time. French laws made needlework an official part of the curriculum because of the unique moral values—"perseverance and calm"—that it imparted to girls. And an accomplished needle could earn income for a working-class girl and her family and serve as a moral shield against sin and vice. As Sarah Curtis has argued, Catholic girls' schools in France provided the model for female primary education in general at the time.[52]

Vialar's confessor and close associate, Abbé Bourgade, created one of the earliest boys' schools around 1842. Previously, the sons of bourgeois creoles were educated in Europe—if the family could afford the expense, which often they could not. Under some circumstances, parents might importune consuls in Tunis for financial assistance, as occurred in 1825 when Ronzetti, a French protégé from Rome who was married to a French woman, sought aid to educate young Angelo in Paris.[53] Sir Richard Wood's two sons, Cecil and Dick, were sent from Tunis for schooling in France, England, and Germany but at his personal expense.[54]

With the arrival of the Frères des Écoles Chrétiennes (FEC) in 1855—a full decade and a half after the SSJ—some families enrolled sons in their institutions located near the Church of Sainte-Croix. The SSJ and the FEC were not competitors but rather complemented each other, since the brothers taught older boys and were not involved in medical work, while the SSJ enrolled only very young boys in some of their schools. In 1858, the FEC opened a primary school for boys with instruction in three languages—Arabic, French, and Italian—and provided free tuition. Of the sixty students enrolled in the FEC class of 1865, several were Muslim Tunisians and a number were from Jewish families, mainly Italian, but a few were Tunisians. To meet growing competition from other institutions, the brothers eventually added classes in music, voice, and instrument to the curriculum, reflecting a pedagogical trend in France that saw musical instruction as key to learning citizenship.[55] Therefore, some transnational Catholic orders were attuned to new learning methods, implementing them in Tunisia long before colonialism.

Spatial analysis of the first FEC school shows that it was established in a structure previously serving as a bagnio and later a refuge for the Spanish Trinitarians after their expulsion from Spain during the French Revolution. Another FEC school was organized in a house leased from a Jewish family, the Raimondos, who rarely bothered to collect the rent. However, in the 1870s, the new owners of "Dar Raimondo" demanded payment with back interest. Muhammad al-Sadiq Bey intervened, granting the building to the FEC on condition that it be employed solely for educational purposes. The beylical decree, dated February 1874, provides clues about the neighborhood and how its denizens reckoned spatial relationships: "it [Dar Raimondo] is situated in the suq al-bramliya [the market of the coopers] near the Sea Gate . . . occupies the second storey above shops and store rooms . . . [some of which are] the shops of Cardoso; to the east is the house of the Maltese Farrugia . . . to the west is the house of the Greek, Basile, and after that a house belonging to the priests of the Catholic Church."[56] In addition to financial support, Muhammad al-Sadiq Bey invited the FEC brothers to attend official state functions and receptions and requested that they furnish instructors to teach the children in his palace in La Marsa. In the same quarter, a building (or part of one) on Shari' al-Qasba owned by the wife of the Zaytuna's Maliki mufti, was leased to the FEC for its school.[57] As a severe housing shortage gripped the city, some Muslim families preferred to rent apartments or sections of domestic compounds to foreigners, since they could charge higher rents and could probably recover rental properties more easily when needed—which is how today's rental market in Tunis operates.[58] This FEC school remained in the same spot until quite recently, when it was forced to close its doors—nor for want of students but rather for lack of vocations and therefore of brothers to staff the institution.

The Husaynid family functioned as a real estate brokerage firm, handing out rental properties and acting as landlords for diverse missions in the same way that the rulers lent prime seaside villas to select members of the consular corps or creole class. From the reign of Ahmad Bey until the Protectorate, the dynasty's generosity and tolerance transformed the practice of Christianity from largely private, house-based worship in towns, such as Sousse, into a public presence with large structures, bells, and processions.[59] Later on, Catholic missions began purchasing buildings with funds provided by local families or consulates as well as by the Propaganda Fide in Rome. The residences occupied by religious women and men are of paramount importance because built space signaled modes of life as well as integration into a particular neighborhood, which in turn shaped sociocultural proximity or distance. In densely populated North African cities, the availability of housing constituted the critical element in successful or failed missionary implantation. In Morocco during the same period, the 'Alawi dynasty dealt with troublesome Anglo-American evangelicals by withholding permission to rent buildings outside of Tangier, which kept missionaries holed up in the port thus restricting contacts with subject Muslims or Jews and impeding proselytizing.[60]

A final dimension of the real estate relationship linking the palace with the missionaries was that the beys, as landlords to the Church, were called upon to mediate between Europeans in battles over property use. In 1854, Ahmad Bey acted to protect the enclosed Capuchin monastery in La Goulette from a residential structure built by a Dr. Castelnuovo that hovered over the monastery's walls, violating its privacy.[61] Indeed the constant solicitations made to the rulers for property titles or interventions in rental disputes—including reductions in the rent paid by the SSJ in Tunis for one of its leased buildings—are striking. In 1854 the French consul responded to yet another petition from the SSJ and Capuchins for more concessions by observing that "the bey has already done many things for the Catholics and I risk abusing his good will by requesting additional favors."[62]

THE SISTERS AND LOCAL SOCIETY

When Emilie de Vialar visited Tunisia for the last time in 1845, she had developed consummate diplomatic skills; she maintained relations and correspondence, however litigious, with military officers, the governor-general, and churchmen in Algeria as well as with Parisian bureaucrats and French clerics. She even made a pilgrimage to Rome for a personal interview with the Pope to promote her congregation (and denounce her nemesis, Dupuch). In addition, Vialar had acquired some familiarity with Islamic property law, most importantly with the legal category of *habus* that she had encountered in Algiers when purchasing the order's first house.[63] And she had also perfected strategies for enrolling increasing numbers of students in her schools. Opening houses in La Marsa, Carthage, and Sidi Bou Sa'id brought additional supporters, funds, and pupils because city notables met and socialized in these resorts. In August 1843, as Vialar was recruiting pupils, she ran into Peloso, formerly the Roman consul to Algiers, whom she had met while still in Algeria; now residing in Tunis, Peloso agreed to send his two daughters to the SSJ school in La Marsa.[64]

Court dignitaries opened doors for the sisters as well. Among the most influential was Count Joseph Marie Raffo, whose advocacy of the SSJ proved decisive: "and tho [sic] he [Raffo] is very rich, his charities to the poor and benevolent institutions are very numerous."[65] Raffo used his influence to gain permission for a new church on the site of an ancient Trinitarian hospital in the madina; in 1852, he obtained the ruler's consent for the Mission Apostolique to create religious establishments in coastal cities. But it was in the realm of girls' education that Raffo made the largest contribution. In 1843 he offered the sisters a "superb palace with a magnificent garden" in La Marsa, complete with a private chapel (the palace may have belonged to the Husaynid family).[66] However, his support eventually posed grave problems.

A widower, Raffo had previously sent his five daughters to Paris for schooling by the Sacré Coeur, but he withdrew his daughters from the French establishment and enrolled them, along with seven nieces resident in Tunisia, with the SSJ in La Marsa. Two years later, widower Raffo's attentiveness caused distress to the school. Enamored of young, attractive Sister Emilie Julien, who oversaw education, the count courted her relentlessly and brought pressure to bear upon her father in France to persuade Emilie to abandon religious for marriage vows. Horrified, Vialar immediately removed the tempting Sister Emilie and another young Italian, Sister Elisabeth, from the establishment and dispatched them to the mother house in Gaillac.[67]

During the spring of 1871, the British traveler Lady Herbert made a point of visiting the SSJ establishments in the Tunis region, since she had visited the order's house in Jerusalem before traveling to North Africa. "The Sisters of St. Joseph 'of the Apparition' . . . have a large orphanage here, together with a hospital and day schools. They have nineteen sisters at work, but their convent is small and must be very hot in summer."[68] It was Easter week when Lady Herbert toured the city, which provided an opportunity to underscore differences in religiosity marking northern Europeans off from Mediterranean Catholics: "This being Holy Saturday, quantities of cannon were fired off when the bells were rung at the 'Gloria in Excelsis,' and some so near the church that it seemed as if they were about to bombard it. The devotion of Catholics here is very striking, but very demonstrative, as with most Southern nations."[69]

PROTESTANTS AND EVANGELICAL MISSIONS

As the Sisters of Saint-Joseph took root in Tunisia, Protestant societies for "saving heathens" were expanding across the British Empire. In 1834, the Society for Promoting Female Education in China, India, and the East was established in London.[70] Soon after it became a British colony, Malta emerged as a Mediterranean center for evangelical expansion closely tied to international abolition movements; in 1815, the Church Missionary Society was established on the island.

The first Protestant mission in Tunisia—as far as we know—was the Board of Foreign Missions of the Methodist Episcopal Church in 1819, which opened the way for others. The Christian Missions in Many Lands established some sort of presence in 1836, and a decade later in 1845 the Foreign Mission Board of the Southern Baptist Convention sent a delegation. In the same period, the London Society for Promoting Christianity amongst the Jews designated Mr. Ewald as its first missionary to Tunisia; the society handed out free copies of Hebrew bibles to Jews, most of whom were illiterate. Other societies distributed free English-language bibles in the markets of Tunis, whose pages usually served to wrap up meat or vegetables.[71]

Evangelical newcomers competed with the Church of England, which had long enjoyed British protection and for centuries represented the main Protestant presence in the country. The congregation remained small into the 1840s, consisting of about fifteen people, including the American consul general, Heap, the British Gibsons, and the Swedish Tulin family. Sunday services were held in the mission house presided over by Reverend Ewald.[72] In 1834 clergy arrived from England to assume responsibility for the first Anglican church, Saint Augustine's, built just outside the Tunis city walls where the central food market is found today. Only in 1901 was the Church of Saint George constructed near Bab Carthagena in the environs of the seventeenth-century Protestant cemetery, which for centuries had provided a resting place for French Huguenots who had relocated to Tunis to escape persecution in France and pursue commercial affairs. Eventually the Anglican Church of Tunisia was placed under the Bishop of Gibraltar's authority and in the twentieth century under the Episcopal diocese of Egypt.[73]

Members of French or Swiss Reformed churches arrived in Tunisia, frequently after initially settling in Constantine; some were quickly disabused of the idea of permanent residency in Algeria, while others stayed on. Thus, the expanding Protestant presence in Tunisia and Algeria in the nineteenth century promoted systematic across-the-border exchanges; the Methodist Church of Tunis, for example, was integrated into the Algerian Methodist hierarchy. Tunisia's growing attraction for migrants and missionaries meant that the country became home to an assortment of odd social types, the Reverend Nathan Davis being a case in point. Born a Polish Jew, he subsequently converted to the Church of England on whose behalf he engaged in missionary activities, as he later did for the Church of Scotland. Davis's origins made him the perfect agent for Protestant societies seeking to convert North African Jews. But he also published accounts of Tunisia in Maltese newspapers, which may have encouraged emigration to the shores of Africa, and he cultivated a relationship with Ahmad Bey to whom he dedicated one of his books. As an eccentric man of the cloth, Davis parallels Abbé Bourgade but pales in comparison to the French cleric in terms of originality of thought and action.[74]

BOURGADE: A MOST CURIOUS CLERIC

Emilie de Vialar kept curious company. In Tunis, Abbé François Bourgade (1806–1866) served as the SSJ order's chaplain, confessor, and administrator of educational and health institutions but he also had an Algerian past. Bourgade had been Vialar's spiritual director—her "providential friend," as she put it—earlier in Algeria. The son of a peasant, Bourgade was ordained in 1826; like Vialar he was enticed to Algiers in 1835, where he assumed the position of vicar of the cathedral, which was a former mosque seized from the Muslim community.[75] Involved in hospitals, sanatoria, and houses of refuge, he soon encountered Vialar, whose brand of spiritual and missionary fervor matched his. In 1840 he was declared persona non grata by Bishop Dupuch because of his unconventional behavior and close friendship with the rebellious Vialar. Bourgade next went to Rome, where he enjoyed the patronage of the Roman Curia, which won him the title of apostolic missionary as well as appointment as extraordinary confessor to Vialar's order.[76] When the SSJ relocated to Tunisia, Bourgade followed close behind and it appears that Vialar pressured the French consulate in Tunis to find the priest a paid post so he could remain. In 1842 Bourgade was named "directeur général de l'Oeuvre Aumônier de la Chapelle Imperiale de St.-Louis à Carthage," the first French priest appointed to the post of apostolic prefecture long monopolized by Italian priests.[77] Among the abbot's stated objectives was "to expand knowledge of our language in the Regency," and to this effect he created the first French college in the country.[78]

In a strange sort of way, Bourgade and those associated with him anticipated the resolutely secular Alliance Française, which established one of its first overseas centers in Tunis soon after the Protectorate expressly to promote the French language and thus combat "the Italian menace." Bourgade's and Vialar's activities in Tunis not only reflected France's growing clout in the country but also increased it, although not necessarily out of a sense of national commitment. Aiding their work immensely were the close relationships cultivated with the palace and political elite. Bourgade entertained amical ties with Ahmad Bey, to whom he dedicated one of his books, as well as with his successor, Muhammad Bey; Muslim scholars and consular officials counted among the cleric's close acquaintances.[79]

Bourgade and Vialar arrived at a moment when remarkable educational experiments were already underway in Tunis; their own actions enriched the mix. An English primary school had been in operation since circa 1830 near today's Rue des Maltais, but little is known about the effort; after the FEC opened their institutions catering largely to Catholic Maltese boys, the English establishment closed its doors. This was a pattern seen throughout the century in Tunisia and elsewhere in the Mediterranean and Ottoman worlds; educators and families experimented with new teaching and learning environments that often foundered due to lack of funds or pupils or because of competition from more robust schools. The brother and sister Pompeo and Esther (b. 1815) Sulema, Jewish political refuges from Leghorn, deserve credit for one of the earliest primary schools for Italian boys in 1831, although apparently two Neapolitan refugees had founded the first Italian school in Tunis in 1821, which like its English counterpart did not last long. When Bourgade created the Collège Saint Louis in 1842, Esther and Pompeo became closely associated with this institution. Admitting Maltese, French, Italian, and Tunisian pupils, irrespective of social class, nationality, or religion, the college's curriculum reflected the students' diverse ethnoreligious backgrounds; lessons were given in Arabic and Italian, with foreign-language instruction in French, Latin, and Greek.[80]

The staff and teachers mirrored the Mediterranean diversity of the students and the capital city. Pompeo Sulema served as professor of calligraphy and collaborated with Bourgade in archeological research into Punic stele, drawing facsimiles of inscriptions for the abbot.[81] A sort of early international school, the college trained the next generation of educators in the capital, for example, Eymon Zephirin, who later taught at Sadiqi College, founded by Khayr al-Din in 1873. An intriguing aspect of the long friendship between Esther Sulema and Bourgade is that she converted to Catholicism and was baptized in April 1843 taking the name Giulia Maria Giovanna. Love motivated her conversion since, immediately after the baptismal ceremony in the Sainte-Croix Parish Church, she married a French Catholic trader, David Ménard, established in Tunis.[82]

Schools like Bourgade's college increasingly became lighting rods for internationalized struggles among local communities and the European states protecting them; the openly bitter animosity between France and Italy dates from this period. The Collège Saint Louis flourished until 1863, when it closed and the Frères des Écoles Chrétiennes took over its pupils. That same year, Muhammad al-Sadiq Bey bequeathed to the Italian state a piece of land for a new school; three years later the Collegio Italiano opened in 1866. Among its teaching staff was again Pompeo Sulema, whose career reveals another social pattern among expatriates residing in Tunis—instructors moved around from institution to institution. During the 1870s, this college served as an institutional core for increasingly strident Italian claims upon Tunisia; as a counterweight to French influence, the Italian state began subsidizing Italian primary schools in Tunisia. Until this time, prosperous Italian merchants, notably the Jews, sent sons to the University of Pisa for education, although Leghorn also attracted students from the Maghrib and Egypt. Under the Protectorate, the Italian college and institutions like it nurtured an Italian cultural and political identity among the large Sicilian community and promoted popular opposition to France's dominance in a French possession whose foreign population remained overwhelmingly Italian.[83] Italian schools and other educational, cultural, or social welfare institutions remained a thorn in the side of the French Protectorate well into the twentieth century and a major source of international animosity between Italy and France.

In 1878, the Alliance Israélite Universelle (AIU) opened its first boys' primary school in Tunis for both indigenous and Italian Jews; by the eve of the Protectorate, there were eight such schools, but schooling for Jewish girls had to wait until 1882.[84] From AIU headquarters in Paris, teachers who were European, mainly French, and who were trained in modern pedagogy were dispatched to North Africa and the Ottoman Empire to teach French, mathematics, natural science, and geography, a curriculum patterned upon France's system. The objective was to inculcate a new modern understanding of Judaism among North African and Middle Eastern Jewry—not to instruct pupils in Jewish religious learning per se.[85] Even before 1881, French state protection was extended to the AIU schools to offset Italian initiatives—the Franco-Italian educational cold war was on. Schooling solely along religious or national lines—and in the case of Italy, irredentist claims—was contrary to the vision held by Vialar, Bourgade, and their circle of like-minded collaborators for educating Tunisia's heterogeneous populations. Nevertheless, since most pupils could not pay tuition, the realization of their pedagogical vision suffered the vicissitudes of private and state funding.

For a period, Bourgade's college received substantial financial backing from the French king, some six thousand francs annually, which increased enrollments to three hundred students. Not satisfied, the cleric embarked on money-raising drives in France, using the local press to appeal for donations. In November 1845, both *La Presse* and *La Gazette du Midi* noted the favorable teaching results achieved by the Collège de St. Louis.[86] Bourgade petitioned the archbishop in Lyon for financial support but he declined to furnish funds, although later in the 1860s substantial sums were sent for the purchase of buildings in Tunis; the archbishop's lack of enthusiasm was probably directed at Bourgade personally rather than his projects per se. In 1846 Bourgade published a two-page appeal in Paris, *Au sujet du Collège et de l'Hôpital St. Louis à Tunis,* whose objective was to "bring together these diverse populations of Tunis" through two principal means, education and charity. According to the cleric, the hospital cared for between sixty and eighty indigenous patients, some of whom came from distant corners of Tunisia for treatment of eye diseases or serious wounds. A touch of the exotic and pull at the heart—and hopefully purse—strings was his vivid evocation of the "Bedouin woman from the countryside with her dying child in her arms." As for the school, "we admit young Tunisian boys in our establishments without ethnic or religious distinction, providing the benefits of education and an example of Christian morals. . . . In our eyes they are neither Muslim nor Jewish but dear children upon whom we lavish paternal care."[87]

The fund-raising appeal was significant for several reasons. It introduced metropole Catholics to Tunisia by providing purportedly accurate population statistics, including the numbers of Jews, Christians, and Muslims. It also extolled the missionary activities of the SSJ—the order's girls' schools, its infirmary, and home visits to the sick—as a compelling marketing device, an early example of what became boilerplate fund-raising discourse.

Bourgade voyaged frequently between Tunis and Marseilles to collect donations in Europe and constantly beseeched French consuls for travel subsidies. By 1851 the consul, having repeatedly been "reprimanded by the French government for giving free boat passages to clerics, especially to the Abbé Bourgade," refused his request for yet another free ride. This stands in stark contrast to the Ministry of the Navy, which granted SSJ members free passage on French naval vessels from 1844 on, a decision that greatly advanced the order's expansion into the eastern Mediterranean.[88] Under the July Monarchy, Bourgade's work flourished. He was awarded the Légion d'Honneur and Louis Philippe's wife, Queen Marie-Amélie, underwrote many of his charitable activities in Tunisia. But the 1848 revolution deprived Bourgade of royal patronage and financial support. Eventually, the abbot's behavior got him in trouble with the French consulate and Italian Capuchins, particularly with Bishop de Rosalia. In 1858 Bourgade's papal authorization was revoked, causing "a huge outcry in the Catholic community" in Tunisia. Deprived of salary and suffering from a serious liver disease, he went to Paris to continue missionary work there.[89]

Several years later, he resurfaced as the publisher-manager of a new newspaper, L'Aigle de Paris (Birjis al-Bariz) (The Eagle of Paris), which began as an Arabic bimonthly and subsequently went into an Arabic-French edition around September 1860. In the first bilingual issue, Bourgade launched a series for teaching Arabic to French speakers, "Leçon d'Arabe." He collaborated with Sulayman al-Harairi, the Arabic notary and secretary at the French consulate in Tunis, for the Arabic editions, which were distributed by bookstores in France, Algeria, and the "Orient" by the well-known Parisian publisher, Challamel.[90] In the December 1859 edition, Bourgade claimed that his journal "encountered sympathy everywhere . . . among those who subscribe are the Bey of Tunis and his court as well as the Hanafi grand mufti of Tunis." Even Amir 'Abd al-Qadir, by then in exile in Damascus, allegedly was a regular subscriber and reader. But what to make of the newspaper's following claim? "The paper's success in the Levant has alarmed the British who convened a meeting in London to neutralize the journal's influence. . . . To counteract Protestant England, we will run off a large number of copies and distribute the newspaper from India to the west coasts of Africa."[91] Was Bourgade attempting to shake the political money tree in Paris through the use of anti-English, anti-Protestant discourse focused specifically upon France's age-old nemesis? The fund-raising aspirations of the newspaper were patent, since it carried a notice regarding how and where to make contributions. However earnest the pleas or shrewd the appeals, Bourgade, destitute and sick, died in misery in Paris in 1866.

Nevertheless, the originality of the cleric's eclectic interpretation of the Catholic civilizing mission is beyond dispute. In his worldview, Islam was not a demonic belief but rather a "preface to the Gospel, which left to God's providence, would eventually bear fruit in Christian truth."[92] Because of this vision of Muslims and Islam, Bourgade promoted a rapprochement through "formal dialogue in narrative and Socratic form," which explains why he was so keen to publicly debate prestigious members of the Tunis 'ulama' in theological discussions held during the summer evenings in Carthage.[93] At some time after 1858, Bourgade encountered Lavigerie in Paris and awakened his interest in the Chapel of Saint Louis; the future archbishop's knowledge of Islam may have initially come from Bourgade's writings on the subject. These works contained imaginary conversations between Muslim scholars and Bourgade during which the priest demonstrated contradictions in Islamic scriptures that naturally confirmed Christian dogma, a traditional dialogic genre dating back centuries. Lavigerie recommended Bourgade's books to his missionaries, although his views of Islam differed substantially from those of the idiosyncratic cleric.[94]

What united Abbé Bourgade and Sister Vialar was a shared commitment not only to proselytizing in Muslim lands but also to a specific combination of spirituality and social activism inspired by the founder of the Redemptorist Congregation, the Neapolitan priest Alphonsus de Liguori (1696–1787), who labored to save the poor and outcast in Naples. In a very real sense, the abbot's and sister's social welfare campaigns in Tunisia among similar populations transplanted de Liguori's work to the Mediterranean's African rim and brought it into the nineteenth century. And, in contrast to Lavigerie, they believed that "mission was dialogue," which led them to eschew muscular or confrontational tactics in favor of communication with Muslims instead.[95] Bourgade appears to have been the first to publicly pose the problem of Muslim women in Tunisia in an essay published in French in 1847, then in Arabic two years later. This tract may have inspired the bey's chief secretary, Bin Diyaf, to compose his unpublished treatise, "Risala fi-l-mar'a" (Essay on Woman) in 1856 as a riposte to European criticisms of the place of women in Islam.[96]

Bourgade, Vialar, and their diverse associates do not fit comfortably into conventional narratives of North African–European encounters in this period. This is what makes them so fascinating, and significant, as religious adventurers and entrepreneurs. Moreover, the abbot was "one of the most controversial figures in the French cultural presence in nineteenth-century Tunis."[97] He appears to have had Masonic links or at least to have frequented Italian expatriates who belonged to Masonic lodges, for example, the Tuscan Jew Pompeo Sulema. Bourgade set up a small Arabic printing press at his college—one of the first of its kind in

Tunis—in order to "explain Christianity" to Muslims, although the Italian Jew Giulio Finzi had created a lithographic press in Tunis circa 1829. Bourgade's printing operation was established with the assistance of two Prussian lithographers who employed their professional skills for other purposes—churning out high-quality, counterfeit Tunisian banknotes, which inundated the country with worthless currency and greatly undermined the state treasury.[98]

At the same time, Bourgade became enamored of archaeological artifacts unearthed from Christian and pagan sites whose promotional potential were not lost on him. He collected inscriptions from Punic stele scattered around Carthage, about which he published a short work dedicated to Ahmad Bey, *Toison d'or de la langue Phénicienne*.[99] He appears to have been the first to organize a small museum at the Saint Louis Chapel where Roman and early Christian finds were housed. Bourgade's fascination with archaeology was taken up several decades later by Lavigerie, who directed the White Fathers to undertake extensive excavations but who also wed fanatically religious and nationalist propaganda with ostensibly scientific research into the past. The role played by early amateur archeologists—well-heeled travelers steeped in the literature of classical antiquity or highly educated military officers in the Algerian army—in the discipline's emergence has already been noted. Yet the part played by missionaries invites further scholarly investigation into the complex politics of archaeology: the intersections between missionary campaigns, excavations in Muslim lands containing large pre-Islamic Christian archeological sites, later French colonial claims to restore the Roman past, and the evolution of the museum then in a process of rapid institutionalization. Soon thereafter, some Tunis notables developed a keen interest in the field and organized a new historical, archeological, and geological society around (or even before?) the Protectorate; from 1885 on, Tunisians participated in the organization of the newly created Bardo museum.[100] Nevertheless, the excavations in Carthage and elsewhere could not have taken place had not Husaynid rulers given missionaries like Bourgade and amateur enthusiasts such as Pompeo carte blanche to move about largely unfettered.

CHOLERA AND CONVERSION

The outbreak of cholera morbus in Europe and the Mediterranean world constituted "the great disease drama of the nineteenth century" due to its novelty in that part of the globe. Its ravages elicited puzzlement, as much as panic, because doctors had rarely, if ever, encountered the affliction; since Arab and European medicine bore a close resemblance in the early part of the century, medical practitioners from both traditions were helpless.[101] While Tunisia was spared until the 1849–1850 epidemic, reports of earlier outbreaks in Europe and the Mediterranean—in 1831 and 1832 cholera reached France and Great Britain—had deeply troubled Husaynid and consular authorities. In 1835 cholera appeared in Genoa, Leghorn, and Marseilles and subsequently reached Algeria due to the massive deployment of troops into the colony. Sir Thomas Reade rightfully observed during the 1835 scare that "the few medical persons who are here are little to be depended upon and I believe not one of them ever had an opportunity of seeing cholera cases." As a precautionary measure, the consul recommended that London replace the current vice-consul, Cunningham, with a "half pay surgeon of the Navy or Army, with permission for him to practice his profession [here in Tunis]."[102] But the proposal fell on deaf ears, not least because the European medical establishment was greatly divided about cholera's causes. However, the main obstacle was the colossal sway of imperial mercantile interests advocating only a "'gentle' control of cholera" in the interests of international commerce.[103]

As dire predictions regarding cholera's potential to wreak havoc were being debated in Tunisia during the 1830s, the SSJ sisters tended to cholera and typhus victims in Algeria and gained valuable hands-on training. Indeed, the congregation's history is intertwined with the disease's progression from Algeria to Tunisia.[104] A few years later, the order opened the first public health clinic in Tunis and introduced something quite novel—home nursing visits for those too ill to visit clinics. The fact that the Tunis Board of Health had been organized in 1835 under Mustafa Bey explains the reception that Sister Vialar and Abbé Bourgade received because they arrived during a period of growing public fright over disease.

By 1849 it was apparent that Tunisia would not be spared. Bin Diyaf's chronicle devotes long passages to cholera, whose "origins lie among the diseases of India" and that causes "those infected to turn yellow and then black in color and death occurs within hours or after a few days."[105] As the century's imperial disease par excellence, cholera came overland from Algeria, spread by tribes and French military units on campaign. Ahmad Bey insisted that the quarantine on all ships coming from Europe be rigorously observed and ordered that three military barracks in the capital be transformed into hospitals, one for each religious community. After military units dispatched to the provinces failed to erect a *cordon sanitaire* around infected regions and stem the flow of diseased or panicked people, the muftis, qa'ids, and other officials abandoned Tunis, leaving an administrative vacuum. Ahmad Bey fled to Carthage, then to his new palace in Muhammadiya, and finally Porto Farina in the north. Since the *hara* was one of the least salubrious quarters, cholera struck impoverished Tunisian Jews with deadly force. Another notoriously foul neighborhood was the environs of the Saint-Antoine cemetery, where Christians had long buried their dead on a plot of land freely bestowed by the Tunisian state; the practice of common graves and shallow burials had produced a serious health menace.[106] Imprecise mortality statistics suggest that at least 7,600 people died of cholera, out of 16,675 stricken in Tunis, a city whose population counted no more than 100,000 inhabitants. European physicians, some employed by the palace, were accused by the terrified populace of deliberately introducing the disease, a reaction duplicating popular responses to medical practitioners in Europe and elsewhere at the time.[107]

While those with the means took flight, the SSJ remained, closed its schools, and sent teaching staff to tend to the ill and bury the dead, which resulted in the death of several sisters. It was for this medical valor that Ahmad Bey bestowed the "medal of glorious achievement" upon the SSJ and showed great largesse toward the wider Christian community of Tunis during the famine following the epidemic. Soon after the outbreak, the Board of Health expanded its powers and scope, which may have encouraged the founding of additional SSJ hospitals and clinics in the capital region and the provinces.[108]

The clinic adjacent to the Sidi Saber School counted eight beds and two nursing sisters. Other sisters made home visits that were initially restricted to Europeans with certificates (or passports?) attesting to national status; although this soon changed, it may have meant that the poorest and thus most vulnerable populations were the least served. The clinic's first physician was a Maltese named Laferla, and medical assistance was free; an administrative council oversaw its work. Expenses were met through public subscriptions and the organization of balls, fetes, and raffles. Adept at fund-raising, Abbé Bourgade collected nearly three thousand piasters in an appeal addressed to the inhabitants of Tunis. In this 1843 drive, the largest donors were members of the consular corps and wealthy merchants. But a number of individuals in service to Ahmad Bey, for example, Borsani, the bey's chief jeweler, and the Italian Austrian Antonio Bogo, one of his closest ministers, made donations, as did the ruler himself.[109] The part that fund-raising drives played in creating a sense of collective, civic identity cutting across national and, to an extent, religious boundaries among certain social classes merits further investigation.

In 1848 one of the SSJ medical establishments was transferred to a more spacious building—a former military barracks—donated by the ruler. In addition to providing a home for orphans, the institution counted twenty-five beds and provided free medical care to all, although most patients were from Europe or Algeria. In view of the opprobrium associated with hospitals, it served the needs of the most desperate—Maltese, Sicilians, and Spanish. Anne-Marie Planel's meticulous analysis of scanty hospital records opens a small window onto the lives of the poor and afflicted who ended their days in the facilities for lack of alternatives. Single, male immigrants employed as unskilled laborers predominated on patient lists, but after 1860 women of humble station—servants, laundresses, or those suspected of prostitution—figured in the registers, as did illegitimate infants and children.[110]

Although a separate beylical hospital exclusively for Muslims and Jews existed in the Qasba quarter, by the 1870s, the SSJ outpatient facility attracted a large Tunisian clientele, perhaps as many as eighty patients per day. However rudimentary or insufficient to the task, public health services attempted to deal with recurrent cholera outbreaks, the devastating 1868 typhus epidemic, and famines that carried off many, including SSJ nursing staff.[111] In the original cohort of sisters relocating to Tunisia with Vialar in 1840, Rosalie Lagrange (d. 1868) worked as a nurse for thirty-six years in the SSJ dispensary and in the Saint Louis Hospital. In addition, she made home visits to the sick irrespective of class or religion, going from miserable abodes in the city's poorer neighborhoods to the palaces of the bey or ministers. During the 1867–1868 epidemics, directly tied to the 1864 rebellion, Sister Rosalie was called to Bizerte to treat afflicted Muslim families there.[112] A description of medical practices in Sousse, where Sister Joséphine ran a public health dispensary for decades, provides some ethnographic details about a typical clinic. It was "a simple white-washed room with benches and a small armoire. Sister Joséphine went from patient to patient, administering eye drops or lancing boils, with the sure hands of a practiced surgeon, she fixed dislocated arms and legs, bandaged an arm or put a cast on a broken leg . . . and oversaw the nursery which admitted sickly infants deprived of nourishment for whom she miraculously found milk."[113]

One of Tunisia's principal attractions for Sister Vialar was precisely the scarcity of modern clinics, pharmacies, and hospitals. As she organized services and institutions, the SSJ founder mobilized a three-pronged program that integrated physical well-being, intellectual and moral health through schooling, and spiritual redemption. She paired schools with clinics throughout the country and, significantly, pioneered home medical visits that probably reached more Tunisians than hospitals or clinics. And she dug into her own private fortune, or what was left of it, to finance projects; although in addition to local fund-raising in Tunisia, she turned to the Oeuvre de la Propagation de la Foi in Lyon for subsidies. Medical assistance and schooling were, however, directly tied to the danger of conversion. For the Christian children in their primary schools, the SSJ's education acted as armor against the ever-present perils of conversion to Islam, as it was "not rare to see a certain number of young people abandon the title of Christian to become Muslims."[114] And as Abbé Bourgade's newspapers aimed to explain Christianity to Muslims and Jews, SSJ clinics promoted more than public health.

As always, there was a spiritual price to pay for medical assistance. The sisters performed secret baptisms for Muslims or Jews judged in danger of imminent death, a condition that would most often apply to infants or children, given their exceptionally high mortality rates. The SSJ carefully, if discreetly, recorded the exact number of baptisms in reports sent back to Rome or Lyon. Clandestine baptisms must not have been that secret since Cardinal Lavigerie later issued a confidential memorandum in 1880, "Circulaire sur le baptême des Musulmans," addressed to diocesan clergy and especially missionaries in Tunis. In it, Lavigerie reminded priests and sisters alike that the Holy See's decree of 1763 regarding infidel children was still in effect. Jewish or Muslim "children remaining under parental authority cannot be baptized." Moreover, the "Diocesan Statutes" of Tunisia explicitly stated that "no Jewish or Muslim child can be baptized without the express permission of its parents. . . . Only abandoned infants in clear danger of death or those completely deprived of family can be baptized." As for adults, "Protestant, Jewish or Muslim adults can only be baptized with our special authorization."[115] It is unclear from the documentation whether Muslims and Jews were aware of the baptisms performed by the sisters. Bourgade inventoried 115 baptisms of children in danger of death during six months in 1842 in his report to the Propaganda Fide but cautioned against making them public knowledge; the majority of the children were Muslim, the rest Jewish. In the 1850s, Vialar claimed that one sister alone had baptized hundreds of children, although she too added the caveat about the need for absolute confidentiality so as not to disaffect the Muslims and Jews who flocked to the clinics.[116]

The circumstances that might have prompted Lavigerie to later reissue regulations governing conversion are suggested by an 1845 incident that caused a public outcry. A Muslim boy in Sousse "took it into his head to turn Christian" and went to Malta (or was taken?), where he was baptized by Capuchin friars who publicized the case. Subsequently, the young man returned to his hometown onboard a Maltese vessel whose master, Paulo di Busuttil, had adopted him. News of his presence in Sousse triggered efforts to seize the lad and restore him to his family but he carried a British passport, which prompted the British agent to intervene on his behalf. In an apparently emotional reunion with his mother, the boy informed her that he would not change his mind, that "'he should die a Christian.'" Ahmad Bey and local officials in Sousse calmed offended Muslim sensibilities but still recognized the validity of his British passport, despite the fact that "the boy is no more a British subject than a Chinese."[117] How this shaped local Muslim opinion is unknown, but one wonders if any connection could be established between this notorious event and the following incident. In 1848, the French consul Rousseau contacted Ahmad Bey regarding unspecified assaults upon a Catholic establishment: "As your Highness knows from a verbal communication, violent attacks and outrages have been committed against one of the fathers belonging to the Capuchin convent. I trust that you will see that justice is done and reparations made."[118]

Hostility toward the men of God also came from within the Catholic fold. In chapter 6 we encountered the inebriated Nicola Malinghoussy who had a run-in with Catholic sisters and priests in 1870. Two sisters from the Tunis convent, Germaine Audouard, the mother superior, and Jeanne Loudet, were convoked by the French vice-consul in La Goulette to testify regarding Nicola's threats to murder Père Félix and Père Lecteur for reasons unknown.[119] Apparently the sisters had earlier taken Nicola in, perhaps due to his penchant for alcohol. But Nicola stormed from the convent armed with a dagger stolen "from the home of Giorgio the Greek," informing the horrified women that he was headed for the port to murder the priests and flee on a ship. Sister Germaine wrested the dagger from Nicola and hurried out to the port to warn the priests. Who appeared shortly thereafter at the convent in La Goulette? Nicola, "slightly excited due to drink." As the mother superior attempted to soothe him, Nicola declared that he "would consume enough alcohol to kill the priests and walk around La Goulette with the heads of each carried in his hands."[120] The murder came to naught and, as we know, Nicola was incarcerated in a ship-prison and eventually transported. Yet the drama, however sensational, demonstrates that enmity toward missionaries did not only come from nonbelievers and provides a glimpse into the social realities with which female religious had to contend in the course of daily life.

"GOING NATIVE"?
CLOTHING, HOUSING, AND LANGUAGE

Recent scholarship on the British Empire stresses that Asian and African peoples defined and thus limited the spheres in which European Christian missionaries carried out their work. One major element in negotiations over boundaries consisted of local gender systems, particularly normatively gendered spaces that shaped how and where healing, instruction, and other activities would transpire. In light of this, physicality and appearance were crucial to the practices of everyday life and to the success or failure of missions. How missionaries dressed, what they ate, and how they organized residential spaces and behaved in public fundamentally influenced how they were received across the globe.[121] As discussed in chapter 1, the primary marker of identity in the streets of Tunis was first and foremost dress, which provided immediate information on the religion, social class, profession, and ethnic belonging of individuals sharing different kinds of spaces. The SSJ chose a habit that did not differ markedly from what middle-class provincial French women wore; the sisters later added a sort of veil worn underneath their white bonnets. In dark blue robes and head coverings, they were not out of place in Tunisia where Muslim women wore a dark or white ha'ik (cloak) over their garments when outside the home. One male observer remarked that "one sees [Tunisian Muslim women] in the streets, especially toward evening, when they go together to the Moorish bath which is their greatest distraction; they are veiled and covered in haiks of somber colors—grey, black, and brown—which makes them appear from afar like penitents in a European religious order."[122] Maltese Catholic women dressed in black habbarahs, long robes covering their bodies. At the Capuchin Church in Tunis on Good Friday, Lady Herbert noted in 1871 that "the church was crammed to suffocation with Maltese women in their black 'habbarahs,' as at Cairo."[123] Because of its potent moral signifying value, clothing might integrate, if only partially, the religious migrants cum missionaries into a community or set them apart.

In the 1840s, Ahmad Bey directed the Capuchins to don the red cap, or shashiya, the Tunisian equivalent of the fez, as their clerical headgear in order to deflect undue attention, something that they obligingly did. "The Bey requested that they wear the chéchia so that they could mix with the crowds with more discretion."[124] As parishes were opened outside the capital—Sousse in 1836, La Goulette in 1838, Sfax in 1841, Bizerte in 1851, and Munastir in 1862—the Capuchins traveled widely and frequently to tend to the faithful. One wonders if the adoption of Tunisian headgear was in response to periodic outbreaks of animosity directed toward some friars. It is significant that the bey urged the Capuchins to "go native" so that they could move about in public more or less undetected. This seemingly trivial piece of evidence suggests that the ruler of the Husaynid state wanted the order to remain in the country—otherwise, why urge a change in dress code? On the other hand, as the French fleet frequented La Goulette on a regular basis, it was incumbent that the beys protect missionaries from harm. Ordinary people may have incorporated missionaries into their own cultural universe, seeing them as holy men and woman—as part of the North African tradition of veneration for living saints, or *murabit,* particularly for individuals blessed with healing abilities. In Algerian Saharan missions of Metlili, the White Fathers were regarded as "Christian marabouts" by the members of the nomadic Chamba tribe.[125] Sister Joséphine Daffis, who spent fifty-four years in her clinic in Sousse, was referred to by city inhabitants as *tabiba* (female doctor) or *ummi* (my mother). Little did her patients' families know that she had secretly baptized so many Muslim and Jewish children. When Lavigerie created the Society of Missionaries in Algeria, he took the matter of dress seriously. By adopting local society's material way of life, food, language, and apparel, missionaries would overcome the Muslim Algerians' contempt for Christianity, at least in his thinking. The White Fathers clung to their "traditional Muslim dress" long after male North Africans had given up the *gandura* and *burnus* and by so doing ironically increased their physical difference from the local populace.[126]

Of signal importance, too, were the spaces in which missionaries dwelled. The earliest missionaries resided in buildings, most often houses, lent or rented to them by the palace or Tunis notables. In 1868, the French consul gave the SSJ a grand residence for another school in the madina, Dar Chamama, which had belonged to the Jewish courtier Nassim who fled for Paris that year, taking a sizeable portion of the treasury with him. Outside the capital, members of the SSJ at first lived in the homes of vice-consuls or local merchants until they could purchase properties later in the century, although how interior domestic life was organized is not fully known. As Tunis extended beyond the Bab al-Bahr, other types of housing became available on reclaimed land between the city and the *buhaira*. When the Carmélites d'Alger were established in Carthage in 1885, the order elected to inhabit *"une maison Mauresque"* (a Moorish house), which had become the residential norm for missionaries, despite the fact that other kinds of housing—more "European" in nature—existed by then, a pattern that persisted into the early twentieth century.[127]

A fundamental element in "going native" was learning the Arabic of the Tunis region or provincial variants. Apparently Abbé Bourgade had acquired enough Arabic to read the Quran, to communicate, and undertake translations. It seems unlikely that Sister Vialar knew Arabic, although some SSJ sisters must have had some familiarity with the spoken language. The La Marsa novitiate was important because some of its earliest novices were from communities speaking some Arabic, in addition to Italian or Maltese. This stands in contrast to the situation in Algeria that Lavigerie encountered when he was named archbishop in 1866. Only a handful of clergy were conversant with Arabic, which is why the White Fathers and White Sisters subsequently placed great emphasis upon mastering the language.

The speed with which the SSJ attracted pupils can perhaps be attributed to language policy. For decades, Italian predominated in classrooms, since "the bad Italian of Barbary" had long served as Tunisia's diplomatic lingua franca and by the 1870s was the language spoken by most immigrants. It is uncertain if Maltese or Arabic were employed for teaching; although in primary schools, depending upon the mix of pupils, various languages would have been necessary to communicate. However, catechism classes were taught in Maltese at times and only later did French become another language of instruction. Forms of Italo-Sicilian were used in the classroom until late in the century and did not go unnoticed by the Alliance Française or colonial officials. In 1885 Paul Mellon, among the founders of the alliance, remarked, "The truth is that the Brothers and the Sisters employ both Italian and French as language of instruction, even giving Italian more emphasis in order to retain in our schools Sicilians and Italians who are the object of anti-French campaigns," campaigns that increasingly commingled nation and empire with Catholicism's diverse representatives in North Africa.[128]

DISCORD AND EXPANSION

The Church in Tunisia reflected larger struggles between church and state in France, between the French Catholic Church and Rome, and among Catholic nations with imperial ambitions in the Maghrib. In 1843 the Holy See named an Italian Capuchin, Fidèle Sutter, as apostolic vicar, which appeared to erode

France's long-standing role as protector of the Roman Catholic Church in Ottoman lands. The dramatic upsurge in new French congregations devoted to overseas work only complicated things. It was not clear if French national law regulating education applied in missions; for example, the Loi Falloux of 1850 stated that primary-school teachers had to have a teaching certificate—*brevet de capacité*—although Catholic congregations were not necessarily subject to this requirement.[129] For most of the century, Italian clergy and missions were at odds with other Catholic groups, particularly the French. This mare's nest of Catholic enmity may partially explain why the SSJ carried on its work in a Muslim state without too much interference at first—much in contrast, once again, with French Algeria, where the order had been expelled because of Sister Vialar's refusal to submit to the will of the Catholic hierarchy. In Tunisia, a single hierarchy did not exist. And unlike Algeria, Maltese pastors were recruited to tend to the faithful in Tunisia because it was reasoned that "Maltese priests alone could dampen their lawlessness."[130]

In 1846 Maltese residents sought permission for a "national" church in Tunis separate both from Rome and from France. In a long petition addressed to the British consulate in Italian and signed (or x-ed by illiterates) by several hundred Maltese, the petitioners stated that "because our numbers increase on a daily basis, it is necessary to create a second parish church specifically for the Maltese . . . since the vast majority of the Maltese do not know the Italian language which is used for preaching and daily instruction."[131] The petition's proposals are revealing: first, that the new church be placed under the protection of the British sovereign and the local consulate; second, that the church be dedicated to San Paolo Naufrago, a saint greatly venerated by the Maltese; and third, that the church be governed by a committee of five elected deputies with permission from Ahmad Bey. While the petition failed and a uniquely Maltese church never saw the light of day, it is significant that the bey and British consul were seen as patrons for a parish organized along the lines of Maltese language, identity, and religiosity. Faced with the impossibility of establishing their own church, the Maltese faithful aided SSJ expansion by petitioning the mother house to send sisters and by organizing communal fund-raising.

In Sfax, local families made such a request in 1852; six SSJ sisters arrived to set up a primary school and create an outpatient health clinic for the city's Muslim and Jewish inhabitants. The same process was at work in Djerba, which despite its relatively small Catholic population—only 300 Maltese and Italian out of 40,000 inhabitants—asked for three sisters to run a girls school. While the SSJ did not arrive in Mahdiya until 1882, the history of the town's first church building illustrates patterns discussed earlier. Originally an olive oil refinery, the structure was given to Sutter by the bey in 1861. The Capuchin priest from Calabria, Père Vitaliano da Tiriolo, initiated the custom of public processions outside church walls. Not only did "Muslims and Jews take part with respect" in the pageantry to honor the Virgin but sailors and fishermen, the port's most marginal and socially suspect groups, were incorporated into the ceremonies. Until the early twentieth century, long-distance fishermen from villages in the Apulia, notably Trani and Barletta, left home in autumn for six- to nine-month sojourns in Tunisian waters. Their inclusion in religious feasts suggests that the parish aimed to integrate potential troublemakers into town life, if only seasonally.[132]

As critical to the creation of new schools or parishes were lay women, such as Annetta Muniglia in Sousse, who acted as benefactors by donating money or providing church furnishings with their own labor: "the women of Sousse paid for the drapes for the windows and great doors of the church."[133] Another campaign produced sufficient funds to purchase land for a Catholic cemetery in Sousse. These activities invested newly arrived Maltese and Sicilian families in the local community by drawing upon collective, freely given, although gendered, labor to construct schools, clinics, cemeteries, or churches and to furnish the interiors of religious buildings. Philanthropic campaigns in foreign Catholic parishes implicated Tunisia in transnational charitable networks, since diaspora members urged relatives "back home" to contribute. These activities transformed small, isolated groups from population islands into nodes attached to larger transversal and trans-sea networks and may have encouraged additional immigration.

In Sousse, the town's sole priest, Père Agostino, took the initiative and begged Emilie de Vialar to send teaching and nursing sisters for a school and clinic. Three SSJ members arrived, among them Joséphine Daffis. Daffis, from a noble family of Toulouse, entered the congregation in 1830 and accompanied Vialar first to Algeria and then Tunisia in 1844; by the time that she settled in Sousse, she had acquired substantial hands-on medical experience. Yet the Catholic community in Sousse was small and poor; after three years of paying rent for the school, its financial backers withdrew. Sister Joséphine set out to purchase a building and here her reputation for healing proved decisive. The French consul supported her appeals to the bey, who granted the sisters *habus* properties—three storage buildings and a small house—through a legal mechanism known as *inzal,* a perpetual lease. In 1858 Joséphine became the mother superior in Sousse as well as administrator of the school and hospital. A visitor to the school in 1860 found five religious instructing fifty girls from wealthy as well as poor families, the latter admitted free, with the usual mix of mainly Maltese or Italian pupils and a smattering of French.[134]

Characterized by a priest in Sousse as a *femme-apôtre* (female apostle), Joséphine was revered as a physician by city inhabitants. And small wonder. For years she practiced pharmacology and medicine, including surgery, and successfully amputated the gangrenous arm of a Tunisian patient, saving his life. During the 1864 insurrection, she refused to abandon her clinic and patients to flee Sousse with the rest of the Europeans. After the 1881 invasion and occupation, a gendered division of labor was immediately reimposed. When Joséphine attempted to pursue medical practice at the French military hospital in Sousse, she found herself demoted; the male physicians condescendingly described her as "a mother, a strong mother" but proscribed her from practicing.[135] As for the 1890 ceremony honoring her, it was symbolically significant that the French decoration was bestowed first; only afterward was the beylical medal making Daffis *commandeur du Nishan al-Iftikhar* awarded. When Monsieur Tauchon, the *contrôleur civil*, conferred the Légion d'Honneur, he revealed another motive for the award—the Italian menace. "Worthy of the highest esteem because of all she has done for the honor of her country and her religious order," the official opined that Joséphine deserved special commendation because she had instructed children of diverse religious and ethnic backgrounds without distinguishing among them; that she had instructed Italian pupils was deemed especially meritorious. Her funeral several years later in 1894 offered the occasion for another magnificent public event, with flags flying at half mast.[136] Mercifully, Sister Joséphine departed this earth when she did. Only nine years later, Protectorate officials began seizing Church properties, closing schools and clinics, and even banned the popular celebration of Corpus Christi from the streets in conformance with church-state disestablishment laws; significantly, the processions in honor of the Virgin of Trapani were not banned by colonial officials, who feared further antagonizing the large Sicilian community in Tunisia.

The missionary archive casting the SSJ and other congregations as the object of universal appreciation in fact needs to be tempered by other sources, however sparse. There existed deeply felt religious antagonisms. One of the most evocative ethnographic accounts comes from Sister Joséphine's town, Sousse, which still suffered several years later from the fallout of the 1864 rebellion and the fierce state repression that followed. One Sunday afternoon in the summer of 1867, as European families promenaded around the Place du Commerce near the port and Christian quarter, a wandering holy man (who was no doubt mad) arrived in the square. Removing his clothes, the naked man began washing himself with soap and water in public, much to horror of the assembled crowd. This spectacle endured for nearly two hours, during which the dervish took delight in washing his private parts. Addressing the Muslim men in the throng, he shouted: "Do as I do [and] wash thoroughly your women; the French are going to come and take over the country; the French like to have your women clean in order to sleep with them; the French always have the upper hand."[137] The same report noted that a French national had been incarcerated, probably by the vice-consul, for a grave affront to the Muslim community—he had ripped the face veil off of a Tunisian woman in the streets, a deliberately provocative gesture of cultural disrespect. In crowded popular quarters of the capital or provincial ports where diverse classes of Europeans rubbed shoulders with Tunisians, incidents such as these betrayed growing resentment against the increasingly numerous, powerful, and visible Christians.[138]

COLONIAL SEQUELS

By 1881, the SSJ boasted a network of clinics and schools. In La Goulette, the order's schools counted, among its 148 female pupils, 1 Tunisian Muslim girl and 16 Jewish girls. By 1890, enrollments had risen dramatically to 236 pupils whose backgrounds reflected decades of trans-Mediterranean settlement. Italians outnumbered French students by 2 to 1; most numerous were the Maltese, with 177 girls.[139] The graduates' social destinies are important but little is known about what life held—whether in the pre-1881 era or later. It seems that girls of working-class backgrounds became dressmakers and seamstresses, reputable professions guaranteeing stable income; until recently, many Maltese women in Tunis earned their living this way. Others returned home to aid families until suitable marriages could be arranged. The poorest found positions as household servants, although domestic service was not highly regarded as a profession due to the attendant sexual dangers.[140]

While it would be somewhat of a stretch to characterize La Goulette as the Alexandria of the Barbary Coast, the port was home to over 4,000 inhabitants, of which 1,500 were Catholics, making the proportion of Christian newcomers to natives one of the highest in the larger region. By the early Protectorate, the humble Capuchin chapel had given way to a large and elegant church and the Catholic mission owned—instead of merely renting—several buildings. Judging by enrollments, the Frères des Écoles Chrétiennes ran successful boys' schools in La Goulette, Tunis, and elsewhere. The pupils, who lined up daily for class or squirmed uncomfortably on the hard, wooden benches, came from backgrounds that revealed once more the social geography of population movements in the central Mediterranean. During the early Protectorate, admission to public schools was restricted by a new criterion, race, which glossed religion and ethnicity and severely limited native and some non-French children's access to academic institutions; vocational training was proposed instead. Nevertheless, the Alliance Israélite Universelle schools for girls in Tunis after 1892 offered academic schooling for both Jewish and non-Jewish girls.[141]

But the Protectorate brought with it more than the French army or metropole bureaucrats. Appointed archbishop of Algiers in 1866, Lavigerie's unbridled zeal for proselytizing to Muslims had set him against civilian and military officials alike. Seeking a more congenial environment, he moved to Tunis in 1881 and was elevated the next year to the position of cardinal of the See of Carthage; but he soon provoked more controversy by publicly attacking Islam. His main opponents were not only Muslims but also fellow Catholics because, true to his character, the cardinal administered churches, religious orders, and educational institutions in imperious fashion. As France's army was invading, the cardinal labored furiously, along with the French consul, to prevent Italian nuns of the Salesian order from establishing a house and school in La Goulette. These machinations nearly triggered serious diplomatic crises, since jurisdictional issues immediately arose—were the Italian Salesian sisters under France's protection, as was the case for Italian nuns in Cairo and elsewhere in the Levant? Or were they protected by the Italian consulate in Tunis?[142] Lavigerie's actions and inflammatory rhetoric caused relations with the Italian clergy, mainly the Capuchins, to deteriorate and in consequence a large contingent of brothers and priests departed for Italy.

Embittered relations with Italian congregations dated back to the 1870s and came to roost on the Chapel of Saint Louis, which had fallen into disrepair. Lavigerie relentlessly pursued chapel politics to wrest guardianship from the Capuchins through accusations to the Holy See that the Italian clerics had neglected the edifice. In a trompe l'oeil diplomatic maneuver, Lavigerie petitioned Rome for permission to restore, expand, and not coincidentally, to assert uncontested authority over the chapel by staffing it with members of his newly created order. Soon the first White Fathers arrived in Tunis to care for the Chapel of Saint Louis, which was greatly enlarged. The politically motivated drive to create a monumental chapel came at a cost. The elaborate church that eventually replaced the older, modest edifice symbolized French-Christian aggression, departing from earlier missionary traditions of a shared built environment. The French consul, Roustan, was acutely aware of how Muslim notables interpreted this immense structure: "St. Louis on Byrsa hill dominates the palace of the bey and the summer villas of his chief ministers; they do not appreciate the fact that the French flag planted on top of the chapel waves above their heads. The chapel resembles much too much a citadel. Foreigners always use it as a means to stir up anti-French sentiment."[143] In 1892 Lavigerie ended his days in Algiers while on a visit; his remains were laboriously transported back to Carthage for sumptuous burial in the fortresslike cathedral towering over Husaynid residences below. After North Africa's independence, his body was transported once again, this time to Rome for reburial.[144]

Nearly four decades after first finding refuge in Tunisia, the SSJ was joined by other female orders and, by the turn of the twentieth century, at least twelve Catholic female and five male congregations had been established. At Lavigerie's insistence, the White Sisters had opened a school for girls of all nationalities in La Marsa in 1883. Two years later, the cardinal directed them to open Le Refuge Saint Augustin, exclusively devoted to the care of "fallen or abandoned girls older than fifteen years." The institution, strategically hidden in a corner of La Marsa on a hill near the sea, limited social contact between its inmates and the fashionable summer resort, which itself enjoyed a reputation for light morals. Equally important, La Marsa was far enough from La Goulette, which as a port operated as a turnstile for imported vice, and distant from Tunis, with its own morally suspect neighborhoods and their secrets. In its first year, the refuge sheltered a handful of Italian and Maltese girls as well as one Tunisian Muslim, but six years later ninety-five girls lived and worked together in the institution, which then became an orphanage. To support themselves, the young female inmates labored as laundresses for male clerics, teachers, and the boarders at the Collège Charles in Tunis.[145]

The refuge raises intriguing questions—was this the first institution specifically for "fallen" girls? Although available documentation is sparse, the SSJ had cared for girls in precarious situations in earlier decades, as indicated by elliptical allusions in consular correspondence and in notes exchanged between Tunisian and European officials. Did Lavigerie borrow this idea from the SSJ? And why did Lavigerie instruct the White Sisters to create a primary school in La Marsa that competed with the long-established SSJ institution? Was the imperial prelate promoting the work of nuns whom he considered "his own" to the detriment of the SSJ? While answers to these questions await their historian, it is irrefutable that the first female missionaries to take root in the land of Saint Augustine and Saint Louis did so thanks to the patronage of Muslim princes.

Religious women were a force to be reckoned with, not least because the presence of celibate, single women in French colonies vastly complicated the play of local politics. If Catholic female religious were lauded for their hard work and devotion in overseas missions, they often antagonized the Church hierarchy, local male officials, and the French state. The combustive mixture of the SSJ founder's gender, education, and social class explains not only Emilie de Vialar's tumultuous relations with the bishop of Algiers but also how her congregation came to Tunisia. Essential to local assimilation, however incomplete, was the nature of the Husaynid state, a diverse household bureaucracy whose patronage furnished the resources required for mission work—buildings, land, funding—as well as freedom of movement and action. And the fact that many missionaries—both female and male—spent most of their adult lives in Tunisia—in some cases, like Sister Joséphine, over six decades—assured at least partial "Tunisification."

Another critical factor was timing. When the SSJ order arrived, Tunisia was soon to suffer the visitations of a terrible disease. In addition, the Husaynid state urgently needed agents and institutions to maintain social harmony among expatriate communities, mainly Catholics, who by midcentury numbered at least 9,000—all the more so because this was precisely the period when state reorganization, combined with uncontrolled immigration, introduced instabilities into the system. That Ahmad Bey occupied the throne when the congregation was expelled from Algeria constituted one of the most fortuitous elements in this female missionary saga. But the entrée that powerful creoles, such as the Raffo family, enjoyed with the palace proved immensely beneficial to the sisters, as did the fact that European notables looked to the missionaries to tame the lumpen proletariat that disembarked with each arriving ship. Finally, the strategy of recruiting local women for the novitiate embedded the SSJ more firmly into certain social circles.

Another set of questions revolves around the circulation of knowledge about North Africa, Islam, and Tunisian society. Did the SSJ contribute to the fund of negative stereotypes held by Europeans at the time about the "Arab family" or Muslim sexual deviance? Unfortunately, there is not much evidence concerning the order's contribution to Orientalist literary or artistic production about the "East." But the SSJ might have contributed to another strand in that tradition— what Jane Schneider calls "Orientalism in one place."[146] Most of the congregation's early labors focused upon impoverished Sicilian and Maltese families universally scorned by northern Europeans as "barbarous." Perhaps the sisters' work, mission reports, and fund-raising in Europe helped to disseminate the idea that southern Mediterranean Christians, regarded as "not-quite-Europeans," were in need of redemption. Finally, Abbé Bourgade's influence upon thinking in the metropole or in colonial circles across France's empire, particularly his views of and writings on Islam, merits further research.[147]

What can be concluded about the missionaries' long-term importance to North Africa's history? While highly speculative due to the archive and current state of secondary scholarship, questions can be raised concerning the social impact that female missionaries exerted upon a society organized around the principle of male-female segregation, which restricted many (particularly urban) women's access to certain kinds of spaces and placed limits on specific types of physical mobility. Women without men, the sisters resided alone, without family or protectors; they worked in public arenas and traveled unaccompanied by male kin. As lifelong celibates and desexed females, the Catholic sisters enjoyed a liberty of movement not available to other women as well as intimate contacts with families and households that male missionaries or colonial officials never claimed. Because of this, Catholic missionary women established girls' schools, clinics, and orphanages and made home visits; frequently they were the only Europeans with whom indigenous women interacted. Did the SSJ and later congregations suggest, however tentatively, novel spheres of female action? Directly related, the existence of girls' schools segregated by sex and run by all-female staff in the era before colonialism might have rendered female schooling more acceptable during the Protectorate, or less problematic, for certain segments of Tunis society, all the more so since the missionaries were not associated with a brutal military invasion and occupation. However, by promoting conversion among minority groups in Algeria, the missionaries introduced cultural alienation and deep communal divisions, as tragically manifest in the Kabylia.

This story also points to the imperative of interrogating temporal boundaries, such as the notion of "precolonial," which often serves as the chronological antechamber to modern, imperial European history. Despite what colonial cheerleaders such as Jules Ferry and Paul Cambon claimed, the French Protectorate was hemmed in by webs of alliances, bargains, and deals concluded between the Husaynid state, creole residents, missionaries of various stripes, and the highly diverse communities that regarded Tunisia as home long before 1881. The ultimate irony came with the disestablishment laws separating church and state in France and in French colonies from 1905 on. Much church property in Tunisia—land and structures—had been bestowed as gifts, loans, or rentals by the palace or notables to various Catholic missions. When Third Republic anticlerical colonial bureaucrats set out to seize Church properties, they faced a daunting legal challenge because property titles were frequently held, in one way or another, by the dynasty.[148] Interpreted differently and applied unevenly in various parts of the empire, the disestablishment laws demonstrated more than anything the force of precolonial pacts between a Muslim state and Catholic congregations. By 1914, French missionary education had been more or less reinstated in Tunisia expressly to offset the dangers posed by the large Italian community; the Italian threat was judged even more perilous than the dangers posed by Catholic missionaries, especially in the realm of education.[149]

North Africa's highly diverse missionary encounters should make us wary of tidy mappings or facile generalizations. In Algeria, relationships between missionaries, local indigenous notables, colonial officials, and settler populations ranged from resolutely hostile to cozy to indifferent. For Tunisia, the wild card was the bruising political tug-of-war over the country's destiny, which only worsened with formal colonial rule and which resonated among the men and women of God, sometimes negatively affecting their work, at others reinforcing it.[150] Another layer of complication resulted from the sometimes bitter competition among missionary societies in the field as well as conflict among ecclesiastical authorities in Europe. In sum, interpreting the SSJ's work, reception, and social insertion into a precolonial Muslim state through a binary *optique* fails to translate the multiple registers of local assimilation or how the sisters' actions resonated among Muslims, Jews, fellow missionaries, or immigrants. Daily social commerce between the heterogeneous segments of society demonstrates the fallacy of formulations such as "Christian versus Muslim." Last but not least, the tale of a Muslim dynasty that afforded refuge to Catholic sisters expelled from a purportedly Christian and European colony whose grand mission was to civilize is frankly a story for our times.

The next chapter takes us away from the clinic and schoolroom, missions and missionaries, cholera and conversion, to visit the beach and hydrotherapy stations against the backdrop of growing health tourism to North Africa. It employs a household-based approach to examine forms of mainly elite sociability associated with the sea and healing waters. Households were not only economic and procreative units but also managed leisure, health-seeking activities, and social communication in ways that implicated members in transversal alliances stretching beyond the limits of kin-defined networks. Women's quarters were important spaces of materiality and of display, where gifts from foreign diplomats or monarchs might be on view; and households were far from immobile but moved about according to the season, which held political consequences.

8

Where Elites Meet

Households, Harim Visits, and Sea Bathing

What a joy it would be to the Prince of Wales to have one [a harim].
CAROLINE, PRINCESS OF WALES (1816)

Strolling along the Corniche in La Marsa, one immediately notices a curious structure partially set in the water. Topped by a whitewashed dome, with balconies and verandas facing the Mediterranean, it is linked to the beach by a small walkway. To the right, another much smaller edifice sits abandoned and half in ruins; fishermen now use it to store nets. A stone's throw away, the wholly submerged remains of a third structure are barely visible at low tide. Today the largest pavilion, built during the reign of Ahmad Bey, has been converted into a three-star restaurant, Qubbat al-Hawa', which serves alcohol until the wee hours of the morning and attracts a high-end clientele. Whatever their present state, these buildings constitute the architectural remains of a seaside culture of sociability that combined politics and leisure, harim visits and diplomacy, business and water therapy.[1]

By the late nineteenth century, gracious neo-Moorish buildings known as *bayt al-bahr* (sea house) sprang up along the shore from La Marsa to the thermal station Hammam Lif and served as bathing pavilions for elite households as well as for the Husaynid princesses. While elevated rank imposed various degrees of seclusion, the women for whom these pavilions were constructed enjoyed sea bathing for its health-conferring benefits. Not far away stood elegant palaces that housed the capital city's great families along with extended kin, clients, and servants during the hottest months of the year. Included in this culture of Mediterranean sociability, often in surprisingly intimate ways, were European notables who participated in the same social forms and seasonal rhythms as their Muslim peers, which brought them into the heart of Tunisian family life—the household, or *dar*, including the harim.

288

FIGURE 15. Women's bathing pavilion, La Marsa beach, c. 1890. One of the many bathing houses that used to dot the shore, employed by women from the palace or notable families in order to take sea baths in privacy. (Charles Lallemand, *Tunis au XIXe siècle* [Paris: La Maison Quantin, 1890].)

This chapter salvages a social universe obscured by colonial narratives and subsequently buried by the triumphant nationalism of the postcolonial era. Anthropologists argue that in house-centered societies, like Tunisia, "the house and the domestic group are social units defining community organization, the forms of social exchange, the inheritance system, and the transmission of knowledge."[2] Moreover, recent work demonstrates that the household was a space where large-scale historical processes not only resonated but were incubated.[3] If much of the physical evidence and archival materials for this seaside culture were deliberately destroyed after 1956, nevertheless, an ethnographic recreation of the forms, spaces, and meanings of this nearly vanished world is possible through an approach that is primarily household based. From this perspective, the household emerges as a critical site of sociability in this particular cultural and historical context, although conventional scholarly wisdom held otherwise.

Since the French scholar Maurice Agulhon first elaborated the notion of *sociabilité* in the 1960s, historians have probed the significance of diverse associational forms—from Masonic lodges and clubs to cafés and confraternities—that allegedly lay outside of family structures and thus operated as midwives of modernity.[4] Juxtaposed, often implicitly, against these sites for extrafamilial modernities was "southern sociability," assumed to be a distinguishing feature of kin-based Mediterranean societies where the clan's ascendancy inhibited associational life, a defining feature of modernity itself. A second related assumption specific to Muslim societies held that households with harims were inaccessible to the outside world and thus excluded from wider networks or social processes transcending the boundaries of kinship.[5] As we well know, in Orientalist discourse, "harim" conjured an imagined, eroticized border encircling domestic compounds and its "caged" members, and as such was impervious to the forces of modernity.[6]

This chapter argues that specific kinds of sociabilities were characteristic of Husaynid political culture and that the women of elite households, together with their kin, friends, and clients, were critical to the system's smooth functioning. Not focusing solely upon harims moves the discussion forward—away from its current fixation on foreign representations of Muslim women and toward an appreciation of the myriad ways that elite households shaped, and were shaped by, various kinds of exchanges and circuits. A range of social practices implicated creoles and resident Europeans in the "palace-harim complex" and therefore in the capital city's elite society. Thus, harim visits—highly ritualized social calls excluding most, but not all, men due to norms of sexual segregation—are recast as sites of diplomacy, gift giving, and information gathering. Ties of amity forged by these rituals resulted in handsome bonuses—not least in the form of long-term loans of princely seaside villas to select clients.

For our purposes, sociability is loosely defined as social networks, both homogenous and heterogeneous in nature, generated by households as they entertained guests, negotiated marriages, acted as patrons, conducted business, celebrated festivals, or indulged in therapeutic activities such as hydrotherapy, which also had religious associations.[7] These are the major questions: How did diverse kinds of exchanges, mediated by households, structure the exercise of power? How did landlord politics, patronage, and seaside diplomacy implicate non-kin notables in the palace-harim complex? In what ways did ordinary people participate in local cultural and social forms attached to the sea? How did resident Europeans, and increasingly tourists and travelers, engage in local healing practices associated with thermal waters and sea bathing? And what historical processes folded these older practices and spaces into the emerging, quite lucrative business of transnational health travel? Finally, how might a close ethnographic look at different expressions of sociabilities force us to rethink conventional chronological markers or divides, such as precolonial and colonial?

A CULTURE FROM THE SEA

Some of the most ubiquitous symbols employed in Tunisian folk art are inspired by the sea. Taxi-cab drivers hang fish medallions on their windshields as insurance policies to ward off the evil eye and (hopefully) prevent accidents. The small wooden vessels that ply the waters at night in search of an increasingly elusive catch are decorated with brightly colored symbolic motifs. Shopkeepers in the Tunis madina used to do a good business selling Mediterranean talismans—in the form of fish—for home use. And the greatest culinary honor bestowed upon dinner guests is still an extravagant seafood couscous. While disappearing under the onslaught of globalization, with its attendant cultural and economic maladies, this culture struggles to survive. It is most clearly perceived in the seasonal shift from the social life of the cold, wet winters to the tempo of June, when families begin to gather at the beach and the denizens of coastal villages ask neighbors if they have taken their first sea bath yet.

In the nineteenth century, during the torrid summer months, the palace and haute bourgeoisie performed tightly choreographed rites that entailed packing up entire households and relocating to residences on the sea, moving scores, if not hundreds, of people. To staff summer villas, wealthy families transported cohorts of relatives, retainers, hangers-on, and servants (and slaves before abolition). But it was not only the ruling family or court elite who fled to the beach during the summer. Powerful 'ulama' families, both Maliki and Hanafi, spent the winter season in palaces clustered in identifiable neighborhoods, or hawmat, in the madina; the areas around nahj al-basha (street of the pasha) or nahj al-hukkam (street of the judges) boasted high concentrations of religious notables. But in summer this all changed; when the first scorching winds burst upon Tunis, families—such as the Bayrams or Ben 'Achours (or Ibn 'Ashurs)—fled to villas situated on the shore, particularly to Sidi Bou Sa'id. (Indeed, today many of these residences, formerly occupied only in summer months, are year-round family dwellings, the case of the Ben 'Achour clan's lovely compound in La Marsa.)[8]

Relocation to the coast allowed these families to forge or preserve bonds with other households, including the all-important matter of marriage alliances, in ways different from customary winter sociability in the capital. This summer princely progress so key to elite identity was reflected in local Islamic marriage contracts and prenuptial agreements designating where the bride would reside during specific seasons. The contract for a bride from Tunis wed to a Qayrawani (i.e., a man from the city of al-Qayrawan in the interior) "stipulated that the husband consent to bring his wife to Tunis every six months and rent a vacation house for her in one of the beach suburbs of the capital."[9]

In short, "going to the beach" constituted one of the most visible signs of high social rank, a tradition that persisted well into the colonial period. The use of carriages by elite women was described in 1844: "the Moorish women always travel in close carriages (rather carts on springs, and so low that scarcely a boy of six years old can stand upright in them) generally covered with white canvass."[10] Four decades later, the Austrian traveler Baron Ernst von Hesse-Wartegg, who spent considerable time in Tunisia, noted around 1880 that, "in spring, when the hot days begin, I have often seen long rows of hermetically-closed carriages with armed eunuchs on the boxes and guards on horseback, leave town [Tunis] to go to the watering-places or country seats of the neighborhood—these were the harims of the rich, changing domicile for some months."[11]

The court's seasonal mobility might be conceptualized as one symbolic performance of authority taken from a larger repertoire. As mentioned in chapter 1, two major manifestations of "power in motion" existed in Tunisia: The first was the mahalla, which tied populations of mountains, steppes, and oases to the dynasty and capital city through justice, taxation, and often brutal resource expropriation. The second displacement was the movement of the Husaynid family, the government—including scribes and ministers—and urban notables to seaside palaces where they resided for months. Well before the Protectorate, the summer relocation drew along in its wake increasing numbers of Europeans and other foreign residents. While women never accompanied the mahalla (as far as we know), they were intimately involved in the summer holiday royal progress.

Upper-class Muslim women eagerly welcomed the Mediterranean season because it conferred more liberty of movement.[12] These months were marked by celebrations of joyful events in the life cycle of the family—births, circumcisions, betrothals, and marriages—often accompanied by performances of Andalusian music. The term *khala'a* (pastoral pleasures), a specifically Tunisian glossing of a word that in classical Arabic usage has libertine associations, meant summertime festivities that frequently resounded with music.[13] In addition to family gatherings often lasting into the night and visits to saints' shrines, sea bathing was a favorite pastime for women. The *bayt al-bahr* translated gendered leisure and healing practices into concrete form. Wooden shelters—or, in the case of the aristocratic or princely families, splendid marble and stone structures—set into the water with trapdoors in the middle over the sea permitted women to bathe unseen. Some structures, such as Dar Mohsen in Sidi Bou Sa'id, boasted two stories with a kitchen, library, and other amenities. Dar Agha, a nineteenth-century summer palace in a neighborhood of Carthage, eventually boasted several wooden sea houses; the extended family retreated to the pavilions to spend the day together enjoying sea baths or sailed across the Bay of Tunis in skiffs for the thermal waters at Korbous.[14] The French artist Charles Lallemand painted the lovely colored image in 1890 of the bathing house in La Marsa now converted into a tourist restaurant: "The women of La Marsa and Sidi Bou Sa'id take sea baths here far from inquiring eyes. They arrived in carriages with the shades pulled down. In the middle of the building is a swimming pool through which the sea water enters freely. The princesses of the bey's family have a similar bathing house not far away from this one."[15]

Ordinary Tunisians, both Muslim and Jewish, also practiced sea bathing and hydrotherapy or, in the desert oases, visited hot springs for healing a range of diseases, including infertility. In many cases, they frequented the same thermal stations as had the Romans. At La Goulette, women who could not afford seaside pavilions bathed at night on the sandy beach fully dressed in light apparel. The state decreed some spa towns, such as Kelibia, to be tax-free zones where onerous impositions on exchanges of goods and services, the *mahsulat,* did not apply, attracting sellers and buyers from all over.[16] Therefore local and regional trade were linked to the business that water healing represented.

The three most ancient and important thermal stations in the Tunis region were Hammam Lif (or Hammam al-Nif), eleven miles from the capital; Korbous, thirty-four miles away; and Nabeul, on the eastern flank of the Cap Bon. However, distance was calculated differently than over land, since many cure seekers used small boats to reach hydrotherapy spots. Hammam Lif sits at the foot of Bu Qarnayn, or the two-horned mountain. Frequented since Punic times, the small village of Naro, as the Carthaginians called it, was renamed Aquae Persianae by the Romans. In the eighteenth century, 'Ali Pasha, bey of Tunis, constructed a princely pavilion at Hammam Lif, which subsequently boasted a bathing pool and a caravansary for merchants and caravans traveling across the Maghrib as well as for hydrotherapy seekers; once again trade was combined with water cures. In 1756, a member of the Bayram family, Muhammad ibn Hassin, undertook a scientific study of Tunisia's different thermal stations, classifying them according to their efficacy in healing.[17]

Beginning in 1826, Husayn Bey expanded the Hammam Lif palace and facilities in order to take cures for extended periods of time with the court in attendance. Completed several years later, the new ensemble included two-storey buildings, a monumental entrance, and gardens with a kiosk.[18] Husayn Bey paid dearly for his thermal treatment, since early in 1829, while he was absent, some of his courtiers in Tunis robbed the state treasury and later that same year fomented a cabal to overthrow him. By the mid-nineteenth century, Hammam Lif boasted the beylical palace, an array of outbuildings, and "a grand bathing establishment situated near the Roman baths."[19] Both Tunisian and European cure seekers from the capital city brought along servants as well as provisions and rented out small houses or rooms in the neighborhood from the locals, often for extended periods of time.[20] After his first stroke, Ahmad Bey spent much of his time residing in the Hammam Lif palace that belonged to a court favorite, Mustafa Sahib al-Tabi', or in his own palace in La Goulette, presumably taking the waters to speed recovery.[21] The same bey also built another palace in La Marsa—which still exists today, although in a state of advanced ruin—and the bathing pavilion Qubbat al-Hawa'.[22] This palace had a separate wing for the princesses, who could reach the bathing house from their private quarters in only minutes by carriage. While the architectural origins for the *bayt al-bahr* remain unknown, the La Marsa palace's architecture is emblematic of the decorative, spatial, and structural features that marked the period, betraying an aesthetic sensibility composed of diverse cultural elements.

Located on the western edge of the Cap Bon, Korbous, or Aquae Calidae Carpitanae, had been the spa of choice for wealthy Romans from Carthage because its sulphur springs, averaging between 120 and 140 degrees Fahrenheit, were believed highly efficacious. By the early nineteenth century, Korbous was a place of no great importance because it could only be reached with difficulty by land. Local people served as guides along the winding trails leading to the thermal waters and made a living by renting rooms to temporary visitors. Then Ahmad Bey constructed a palace bathing complex that provoked a moderate boom in the village's fortunes as the ruler's presence brought improvements in road transportation, making the springs more accessible. Tunisians and resident Europeans employed the waters of Korbous to treat rheumatism, arthritis, dermatitis, and digestive problems. While documentation on health seekers in the precolonial period is scarce, the well-known poet from Tunis, al-Baji al-Mas'udi (1810–1880), sought a cure there, apparently staying for an extended period of time, which moved him to compose nostalgic verses lauding the capital city while in "exile" only a few miles away.[23]

But the sacred was never far removed from health-seeking behavior and social praxis. As was true of most springs in North Africa, the waters of Korbous enjoyed the protection of a renowned saint, Sidi Abu 'Ammara, whose zawiya (tomb-shrine) was the object of veneration and pilgrimage; women in particular sought the saint's blessings for infertility. While the tombs of the saintly lineage remain in Korbous, today the village serves a very restricted clientele of local cure seekers and the beylical palace is in sad disarray. Set on a hill overlooking the town with a splendid view of the Gulf of Tunis, the zawiya's present tattered condition hints at serious erosion in spiritual reputation.

The third main hydrotherapy station is Nabeul, the most distant from the capital. While documentation on precolonial practices is not abundant, evidence from the early Protectorate demonstrates the persistence of older patterns of leisure. In his 1892 report to Justin Massicault, the French resident general (1886–1892), Louis Créput, an official with the Contrôle Civil de Nabeul, noted that "the climate of Nabeul is so temperate and so mild that the town serves as a summer resort for Jewish and Muslim families from elsewhere who come to take the waters. The trip between the town and the sea is done via a taxi service which has discount prices of 15 centimes per person. Several outdoor public establishments—both Jewish and Muslim—serve drinks and confer upon the beach an animated atmosphere that frequently lasts into the night."[24]

In contrast to the sociospatial organization that colonial officials and resort promoters later imposed upon thermal spas like Korbous or Nabeul, hammam signified a number of interrelated things in the cultural vocabulary of the time.

It could mean a steam bath, a bathing pool, a thermal spa, or simply a watering place. Weekly visits to public baths constituted religious duties that were tied to Islamic and Jewish purity and pollution taboos and were required for bodily health, spiritual well-being, and morality. But visiting urban bathhouses was also a social ritual, as were sea bathing and taking thermal waters. Thus the religious and social—and the purified and political—were enmeshed in complex ways. In addition, the fact that Europeans and others rented rooms or cottages from the local inhabitants of thermal sites, such as Hammam Lif and Korbous, indicates that a form of health tourism existed in Tunisia well before colonialism. The rentals of simple abodes near springs or the sea paralleled the exchanges of sumptuous pleasure properties among elites, suggesting that thermal stations represented places where religion or social class did not prevent seasonal mixing, as demonstrated by Créput's 1892 report on Nabeul.

CREOLE AMUSEMENTS, SEASIDE DIPLOMACY, AND HARIM VISITS

Summer vs. winter lifestyles very different

To appreciate the role played by seasonality in shaping relations between the Husaynid family, the court, and creole or foreign notables, we need to return to the three most important spatial coordinates in the capital city region: first, Tunis proper; second, the Mediterranean villages; and third, the small town and palace complex of Bardo.[25] At the Bardo, European consuls made formal visits in the ruler's audience chamber; but the presence of the *mahkama,* or hall of justice, which attracted hordes of subjects and supplicants, made getting the bey's undivided attention somewhat daunting.[26] Thus, a geographical element that heightened the political importance of summer residence was the fact that it was easier to gain access to, and coax favors from, rulers or palace retainers in the cozy atmosphere of the Mediterranean suburbs than during the winter court season.

What emerges from this mapping exercise are the residential strategies pursued by Europeans, who duplicated the summer rituals of the court and Tunis elites by clustering in close proximity to, or frequently in, villas owned by the palace. In 1831, Sir Thomas Reade, the British consul general, wrote, "The house which I reside in at present is in the country, in the midst of those occupied in the Hot months and in some instances even in the winter by the other consuls, and is only one hour and one half from the Bey's palace, and not more than half the distance that Tunis is from the anchorage, which is certainly a great advantage."[27] A fellow Englishman, Sir Grenville Temple, who called upon the Reade family in their "spacious summer palace" in 1833, noted that their villa was "surrounded by a number of other country seats inhabited by the first Moorish families, or by European consuls; all these houses are connected with pretty and shady gardens."[28] Another visitor to the Reade household in the 1840s observed that "when Hussain Bey died 1835, he loved the English and heaped privileges upon them. The royal palace of the Abdellia [sic], situated in La Marsa . . . was ceded to Sir Thomas Reade as a country residence, for a moderate rent. . . . Once the bey honored Reade by dining with him at the Abdellia, an honor never before nor since accorded any European consul."[29] Other diplomats voiced identical sentiments about the desirability of summer lodgings in proximity to Husaynid households, since these were strategically situated for wheeling and dealing.

The dynasty held in one form or another much of the beachfront real estate, which was graced by magnificent palaces, villas, and pavilions ornamented with fountains, patios, and luxuriant gardens of bougainvillea, jasmine, and palmiers. The assortment of palaces resulted in part from a widely held local belief that, if a ruler died in a particular residence, it would bring misfortune upon his successor to inhabit the same space, which had become *mshuma* (dishonored).[30] With palaces under continual construction, there were plenty to spare, so the beys or princes leased or more often simply loaned for extended periods the most elegant of these palaces to the most powerful Europeans. A similar practice, though under somewhat different circumstances, was already noted in the eighteenth century: rulers attempted to persuade foreign diplomats or military officers with needed skills to accept positions at court by offering tempting inducements. In 1793, Hammuda Bey proposed to take the French consul, Devioze, who had resided in Tunis some twenty years, under his "special protection *[garde]* and provide a residence either in my palace or in one of my seaside villas *[maisons de plaisance]*."[31]

Long- or short-term loans of palatial residences greased the wheels of diplomacy and may have, in at least one instance, averted military hostilities. Remember the Exmouth expedition that anchored off La Goulette in 1816 just after Caroline, Princess of Wales, and her Italian tutor had arrived for their tour of classical sites? In what can only be characterized as hospitality under fire, Muhammad Bey "feted [the princess] in accordance with her rank . . . even appointing his son to accompany her on visits around the country."[32] The ruler housed Caroline and her retinue at the Dar al-Bey in the madina, where a beautiful palace reserved for the most distinguished visitors had been decorated specifically for the royal visitors. Indeed, the Princess of Wales enjoyed a magnificent luncheon with the women of the bey's harim, which she found greatly amusing. Dignitaries such as the Duc de Montpensier, the Prince de Joinville, and the Duc d'Aumale, who made official visits between 1845 and 1846, were housed in the same palace as Caroline.[33] Indeed, even today, the most magnificent ambassadorial accommodations by far is the French residence La Camilla, a former beylical palace in La Marsa with a superb sea view that was "loaned" to France before 1881.

This gifting of housing was a shrewd policy because it created ties of indebtedness and social obligation; the beys were, in effect, landlords to the Europeans. Decades later as the Protectorate was being imposed, a visitor to the Husaynid court observed that, "besides the above-named palaces, there are in Tunis and its environs several others of colossal dimensions and great beauty. But on inquiry they turn out to be the palaces of former beys, given by their successors to the foreign consuls or to Tunisian favourites."[34] And, as seen in the preceding chapter, the Husaynids employed an identical strategy for Catholic missionaries from the 1840s on, providing them with preexisting buildings for schools and clinics. As was true for diplomats and diplomacy, the summer months in Mediterranean villages afforded opportunities to carry on theological debates, sort of interfaith dialogues. Throughout his years in Tunisia, Abbé François Bourgade "maintained amicable relations with the 'ulama' and highly placed officials from the bey's court at their villages in La Marsa and Sidi Bou Sa'id," where he claimed to have participated in "theological discussions of which educated Muslims are so fond."[35] However, hospitality was not one-sided. From Ahmad Bey's reign on, rulers and members of their entourage sometimes attended balls and other grand occasions organized by European associates. When the new French consulate located outside city walls was inaugurated with great pomp in December 1861, Muhammad al-Sadiq Bey and the heir apparent took part in the festivities hosted by the French consul, Léon Roches.[36] The practice of landlord diplomacy and the bestowal of high-end housing, an established Husaynid strategy for managing bigger, meaner foreign states and statesmen, persisted after 1881.

With improvements in the roads linking the capital with coastal suburbs, more Europeans acquired seaside residences. Far from the heat and hubbub of Tunis proper, consular families, members of court, and government officials routinely met. Combining diplomacy with entertaining in a manner reminiscent of tony spas, like Vichy, these gatherings functioned as informal salons.[37] In her letters, Sir Richard Wood's wife Christina portrays the summer season during the 1860s as a moment for intense socializing, which resulted in the circulation of critical information. In July 1861, she "dined at Marsa with the Raffos on Sunday," obtaining insider news from Countess Raffo, whose husband was among the highest officials in the government. The latest political gossip from Europe and the Ottoman Empire, diplomatic postings, and the intimate doings of Tunis elites were reported over sumptuous dinners.[38] Balls, costume parties, and musical evenings served as antidotes to the ennui of daily life.[39]

As might be expected in a semienclosed social universe, personal rivalries, petty bickering, and scandalous behavior—or accusations of such—marked relationships and may have influenced diplomacy as well. The best documented case in the genre of *liaisons dangereuses* was the salon overseen during the 1860s and 1870s by Madame Luigia Traverso Mussalli, the wife of Elias Mussalli and alleged mistress to two French consuls, Léon Roches (in post from 1855 to 1863) and

Théodore Roustan (in post from 1874 to 1882). Emblematic of Euro-Tunisian society, Mussalli and his purportedly wayward wife merit a digression. As discussed in chapter 2, Mussalli, from a Syrian Christian family, had served Egyptian rulers before his engagement as a valued interpreter to Ahmad Bey from 1847 on, a position that soon catapulted him into the Ministry of Foreign Affairs. Mussalli profited handsomely from his post by embezzling state funds until his dismissal in 1872. But his office was restored after his wife, Luigia, intervened on her cuckolded husband's behalf with her lover, Roustan, who in turn importuned Muhammad al-Sadiq Bey's personal physician, Francisco Mascaro, who had the ruler's ear—and so the lines of patronage, intrigue, and behind-the-scenes lobbying went.[40] Regarded as a great beauty, Luigia, the daughter of a Genoese merchant, was born in Tunis in 1835; her household served as a political club for one of two principal factions in the capital, the pro-French party whose ranks included numerous Italians loyal to France. Luigia presided over meetings, discussions, and soirées and appeared in public with Roustan at official diplomatic functions, apparently with her husband's assent or studied indifference.[41] Discussed in Luigia's salon were ways of achieving France's imperial designs on Tunisia through anti-Italian strategies that included marginalizing Italian Catholic missionaries.[42]

In addition to gossipy dinners, other attractions and distractions abounded, although the pursuit of leisure was deeply gendered as well as subject to class. Men from consular or mercantile families went on shooting parties, sometimes with members of the court, in marshlands near the shore rich in fowl and game. The British diplomat John Gibson, who caught malaria while on one such hunting expedition—from which he expired in 1833—was emblematic of upper-class male leisure-time activities: "no person entered more completely into all the Enjoyments or amusements this country affords than he did during the seven years that he lived here; he kept a large stud of horses, three carriages, innumerable dogs, and followed all the field sports with peculiar ardor."[43] At times, European women rode horseback in the countryside around Tunis; Princess Caroline, arguably the first modern female tourist in North Africa, mounted on horseback during her 1816 visit. And as seen in chapter 4, frequenting popular cafés and taverns was another gendered pastime beloved of those of modest social rank, while the more respectable establishments, such as Parisian-type hotels and dining rooms springing up near the Sea Gate, served as spaces of conviviality for the well-heeled.

GENDER AND SOCIAL VISITING

How did gender shape social life for women? As discussed in chapter 3, resident European women regularly called upon the Husaynid women at the Bardo or summer palaces. However, entertaining visitors constituted one social duty among a constellation of obligations incumbent upon the dynasty's women. Among the most essential functions were charity and patronage.[44] When Husayn Bey's favorite wife, Lalla Fatima, died tragically in 1827 after childbirth, she was mourned by all classes of people in the regency, including foreigners and, above all, the poor upon whom she had showered gifts. A eulogy for Baya Fatima reveals that women of beylical households were taught the art of protocol so important to state functions. In addition to devoting herself to benevolent work, Baya Fatima knew the intricate ranking system for the city's notables and involved herself directly in the socially critical matter of banquets (walima).[45] Wealthy women invested in land, real estate, or commercial enterprises, such as urban coffee-houses, so entrepreneurial pursuits occupied their time, as did family, household, and religious duties. But little is known with certainty about the inner workings of the palace or the daily lives of harim women. Episodic panegyrics for Husaynid women are scattered throughout Bin Diyaf's chronicle, for example, Ahmad Bey's sister is briefly described as "the chaste, revered Lady Fatuma" but that is all.[46]

Let's return to Mme. Berner's narrative of 1835 (see chapter 3), the year she and a bevy of friends called upon the princesses at the Bardo palace. Despite the obvious problems inherent in records of harim socializing, this kind of evidence offers a rich, ethnographic view of the material aspects of life in princely residences—details of clothing, dress, food, furniture, and furnishings—which supply clues about taste, aesthetics, and the critical matter of gift giving. In addition, the protocols and cultural norms governing visiting emerge from these accounts. Of course, standard Orientalist tropes are invoked, the notion of the "caged ladies" first and foremost. Another leitmotif is the corpulence of upper-class women, a cultural commentary found in French accounts of "Eastern" women during the 1798 Egyptian occupation, as in most European travel literature of the period.[47]

Upon arrival at the Bardo, Mme. Berner's cohort of ladies was first greeted by one of the Husayn Bey's chief ministers who conducted them as far as the harim's second interior court, where he took leave. In Berner's words, "The wife of the Bey, richly but not tastefully dressed, sat opposite to us on the Ottoman, but rose on our entrance and requested us to take places near her, with the words, 'May your entrance be blessed and may you remain as long as it pleases you.'" The marriage of the bey's second daughter to a high-ranking court official was then being celebrated and the European ladies were invited to attend some of the weeklong festivities. According to Mme. Berner, "The constant entertainment consisted again only of sweetmeats and pastry, coffee, chocolate, lemonade but the Bey was this time far more talkative, and played the host in the most affable manner—saying frequently that we were here in our own house, and might do whatever we pleased. He himself took the light, to show us the bridal bed, which was of white satin, tastefully embroidered with gold."[48]

Of note is something that Berner mentions in passing—that the ruler was "this time far more talkative," which indicates that she had entered into conversation with Husayn Bey in the course of an earlier visit, a likely occurrence since her husband had served for years as Danish consul—until his untimely death incurred while sea bathing. Thus, other social calls must have been paid by resident European women to Husaynid harims but were not recorded. Moreover, that these accounts were not published is significant; it suggests that palace visits were seen at the time, by the social actors involved, as mundane, not worthy of committing to print. This may lend more credence to these earlier as opposed to later narratives composed with European audiences, avid for titillating details of the Orient, in mind.

Around the same time, Lady Temple, who had taken residence with her husband in Tunis, was invited to the Bardo in 1833, where she was presented to "her Highness the *Lillah Kabira* [the ruler's chief wife] in a *patio,* adorned in the usual oriental style with fountains."

> The *Lillah* herself, though much larger than we should in Europe consider becoming, was however amongst the least of the set. She was not pretty, but the expression of her face was most agreeable and good-humoured, and I felt quite sorry for her when I heard shortly afterward that she had been put aside by the Bey to make way for a young girl of thirteen. The Lillah asked if I had no children, when hearing that I had a little boy, inquired why I had not brought him and seemed really sorry. When we had finished our luscious repast, she ordered all the remaining cakes to be put into a basket and desired that I would take them for my child. She had her own little boy of about two years old in her arms.[49]

These visits were followed with another social call sometime in 1844 by the women and children from Sir Thomas Reade's family, including a Miss Smith, probably the governess, who provided the account of their visit. This time, however, the European ladies went to the summer palace in La Marsa, belonging to the heir apparent, Sidi Muhammad, whose harim was guarded by black eunuchs often supplied from Egypt.

> They [the princesses] generally reside at the Bardo, except two or three months in the summer when Sidi Mohammed takes his family to his country-house, situated near the sea at Marsa, from whence they have beautiful views of the sea, the coast, Cape Bon, the isle of Zembra, etc., for although the ladies' windows or jalousies are so constructed, that it is impossible for them to be seen by people outside, yet they can themselves see from within very tolerably all that passes.... It was at this marine villa that we saw the Lillah [chief wife].... We entered by a great arched door ... into a square courtyard, in which we were pleased with the sight of peacocks, turkeys, Barbary doves and other birds.... We entered a marble *patio,* or upper court open to both the serene face of the dark court blue heavens, in which played refreshingly two or three marble fountains, the noise of the falling

water gracefully enchanting the ear, and the scattered spray diffusing a delightful coolness through the place. When the heat is very great this place is covered with an awning of silk and other stuff. From an apartment opposite to this window, at the door of which hung a curtain, the Lillah met us, and, kissing us on each cheek, ushered us into the room, where we found several ladies, relatives and visitors sitting in the Oriental fashion, on a couch or divan, placed around the room, and its only furniture. . . . All the Lillahs behaved in a quite lady-like manner, a sister of Sidi Mohammed particularly so, although of course they were very inquisitive, examining our dresses and asking us a thousand questions, more particularly on the *article* of marriage.[50]

On this occasion, the European and Tunisian women ventured outside where tents were pitched near the beach so that they could promenade together, "passing through the olive groves and vineyards to the seaside." During warm summer evenings, palace women were at liberty to walk in the gardens "when everybody [was] sent out of the way, their black guards in the meanwhile surrounding the walks to prevent any person approaching."[51]

Miss Smith's description of the chief wife's private apartment contains invaluable descriptions of materiality, which can be verified by comparing her account with those of other visitors. According to Smith,

The Lillah . . . then arose inviting us to go up stairs into her gallery, which we found was a very long narrow room paved with marble and splendidly furnished. One side was formed of a continuation of latticed windows with a divan, or ottoman, running the whole length of the apartment, on the other side was a recess; the walls were partly covered with a few pictures, mirrors and several clocks, for the Moors are fond of having a great number of clocks and watches hanging up together; there were also marble tables, on which were thickly strewn rich ornaments and other fantastic nicknackery; besides there were European sofas and chairs, chandeliers and lamps, for at most of the respectable Moorish houses as also at the Bardo, European furniture is now fashionable, and will undoubtedly continue so.[52]

Thus, even before the mid-nineteenth century, the ruling family and state elites partially furnished their palaces in Louis XVI style—much to the disappointment of first-time callers who, needless to say, eagerly anticipated the exotic or outlandish. And costly presents from European monarchs—gilt mirrors, oil paintings, gold watches, bejeweled clocks, rich textiles—graced interior apartments, including the women's quarters. As James Richardson noted after visiting Ahmad Bey's private apartments in 1844,

In the new suites of rooms added to the Bardo, particularly those belonging to his highness, the Bey has followed as much as possible European taste and imitated the Royal apartments of European sovereigns. One spacious hall, commonly called the *Saloon,* is especially deserving of notice being superbly garnished with sofas, chairs, tables, curtains, looking-glasses, and pictures, oil-paintings and prints in immense profusion.... A number of the portraits of foreign princes hang up in these state-rooms. There is also a very good likeness of the Bey himself drawn by Mr. Ferriere, British vice-consul. The Bey's bedroom—in which there is a regular European bed and bedstand—is also adorned with various portraits, and amongst the rest there is a portrait of Sir Thomas Reade, one of the Bey's principle supporters and counselor in any difficulties with foreign governments which arise.[53]

These were not mere decoration since their display translated into concrete expression the strength of diplomatic amities between the Husaynids and other powers from the early years of the century.[54]

In 1825, Sidi Mahmud Kahiya, who had represented Husayn Bey in Paris during Charles X's coronation, returned to Tunis on a French frigate bearing gifts from the new monarch: "French manufactures in silk, brocade, broad clothes, cashmere, cambric, porcelain, besides some vases and plateaux in silver gilt and eight superb lace dresses for the ladies of the Harem."[55] But rare commodities flowed both ways. When Sidi Mahmud had first arrived in France, he brought coffers and cages overflowing with gifts, among them horses, lions, ostriches, gazelles, racing camels, perfume essences, tiger and lion skins, silk textiles, and a saddle richly ornamented in gold. Included in diplomatic exchanges of pricey material objects were female attire, some intended for the Husaynid princesses— the lace dresses referred to above—and others for the queen of France. Among the gifts sent in 1825 to the French king was "a Moorish costume" made from silk and gold material and worn by elite Tunisian women. Court attendants in Paris were charmed but admitted that "it is difficult to imagine the august Marie-Thérèse-Charlotte of France . . . dressed in pants ornamented with silk and gold."[56] (The pants, or culottes, were the sirwal worn by Tunisian women under tunics.)

Gendered gift giving reinforced ties of friendship between heads of state and, in one case in 1828, defused a diplomatic crisis over the use of carriages in Tunis. In this period, only the Husaynid ruler enjoyed the right of traveling about in a four-wheeled carriage, a visible sign of sovereignty. When Sir Thomas Reade imported a four-wheeler in a deliberate challenge to older protocol, the stage was set for a confrontation. Husayn Bey saved face and avoided a showdown by decreeing that use of the contentious vehicle was a mark of favor bestowed upon Lady Reade, an act of munificence. Quick to take umbrage at his rival's success, the French consul, de Lesseps, immediately demanded the right to this kind of conveyance. Husayn Bey soothingly informed him that as soon as Lady de Lesseps arrived, she would be allowed to drive about in a wheeled carriage as well.[57]

While seaside socializing was part of the normal summer routine for palace women and their intimates, the Husaynid court also organized a well-oiled and orchestrated performance of harim tours crafted for important visitors from across the sea. (As seen in chapter 3, the Bardo palace employed an unnamed

Italian woman to act as guide and interpreter for female callers during the 1830s and 1840s.) Lady Herbert's 1871 tour, however, more or less constituted palace or harim hopping, as she visited princesses or notables, such as the Bin 'Ayyad, at their residences—five or six palace households—from the Bardo to the Mediterranean suburbs. At each stop, hospitality was lavished upon Lady Herbert and the British consul's wife, Christina Wood, who conducted the tour since she was a close friend of Muhammad al-Sadiq Bey's female relatives and spoke some Tunisian Arabic. Correspondence between women in this milieu demonstrates true affection. A letter sent in 1860 by Camille Roches, wife of the French consul, to one of the bey's wives reveals strong emotional attachments. Abruptly called back to France due to a family tragedy, Mme. Roches wrote from Bordeaux: "Dear Princess: the hastiness of my departure from Tunis prevented me from calling to bid you farewell in the manner that I would have desired . . . my sorrow is rendered less bitter because of the sympathy of friends . . . I thank you profoundly."[58]

Being male did not necessarily exclude the curious from the harim's sacrosanct space. When Baron von Hesse-Wartegg was received at the Bardo in the summer of 1881, he too was ushered into the private women's quarters to admire the beautifully wrought decor—all of the ladies were then absent at the beach palaces. Allowing foreign dignitaries into the women's apartments may have been a way of bestowing particular favor.[59] When Ahmad Bey visited France in 1846, he had marveled at the wonders of the Versailles palace and had been admitted into the domestic intimacy of the king's family apartments—why wouldn't the Husaynids return the compliment and display the luxuries of their private dwellings, observing, of course, the dictates of gender segregation?[60]

As a system, ritualized visiting had implicitly political dimensions. For, as historians of British India have demonstrated, elite households and harims represented critical funds of insider information because of the large number of servants and retainers, the case in European courts as well.[61] In 1835 the British consul alleged that several mamluks "in the bey's seraglio" were being secretly paid by the French government to pass along classified rumors about what transpired in the heart of the palace.[62] Moreover, since the ruling bey's mother was the most powerful female figure in the Husaynid household, establishing friendships with her could result in considerable advantage—recall that Ahmad Bey regularly consulted his mother. The 1844 visit to the heir to the throne's harim at the seashore was more than a casual event; Miss Smith stated that "we promised to give them [i.e., consular officials] a faithful report of all that we saw and heard." Her concluding remark says it all: "I am sorry that my account of the harem of Sidi Mohammed is so uninteresting, but I have made the best I could of the few incidents."[63] Palace socializing facilitated covert intelligence gathering. Hesse-Wartegg admitted to collecting information on Husaynid households by interrogating women living in Tunis: "Though I cannot boast of having penetrated during my stay in Tunis into a harem while it was inhabited by its tenants, I was fortunate enough to hear everything worth knowing from European ladies who, by a long residence in Tunis, as well as through their intimate relations with the established feminine world, were better entitled than anybody else to give me the necessary particulars."[64]

But intelligence gathering flowed in both directions. If the beys opened up their harims to visitors, who subsequently passed along what they had seen and heard, the fact that the beylical family lodged foreigners for long periods of time in upscale housing rewarded the ruling class with information about what their "tenants" were up to. Moreover, many Europeans engaged local servants, Tunisian subjects or Maltese expatriates, who must have relished, and profited from, their position as gossip brokers.

As tourism to French Algeria greatly expanded, precolonial Tunisia was added to the list of attractions on the circuit for bourgeois travelers. Since she enjoyed uncommon access to domestic residences during her 1871 tour, Lady Herbert inventoried the rental housing market in Tunis for upper-class associates back in London who were considering "taking houses there for the winter." Well-traveled—by this time she had visited Egypt and Palestine—and well-heeled, Lady Herbert knew a prime tourist spot when she saw it:

> Between this spot [Carthage] and Goletta were a number of villas and country houses, or rather sea-side watering-places of the Bey's family or his ministers; and I can conceive no more enjoyable spot in the summer-time that this sea-shore with its big shady rocks, beautiful sands, lovely shells, and glorious blue sky.... Mrs. Wood told me that it was her children's greatest delight to come here for the day from their country house at Marsa which is only a few miles off, and I did not wonder at their taste.[65]

Lady Herbert had not only come to hobnob with princesses; her trip was motivated by the search for relief from rheumatism. "Being anxious to judge for myself as to this country and especially to test the efficacy of certain warm springs, which had been strongly recommended to me by a Paris doctor for rheumatism, I started last January [1871] with my eldest daughter."[66] That Lady Herbert ventured across the sea to take thermal waters on the recommendation of a French physician indicates that aristocratic grand tours of the Mediterranean were on the cusp of becoming middle-class health tourism.

WHERE ELITES MEET: THE SEA AND THE BATH

The cult of seaside holidays, a largely English social and cultural invention, merged with the growing awareness of the benefits of salt or mineral waters by the European, particularly German, scientific world in the very late eighteenth century.[67] Malta became popular among English health seekers when the Dowager Queen Adelaide, widow of William IV, journeyed to the island to spend the winter of 1836 there, "with decided advantage to her physical condition."[68] As beach resorts and bathing caught on among European middle classes during the nineteenth century, regulations governing behavior mushroomed across the Mediterranean world and Europe. For example, the British-controlled Ionian Islands enacted statutes in 1836 regulating hours and places of public bathing. Some provisions were inspired by safety concerns but the final clause aimed at public morality—"bathing by men is forbidden anytime that women are present"—which reflected the situation in Great Britain at the time, where bathing was also sexually segregated by law.[69] In France, sea bathing became the rage by the 1860s, driven by the social imperative of summer holidays away from Paris that turned quiet villages on the Normandy coast, such as Deauville and Trouville, into elegant watering spots.

Sea bathing was a well-established practice among creoles and resident Europeans, as it was for Tunisians. During his 1835 stay, Sir Grenville Temple toured Sidi Bou Sa'id, where he found "many good houses, to which the Moors resort in summer for the advantages of sea bathing. The Bey has also a palace here."[70] In 1834, the English vice-consul, William Carleton, stated that he frequently went to La Marsa beach to bathe and had been so doing for years.[71] Expanded immigrant settlement after the 1830s transformed small, sleepy suburbs into bustling towns. When Sister Emilie de Vialar returned to Tunisia in 1843, she went to La Marsa to visit her order's house and school where a conflict over sea bathing had erupted. Some sisters were scandalized by the fact that the town's inhabitants took sea baths, while other sisters wanted to partake of the healing waters, which raised the issue of modesty. Vialar resolved the problem by declaring that bathing could only take place in "a completely enclosed tent in the form of a pavilion that reached all the way to the water's edge which [the sisters] should only use when La Marsa's bathers were absent."[72] The school's female pupils must have been allowed to swim, since later a member of the order lost her life attempting to save a drowning girl. Vialar's solution to the issue of decorum calls to mind the princesses' bathing houses set right in the water, although on a much less glorious scale.

In July 1858, Charles Cubisol, French vice-consul in La Goulette, investigated disagreements over proper beach comportment in a report called "Établissement des bains de mer sur la plage" (Bathing Establishments on the Beach). Important here is that the port, whose population included thousands of "Europeans, Moors, Maltese or Jews, of which many were fishermen or boatmen," was rapidly being peopled by indigent Mediterranean islanders.[73] As we have seen, immigration partially transformed the older system of aligning residential neighborhoods with religious affiliation or legal jurisdiction. As occurred in Tunis when the older coffeehouse merged with the tavern, creating a novel social space where forms of leisure and sociability became a source of discord because codes of conduct had yet to be worked out, so too at the beach. After midcentury, the question of appropriate use of these spaces increasingly prompted conflict—in one case over different ways of dressing and behaving at the beach while bathing.

In the "La Goulette affair," some bathers had placed tents—the precursor to the bathing machine—on the sand in such a way as to impede others from direct access to the water, provoking alarm over privacy. (A popular device first developed in late eighteenth-century England, the bathing machine was a covered wooden cart in which bathers changed into beach attire without offending public morals. The cart was then hauled down to the water's edge, where sexually segregated bathing for health purposes took place.) Muhammad Bey had bequeathed this beach property to La Goulette's mainly foreign inhabitants, and the port's governor, Khayr al-Din, was called upon to mediate. In his letter to the feuding bathers, Khayr al-Din stipulated that individuals could not encroach upon places designated as public in accordance with the recognized principle of "communal rights of access." What is fascinating about this seemingly trivial matter is that, while Tunisians also bathed there, it appears none were involved in the dispute. In effect, the Husaynid state, through Khayr al-Din's arbitration, spelled out beach-use regulations for Europeans, who held different notions of decency, as well as about what constituted public and private spaces.[74]

As was true in Europe at the time, those at the top of the social pyramid sought water therapies in more exclusive circumstances than public beaches—from the privacy of villas. Christina Wood's 1861 letters to her husband, Richard, while he was on mission in Syria, demonstrate the extent to which Tunisian and Europeans of the same class socialized together, maintaining, of course, gender segregation. In the summer of 1861, Mrs. Wood wrote that "we have been all as well as possible . . . profiting by the baths." A few days later she states, "We are all quite flourishing since we are installed here. The children are very much improved and live in the open air. . . . Baby is quite well and lively again, she takes her salt water baths . . . I go every morning [to the beach] but have only taken a few baths."[75] Christina provided details on dinner parties and visits with Tunisian and European neighbors, including the Husaynid princesses. The seaside residence that the Woods occupied in the summer months belonged to the ruling family but had been put at their disposition.

The increased time at the beach had repercussions in the realm of justice. As consuls dallied for longer periods at summer villas, they were less involved in daily administrative minutiae. Upon his arrival from Damascus in 1856, Wood expanded the consular staff, and presumably its reach into the lives of protégés, but paradoxically created more distance between the consul and his most numerous charges, the Maltese. Somewhat of an operator, Wood cajoled the bey into paying—out of the ruler's own pocket—for a new wing of the consul's country estate in La Marsa, then under construction, when funds were predictably not forthcoming from London. This did not go unnoticed by Anglo-Maltese protégés, if the vitriolic tract written in 1868 by the Maltese physician Dr. Luigi Demech is credible: "[Wood] spends a portion of the year in the enjoyment of the amenities of his country-house at the Marsa, a gift due to the munificence of his friend, the Bey. That delightful country-house, about 15 miles distant from town, keeps him away for six months from this office, in which he appears but once a week, and for a few hours in order to transact some business with the Bey, whose minister and advocate he has become."[76] While Demech's denunciations of Wood should be interpreted with caution, prolonged absences from Tunis must have compromised the consul's ability to stay attuned to the needs, activities, and whereabouts of protégés, a task left to subalterns.

In addition to saltwater baths, thermal cures were popular, especially at the Hammam Lif springs readily accessible by rowboats. Again in 1861, Christina Wood described one typical outing in a skiff with the Cubisol family, including "all the children." When the party returned home, news of their excursion reached Muhammad al-Sadiq Bey, then in his nearby residence. The ruler sent a note to the Wood family, which Christina recorded as saying "that the next time [we go to Hammam Lif] we must go in his boat."[77] The bey also offered the use of his carriages and horses for transport to the La Marsa beach and at the same time offered the wife of a French dignitary a fine diamond necklace. In the same period, the Swiss humanitarian and founder of the Red Cross, Henri Dunant, took the waters at Hammam Lif, which "fortified the nervous system" and was particularly beneficial for stomach illnesses as well as for "melancholy, hypochondria, heart palpitations, sciatica, paralysis, gall stones, skin problems, and weakness of the spine."[78] Tunisians and Europeans apparently had great faith in Hammam Lif, since prodigious cures were attributed to its springs. By 1882, a French national operated a *bains de mer* at Hammam Lif, although the record does not indicate if he was only the manager or the proprietor nor does it tell us whether he acquired the sea-bathing establishment by virtue of ties to the palace or the French consulate or both.[79]

Finally, Mrs. Wood commented to her absent husband upon the kinds of intimate social exchanges possible during the summer months: "Our neighbors, the Caid's [qa'id] family are too kind and good-natured and very quite good people. . . . Si Hussein called to see me today and left me a letter to enclose for you. He really is a great friend of yours and a first-rate fellow worked to death in his new office, he complains that he has not a moment for exercise." Mrs. Wood reported that she had "made great friends with the ladies [of the qa'id's family] and am making great progress in Arabic," which the "ladies" were teaching her.[80] This represents a nice reversal of the conventional nineteenth-century practice of foreign governesses teaching European languages to the members of elite Ottoman households.[81]

Despite its relative inaccessibility, Korbous too became increasingly attractive for hydrotherapy. From the 1820s, if not earlier, members of the diplomatic and creole community utilized its hot mineral waters for medicinal purposes, and locals had always looked to the site for physical and spiritual healing. Louis Gaspary, a member of the large Gaspary clan in La Goulette, noted in April 1824 that "my mother-in-law is counting on going to Korbous at the beginning of May and she would be very happy if Madame Guys [the French consul's wife] would honor her by going there with her." Transport was by small craft because this was considerably quicker and safer than by land; yet bad sailing weather in April and May delayed the trip. However, by late May, Gaspary reported having "just arrived back from Korbous where I left Mme. Guys 'bien portante'. Our trip there was short and happy; she is with her daughter; they went by a little boat."[82] Two months later, in June 1824, the ladies were still at the station whose waters had very much improved Mme. Guys' health. They were provided for by Gaspary's brother, who went back and forth by skiff from La Goulette, carrying messages, food, and provisions.

This early, rare account raises some questions, particularly when compared to later practices under the colonial regime.[83] One wonders where Mesdames Gaspary and Guys resided—they were absent from home for weeks. Moreover, their two-month stay occurred prior to Ahmad Bey's building program and well before Europeans could own property. While the sources do not state it explicitly, the women must have lived in Tunisian houses because, at the time, there were neither hotels nor other amenities in Korbous; leasing domestic space to cure-seekers was a major source of livelihood for villagers—as it still is today. The Gasparys had been going to Korbous on a regular basis, evidenced by the vice-consul's mention of his mother-in-law "counting on going" there. Whether they took their baths with Tunisian women remains uncertain, although it seems likely, and they must have been treated by local female healers.

Beylical decrees issued in 1787, and reconfirmed periodically, affirmed the rights of Shaykh 'Ammara's descendants over the baths, springs, and bathing pool at Korbous; some specifically mention female members of the saintly lineage. In 1835, Mustafa Bey's decree names the shaykh's sister, Mas'uda, in the list of family members "responsible for the administration and surveillance of the *zawiya* at Hammam Kurbus as well as the buildings and baths." Another woman, Khadija, is mentioned in 1840 as a part of the saintly clan. What precise role women from the holy lineage played in the management of the springs or in water treatments—intimately linked to spiritual healing and the sacred— remains uncertain; but their presence in the documents is suggestive. A later decree from 1875 mentions a café at the site for the first time.[84]

Richard Wood frequented Korbous for healing, an appreciation surely acquired in Istanbul where he was raised. In November 1858, Wood wrote from the Cap Bon to his French colleague, Léon Roches, to apologize for his absence from Tunis. Suffering grievously from rheumatism, Wood had felt obliged to go off "to the Baths of Korbous" due to worsening health problems.[85] In January 1874, Cubisol went to Hammam Lif for a winter thermal session, leaving his post to "take the waters" while a huge political crisis erupted in Tunis.[86] This shows that seeking a cure was regarded as a credible reason for not being on duty or perhaps a convenient excuse. That both Cubisol and Wood repeatedly took the waters at local thermal stations suggests faith in the curative potency of springs and in indigenous caregivers. As early as 1858 a French national, Leprieur, had undertaken scientific analyses of the waters at Korbous; and the publication of Dr. Guyon's work on Tunisian thermal stations in 1864 sparked great interest in the medical community, although most studies came after 1881.[87]

Travel to ameliorate failing health has an ancient pedigree in the Mediterranean, as elsewhere. As mentioned above, Husayn Bey expanded the Hammam Lif bathing facilities in order to spend more time there. Was he influenced by his European physicians in a period when doctors increasingly prescribed hydrotherapy? Research on late-eighteenth-century German states has shown that the personal physicians of many princes promoted systematic use of spas for healing therapies.[88] Did Wood, Cubisol, and other cure seekers follow a twenty-one-day cure at the Korbous spa, as was customary in Tunisian and Mediterranean healing? This had become the standard treatment cycle in Europe, one whose origins apparently dated back to antiquity.[89] In addition, the temporalities of hydrotherapy is intriguing, although evidence is thin. A medical guide published in 1912 stated that the season in Korbous "runs from November to the end of May." However, this had a European clientele in mind; it was hoped that spa-goers would frequent French stations during the summer and then be lured across the sea to Tunisia.[90] Did the increased use of Hammam Lif and Korbous for winter cures indicate that the purely therapeutic nature of thermal springs was progressively being disentangled from the larger social and religious matrix in which older practices had traditionally been enmeshed?

As ever greater numbers of Europeans traveled to North Africa, a reverse current of health-seeking tourism moved in the opposite direction. High-ranking state officials and even religious notables began frequenting European spas on a regular basis. The religious scholar and Hanafi shaykh Muhammad Bayram V, who suffered from a serious "nervous affliction," consulted physicians in Paris and sought cures in prestigious European centers.[91] However, the political and therapeutic were never far apart. After Khayr al-Din's fall from grace in 1876, he received the ruler's permission to go to France in 1877 and 1878—even though he was theoretically under "palace arrest" in Tunis—for cures at Vichy and Saint-

Nectaire.[92] Thus health offered an expedient rationale for quitting the country, only a few years before French troops invaded and colonial officials forced the newly enthroned 'Ali Bey to sign away his kingdom at the beachside palace where the La Marsa Convention was signed in June 1883.

COLONIAL WATERS

In the 1990s, Dane Kennedy demonstrated that, after the 1857 Mutiny in South Asia, Indian hill stations became increasingly critical to the practices of the British Empire and as such suffered profound cultural permutations. Originally mountains sacred to both Muslims and Hindus, then playgrounds for Britons on tour, these whimsical high-altitude outposts were ultimately transformed into the administrative-political heart of the empire; here officials, soldiers, and families enjoyed hygienic isolation and cultural quarantine from the "natives" below.[93] Scholars are now tracing similar processes in the French Empire, whereby indigenous healing practices were appropriated to promote health tourism, which drew sociospatial boundaries grounded in racial hygiene between science and superstition, colonizer and colonized. Yet the "colonial situation" can only be fully intelligible if earlier social arrangements are reconstructed, however daunting due to problems of documentation.[94]

In 1905 the Protectorate compelled the Tunisian state to cede the springs at Korbous to a French company, the Compagnie des Eaux Thermales, which eventually "acquired" ownership of the bathing pools as well as huge shares of the villagers' houses, land, and water. But this did not happen without a bitter, protracted struggle waged by the Korbous saintly lineage and local property holders, which delayed the takeover for years. Significantly, even as pressures mounted on the palace and the Idarat al-Ahbas (Administration of Muslim Foundations) to hand over land titles to Eaux Thermales, other French officials at the Direction de Santé held that "indigent Muslims at Korbous should be able to get care for free because Korbous is important to all of the country's Muslims"—which hinted that the fight over the healing water would not be an easy battle to win.[95]

Spatially segregated hydrotherapy by "race" envisioned by spa promoters had origins not in the early colonial period but came later, after 1900. While the Korbous company attempted to insulate middle-class European patients from resident spa users through the scare tactic of "syphilis-infected natives," it failed to completely banish Muslims or Jews—or even indigent Europeans—from the station's small confines. In part this was because the capital city's inhabitants, of whatever background, had frequented local beaches and thermal springs together for nearly a century prior to the creation of what Eric Jennings so aptly terms "recompression chambers" for ailing French nationals returning home from the empire's enervating tropics. And in the colonial era, upper- and middle-class

Tunisians continued to seek cures in Korbous, even if they "kept their distance from [foreign Europeans]."[96] Until 1903, when the church-state disestablishment laws were enacted, Catholic missionaries were allowed entry to spas free of charge. Colonial spas did, however, sever the sacral dimensions of thermal cures from the purely therapeutic, while also partially erasing the contributions of age-old Tunisian healing arts associated with water.[97]

Social historians have demonstrated that regular bathing only caught on in France in the late nineteenth and early twentieth centuries, although hydrotherapy had been prescribed for nervous disorders for over a hundred years.[98] While rarely, if ever, acknowledged, colonial spas drew inspiration from older North African and Mediterranean practices and beliefs tied to the sea and its health-conferring benefits for body, spirit, and society. One wonders if Europeans who frequented Tunisia, with its ancient culture of weekly *hammam* visits, sea baths, and thermal cures, introduced more modern notions of hygiene when they returned to Europe—or at least eased the acceptance of novel ideas regarding water and the body.[99] Clearly, health tourism appropriated local forms of knowledge and the traditional built environment; the Korbous Company drew heavily upon Tunisian and Islamic architectural forms when expanding the site's buildings, probably with an eye toward the promotional lure of the exotic.[100]

This was just one dimension of projected colonial investment in seaside tourism. Louis Créput's 1892 report on Nabeul, mentioned earlier in the chapter, suggests that, as the *contrôleur civil,* Créput was reconnoitering the village for the resident general with a view to establish not only a hydrotherapy station but also a tourist complex that would "revive" local handicrafts by imposing European aesthetic and technical standards upon indigenous artisans.[101] Yet, travel for cures differed significantly from other kinds of travel because the former required long-term, seasonal residency, which necessitated clinics and, frequently, rental agreements with North African landlords; also needed were cemeteries in case the treatment failed to work. The medical treatises extolling the benefits of North African waters that appeared from the mid-nineteenth century on were initially guidebooks of a sort and merged with full-blown tourist guides by Hachette, Cook, or Baedeker by the century's end.[102]

Another blurring of genres folded older travel accounts into the emergent mass tourist guides, a trend detected around the time of Lady Herbert's narrative of harim visits and cures. While emblematic of the older class-bound genre, Lady Herbert's work anticipated the modern guidebook because it contained practical suggestions, notably how to rent suitable houses for the season from local families as well as the location of especially potent thermal springs. In Algiers at the same time, British ladies, whose class did not get them invited into elite households, were instead offered sightseeing options not available to men—visiting "native" women and Muslim families at home in the intimacy of the household.

Was the growth of gendered travel packages a variation on the older harim visit but aimed at the middle classes?[103] Not too long after Lady Herbert's excursion, a few elite Tunis women began traveling to Europe. *Le Petit Tunisien Indépendent* reported in 1886 that the family of Mustafa ibn Isma'il, a high-ranking court notable, had returned from an extended stay in Paris where he too may have consulted doctors. The traveling household included several princesses and "six Mauresques" in service to the family while in Paris. The ladies wore "French clothes"—at least while boarding ship in Marseilles for La Goulette—and were under the close guard of a eunuch.[104]

This chapter has attempted to salvage a social universe whose only visible expression today consists of the crumbling bathing pavilions and palaces that once adorned coastal villages. Visits between households, whether in Tunis or at the beach, created webs of obligation that structured the precolonial order of things. The dynasty and court notables employed seaside diplomacy, harim tours, and other expressions of hospitality to introduce resident foreigners or visiting dignitaries into the prevailing culture, one ultimately grounded in Islamic norms regarding purity and pollution. In this analysis, the Mediterranean villa, dismissed as a mere space of frivolous entertainment, emerges as a site for nurturing strategic alliances, which in turn constituted a delicate exercise in relations between states. The older literature on the governing class characterized that class as passive and thus ineffective when confronted with increasingly aggressive demands by European statesmen after 1830.[105] Yet, the palace adroitly monitored chosen European families through the loan of palatial residences and a dramatic repertoire of well-rehearsed social calls, gifts, and favors. Thus, as disseminators of scarce resources and catchment basins for information, elite households, especially at the seaside, were critical to the conduct of foreign affairs.

Revisiting the gendered sociabilities associated with households and harims from an ethnographic perspective suggests the existence of widely variant local expressions and meanings that only close historical contextualization can call forth. The large Reade family resided in Tunis for nearly twenty-five years—from 1825 to 1849—and their house in La Marsa was a gift from the palace; but equally important was the fact that they resided in domestic spaces identical to those called home by Tunisians, as did the Wood family. Periodic social calls paid by women and children from resident European households to the Husaynid princesses did not have the same valence as the slightly later harim encounters, which fall into a distinctive category of short-term travel tours, often with a view to publication. After all, Christina Wood never published accounts of her social rapports with harim women.[106] Directly related, one unanticipated finding is the existence of a seasonality of sociability, including diplomatic exchanges governed by winter-summer rhythms, each associated with particular spaces and varying intensities of interaction—and of course, quarrels and backstabbing. One needs to speculate, however, on the politics of the court's extended stays in seaside villages from the mid-1850s on, separated from Tunis and the Bardo. Did the fact that the beys were surrounded, indeed beleaguered, by diplomats and concession hunters mean that Mediterranean palaces had become a sort of gilded cage?

One implicit question revolves around periodicity and the assumed rupture between the precolonial and colonial periods. Scholars arguing for the durability of "the precolonial" after, even long after, the advent of full-scale imperial rule in Asia or Africa rely upon political and economic institutions to buttress their positions. Forms of sociability such as visiting, leisure, and health-seeking practices offer novel points of entry to rethink these issues. The notion that the precolonial and the premodern were more or less equivalent because kin-based systems of sociability impeded wider social contacts and the flow of ideas seems inadmissible for nineteenth-century Tunisia.[107] The staying power of these arrangements and alliances during the two decades following 1881 allowed Tunisian reformers, however embattled, to continue their program of judicious modernization initiated by Khayr al-Din in the 1870s. However in 1900, a right-wing colonial lobby intent upon spoliation through legal manipulations and land seizures came to power and looked to Algeria as a model for how to best exploit Tunisia and the Tunisians. Two years later, the new "Islamophobe" resident general, Stephen Pichon, secretly attempted to subvert traditional succession to the Husaynid throne, something never attempted during the previous decades of colonial rule.[108]

Nevertheless, the persistence of much older social practices hampered the colonial project of creating racially segregated spaces of leisure and health for an exclusively bourgeois European clientele in Tunisia's watering spots. We have already seen that the Korbous hydrotherapy scheme was partially thwarted because of fierce local opposition and the fact that people of ordinary status and indeterminate nationality had long sought cures there. As importantly, the continued presence of the large Italian community, some of whose ancestors hailed from the ranks of the nineteenth-century creole class and enjoyed ties to the palace, imposed some limits after 1881 on the more brutal types of colonial oppression wrought upon Algeria.

Even after 1900, beachside socializing between Tunisian and European notables endured and took place in the once-elegant Hotel Zephyr in La Marsa, a stone's throw from the shore and situated so as to catch light breezes off the sea. My neighbor and friend, Naila Rostom, from the old Tunisian-Turkish aristocracy, recalled the nightly gatherings at the hotel. According to Naila, whose family memory stretched back to the early twentieth century, "during balls and soirées at the Zephyr, the champagne flowed in torrents." Fresh fish plucked from waters nearby and prepared for midnight suppers were "immense"—not like they are now, or so memory would have us believe.[109]

Independence brought the partial demise of this society. Habib Bourguiba, president of the new republic, personally oversaw the destruction of many palaces and pavilions, unleashing bulldozers and crews armed with dynamite upon ornate neo-Moorish structures and lush gardens. According to the last bey's chief gardener, Bourguiba "ran around like a happy child and said 'here! destroy! blow this up.'"[110] That the president did not demolish such blatantly colonial monuments as the Tunis train station or central post office was noteworthy. The palaces were visible reminders of the Husyanid dynasty, which had endured for two and a half centuries, and of the great families of Tunis, including Naila Rostom's lineage. Nationalist fervor and personal vendetta conspired to bury much of a princely seaside culture under its own ruins. In 2001, Tunisia's ruling family seized the Hotel Zephyr, leveled it, and constructed an American-style shopping mall in its place.

From the seaside we move to the final chapter, which reconstructs the life story of a major figure in the Husaynid court, Khayr al-Din, and grapples with the question of thinkers, intellectuals, educators, and reformers against the backdrop of population displacements. It asks how transnational communities of thought came to be, within the larger crucible of mobilities and modernities. Using a biographical approach, the chapter returns full circle to the critical shifts in multiple axes of communication across the nineteenth-century Mediterranean world.

Khayr al-Din al-Tunisi and
a Mediterranean Community of Thought

I gathered together what I had deduced from years of thought and reflection
along with what I had witnessed during my travels to European countries.

KHAYR AL-DIN AL-TUNISI

In the Bardo museum there once hung a dramatic portrait of Khayr al-Din
(c. 1822–1890) in the manner of Jacques-Louis David's monumental *Napoleon at*
the Saint Bernard Pass. His right hand clasping an ornate sword, his left firmly
grasping the reins, Khayr al-Din is mounted in full military dress upon a pranc-
ing white steed in a style reminiscent of the French emperor. (This image now
appears on twenty-dinar notes that characterize Khayr al-Din as "the Tunisian.")
Other portrayals, however, present him in a serene mood after classic Van Dyck
arrangements, or perhaps David's 1812 *Napoleon in His Study*. In one portrait,
Khayr al-Din stands serenely next to a table graced by an open book, hinting at
a scholarly disposition; in another, he is seated with arms akimbo, regarding the
viewer directly. Shorn, for the most part, of objects or poses associated with state
office or military rank, these likenesses suggest a man of quiet thought, even of
erudition.[1]

We have already come across Khayr al-Din during the crises generated by
immigration to Tunisia—the municipal reforms, the Fundamental Pact, and in
the interminable disputes created by legal pluralism. Also considered were the
ways in which the Tunisian political elite, European creoles, and consular authorities policed the immigrants or manipulated them to advantage. Nevertheless, the
tangled daily encounters between the capital city's inhabitants and the migrants
of various sorts have received the most attention. How "people on the move" in
the nineteenth century influenced Muslim intellectuals or circuits of thought
might not, at first glance, appear germane. Yet the massive dispersal of Europe's
outcasts, operators, and empire builders to Ottoman lands introduced new, or
at least somewhat different, worldviews, categories of thinking, and ways of

doing things to all ranks of society. The time-space compression deeply affected communication, diplomacy, and state rituals. Older, quite elaborate delegations bearing sumptuous gifts that cemented relations between the Husaynids and their Ottoman overlords were replaced in the 1870s by terse telegrams dispatched from Tunis to the Porte. Dramatic and mundane disturbances resonated in unexpected places—in street culture, the reorganization of cities, the cafés of burgeoning port cities, on ships crossing the sea, and in debates about Islamic reform as well as Europe's dangerous scientific and intellectual attractions. No one was more aware of these disturbances than Khayr al-Din, a Circassian, an Ottoman, an official in service to the Husaynids, and in his final days, a Tunisian.

Khayr al-Din was one of the principal architects of the 1857 'Ahd al-Aman (Fundamental Pact), the Tunisian version of the Ottoman Tanzimat that attempted from 1839 on to reorder society, state, and law, largely in response to immigration and creeping imperialism. His greatest work, however, was a political treatise appearing in Tunis in 1867, *Aqwam al-masalik li ma'rifat ahwal al-mamalik (The Surest Path to Knowledge of the Condition of Countries)*, that advocated profound transformations in statecraft. He also established one of the Maghrib's earliest institutions of modern education, Sadiqi College, in 1875. However, the threads winding through Khayr al-Din's biography from beginning to end were his cease-less travels that drew him into ever expanding circles of Ottoman and European intellectuals, Muslim reformers, and social engineers stretching from Tunis to Constantinople, Paris, Algiers, Cairo, and beyond. It is these travels, and the multiple displacements thereby occasioned, that concern us. Who was Khayr al-Din and how does his story figure into larger narratives of trans-Mediterranean odysseys? Can the different portraits of Khayr al-Din as mamluk, military officer, educator, and thinker-reformer be reconciled? How did Khayr al-Din's long resi-dence in Tunis, a purely fortuitous event, shape his life trajectory? What contribu-tion did he and his circle make to modernities in the Muslim Mediterranean?

This chapter reimagines Khayr al-Din's life in relation to broadly based com-munities of thought that had long existed but assumed a different guise around the middle of the nineteenth century. The notion of trans-sea bearers of knowl-edge opens up new perspectives in which intellectuals are generously defined—rather than hermetically sealed by assumed boundaries between states, religions, and cultures. A dual biography—one focusing upon individuals *and* the rapidly changing spaces through which they moved—allows for reconstructing the webs in this commonwealth of ideas and practices. But at which moments do we pause, which times, or works, do we privilege, in life stories? One strategy is to track individuals like Khayr al-Din as they moved about, taking into account not only the great texts for which they are remembered but also correspondence in the back drawers of their desks. Such an approach reveals unsuspected axes of exchange or semiconcealed transactions that determined, in large measure, the

FIGURE 16. Portrait of Khayr al-Din (Khéreddine), c. 1851. The portrait can be dated because this was the year Khayr al-Din was promoted in military rank to commander of the cavalry by Ahmad Bey. The cavalry unit under his command was quartered outside of Tunis in the village of La Manuba, and Khayr al-Din built a palatial residence there. (Institut National de Patrimoine, Tunis.)

arc of Khayr al-Din's story. Remapped, his life becomes a geography of biography; he himself becomes a sort of borderland intellectual.[2]

A progeny of the moribund mamluk system, Khayr al-Din advocated new and, in the eyes of many devout Muslims, shocking ideas regarding the Ottoman Empire's pressing need for enlightened forms of government, liberty, and modern education. In the introduction to his political treatise, Khayr al-Din repeatedly observed that the "world has become a smaller place"; in consequence, Muslim statesmen, religious leaders, and believers needed to adjust their thinking accordingly.[3] But the most crucial element determining Khayr al-Din's life trajectory was pure contingency—he was taken from Istanbul to Tunis at the very moment when the central Mediterranean corridor had turned into highly dynamic migratory frontiers of a particular sort. Had fate landed the young man in Baghdad or Aleppo would his story have unfolded as it did? And would a palace mamluk have composed one of the most original political essays from the nineteenth-century Islamic-Ottoman world? That the author of *The Surest Path* emerged from within the mamluk tradition, which even its heyday did not breed men of the pen, suggests profound ruptures in a number of realms as older axes of exchange linking the Maghrib to the Ottoman heartlands were undermined or reoriented.[4]

KHAYR AL-DIN AL-TUNISI:
SOURCES AND INTERPRETATIONS

Khayr al-Din's biography—or certain segments of it—has been told so frequently that fresh reinterpretations seem doomed to failure.[5] Most of Khayr al-Din's adult life was spent in Tunis—from c. 1839 to 1877—when he was not on a ship bound for Istanbul or European capitals on official missions. Predictably, in accordance with literary convention, his political treatise offers little autobiographical information. His memoirs, composed in French just before his death in Istanbul in 1890, were dictated to a succession of secretaries, notably Adolphe Jacot, from Switzerland, sometime around 1888. *À mes enfants: Ma vie privée et politique* (For My Children: My Private and Political Life), while ostensibly for his children, was a refutation of the completely unfounded charges of incompetence—or worse—leveled against Khayr al-Din after his long career as a statesmen abruptly ended in 1877 due to court intrigues in Tunis. Yet this work reveals little personal information, in part because of the cultural disinclination to divulge intimate family details; his relationships with his wives and children, for example, remain obscure. In addition, as a mamluk Khayr al-Din was severed from his birth family in the Caucasus, which deprives historians of documentation to build context. Tunisian and European state archives provide most of the evidence comprised of his official correspondence either in Arabic or French. Thus Khayr al-Din's life has been narrated as a series of public posts, which holds true for most figures from the period, as the practice of keeping diaries or writing personal memoirs had not yet taken hold.[6]

One of the first biographies of Khayr al-Din, written by the Orientalist scholar Theodor Menzel and published in 1908, cast him primarily as an Ottoman statesmen who had incidentally spent time in Tunisia, despite his nearly four decades in the country. This insistence upon his Ottoman identity arose from Menzel's interest in the initial and concluding chapters of Khayr al-Din's story. Subsequent interpretations portrayed Khayr al-Din as an agent of France or conversely of the Ottoman sultan, as a Tunisian as opposed to an Ottoman reformer, or even as a protonationalist.[7] Lionized as a remarkably capable administrator and diplomat by contemporaries, Khayr al-Din was rarely characterized as an intellectual or thinker, even less as a "self-naturalized" Tunisian.

It is worthwhile to briefly revisit the older interpretive framework in which figures like Khayr al-Din were inserted. In that scholarship, intellectual history represented a sort of *isnad* (chain of authorities) tracing the transmission of ideas among individuals or groups in ideological genealogies.[8] The responses of Mediterranean Muslim societies to Europe's growing hegemony were classified into two mutually exclusive camps: either "liberal," reform-minded modernizers; or a residual, monolithic category of "conservative 'ulama'" resolutely opposing the new and foreign.[9] The trunk lines of new ideas, the pulses of modernity, ran primarily from Paris, London, and Berlin to Istanbul or Cairo; the bulk of the traffic ran, naturally, from west to east or north to south. The most critical exchanges took place in European capitals or the Ottoman center, less frequently in provinces such as Tunisia or in recently colonized places like Algeria. Moreover, Islamic reform was rarely connected to modern travel, passports, and fixed steamship schedules or urbanization projects in the style of George-Eugène Haussmann that ripped open the bellies of ancient cities, notably Istanbul and Cairo. The extent to which complex population movements configured debates, literary production, and mode of thought among thinkers in majority Muslim societies was ignored. Theoretical problems associated with the very category of "the intellectual," derived from French history, were avoided by employing the rubrics of "reformer," "statesmen," or "modernizer."[10] Khayr al-Din's life and times tell us otherwise.

FROM THE BLACK SEA TO THE CENTRAL MEDITERRANEAN CORRIDOR

European imperial expansion across Africa and Asia quickened from the early nineteenth century on. In the Caucasus, the Abkhazia, a Circassian people of the eastern Black Sea, suffered assaults upon their mountains from their formidable Russian neighbor to the north. It was here that Khayr al-Din was born, most likely around 1822 to a family of warrior notables. His father, Hassan Leffch (or Lash), a local chieftain, was killed in battle during one of Russia's invasions of Sukhum.[11] Orphaned, Khayr al-Din was sold into slavery as a small child, not an unusual fate given that his people had supplied slave markets for centuries. As fortune would have it, he ended up in Istanbul in the household of the Cypriot Ottoman notable Tahsin Bey, the *naqib al-ashraf* (head of the descendants of the Prophet) and *qadi al-ʿaskar* (chief judge of the army) of Anatolia as well as a poet of some reputation. Residing in Tahsin Bey's palace in Kanlica on the Asian side of the Bosporus, Khayr al-Din received a first-rate education, equal to that given his master's children, which included instruction in Islam, Turkish, and perhaps French; but he was not raised as a mamluk. Rather the young Circassian served as childhood companion to Tahsin Bey's son for a number of years. After this son's tragic premature death, Tahsin Bey sold Khayr al-Din to a Tunisian envoy in Istanbul who was on a diplomatic mission for Ahmad Bey. (We can only speculate upon the emotional impact that this uprooting might have exerted upon Khayr al-Din.) Soon thereafter, they boarded a ship bound for Africa; the young man was about seventeen years old at the time.

Sometime between 1839 and 1840, Khayr al-Din was placed in Ahmad Bey's court as a *mamluk bi-l-saraya* (inner palace retainer) and he continued his studies, both religious and profane, eventually mastering Arabic. A pious Muslim, he was versed in the Islamic sciences but preserved some knowledge of Ottoman Turkish, which advanced his career, since few indigenous notables, or even mamluks, had facility in that language. By the time he arrived in Tunis, Circassian and Georgian mamluks were becoming rarer due to political events in the Caucasus and, by the 1820s and 1830s, Great Britain's global antislavery campaigns.[12] A certain number of mamluks were of Greek-Balkan origins. Khayr al-Din's first wife, Janina, whom he married in 1862, was the daughter of one of the most powerful Greek courtiers, Mustafa Khaznadar (1817–1878); her mother, Kalthum, was Ahmad Bey's sister and of Sardinian origins.[13]

The giving of women, some of Christian Mediterranean origins, from the beys' family to mamluks in marriage—known as ennobling—reinforced the fictive kinship undergirding the mamluk system.[14] The importance of women as mediators became apparent with Janina's death in 1870. It was she who had kept the fraught relations between her father, the *khaznadar* (head of the state treasury), and her husband on a cordial basis; with her passing, Khayr al-Din and Mustafa Khaznadar immediately had a falling out.[15] Khayr al-Din's years of daily schooling and contacts with Husaynid family members were also critical to creating kinlike bonds. Compared to other Ottoman lands, therefore, Tunisia had evolved its own political traditions and practices forged in part by geographic positioning. Indeed, it might be argued that the older Ottoman model was transformed in the nineteenth century because of the increasing recruitment of mamluks from adjacent lands. One of the mechanisms assuring a lifetime of loyal service was the severing of familial and communal ties between a young mamluk and his distant birthplace, which was no longer always the case.

Thus far Khayr al-Din's biography appears somewhat banal in the annals of North African–Ottoman history—a bright young man rapidly ascends the politicomilitary hierarchy through a combination of luck, intelligence, patronage, palace education, and marriage. But the story becomes curious when one considers that the mamluk system was also unraveling because indigenous Tunisians were admitted to the bureaucracy and even certain sectors of the military establishment.[16] The initial blow had come with the 1811 destruction of the seditious Turkish militia in Tunis—or its remnants—long before the Ottoman sultan Mahmud II disbanded his own unruly janissaries in 1826. As seen in chapters 4 and 6, some mamluks violated the moral pact of fidelity to their master's households by seeking refuge with European consuls and petitioning for the legal status of protégé. In 1831 a Greek courtier from Scio sought haven in the French consulate in Tunis, claiming France's protection because of his Christian origins; two other mamluks from Naples followed his example.[17]

Erudition was rare among his peers and Khayr al-Din might be compared with another equally atypical palace retainer, Husayn Khoja (died c. 1857–1858), originally Giovanni Certa from Sicily (or Naples, according to another source). Husayn was well educated by the standards of the day: "He was interested in history and was a bibliophile. When late in his career he was obliged to sell his property in settlement for debts, Ahmad Bey purchased his book collection and presented them as a waqf to the Zaytuna [mosque-university]."[18] A major difference, however, was that Husayn Khoja, unlike his Circassian counterpart, was an autodidact. His learning was disassociated both from his government posts, first as *bash mamluk* and then minister, and from his considerable, although precarious, personal social capital. Indeed one of Husayn Khodja's strategies for ensuring his court position was to "staff the palace with his compatriots" from Italy, an option not available to Khayr al-Din for obvious reasons.[19] What made Khayr al-Din's experience different was that, out of the remnants of the waning mamluk system, he translated his education and travels into remarkable erudition.

AL-MAKTAB AL-HARBI: THE MILITARY ACADEMY

That Khayr al-Din was brought to Tunis in c. 1839–1840 was fortuitous. Ahmad Bey had just embarked on ambitious state reforms, modeled on similar programs in Turkey and Egypt, whose centerpiece was the Bardo Military School (al-Maktab al-Harbi), which constituted both a rival and successor to the mamluk tradition while also anticipating Sadiqi College, which Khayr al-Din later organized.[20] Khayr al-Din rose quickly through the ranks of the elite cavalry unit attached to the academy that formed the nucleus of Ahmad Bey's new army. While Khayr al-Din neither enrolled in nor taught at the school, he maintained close contacts with its teaching staff, which was composed of select members of the 'ulama' corps as well as European military instructors, many of whom had previously served in Cairo or Istanbul. One wonders if Ahmad Bey's emissary had expressly purchased the young man in Istanbul to help staff Tunisia's modernization program.

Among the most preeminent of the teachers was Shaykh Mahmud Qabadu (1812–1871), a recognized scholar of Quranic studies who had just returned to his native land after a long absence. The shaykh's life trajectory illustrates older currents of religiointellectual exchange and merits a digression. Qabadu had departed Tunisia years before on a spiritual journey to the Madaniyya Sufi center in Tripolitania. He eventually ended up in Istanbul where he joined the entourage of the *shaykh al-Islam* 'Arif Bey, a partisan of the Tanzimat, during the period of Khayr al-Din's residence with Tahsin Bey. In 1842 Ahmad Bey dispatched his private secretary to Istanbul to prevail upon Shaykh Qabadu to accept a post as professor of Arabic and Islam at the newly created military academy. Regarded as one of the first advocates of modern science, Qabadu also taught at the Zaytuna mosque-university, served as qadi to the Bardo (chief judge) and after 1868 as Maliki mufti, and was acclaimed as a leading poet.[21] In a treatise composed around 1850, he argued that the wellspring of European might was modern science, which was not necessarily proscribed to believers, and he packaged his ideas within strategically chosen framing devices legitimating the notion of foreign borrowing. Qabadu's treatise reconciling aspects of Western science with Islam served as the introduction to a work on the art of warfare published in Paris in 1838 (Jomini's *Précis de l'art de la guerre*) and was subsequently translated into Arabic for the military school's teachers and students. He later became a key member of the editorial staff of the first government publication, *al-Ra'id al-Rasmi*, in 1860.[22]

Qabadu's wanderings before returning to his natal land reveal that older transversal circuits linking Tunisia with the Ottoman heartlands still flourished, even as north–south forces pulling the Maghrib into Europe's orbit assumed greater consequence. Some historians have minimized the importance of Qabadu's participation in the Tunisian Tanzimat, arguing that only the political class (as opposed to Muslim scholars) was exposed to challenges from outside. This view, however, undervalues the impact of travel upon knowledge and worldviews and fails to grasp how the social worlds of political elites and religious notables increasingly intersected and overlapped. Although Qabadu never ventured to Paris, his long residence in Istanbul surely introduced him to the appeals and perils of European thought. As importantly, Qabadu and Khayr al-Din collaborated closely in the critical matter of reform; that a mamluk became an intellectual intimate of a prestigious member of the religious establishment constitutes an index of profound shifts. Khayr al-Din's ardor for education was a product of his frequent interactions with Qabadu and other Tunis scholars, although it is possible that he was initially exposed to new forms of schooling during his youth in Istanbul.

One key element frequently absent from discussions of Tunisian reforms is the Italian contribution, which, as we have seen, not only introduced novel types of entertainment, sociability, and political identity—theaters, Masonic lodges, and anarchist circles—but also schooling institutions. Thus, Ahmad Bey's military academy should not be viewed as distinct from other types of educational experiments then taking place in Tunis; they exerted reciprocal influences. Moreover, the newcomers introduced odd behaviors in the practices of daily life in Tunis, for example, placarding city walls with highly charged political tracts during periods of intense communal conflict. The first publication printed in Tunisia—as opposed to imported from Europe or the Middle East—was in Italian, *Il Giornale di Tunis e di Cartagine,* which appeared in 1838 but was immediately banned. Only in 1860 did the official government press begin to publish *al-Ra'id al-Rasmi* (The Official Guide), a sort of *Journal Officiel,* in a bilingual Arabic and Italian edition. After 1883, it appeared in bilingual Arabic and French editions.[23]

The tardy appearance of the press in Tunisia was directly connected to migration and French Algeria. Until 1860, the Husaynid rulers steadfastly opposed private or even state presses, such as the Egyptian Bulaq Press, on pragmatic grounds inspired by genuine fears that publishing inflammatory news from Europe by politically divided and fractious foreign residents would provoke additional problems with the Great Powers. For Tunisia, mention must also be made of the fact that Malta served as an entrepôt for distributing Arabic-language missionary tracts between 1825 and 1842 organized by the Church Missionary Society; thus, apprehensions over proselytizing may have also been at work. In 1860 Richard Holt, a British subject, obtained permission, through Sir Richard Wood's patronage, to publish the first newspaper, containing mainly commercial information, shipping schedules, statistics, and news extracts from European newspapers; expressly excluded in the agreement between the bey and Holt was the printing of any political information. The Sardinian consul had earlier sought similar concessions but was turned down because Italians in Cagliari had created a journal there, specifically for distribution in Tunisia, whose sole object was to fan the flames of opposition to France's domination of Algeria. The presence of Algerian refugees, the Algerian question, and bilateral treaties impeded Tunisia's embrace of the press, since diplomatic agreements made it impossible for the government to suppress an offending publication owned by Europeans once it was printed in the country. In 1879, private as opposed to state-owned printing was authorized in-country, produced on imported lithographic and then typographic presses in which the Jewish Finzi family played a leading role.[24]

Moreover, the question of a modern census has scarcely been broached in the scholarship; yet Ahmad Bey's eagerness to embrace reforms akin to the Ottomans and Muhammad 'Ali Pasha in Egypt renders the absence of a census perplexing. The first partial census was only undertaken in 1906; the lack of enthusiasm by both the Husaynids in the precolonial period and French officials during the early Protectorate for counting heads was no doubt due to the presence of large, politically divided expatriate communities. Thus another singular element to this story is that some of the conventional indicators for calibrating modernity—the census and an indigenous publishing industry—came slightly later to Tunisia relative to Egypt or Turkey *because* of the nature of precolonial settlement. But books and other materials had long been available through a number of channels; from the late fifteenth century on, books printed in Europe had been introduced to the Middle East. By the nineteenth century, traders, diplomats, and pilgrims brought printed Arabic works home to Tunis from Cairo or Istanbul; travelers like Khayr al-Din purchased books in Paris, including Arabic works. In letters that Bin Diyaf sent between 1853 and 1857 from Tunis to his friend, Khayr al-Din, then negotiating with the French government, Bin Diyaf thanked him for sending a section "of Ibn Khaldun published in Paris."[25] In addition, the reading public of Tunis, while not large, subscribed to newspapers in Arabic, Hebrew, Italian, French, and English published elsewhere and brought in by ship; apparently, Muhammad al-Sadiq Bey and the Hanafi mufti in Tunis both subscribed to the bilingual Arabic-French newspaper, *Birjis al-Bariz*, or *L'Aigle de Paris*, published in Paris, or so François Bourgade claimed.[26] Indeed one could argue that, because of its strategic location in the central Mediterranean corridor, Tunis functioned as sort of catchment basin for knowledge, news, and information, some printed, most orally transmitted, that crossed the Mediterranean, which greatly influenced local expressions of the larger community of thought.

In his 1867 treatise, Khayr al-Din noted the immense impact of Gutenberg's printing press upon the course of European history. Indeed as he was laboring over his intellectual masterpiece during the 1860s, the printing press and publishing took off in Tunisia. Thus the acceleration of physical displacements from the early nineteenth century on, due in large measure to rapidly advancing transportation technology, imperialism, and heightened entanglements with Europe, exposed Tunisian notables to new or different modes of thought through print culture long before the creation of the first in-country Arabic presses.[27]

KHAYR AL-DIN:
FROM DIPLOMATIC ENVOY TO BIBLIOPHILE

Between 1846 and 1877—over thirty years—when not "at home" in Tunisia, Khayr al-Din traveled ceaselessly, repeatedly visiting the Ottoman capital and many European countries: France, Great Britain, Sweden, Prussia, Poland, Holland, Belgium, and Denmark.[28] Until 1846, Khayr al-Din had never ventured to Europe, although he entertained numerous contacts with Europeans residing in Tunisia. That year, he accompanied Ahmad Bey as his aide-de-camp on a two-month trip to France. Significantly the journey from Tunis to Toulon on the French steamship *Dante* lasted only three days—instead of three weeks. The Tunisian delegation spent eight days traveling in carriages from Toulon to Paris, which exposed them to cities and the countryside. As the first state visit by a Muslim ruler to a European court, Ahmad Bey's sojourn in France exerted a lasting impact upon him and his entourage, which included the well-traveled court official Hassuna al-Murali and also Bin Diyaf. Significantly, Ahmad Bey and Louis Philippe conversed in Italian, the only language they shared, although Captain Pourcet, who accompanied the visitors throughout France, disdainfully observed that the bey "spoke the bad Italian that is used on the coast of Barbary."[29] During their stay, the Tunisians appear to have interpreted Paris partially through the lens of Rifa'a Rafi' al-Tahtawi's *Takhlis al-ibriz fi talkhis Bariz* (A Profile of Paris), first published in 1834; indeed one has the impression that they employed al-Tahtawi's work as a sort of travel guide.

The places in France that Ahmad Bey and his entourage visited are significant for understanding some of the changes and reforms effected, or attempted, in Tunisia subsequent to the voyage. Concerts at Saint Cloud, fireworks at the Château de Vincennes, visits to the Hôtel de Ville, Chambre de Députés, Versailles, Gobelins, Imprimerie Royale, Hôtel de Monnaie, École Polytechnique, and the Jardin des Plantes. In short, displays of military and technological might were mixed with art, science, modern political institutions, and royal splendor.[30] They attended a theatrical production held in the gardens attached to Louis Philippe's palace; the play touched upon women's right to marry freely and was well received by the Tunisian audience.[31] From this first exposure to the stage, Khayr al-Din developed an enduring passion for the theater. The nineteenth-century troupes, particularly from Italy, often came to Alexandria or Cairo at the bequest of the Egyptian dynasty; and while the theater in Tunisia arose at the same time, it did not generally enjoy state sponsorship as in Egypt. For Egyptian modernizers, such as al-Tahtawi and Naqqash, the theater offered the possibility of mass popular civic instruction, effectively teaching modernity despite widespread illiteracy. In addition to the theater, a tour of the Bibliothèque Royale's Oriental collection greatly impressed the Tunisians, notably the many rare Arabic manuscripts on display, which later resulted in an exchange of manuscripts between Paris and Tunis. In short, as ever larger numbers of North African or Middle Eastern notables arrived in Paris during nineteenth century, the government rolled out a calculated spectacle of entertainment and sightseeing designed to exhibit France's power. Indeed, the capital functioned as theater and stage to awe foreign dignitaries.

In December 1846 the travelers returned home. It was not only Khayr al-Din who appreciated the value of foreign lands as a source of enlightenment; Bin Diyaf's biographies of notables extolled the merits of travel.[32] Khayr al-Din subsequently crossed the Mediterranean on numerous occasions, for the most part in service to the Husaynids, and these years of traveling proved critical to his own intellectual journey. But the 1846 trip was of tremendous importance because it expanded the cultural space deemed acceptable for Muslim rulers. Having traveled beyond the land of Islam, Ahmad Bey was blessed upon his return to Tunis by the grand mufti; thus the older Islamic practice of *rihla* (travel, often for religious purposes) was acquiring new meanings and expressions.[33] It should be noted, however, that Khayr al-Din's experiences in, and thus visions of, France were colored by what he did *not* see. The 1846 state visit missed by only two years the great populist upheavals of 1848–1849; the disorders and ferocious repression of the Bonapartist coup of 1851 were over for the most part when Khayr al-Din returned in 1853. Nor was he present in Paris during the terrible Prussian siege of 1870–1871, followed by the 1871 commune.

Population displacements siphoned the larger Mediterranean world into North Africa in new ways by midcentury; Khayr al-Din's extended stay in Europe was the direct product of positioning along a migratory frontier, which brings us to the infamous Bin 'Ayyad affair. In November 1853, Khayr al-Din was back in Paris ostensibly to negotiate an international loan for the Husaynids to pay for a military contingent to aid the sultan in the Crimean War. He ended up spending years there during an interminable affair provoked by a Tunisian notable, Mahmud bin 'Ayyad (1810–1880) who manipulated headship of Tunisia's newly created national bank to embezzle most of its assets; the bank vaults emptied, he fled the country in 1852. Because Bin 'Ayyad had, with great foresight, purchased property and established permanent residence in France, he acquired citizenship through naturalization in September 1852. The fact that Bin 'Ayyad had been a beylical subject when he made the bank heist, but was a French citizen when the Tunisian state demanded return of its purloined assets, created intractable jurisdictional questions for the court of arbitration. Recovery of the swindled funds turned into a legal labyrinth, which prolonged Khayr al-Din's stay in Paris as he argued the Tunisian government's case before a French tribunal.[34] The Tunisians lost their case.

The Bin 'Ayyad imbroglio illustrated in dramatic relief the problem of justice begot by settlement in North Africa, challenges that bedeviled Khayr al-Din and Tunisia—indeed much of the Ottoman-Mediterranean world—until the Great War. The affair signaled another ominous trend, one shared by Egypt and by the Ottomans—state bankruptcy to European creditors.[35] One direct result of the financial crisis was that the Husaynids, bankrupt by 1869, sacrificed their long cherished political autonomy from the Porte to offset a menace greater than

greedy European bankers—imperial armies and navies. The 1871 *firman* reinstated the Regency of Tunis as part of the Ottoman Empire; its ruler, Muhammad
al-Sadiq, was "demoted" to the rank of *wali* (governor) and in exchange the
Husaynids achieved formal recognition as a hereditary dynasty. Although there
are no studies of Khayr al-Din's tribulations with the French legal system, what
this long, drawn-out, bitter experience meant for the evolution of his worldview
is a question worth posing.

The years in France allowed Khayr al-Din to examine not only a state organized along different principles but also institutions of knowledge and learning.
A close reading of his great treatise reveals that he spent spare time in libraries,
schools, museums, and bookshops. He continued to enjoy the theater, although
the types of performances he attended remain uncertain; and he participated in
Parisian literary salons in which he closely followed international events. It is
unknown where he lived or if he visited the large numbers of Ottoman officials
and students in Paris at the time, including Mehmed Cemil Pasha, the Porte's
ambassador.[36] Later, as his rheumatism worsened and his political star faded in
Tunis, Khayr al-Din took refuge in French fashionable spas, where he might have
encountered not only European elites but also Middle Eastern notables from
Egypt, Turkey, and Persia.[37]

Toward the end of his life, Khayr al-Din stated in his memoirs: "My residence
in France as well as my numerous travels allowed me study the nature and origins
of European civilization and the institutions of the great powers of Europe."[38] His
prolonged stay also allowed him to perfect his written and spoken French. In any
case, he must have cut a fine figure; he was tall and robust—a full head taller than
the average Tunisian at the time—and was always impeccably dressed in military
uniform. Between 1853 and 1857, he only returned to Tunis on one occasion; it
was perhaps during this period that he commissioned the portrait in the style of
David's Napoleon. He left Paris in 1857, spending time in London before sailing
home.

MINISTER OF THE NAVY

In gratitude for his service, Muhammad Bey named Khayr al-Din minister of
the navy in 1857, a post he occupied until 1862. This phase in his life has received
less attention because scholars prefer his more glorious years as prime minister
(1873 to 1877), but it might yield unsuspected insights.[39] As minister and governor of the largest port, Khayr al-Din faced head-on the dilemmas created by
unregulated in-migration. Because of his education as well as travels, he realized
the urgency of the problem and that, given Tunisia's strategic importance, solutions would be daunting, if not impossible. Louis Jean-Baptiste Filippi, Sardinian
consul general and longtime resident of Tunis, made an astute observation in the

late 1820s regarding the duties incumbent upon the governor of the port: "the functions which he assumes are often very difficult because of the large number of relations in La Goulette between foreigners and the Moors."[40] Three decades later, those relationships had become all the more snarled.

In *The Surest Path*, Khayr al-Din argued that the Tanzimat's failure was due to a great many obstacles, principally the manipulation of the *shurut* or *imtiyazat* (capitulatory agreements, i.e., the Capitulations) to exempt European nationals residing in Ottoman lands from local laws.[41] His acute understanding sprang from his years in Paris during the Bin 'Ayyad proceedings and his post of minister of the navy, which included oversight of La Goulette. In 1861 he held discussions with the French Ministry of Foreign Affairs over the hotly disputed issues of frontiers between French Algeria and Tunisia, tariffs, and, most significantly, the legal jurisdiction and competence of Tunisian courts—the heart of the matter. During his tenure as navy minister, a third wave of Italian politicos, the Carbonari, surged into the country.[42]

Khayr al-Din proposed the creation of a Tunisian passport for his countrymen, an instrument fixing identity and thus legal jurisdiction that differed from the older permits or papers granted by the beys to allow people and goods to enter or leave the country.[43] Once again, the Bin 'Ayyad case influenced his thinking since it had revolved precisely around issues of legal pluralism and justice; although one did not have to travel as far as Paris to encounter similar problems occurring on a daily basis in Tunis. But it is also significant that Khayr al-Din had begun to think of himself as "Tunisian"—or, more precisely, of Tunisia as his adopted country. Thus his concern with documents establishing a new kind of identity may have reflected his own interior passage from a mamluk serving the Husaynid dynasty to an individual attached to a particular place.[44] In addition to travel documents, Khayr al-Din initiated an ambitious public works project focusing upon improvements to the port to facilitate trans-Mediterranean shipping and maritime links, thereby increasing the country's share of international commerce. Conversely, he adamantly opposed the construction of a rail line from French Algeria to Tunisia, clearly realizing its military risks (a decade later he reversed the decision, perceiving the benefits of a railroad linking Tunis to the Algerian frontier to outweigh the hazards).[45]

At La Goulette, Khayr al-Din oversaw the prison, hospital, the arsenal employing numerous Europeans, mainly engineers, and the customs administration regulating the importation of goods. Increased maritime contacts were far from benevolent; one critical task was to further modernize the quarantine system. In 1853, the government mandated observation of all vessels arriving from Malta, even those with clean bills of health. This was inspired by Ahmad Bey's well-founded apprehensions about the dangers to public health posed by the British island colony of Malta, "in consequence of the continual and rapid arrival there of steam and sailing ships from ports in England where the Asiatic cholera has unhappily made its appearance."[46] Another project was the reconstruction of the Carthage light house.

The spaces where individuals choose to dwell, the ways in which domestic interiors were embellished, provide clues about mental states and cultural referents.[47] Khayr al-Din began work on a summer palace for his family, locating it in orchards with a commanding sea view; still standing, the villa and its illustrious owner are memorialized by a train stop, Khéreddine, between Carthage and La Goulette. Built in the Italianate style of the period, the immense palace combined a large number of North African decorative and architectural elements; one entire exterior wall was graced by fretted windows facing the water, or *mashrabiyas*. Khayr al-Din appointed his residence with European and Tunisian furnishings, Italian frescos, and bottles of Vichy water, cheeses, good cigars, French vermouth, and large quantities of books for his personal library. (The vermouth was probably for medicinal purposes.) Lists of books sent from Paris during the 1875–1879 period show a mind attracted to an eclectic array of subjects—there were European works on classical antiquity, travel accounts, and classical Arabic texts in medieval Islamic law and prophetic traditions. He closely followed international events by subscribing to French- and Arabic-language newspapers sent from the Middle East and Europe: *Journal des débats, Le petit Marseillais, al-Jawai'ib* (from the Mashriq), and *al-Akhbar* (published in Algeria), to name but a few. Outside the Carthage home were European-style gardens, tended by a French gardener, as well as a small zoo filled with exotic birds and animals from the Sahara and farther afield.[48] The culture and habit of collecting and displaying curiosities—then a social indicator of elite status in Europe—was taking root in Tunisia.

The Mediterranean house was not Khayr al-Din's first. In 1853, after receiving the highest military grade from the bey—commander of the cavalry—Khayr al-Din built a palace in the suburb of La Manuba to the east of the capital, where his unit was quartered but which was also strategically close to one of the Husaynid's summer palaces. High-ranking mamluks constructed lavish residences in the madina, particularly in the area of the Qasba with its enduring association with the Ottoman Empire.[49] Khayr al-Din's father-in-law, Mustafa Khaznadar, boasted a Renaissance-style palazzo built by Italian architects and filled with both oriental and European furnishings, located in the Halfaouine quarter in Tunis's ancient core.[50] Khayr al-Din had a grand residence in the madina (in the quarter of Place du Tribunal), and it too resembled a Sicilian palazzo; although after becoming minister of the navy, he spent more and more time in his seaside home.[51] Nevertheless, Khayr al-Din's various dwellings reflect different dimensions of his social positioning.

As seen in chapter 8, coastal villages attracted many foreign consuls and expa-

330 KHAYR AL-DIN AL-TUNISI

triate notables after midcentury, along with the Husyanid family and members of court. In villas and gardens far from the capital's heat and hubbub, Khayr al-Din mingled with this cosmopolitan, if fractious, world. Combining diplomacy with deal making, these gatherings functioned as informal salons not unlike those in Paris that Khayr al-Din had so appreciated. When not attending to state business, Khayr al-Din expended much time and energy attempting to unravel the legal knot of property rights, occupancy, and ownership in La Goulette, judging by the number of indignant petitions and letters he received demanding resolution of endless quarrels over housing, beach use, leases, and rents.[52]

THE PATH TO *THE SUREST PATH*

The year that Khayr al-Din assumed command of the navy was marked by a momentous event directly tied to the expanding foreign presence as well as reforms in the Ottoman Empire. In 1857 Khayr al-Din and others in his circle drafted the Fundamental Pact, a precursor to the constitution proclaimed four years later, that earned Khayr al-Din an approving article, accompanied by his likeness, in one of France's leading newspapers, *L'illustration, journal universel.*[53] And Khayr al-Din was instrumental in drawing up the 1861 constitution, which attempted to institutionalize the principles proclaimed in 1857; one proposal put forth that did not figure in the final version was representation for Tunisian, as opposed to Italian, Jews.[54] While these radical transformations came largely to naught after the outbreak of the 1864 revolt, the Tunisian constitution is the Arab world's oldest. Some provisions attempted to establish a constitutional monarchy with a parliament; others were inspired by in-migration and the need to reorder society within the larger matrix of relations with Europe and the Ottoman Empire.[55] In his memoirs, Khayr al-Din enumerated the reforms that he regarded as his life's accomplishments; of those listed, most represented efforts to adjust policies and practices to come to grips with "strangers in the city."[56]

One constitutional innovation was the Supreme Council (Majlis al-Akbar), a parliamentary body fashioned after institutions in France and England. In 1861, Muhammad al-Sadiq Bey appointed Khayr al-Din to head the council, but a year later he resigned this post and that of minister of the navy. As he explained years after the fact, "since my efforts did not produce positive results, and not wishing that my presence on the council would contribute to the spoliation and ruin of my adopted country, I resigned my position."[57] Powerless to check the plundering of Tunisia's resources by Mustafa Khaznadar, his father-in-law and the bey's favorite, as well as by unscrupulous courtiers and their European allies, Khayr al-Din retired from public life to protest government corruption.[58] This decision brought a respite from administrative duties and provided a sabbatical for writing, reflecting, and more travels abroad. Thus another contingency—his disaffection from the court—leads us to ask, would his treatise have come to be had he not renounced the onerous duties of state?

Between 1862 and 1869, he traveled constantly to Europe and Constantinople; in 1867 he went to Paris expressly to visit the universal exposition, which would prove immensely influential to his educational reforms in the next decade.[59] When in Tunis, he retreated to his La Manuba residence to labor over a work of political philosophy whose objective was to "encourage statesmen and scholars to resolutely seek ways to improve the conditions of the Islamic *umma* . . . through expanding the spheres of science and knowledge, promoting agriculture, commerce, and industry while banishing idleness. And the basis for all of this is good government."[60] He composed his work with the assistance of Bin Diyaf as well as leading 'ulama', notably Shaykh Muhammad Bayram V, who were trained in classical Islamic traditions at the Zaytuna. Once again, this kind of collaboration was unusual for a mamluk in the same way that writing a learned treatise was an endeavor rarely undertaken by men of Khayr al-Din's background. As significantly, however, the arguments advanced regarding the legitimate exercise of power within a Muslim state departed substantially from the 'ulama''s traditional worldview, which made religious scholars the mediators between rulers and ruled via their guardianship of holy law. Indeed, in the opening pages of *The Surest Path,* Khayr al-Din criticized the religious establishment for lack of knowledge about the outside world.[61] Khayr al-Din's audience was first the *umma* (community of believers), and notably his fellow reformers, but he had at least two additional audiences in mind—Europeans and the political elite in Istanbul.

The publishing and translation odyssey of Khayr al-Din's masterpiece illustrates some of the contours of trans-Mediterranean intellectual traffic. After the first appearance of the work in Tunis in 1867–1868, other editions followed, including one published by Istanbul's Arabic press and serialized in newspapers (the original ran to a hefty five hundred pages). Khayr al-Din arranged for the shorter *muqaddima,* or introduction (inspired by Ibn Khaldun's work), to be immediately translated into French under his supervision; it came out the next year in Paris under the title *Réformes nécessaires aux états musulmans.*[62] As soon as the French edition appeared in 1868, the Persian ambassador to Paris requested a copy and immediately set about translating it into Farsi.[63] Translations of the *muqaddima* into Ottoman Turkish and English subsequently followed; although a complete Turkish edition was only published in Istanbul in 1878, the year that Khayr al-Din was called back to the capital by Sultan 'Abd al-Hamid. A bit later in time, the Indian Muslim leader, Sir Sayyid Ahmad Khan, found Khayr al-Din's ideas and arguments profoundly compelling.[64]

Previous scholarship mined *The Surest Path* principally for its political concepts. An alternative reading reconstructs Khayr al-Din's activities when off duty—the hours spent in libraries, botanical gardens, zoological parks, museums, schools, and theaters. This approach connects lived experience with Khayr al-Din's call for modern schooling and sound government; his contention that the number of volumes in the national library indicated the degree of freedom enjoyed by France's inhabitants shows what he did while in Paris. To underscore the scientific nature of his arguments, he meticulously inventoried the number of volumes held at the Bibliothèque Royale and also books per inhabitant in the United Kingdom.[65] His long years of collaboration with French and Italian military officers in Tunis had aroused an interest in engineering and technological inventions; he found the Braille method and sign language utterly fascinating. Lending libraries, as monuments to print culture, elicited enthusiasm. Khayr al-Din's impassioned pleas for modern education in Tunis reflected practical, on-the-ground experience. In Paris, he had visited a number of boarding schools searching for a suitable institution for his wife's brothers, which may have influenced his thinking on the organization of Sadiqi College.[66] Approached from this angle, *The Surest Path* becomes a manifesto for his lifelong passion—knowledge and education.

PRIME MINISTER AND EDUCATOR

Five years after Khayr al-Din's masterpiece appeared in Tunis, Muhammad al-Sadiq Bey's government underwent a minor revolution. Khayr al-Din was named prime minister in 1873, replacing his own disgraced (now former) father-in-law in office. Holding the second most powerful position allowed him to overhaul the bureaucracy, above all, to rationalize finances—an urgent matter since the state was under receivership to European creditors—as well as to translate his ideas on learning into concrete institutions. Another delicate diplomatic task revolved around changes in religious affiliation and legal identity. He sought to regularize conversions to Islam by resident Christians, which unleashed quarrels with European consuls opposed to protégés assuming a new religious and jurisdictional status.[67] In addition, working with judiciously selected 'ulama', he transformed the management of Islamic pious endowments and the curriculum for the Zaytuna in 1875. That year a public lending library featuring a special collections section was opened in Tunis. Khayr al-Din collected over a thousand rare manuscripts, scattered around the country and housed haphazardly in mosques, and had them deposited in the library; he also donated fine manuscripts to the public library from his own collection and stipulated that readers observe European-type rules concerning their use. Directly connected was his greatest achievement, a stone and mortar embodiment of *The Surest Path* that took the form of Khayr al-Din's Sadiqi College, (al-Madrasa al-Sadiqiya) named after the ruler and "founded upon the model of European lycées." However, the college should not be divorced from the larger historical context of educational innovation in Tunis dating from previous decades.[68]

Khayr al-Din's pedagogical philosophy was the fruit of attentively scrutinizing various methods for organizing and transmitting knowledge. By the 1870s, he had experienced several types of schooling: the household education of Tahsin Bey, the Husynid palace school, and the new military academy. In addition, after 1869 the Ottoman Empire embarked upon radical public educational reforms, which surely did not escape Khayr al-Din's notice.[69] By then, a philological society existed in Tunis, with the task of composing Arabic-French dictionaries, and the government press had begun publishing Arabic manuscripts from the Zaytuna library collection. Archeological excavations were underway; a new sense of the past was emerging. But the theft and sale of priceless artifacts from Carthage and elsewhere, principally by resident consular families, had begun in the 1840s, if not earlier, and turned into wholesale looting under the Protectorate.[70] Of course, many of these undertakings, backed by European interests, were far from benign since they advanced the claims of rivals for control of Tunisia.

In 1875, Sadiqi College welcomed its first class of students in a building that had once served as a barracks located on the madina's principal thoroughfare between the Zaytuna mosque-university and the Sea Gate—in the same neighborhood as some of the other schools discussed in chapter 7. Studies were free and followed an eight-year cycle. Specifically designed to educate competent civil servants and teachers, the Sadiqi experiment survived and even thrived—in large measure due to its spirit of cultural and political compromise. Not only were Arabic grammar, Islamic law and Quranic recitation required—in addition to mathematics, chemistry, and languages—but the religious sciences benefited from being taught at optimal times in the school day (when there were no required prayers). Privileging Islamic knowledge in the curriculum indicated that Khayr al-Din made concessions "to avoid bruising the sensibilities of the 'ulama' any more than was necessary."[71] Under the French Protectorate, Sadiqi College served as a model for the first academic nonmissionary school for Muslim girls in French North Africa, which opened its doors in 1900.[72] Yet prior to colonialism, Sadiqi College was regarded as a template for learning in unexpected places.

Exchanges in the central Mediterranean corridor sometimes ran in counterintuitive directions, *from* Tunis to Algiers. Sadiqi College soon came to the attention of French educators in Algeria intrigued by its language instruction and policies for recreation, exercise, and discipline. In 1876, L. Charles Féraud, head interpreter for the Algerian army, arrived in Tunis to collect Roman epigraphy for the *Revue Africaine,* Algeria's leading scientific journal. Féraud had just read *Réformes nécessaires* with boundless enthusiasm, so he shelved the antiquities project to observe the college firsthand: "Among the things that attracted my attention during my stay in Tunis, I rank first in importance the intellectual developments among the Tunisians during the past years."[73] Comparing the facilities and curriculum favorably to institutions in France, Féraud noted that two Algerian Muslims served on the teaching staff—Sidi Tahar ibn Salah, a former student from the Collège de Constantine, and the school's doctor, Sidi Qaddur ibn Ahmad, educated in the Algiers medical school. What really struck him were the methods for teaching French to Arabic speakers, which explained "the facility with which they [the Tunisian students] learn to read and write the French language."[74]

Féraud's report triggered a wave of interest in the new institution, but Khayr al-Din's own actions publicized the college as well. Khayr al-Din subscribed to the emerging pedagogical practice of pupil competitions, and in 1876 Sadiqi students won a prize in the Exposition Scolaire d'Alger, enhancing the college's reputation. In 1878, Daniel Grasset, principal of the Lycée d'Alger, inspected the institution, subsequently submitting a formal report titled *L'instruction publique en Tunisie* to none other than the governor-general of Algeria.[75] Grasset visited classes, toured the Sadiqi College library and ate at the dining hall, sticking his nose into every nook and cranny in the manner of a metropole *inspecteur*. Some things were found lacking—the science labs had not yet materialized. Nevertheless, Grasset proposed that some curricular innovations—especially bilingual instruction, methods of foreign-language acquisition, and disciplinary practices—employed in Tunis be adopted in Algeria. And he urged the colonial government to employ Sadiqi graduates in teaching positions in Algeria—a less-than-innocent proposition.[76] The year of Grasset's visit, Khayr al-Din sent samples of the best student work to Paris to compete for school prizes in the universal exposition, an idea whose origins may be traced to his tour of the 1867 exposition. Increased awareness of Sadiqi's achievements, particularly in language instruction, sparked colonial interest in Islamic pedagogy among scholarly societies in Algeria. The Algerian Muslim erudite and educator Mohammed Bencheneb (1869–1929), published several translations of Arabic pedagogical treatises in the *Revue Africaine* at the century's close. As the dyspeptic Baron von Hesse-Wartegg, who spent considerable time in Tunis and was generally critical of things Muslim, observed in 1881: "No school in the East can be compared in excellence to the College Sadiqi."[77]

THE WOMAN QUESTION?

One immensely important but unresolved question concerning Khayr al-Din's views revolves around women. Foreign settlement, tourism, and female missionary activity meant that women were increasingly conspicuous in the streets of Tunis. Khayr al-Din had spent years in Europe, where women occupied most public spaces, participated in official functions, and were increasingly vociferous in demanding the rights denied them. And his closest collaborator, Bin Diyaf, had composed an unpublished "Treatise on Woman" in 1856, one of the first of its kind in the Arab Muslim world. While it is uncertain if Bin Diyaf shared the essay with his close associates, it seems unlikely that this surprisingly conservative reflection on the status of women in Islam would have been unknown to them. Composed in the same period as the Fundamental Pact, nevertheless there was no attempt to rethink women's place even as the sociolegal status of foreigners, nonsubject residents, and religious minorities was being debated. A profound reevaluation of women and Islamic law would have to wait until the turn of the century, when Egyptian writers such as Qasim Amin took up the challenge. Khayr al-Din's silence in his own treatise may have been a strategic choice; why explicitly raise this difficult, complex issue when attempting to convince potentially hostile audiences of the pressing need to overhaul the state?[78]

Do Khayr al-Din's relationships with his wives afford any intimation regarding his thinking? In May 1862, at the age of about forty, he married his first wife Janina, whose mother was a Husaynid princess, an event celebrated with great pomp and announced in the official newspaper, *al-Ra'id al-Rasmi*. Several months later that year, he resigned his post and began work on his political treatise in their La Manuba residence, where he spent much time *en famille* and tended to his garden of rare plants. During eight years of marriage, his wife produced three children, including a son, Muhammad al-Sa'id, who died the same year as Janina, in 1870. His two daughters, Mahbuba (b. 1864) and Hanan (b. 1866) were married to members of the powerful baldi Zarruq clan of Tunis. One source claims that Khayr al-Din desired that his wife be referred to as "Madame" when she received European women, mainly the wives of creoles or consuls, at their home for social calls.[79] About a year after Janina's untimely death, he married two sisters of Turkish origins, both of whom gave birth to sons in 1872. Soon thereafter, he repudiated them to marry Kmar (Qamar in Arabic, "Moon"), also of Turco-Circassian origins in 1873, a union that resulted in two sons and a daughter. It seems probable that Khayr al-Din married the two sisters for the sole purpose of producing male progeny but wed Kmar, his fourth wife, out of love. In any case, his last marriage was monogamous; Kmar died in Istanbul several years after her husband's death.[80]

Khayr al-Din's children's lives reflect their father's peregrinations and attachments to Turkey, Tunisia, and France. In view of Khayr al-Din's devotion to the Ottoman Empire, it is tragically ironic that his son, Salah Damad (b. 1876 from his union with Kmar), who married into the Ottoman imperial family, was executed in 1913 for involvement in the assassination attempt on Grand Vizier Mahmut Şevket. One son, Muhammad al-Hadi, settled in Paris where he became an artist; another, Mahmud (b. 1872), in contrast to his seditious brother, had a distinguished career in the Ottoman army. The third son, Tahar, returned to Tunis in 1921 to serve as minister of justice to the Husaynid government, which had been under France's rule for three decades.

FIGURE 17. View of Galata Bridge, Istanbul, c. 1880. This image was taken around the time of Khayr al-Din's final years in Istanbul and features the newly constructed Galata Bridge, completed in 1875, that spanned the Golden Horn. Perhaps Khayr al-Din crossed the bridge. (Library of Congress Prints and Photographs, LC-US762–81746.)

EXILE OR RETURN HOME?

In many areas, above all, education, Khayr al-Din and his cohort of visionary reformers could legitimately claim to have accomplished a great deal—despite daunting opposition from many quarters. Yet their ultimate aspiration—transforming the state along modern lines to ensure Tunisia's political independence—remained unfulfilled. In July 1877, Khayr al-Din resigned his post as prime minister after a serious falling out with the ruler. Fearing reprisals, he left the country as a precautionary measure and resumed his cures in Vichy for severe rheumatoid arthritis. Upon his return to Tunis in June 1878, he found himself a pariah, fated, in his words, to "wander from the African loneliness of La Mannouba [sic] to the solitary mountains of Auvergne."[81] The restructuring of justice, taxation, finances, and bureaucracy had provoked the ire of those court officials and European diplomats or traders whose interests lay in the older corrupt, inefficient way of running the state. As he remarked bitterly in his memoirs, "However much I could take satisfaction in the things that I had accomplished for my adopted country, its future was in doubt."[82]

Khayr al-Din could well have ended his days under palace arrest, deprived even of the company of dear friends, had not a telegram from Istanbul arrived in the summer of 1878. It contained an invitation from the sultan to journey back to the place of his upbringing to confer with officials at the Porte; the next day a telegram accepting the offer was dispatched. Several weeks later, Khayr al-Din sailed to Marseilles, where he boarded another ship for the eastern Mediterranean. He arrived in the Ottoman capital alone in September 1878, for his family was not allowed to leave until later. One wonders at Khayr al-Din's thoughts as the ship pulled away from La Goulette—forty years after he had first laid eyes upon the Gulf of Tunis. Perhaps he searched for his villa on the slopes of Carthage as the steamer headed to Malta and then France; he could not have known that this was a last glimpse of his adopted country. Khayr al-Din had returned to Istanbul on a number of occasions—in 1842, 1859, 1871—but always as an emissary of Husaynid rulers.[83] This time was very different; his presence set off endless rumors and speculation. As the British ambassador in Istanbul, Layard, noted,

> General Khairredin [sic] . . . was received on his arrival with unusual distinction. . . . He was immediately received by the Sultan. The Grand Vizer stated to me that his Majesty had no political object in inviting General Khairredin to visit him, being only desirous of seeing so distinguished a Mussulman statesman. There is a rumor here that HM has offered the General a high post in his service, and that it has been refused. . . . It is most probable that the Sultan will consult him as to public affairs, and should such be the case I trust that his enlightened and liberal views may make a favorable impression upon HM and do good. . . . I am most struck by his liberal and practical views on reforms necessary for this Empire. . . . He will be a very useful advisor to the Sultan.[84]

To the surprise of many, Sultan 'Abd al-Hamid named Khayr al-Din grand vizier in December 1878. The enslaved orphan child from the edges of the Ottoman Empire had acceded to the second most powerful office in the realm. Nevertheless, this came with a price, since malicious tongues rebuked him for his imperfect command of Turkish, among other things.[85] But he only occupied the post for six months; the same political dynamic occurred in Istanbul as had in Tunis. Dismayed by Khayr al-Din's firm conviction that fundamental changes were needed in the prevailing structures of power, including the creation of a parliament with ministerial responsibility, the sultan dismissed him in July 1879, despite pleas on his behalf—surely not disinterested—from Great Britain's ambassador to the Porte and the British foreign secretary.

After his forced retirement, Khayr al-Din rarely left the spacious mansion that the sultan had bequeathed upon him and he never ventured much beyond Istanbul.[86] From correspondence exchanged with his longtime friend Vallet, a French diplomat, it seems that in 1878 he would have preferred to return home to Tunis: "However beautiful the shores of the Bosporus might be, I do not wish to attach or tie myself down here."[87] But the 1881 French invasion ended hopes of return to Tunisia. Not a few Tunisian statesmen, such as Muhammad al-Sanusi, sought refuge in Istanbul from this period on, enlarging the circle of those already established in the Ottoman capital and providing companionship. Ill health rendered Khayr al-Din's last years difficult. Embittered by his exile, he spent his remaining days dictating his memoirs in French to a succession of secretaries, including Pietro Maccaro, a former Garibaldi partisan who converted to Islam and took the name Muhammad al-Sa'id.[88]

Given Khayr al-Din's fluency in French, apparent from his correspondence, why did he not pen the memoirs himself? It may well have been that his advanced state of rheumatoid arthritis made writing too painful. However, these last writings were partially intended for French readers, or at least a Francophone audience. Khayr al-Din may have employed secretaries skilled in the language to ensure absolute accuracy—after all, he was defending himself against scurrilous attacks regarding his actions as prime minister in Tunis. Obstinate to the last, he attempted to redirect the course of change in the imperial center by drafting unsolicited state reform programs that he submitted to the increasingly paranoid Sultan 'Abd al-Hamid, to no avail.

Khayr al-Din died in 1890 surrounded by his family in their Bosporus *konak* (villa) in Kuruçeşme. The funeral was celebrated with pomp, his remains laid to rest in a specially built mausoleum in the Eyüp Mosque on the Golden Horn. A large crowd accompanied the funeral procession, among them the Ottoman Empire's highest officials and a bevy of European dignitaries. If his last view of Tunis had been twelve years earlier as the ship pulled out of La Goulette bound for Europe and then Istanbul, that had not been his final trans-Mediterranean journey; Khayr al-Din's remains were repatriated to the Republic of Tunisia in March 1968—but that is another story.[89]

FINAL THINGS

Narrating Khayr al-Din's life as a geography of biography brings unsuspected connectivities to light, at least in cameo. Global, transnational, and quite local transformations in technologies of movement and measurement, identities and belongings, undermined older, comfortable ways of experiencing, seeing, and doing. That the voyage from Tunis to Istanbul or Marseilles was drastically reduced, with travel calculated in hours and minutes—not days or weeks—was essential to trans-Mediterranean communities of thought. But the story might have unfolded differently if, as a young man, Khayr al-Din had served masters in remote outposts of the late Ottoman Empire. Thinking about him as simultaneously a traveler, intellectual, educator, and statesman situates his trajectory at the historical juncture where fictive kinship ties to a princely household and dynasty gave way to affinity with a people and their history.

In the mamluk tradition at its best, Khayr al-Din gave unwavering loyalty to the Husaynids and sultans—until their policies violated his notion of just governance informed by his own lived experience, Islamic moral precepts, and chosen European political principles. As author of *The Surest Path*, he worked closely with Tunis notables and 'ulama' in an unusual collaboration that produced a remarkable document and equally remarkable institution—Sadiqi College, whose educational philosophy was unique and at the same time borrowed from similar experiments underway in Istanbul, Cairo, Paris, and Algiers. Khayr al-Din's political career was a consequence of timing and the curious nature of Tunisia's relationship with the Ottoman Empire, Europe, and the Mediterranean world. Indeed, the regency's autonomy vis-à-vis Istanbul allowed Khayr al-Din to pursue the path that he did. As prime minister, however, he further dismantled the mamluk system—the very imperial culture that had propelled him into the Tunisian-Ottoman elite.[90]

His circle of associates subscribed to the notion of travel as a source of wisdom about the world; the cosmopolitanism of Tunis, which was not an identity so much as a manner of social existence, primed him for diplomatic missions that appeared, for a time, to secure Tunisia a place, however minor, among Mediterranean powers. As a borderland intellectual, he operated at multiple points of intersection: between the Maghrib and the Ottoman Empire; Europe and North Africa; the central Mediterranean corridor and the sea writ large; the universes of the philosopher-educator and statesman. In light of his multifaceted border crossings, Khayr al-Din might be seen as a latter-day Ibn Khaldun or a Hasan al-Wazzan, Leo Africanus to Renaissance Europeans.[91] And *The Surest Path* could be recast as a modern expression of the *rihla* through which Khayr al-Din attempted to legitimate distant or foreign knowledge. His text also anticipated another genre penned by Muslim or Arab intellectuals that appeared at the fin de siècle—published appeals, frequently in French, addressed to likeminded supporters in Europe, for assistance with the modernizing project.[92]

Nevertheless, Khayr al-Din seemed to have underestimated the opposition among European powers to a fundamental reordering of state and society in Tunisia, although many of his decisions were shaped by the political fact that the country had long shared a turbulent border with French Algeria, the perils of which were obvious. Seduced by Europe, above all by France and French culture, he reluctantly admitted that the existence of a truly modern Muslim polity was far from welcome, while acutely observing that, "due to its geographic location, more than its territorial importance, Tunisia is well placed to tempt European pow-ers."[93] Whether the transformations achieved by the 1870s hastened or delayed the imposition of the Protectorate is open to debate. What is certain is that colonial officials inherited a state in which the process of modernity, inspired in part by new ideas on governance, notably French social engineering, but adapted to Tunisia's historical circumstances, was well advanced.[94]

While this chapter has not mapped out all the coordinates of Khayr al-Din's biography, the arc of his life illuminates the dialogic nature of movement and stability, connectivities and ruptures.[95] The element of chance that is so striking resonates with Bakhtin's reflections on aleatory encounters: "The road is a par-ticularly good place for random encounters.... The spatial and temporal paths of the most varied people—representatives of all social classes, estates, religions, nationalities, ages—intersect at one spatial and temporal point. People who are normally kept separate by social and spatial distance can accidentally meet; any contrast may crop up, the most various fates may collide and interweave with one another."[96]

To bring some closure to our peregrinations though the time and space of nineteenth-century North Africa, the epilogue takes up the problem of ruptures from a slightly different perspective to address a principal theme of this book: the persistence of multiple social forces at work in Tunisia, Algeria, and the cen-tral Mediterranean corridor from circa 1800 that powerfully shaped the nature of the colonial state. Most studies of nineteenth-century imperialism privilege the imposition of formal colonial rule—when armies invade, treaties are forced upon unwilling local leaders, laws and institutions are imposed, and foreigners arrive to take control of land, resources, and the instruments of coercion. From this comes the chronological scaffolding for imperial histories: the construction of a temporal binary of before and after, precolonial and colonial. A temporal binary calls forth another dichotomous taxonomy—"Europeans" (or colonizers) and "Muslims" (or colonized), something that this volume has attempted to challenge.

This is not to say that foreign rule represented anything less than a shattering experience. As the French army advanced toward Tunis from Algeria and the navy bombarded Tunisian ports during the summer of 1881, city inhabitants went down to La Goulette in the hope of espying an Ottoman fleet on the horizon bringing deliverance. Some within diaspora communities celebrated the imposi-tion of the Protectorate; others were utterly dismayed, sensing that the good old days were soon to be over. And so they were in many respects. In the south, tribal rebellions erupted that took years to put down and Tunisian refugees poured over the border into Ottoman-ruled Tripolitania.[97] Paradoxically, thousands more from Sicily flocked to a country now under France's protection, driven from their own homeland by the years of drought and famine marking the 1880s and drawn by the promise of work. Nevertheless, many ways of doing things, of carrying on with daily life, making a living, seeing the world, and negotiating one's way through the maze of competing legal authorities, remained more or less the same, at least for a while.

Epilogue

Fetched Up on the Maghrib's Shores

On ne s'exile pas de gaieté de cœur.
[One does not leave home with a joyous heart.]
MICHEL AUGUGLIORO, *LA PARTENZA: LA SAGA D'UNE FAMILLE*
SICILIENNE DE TUNISIE, PREMIÈRE PARTIE, 1887–1909

Exactly how the tragedy came to pass remains uncertain, although the plan was probably hatched in one of La Goulette's popular cafés where young men with too much time on their hands gather to while away the hours. Sometime during the evening of Sunday, January 18, 2009, and the following day, a band of thirty-five would-be labor migrants, all apparently Tunisian nationals from the port's modest neighborhoods, stole a fishing boat. Driven by dreams of reaching the "European El Dorado," the group set out at night for Italy via the islets of Pantelleria and Lampedusa. They never made it past coastal waters off La Goulette and La Marsa. The boat capsized in bad weather and, since most could not swim, twenty-six people disappeared; five swam ashore to La Marsa, where they alerted authorities, who fished four men alive from the sea. Despite massive maritime and air rescue efforts, the bodies of the others were never found.[1]

Of course, this was only one among countless such incidents, occurring not only in the Mediterranean but also across the globe, whose frequency tends to normalize, even trivialize, the personal and collective dramas inherent in expatriation. Recently the European Commission estimated that four thousand people have perished in the Mediterranean while attempting to reach Europe since 2003; what was once a maritime thoroughfare for people in search of social betterment on both sides of the sea has become a sepulcher for some. In 2008, Italy experienced a 75 percent increase in clandestine immigration with the arrival of an estimated thirty-seven thousand people without papers, mainly but not exclusively from Africa.[2] Italy, whose nationals departed by the millions during the long nineteenth century, has become an unwilling New World migratory frontier in part because of proximity to the Maghrib, now perceived as Europe's dangerous southern frontier. Behind the boat people—propelling them from homes, villages, cities, and countries—are the potent forces of war, violence, expropriation, transnational capitalism, and ecological/environmental devastation. That contemporary population movements take place with a singular density, a distinctive intensity, in the Mediterranean, and particularly in the central corridor, merely substantiates age-old patterns of displacements.

It is useful to juxtapose the January 2009 calamity with a mass emigration in the late nineteenth century, around the time of the Protectorate, when nearly a third of the total population of tiny Pantelleria, some three thousand people, relocated to the Cap Bon, where they cultivated orchards and fished—and shoved aside local farmers. The key elements appear roughly similar—the desire to make a living, achieve mobility, or simply escape unfavorable circumstances—framed by states, laws, communications, and the contingencies of the moment. These paired incidents are not merely resonant of universal problems associated with "strangers in the city" but illustrate how earlier migratory flows directly shaped subsequent south-to-north movements in the twentieth and early twenty-first centuries. Yet the dots need to be connected by pulling together arguments or findings from our extended ethnographic voyage, whose focus upon mobilities challenges some of assumed verities about the many histories of North Africa, the Ottoman Empire, and Europe.

How best to characterize the people who had long called Tunisia home—some since the 1820s or 1830s? The terms "cultural creoles," "Crypto-Europeans," or "Euro-Tunisians" are a few of the conceptual envelopes used throughout this study—and messy ones indeed—which is the point. The fact that we lack a satisfactory language to talk about these folks is suggestive of the problem itself. It is also important to cast them not only in the roles of mere brokers or social intermediaries, which tend to be static concepts, but instead to see them as new social formations arising from constantly improvised communities forged by successive dislocations, settlement, and assimilation to varying degrees. By disaggregating and reimagining those processes and forces, a new kind of a borderland—or perhaps borderlands—comes into view that renders notions of "Europe" and "North Africa," "Muslim" and "Christian," more problematic.[3] Do we really know where Europe began and ended in the nineteenth century, who and what was a European, where Islam and Muslims were situated, and where the boundaries between religions, cultures, states, and empires fell as borderlands become borders?

Looking at empire from a small place, with attention to mutable and contingent processes after 1800, demonstrates the ways in which forces of various magnitudes bled into one another. In the course of the nineteenth century, the Mediterranean became a space largely dominated by British and French navies,

armies, merchant fleets, and communication technology, but it did not constitute "a colonial sea," a perspective that empowers the Great Powers in ways,
and to degrees, that facts on the ground belie. Yet the weight of the archive,
European and colonial, and the rhetoric of empire continue to depict the leading
Euro-Mediterranean powers as purposefully hegemonic, even though seemingly
insignificant social realities, when assembled, temper that view. Always and
everywhere, the countervailing winds of the unexpected, unintended, and unde-
sired were at work. The rules of the game may have drastically changed after 1830,
but they were by no means unilaterally rewritten by the victorious. In response
to pressures "from below," consular officials in North African ports "made it up"
when policies were not forthcoming from Paris or London; the Foreign Office and
Quai d'Orsay often proved supremely indifferent to the actions and daily lives
of representatives, merchants, and protégés who were theoretically governed by
treaties (backed by the threat of gunboat diplomacy).[4] Making it up represented
a sort of system of rule or governance in itself; yet, the laws, practices, and procedures for stabilizing the unstable in the Maghrib and in the Mediterranean
were worked out through incessant negotiation, concession, and sparring, which
brought together emerging and older ways of doing things. Moreover, a comparative examination of late nineteenth-century imperial expansion into places such
as Malaysia suggests that the Mediterranean furnished a template for the second
wave of European empire building.

Our examination from below of the contraband economies has flushed out
a subterranean world of transactions running counter to the aims of imperial states—and to those of North African elites such as Khayr al-Din as well.
Unregulated exchanges of people and things spliced together ports and hinter-
lands, producers and consumers, exploiters and the exploited, the distant and
local. As increasingly aggressive consuls and merchants struggled to construct
exclusive spheres of economic influence for home governments, some of their
own countrymen doggedly undercut those efforts. And while the colonial administration frantically passed decrees after 1840 restricting Algeria's access to the
contraband economy, enterprising free-traders and adventurers thwarted those
ambitions. Forbidden exchanges constituted undeclared commercial warfare,
under-the-table credit and banking operations, out-the-back-door commerce,
or behind-the-scenes maneuvers by local authorities charged with curtailing
the illicit and illegal. By 1896, the transregional smuggling economy—stretching
from eastern Algeria, the Gulf of Tunis, coastal Tunisia, and the Sicilian-Maltese
triangle—was so pervasive and successful a free-trade zone that colonial law-
makers in both Tunisia and Algeria imposed a legal-administrative grid on the
web of exchanges forged by folks like Giovanna Tellini and her associates.

Given the demographic, economic, and other pressures building on the adjacent islands, immigration would have occurred even without the new imperial-

ism unleashed by 1830. Remember the Maltese? In the late 1820s, they had begun to people Tunis in ways different from the past; their decisions to leave home, however tentatively, created some of the first nodes in the Maltese diaspora that eventually stretched to Australia. These relatively early displacements, mainly from islands, to colonial Algeria and precolonial Tunisia need to be considered in relation to the slightly later mass emigrations from Italy and elsewhere, principally to the Americas.[5] There was a long tradition of mainly northern Italian labor migration to southeastern France, but we might ask whether the incipient north-to-south movements in the central Mediterranean primed the pump for the slightly later mass transatlantic migrations. Did a sojourn in Tunis or Algiers render crossing the ocean somehow less daunting? Clearly, large numbers of people came and went—after failing to make it, being expelled, or imagining that more promising opportunities lay over the horizon. The stories of those who alighted for a time in the Maghrib, only to subsequently move on, have rarely been told or incorporated into the historical narrative but are nevertheless important; surely these people took some part of the North African experience with them—wherever their final destiny. Moreover, the fact of accelerated comings and goings represented a force, among many, for modernity.

However, this volume argues against the notion that colonial states or immigrants were the principal bearers of modernity to the Maghrib. The sheer number and diversity of the newcomers, the legal, social, economic, and moral problems posed by their more or less permanent presence, prompted indigenous states and political elites to devise solutions to the transformations unleashed by more people moving about more often. It may even be that laws and concepts for inclusion and exclusion, for achieving legibility, were fashioned on the margins, as suggested by efforts to fit "expatriate" Algerians or women who abandoned the faith of their husbands into emerging legal categories. After 1881, the colonial state shamelessly poached on the reforms already underway in Tunisia, while blocking or hindering changes in the configuration of state and society that were characteristic of modernity. Thus the unsuspected local histories of modernities in North Africa start to come into view. Reconsidered, the clean breaks and ruptures associated with formal imperial rule reemerge instead as moments of transition that call into question stock-in-trade temporalities such as "precolonial" and "colonial."[6] Finally, if the Maghrib was peopled not only by France's "nationals" but also by Spanish, Italians, and Maltese, what was French about French North Africa?

THE POISONED CHALICE OF THE PAST

In the older literature on modern empires, the settlement of "European" expatriates was seen as a boon for imperial projects. Subsequent research reconcep-

tualized these people as poor whites, hybrids, and cultural hyphens and theo-
rized about how they violated, complicated, or pushed at the boundaries—legal,
political, sexual, moral—of colonial or protocolonial rule.[7] The trajectories of
"people on the move" reveal that some subsistence migrants turned into Tunis
residents—neighbors or troublesome renters, business partners or labor competitors, debtors or creditors—along lines that defied neat mapping by conventional
categories such as religion; in some cases, social class exerted the greatest torque
in the construction of hierarchies and inequalities. At first, many recently arrived
people labored as masons, wet nurses, fishermen, domestic help, or smugglers;
they later farmed small plots, and became mechanics, seamstresses, boat makers,
or music instructors. Expatriate communities boasted solid bourgeois families
as well as lumpen proletariat clinging to the bottom rungs of the social order
for generations, although some rose to the top. Collective memory in today's
Tunisia recalls the Sicilians and Maltese as "being very poor."[8] Some were refused
membership in the charmed circle of the "Europeans," at least until the twentieth
century. Others gradually became European or not-quite-French through education that owed much to precolonial experiments in schooling and later through
military service; a few acquired French nationality, which was severely restricted
until the interwar period.

Long after 1881, the poisoned chalice of Tunisia's migrant past continued to
vex the Protectorate. The spoils of a half century of heterogeneous migratory currents, immigrant (or continually creolizing?) communities counted large pockets
of border crossers in every sense of the term, including some who openly transgressed religiosexual boundaries. A somewhat imprecise statistic from 1896, when
the Franco-Italian conventions were signed, encapsulates the demographic and
therefore political dilemma facing France: 88 percent of resident "Europeans" were
Italians, estimated at about fifty-five thousand.[9] Moreover, the labor migrants in
both Tunisia and Algeria fulfilled the same functions as do Maghribis (and others)
in today's Europe. French North Africa's colonial infrastructure—mines, roads,
forests, ports, and irrigation—was built by tens of thousands of non-French workers. The emerging modern service sector also provided a living for subsistence
migrants who were climbing up the social ladder; but whatever meager benefits
accrued to indigenous laborers, both male and female, from these developments
must be weighed against the destruction of local production, corporative associations, and subsistence agriculture. By the end of the century, colonial officials
sounded the alarm about the declining state of the capital city's most illustrious
guilds, some with origins in the ninth or tenth centuries.[10] The demise of the textile and other industries, mainly centered in the Tunis region, devastated guilds,
artisans, and families as well as urban life in general, providing fertile recruiting ground for various expressions or strands of Tunisian or other nationalisms.
This raises the critical issue of identities, which from a diachronic perspective are

always multilayered, fungible, and protean, although conventional interpretations have favored static concepts, principally ethnicity/language or religion, when tracing identity formation.

As shown, a single Italian community did not exist before the Protectorate but rather there were congeries of anarchists, Masons, socialists, Garibaldians, bourgeois secular Jewish traders, and pious Catholic noblemen whose ranks fed pro- and anti-French factions as well as the pro-Church and anticlerical factions. French rule helped to solidify a more pervasive sense of Italian-ness among the Sicilians, Tuscans, and Neapolitans residing in Tunisia—one of the many places where the nation was constructed in diaspora. Did a discernible sense of "Mediterranean-ness" eventually emerge among these various and sundry communities? There is little evidence of this in the period under consideration. Yet the existence of a shared social communications order expressed in the dialect of quotidian exchanges can be detected. "All of Tunis was talking about it," an oft-repeated phrase employed by city dwellers of whatever origins supports this contention, as do other sources. Although migrant or minority spaces regarded as culturally different had acquired designations reflected in neighborhood vernacular, such as the "street of the Maltese" or "quarter of the Sicilians"; this did not preclude broader patterns of *convivencia,* for a while at least.[11]

CONNECTING THE DOTS

Tunisia's geographical positioning, together with the urgent need to offset the Italian menace by attracting French men and women into commercial and agricultural sectors, meant that the velocity of people moving in and out of the country remained high well into the interwar period. After World War I, thousands of French nationals arrived in both Morocco and Tunisia; in the latter, the growing Italian presence increased pressures to seize Tunisian state and/or *habus* lands for colonization, wreaking havoc in the traditional agrarian society as the world economic crisis struck.[12] By the late 1930s, Morocco counted some 150,000 European settlers; on the eve of the 1923 Morinaud Law of naturalization, 54,000 French citizens resided in Tunisia, as did tens of thousands of non-French people. Algeria's European populations, naturalized and non-French, had climbed to 833,000 by 1926.[13] However, the principal axis of population movements underwent a radical shift by the beginning of the twentieth century.

The historical strands of successive North African labor migrations to France and Europe are now well documented. But the at times tragic dialogic relationship between the historically later south-to-north flows and the nineteenth-century settlement of Algeria and Tunisia (and slightly later Morocco), tend to be insufficiently emphasized. Around World War I, a reverse migratory stream took shape; it was composed largely of temporary laborers, impoverished Arab or Berber men whose land and villages in Algeria had been appropriated by the settlers. During the world wars, tens of thousands of North African laborers circulated between the Maghrib and France's factories, in addition to conscripted colonial soldiers who fought under the tricolor in the trenches; many never returned home.

The end of empire spawned another movement of people from south to north. The forced exodus of Europeans who had lived in French North Africa, many for generations, constituted one of the largest population transfers of the post–World War II era. In a decade, over one and a half million people were "repatriated" to a France (or Spain, Israel, or Latin America) they neither knew nor necessarily identified with.[14] Between 1955 and 1959, 170,000 Europeans—roughly two-thirds of the total resident in the country—left Tunisia. In the first year and a half after Tunisian independence, nearly 8,000 French functionaries departed. Reduced to the legal status of resident aliens, the Italians of Tunisia counted 67,000 people; a third left before the end of the 1950s, although a few still remain. Of the Tunisian Jews who numbered 85,000 just before independence, nearly 15 percent relocated to Israel, but the majority chose France as their new homeland. In addition, thousands of Algerians who had served France were also forced out during the last anguished days of the Algerian War.

This exodus was followed by yet another influx of North African workers (and others from elsewhere in the former French Empire) in search of a decent livelihood across the sea, a population movement that endured until the early 1970s when fortress Europe began to shut its doors. But it should be noted that it was not only North African laborers who were siphoned into western Europe; increasingly a *fuite de cerveau* (brain drain) skimmed off highly educated, talented individuals. Connecting these dots reveals how and why North Africa became Europe's southern frontier. The historical antecedents of many Franco-Maghribi communities, some third- or fourth-generation but still second-class "citizens," lie in the nineteenth century when Alsatian, Maltese, Sicilian, or Spanish laborers and peasants sought fortune on the Mediterranean's African shores. The recent rebirth of Marseilles, a city not previously held up as a model of tolerance or harmonious coexistence, has emerged as the unlikely crucible for living the art of intimacy, which was celebrated in 2008 by a Fête de la Méditerranée.[15]

Perhaps a historical vision generous enough to see the complex filiations between those earlier displacements and contemporary migratory movements can check xenophobic, racist thinking about the strangers in our midst. Such a vision might offer an antidote to the so-called clash of civilization thesis and the crude binaries currently deployed to justify imperial interventions in today's North Africa and Middle East. For a world where at least two hundred million humans, 3 percent of the globe's population, now live outside their countries or societies of origin, this is my sincerest hope.

NOTES

ABBREVIATIONS

Archives, Libraries, and Collections

AMAE	Archives du Ministère des Affaires Étrangères, Paris
ANT	Archives Nationales de Tunisie, Tunis
ASHAT	Archives du Service Historique de l'Armée de Terre, Château de Vincennes
BDT	Bibliothèque Diocésaine de Tunis, Sidi Saber
BL	British Library, London
BNF	Bibliothèque Nationale de France, Paris
BNT	Bibliothèque Nationale de Tunisie, Tunis
CADN	Centre d'Archives Diplomatiques, Nantes
CAOM	Centre des Archives d'Outre-Mer, Aix-en-Provence
CCM	Chambre de Commerce et d'Industrie de Marseille-Provence, Série MQ 52, Commerce International, Tunisie
CNRS	Centre National de Recherche Scientifique
IBLA	Institut des Belles Lettres Arabes, Tunis
IRMC	Institut de Recherche sur le Maghreb Contemporain, Tunis
ISHMN	Institut Supérieur de l'Histoire du Mouvement National, Tunis
LC	Library of Congress, Prints and Photographs, Washington, D.C.
MMSH	Maison Méditerranéenne des Science de l'Homme, IREMAM Collection, Aix-en-Provence
NAUK	National Archives of the United Kingdom, London, Foreign Office Documents
OBL	Oxford University, the Bodleian Library
ORL	Oxford University, Rhodes House Library, Scicluna Collection
RW	Oxford University, St Antony's College, Private Papers Collection, Archives of Sir Richard Wood
USNA	U.S. Department of State, National Archives, Washington, D.C.

Journals

AESC	*Annales: Economies, Sociétés, Civilisations*
AHR	*American Historical Review*
CT	*Cahiers de Tunisie*
EI1; EI2	*Encyclopedia of Islam*, 1st and 2nd eds.
FHS	*French Historical Studies*
IBLA	*Revue de l'Institut des Belles Lettres Arabes*
IJMES	*International Journal of Middle East Studies*
JAH	*Journal of African History*
JAOS	*Journal of the American Oriental Society*
JESHO	*Journal of the Economic and Social History of the Orient*
JMH	*Journal of Modern History*
JNAS	*Journal of North African Studies*
JWH	*Journal of World History*
RA	*Revue Africaine*
RHM	*Revue d'Histoire Maghrébine*
RMMM	*Revue des Mondes Musulmans et de la Méditerranée*
ROMM	*Revue de l'Occident Musulman et de la Méditerranée*
RT	*Revue Tunisienne*
RTSS	*Revue Tunisienne des Sciences Sociales*
SSH	*Social Science History*

Frequently Cited Works

Bin Diyaf, *Ithaf*

Ibn Abi al-Diyaf, Ahmad. *Ithaf ahl al-zaman bi-akhbar muluk tunis wa 'ahd al-aman.* 8 vols. Tunis: al-Dar al-Tunisiya lil-Nashr, 1989. In citations, the notation "3/5," for example, refers to volume 3, chapter 5; sequentially numbered biographical entries are indicated by notations such as "no. 189."

Brown, *Surest Path*

Brown, Leon Carl. *The Surest Path: The Political Treatise of a Nineteenth- Century Muslim Statesmen; A Translation of the Introduction to "The Surest Path to Knowledge Concerning the Condition of Countries" by Khayr al-Din al-Tunisi.* Cambridge, Mass.: Harvard University Press, 1967.

Feise, "Observations"

Feise, Godfrey. "Observations on the Regency of Tunis, 1812, 1813." Ms. no. 15.417, the British Library, London.

Planel, "De la nation"

Planel, Anne-Marie. "De la nation à la colonie: La communauté française de Tunisie au XIXe siècle d'aprés les archives civiles et notariées du consulat général de France à Tunis." 3 vols. PhD dissertation, École des Hautes Études en Sciences Sociales, Paris, 2000.

"Procedura"

Agenzia e Consolato Generale di S. M. Il Re d'Italia a Tunisi, anno 1868, no. 31, Procedura Penale Contro Giovanna Tellini e Biagio Veglione, in carton 381, Tunisie, 1er versement, CADN.

Raymond, *Chronique*
    Raymond, André, trans. *Commentaire historique d'Ibn Abi l-Diyaf. Présent aux hommes de notre temps. Chronique des rois de Tunis et du pacte fondamental. Chapitres IV et V.* 2 vols. Tunis: Alif, 1994.
Richardson, "Account"; Richardson, "Addenda"
    Richardson, James. "An Account of the Present State of Tunis," 1845, FO 102/29, NAUK. This work exists in two forms: one remains in manuscript in the Foreign Office Tunisia series; but it also appeared in Confidential Print no. 137, for the Foreign Office by T. R. Harrison, London, 1847. The two abbreviations distinguish the "Account" from the appended "Addenda on the Tunisian Harem."
Xuereb, OBL
    "Correspondence Arising out of the Trial in the Bey's Court at Tunis, of Paolo Xuereb, a Maltese, for the Murder of a Moor, 1843 – 1844." Oxford University, Bodleian Library, Confidential Print no. 146.

INTRODUCTION

1. Daniel Panzac, *Les corsaires barbaresques: La fin d'une épopée, 1800–1820* (Paris: Éditions du CNRS, 1999), 97–103, 228–44; and Claude Antoine Rozet *Voyage dans la Régence d'Alger; ou, description du pays occupé par l'armée française en Afrique; contenant des observations sur la géographie physique, la géologie, la météorologie, l'historie naturelle* (Paris: A. Bertrand, 1833), 26–27. Exmouth's real objective was to reaffirm Great Britain's Mediterranean hegemony to counter the American threat after the naval expeditions of 1815. The 1816 attack was followed in 1819 by a joint Anglo-French expedition to enforce compliance with the 1818 Treaty of Aix-la-Chapelle by the North African states.

2. Eugène Plantet, *Correspondance des beys de Tunis et des consuls de France avec la cour, 1577–1830,* 3 vols. (Paris: Félix Alcan, 1899), 3: 548–49.

3. Bin Diyaf, *Ithaf,* 3/3: 147–48, pays little attention to the naval expedition but narrates Princess Caroline's visit in detail. Khelifa Chater, *Dépendance et mutations précoloniales: La Régence de Tunis de 1815 à 1857* (Tunis: Publications de l'Université de Tunis, 1984), 241–63, raises questions regarding the true motivations for Exmouth's second assault upon Algiers.

4. Bin Diyaf, *Ithaf,* 3/5: 267; and Reade, January 18, 1837, FO 77/30, NAUK.

5. The notion of peoplings was advanced long ago in Bernard Bailyn, *The Peopling of British North America* (New York: Vintage, 1986). Its use here for a region, or series of linked regions, with millennia of contact, is meant to evoke constant, although historically differentiated, human sedimentation.

6. Michael J. Reimer, *Colonial Bridgehead: Government and Society in Alexandria, 1807–1882* (Boulder: Westview Press, 1997), 159–61. See also Kenneth Brown and Hannah Davis Taieb, eds., *Alexandria in Egypt,* special issue, *Mediterraneans* 8, 9 (1996); and *Alexandrie entre Deux Mondes,* special issue, *ROMM* 46 (1987).

7. John R. McNeill, *Mountains of the Mediterranean* (Cambridge: Cambridge University Press, 1993); and Russell King, Lindsay Proudfoot, and Bernard Smith, eds., *The Mediterranean: Environment and Society* (New York: Oxford University Press, 1997).

8. N. Van Hear, *New Diasporas: The Mass Exodus, Dispersal and Regrouping of Migrant Communities* (Seattle: University of Washington Press, 1998), 6, offers a standard definition of a diaspora; missing, however, are critical exchanges between diasporic nodes and local or host communities and the impact exerted upon sending societies.

9. James C. Scott, *Seeing Like a State: How Certain Schemes to Improve the Human Condition Have Failed* (New Haven: Yale University Press, 1998). Phillippe Farques, "Migration et identité: Le paradoxe des influences réciproques," *Esprit*, no. 361 (2010): 6–16.

10. Paul Sebag, *Tunis: Histoire d'une ville* (Paris: L'Harmattan, 1998). Daniel Panzac estimates the percentage of permanent European residence in nineteenth-century Cairo at 5.8 percent in "The Population of Egypt in the Nineteenth Century," *Asian and African Studies* 21 (1987): 31.

11. Paul Melon, *Problèmes algériens et tunisiens: Ce que disent les chiffres* (Paris: Challamel, 1903). David Prochaska, *Making Algeria French: Colonialism in Bône, 1870–1920* (Cambridge: Cambridge University Press, 1990), 62–71, 86, shows that by 1850, in Bône alone, of approximately 7,000 resident Europeans, at least 2,500 were Maltese, if official statistics have any credence—which is unlikely.

12. Planel's three-volume "De la nation," is the most comprehensive study of precolonial expatriate society with a focus upon French nationals or protégés.

13. Terence Ranger, "Europeans in Black Africa," *JWH* 9, 2 (Fall 1998): 255–68.

14. Carlo Ginzburg, *Myths, Emblems, Clues,* trans. John and Anne C. Tedeschi (London: Hutchinson Radius, 1990); and Chiara Frugoni, *A Day in a Medieval City,* trans. William McGuaig (Chicago: University of Chicago Press, 2005). See also William Julius Wilson and Anmol Chaddha, "The Role of Theory in Ethnographic Research," *Ethnography* 10, 4 (2009): 549–64.

15. Nezar AlSayyad, ed., *Hybrid Urbanism: On the Identity Discourse and the Built Environment* (Westport: Praeger, 2001).

16. Donna Gabaccia, *Italy's Many Diasporas* (Seattle: University of Washington Press, 2000), argues that, in labor-exporting societies marked by expatriation over several generations, each phase in serial diasporas displayed its own unique characteristics.

17. The theoretical literature on networks is too vast to cite here. The Social Science History Association has the study of networks at the center of its inquiry; Susan Cotts Watkins, "Social Networks and Social Science History," *SSH* 19, 3 (Fall 1995): 295–311.

18. Fernand Braudel's *La Méditerranée et le monde méditerranéen à l' époque de Philippe II* (Paris: A. Colin, 1976) presents the Mediterranean as place of seismic encounters on some levels, yet as a curiously immobile space on others; his magisterial synthesis may have discouraged historians of later centuries from attempting a study on this scale. Then, too, the discovery of new worlds and the dominance of the nation-state as a unit of analysis diverted attention away from the Mediterranean's later histories, which were left primarily to nautical experts or naval historians concerned with the sea as a field of technological power. See Gelina Harlaftis and Carmel Vassallo, *New Directions in Mediterranean Maritime History,* Research in Maritime History no. 28 (St. John's: International Maritime Economic History Association, 2004); and W. V. Harris, ed., *Rethinking the Mediterranean* (Oxford: Oxford University Press, 2005).

19. Frederick Arthur Bridgman, *Winters in Algeria* (New York: Harper, 1890), 1; and

Miriam Cooke, Erdag Göknar, and Grant Parker, eds., *Mediterranean Passages: Readings from Dido to Derrida* (Durham: Duke University Press, 2009), introduction.

20. Felipe Fernández-Armesto, *Pathfinders: A Global History of Exploration* (New York: W. W. Norton, 2006), 149. The literature on the Mediterranean, especially port cities, is staggering; a bibliographic introduction is found in Claude Nicolet, Robert Ilbert, and Jean-Charles Depaule, eds., *Mégapoles méditerranéennes: Géographie urbaine rétrospective* (Paris: Maisonneuve & Larose, 2000), 986–1060.

21. A much touted popular work, John Julius Norwich's *The Middle Sea: A History of the Mediterranean* (New York: Vintage, 2006), is emblematic of how nonscholarly histories erase North Africa: pre-Roman Carthage merits a few pages; Ifriqiya is next discussed in 1881 when France occupied Tunisia. A different mystification came at the nineteenth century's close with the writings of Louis Bertrand who, after settling in French Algeria, argued that the Mediterranean's inherently "mongrel" nature allowed for greater assimilation of the European settlers. Julia Clancy-Smith, "Le regard colonial: Islam, genre et identités dans la fabrication de l'Algérie française, 1830–1962," *Nouvelles Questions Féministes* 25, 1 (2006): 25–40; and Azzedine Haddour, "Algeria and Its History: Colonial Myths and the Forging and Deconstructing of Identity in *Pied-Noir* Literature," in *French and Algerian Identities from Colonial Times to the Present: A Century of Interaction,* ed. Alec G. Hargreaves and Michael J. Heffernan (Lewiston: Edwin Mellen Press, 1993), 76–94. See also William Cunningham Bissel, "Engaging Colonial Nostalgia," *Cultural Anthropology* 20, 2 (2005): 215–48.

22. Many studies of global migration—Dirk Hoerder's *Cultures in Contact: World Migrations in the Second Millennium* (Durham: Duke University Press, 2002) is an example—pay scant attention to religion and migration, aside from pilgrimage. If some scholarship only sees Muslims out there, other research slights religion's significant role in humankind's displacements.

23. James Hammerton, "Gender and Migration," in *Gender and Empire,* ed. Philippa Levine (Oxford: Oxford University Press, 2004).

24. Peregrine Horden and Nicholas Purcell, *The Corrupting Sea: A Study of Mediterranean History* (Oxford: Blackwell, 2000) triggered a long, vigorous debate on Braudel's legacy for Mediterranean studies, notably the issue of human agency. See also David Abulafia, ed., *The Mediterranean in History* (London: Thames & Hudson, 2003).

25. J. Donald Hughes, *Pan's Travail: Environmental Problems of the Ancient Greeks and Romans* (Baltimore: Johns Hopkins University Press, 1994), 11. See also Irad Malkin's introduction in *Mediterranean Historical Review* 18, 2 (December 2003): 1–8.

26. Michael N. Pearson, "Littoral Society: The Concept and the Problems, *JWH* 17, 4 (2006): 353–73. Historians have problematized the notions of "region" that are cultural-spatial constructs deeply inflected by power with little that is "natural." *AHR* Forum, "Bringing Regionalism Back to History," *AHR* 104, 4 (October 1999): 1156–1220.

27. Lucette Valensi, *Le Maghreb avant la prise d'Alger, 1790–1830* (Paris: Flammarion, 1969).

28. Fawzi Mellah, *Clandestin en Méditerranée* (Paris: Le Cherche Midi, 2000).

29. Most studies of nineteenth-century Mediterranean port cities begin and end on the docks. Studies comparable to Pablo E. Pérez-Mallaína's *Spain's Men of the Sea: Daily*

Life on the Indies Fleet in the Sixteenth Century, trans. Carla Rahn Phillips (Baltimore: Johns Hopkins University Press, 2005), do not exist. Janet J. Ewald, "Crossers of the Sea: Slaves, Freedmen, and Other Migrants in the Northwestern Indian Ocean, c. 1750-1914," *AHR* 105, 1 (2000): 69-91, advances understanding of connections between high-seas and port cultures.

30. Adam McKeown, "Global Migration, 1846-1940," *JWH* 15 (June 2004): 155-89.

31. Robert Schor's "La France et les migrations méditerranéennes au XXe siècle," in *La France et la Méditerranée: Vingt-sept siècles d'interdépendance* (Leiden: E. J. Brill, 1990), 272-307, signaled reawakened scholarly interest in the Mediterranean and migrations, after decades of focus upon the nation-state.

32. This migratory frontier is now the subject of scholarly inquiry; see James H. Meyer, "Immigration, Return, and the Politics of Citizenship: Russian Muslims in the Ottoman Empire, 1860-1914," *IJMES* 39 (2007): 15-32.

33. Leila Tarazi Fawaz and Christopher A. Bayly, eds., *Modernity and Culture: From the Mediterranean to the Indian Ocean* (New York: Columbia University Press, 2002), 9; and Edhem Eldem, Daniel Goffman, and Bruce Masters, *The Ottoman City between East and West* (Cambridge: Cambridge University Press, 1999).

34. A number of dissertations and monographs have appeared, among them Ilham Khuri-Makdisi, *The Eastern Mediterranean and the Making of Global Radicalism, 1860-1914* (Berkeley: University of California Press, 2010).

35. Leila Tarazi Fawaz, *Merchants and Migrants in Nineteenth-Century Beirut* (Cambridge, Mass.: Harvard University Press, 1983); Akram Khater, *Inventing Home: Emigration, Gender, and the Middle Class in Lebanon, 1870-1920* (Berkeley: University of California Press, 2001); Sarah Gualtieri, "Gendering the Chain Migration Thesis: Woman and Syrian Transatlantic Migration, 1878-1924," *Comparative Studies of South Asia, Africa and the Middle East* 24, 1 (2004): 67-87; Roberto Marín-Guzmán and Zidane Zéraoui, *Arab Immigration in Mexico in the Nineteenth and Twentieth Centuries: Assimilation and Arab Heritage* (Austin: Morgan Printing, 2003); and Susan G. Miller, "Kippur on the Amazon: Jewish Emigration from Northern Morocco in the Late Nineteenth Century," in *Sephardi and Middle Eastern Jewries: History and Culture in the Modern Era,* ed. Harvey E. Goldberg (Bloomington: Indiana University Press, 1996), 190-209.

36. Julia Clancy-Smith, "Changing Perspectives on the Historiography of Imperialism: Women, Gender, and Empire," in *Middle East Historiographies: Narrating the Twentieth Century,* ed. Israel Gershoni, Amy Singer, and Y. Hakan Erdem (Seattle: University of Washington Press, 2006), 70-100.

37. Recent novels portray, if nostalgically, this borderland society; see Claude Risso, *Le Maltais du Bab el-Khadra* (Paris: Michel Lefon, 2003). However, Michel Auguglioro, *La Partenza: La saga d'une famille sicilienne de Tunisie, 1887-1909* (Tunis: Éditions Cartaginoiseries, 2008) captures the hardships that pushed his family out of Sicily.

38. Émile Temime, *Migrance: Histoire des migrations à Marseille* (Aix-en-Provence: Édisud, 1990); Émile Temime, "La migration européenne en Algérie au XIXe siècle: Migration organisée ou migration tolérée?" *ROMM* 43 (1987): 31-45; and Gérard Noiriel, *The French Melting Pot: Immigration, Citizenship, and National Identity,* trans. Geoffroy de Laforcade (Minneapolis: University of Minnesota Press, 1996).

39. Michael Heffernan, "French Colonial Migration," in *The Cambridge Survey of World Migration,* ed. Robin Cohen (Cambridge: Cambridge University Press, 1995), 33–38.

40. Joël Cuénot, *Tunisie: Ma mémoire d'enfant* (Tours: Éditions Joël Cuénot, 1988); and Andrea L. Smith, *Colonial Memory and Postcolonial Europe: Maltese Settlers in Algeria and France* (Bloomington: Indiana University Press, 2006).

41. Daniela Melfa, *Migrando a sud: Coloni italiani di Tunisia (1881–1939)* (Rome: Aracne editrice, 2008); and Salvatore Bono, *Un altro Mediterraneo* (Rome: Salerno Editrice, 2008).

42. Edmund Burke III and David Prochaska, eds., *Genealogies of Orientalism: History, Theory, Politics* (Lincoln: University of Nebraska Press, 2009); and Zeynep Çelik, *Empire, Architecture, and the City: French-Ottoman Encounters, 1830–1914* (Seattle: University of Washington Press, 2008).

43. Julia Clancy-Smith, "Locating Women as Migrants in Nineteenth-Century Tunis" in *Contesting Archives: Historians Develop Methodologies for Finding Women in the Sources,* ed. Nupur Chaudhuri, Sherry Katz, and Mary Elizabeth Perry (Urbana: University of Illinois Press, 2010).

44. A study of how debt and indebtedness not only drew city inhabitants of highly diverse backgrounds together but also constituted a sort of language of daily exchange is worthy of pursuing, as is the issue of housing, identities, and social conflict. For example, French military records yield rich information on deserters from the huge colonial African army and navy who fled to precolonial Tunisia; the departmental archives of the Wilaya of Constantine contain the prehistories of some of the people who abandoned Algeria for Tunisia.

CHAPTER 1

Epigraph: Peregrine Horden and Nicholas Purcell, *The Corrupting Sea: A Study of Mediterranean History* (Oxford: Blackwell, 2000), quote from the frontispiece showing a medieval vision of the corrupting sea with a female Africa, Eve, and Adam, who represents Europe; the scene of the fall is located near the Strait of Gibraltar and a devil's head, labeled "the cause of sin," is situated in the Mediterranean Muslim Levant.

1. Roy Armes, *Postcolonial Images: Studies in North African Film* (Bloomington: Indiana University Press, 2005), 141–49.

2. "Legal wilderness" does not mean that North African states failed to respect international laws or treaties. Christian Windler's *La diplomatie comme expérience de l'autre: Consuls français au Maghrib (1700–1840)* (Geneva: Droz, 2002) demonstrates that Muslim rulers observed a body of commonly shared laws and customs with Europe; see also Sibel Zandi-Sayek, "Struggles Over the Shore: Building the Quay of Izmir, 1867–1875," *City and Society* 12, 1 (2000): 55–78.

3. Paul Sebag, "La Goulette et sa forteresse de la fin du XVIe siècle à nos jours," *IBLA* 117 (1967): 13–34; Charles Monchicourt, "Essai de bibliographie sur les plans imprimés de Tripoli, Djerba et Tunis-Goulette au XVIe siècle," *RA* 66 (1925): 388–418; and Arthur Pellegrin, *Histoire illustrée de Tunis et de sa banlieue* (Tunis: Editions Saliba, 1955), 159.

4. Richardson, "Account," 45.

5. La Goulette has been eclipsed by its sister cities, whose glorious achievements conferred third-class status—at best—upon the port; most histories focus on Tunis or Carthage. La Goulette sustained heavy damage during World War II bombardments, which destroyed many records, rendering historical reconstruction difficult. Numerous monographs are devoted to Tunis proper—for example, Alexandre Lézine, *Deux villes d'Ifriqiya: Études d'archéologie d'urbanisme de démographie, Sousse, Tunis* (Paris: Librarie Orientaliste, 1971), and Slimane Mostafa Zbiss, *La médina de Tunis* (Tunis: Institut National d'Archéologie et d'Art, 1981)—but concentrate on Islamic monuments and architecture; city dwellers are largely absent, the changing social uses of urban spaces unexplored. With Paul Sebag, *Tunis: Histoire d'une ville* (Paris: L'Harmattan, 1998), and Abdelhamid Larguèche, *Les ombres de la ville: Pauvres, marginaux et minoritaires à Tunis (XVIIIème et XIXè siècles)* (Tunis: Centre de Publication Universitaire, 1999), indigenous city inhabitants receive their due.

6. François Levernay, "The Guide and Yearbook of Egypt," in *Alexandria, 1860–1960: The Brief Life of a Cosmopolitan Community,* ed. Robert Ilbert and Ilios Yannakakis with Jacques Hassoun, trans. Colin Clement (Alexandria: Harpocrates Publishing, 1997), 202.

7. Logbook, Algiers, 1829–1830, FO 113/5, NAUK. After 1827, the British consul protected the few remaining French nationals serving as diplomatic middleman between the dey and Paris.

8. Nora Lafi, "Les relations de Malte et de Tripoli de Barbarie au XIXe siècle," *ROMM* 71 (1994): 127–42; and Nora Lafi, *Une ville du Maghreb entre ancien régime et réformes ottomanes: Genèse des institutions municipales à Tripoli de Barbarie (1795–1911)* (Paris: L'Harmattan, 2002).

9. Khelifa Chater, *Dépendance et mutations précoloniales: La Régence de Tunis de 1815 à 1857* (Tunis: Publications de l'Université de Tunis, 1984), 29–40; and Lucette Valensi, "Islam et capitalisme: Production et commerce des chéchias en Tunisie et en France aux XVIIIe et XIXe siècles," *Revue d'Histoire Moderne et Contemporaine* 17 (1969): 376–400.

10. Reade, January 1835, FO 77/26, NAUK; and Louis Frank, *Histoire de Tunis,* introduction and annotation by J. J. Marcel, 2nd ed. (Paris: Firmin-Didot, 1851), 7, 49.

11. Pierre Grandchamp, "Le différend tuniso-sarde de 1843–1844," *RT,* nos. 13–14 (1933): 127–209.

12. For average sailing times, Logbook, 1828–1830, FO 77/20–21, NAUK; Agnès Cavasino, *Emilie de Vialar, fondatriçe: Les Soeurs de Saint-Joseph de l'Apparition, une congrégation missionnaire* (Fountenay sous Bois: Congrégation des Soeurs de Saint-Joseph de l'Apparition, 1987), 121–22; and Roch, captain of *La Sainte Anne,* May 4, 1846, carton 206, dossier 87, ANT.

13. Henri Cons, *La Tunisie, esquisse géographique,* Extrait du Bulletin de la Société Languedocienne de Géographie (1883), 4.

14. Daniel Panzac, *Barbary Corsairs: The End of a Legend, 1800–1820,* trans. Victoria Hobson (Leiden: E. J. Brill, 2005), 253.

15. Gaspary, March 1842, carton 410B, CADN.

16. Raymond, *Chronique,* 2: 8–9, 77.

17. Reade, September 22, 1831, FO 77/22, NAUK; and Daniel Panzac, *Quarantaines*

et lazarets: L'Europe et la peste d'Orient (XVIII–XXe siècles) (Aix-en-Provence: Édisud, 1986), 33–56.

18. Feise, "Observations," 1–5.

19. Panzac, *Corsairs*, 322–23; and Panzac, *Quarantaines*.

20. Joel Montague, "Notes on Medical Organization in Nineteenth-Century Tunisia: A Preliminary Analysis of the Materials on Public Health and Medicine in the Dar El Bey in Tunis," *Medical History* 17, 1 (January 1973): 75–82.

21. Reade, September 7, 1835, FO 77/26, NAUK.

22. Baynes to Ahmad Bey, October 26, 1853, carton 227, dossier 411, ANT. On the quarantine in French Algeria during the 1840s, see Évariste Bavoux, *Alger: Voyage politique et descriptif dans le nord de l'Afrique*, 2 vols. (Paris: Chez Brockhaus et Avenarius, 1841), 2: 257–70.

23. Reade to bey, 1827, carton 225, dossier 408, ANT.

24. Reade, January 16, 1835, FO 77/22, NAUK.

25. September 1858, carton 227, dossier 411, ANT.

26. Cubisol, November 4, 1873, carton 413, CADN.

27. Letter from French traders, Tunis, to the Chambre de Commerce in Marseilles regarding regulations for disembarking in port, c. 1843, carton 79, CCM; and Jo Stanley, "Women at Sea: An Other Category," *Gender and History* 15, 1 (April 2003): 135–39.

28. Reade, 1829, FO 77/20, NAUK.

29. Gaspary, March 17, 1824, carton 407, CADN.

30. Gaspary, February 20, 1822, carton 406B, CADN.

31. Gaspary, September 3, 1842, carton 382, CADN.

32. Logbook, 1828–1830, FO 77/20, 77/21, NAUK.

33. Gaspary, February 19, 1839, and February 23, 1839, carton 409B, CADN.

34. Anonymous ms., c. 1835, carton "Confins Algéro-Tunisiens," Algérie, F 80 1697, CAOM; Planel, "De la nation," 1: 22–23; Raymond, *Chronique*, 2: 29; and Larguèche, *Ombres*, 208–12.

35. François Dornier, *La vie des Catholiques en Tunisie au fil des ans* (Tunis: Imprimerie Finzi, 2000), 215–16. The Gaspary family resided in La Goulette until 1978; their house had its chapel as late as 1942.

36. Gaspary to Adolphe Tulin, Swedish and Norwegian consul, September 3, 1842, carton 410B, CADN.

37. Gaspary, March 4, 1837, carton 409A, CADN.

38. Silvia Finzi, ed., *Architetture italiane di Tunisia* (Tunis: Finzi, 2002).

39. Léon Denis, *Tunis et l'île de Sardaigne: Souvenirs de voyage* (Tours: Imprimerie E. Arrault, 1884), 5.

40. Sebag, "La Goulette," 25, noted that Husaynid rulers considered engaging European engineers to drain the buhaira and bring the waters of the Mediterranean to the gates of Tunis. Hammuda Bey was discouraged by Dutch engineers, who greatly feared that drying the lake would release deadly miasmas and cause a frightful epidemic. The quote is from Richardson, "Account."

41. After 1881, Bab al-Bahr was renamed Porte de France.

42. Jamila Binous, Fatma Ben Bechr, and Jellal Abdelkafi, *Tunis* (Tunis: Sud-Editions,

1985); and Paul Lowy, "Evolution des grandes médinas tunisiennes," in *Présent et avenir des médinas (de Marrakech à Alep)* (Tours: Institut de Géographie, 1982), 103–20.

43. Zeynep Çelik, *The Remaking of Istanbul: Portrait of an Ottoman City in the Nineteenth Century* (Seattle: University of Washington Press, 1986); Ahmed Abdesselem, *Les historiens tunisiens des XVIIe, XVIIIe et XIXe siècles: Essai d'histoire culturelle* (Paris: Librairie Klincksieck, 1973), 95; and J. S. Woodford, *The City of Tunis: Evolution of an Urban System* (Cambridgeshire: Middle East and North African Studies Press, 1990), 119–20.

44. Major Sir Grenville T. Temple, *Excursions in the Mediterranean. Algiers and Tunis*, 2 vols. (London: Saunders and Otley, 1835), 1: 172–74.

45. Faiza Matri, *Tunis sous le Protectorat: Histoire de la conservation du patrimoine architectural et urban de la médina* (Tunis: Centre de Publication Universitaire, 2008), 142–64.

46. Isabelle Grangaud, "Masking and Unmasking the Historic Quarters of Algiers: The Reassessment of an Archive," in *Walls of Algiers: Narratives of the City through Text and Image*, ed. Zeynep Çelik, Julia Clancy-Smith, and Frances Terpak (Los Angeles: Getty Research Institute; Seattle: University of Washington Press, 2009), 179–92.

47. Mohamed El Aziz Ben Achour, *Catégories de la société tunisoise dans la deuxième moitié du XIXème siècle* (Tunis: Institut National d'Archeologie et d'Art, 1989), 75–82.

48. Sebag, *Tunis*, 261–310; and Paul Sebag, *La hara de Tunis: L'évolution d'un ghetto nord-africain* (Paris: Mémoires du Centre d'Études de Sciences Humaines, 1959).

49. Julia Clancy-Smith, "A Woman without Her Distaff: Gender, Work, and Handicraft Production in Colonial North Africa," in *A Social History of Women and the Family in the Middle East*, ed. Margaret Meriwether and Judith Tucker (Boulder: Westview Press, 1999), 25–62; and Arthur Pellegrin, *Le vieux Tunis: Les noms de rue de la ville arabe*, 2nd ed. (Tunis: Espace Diwan, n.d.), 5–30.

50. Frances E. Nesbitt, *Algeria and Tunisia Painted and Described* (London, 1906), 159. Renaudot, the French agent to Algiers, claimed that under the last Algerian ruler, Dey Husayn, "the women of Algiers enjoyed the privilege of having the doors to the city opened at night each time they wanted to go out to the countryside." Cited in Robert Jungmann, *Costumes, moeurs et usages des Algériens* (Strasbourg: J. Bernard, 1837), 17. The same practice is reported for Iranian cities; whether it occurred in Tunis is worthy of further study. Rudi Matthee, "Prostitutes, Courtesans, and Dancing Girls: Women Entertainers in Safavid Iran," in *Iran and Beyond: Essays in Middle Eastern History in Honor of Nikki R. Keddie*, ed. Rudi Matthee and Beth Baron (Costa Mesa: Mazda Publishers, 2000), 121–50.

51. Mustapha Chelbi, *Musique et société en Tunisie* (Tunis: Editions Salammbo, 1985), 96. Julia Clancy-Smith, "'Women on the Move': Gender and Social Control in Tunis, 1815–1870," in *Femmes en villes*, ed. Dalenda Larguèche (Tunis: Centre de Publications Universitaires, 2006), 209–37.

52. Feise, "Observations," 8–9, 16.

53. Ibid.

54. Alessandro Triulzi, "Italian-Speaking Communities in Early Nineteenth Century Tunis," *ROMM* 9, 1 (1971): 167–77; Mohamed El Aziz Ben Achour, "Islam et contrôle social

à Tunis aux XVIIIe et XIXe siècles," in *La ville arabe dans l'Islam,* ed. Abdelwahab Bouh-diba and Dominique Chevallier (Tunis: CÉRÈS, 1982), 137–47; and Dalenda Larguèche, "Loisirs et mutations socio-culturelles en Tunisie à l'époque ottomane," unpublished ms.

55. Leon Carl Brown, *The Tunisia of Ahmad Bey, 1837–1855* (Princeton: Princeton University Press, 1974), 194; and Ahmed Abdesselem, "La sémantique sociale de la ville d'après les auteurs tunisiens des XVIIIe et XIXe siècles," in *La ville arabe dans l'Islam,* ed. Abdelwahab Bouhdiba and Dominique Chevallier (Tunis: CÉRÈS, 1982), 45–65.

56. Ben Achour, *Catégories,* 33.

57. Ibid., 29–34, 142–51.

58. Sebag, *Tunis,* 271–80; Haim Saadoun, "Tunisia," in *The Jews of the Middle East and North Africa in Modern Times,* ed. Reeva Spector Simon, Michael Laskier, and Sara Reguer (New York: Columbia University Press, 2003), 444–57; Lucette Valensi, "Esclaves chrétiens et esclaves noirs à Tunis au XVIII siècle," *AESC* 4 (1967): 1267–88; and Chater, *Dépendance,* 147–48, 549. Pierre Soumille, *Européens de Tunisie et questions religieuses (1892–1901)* (Paris: Éditions du CNRS, 1975), 10, states that even as late as 1892 the Protectorate was poorly informed about the exact number of Maltese, Sicilians, and other non-French nationals residing in Tunisia; the 1906 census did not include the Muslim population.

59. Reade, December 30, 1836, FO 77/29, NAUK.

60. Ferriere, March 31, 1848, FO 102/32, NAUK; and Prax, 1847, "Le commerce de Tunis avec l'intérieur de l'Afrique," F 80 1697, CAOM. On French nationals or protégés, see Planel, "De la nation," 1: 92–94; and Romain H. Rainier, *Les Italiens dans la Tunisie contemporaine* (Aix-en-Provence: Publisud, 2002), 23.

61. Andreas Tunger-Zanetti, *La communication entre Tunis et Istanbul, 1860–1913: Province et métropole* (Paris: L'Harmattan, 1996), 29–44.

62. Asma Moalla, *The Regency of Tunis and the Ottoman Porte, 1777–1814: Army and Government of a North-African Ottoman Eyâlet at the End of the Eighteenth Century* (London: Routledge, 2005) 134–35; Miguel de Epalza and Ramón Petit, eds., *Recueil d'études sur les Moriscos Andalous en Tunisie* (Madrid: Instituto Hispano-Arabe de Cultura, 1973); and Ben Achour, *Catégories,* 33.

63. Julia Clancy-Smith, *Rebel and Saint: Muslim Notables, Populist Protest, Colonial Encounters (Algeria and Tunisia, 1800–1904)* (Berkeley: University of California Press, 1994).

64. On Tunisian Jews, see Paul Sebag, *Histoire des Juifs de Tunisie des origines à nos jours* (Paris: L'Harmattan, 1991); Abraham L. Udovitch and Lucette Valensi, *The Last Arab Jews: The Communities of Jerba, Tunisia* (New York: Harwood Academic, 1984); Robert Attal and Claude Sitbon, eds. *Regards sur les Juifs de Tunisie* (Paris: Albin Michel, 1979); and Simon, Laskier, and Reguer, eds., *Jews of the Middle East and North Africa,* 63–85. The Jewish population expanded throughout the nineteenth century and peaked during World War II when numbers reached between 71,000 and 85,000 due to the presence of Jewish refugees who fled Europe for North Africa; see Michel Abitbol, "Tunisia," in *Encyclopedia of the Holocaust,* 4 vols. (New York: Macmillan, 1990), 4: 152; and Michel Abitbol, *The Jews of North Africa during the Second World War* (Detroit: Wayne State University Press, 1989).

65. Alex Weingrod, "Saints and Shrines, Politics, and Culture: A Morocco-Israel Comparison," in *Muslim Travellers: Pilgrimage, Migration, and the Religious Imagination,* ed. Dale F. Eickelman and James Piscatori (London: Routledge, 1990), 221–22.

66. Dornier, *Catholiques,* 529; and Jean Ganiage, *Les origines du Protectorat Français en Tunisie (1861–1881)* (Tunis: Maison Tunisienne de l'Édition, 1968), 600–601.

67. Ganiage, *Origines,* 134–41; Saadoun, "Tunisia," 446–47; and Sebag, *La hara,* 14–19.

68. Albert Memmi, *La statue de sel* (Paris: Éditions Gallimard, 1953).

69. Brown, *Tunisia,* 100–102, 41–53.

70. Interview with Madame Hasiba Agha, who kindly showed me around Dar Mabruk, November 3, 2007, Kram.

71. Ben Achour, *Catégories,* 171–256; Brown, *Tunisia,* 29–33, 79–92; and Mohamed-El Aziz Ben Achour, *La cour du bey de Tunis* (Tunis: Espace Diwan, 2003), ix–xxii.

72. Christian Windler, "Consuls français et drogmans dans les régences du Maghreb au XVIIIe siècle: Traduire dans un orient étrangement proche," in *Istanbul et les langues orientales,* ed. Frédéric Hitzel (Paris: L'Harmattan, 1997), 439–40; Nabil ben Khelil, *Maisons de Carthage* (Tunis: Dar Ashraf, 1996), 88–93; and Nadia Sebaï, *Mustapha Saheb Ettabaa: Un haut dignitaire beylical dans la Tunisie du XIXe siècle* (Carthage: Éditions Cartaginoiseries, 2007), 24–25. Family history cannot be disassociated from the domestic residences still held by a few notable families, since the *dar* (house) constitutes an archive of collective memory. The occasion of marriage with a princess often led to the construction of a residence by the sea.

73. Ben Achour, *Catégories,* 226–27. The "Tunsification" of the Turkish elite owed much to the sexual politics of intermarriage with local families, which contrasts with Ottoman Algeria; see Brown, *Tunisia,* 65–92, 105–7.

74. Bin Diyaf, *Ithaf,* 3/3: 135.

75. Raymond, *Chronique,* 2: 3–4.

76. Chater, *Dépendence,* 67–83; and Mohamed-El Aziz Ben Achour, *Cour,* 76–82. Nineteenth-century Tunisian rulers employed various terms, such as *sahib al-mamlakat al-tunisiya* (possessor of the kingdom of Tunis), among other titles and honorifics expressive of ideologies of legitimacy.

77. Mohamed-Hédi Cherif, *Pouvoir et société dans la Tunisie de H'usayn Bin 'Ali, 1705–1740,* 2 vols. (Tunis: Publications de l'Université de Tunis, 1986), 1: 188–89; Abdesselem, *Historiens,* 61; and Raymond, *Chronique,* 2: 92, 118.

78. Leïla Ladjimi Sebaï, *Dar al Kamila: Résidence de France à La Marsa* (Tunis: Dunes Éditions, 2004), 10–23.

79. Dalenda Larguèche, "The *Mahalla:* The Origins of Beylical Sovereignty in Ottoman Tunisia during the Early Modern Era," in *North Africa, Islam, and the Mediterranean World: From the Almoravids to the Algerian War,* ed. Julia Clancy-Smith (London: Frank Cass Publications, 2001), 105–16.

80. Abdeljelil Temimi, "Problems of Interpretation of North African history: The Impact of Information on the Policies of Hammuda Pasha (1810–13)," in *North Africa: Nation, State, and Region,* ed. George Joffé (London: Routledge, 1993), 49–55. The Jalluli correspondence, hundreds of letters, carton 225, dossier 408, ANT, is in both Arabic and Italian. The correspondence of the Farrugia brothers, written mainly in Italian, for the

period 1821 to 1850 numbers nearly nine hundred documents, carton 224, dossier 415, ANT.

81. Antonio Farrugia to Ahmad Bey, April 17, 1841, carton 224, dossier 415, ANT.

82. Colonial Office to Foreign Office, London, July 11, 1836, FO 77/29, NAUK.

83. Tunger-Zanetti, *Communication*; and Arnold H. Green, *The Tunisian Ulama, 1873–1915: Social Structure and Response to Ideological Currents* (Leiden: E. J. Brill, 1978), 47–48.

84. Bin Diyaf, *Ithaf,* 3/4: 199.

85. Reade to Hay, July 13, 1835, FO 77/26, NAUK.

86. Brown, *Tunisia;* G. S. Van Krieken, *Khayr al-Din et la Tunisie (1850–1881)* (Leiden: E. J. Brill, 1976); and Odile Moreau, *L'Empire Ottoman à l'âge des réformes: Les hommes et les idées du "Nouvel Ordre" militaire, 1826–1914* (Paris: Maisonneuve & Larose, 2007).

87. Planel, "De la nation," 1: 27–32.

88. Sebag, *Tunis,* 327.

89. One original meaning of "creole" referred to Louisiana's white inhabitants of mixed Franco-Spanish heritage; yet the term is also employed for mixed-race communities speaking "hybrid" languages. Ehud R. Toledano, "African Slaves in the Ottoman Eastern Mediterranean: A Case of Cultural 'Creolization?'" in *The Mediterranean World: The Idea, the Past and Present,* ed. Eyüp Özveren, Oktay Özel, Suha Ünsal, and Kudret Emiroğlu (Istanbul: Iletişim Yayinlari, 2006), 107–24. Doris Garraway, *The Libertine Colony: Creolization in the Early French Caribbean* (Durham: Duke University Press, 2005), 18, defines creolization as the "process of cultural transformation productive of new ways of acting, thinking, and imagining community and identity."

90. Homi K. Bhabha's notion of "hybrid" in "Of Mimicry and Man: The Ambivalence of Colonial Discourse," in *Tensions of Empire,* ed. Frederick Cooper and Ann Laura Stoler (Berkeley: University of California Press, 1997), 152–62, is essentially ahistorical, its utility for diachronic analysis problematic.

91. In 1709, for example, the Swedish ruler King Charles XII fled to Istanbul after his defeat by the Russian army at Poltava; see Elisabeth Özdalga, *The Last Dragoman: The Swedish Orientalist Johannes Kolmodin as Scholar, Activist and Diplomat* (Istanbul: Swedish Research Institute in Istanbul, 2006).

92. Planel, "De la nation," 1: 43–44.

93. Windler, *Diplomatie,* 358–64.

94. Yvan Debbasch, *La nation Française en Tunisie (1577–1835)* (Paris: Sirey, 1957), 242–43, note 9.

95. Ibid., 243–44, and 243, note 5.

96. Planel, "De la nation," 1: 27–36.

97. Ibid. Raffo died in Paris in 1862 and his son died in Florence in 1878, which would seem to indicate that the family had lost strong attachments to Tunis and creole society. But Raffo's grandson, Giuseppe (1847–1904), lived out his life in Tunis, where he married Farida Wood in 1874, the oldest daughter of Richard Wood, British consul to Tunis. See Ganiage, *Origines,* 597; Windler, *Diplomatie,* 425–26; and Richardson, "Account," 29. The quote is from Nicholson to Secretary of State, July 7, 1860, Despatches, Tunis, volume 8, USNA.

98. Planel, "De la nation," 3: 738.

99. Mustafa Bey to Reade, August 26, 1835, FO 77/26, NAUK.

100. Philippa Day, ed., *At Home in Carthage: The British in Tunisia* (Tunis: Trustees of St. Georges Church, 1992), 15.

101. Richardson, "Account," 42.

102. Reade to foreign secretary, December 5, 1834, FO 77/25, NAUK.

103. The case of Nicolas Béranger (1631–1707), a failed Marseilles trader who went to Tunis, where he headed the council of French traders for twenty-three years, was fairly typical. As a sign of favor, the bey accorded him a farm, which, however, was conferred solely upon him; with his death, the property devolved to the ruler. Pierre Grandchamp, "Autour du Consulat de France à Tunis (1577–1881)," *RT*, nos. 53–54 (1943): 33–35.

104. Abdelhamid Hénia, *Propriété et stratégies sociales à Tunis (XVIe–XIXe siècles)* (Tunis: Facultés des Sciences Humaines et Sociales de Tunis, 1999), 311–21.

105. In *Ithaf,* 4/6: 12, Bin Diyaf observed that Ahmad Bey had "learned to speak Italian but not to write it," which underlines the importance of resident Europeans or creoles with written competence in Italian and other European languages.

106. Bin Diyaf, *Ithaf,* 3/5: 267. Mustafa Bey to Reade, August 26, 1833, FO 77/26, NAUK; Richard Clogg to Foreign Office, June 29, 1831, FO 77/22, NAUK; and Richardson, "Account." Born in England, Reade resided in Cheshire prior to his posting in Tunis.

107. Arthur Marsden, *British Diplomacy and Tunis, 1875–1902* (New York: Africana, 1971), 28–30.

108. Léon Roches, *Trente-deux ans à travers l'Islam (1832–1864),* 2 vols. (Paris: Firmin Didot, 1884–1885), a somewhat fanciful autobiography; and Ganiage, *Origines,* 598–99.

109. Reade to Hay, August 6, 1834, FO 77/25, and September 7, 1835, FO 77/26, NAUK.

110. Zbiss, *La médina,* 14.

111. Dornier, *Catholiques,* 35, 167.

112. Ibid; Windler, *Diplomatie,* 178–87; and Pierre Soumille, "Le cimetière européen de Bab-el-Khadra à Tunis: Étude historique et sociale," *CT* 19 (1971): 129–77. There were other much older Catholic establishments, for example, small chapels created in trading posts along the Tunisian coast at Tabarka and elsewhere for Provençal coral fishermen.

113. Nabil Matar, ed. and trans., *In the Lands of the Christians: Arabic Travel Writing in the Seventeenth Century* (London: Routledge, 2003), xxix–xxx; and Nabil Matar, *Turks, Moors, and Englishmen in the Age of Discovery* (New York: Columbia University Press, 1999), 23–24.

114. Reade to Hay, December 23, 1831, FO 77/22, NAUK.

115. Ferriere to bey, December 6, 1855, carton 227, dossier 411, ANT.

116. Julia Clancy-Smith, "Marginality and Migration: Europe's Social Outcasts in Pre-Colonial Tunisia, 1830–81," in *Outside In: On the Margins of the Modern Middle East,* ed. Eugene Rogan (London: I. B. Tauris, 2002); and Julia Clancy-Smith, "Gender in the City: Women, Migration and Contested Spaces in Tunis, c. 1830–1881," in *Africa's Urban Past,* ed. David. M. Anderson and Richard Rathbone (Oxford: Currey, 2000).

117. Daniela Melfa argues that a multiplicity of "Little Sicilies" existed not only in the Tunis region but also scattered along the coast, each with its own peculiar micro-local culture. See Daniela Melfa, "Regards italiens sur les Petites Siciles de Tunisie," *IBLA* 70, 1 (2007): 3–27; Janice Albertini Russell, "The Italian Community in Tunisia, 1861–1961: A Viable Community" (PhD dissertation, Columbia University, 1977), 40, 47.

118. Bin Diyaf, *Ithaf,* 3/5: 267, and 4/6: 89–90; also, Ben Achour, *Catégories,* 31–32.

119. For example, when in 1823 a baker from the Italian Piedmont was caught with a Muslim woman, both were executed. Bin Diyaf, *Ithaf,* 3/3: 186.

120. On the Sardinian crisis, see Bin Diyaf, *Ithaf,* 3/4: 232–34.

121. Michael Zakim, "Sartorial Ideologies: From Homespun to Ready-Made," *AHR* 106, 5 (2001): 1553–86; and Susan Hiner, "'Cashmere Fever' in Nineteenth-Century France," *Journal of Early Modern Cultural Studies* 5, 1 (2005): 76–98. For an overview of state interventions into clothing, particularly headgear, Annelies Moors, "The Gender of (post-) Colonial Governance: Contextualizing Dress Regulations in the Middle East and Europe," in *Changes in Colonial and Post-Colonial Governance of Islam: Continuities and Ruptures,* ed. Veit Bader, Annelies Moors, and Marcel Maussen (Amsterdam: University of Amsterdam, 2010).

122. Lucette Valensi, *On the Eve of Colonialism: North Africa before the French Conquest, 1790–1830,* trans. Kenneth J. Perkins (New York: Africana, 1977), 35. See also Muhammad Bayram al-Khamis, *Safwat al-i'tibar bi mustawda' al-amsar wa-al-aqtar,* 5 vols. (Tunis: Bayt al-Hikma, 2000), 2: 137; and Ben Achour, *Catégories,* 29–34.

123. Marcel Gandolphe, "La vie à Tunis, 1840–1881," in *Histoire de la ville de Tunis,* ed. Charles-Henri Dessort (Algiers: Pfister, 1926), 166.

124. Donald Quataert, "Clothing Laws, State, and Society in the Ottoman Empire, 1720–1829," in *IJMES* 29, 3 (1997): 403–25.

125. Chater, *Dépendence,* 297–98.

126. Richardson, "Account," 139.

127. Sonia Fellous, ed., *Juifs et Musulmans en Tunisie: Fraternité et déchirements* (Paris: Somogy Éditions d'Art, 2003), plate 3.

128. "Procedura," carton 381, CADN.

129. Nathan Davis, *Tunis, or Selections from a Journal During a Residence in That Regency* (Malta: Muir, 1841), 45; and Robert Urie Jacob, *A Trip to the Orient: The Story of a Mediterranean Cruise* (Philadelphia: Winston, 1907), 89. See Charles Lallemand, *Tunis au XIXe siècle* (Paris: Maison Quantin, 1890), for textual and visual descriptions of indigenous clothing.

130. Richardson, "Addenda," 58.

131. Richardson, "Account," 58.

132. David Prochaska, "History as Literature, Literature as History: Gagayous of Algiers," *AHR* 101, 3 (June 1996): 671–711; and Kmar Mechri-Bendana, "Kaddour Ben Nitram et Sabirs: Les traces d'une culture plurielle," in *Pratiques et résistance culturelle au Maghrib,* ed. Noureddine Sraïeb (Paris: Éditions du CNRS, 1992), 283–91. Nevertheless, the Protectorate published grammars of Tunisian dialect for training colonial officers; see the fourth edition of *Cours normal et pratique d'arabe parlé: Dialecte tunisien* (Tunis: Bouslama, 1913).

133. Moalla, *Regency,* 100–102; and Raymond, *Chronique,* 2: 17–18.

134. Dessort, *Histoire,* 107–8, which supports Toledano's research on the diversity of harim languages in Istanbul and Cairo.

135. Windler, "Consuls français," 433–49, Peyssonnel quote p. 442. An eighteenth-century legal document from the French consulate in Tunis reveals that "a jargon of

Italo-Maltese-Provençal" was committed to writing; see Pierre Grandchamp, "Esclaves musulmans rachetés en Chretienté," *RT,* 13 (1943): 239.

136. Stephen Wilson, *Feuding, Conflict and Banditry in Nineteenth-Century Corsica* (Cambridge: Cambridge University Press, 1988), 4; Marinette Pendola, "La lingua degli Italiani di Tunisia," in *Memorie italiane di Tunisia,* ed. Silvia Finzi (Tunis: Finzi Editore, 2000), 13–18; and Jocelyne Dakhlia, *Lingua Franca: Histoire d'une langue partagée en Méditerranée* (Paris: Actes Sud, 2008).

137. Joseph Greaves, *The Journal of Mr. Joseph Greaves, on a Visit to the Regency of Tunis,* in *Christian Researches in Syria and the Holy Land 1823 and 1824 in Furtherance of the Objects of the Church Missionary Society,* by Rev. William Jowett (London: Seeley & Son, 1825), 476.

138. Gaspary, November 8, 1837, carton 409A, CADN.

139. A. Cour, "Notes sur les chaires de langue arabe d'Alger, de Constantine et d'Oran (1832–1879)," *RA* 65, 318 (1924): 20–64.

140. Linda Colley, *Captives: Britain, Empire and the World, 1600–1850* (London: Jonathan Cape, 2002); Walter E. Mignolo, "Globalization, Civilization Processes, and the Relocation of Languages and Cultures," in *The Cultures of Globalization,* ed. Frederic Jameson and Masao Miyoshi (Durham: Duke University Press, 1998), 32–53; and Pier M. Larson, *Ocean of Letters: Language and Creolization in an Indian Ocean Diaspora* (Cambridge: Cambridge University Press, 2009).

CHAPTER 2

1. Reade to Husayn Bey, 1827, carton 225, dossier 408, ANT. Bin Diyaf makes no mention of this in *Ithaf.*

2. Reade, June 1829, FO 77/20, NAUK; and Bin Diyaf, *Ithaf,* 3/4: 207–8.

3. Bin Diyaf, *Ithaf,* 3/5:267; and Reade, January 18, 1837, FO 77/30, NAUK.

4. Leslie Page Moch, *Paths to the City: Regional Migrations in France* (Beverly Hills: Sage Publications, 1983); and Mary W. Helms, *Ulysses' Sail: An Ethnographic Odyssey of Power, Knowledge, and Geographical Distance* (Princeton: Princeton University Press, 1988), 50.

5. Bin Diyaf, *Ithaf,* 4/6: 12.

6. Gaspary, November 11, 1815, carton 406B, CADN.

7. Dornier, *Les Catholiques en Tunisie au fils des ans* (Tunis: Finzi, 2000), 43; and Stephen A. Toth, *Beyond Papillon: The French Overseas Penal Colonies, 1854–1952* (Lincoln: University of Nebraska Press, 2006).

8. Abdelhamid Larguèche, "The City and the Sea: Evolving Forms of Mediterranean Cosmopolitanism in Tunis, c. 1700–1881," in *North Africa, Islam, and the Mediterranean World: From the Almoravids to the Algerian War,* ed. Julia Clancy-Smith (London: Frank Cass, 2001), 117–28; and Lucette Valensi, *On the Eve of Colonialism: North Africa Before the French Conquest, 1790–1830,* trans. Kenneth J. Perkins (New York: Africana, 1977), 48–49.

9. Osmân Agha de Temechvar, *Prisonnier des infidèles: Un soldat ottoman dans l'Empire*

Habsbourg (Paris: Sindbad, 1998); and Salvatore Bono, *Schiavi musulmani nell' Italia moderna. Galeotti, vu' cumpra', domestici* (Napoli: Edzioni scientifiche italiane, 1999).

10. Gaspary, June 28, 1816, carton 406B, CADN. On Leghorn's rise to commercial preeminence in the seventeenth and eighteenth centuries, see Molly Greene, "Resurgent Islam, 1500–1700," in *The Mediterranean in History,* ed. David Abulafia (London: Thames & Hudson, 2003), 219–50.

11. Daniel Panzac, *Les corsaires barbaresques: La fin d'une épopée, 1800–1820* (Paris: Éditions du CNRS, 1999); and Aurélia Martin Casares, "Esclavage féminin: Femmes maghrébines à Grenade au XVIIe siècle," in *Histoire des femmes au Maghreb: Culture matérielle et vie quotidienne,* ed. Dalenda Larguèche (Tunis: Centre de Publication Universitaire, 2000), 77–87.

12. Pierre Boyer, "Alger et les corsaires français, 1808–1814," in *Navigations et migrations en Méditerranée: De la préhistoire à nos jours,* ed. Jean-Louis Miège (Paris: Éditions du CNRS, 1990), 377–90.

13. Nabil Matar, ed. and trans., *In the Lands of the Christians: Arabic Travel Writing in the Seventeenth Century* (London: Routledge, 2003), xiii–xlviii; and Gerald M. MacLean, *The Rise of Oriental Travel: English Visitors to the Ottoman Empire, 1580–1720* (New York: Palgrave Macmillan, 2004).

14. Edmund Burke III, "The Mediterranean before Colonialism: Fragments from the Life of 'Ali bin 'Uthman al-Hammi (Late 18th–19th Centuries)," in *North Africa, Islam, and the Mediterranean World: From the Almoravids to the Algerian War,* ed. Julia Clancy-Smith (London: Frank Cass Publications, 2001), 129–42. See also Régis Bertrand, "Les cimetières des 'esclaves turcs' des arsenaux de Marseille et de Toulon au XVIIIe siècle," *RMMM,* nos. 99–100 (2002): 205–17.

15. Reade, July 25, 1837, FO 77/30, NAUK.

16. Bin Diyaf, *Ithaf,* 7/8: 66–68, biographical notice no. 279; and Leon Carl Brown, *The Tunisia of Ahmad Bey, 1837–1855* (Princeton: Princeton University Press, 1974), 252.

17. Henri Hugon, "Une ambassade tunisienne à Paris en 1825 (Mission de Si Mahmoud Kahia)," *RT,* nos. 13–14 (1933): 93–126, quote p. 98.

18. On Mahmud, see Bin Diyaf, *Ithaf,* 3/4: 200; Raymond, *Chronique,* 2: 150; and Henri Cambon, *Histoire de la Régence de Tunis* (Paris: Berger-Levrault, 1948), 97.

19. Hugon, "Ambassade," 100–101.

20. Alessandro Triulzi, "Italian-Speaking Communities in Early Nineteenth-Century Tunis," *ROMM* 9, 1 (1971): 153–84.

21. Raymond, *Chronique,* 2: 80.

22. The Moroccan sultans sent few envoys; the first diplomatic mission to France was led by Muhammad al-Saffar. Susan Gilson Miller, *Disorienting Encounters: Travels of a Moroccan Scholar in France, 1845–1846* (Berkeley: University of California Press, 1992).

23. Bin Diyaf, *Ithaf,* 4/6: 54–55. See also Daniel Schroeter, *Merchants of Essaouira: Urban Society and Imperialism in Southwestern Morocco, 1844–1886* (Cambridge University Press, 1988); and Mohamed El Mansour, "Maghribis in the Mashriq during the Modern Period: Representation of the Other within the World of Islam," in *North Africa, Islam and the Mediterranean World: From the Almoravids to the Algerian War,* ed. Julia A. Clancy-Smith (London: Frank Cass, 2001).

24. Fanny Colonna, "Les 'Détenus Arabes' de Calvi, 1871–1903," in *Golden Roads: Migration, Pilgrimage and Travel in Mediaeval and Modern Islam,* ed. Ian Richard Netton (Richmond, UK: Curzon Press, 1993), 95–109.

25. François Renault, *Cardinal Lavigerie: Churchman, Prophet and Missionary* (London: Athlone Press, 1994), 164–66; and Richard C. Keller, *Colonial Madness: Psychiatry in French North Africa* (Chicago: University of Chicago Press, 2007), 41–42.

26. Zeynep Çelik and Leila Kinney, "Ethnography and Exhibitionism at the Expositions Universelles," *Assemblage* 13 (1990): 34–59.

27. Christian Windler, *La diplomatie comme expérience de l'autre: Consuls français au Maghreb (1700–1840)* (Geneva: Droz, 2002), 210. See also Molly Greene, *Catholic Pirates and Greek Merchants: A Maritime History of the Early Modern Mediterranean* (Princeton: Princeton University Press, 2010).

28. Stanley Mayes, *The Great Belzoni: The Circus Strongman Who Discovered Egypt's Ancient Treasures* (1959; London: Tauris Parke Paperbacks, 2003), 11.

29. Michael J. Reimer, *Colonial Bridgehead: Government and Society in Alexandria, 1807–1882* (Boulder: Westview Press, 1997), 53–63; and Anna and Pierre Cachia, *Landlocked Islands: Two Alien Lives in Egypt* (Cairo: American University in Cairo Press, 1999), 6.

30. Both Conti's and Mussali's careers carried over into the Protectorate, which means that this group served as a bridge between the precolonial and early colonial eras. Mongi Smida, *Consuls et consulats de Tunisie au 19e siècle* (Tunis: Imprimerie de l'Orient, 1991), 27–30.

31. Rifaʿa Rafiʿ al-Tahtawi, *Takhlis al-ibriz fi talkhis Bariz aw al-diwan al-nafis bi-iman Baris* (Cairo: al-Hayʾa al-Misriya al-ʿAmma lil-Kitab, 1993), 120.

32. Pierre Masson, *Histoire des établissements et du commerce français dans l'Afrique barbaresque (1560–1793)* (Paris: Hachette 1903), 585.

33. Pierre Grandchamp, "A propos du séjour à Tunis de Caroline de Brunswick, princesse de Galles (4–12 avril 1816)," *RT* (1934): 59–70; Bin Diyaf, *Ithaf,* 3/3: 147; and Jane Robins, *The Trial of Queen Caroline: The Scandalous Affair that nearly Ended a Monarchy* (New York: Free Press, 2006), 69–71, quote p. 70..

34. Frances Terpak, "The Promise and Power of New Technologies: Nineteenth-Century Algiers" in *Walls of Algiers: Narratives of the City Through Text and Image,* ed. Zeynep Çelik, Julia Clancy-Smith, and Frances Terpak (Los Angeles: Getty Research Institute; Seattle: University of Washington Press, 2009), 87–133; and Adolphe Otth, *Esquisses africaines, dessinées pendant un voyage à Alger et lithographiées par Adolphe Otth* (Berne: J. F. Wagner, 1839).

35. Julia Clancy-Smith, "Exoticism, Erasures, and Absence: The Peopling of Algiers, 1830–1900," in *Walls of Algiers: Narratives of the City Through Text and Image,* ed. Zeynep Çelik, Julia Clancy-Smith, and Frances Terpak (Los Angeles: Getty Research Institute; Seattle: University of Washington Press, 2009), 19–61. See also, Marc Barioli, *La vie quotidienne des Français en Algérie 1830–1914* (Paris: Hachette, 1967), 12–13; and Pierre Nora, *Les Français d'Algérie* (Paris: René Julliard, 1961).

36. François-René de Chateaubriand, *Voyage de Tunis,* ed. Samira M'rad-Chaouachi (Tunis: Cérès Éditions, 2007); and David Brafman, "Facing East: The Western View of

Islam in Nicolas de Nicolay's *Travels in Turkey,*" *Getty Research Journal,* no. 1 (2009): 153–60.

37. Ewa Morawska and Willfried Spohn, "Moving Europeans in the Globalizing World: Contemporary Migrations in a Historical-Comparative Perspective," in *Global History and Migrations,* ed. Wang Gungwu (Boulder: Westview Press, 1997), 23–61, on information and assistance networks.

38. *Maltese Times or Broadsheet of the Mediterranean,* no. 2, April 10, 1840, 6; and no. 4, April 20, 1840, 14, BL.

39. *Harlequin or Broadsheet of the Mediterranean,* no. 97, November 16, 1839, 7, BL.

40. Ibid., 4.

41. Una Monk, *New Horizons: A Hundred Years of Women's Migration* (London: Her Majesty's Stationary Office, 1963); and James Hammerton, *Emigrant Gentlewomen: Genteel Poverty and Female Emigration, 1830–1914* (London: Croom Helm, 1979).

42. John R. McNeill, *Mountains of the Mediterranean* (Cambridge: Cambridge University Press, 1993), 2–11; and Jane and Peter Schneider, *Festival of the Poor: Fertility Decline and the Ideology of Class in Sicily, 1860–1980* (Tucson: University of Arizona Press, 1996), 17–88.

43. Charles A. Price, *Malta and the Maltese: A Study in Nineteenth Century Migration* (Melbourne: Georgian House, 1954), v. Carmel Vassallo has done the most recent work on Maltese commercial networks in *Corsairing to Commerce: Maltese Merchants in XVIII Century Spain* (Msida: Maltese University, 1997).

44. Lucette Valensi, "Calamités démographiques en Tunisie et en Méditerranée orientale aux XVIIIe et XIXe siècles," *AESC* 24, 6 (1969): 1540–62.

45. Philip Dwyer, *Napoleon: The Path to Power* (New Haven: Yale University Press, 2008), 359.

46. Pierre Grandchamp, "Esclaves musulmans rachetés en Chretienté," *RT,* nos. 53–54 (1943): 238–45. The Jesuits played a role in ransoming Tunisian Muslim slaves held in Malta and perhaps elsewhere in the Mediterranean. Nabil Matar, *Britain and Barbary, 1589–1689* (Gainesville: University Press of Florida, 2005), 117–120. Martine Vanhove, "A Malte, une langue inscrite dans l'histoire," *Le Monde Diplomatique* 54, 643 (October 2007), 31, claims Malta held ten thousand Tunisian and Algerian slaves in the eighteenth century.

47. Carmel Cassar, *Witchcraft, Sorcery, and the Inquisition: A Study of Cultural Values in Early Modern Malta* (Msida: Minerva Publications, 1996), 3; and Aurélia Martin Casares, "Esclavage féminin: Femmes maghrébines à Grenade au XVIIe siècle," in *Histoire des femmes au Maghreb: Culture matérielle et vie quotidienne,* ed. Dalenda Larguèche (Tunis: Centre de Publication Universitaire, 2000), 77–87.

48. *Memoir on the Finances of Malta, under the Government of the Order of St. John of Jerusalem, during the Last Years of its Dominion and as Compared with Those of the Present Time* (Malta: Printed at the Government Press, 1836), 56–60.

49. Anne Brognini, "Malte et la Méditerranée aux XVIe et XVIIe siècles: Développement de la consommation et essor des échanges," in *Consommations et consommateurs dans les pays méditerranéens (XVIe–XXe S.),* ed. Lilia Ben Salem, special issue of *RTSS* 42, 129 (2005): 199–216.

50. Peter Earle, *Corsairs of Malta and Barbary* (London: Sidgwick & Jackson, 1970), 97–100; Jacques Godechot, *Histoire de Malte* (Paris: Presses Universitaires de France, 1970); O. Vidala, *Les Maltais hors de Malte: Étude sur l'émigration maltaise* (Paris: Rousseau, 1911); and Charles Owens, *The Maltese Islands* (London: David & Charles, 1969).

51. *Memoir on the Finances of Malta*, 56–60. Each *salm* equaled 441 pounds.

52. Price, *Malta*, 1–8; Jean Mathiex, "Le ravitaillement moghrebin de Malte au XVIIIe siècle," *CT* 2 (1954): 191–96, quote p. 191; and Ernest Fallot, "Malte et ses rapports économiques avec la Tunisie," *RT* 3 (1896): 17–38.

53. Daniel Panzac, *Quarantaines et lazarets: L'Europe et la peste d'Orient (XVIIe–XXe siècles)* (Aix-en-Provence: Édisud, 1986). The long quarantine often observed in the breach, imposed on ships from Malta by other Mediterranean ports between 1813 and 1826—thirteen years—may have encouraged clandestine trade and emigration.

54. Price, *Malta*, 2–3.

55. *Memoir on the Finances of Malta*, 63–66; and George Percy Badger, *Description of Malta and Gozo* (Malta: M. Weiss, 1838), 73.

56. Adrianus Koster, *Prelates and Politicians in Malta: Changing Power-Balance between Church and State in a Mediterranean Island Fortress, 1800–1976* (Assen: Van Gorcum, 1984), 38–39, 53–54.

57. Badger, *Description*, 71–72.

58. Reade, March 22, 1835, FO 77/26, NAUK; and Bin Diyaf, *Ithaf,* 3/5: 257–58.

59. Badger, *Description*, 74, for quote.

60. Ferriere, June 28, 1847, "Memorandum relative to some points that appear to require investigation and regulation in the British Consulate at Tunis," FO 335 (96) 10, NAUK.

61. Frank M. Snowden, *Naples in the Time of Cholera, 1884–1911* (Cambridge: Cambridge University Press, 1995), 11–16.

62. Schneider, *Festival;* Paul Melon, *Problèmes algériens et tunisiens: Ce que disent les chiffres* (Paris: Challamel, 1903), 145, for 1890 estimates.

63. Giuseppe Tomasi di Lampedusa (1896–1957), *The Leopard*, trans. Archibald Colquhoun (New York: Pantheon, 1960), 65–74.

64. Denis Mack Smith, *A History of Modern Sicily after 1713* (New York: Viking Press, 1968), 373–402.

65. Gaston Loth, *Le peuplement italien en Tunisie et en Algérie* (Paris: Colin, 1905); and Jules Saurin, *Le peuplement français en Tunisie* (Paris: Challamel, 1910).

66. Gérard Crespo, *Les Italiens en Algérie, 1830–1960: Histoire et sociologie d'une migration* (Calvisson: J. Gandini, 1994), 30–33. Between 1850 and 1860, immigration into Algeria, whether from Italy or Spain, stagnated. From the 1860s on, Algeria experienced another migratory surge due to events in Sicily; Tunisia experienced the same migratory surge. The opening of mines, particularly the Jabal Halluf lead mine, by the Protectorate attracted numerous Sardinian miners.

67. Pierre Ficaya, *Le peuplement italien en Tunisie* (Paris: Les Presses Modernes, 1931), 28, 20.

68. Silvia Finzi, "Le Travail des Sardes dans les mines tunisiennes à travers les souvenirs d'enfance de la fille d'un mineur," in *Mestieri e professioni degli Italiani di Tunisia/*

Métiers et professions des Italiens de Tunisie, ed. Silvia Finzi (Tunis: Editions Finzi, 2003), 270–75; and Fanny Colonna and Zakiya Daoud, eds., *Etre marginal au Maghreb* (Paris: Alif, 1993).

69. Ficaya, *Peuplement,* 19.

70. Triulzi, "Italian-Speaking Communities," 153–84; and Michel Ersilio, *Esuli italiani in Tunisia (1815–1861)* (Milan: Instituto per gli Studi di Politica Internazionale, 1941).

71. Joseph Greaves, *The Journal of Mr. Joseph Greaves, on a Visit to the Regency of Tunis,* in *Christian Researches in Syria and the Holy Land 1823 and 1824 in Furtherance of the Objects of the Church Missionary Society,* by Rev. William Jowett (London: Seeley & Son, 1825), 467–68.

72. Abdelhamid Larguèche and Habib Kazdaghli, "Elia Finzi, imprimeur de père en fils," in *Mestieri e professioni degli Italiani di Tunisia/Métiers et professions des Italiens de Tunisie,* ed. Silvia Finzi (Tunis: Editions Finzi, 2003), 278–84.

73. Jasper Ridley, *Garibaldi* (New York: Viking Press, 1974), 37–38.

74. Paul Sebag, *La Hara de Tunis: L'évolution d'un ghetto nord-africain* (Paris: Mémoires du Centre d'Études de Sciences Humaines, 1959), 14–19; and Jean Ganiage, *Les origines du Protectorat Français en Tunisie (1861–1881)* (Tunis: Maison Tunisienne de l'Édition, 1968), 43, 134–41, 583.

75. A. Larguèche and Kazdaghli, "Elia Finzi." In the politics of mobilities in the central Mediterranean corridor, a pattern emerges that is confined neither to the nineteenth century nor to political activists. Bettino Craxi, Italy's Socialist prime minister, fled to Tunis in the 1990s after indictment for corruption charges involving billions of lire in bribes; he died there in 2000.

76. Dwyer, *Napoleon,* 53–75.

77. Stephen Wilson, *Feuding, Conflict and Banditry in Nineteenth-Century Corsica* (Cambridge: Cambridge University Press, 1988), 1–14; and Léon Denis, *Tunis et l'île de Sardaigne: Souvenirs de voyage* (Tours: Imprimerie E. Arrault, 1884), 38–49. Denis spent time in Sardinia in 1879 and noted the extreme poverty of its illiterate inhabitants but presented Muslim Tunisians in relatively favorable terms; Denis described the Sardinians as "ugly and dirty . . . their features have an African aspect to them" (38). By then a direct, regular steamship service linked Tunis to Cagliari.

78. Habib Kazdaghli, "Communautés méditerranéennes de Tunisie: Les Grecs de Tunisie; du Millet-i-Rum à l'assimilation française (XVIIe-XXe siècles)," *RMMM,* nos. 95–98 (2002): 449–76.

79. Thomas W. Gallant, *Experiencing Dominion: Culture, Identity, and Power in the British Mediterranean* (Notre Dame: University of Notre Dame Press, 2002), 6–14.

80. Reade, July 20, 1830, FO 77/21, NAUK.

81. On Tunisia and the treaty of 1830 with France following the invasion of Algeria, see Windler, *Diplomatie,* 388–89; for Tunisian reactions, Bin Diyaf, *Ithaf,* 3/4: 209–28.

82. Annie Rey-Goldzeiguer, "Les enjeux des relations franco-tunisiennes pour les élites tunisennes et françaises 1830–1875," in *Les relations tuniso-françaises au miroir des élites (XIXè, XXème siècles),* ed. Noureddine Dougui (Tunis: Publications de la Faculté des Lettres, Manouba, 1997), 15–36; and Philippe Daumas, *Quatre ans à Tunis* (Algiers: Tissier, 1857).

83. Alf A. Heggoy, *The French Conquest of Algiers, 1830: An Algerian Oral Tradition* (Athens: Ohio University, 1986), 32.

84. Évariste Bavoux, *Alger: Voyage politique et descriptif dans le nord de l'Afrique,* 2 vols. (Paris: Chez Brockhaus et Avenarius, 1841), 2: 334–36; André Rampal, "Les stations navales et les migrations en Méditerranée au début du XIXe siècle," in *Navigations et migrations en Méditerranée: De la préhistoire à nos jours,* ed. Jean-Louis Miège (Paris: Éditions du CNRS, 1990), 333–41; and Guy Tudury, *La prodigieuse histoire des Mahonnais en Algérie* (Nimes: C. Lacour, 1992).

85. Joanny Pharaon, *De la législation française, musulmane et juive à Alger* (Paris: Théophile Barrois Fils, 1835); and A. Cour, "Notes sur les chaires de langue arabe d'Alger, de Constantine et d'Oran (1832–1879)," *RA* 65, 318 (1924): 20–64.

86. Leslie Page Moch, *Moving Europeans: Migration in Western Europe since 1650,* 2nd ed. (Bloomington: Indiana University Press, 2003).

87. Joshua Cole, *The Power of Large Numbers: Population, Politics, and Gender in Nineteenth-Century France* (Ithaca: Cornell University Press, 2000).

88. Capitaine Carette, *Algérie,* in *L'univers pittoresque: Histoire et description de tous les peuples, de leurs religions, moeurs, coutumes, industrie, &* (Paris: Firmin Didot, 1850), 275.

89. Jean Meyer, Jean Tarrade, Annie Rey-Goldzeiguer, and Jaques Thobie, *Histoire de la France coloniale: Des origines à 1914,* 3 vols. (Paris: Armand Colin, 1990), 1: 371; and Marianne Roux, "Le départ des colons français pour L'Algérie au XIXème siècle" (diplôme d'études approfondies, Université de Paris I, 1993).

90. Michael Heffernan, "French Colonial Migration," in *The Cambridge Survey of World Migration,* ed. Robin Cohen (Cambridge: Cambridge University Press, 1995), 33–38; and Crespo, *Italiens,* 91–92.

91. Lucien de Montagnac, *Lettres d'un soldat: Neuf années de campagnes en Afrique; Correspondance inédite du Colonel de Montagnac* (Paris: Plon, 1885), 13.

92. Joseph Chailley-Bert, *L'émigration des femmes aux colonies: Allocution de M. le comte d'Haussonville et discours de M. J. Chailley-Bert à la conférence donnée le 12 janvier 1897 par l'union coloniale française* (Paris: A. Colon, 1897).

93. J. A. Bolle, *Souvenirs de l'Algérie* (Angoulème: Broquisse, 1839), 21–24.

94. Charles-André Julien, *Histoire de l'Algérie contemporaine,* 2nd ed., vol. 1, *La conquête et les débuts de la colonisation (1827–1871)* (Paris: Presses Universitaires de France, 1979), 106–63; and Rampal, "Les stations," 336.

95. Barioli, *Vie,* 15; Julien, *Histoire,* 1: 120, 158; and Julia Clancy-Smith, "Le regard colonial: Islam, genre et identités dans la fabrication de l'Algérie française, 1830–1962," *Nouvelles Questions Féministes* 25, 1 (2006): 25–40.

96. Julien, *Histoire,* 1: 297.

97. Carette, *Algérie,* 176. Legal marriages were rare among immigrants; at least one-third of the children born to French nationals were *enfants naturels,* or illegitimate. The first major published study of prostitution was Edouard Adolphe Duchesne's *De la prostitution dans la ville d'Alger depuis la conquête* (Paris: J. B. Baillière, 1853).

98. Christelle Taraud, *La prostitution coloniale: Algérie, Tunisie, Maroc (1830–1962)* (Paris: Payot, 2003).

99. Alexis de Tocqueville, *Writings on Empire and Slavery*, ed. and trans. Jennifer Pitts (Baltimore: Johns Hopkins University Press, 2001), May 7, 1841, "General Appearance of the Country," 36–37.

100. Ibid.

101. Alexis de Tocqueville, *Oeuvres complètes*, vol. 3, *Écrits et discours politiques* (Paris: Gallimard, 1962): 322–24, 354–55.

102. Carette, *Algérie*, 39, 41, quote p. 275.

103. Tocqueville, *Oeuvres*, 3: 375–76.

104. British consul, Algiers, April 17, 1858, FO 113/5, NAUK.

105. Papers of Edward William Auriol Drummond-Hay (1785–1845), consul general in Tangiers, 1829–1845, ms. e.354 (c. 1835), OBL (including quotes in paragraph).

106. French consul, Carthagena, Spain, to minister of foreign affairs, Paris, April 10, 1865, F 80 1804, CAOM.

107. Ibid.

108. Ibid. (including quotes in paragraph).

109. Akram Fuad Khater, *Inventing Home: Emigration, Gender, and the Middle Class in Lebanon, 1870–1920* (Berkeley: University of California Press, 2001), 23, 29.

110. Minister of war, Paris, January 31, 1861, to Randon, Algiers, F 80 1804, CAOM.

111. Minister of war, Paris, report of 1866, to Randon, Algiers, F 80 1804, CAOM.

112. British consul, Algiers, June 12, 1832, FO 113/5, NAUK.

113. French consul, Malta, July 3, 1872, to minister of foreign affairs, Paris, citing the official gazette of the Maltese government, F 80 1804, CAOM.

114. Lady Mary E. Herbert, *A Search After Sunshine, or Algeria in 1871* (London: Bentley, 1872), 115.

115. Hammerton, "Gender," 156–80, quote pp. 158–59.

116. Jean Reynaud, "La résidence des femmes françaises en Levant au XVIIIème siècle," *Revue de la Chambre de Commerce de Marseille* 35, 581 (November 1948): 21–24, quote p. 22.

117. Minister of the navy, memorandum, June 17, 1837, F 80 586, CAOM.

118. Jacqueline Baylé, *Quand l'Algérie devenait française* (Paris: Fayard, 1981), 161–63.

119. Marcel Emerit, *Pauline Roland et les déportées d'Afrique* (Algiers: Editions de l'Empire, 1945).

120. Baylé, *L'Algérie*, 161–63.

121. Reade, March 23, 1835, FO 77/26, NAUK.

122. Roches, Tunis, to Monge, Bizerte, July 19, 1858, carton 485, CADN.

123. Gaspary, June 28, 1839, carton 409B, CADN; and British consul, Algiers, September 1, 1856, FO 113/6, NAUK.

124. Bolle, *Souvenirs*, 11–12.

125. French consul, Malta, to minister of foreign affairs, Paris, July 2, 1872, F 80 1804, "Colonisation," CAOM.

126. Roustan to Khayr al-Din, December 11, 1876, carton 68, dossier 813, ANT.

127. French consul, Malta, to minister of foreign affairs, Paris, July 3, 1872, F 80 1804, "Colonisation," CAOM.

128. Jennifer E. Sessions, "L'Algérie Devenue Française: The Naturalization of Non-

French Colonists in French Algeria, 1830–1849," *Proceedings of the Western Society for French History* 30 (2004): 165–77.

129. Gaspary, December 4, 1842, carton 410B, CADN.

130. Gaspary, January 1847, carton 411A, CADN.

131. Melon, *Problèmes,* 28–29, for counting in nineteenth-century Algeria before and after 1889 naturalization, which rendered the statistical-legal category of *étrangers* hopelessly complex.

CHAPTER 3

1. Bin Diyaf, *Ithaf,* 3/4: 233–37. The *nawba,* a military fanfare of Turkish music, signaled the ruler's daily routine; during Ramadan, it announced the last meal before dawn, *sahur.* For a different version of the events, see Reade, February 3, 1833, FO 77/24, NAUK.

2. Hamilton Sipho Simelane, "The State, Chiefs and the Control of Female Migration in Colonial Swaziland, c. 1930s–1950s," *JAH* 45, 1 (2004): 103–24, argues that labor migration is never solely about work but interwoven with other motivations; for women, it offered the means to escape patriarchal control, frequently the threat of forced marriages.

3. Miriam Cooke and Bruce B. Lawrence, eds., *Muslim Networks from Hajj to Hip Hop* (Chapel Hill: University of North Carolina Press, 2005), 1.

4. Susan Cotts Watkins, "Social Networks and Social Science History," *SSH* 19, 3 (Fall 1995): 295–311.

5. Jean Ganiage, *Les origines du Protectorat Français en Tunisie* (Tunis: Maison Tunisienne de l'Édition, 1968); Leon Carl Brown, *The Tunisia of Ahmad Bey, 1837–1855* (Princeton: Princeton University Press, 1974); and Khelifa Chater, *Dépendance et mutations précoloniales: La Régence de Tunis de 1815 à 1857* (Tunis: Publications de l'Université de Tunis, 1984). There are few studies of even colonial industries; one of the first modern extractive industries was the French phosphate company in the southwest near Gafsa. Noureddine Dougui, *Histoire d'une grande entreprise coloniale: La compagnie des phosphates et du chemin de fer de Gafsa, 1897–1930* (Tunis: Publications de la Faculté de la Manouba, 1995).

6. Lucette Valensi, "Islam et capitalisme: Production et commerce des chéchias en Tunisie et en France aux XVIIIe et XIXe siècles," *Revue d'Histoire Moderne et Contemporaine* 16 (1969): 376–400; Mohamed El Aziz Ben Achour, *Catégories de la société tunisoise dans la deuxième moitié du XIXème siècle* (Tunis: Institut National d'Archéologie et d'Art, 1989), 374–78; Mustapha Kraïem, *La Tunisie précoloniale,* 2 vols. (Tunis: Société Tunisienne de Diffusion, 1973), 2: 37–40; and Julia Clancy-Smith, "A Woman without Her Distaff: Gender, Work, and Handicraft Production in Colonial North Africa," in *A Social History of Women and the Family in the Middle East,* ed. Margaret Meriwether and Judith Tucker (Boulder: Westview Press, 1999), 25–62. For the Tunis guilds, there is nothing comparable to André Raymond's *Artisans et commerçants au Caire au XVIIIe siècle,* 2 vols. (Damascus: Institut Français de Damas, 1973–1974).

7. Charles Lallemand, *Tunis au XIXe siècle* (Paris: La Maison Quantin, 1890), 51.

8. Paul Sebag, *Tunis: Histoire d'une ville* (Paris: L'Harmattan, 1998), 261–310; and Jerome S. Woodford, *The City of Tunis: Evolution of an Urban System* (Cambridgeshire: Middle East and North African Studies Press, 1990), 154–55.

9. Dalenda Larguèche, ed., *Histoire des femmes au Maghrib: Culture matérielle et vie quotidienne* (Tunis: Centre de Publication Universitaire, 2000); Dalenda Larguèche and Abdelhamid Larguèche, *Marginales en terre d'Islam* (Tunis: Cérès Productions, 1992); Julia Clancy-Smith, "Envisioning Knowledge: Educating the Muslim Woman in Colonial North Africa, 1900–1918," in *Iran and Beyond: Essays in Middle Eastern History in Honor of Nikki Keddie*, ed. Beth Baron and Rudi Matthee (Los Angeles: Mazda Press, 2000), 99–118.

10. Lucette Valensi, *Fellahs tunisiens: L'économie rurale et la vie des campagnes aux 18e et 19e siècles* (Paris: Mouton, 1977).

11. For the 1863 convention, see J. C. Hurewitz, ed., *The Middle East and North Africa in World Politics: A Documentary Record*, 2 vols. (New Haven: Yale University Press, 1975), 1: 352–55.

12. Mohamed El Aziz Ben Achour, introduction and commentary, in *La cour du bey de Tunis* (Tunis: Espace Diwan, 2003), xix–xxi; Taoufik Bachrouch, *Le saint et le prince en Tunisie* (Tunis: Faculté des Sciences Humaines et Sociales de Tunis, 1989); and Lucien Moatti, *La mosaïque médicale de Tunisie, 1800–1950* (Paris: Éditions Glyphe, 2008), 21–68.

13. Charles Monchicourt, *Documents historiques sur la Tunisie: Relations inédites de Nyssen, Filippi et Calligaris (1788, 1829, 1834)* (Paris: Société d'Éditions Géographiques, Maritime et Coloniales, 1929), 92–95.

14. I use the terms "harim" and "household" almost interchangeably, although strictly speaking the harim was one section of a larger domestic compound. Asma Moalla, *The Regency of Tunis and the Ottoman Porte, 1777–1814: Army and Government of a North-African Ottoman Eyâlet at the End of the Eighteenth Century* (London: Routledge, 2005), 79–80; and Ben Achour, *Catégories*, 226–27. See also Ehud R. Toledano, "African Slaves in the Ottoman Eastern Mediterranean: A Case of Cultural 'Creolization?'" in *The Mediterranean World: The Idea, the Past and the Present*, ed. Eyüp Özveren, Oktay Özel, Suha Ünsal, and Kudret Emiroşlu (Istanbul: Iletişim Yayinlari, 2006), 107–24. In Toledano's view, the racially, ethnically, and linguistically heterogeneous nature of harims was significant because the process of creolization took place in major urban elite households.

15. See Amy Elouafi Aisen, "Being Ottoman: Family and the Politics of Modernity in the Province of Tunisia" (PhD dissertation, University of California, Berkeley, 2007), for a study of the eighteenth- and early nineteenth-century court, particularly the Husaynid women, about which little is known.

16. Reade, September 22, 1831, FO 77/22, NAUK; and Louis Frank, *Histoire de Tunis*, introduction and annotation by J. J. Marcel, 2nd ed. (Paris: Firmin-Didot, 1851), 51. Naval officers represented important sources of information for the palace; the consuls often provided newspaper accounts from Europe in translation to government officials.

17. Ben Achour, *Catégories*, 74–75.

18. Karen Tranberg Hansen, "Body Politics: Sexuality, Gender, and Domestic Service in Zambia," in *Expanding the Boundaries of Women's History*, ed. Cheryl Johnson-Odim and Margaret Strobel (Bloomington: Indiana University Press, 1992), 1–24, argues that gender conventions governing domestic service in migrant labor markets are unstable over time; for example, the abolition of slavery in 1834 in Zambia meant that impoverished European women began dominating the domestic service sector. Homa Hoodfar, *Between Marriage*

and the Market: Intimate Politics and Survival in Cairo (Berkeley: University of California Press, 1997), 113–14, notes that Cairene maids today tend to earn much more than school teachers but that domestic service is regarded as lower in status and thus less desirable.

19. Anne Walthall, ed., *Servants of the Dynasty: Palace Women in World History* (Berkeley: University of California Press, 2008), 1–21; and Leslie P. Peirce, *The Imperial Harem: Women and Sovereignty in the Ottoman Empire* (New York: Oxford University Press, 1993).

20. Even today most domestic-service laborers have no written contracts, although modern cleaning services resembling "Merry Maids" businesses are emerging and workers generally enjoy contracts. Leila Blili Temime, *Histoire de Familles: Mariages, répudiations et vie quotidienne à Tunis, 1875–1930* (Tunis: Editions Script, 1999), 167–69; and Suraiya Faroqhi, *Subjects of the Sultan: Culture and Daily Life in the Ottoman Empire* (London: I. B. Tauris, 2000), 112–13. There is a considerable scholarship on domestic service in modern European history; for example, Deborah Oxley, *Convict Maids: The Forced Migration of Women to Australia* (Cambridge: Cambridge University Press, 1996).

21. Bin Diyaf, *Ithaf,* 3/4: 233–37, quotes p. 235.

22. Feise, "Observations," 9. His calculations seem a bit high compared to Daniel Panzac, *Les corsaires barbaresques: La fin d'une épopée, 1800–1820* (Paris: Éditions du CNRS, 1999), 98, which estimates the number at around sixteen hundred.

23. Feise, "Observations," 9.

24. Ibid., 5. Compare Feise's account with Nabil Matar, *Britain and Barbary, 1589–1689* (Gainseville: University Press of Florida, 2005), 117–120, on enslaved Muslims, generally North Africans, in Europe. While the Knights of Santo Stefano rescued Christians held captive by Muslims, they enslaved North Africans in large numbers; see Molly Greene, "Resurgent Islam, 1500–1700," in *The Mediterranean in History,* ed. David Abulafia (London: Thames & Hudson, 2003), 219–50.

25. Anonymous ms., c. 1835, carton "Confins Algéro-Tunisiens," Algérie, F 80 1697, CAOM.

26. Richardson, "Account," 29.

27. Khaled Fahmy, *All the Pasha's Men: Mehmed Ali, His Army, and the Making of Modern Egypt* (Cairo: American University in Cairo Press, 2002).

28. Bin Diyaf, *Ithaf,* 3/5: 262–64.

29. Eve Troutt Powell's *A Different Shade of Colonialism: Egypt, Great Britain, and the Mastery of the Sudan* (Berkeley: University of California Press, 2003) invites us to consider similar issues for Tunisia.

30. Panzac, *Corsaires,* 98–99; Lucette Valensi, "Esclaves chrétiens et esclaves noirs à Tunis au XVIII siècle," *AESC* 4 (1967): 1267–88; and Abdelhamid Larguèche, *L'abolition de l'esclavage en Tunisie à travers les archives, 1841–1846* (Tunis: Alif, 1990). See also Yonne J. Seng, "Fugitives and Factotums: Slaves in Early Sixteenth-Century Istanbul," *JESHO* 39, 2 (1996): 136–69. Several families residing in Tunis at midcentury were descended from Christian slaves manumitted over thirty years prior.

31. Ehud R. Toledano, *The Ottoman Slave Trade and Its Suppression* (Princeton: Princeton University Press, 1982).

32. Nadia Sebaï, *Mustapha Saheb Ettabaa: Un haut dignitaire beylical dans la Tunisie du XIXe siècle* (Carthage: Éditions Cartaginoiseries, 2007), 25–26.

33. Gaspary, October 3, 1823, carton 406B, CADN.

34. Reade, September 17, 1831, FO 77/22, NAUK. A şavuş was a sergeant in the Ottoman army.

35. Eugène Plantet, *Correspondance des beys de Tunis et des consuls de France avec la cour, 1577–1830*, 3 vols. (Paris: Alcan, 1899), 3: 684–86.

36. Valensi, "Esclaves," 1267–88; and Chater, *Dépendance*, 147–48, 549. Tunis had the largest community of manumitted slaves numbering between six and seven thousand by 1861.

37. Abdelhamid Larguèche, *Les ombres de la ville: Pauvres, marginaux et minoritaires à Tunis (XVIIIème et XIXè siècles)* (Tunis: Centre de Publication Universitaire, 1999), 393–419; and Temime, *Histoire*, 167–69.

38. Bin Diyaf, *Ithaf,* 3/4: 202–3; and anonymous ms., c. 1835, carton "Confins Algéro-Tunisiens," Algérie, F 80 1697, CAOM.

39. Valensi, "Esclaves," 1279; and A. Larguèche, *Abolition,* 20.

40. Laurent Gay, médecin du bey, "Mémoire sur la médicine, la peste et la vaccine dans la Régence de Tunis," ms. no. 1821, F 80 1697, CAOM.

41. Reade, January 26, 1836, FO 77/29, NAUK.

42. Richardson, "Addenda," 54. His stated purpose for collecting firsthand harim accounts was "to present a proper idea of Tunisian female aristocracy to the reader" (60).

43. Logbook, 1829–1830, FO 77/21, NAUK.

44. Philippa Day, ed., *At Home in Carthage: The British in Tunisia* (Tunis: Trustees of St. Georges Church, 1992), 15.

45. Female slaves in the Husaynids' harims were not necessarily manumitted by 1846; only in 1887 did 'Ali Bey free them. François Renault, *Lavigerie, l'esclavage africain, et l'Europe, 1868–1892*, 2 vols. (Paris: E. de Boccard, 1971), 2: 9–18.

46. A. Larguèche, *Abolition,* 29, 56–63; and Renault, *Lavigerie,* 1: 110–53; and 2: 9–18. See also Y. Hakan Erdem, *Slavery in the Ottoman Empire and Its Demise, 1800–1909* (New York: St. Martin's Press, 1996).

47. Richardson, "Account," 29.

48. Brown, *Tunisia,* 321–25.

49. Richardson, "Account," 142.

50. According to the Mamelouk family, their ancestor was one of the last English captives seized at sea around 1830; the young man, named Ramdan, was raised at the Bardo palace. Author interview with Mohamed Mamelouk, Tunis, November 2008. Compared to the hefty harim literature for Egypt or Turkey in the same period, the sources for nineteenth-century Tunisia are surprisingly slim. Diane Robinson-Dunn, *The Harim, Slavery and British Imperial Culture: Anglo-Muslim Relations in the Late Nineteenth Century* (Manchester: Manchester University Press, 2006).

51. Richardson, "Addenda," 60.

52. Ibid. Mme. Berner's account only exists in the "Addenda," although Richardson may have interviewed her while in Tunis.

53. Major Sir Grenville T. Temple, *Excursions in the Mediterranean: Algiers and Tunis,* 2 vols. (London: Saunders and Otley, 1835), 1: 196.

54. Richardson, "Addenda" 63–64. This information is inserted as marginalia.

55. Lady Mary E. Herbert, *A Search After Sunshine, or Algeria in 1871* (London: Richard Bentley, 1872), 260–62, quote p. 261. The aristocratic Herbert was a socially prominent writer, philanthropist, and translator.

56. Karin van Nieuwkerk, *"A Trade Like Any Other": Female Singers and Dancers in Egypt* (Austin: University of Texas Press, 1995), 21–39.

57. Richardson, "Addenda," 63–64.

58. Bin Diyaf, *Ithaf,* 4/6: 12; and Richardson, "Addenda," 42.

59. Reade to prime minister, October 12, 1880, carton 228, dossier 414, ANT, (both quotes in paragraph).

60. A. Larguèche, *Abolition,* 35. Sebag, *Tunis,* 269–70, estimates their numbers at "several thousand." See also Mohammed Ennaji's *Soldats, domestiques et concubines: L'esclavage au Maroc au XIXe siècle* (Tunis: Cérès Éditions, 1994).

61. Larguèche and Larguèche, *Marginales,* 31–31, and appendix 3, 82.

62. Temime, *Histoire,* 168–69. In some aristocratic urban families, service did not always mean dismal servitude; servants were raised as family members and the Arabic *rabiba* or *mrubbiya* (foster or stepdaughter) expressed kin relations.

63. Ernst von Hesse-Wartegg, *Tunis: The Land and the People* (New York: Dodd, Mead, & Company, 1882), 81.

64. Moatti, *Mosaïque,* 22–24, 217–18, 224, 276–77; and Gay, "Mémoire."

65. Plantet, *Correspondance,* 3: 588.

66. Richardson, "Addenda," 60.

67. Planel, "De la nation," 3: 734; and Wood, July 18, 1872, carton 382, CADN. French cooks in the Bardo's palace kitchens raise important questions about changing tastes in food.

68. Anonymous ms., c. 1835, "Confins Algéro-Tunisiens," 85, F 80 1697, CAOM.

69. Planel, "De la nation," 3: 738; and Ganiage, *Origines,* 583.

70. Wood to Raffo, October 17, 1856, carton 227, dossier 411, ANT.

71. Italian consul general to Botmiliau, May 14, 1869, carton 381, CADN. The image of the sly servant is a prevalent one; see Elsbeth Locher-Scholten, "So Close and Yet So Far: The Ambivalence of Dutch Colonial Rhetoric on Javanese Servants in Indonesia, 1900–1942," in *Domesticating the Empire: Gender, Race, and Family Life in the Dutch and French Empires,* ed. Julia Clancy-Smith and Frances Gouda (Charlottesville: University Press of Virginia, 1998), 131–53.

72. British vice-consul Ancram to Ahmad Bey, January 3, 1838, carton 226, dossier 409, ANT.

73. Wage-labor opportunities in Malta for women were limited until home cottage industries emerged to serve the port's increasing maritime traffic. Women manufactured cigars using imported tobacco; subject to very low duties relative to the rest of the Mediterranean, the sale of cigars to crews and passengers proved one source of income. In addition, a pasta factory operated in Valletta, employing a mainly female workforce. *Memoir on the Finances of Malta, under the Government of the Order of St. John of Jerusalem, during the Last Years of Its Dominion and as Compared with Those of the Present Time* (Malta: Printed at the Government Press, 1836), 72; and George French Angas, *A Ramble in Malta and Sicily in the Autumn of 1841* (London: Smith, Elder, and Co., 1842), 15.

74. Logbook, April 3, 1829, FO 77/20, NAUK.

75. *Le Petit Tunisien Indépendent,* Tunis, Friday, March 12, 1886, p. 7. Sardinian, Sicilian, or Maltese nannies and wet nurses were employed by Tunis notables well into the twentieth century, until the eve of independence if not later.

76. Abdessatar Amamou, "Rencontre avec Abdessatar Amamou," *La Presse* (Tunis), Friday, May 14, 2003, p. 1. Raffo was the eleventh child of Terrasson, born in 1795; Ahmad was born in December 1806.

77. In *Samt al-qusur (Les silences du palais,* 1994), the filmmaker Moufida Tlatli explored the milieu of female servants, and the sexual favors expected of them, in the bey's household.

78. Logbook, February 12 and February 18, 1829, FO 77/16, NAUK.

79. Gaspary, October 24, 1820, and May 25, 1822, carton 406B, CADN.

80. Planel, "De la nation," 1: 81–83.

81. Gaspary, June 30, 1839, carton 409B, and December 21, 1842, carton 410B, CADN.

82. Angelo Saliba, died Tunis July 5, 1850, probate settled January 16, 1851, FO 335/99/8, NAUK.

83. Roches, February 18, 1860, carton 207, dossier 96, ANT.

84. Cubisol, December 29, 1868, carton 413, CADN.

85. "Notes des effets réclamés," December 28, 1868, carton 413, CADN.

86. Correspondence between the French and British consulates, July 14, 1869-November 2, 1869, carton 382, CADN.

87. Christina Wood, Personal Papers, Box 1, Letter WD269–271, RW.

88. Cubisol to De Billing, September 24, 1874, carton 413, CADN.

89. Cubisol, September 24, 1874, carton 413, CADN.

90. "Procedura," February 27, 1868, testimony of Gianmaria Hiberras.

91. "Procedura," March 17, 1868, testimony of Isacco Sfez.

92. Billings to Khayr al-Din, September 11, 1874, carton 207, dossier 108, ANT.

93. August 21, 1826, carton 78, CCM.

94. Sebag, *Tunis,* 268.

95. Luigi Demech, *The British Consulate in Tunis: Critical Remarks* (Malta: Albion Press, 1868), 42. After 1840, the French consulate operated a post office for nationals sending or receiving mail from France and Algeria; by the late 1860s, most consulates boasted more or less regular postal services.

96. "Expense Sheet of the Consulate in Tunis," 1833, FO 77/2, NAUK.

97. Feise, "Observations," 9. With a pedigree dating to the fourteenth century, dragomen constituted ubiquitous figures in Ottoman lands, where they filled numerous capacities, most often as translators and intermediaries. A permanent feature of the Ottoman diplomatic system by the eighteenth century, dragomen were non-Muslim "Levantines," often descendants of unions between Eastern Christian Ottoman subjects and European traders. Sultan Mahmud II (1808–1839) opened the post to Muslims to counter the power of the Greek Orthodox, who had long monopolized the position. Alexander H. De Groot, "Protection and Nationality: The Decline of the Dragomans" in *Istanbul et les langues orientales,* ed. Frédéric Hitzel (Paris: L'Harmattan, 1997); and Elisabeth Özdalga, *The Last*

Dragoman: The Swedish Orientalist Johannes Kolmodin as Scholar, Activist and Diplomat (Istanbul: Swedish Research Institute in Istanbul, 2006).

98. Windler, *Diplomatie,* 429.

99. Logbook, April 7, 1829, FO 77/20, NAUK.

100. J. Clark Kennedy, *Algeria and Tunisia in 1845,* 2 vols. (London: Colburn, 1846), 2: 43.

101. Ferriere, "Memorandum," 1847, FO 335 (96) 10, NAUK.

102. Demech, *British Consulate in Tunis,* 31.

103. Wood, 1856, carton 224, dossier 403, ANT.

104. Wood, December 26, 1859, carton 227, dossier 411, ANT.

105. Wood to Muhammad al-Sadiq Bey, May 26, 1863, carton 224, dossier 403, ANT.

106. Ibid.. In 1830 the French expeditionary commander to Algiers pressed the bey to supply indigenous translators.

107. Reade, July 1846, FO 335/92/5, NAUK.

108. Baynes, February 4, 1852, FO 335/101/16, NAUK.

109. Roches to Mustafa Khaznadar, October 16, 1860, carton 207, dossier 96, ANT.

110. The consuls did not only vet or promote middle-class job candidates but also recruited workers from Europe; when the first modern textile manufacturing center was established to supply the Tunisian army, it employed fifteen skilled workers and masters from France. Jean Ganiage, *La population européenne de Tunis* (Paris: Presses Universitaires de France, 1960), 11.

111. Schwebel to Murali, June 28, 1837, carton 206, dossier 85, ANT.

112. Temple, *Excursions,* 1: 28.

113. Gaspary to Tulin, September 3, 1842, carton 410B, CADN and Nathan David, *Tunis, or Selections from a Journal during a Residence in That Regency* (Malta: G. Muir, 1841), "the French Deserter," 15–35.

114. Davis, *Tunis,* 15.

115. Ibid., 35.

116. Salvatore Bono, "Conversions à l'islam à l'époque coloniale," in *Conversions islamiques: Identités religieuses en Islam méditerranéen,* ed. Mercedes García-Arenal (Paris: Maisonneuve & Larose, 2001), 319.

117. Ganiage, *Origines,* 576.

118. Gaspary, 1842, carton 410B, CADN.

119. Ben Achour, *Catégories,* 299–300.

120. Richardson, "Addenda," 64.

121. Cubisol, September 27, 1854, carton 412, CADN; and Charles Matrat, "La Société Pastré Frères, Agence Commerciale de Sidi Mustapha Khaznadar à Marseille," in *Etudes d'histoire contemporaine tunisienne (1846–1871)* (Marseilles: Université de Provence, 1973), 28–100.

122. Bin Diyaf, *Ithaf,* vol. 4, Abdesselem edition, 48, 106–07; and Davis, *Tunis,* 53–54.

123. 'Abd al-Majid Karim and Hadi Jallab, *Qusur al-Muhammadiya wa al-taramway* (Tunis: al-Ma'had al-a'la li-tarikh al-haraka al-wataniya, 1993).

124. Charles Monchicourt, "Les Italiens de Tunisie et l'Accord Laval-Mussolini de 1935," *Bibliothèque des Questions Nord-Africaines* 2 (1938): 3; Jean Ganiage, "Les Européens en Tunisie au milieu du XIXe siècle," *CT* 3, 9 (1955): 389–421; Ficaya, 20–21; and

Marc Donato, *L'émigration des Maltais en Algérie au XIXème siècle* (Montpellier: Collection Africa Nostra, 1985), 108.

CHAPTER 4

1. Bin Diyaf, *Ithaf,* 3/5: 267.

2. Michael E. Bonine, ed., *Population, Poverty, and Politics in Middle East Cities* (Gainesville: University Press of Florida, 1997).

3. Logbook, February 1828, FO 77/20, and December 3 and 4, 1830, FO 77/22, NAUK; and Abdelhamid Hénia, *Propriété et stratégies sociales à Tunis (XVIe–XIXe siècles)* (Tunis: Faculté des Sciences Humaines et Sociales de Tunis, 1999).

4. Logbook, 1828, FO 77/20, NAUK.

5. "Procedura," 21, 41.

6. Logbook, 1829, FO 77/20, NAUK.

7. Ibid.; and "Procedura," 37, 39, 50.

8. Logbook, December 26, 1828, FO 77/20, NAUK; and for the quote, Carleton to the *khaznadar,* September 1862, carton 227, dossier 411, ANT.

9. Ashraf Azzous and David Massey, *Maisons de Sidi Bou Saïd* (Tunis: Dar Ashraf Editions, 2005), 20; and Albert Memmi, *La statue de sel* (Paris: Éditions Gallimard, 1966), 1–2.

10. William L. Cleveland, "The Municipal Council of Tunis, 1858–1870: A Study in Urban Institutional Change," *IJMES* 9, 1 (1978): 38.

11. Mohamed El Aziz Ben Achour, *Catégories de la société tunisoise dans la deuxième moitié du XIXe siècle* (Tunis: Institut National d'Archéologie et d'Art, 1989), 384.

12. Dalenda Larguèche, "Le commerce du café avant l'ère des plantations coloniales: Espaces, réseaux, sociétés (XVe–XIXe siècle)," *Cahiers des Annales Islamologiques* 20 (2001): 203–5; and Abdelhamid Larguèche, *Les ombres de la ville: Pauvres, marginaux et minoritaires à Tunis (XVIIIè et XIXè siècles)* (Tunis: Centre de Publication Universitaire, 1999), 36–39.

13. Abdelhamid Larguèche and Habib Kazdaghli, "Elia Finzi, imprimeur de père en fils," in *Mestieri e professioni degli Italiani di Tunisia/Métiers et professions des Italiens de Tunisie,* ed. Silvia Finzi (Tunis: Editions Finzi, 2003), 278–84. The Finzi family continues to work in the printing business today in Tunisia. See also Michele Brondino, *La stampa italiana in Tunisia: Storia e società, 1838–1956* (Milan: Editoriale Jaca Book, 1998).

14. A. Larguèche and Kazdaghli, "Elia Finzi," 278–79.

15. This information kindly provided by Robert Zecker, University of Minnesota.

16. Ahmed Ben Miled, "Les hôpitaux étrangers à Tunis," *Rivista di Storia della Medicina* (1975): 160–65; Reports of June 30, 1854, and July 14, 1854, carton 349, CADN; and "Procedura," 34–35.

17. Cleveland, "Council"; Julia Clancy-Smith, "Gender in the City: Women, Migration and Contested Spaces in Tunis, c. 1830–1881," in *Africa's Urban Past,* ed. David M. Anderson and Richard Rathbone (Oxford: Currey, 2000), 189–204; Ridha' b. Rajab, "Al-shurta wa aman al-hadira, 1861–1864" (thèse du doctorat, 3ème cycle, Université de Tunis I, 1992); and "Procedura," 46.

18. Feise, "Observations," 8–9, 16.

19. Alessandro Triulzi, "Italian-Speaking Communities in Early Nineteenth Century Tunis," *ROMM* 9, 1 (1971): 167–77; Rainero Romain, *Les Italiens dans la Tunisie contemporaire* (Paris: Publisud, 2002); and Silvia Finzi, *Memorie italiane di Tunisia/Mémoires italiennes de Tunisie* (Tunisi: Finzi Editore, 2000).

20. Major Sir Grenville T. Temple, *Excursions in the Mediterranean: Algiers and Tunis,* 2 vols. (London: Saunders and Otley, 1835), 1: 184; Gaspary, 1847, carton 411, CADN; and Marc Barioli, *La vie quotidienne des Français en Algérie, 1830–1914* (Paris: Hachette, 1976), 18.

21. Moncef Charfeddine, *Deux siècles de théâtre en Tunisie* (Tunis: Les Éditions Ibn Charaf, n.d.), 19–27; and Cynthia Gray-Ware Metcalf, "From Morality Play to Celebrity: Women, Gender, and Performing Modernity in Egypt, 1850–1939" (PhD dissertation, History, University of Virginia, 2008).

22. Omar Carlier, "Le Café Maure: Sociabilité masculine et effervescence citadine (Algérie XVIIe–XXe siècles)," *AESC* 45, 4 (1990): 975–1003; and Jean-Louis Miège et al., *Le café en Méditerranée: Histoire, anthropologie, economie, XVIIIe–XXe siècles* (Aix-en-Provence: Université de Provence/CNRS, 1981).

23. Charles Lallemand, *Tunis au XIXe siècle* (Paris: Maison Quantin, 1890), 45.

24. Feise, "Observations," 6, 13–14.

25. D. Larguèche, "Commerce," 181–210.

26. Logbook, February 4, 1829, FO 77/20, NAUK; Chadly Ben Abdallah, *Fêtes religieuses et rythmes de Tunisie* (Tunis: J. P. S. Editions, 1988), 59–85; and Lallemand, *Tunis,* 44–49.

27. D. Larguèche, "Commerce," 200.

28. "Procedura," 3–5, 43.

29. D. Larguèche, "Commerce," 187–89; and Lallemand, *Tunis,* 44.

30. D. Larguèche, "Commerce," 187–89; and Lallemand, *Tunis,* 48.

31. Feise, "Observations," 11.

32. Ibid., 13–14.

33. Mohamed Houbbaida, "Le vin au Maroc précolonial: De la discrétion à l'exhibition," in *Horizons Maghrébins: Le droit à la mémoire,* special issue, *Manger au Maghrib,* ed. Mohammed Habib Samrakandi and Jean-Pierre Poulain (Toulouse: Presses Universitaires du Mirail, 2006), 97.

34. François Georgeon, "Ottomans and Drinkers: The Consumption of Alcohol in Istanbul in the Nineteenth Century," *Outside In: On the Margins of the Modern Middle East,* ed. Eugene Rogan (London: I. B. Tauris, 2002), 7–30.

35. Roderic H. Davison, "The French Dragomanate in Mid-Nineteenth Century Istanbul," in *Istanbul et les langues orientales,* ed. Frédéric Hitzel (Paris: L'Harmattan, 1997), 272.

36. Asma Moalla, *The Regency of Tunis and the Ottoman Porte, 1777–1814: Army and Government of a North-African Ottoman Eyâlet at the End of the Eighteenth Century* (London: Routledge, 2005), 134–36.

37. Gaspary, 1814–1819, carton 406B, c. 1839–1840, carton 409B, and carton 410A, CADN.

38. Gibson, September 3, 1834, FO 77/25, NAUK.

39. Gaspary, 1816, carton 406B, CADN.

40. Tunisian government circular to the consulates, March 26, 1831, carton 58, dossier 636, ANT.

41. Robert Brunschvig, "Tunis," *EI₁*, 8: 843–44; and Cleveland, "Council."

42. Wood to Muhammad al-Sadiq Bey, January 14, 1862, carton 58, dossier 636, ANT.

43. British vice-consul, Bizerte, September 9, 1829, carton 225, dossier 408, ANT.

44. French consul to bey, September 1874, carton 58, dossier 636, ANT.

45. Pierre Grandchamp, "Esclaves musulmans rachetés en Chrétienté," *RT*, nos. 53–54 (1943): 238–45.

46. Anonymous ms., c. 1835, carton "Confins Algéro-Tunisiens," F 80 1697, CAOM.

47. Deval to bey, April 17, 1835, carton 58, dossier 636, ANT.

48. Government circular to the consulates, March 7, 1837, carton 56, dossier 620, ANT.

49. French consul to bey, March, 16, 1852, carton 483, CADN.

50. Theis to bey, March 16, 1852, carton 58, dossier 636, ANT; and Baynes to bey, March 10, 1852, carton 227, dossier 411, ANT.

51. Baynes to bey, July 2, 1852, carton 58, dossier 636, ANT.

52. Joseph Greaves, *The Journal of Mr. Joseph Greaves, on a Visit to the Regency of Tunis*, in *Christian Researches in Syria and the Holy Land 1823 and 1824 in Furtherance of the Objects of the Church Missionary Society*, by Rev. William Jowett (London: Seeley & Son, 1825), 471.

53. David Prochaska, "History as Literature, Literature as History: Cagayous of Algiers," *AHR* 101, 3 (1996): 671–708.

54. Wood to the *khaznadar*, August 30, 1875, carton 228, dossier 413, ANT.

55. Wood to the *khaznadar*, July 20, 1878, carton 228, dossier 414, ANT.

56. Reade to London, May 31, 1846, FO 335/92/5, NAUK. Mahdiya's British agent was a Tuscan Jewish merchant, Bensasson, who resided with his family there and engaged in commerce.

57. Wood to bey, December 17, 1862, carton 58, dossier 636, ANT.

58. This affair involved Khayr al-Din plus the governor of the province and the French and English consuls, since the rented house cum tavern was the property of a French protégé, while the renter and freelance tavern keeper was Maltese; apparently the governor had first contacted the bey. De Vallat to Khayr al-Din, January 14, 1874, and Wood to Khayr al-Din, January 16, 1874, carton 58, dossier 636, ANT.

59. Wood to Khayr al-Din, July 20, 1878, carton 58, dossier 636, ANT.

60. Louis Créput, "Rapport sur Nabeul," 1882, Recueil 5 (bobine 5), no. 1, p. 13, ISHMN. See also Raymond-Joseph Matignon, *L'art médical à Tunis* (Bordeaux: Paul Cassignol, 1901), 85–87.

61. Numerous consular reports attest to this; for example, Reade's 1846 letter to London detailing the disorders in a tavern owned by a Maltese in Sousse, FO 335/92/5, NAUK. See Feise, "Observations," 11, on the *private* consumption of alcohol by Muslims, which Temple in 1833 confirms in *Excursions*, 1: 188–89.

62. Wood to prime minister, February 26, 1878, carton 56, dossier 620, ANT.

63. Cleveland, "Council," 49.

64. Pierre Grandchamp, "Le fondouk des Français," *CT* 13 (1965): 39–49.

65. A. Larguèche, *Ombres*, 79–82.

66. Dalenda Larguèche, "La Tunisie aux Expositions Universelles de Paris," *Les relations franco-tunisiennes au miroir des élites XVIIIe, XIXe, XXe siècles* (Tunis: Faculté des Lettres de la Manouba, 1994), 71–111.

67. Gaspary, May 17, 1847, carton 411A, CADN; and Cubisol to Béclard, September 27, 1854, carton 412, CADN.

68. *al-Ra'id al-Rasmi*, Tunis, nos. 268–270, 1860–1861, BNT.

69. Régence de Tunis, Protectorat Français, Direction de l'Agriculture et du Commerce, *Notice sur la Tunisie* (Tunis: Imprimerie Générale, 1899), 5–7. Several steamship companies, among them La Compagnie Trans-Atlantique and La Compagnie de Navigation Mixte, operated in Tunis; the growth of modern ship transportation between Europe and North Africa has not been studied.

70. Temple, *Excursions*, 1: 22; and Évariste Bavoux, *Alger: Voyage politique et descriptif dans le nord de l'Afrique*, 2 vols. (Paris: Chez Brockhaus et Avenarius, 1841), 2: 133.

71. Lady Mary E. Herbert, *A Search After Sunshine, or Algeria in 1871* (London: Bentley, 1872), 94–95.

72. Joëlle Redouane, "La présence Anglaise en Algérie de 1830 à 1930," *ROMM*, 38, 2 (1984): 15–36.

73. Eric T. Jennings, *Curing the Colonizer: Hydrotherapy, Climatology, and French Colonial Spas* (Durham: Duke University Press, 2006), 154–77.

74. Roches to bey, January 10, 1860, carton 207, dossier 96, ANT; and Marcel Gandolphe, "La vie à Tunis, 1840–1881," in *Histoire de la ville de Tunis*, ed. Charles-Henri Dessort (Algiers: Pfister, 1926), 166.

75. Greaves, *Journal*, 472.

76. "Confins Algéro-Tunisiens," F 80 1697, CAOM.

77. Le Capitaine XXX, *Une promenade à Tunis en 1842* (Paris: Dentu, 1844), 76–77.

78. Planel, "De la nation," 3: 754, quote p. 586.

79. Planel, "De la nation," 3: 734; Gandolphe, "La vie," 162; and Wood to Botmiliau, July 18, 1872, carton 382, CADN.

80. Planel, "De la nation," 3: 733; and Declaration, signed by Clermont Cerenhe, February 5, 1873, carton 381, CADN.

81. Foreign minister, Paris, to governor-general, Algiers, "Confins Algéro-Tunisiens," F 80 1697, CAOM.

82. Mohamed Bergaoui, *Tourisme et voyages en Tunisie: Les années de la Régence*, 3rd ed. (Tunis: Simpact, 2005), 31.

83. Planel, "De la nation," 3: 585–86, 733–34, 748; French vice-consul, La Goulette, August 25, 1872, carton 413, CADN.

84. Gaspary, carton 411A, CADN.

85. French vice-consul, La Goulette, January 31, 1874, carton 413, CADN; and Planel, "De la nation," 3: 593.

86. Eugène Poiré, *La Tunisie française* (Paris: Plon, 1892), 207.

87. Bergaoui, *Tourisme*, 48–49.

88. Mark R. Cohen, "Introduction: Poverty and Charity in Past Times," *Journal of Interdisciplinary History* 35, 3 (2005): 347–60; and Rachel G. Fuchs, *Poor and Pregnant in Paris: Strategies for Survival in the Nineteenth Century* (New Brunswick: Rutgers Univer-

sity Press, 1992), 1–18. On poverty in precolonial Tunis, especially for Jewish and African minorities, see A. Larguèche, *Ombres;* and Fanny Colonna, ed., *Etre marginal au Maghreb* (Tunis: Alif, 1993).

89. Ayse Bugra, "Poverty and Citizenship: An Overview of the Social-Policy Environment in Republican Turkey," *IJMES* 39 (2007): 33–52, quote p. 33.

90. Jean Ganiage, "Les Européens en Tunisie au milieu du XIXe siècle," *CT* 3 (1955): 389–421.

91. Bin Diyaf, *Ithaf,* 6/8: 118–19.

92. A. Larguèche, *Ombres,* 35–39. It is instructive to compare Tunisian state efforts to deal with the poor and poverty with Cairo, where already by the middle of the nineteenth century hospitals and other institutions of poor relief were employed to confine city populations deemed undesirable as well as to identify groups for forcible return to villages. See Mine Ener, "At the Crossroads of Empires: Policies toward the Poor in Early- to Mid-Nineteenth-Century Egypt," *SSH* 26, 2 (Summer 2002): 393–426.

93. In addition to legal sanctuary, shrines served as social welfare centers; in 1857 Daddu bint Ahmad died there and was buried nearby at the expense of the *bayt al-mal,* as were a number of poor women from the lowest stratum of urban society who were mainly "women without men," that is, without kin. Dalenda Larguèche and Abdelhamid Larguèche, *Marginales en terre d'Islam* (Tunis: CÉRÈS, 1992), 117.

94. Ali Chenoufi, ed. *Le ministre Khéreddine et ses contemporains* (Tunis: Beit al-Hikma, 1990), 75.

95. Muhammad Salih Mzali, introduction in *Min rasa'il Ibn Abi al-Diyaf* (Tunis: al-Dar al-Tunisiya lil-Nashr, 1969), 18.

96. Béclard to Ahmad Bey, October 19, 1854, carton 64, dossier 755, ANT. On Catholic missionary poor relief, see Matignon, *Médical,* 49–52, 68; and Mgr. Baunard, *Le Cardinal Lavigerie,* 2 vols. (Paris: J. De Gigord, 1922), 1: 493.

97. Planel, "De la nation," 1: 49, and 3: 751.

98. Gaspary, November 9, 1818, carton 406B, CADN.

99. Bin Diyaf, *Ithaf,* 3/4: 165; and Nancy Gallagher, *Medicine and Power in Tunisia, 1780–1900* (Cambridge: Cambridge University Press, 1983), 33–39, also chapter 7.

100. Fassy file, 1815–1827, carton 77, CCM.

101. French consul, Tunis, to Marseilles, June 6, 1819, Fassy file, 1815–1827, carton 77, CCM.

102. Jean Ganiage, *La population européenne de Tunis* (Paris: Presses Universitaires de France, 1960), 17.

103. Head *(deputé)* of the French trading community, Tunis, to Marseilles, April 13, 1828, carton 78, CCM.

104. Logbook, 1830, FO 77/21, NAUK.

105. Luigi Demech, *The British Consulate in Tunis: Critical Remarks* (Malta: Albion Press, 1868), 43.

106. Gaspary, September 7 and 9, 1816, carton 406B, CADN.

107. Gaspary, September 24, 1847, carton 411A, CADN.

108. French consul, Tunis, to Marseilles, April 13, 1828, carton 78, CCM.

109. Arthur Pellegrin, "Le vieux Tunis: Les noms de rue dans la ville arabe," in *Voyages*

en Tunisie, 1850–1950, ed. Claude Canceil (Tunis: Editions Nirvana, 2005), 37; and letters exchanged between Rousseau and Ahmad Bey, September 1848, carton 206, dossier 88, ANT.

110. A. Larguèche, *Ombres,* 37.

111. Rachel Sturman, "Property and Attachments: Defining Autonomy and the Claims of Family in Nineteenth-Century Western India," *CSSH* 47, 3 (2005): 611–37.

CHAPTER 5

1. Stevens to Muhammad al-Sadiq Bey, September 14, 1874, carton 228, dossier 413, ANT.

2. David Prochaska, "History as Literature, Literature as History: Gagayous of Algiers," *AHR* 101, 3 (1996): 671, glosses *"faire le kif"* in the Algiers street patois as "seeking pleasure." Mohamed Kerrou and Moncef M'Halla in "La prostitution dans la médina de Tunis aux XIXe et XX siècles," in *Etre marginal au Maghreb,* ed. Fanny Colonna and Zakya Daoud (Paris: Éditions du CNRS, 1993), 207, note that the word "kif" designated nighttime debauchery and drugs. See also Raymond-Joseph Matignon, *L'art médical à Tunis* (Bordeaux: Paul Cassignol, 1901), 87. Kif's legal status after 1881 has not been studied; it appears to have been tolerated.

3. The term "contraband" is shorthand for a constellation of extralegal or illegal exchanges, bargains, and transactions; see Julia Clancy-Smith, "The Maghrib and the Mediterranean World in the Nineteenth Century: Illicit Exchanges, Migrants, and Social Marginals" in *The Maghrib in Question: Essays in History and Historiography,* ed. Michel Le Gall and Kenneth Perkins (Austin: University of Texas Press, 1999), 222–49; and Alan L. Karras, *Smuggling: Contraband and Corruption in World History* (Lanham: Rowman & Littlefield, 2009).

4. Capitaines Rozet and Carette, *Algérie in l'univers pittoresque: Histoire et description de tous les peuples, de leurs religions, moeurs, coutumes, industrie, &* (Paris: Firmin Didot, 1850), 27–28; and Jamil M. Abun-Nasr, *A History of the Maghrib in the Islamic Period* (Cambridge: Cambridge University Press, 1987), 249.

5. Alejandro Portes, "Economic Sociology and the Sociology of Immigration: A Conceptual Overview," in *The Economic Sociology of Immigration,* ed. Alejandro Portes (New York: Russell Sage Foundation, 1995), 30–31.

6. Richard A. Lobban, ed., *Middle Eastern Women and the Invisible Economy* (Gainesville: University of Florida Press, 1998), 3–6; Richard A. Lobban, "Responding to Middle Eastern Urban Poverty: The Informal Economy in Tunis," in *Population, Poverty, and Politics in Middle East Cities,* ed. Michael E. Bonine (Gainesville: University Press of Florida, 1997), 85–112; and Milton Santos, *The Shared Space: The Two Circuits of the Urban Economy in Underdeveloped Countries* (London: Methuen, 1979).

7. Charles P. Issawi, *An Economic History of the Middle East and North Africa* (New York: Columbia University Press, 1992), 19. The convention established a 3 percent ad valorem import duty, 12 percent export duty, and 3 percent transit tax. Issawi saw it as a major turning point because British consular authorities presumably had the means to implement provisions in Ottoman port cities, which was not always the case. James C.

Scott, *Seeing Like a State: How Certain Schemes to Improve the Human Condition Have Failed* (New Haven: Yale University Press, 1998), 1–8; and Willem van Schendel and Itty Abraham, eds., *Illicit Flows and Criminal Things: States, Borders, and the Other Side of Globalization* (Bloomington: Indiana University Press, 2005), 1–37.

8. Janet Roitman, *Fiscal Disobedience: An Anthropology of Economic Regulation in Central Africa* (Princeton: Princeton University Press, 2004), 4; Josiah McC. Heyman, "Ports of Entry as Nodes in the World System," *Identities: Global Studies in Culture and Power* 11, 3 (2004): 303–27; and Marcus Rediker, *The Slave Ship: A Human History* (New York: Viking, 2007). The kinds of historical studies that Rediker had in mind, abundant for the Atlantic world, will have to wait until historians of North Africa take up the challenge.

9. Eyal Ginio, "Migrants and Workers in an Ottoman Port: Ottoman Salonica in the Eighteenth Century," in *Outside In: On the Margins of the Modern Middle East,* ed. Eugene Rogan (London: I. B. Tauris, 2002), 126–48.

10. Reade to bey, July 30, 1836, carton 225, dossier 408, ANT.

11. Léon Denis, *Tunis et l'île de Sardaigne: Souvenirs de voyage* (Tours: Imprimerie E. Arrault, 1884), 5.

12. British agent, Sfax, to Reade, Tunis, October 17, 1831, FO 77/22, NAUK. The agent noted that four pilgrims had died of cholera.

13. Gaspary, 1839–1840, carton 409B, CADN.

14. Ibid. On debtors, see Wood to Conti, October 1879, carton 228, dossier 414, ANT.

15. Richardson, "Account," 146.

16. Wood to Muhammad al-Sadiq Bey, September 14, 1862, carton 227, dossier 411, ANT. In 1741 an Italian theatrical group left Genoa for southern France but was seized by Tunisian corsairs flying the French flag and held in captivity in Tunis. Moncef Charfeddine, *Deux siècles de théâtre en Tunisie* (Tunis: Les Éditions Ibn Charaf, n.d.), 6.

17. P. A. Hennique, *Les caboteurs et pêcheurs de la côte de Tunisie* (Paris: Gauthier Villars, 1888).

18. Richardson, "Account," 174.

19. J. Donald Hughes, *Pan's Travail: Environmental Problems of the Ancient Greeks and Romans* (Baltimore: Johns Hopkins University Press, 1994), 13.

20. E. De Fages and C. Ponzevera, *Les pêches maritimes de la Tunisie,* 2nd ed. (Tunis: Editions Bouslama, 1977), 103; and Jean Ganiage, *Les origines du Protectorat Français en Tunisie (1861–1881),* 2nd ed. (Tunis: Maison Tunisienne de l'Édition, 1968), 597. The ruins of an Italian tuna factory remain on an islet in Munastir's port, now turned into an ultralux tourist complex.

21. Mary Wood's school exercise book, Box 7, RW.

22. Gérard Crespo, *Les Italiens en Algérie, 1830–1960: Histoire et sociologie d'une migration* (Calvisson: J. Gandini, 1994), 30–34; Gaston Loth, *Le peuplement italien en Tunisie et en Algérie* (Paris: Colin, 1905), 269–70; and Lady Mary E. Herbert, *A Search After Sunshine, or Algeria in 1871* (London: Bentley, 1872), 243.

23. Hassine Hamza, "Les pêcheurs saisonniers Italiens à Mahdia (1871–1945)," in *Etre marginal au Maghreb,* ed. Fanny Colonna and Zakya Daoud (Tunis: Alif, 1993), 155–59; Eugène Poiré, *La Tunisie française* (Paris: Plon, 1892), 155–59; Roman H. Rainero, *Les Ita-*

liens dans la Tunisie contemporain (Paris: Éditions Publisud, 2002), 21–24; and De Fages and Ponzevera, *Pêches,* 39.

24. British consul to Muhammad al-Sadiq Bey, October 28, 1879, carton 228, dossier 414, ANT.

25. Ibid.

26. Hamza, "Pêcheurs," 156.

27. British consul to Muhammad al-Sadiq Bey, October 28, 1879, carton 228, dossier 414, ANT.

28. Hamza, "Pêcheurs," 156.

29. The Tunisian National Archives, H series, correspondence with foreign states, contains hundreds of documented cases of seamen caught or suspected of smuggling.

30. Reade, July 25, 1837, FO 77/30, NAUK.

31. Bin Diyaf, *Ithaf,* 4/6: 158.

32. Richardson, "Account," 57–58.

33. Reade, November 14, 1833, FO 77/25, NAUK.

34. Ibid.

35. Baynes to Ahmad Bey, July 4, 1855, carton 227, dossier 411, ANT.

36. French consul to Ahmad Bey, June 26, 1851, carton 483, CADN.

37. Bin Diyaf, *Ithaf,* 3/4: 232–33; André Raymond, *Chronique,* 2: 77–79; and Reade, November 12, 1839, FO 102/6, NAUK.

38. A popular British travel guide portrayed Ghar al-Milh as a smuggling center, perhaps to lure tourists. *Murray's Handbook for Travelers in Algeria and Tunis* (London: John Murray, 1891).

39. French foreign minister to governor-general of Algeria, May 1834, Archives du Gouvernement Générale de l'Algérie, F 80 1420, CAOM.

40. Reade, November 12, 1839, FO 102/6, NAUK.

41. *Harlequin or Broadsheet of the Mediterranean,* no. 97, November 16, 1839, p. 7, BL.

42. Julia Clancy-Smith, *Rebel and Saint: Muslim Notables, Populist Protest, Colonial Encounters (Algeria and Tunisia, 1800–1904)* (Berkeley: University of California Press, 1994), 159–67.

43. Julia Clancy-Smith, "Saints, Mahdis, and Arms: Religion and Resistance in Nineteenth Century North Africa," in *Islam, Politics, and Social Movements,* ed. Edmund Burke, III, and Ira M. Lapidus (Berkeley: University of California Press, 1988), 60–80.

44. Wood to Khayr al-Din, January 17, 1874, carton 228, dossier 413, ANT.

45. Muhammad al-Sadiq Bey to Wood, November 16, 1869, carton 227, dossier 412, ANT.

46. Denis Mack Smith, *A History of Sicily* (London: Chatoo & Windus, 1968), 390; and Reade to Ahmad Bey, January 3, 1840, carton 226, dossier 410, ANT.

47. Feise, "Observations," 6, 13–14; and Ahmed Abdesselem, *Les historiens tunisiens des XVIIe, XVIIIe et XIXe siècles: Essai d'histoire culturelle* (Paris: Librairie Klincksieck, 1973), 92–94.

48. John R. McNeill, *The Mountains of the Mediterranean World: An Environmental History* (Cambridge: Cambridge University Press, 1992), 257–60, points out that in Morocco's Rif mountains, "kif" denotes tobacco blended with marijuana.

49. Bin Diyaf, *Ithaf,* 3/2: 121.

50. Allan Christelow, *Muslim Law Courts and the French Colonial State in Algeria* (Princeton: Princeton University Press, 1985), 85–86, quote p. 85.

51. Ibid., quote p. 85–86. On mental alienation and drug use among North Africans, see Richard C. Keller, *Colonial Madness: Psychiatry in French North Africa* (Chicago: University of Chicago Press, 2007), 144–47.

52. Christelow, *Courts,* 86, note 9.

53. French ship captain, Bougie, March 1856, based upon intelligence from spies since 1855, 1 H 13 (1856), Archives du Gouvernement Général de l' Algérie, CAOM.

54. For Gibraltar, see *The Spanish Red Book on Gibraltar: Documents Presented to the Spanish Cortes by the Minister of Foreign Affairs* (Madrid, 1965), 35–43. The British played a leading role in smuggling English manufactures into Spain from Gibraltar after the 1841 First General Customs Tariff.

55. Wood to Botmiliau, April 11, 1868, and June 10, 1868, carton 382, CADN.

56. Ibid.

57. Ibid.

58. Dalenda Larguèche, *Territoire sans frontières: La contrebande et ses réseaux dans la Régence de Tunis au XIXe siècle* (Tunis: Centre de Publication Universitaire, 2001), 50–62.

59. Jean Mathiex, "Le ravitaillement moghrebin de Malte au XVIIIe siècle," *CT* 2 (1954): 191–96, quote p. 191. See also Desmond Gregory, *Sicily: The Insecure Base; A History of the British Occupation, 1806–1815* (London: Associated University Presses, 1988), 137–40; and Jane C. Schneider and Peter T. Schneider, *Festival of the Poor: Fertility Decline and the Ideology of Class in Sicily, 1860–1980* (Tucson: University of Arizona Press, 1996), 66–69.

60. *Memoir on the Finances of Malta, under the Government of the Order of St. John of Jerusalem, during the Last Years of its Dominion and as Compared with Those of the Present Time* (Malta: Printed at the Government Press, 1836), 31.

61. Ibid., 70–71.

62. Smith, *Sicily,* 380–82, quotes pp. 380–81.

63. Gregory, *Sicily,* 137–40; Smith, *Sicily,* 380–82; Schneider, *Festival,* 66–69; and Jean Ganiage, *La population européenne de Tunis au milieu du XIXe siècle: Étude démographique* (Paris: Presses Universitaires de France, 1960), 19. See also Sabra J. Webber, *Romancing the Real: Folklore and Ethnographic Representation in North Africa* (Philadelphia: University of Pennsylvania Press, 1991), 40–43, and 48. Sometime in the early Protectorate, the Italian consul general bought tracts of land on the Cap Bon and resold small parcels to copatriots from Pantellaria who arrived en masse. The peninsula's rich soils also attracted Algerians who fled to the Cap Bon soon after France's invasion.

64. D. Larguèche, *Territoire,* 50–62.

65. Baynes to bey, October 26, 1853, and December 29, 1853, carton 227, dossier 411, ANT.

66. Xuereb, OBL.

67. Ibid. After the Xuereb affair, Reade's attitude toward his Maltese protégés worsened. Previously he had defended them, at times against charges of misconduct by other European consuls or beylical authorities, if facts were in dispute; but after 1843, Reade rarely sided with the Maltese.

68. Roches to Arnaud, consular agent, Mahdiya, June 25, 1858, carton 485, CADN.

69. De Lagau to Ahmad Bey, June 13, 1839, carton 206, dossier 86, ANT.

70. Roches to Arnaud, consular agent, Mahdiya, June 25, 1858, carton 485, CADN.

71. Documents from 1850–1862, carton 227, dossier 411, ANT, suggest this. Regulations differed dramatically from port to port; in 1850 quarantine was ten days in Tripoli but twenty-one days in Naples, and enforcement varied considerably.

72. Levy, Sousse, to Baynes, January 7, 1851, carton 227, dossier 411, ANT.

73. Carleton, Sfax, to Wood, September 1862, carton 227, dossier 411, ANT.

74. Reade to Mustafa Bey, July 30, 1836, carton 225, dossier 408, ANT. Other acts of violence against Maltese were reported in November 5, 1837, carton 225, dossier 408; and May 11, 1838, August 31, 1838, and December 5, 1838, carton 226, dossier 409, ANT.

75. Reade, July 6, 1835, FO 77/29, NAUK.

76. Alexandre Deval to Mustafa Bey, May 30, 1836, carton 206, dossier 84, ANT.

77. Reade, July 25, 1837, FO 77/30, NAUK.

78. Maltese involvement in contraband is amply documented by archival records in North Africa and Europe. For examples, see Archives de l'armée de terre, Vincennes, Algérie, M 1319/20–23, General Pelet's report of 1834, and the reports in the FO 335 series, 1845–1870, NAUK.

79. Lobban, "Poverty," 97; Kerrou and M'Halla, "Prostitution," 201–21; and Dalenda Larguèche and Abdelhamid Larguèche, *Marginales en terre d'Islam* (Tunis: Cérès Productions, 1992), 13–83. See also Leslie Peirce, "Writing Histories of Sexuality in the Middle East," *AHR* 114, 5 (2009): 1325–39.

80. Christelle Taraud, *La prostitution coloniale: Algérie, Tunisie, Maroc* (1830–1962) (Paris: Payot, 2003), 55–57; Larguèche and Larguèche, *Marginales,* 13; and Mohamed Larbi Snoussi, "La prostitution en Tunisie au temps de la colonization," in *La Tunisie mosaïque: Diasporas, cosmopolitisme, archéologies de l'identité,* ed. Jacques Alexandropoulos and Patrick Cabanel (Toulouse: Presses Universitaires du Mirail, 2000), 389–413.

81. Elyse Semerdjian, *"Off the Straight Path": Illicit Sex, Law, and Community in Ottoman Aleppo* (Syracuse: Syracuse University Press, 2008); Philippa Levine, *Prostitution, Race and Politics: Policing Venereal Disease in the British Empire* (London: Routledge, 2003), 231–56; Kerrou and M'Halla, "Prostitution," 205; and for the quote, Richardson, "Account," 69.

82. Raymond, *Chronique,* 2: 106–7.

83. Bin Diyaf, in *Ithaf,* 3/4: 262, clearly approved of the bey's decision to abolish this blameworthy state office. See also Raymond, *Chronique,* 2: 23; and Kerrou and M'Halla, "Prostitution," 207.

84. Larguèche and Larguèche, *Marginales,* 13–78; and Taraud, *Prostitution,* 186–90. Emancipation in Morocco also pushed African women into prostitution; see Mohammed Ennaji, *Serving the Master: Slavery and Society in Nineteenth-Century Morocco* (New York: St. Martins Press, 1999), 50.

85. Bin Diyaf, in *Ithaf,* 3/4: 197–98, reported with evident opprobrium the 1824 case of a Tunisian Jew wrongly accused of sexual relations with a Muslim woman in Tunis; both were executed, even though many believed the charges were false. The incident was publicized by numerous consular reports and travel accounts.

86. Reade to Foreign Office, letter marked "private," March 10, 1831, FO 77/22, NAUK.

87. Ibid.

88. Ganiage, *Population*, 49, note 3.

89. Larguèche and Larguèche, *Marginales*, 47–50.

90. Dumerque and Krieger to Roustan, March 1, 1877, carton 208, dossier 114, ANT.

91. Ibid.; and Roustan to prime minister, March 2, 1877, carton 208, dossier 114, ANT.

92. Ben Levy to Baynes, August 8, 1852, FO 335/101/16, NAUK.

93. Minna Rozen, "Strangers in a Strange Land: The Extraterritorial Status of Jews in Italy and the Ottoman Empire in the Sixteenth to the Eighteenth Centuries," in *Ottoman and Turkish Jewry: Community and Leadership*, ed. Aron Rodrigue (Bloomington: Indiana University, 1992), 123–66.

94. Wood to the prime minister, letter marked "private," October 12, 1876, carton 288, dossier 413, ANT.

95. Ganiage, *Origines*, 45.

96. Wood to the *khaznadar*, March 29, 1878, carton 228, dossier 414, ANT.

97. Larguèche and Larguèche, *Marginales*, 47.

98. Wood to Musali, May 29, 1862, carton 227, dossier 411, ANT.

99. Taraud, *Prostitution*, 56–57.

100. "Procedura," testimony of Gianmaria Hiberras, February 27, 1868.

101. Ibid.

102. "Procedura," first testimony of Giovanna Tellini, February 27, 1868.

103. "Procedura," Trasferta d'Ufficio, February 27, 1868, p. 1.

104. "Procedura," testimony of Gianmaria Hiberras, February 27, 1868.

105. Ibid.

106. "Procedura," second testimony of Giovanna Tellini, March 12, 1868.

107. "Procedura," Trasferta d'Ufficio, February 27, 1868.

108. "Procedura," second testimony of Giovanna Tellini, March 12, 1868.

109. Ibid. For a gendered analysis of the proceedings, see Julia Clancy-Smith, "Locating Women as Migrants in Nineteenth-Century Tunis," in *Contesting Archives: Historians Develop Methodologies for Finding Women in the Sources*, ed. Nupur Chaudhuri, Sherry Katz, and Mary Elizabeth Perry (Urbana-Champaign: University of Illinois Press, 2010), 35–55.

110. J. Rousseau, 1881, "Correspondance au sujet de la contrabande de tabac," carton 96, dossier 141, ANT.

111. There was a mafia presence in Tunisia by the time of the early Protectorate, although its origins remain uncertain. Letizia Paoli, *Mafia Brotherhoods: Organized Crime Italian Style* (New York: Oxford University Press, 2003), 33, states that mafia groups dated from 1838 and were established on the Sicilian coast to take advantage of maritime smuggling.

112. Wood to prime minister, October 18, 1878, carton 228, dossier 414, ANT.

113. François Renault, *Lavigerie, l'esclavage Africain et l'Europe*, 2 vols. (Paris: Éditions E. de Boccard, 1971), 2: 13.

114. Brown, *Surest Path*, 40.

115. Schendel and Abraham, *Illicit Flows*.

116. In Pierre Chenal's classic 1938 feature film, *La Maison du Maltais*, the hero was a Maltese smuggler; the film was based upon Jean Vignaud's novel, *La Maison du Maltais* (Paris: Plon, 1926). Philip S. Khoury, "Abu Ali al-Kilawi: A Damascus Qabaday," in

Struggle and Survival in the Modern Middle East, ed. Edmund Burke, III, and David N. Yaghoubian, 2nd ed. (Berkeley: University of California Press, 2006), 152–63.

117. De Lagau to Ahmad Bey, June 13, 1839, carton 206, dossier 86, ANT.

118. André Martel, *Luis-Arnold et Joseph Allegro: Consuls du bey de Tunis à Bône* (Paris: Presses Universitaires de France, 1967), 129.

119. Ganiage, *Origines,* 48–55, 454–59; Raymond Burgard, "Julius von Eckardt: Consul général d'Allemagne à Tunis (1885–1889)," *RT* 5 (1931): 124–25.

CHAPTER 6

1. Cubisol to Botmilieu, December 29, 1870, carton 413, CADN. Nicola was most likely a member of the Papal Zouaves, organized in 1860 by General de Lamoricière, who had earlier fought in Algeria, to defend the papal state. The Papal Zouaves, a voluntary army, recruited mainly young Catholic bachelors to aid Pius IX in struggles against the anti-clerical Italian Risorgimento. With Victor Emmanuel's 1870 occupation of Rome, the Papal Zouaves were disbanded.

2. Deposition, Mother Superior Germaine Audouard, December 18, 1870, carton 413, CADN.

3. Cubisol, December 29, 1870, carton 413, CADN.

4. Stephen A. Toth, *Beyond Papillon: The French Overseas Penal Colonies, 1854–1952* (Lincoln: University of Nebraska Press, 2006).

5. Jasper Yeates Brinton, *The Mixed Courts of Egypt,* rev. ed. (New Haven: Yale University Press, 1968); and Byron Cannon, *Politics of Law and the Courts in Nineteenth-Century Egypt* (Salt Lake City: University of Utah Press, 1988).

6. Lauren Benton, *Law and Colonial Cultures: Legal Regimes in World History, 1400–1900* (Cambridge: Cambridge University Press, 2002), traces the complex historical transition from older pluralistic legal orders to state-dominated legal orders, notably in colonial states. See also Anthony Anghie, *Imperialism, Sovereignty, and the Making of International Law* (Cambridge: Cambridge University Press, 2005); Christian Windler, *La diplomatie comme expérience de l'autre: Consuls français au Maghreb (1700–1840)* (Geneva: Droz, 2002); and Marcel A. Boisard's "On the Probable Influence of Islam on Western Public and International Law," *IJMES* 11, 4 (1980): 429–50. The quote is from Richard J. Ross, "Puritan Godly Discipline in Comparative Perspective: Legal Pluralism and the Sources of 'Intensity,'" *AHR* 113, 4 (2008): 991.

7. The category "women" demands differentiation by religion, class, ethnic or racial origins, age, marital status, and lineage. Women from merchant-consul families resident in Tunis enjoyed access to property, secure membership in status groups, and at times patronage from the palace. Social rank offered certain avenues for redress, while perhaps closing off others. Aside from an inheritance controversy involving a wealthy Muslim widow in late-eighteenth-century Patna, Benton's work devotes little space to women and gender in relation to legal pluralism. Benton, *Law,* 140–45.

8. Richardson, "Account," 25.

9. Leon Carl Brown, *The Tunisia of Ahmad Bey, 1837–1855* (Princeton: Princeton University Press, 1974), 93–145.

10. Arnold H. Green, *The Tunisian Ulama, 1873–1915: Social Structure and Response to Ideological Currents* (Leiden: E. J. Brill, 1978), 49–57, quote p. 52; and Abdelhamid Hénia, *Propriété et stratégies sociales à Tunis (XVIe–XIXe siècles)* (Tunis: Faculté des Sciences Humaines et Sociales de Tunis, 1999).

11. Richardson, "Account," 47.

12. Madeline Zilfi's arguments in "A Medrese for the Palace: Ottoman Dynastic Legitimation in the Eighteenth Century," *JAOS* 113, 2 (1993): 184–191, work well for Tunisia.

13. Khelifa Chater, *Dépendance et mutations précoloniales: La Régence de Tunis de 1815 à 1857* (Tunis: Publications de l'Université de Tunis, 1984), 355–61.

14. On the Capitulations, or *imtiyazat*, from the Arabic root *m-y-z*, "to separate or distinguish but also to favor" in the eighth form, with implicit meaning of reciprocity, see the article "Imtiyazat," *EI2*, 3: 1178–95. In nineteenth-century Egypt, extraterritoriality, as practiced on the ground in daily negotiations, "was at variance with the capitulations" as well as with an order-in-council issued by London on the issue. Michael J. Reimer, *Colonial Bridgehead: Government and Society in Alexandria, 1807–1882* (Cairo: American University in Cairo Press, 1997), 86–87; also, Jens Hanssen, *Fin de Siècle Beirut: The Making of an Ottoman Provincial Capital* (Oxford: Clarendon Press, 2005).

15. Richardson, "Account," 26. Bernard Doumerc's "Le Consul Venitien de Tunis (1470–1473)," *CT* 43, 58 (1991): 447–78, and other work on the earlier periods, reminds us of the persistence over centuries of protection shared by Muslim and Christian states.

16. Windler, *Diplomatie*, 210; and J. S. Woodford, *The City of Tunis: Evolution of an Urban System* (Cambridgeshire: Middle East and North African Studies Press, 1990).

17. Daniel Panzac, *Barbary Corsairs: The End of a Legend, 1800–1820* (Leiden: Brill, 2005), 335–37, lists the treaties. See also Ganiage, *Origines*, 14–15.

18. French consul to the consul of Sardinia, Tunis, May 16, 1852, carton 483, CADN.

19. Julia Clancy-Smith, "Europe and Its Social Marginals in 19th-Century Mediterranean North Africa," *Outside In: On the Margins of the Modern Middle East,* ed. Eugene Rogan (London: I. B. Tauris, 2002), 149–82; and Julia Clancy-Smith, "Women, Gender and Migration along a Mediterranean Frontier: Pre-Colonial Tunisia, c. 1815–c.1870," in *Gender and History* 17, 1 (April 2005): 62–92.

20. Logbook, 1828–1830, FO 77/20–21, NAUK.

21. Ibid.

22. Ahmad Bey to Rousseau, 1848, carton 206, dossier 88, ANT.

23. French merchants, Tunis, September 4, 1838, carton 79, CCM.

24. Reade to London, November 2, 1833, FO 77/24, NAUK. Reade also observed that the lawlessness of the Maltese in Tunisia diminished Britain's international stature, as seen in "the unpleasant observations of the consuls of other powers."

25. Windler, *Diplomatie*, 9–34; and Allan Christelow, *Muslim Law Courts and the French Colonial State in Algeria* (Princeton: Princeton University Press, 1985). See Benton, *Law,* 140, note 25, on Weber's characterization of Islamic law.

26. A further example of this is that the deposition of Abu Shanaq of August 1866 in Arabic was admitted as evidence (carton 382, CADN) in the alleged murder of an infant.

27. Antony Anghie, "Finding the Peripheries: Sovereignty and Colonialism in Nineteenth-Century International Law," *Harvard International Law Journal* 40, 1 (Winter 1999): 1–80.

28. Xuereb, OBL.

29. Bin Diyaf, *Ithaf,* 3/4: 232–33.

30. Reade, October 3, 1836, FO 77/29, NAUK.

31. Ferriere, "Memorandum," 1847, FO 335 (96), NAUK, 10.

32. Richardson, "Account," 26.

33. Wood to bey, September 1862, carton 224, dossiers 403/404, ANT. The term "adjustment" meant adjudication, arbitration, or settlement of disputes.

34. Winder, *Diplomatie,* 179. Similar agreements had existed for centuries between Islamic and Christian states; see Boisard, "Influence," 433.

35. Reade, December 23, 1831, FO 77/22, NAUK.

36. Logbook, April 11, 1831, FO 77/23, NAUK.

37. Philippa Day, ed., *At Home in Carthage: The British in Tunisia* (Tunis: Trustees of St. Georges Church, 1992), 15. The Chapel of Saint Louis in Carthage, under France's protection, housed an enslaved African family prior to abolition.

38. Logbook, July 5, 1828 FO 77/20, NAUK.

39. Logbook, August 2, 1828 FO 77/20, NAUK.

40. Schwebel to Murali, May 13, 1837, carton 206, dossier 85, ANT.

41. Brown, *Tunisia,* 246–60.

42. Tulin to Beauval, December 9, 1864, carton 381, CADN.

43. Wood to Conti, 1879, carton 228, dossier 414, ANT.

44. Abdelhamid Larguèche, *Les ombres de la ville: Pauvres, marginaux et minoritaires à Tunis (XVIIIème et XIXè siècles)* (Tunis: Centre de Publication Universitaire, 1999), 185; and Julia Clancy-Smith, *Exemplary Women and Sacred Journeys: Women and Gender in Judaism, Christianity, and Islam from Late Antiquity to the Eve of Modernity* (Washington, D.C.: American Historical Association, 2006).

45. In 1851 a Tunisian subject, Ibrahim Gharbli, indebted to a Maltese, Felice Grima, for a quantity of olive oil, resided for weeks in a *zawiya* to escape repayment; Baynes to bey, January 14, 1851, carton 227, dossier 411, ANT.

46. Carton 201, dossier 25, ANT. On petitions *('arida/'ara'id)* in Egypt, see John T. Chalcraft, *The Striking Cabbies of Cairo and Other Stories: Crafts and Guilds in Egypt, 1863–1914* (New York: SUNY Press, 2005), 74–80.

47. Reade, September 3, 1828, FO 77/20, NAUK.

48. Reade, December 31, 1847, FO 335/96/10, NAUK.

49. Ibid. The coastal towns of Sousse, Munastir, and Mahdiya hosted the second-largest concentration of British protégés, 527, at least according to the statistics.

50. Reade, April 2, 1831, FO 77/22, NAUK.

51. Richardson, "Account," 18; and Chater, *Dépendance,* 355–61.

52. Reade, April 2, 1831, FO 77/22, NAUK.

53. Ferriere, "Memorandum," 1847, FO 335 (96), NAUK.

54. Reade, March 23, 1835, FO 77/26, NAUK.

55. Ibid.

56. Antonio Farrugia, 1844, carton 224, dossier 415, ANT.

57. Le Capitaine XXX, *Une promenade à Tunis en 1842* (Paris: Dentu, 1844), 77.

58. Radhika Viyas Mongia, "Race, Nationality, Mobility: A History of the Passport,"

in *After the Imperial Turn: Thinking With and Through the Nation,* ed. Antoinette Burton (Durham: Duke University Press, 2003), 197–214; John Torpey, *The Invention of the Passport: Surveillance, Citizenship and the State* (Cambridge: Cambridge University Press, 2000); Martin Lloyd, *The Passport: The History of Man's Most Travelled Document* (Stroud: Sutton Publishing, 2003); and Claudia Moatti and Wolfgang Kaiser, eds., *Gens de passage en méditerranée de l'antiquité à l'époque moderne: Procédures de contrôle et d'identification* (Paris: Maisonneuve & Larose, 2007).

59. British Embassy Circular, Constantinople, May 2, 1848, FO 335/99/9, NAUK.

60. Ibid.; and Yvonne J. Seng, "Fugitives and Factotums: Slaves in Early Sixteenth-Century Istanbul," *JESHO* 39, 2 (1996): 137.

61. The life of Louis-Arnold Allegro (1804–1868) is emblematic of the border crossers. Born in Tunis of Spanish parents, he joined a French regiment in Algeria around 1833 and later held the post of beylical consul to Bône, where he married a Muslim Kabyle woman, Khadija, in the 1840s, with whom he had five children. In 1851, he petitioned colonial authorities to conclude a civil marriage with Khadija under French law. André Martel, *Luis-Arnold et Joseph Allegro: Consuls du bey de Tunis à Bône* (Paris: Presses Universitaires de France, 1967), 72–74, quote p. 15.

62. Thomas W. Gallant, *Experiencing Dominion: Culture, Identity, and Power in the British Mediterranean* (Notre Dame: University of Notre Dame Press, 2002), 6–14; and Habib Kazdaghli, "Communautés méditerranéennes de Tunisie: Les Grecs de Tunisie; du Millet-i-Rum à l'assimilation française (XVIIe–XXe siècles)," *RMMM,* nos. 95–98 (2002): 449–76. Confusion over the Ionian Islands persisted; "Confidential Print on Turkey and the Ottoman Empire," no. 878, July 20, 1860, required twenty-seven pages to determine jurisdiction over Greek protégés.

63. Reade, March 23, 1835, FO 77/26, NAUK.

64. Logbook, September 18, 1828, FO 77/21, NAUK.

65. Gaspary, November 8, 1837, carton 409A, CADN.

66. Reade, January 26, 1836, FO 77/29, NAUK, reporting the 1834 incident.

67. Ahmad Bey to French consul, May 28, 1851, carton 483, CADN.

68. Roches to Wood, January 20, 1863, carton 349, CADN. Mansfield directed his letter to Wood, who sent it to Roches due to jurisdictional uncertainty.

69. Wood to Roches, August 9, 1864, carton 349, CADN.

70. July 14, 1842, carton 382, CADN. Affidavits or depositions in cases involving the Maltese were almost always in Italian. Appellate cases and the most serious criminal cases were usually heard by tribunals in Naples, Leghorn, Genoa, Malta, or Aix-en-Provence and, sometimes, Algiers.

71. Luigi Demech, *The British Consulate in Tunis: Critical Remarks* (Malta: Albion Press, 1868), 17–18.

72. A. Larguèche, *Ombres,* 180–251.

73. Raymond, *Chronique,* 2: 29; and A. Larguèche, *Ombres,* 208–12.

74. Logbook, October 6, 1828, FO 77/21, NAUK.

75. Baynes, February 10, 1851, FO 335/99 (9), NAUK.

76. Demech, *Consulate,* 41.

77. Ferriere to Baynes, January 26, 1852, FO 335/101/15, NAUK, regarding twenty dol-

lars bail by the Maltese innkeeper, Michel Galia, as security for a friend accused of a crime.

78. French consul to Ahmad Bey, October 29, 1851, carton 483, CADN.

79. Logbook, 1828–1830, FO 77/20–21, NAUK.

80. French consul to Sardinian consul, November 31, 1853, carton 349, CADN.

81. Gallant, *Dominion*, xiii.

82. Reade, November 24, 1835, FO 77/26, NAUK.

83. Bin Diyaf, *Ithaf*, 3/5: 282.

84. Ibid., 254.

85. Reade to bey, April 24, 1829, FO 77/21, NAUK.

86. Reade, December 30, 1836, FO 77/29, NAUK.

87. Ibid.

88. Ibid., enclosing Mustafa Bey's letter, December 20, 1836.

89. Bin Diyaf, *Ithaf*, 3/5: 267.

90. Reade, January 18, 1837, FO 77/30; and Reade, April 21, 1837, FO 77/30, NAUK.

91. Yvan Debbasch, *La nation française en Tunisie (1577–1835)* (Paris: Éditions Sirrey, 1957), 240–41.

92. Reade, November 2, 1833, FO 77/24, and Reade, November 24, 1835, FO 77/26, NAUK.

93. British consul, Algiers, February 13, 1858, FO 113/5, NAUK.

94. Debbasch, *Nation*, 237–44; and Clancy-Smith, "Women, Gender and Migration."

95. French consul, May 1846, carton 206, dossier 87, ANT.

96. On women's use of, and access to, courts, see Leslie Peirce, *Morality Tales: Law and Gender in the Ottoman Court of Aintab* (Berkeley: University of California Press, 2003); and Judith E. Tucker, *In the House of the Law: Gender and Islamic Law in Ottoman Syria and Palestine* (Berkeley: University of California Press, 1998).

97. Debbasch, *Nation*, 62–65.

98. Benton, *Law*, 26.

99. See Ussama Makdisi, *Artillery of Heaven: American Missionaries and the Failed Conversion of the Middle East* (Ithaca: Cornell University Press, 2008), on the Maronite hierarchy's violent reaction to As'ad al-Shidyaq's conversion to Protestantism. His brother Faris (1801–1887) also became a Protestant but left the Lebanon for Egypt, Malta, England, and Paris. In 1846, Faris met Ahmad Bey during the Tunisian delegation's visit to France and went to Tunis where he embraced Islam, taking the name Ahmad. Faris resurfaced in Istanbul circa 1860 but apparently returned to the religion of his ancestor prior to his death. See also Marc David Baer, *The Dönme: Jewish Converts, Muslim Revolutionaries, and Secular Turks* (Stanford: Stanford University Press, 2010).

100. Mercedes García-Arenal, ed., *Conversions Islamiques: Identités religieuses en Islam Méditerranéen* (Paris: Maisonneuve & Larose, 2001); and García-Arenal, "Conversion to Islam in the Muslim Mediterranean World," in *Individual and Society in the Mediterranean Muslim World: Issues and Sources*, ed. Robert Ilbert and Randi Deguilem (Aix-en-Provence: European Science Foundation, 1998), 12–23. For religious border crossing in the early modern era, see Molly Greene, *A Shared World: Christians and Muslims in the Early Modern Mediterranean* (Princeton: Princeton University Press, 2000), 89–95.

101. Planel, "De la nation," 2: 309–18, discusses Foreign Legion deserters, such as the Prussian Kruger, Muhammad after conversion, who served the Husaynid beys.

102. Salvatore Bono, "Conversions à l'époque coloniale," in Mercedes Garcia-Arenal, ed., *Conversions Islamiques: Identités religieuses en Islam méditerranéen* (Paris: Maisonneuve & Larose, 2001), 316; A. Larguèche, *Ombres*, 178; and Mohamed Kerrou, "Logiques de l'abjuration et de la conversion à l'Islam en Tunisie aux XIXe et XXe siècles," in *Conversions Islamiques: Identités religieuses en Islam méditerranéen*, ed. Mercedes García-Arenal (Paris: Maisonneuve & Larose, 2001), 325–65.

103. Planel, "De la nation," 2: 309, note 88, shows that individuals or couples crossed back and forth between Islam and Christianity in the course of their lives. Very restricted access to divorce for women in England only became available in 1859, in France in 1884. Since British officials in Malta avoided antagonizing the Church, canon law was in force; civil marriage or divorce did not exist. Adrianus Koster, "The Kappillani: The Changing Position of the Parish Priest in Malta," in *Religion, Power and Protest in Local Communities*, ed. Eric R. Wolf (Paris: Mouton, 1984), 185–211.

104. Reade, July 1830, FO 77/22, NAUK.

105. Ibid.

106. Brown, *Tunisia*, 245–46.

107. "Nationality," Confidential Print no. 978, July 22, 1861, OBL.

108. Wood to bey, November 7, 1865, carton 63, dossier 722 bis, ANT.

109. Laura Tabili, "Empire Is the Enemy of Love: Edith Noor's Progress and Other Stories," *Gender and History* 17, 1 (April 2005): 5–28. See also Leïla Blili Temime, *Histoire de familles: Mariages, répudiations et vie quotidienne à Tunis, 1875–1930* (Tunis: Éditions Script, 1999), 63–65. Widowhood in expatriate communities in North Africa deserves study; Muslim and Jewish societies strongly encouraged remarriage as soon as possible. See Kenda Mutongi, "'Worries of the Heart': Widowed Mothers, Daughters and Masculinities in Maragoli, Western Kenya, 1940–60," *JAH* 40, 1 (1999): 67–86.

110. For a fuller discussion, see Julia Clancy-Smith, "Migrations, Legal Pluralism, and Identities: Algerian 'Expatriates' in Colonial Tunisia," in *Identity, Memory and Nostalgia: France and Algeria, 1800–2000*, ed. Patricia Lorcin (New York: Syracuse University Press, 2005), 3–17; and Alain Messaoudi, "Être Algérien en Tunisie (1830–1962): La construction d'une catégorie nationale," *Correspondances* 54 (1999): 10–14.

111. Letters of June 23 and June 26, 1858, carton 485, CADN.

112. Vallat to Khayr al-Din, December 6, 1873, carton 207, dossier 105, ANT.

113. Clancy-Smith, "Migrations"; and Mohammed Kenbib, *Les protégés: Contribution à l'histoire contemporaine du Marco* (Rabat: Faculté des Lettres et des Sciences Humaines, 1996).

114. Lieutenant Prax, "Le commerce de Tunis avec l'intérieur de l'Afrique," F 80 1697, CAOM.

115. Ibid.

116. September 4, 1838, carton 79, "Commerce international, Tunisie," CCM. The *carte de sûreté* was established during the Terror to police the inhabitants of Paris. Citizens, defined as males older than fifteen years, were legally obliged to carry cards with name, age, profession, address, and birthplace; witnesses verified identity.

396 NOTES TO PAGES 236–244

117. French consul to bey, July 19, 1855, carton 484, CADN.

118. Christelow, *Courts,* 165–76. Whether the 1859 decree, bitterly contested by Algerian Muslims, encouraged emigration is a question worth posing.

119. French consul to bey, July 8 and August 3, 1855, carton 484, CADN.

120. French consul to bey, August 25, 1851, carton 483, CADN.

121. R. Arditti, Recueil des textes législatifs et juridiques concernant les Israelites de Tunisie de 1857 à 1913 (Tunis: Borrel, 1915); and Joshua Schreier, "Napoléon's Long Shadow: Morality, Civilization, and Jews in France and Algeria, 1808–1870," *FHS* 30, 1 (Winter 2007): 77–104.

122. French vice-consul, Mahdiya, February 10, 1866, carton 422, CADN.

123. Gérard Noiriel, *The French Melting Pot: Immigration, Citizenship, and National Identity,* trans. Geoffroy de Laforcade (Minneapolis: University of Minnesota Press, 1996), 45–90.

124. June 10, 1874, carton 422, CADN, contains the Arabic deposition.

125. French consul, January 10, 1860, carton 349, CADN.

126. "Projet de convention pour la naturalisation tunisienne à accorder aux immigrants algériens," 1876, F 80 1816, CAOM.

127. Planel, "De la nation," 3: 465.

128. Xuereb, OBL. The affair generated enormous interest and an equally enormous corpus of documentation. When the Italian consul in Egypt had a protégé arraigned in a Muslim court in 1849, months of uproar ensued among the European population; see Reimer, *Bridgehead,* 86–87.

129. Gaspary, March 10, 1844, carton 410A, CADN.

130. Brown, *Tunisia,* 247–51. The Gülhane decree of 1839, established new institutions guaranteeing security to all subjects, regardless of religion, in life, honor, and property; taxes were regularized and military conscription was implemented. The decree was akin to the 1789 Declaration of the Rights of Man, not so much in abstract principles as in practices.

131. Chater, *Dépendance,* 595–96.

132. Bin Diyaf, *Ithaf,* 4/6: 29–30, on subjects seeking foreign protection *(ihtima');* C. R. Pennell, "The British Consular Courts and Moroccan Muslim Identity: 'Christian' Justice as a Tool," *JNAS* 1, 2 (1996): 172–91; and C. R. Pennell, "Law on a Wild Frontier: Moroccans in the Spanish Courts in Melilla in the Nineteenth Century," *JNAS* 7, 3 (2002): 67–78.

133. Bin Diyaf, *Ithaf,* 4/7: 257–81; Kenneth J. Perkins, *A History of Modern Tunisia* (Cambridge: Cambridge University Press, 2004), 18–33; and Khalifa Chater, "Le constitutionalisme en Tunisie au 19éme siècle," *RTSS,* nos. 40–43 (1975): 243–72.

134. Le général commandant, March 11, 1883, carton 1 bis, bobine 504, ISHMN.

135. Gerald MacLean, *The Rise of Oriental Travel: English Visitors to the Ottoman Empire, 1580–1720* (London: Palgrave, 2006); and Suraiya Faroqhi, *The Ottoman Empire and the World around It* (London: Tauris, 2006).

136. Peirce, *Morality,* 1–3, 121–25.

137. Joseph Greaves, *The Journal of Mr. Joseph Greaves, on a Visit to the Regency of Tunis,* in *Christian Researches in Syria and the Holy Land 1823 and 1824 in Furtherance of the Objects of the Church Missionary Society,* by Rev. William Jowett (London: Seeley & Son, 1825), 467–68.

138. Jessica Harland-Jacobs, "'Hands Across the Sea': The Masonic Network, British Imperialism, and the North Atlantic World," *Oceans Connect* 89, 2 (April 1999): 237–53.

139. Noiriel, *Melting Pot*, 67–68, paid scant attention to the influence of colonial laws *upon* the metropole.

140. Mahmud Bayram al-Tunisi, *Mudhakkirati: al-Majmu'a al-Kamila* (Tunis: Dar al-Janub lil-Nashr, 2001), 119.

CHAPTER 7

1. Sarah A. Curtis, *Civilizing Habits: Women Missionaries and the Revival of French Empire* (New York: Oxford University Press, 2010). See also Sarah A. Curtis, "Emilie de Vialar and the Religious Reconquest of Algeria," *FHS* 29, 2 (2006): 261–92; and Sarah A. Curtis, *Educating the Faithful: Religion, Schooling, and Society in Nineteenth-Century France* (DeKalb: Northern Illinois University Press, 2000).

2. François Dornier, *La vie des catholiques en Tunisie au fil des ans* (Tunis: Finzi, 2000), 43.

3. Leon Carl Brown, *The Tunisia of Ahmad Bey, 1837–1855* (Princeton: Princeton University Press, 1974), 326; and Pierre Gandolphe, "St.-Louis de Carthage, 1830 à 1850," *Les cahiers de Byrsa* (Paris: Imprimerie Nationale, 1951), 12. The inspiration for awarding the medal to the SSJ may have come from Count Raffo.

4. Nancy E. Gallagher, *Medicine and Power in Tunisia, 1780–1900* (Cambridge: Cambridge University Press, 1983), 40–64; and Marcel Gandolphe, "Premiers hôpitaux français en Tunisie," *Tunisie Médicale*, 1931, 167–70.

5. Dornier, *Catholiques*, 401.

6. François Renault, *Cardinal Lavigerie: Churchman, Prophet, and Missionary* (London: Athlone Press, 1994); François Renault, *Lavigerie, l'esclavage africain, et l'Europe, 1868–1892*, 2 vols. (Paris: E. de Boccard, 1971); and Aylward Shorter, *The Cross and the Flag in Africa: The White Fathers during the Colonial Scramble (1892–1914)* (Maryknoll: Orbis Books, 2006).

7. See Geoffrey A. Oddie's review of Rhonda Anne Semple, *Missionary Women: Gender, Professionalism and the Victorian Idea of Christian Mission* (Rochester: Boydell, 2003) in *AHR* 110, 1 (February 2005): 225–26; and Andrew Porter, *Religion versus Empire? British Protestant Missionaries and Overseas Expansion, 1700–1914* (New York: Manchester University Press, 2004).

8. Jean and John Comaroff, *Of Revelation and Revolution: Christianity, Colonialism, and Consciousness in South Africa* (Chicago: University of Chicago Press, 1991); and George Orwell, *Burmese Days: A Novel* (New York: Harcourt Brace, 1934).

9. Rita Smith Kipp, *The Early Years of a Dutch Colonial Mission: The Karo Field* (Ann Arbor: University of Michigan Press, 1990); Derek R. Peterson, "Morality Plays: Marriage, Church Courts, and Colonial Agency in Central Tanganyika, ca. 1876–1928," *AHR* 111, 4 (2006): 983–1010; and Patricia Grimshaw, "Faith, Missionary Life, and the Family," in *Gender and Empire*, ed. Philippa Levine (Oxford: Oxford University Press, 2004), 260–80.

10. Karima Direche-Slimani, *Chrétiens de Kabylie: Histoire d'une communauté sans histoire: Une action missionnaire de l'Algérie coloniale* (Paris: Bouchène, 2004).

11. J.P. Daughton, *An Empire Divided: Religion, Republicanism, and the Making of French Colonialism, 1880–1914* (Oxford: Oxford University Press, 2006); and J.P. Daughton and Owen White, eds., *In God's Empire: French Missionaries and the Modern World* (New York: Oxford University Press, 2010). On missionaries in the historiography of the early French Empire, see Sue Peabody, "'A Dangerous Zeal': Catholic Missions to Slave in the French Antilles, 1635–1800," *FHS* 25, 1 (2002): 53–90. See also Julia Clancy-Smith, "Changing Perspectives on the Historiography of Imperialism: Women, Gender, and Empire," in *Middle East Historiographies: Narrating the Twentieth Century*, ed. Israel Gershoni, Amy Singer, and Y. Hakan Erdem (Seattle: University of Washington Press, 2006), 70–100; and Julia Clancy-Smith, "Education: Missionary. North Africa," in *Encyclopedia of Women and Islamic Cultures*, vol. 4, *Economics, Education, Mobility and Space*, ed. Suad Joseph (Leiden: E.J. Brill, 2007), 283–85.

12. A list of Vialar's extensive travels is in Agnès Cavasino, *Emilie de Vialar, fondatriçe: Les Soeurs de Saint-Joseph de l'Apparition, une congrégation missionnaire* (Fountenay sous Bois: Congrégation des Soeurs de Saint-Joseph de l'Apparition, 1987), 324.

13. Planel, "De la nation," makes extensive use of parish records from the Prélature de Tunis. Dornier, *Catholiques*, 44, notes that Capuchin archives were transferred to Rome. Apparently no documents remain in Tunis.

14. Claude Langlois, *Le catholicisme au féminin: Les congrégations françaises à supérieure générale au XIXe siècle* (Paris: Cerf, 1984); Curtis, "Vialar," 264–65; and Cavasino, *Vialar*, 22–56.

15. Le Père Testas, *La vie militante de la bienheureuse Mère Emilie Vialar* (Marseilles: Éditions Publiroc, 1938), 80–83; and Cavasino, *Vialar*, 60–64.

16. Testas, *Vie*, 93–97.

17. Ibid., 98–103, 113–14.

18. Ibid., 112, 130.

19. Arnulf Camps, "M. l'Abbé François Bourgade (1806–1866) in Dialogue with Muslims at Carthage: A Forgotten Discussion on the Universal Meaning of Jesus by a Man Who Passed into Oblivion," in *A Universal Faith? Peoples, Cultures, Religions, and the Christ*, ed. Catherine Cornille and Valeer Neckebrouck (Louvain: Peeters Press, 1992), 73–87; and Paul Gabend, *Un oublié: L'Abbé Bourgade, missionnaire apostolique, premier aumônier de la Chapelle Royale de Saint-Louis de Carthage (1806–1866)* (Auch: Imprimerie Centrale, 1905).

20. Concerted proselytizing came slightly later with Lavigerie's appointment as archbishop of Algiers, when he initiated intense conversion campaigns in the Kabylia, since he and many others wrongly believed that the Berbers retained elements of their ancient Christian belief and thus were more amenable to conversion. Joseph Dean O'Donnell, *Lavigerie in Tunisia: The Interplay of Imperialist and Missionary* (Athens: University of Georgia Press, 1979); and Patricia Lorcin, *Imperial Identities: Stereotyping, Prejudice, and Race in Colonial Algeria* (London: I.B. Tauris, 1995).

21. Testas, *Vie*, x. Today, the congregation has a center and archive in Rome, the Istituto E de Vialar.

22. Author interview with Sister Marie-Joseph Guimard and Sister Jean-Marie Zayed Rabie, SSJ mother house, Tunis, June 2006.

23. Cavasino, *Vialar*, 188.

24. Testas, *Vie*, xvi; Jacques Ducos, *Marie-Jeanne Rumèbe: Soeur Joséphine de Jérusalem missionnaire en Terre Sainte* (Saint Gaudens: Editions Catherine de Coarraze, 1998), 16.

25. O'Donnell, *Lavigerie*, 1.

26. Dornier, *Catholiques*, 37; and Steven A. Epstein, *Speaking of Slavery: Color, Ethnicity, and Human Bondage in Italy* (Ithaca: Cornell University Press, 2001), 33–39.

27. Habib Kazdaghli, "Communautés méditerranéennes de Tunisie: Les Grecs de Tunisie; du Millet-i-Rum à l'assimilation française (XVIIe–XXe siècles)," *RMMM* 95–98 (2002): 449–76.

28. Dornier, *Catholiques*, 167; and Pierre Soumille, "Le cimetière Européen de Bab-el-Khadra à Tunis: Étude historique et sociale," *CT* 19, 75–76 (1971): 129–82.

29. Dornier, *Catholiques*, 39–40.

30. Ibid., 39.

31. Papers of Edward William Auriol Drummond-Hay (1785–1845), book no. 1, ms. e.354, p. 127, OBL.

32. French consul, Deval, to Husayn Bey, April 15, 1833, carton 64, dossier 756, ANT.

33. Jean Ganiage, *La population européenne de Tunis* (Paris: Presses Universitaires de France, 1960), 11.

34. Brown, *Tunisia*, 209.

35. Bin Diyaf, *Ithaf*, 4/6: 92–93; Ahmed Abdesselem, "Contribution à l'étude de la politique et de l'administration d'Ahmed Bey: La délégation de pouvoir en 1846," *CT* 19, 73–74 (1971): 109–118; Magali Morsy, ed., *Essai sur les réformes nécessaires aux états musulmans: Texte français du général Khayr ed-Din, homme d'état du XIXe siècle, réédité et annoté* (Aix-en-Provence: Édisud, 1987), 20; and Pierre Soumille, "Une correspondance inédite entre Ahmed Bey et le Pape Pie IX (1849–1851)," *RHM* 3 (1975): 95–99.

36. Bin Diyaf, *Ithaf*, 4/6: 89.

37. Muhammad Salih Mzali, ed., *Min rasa'il Ibn Abi al-Diyaf* (Tunis: Al-Dar al-Tunisiya lil-Nashr, 1969), 17–18.

38. Dornier, *Catholiques*, 43; Brown, *Tunisia*, 195; and Sibel Zandi-Sayek, "Orchestrating Difference, Performing Identity: Urban Space and Public Rituals in Nineteenth-Century Izmir," in *Hybrid Urbanism: On the Identity Discourse and the Built Environment*, ed. Nezar AlSayyad (London: Praeger, 2001), 42–66.

39. Renault, *Lavigerie*, 142–43.

40. Gandolphe, "St.-Louis," 269–307.

41. Jean Marcille, ed., "Le printemps de Carthage: Souvenirs et images sur les collines de Carthage (période 1841 à 1925)," 5–6, ms., BDT.

42. Ibid.

43. Zeynep Çelik, *Urban Forms and Colonial Confrontations: Algiers under French Rule* (Berkeley: University of California Press, 1997); and Zeynep Çelik, Julia Clancy-Smith, and Frances Terpak, eds., *The Walls of Algiers: Text and Image in the Making of the City* (Los Angeles: Getty Research Institute; Seattle: University of Washington Press, 2009). In Tunisia, Protectorate officials rarely confiscated Islamic structures; the violent 1911 Jellaz confrontation over a Muslim cemetery discouraged colonial assaults on Islamic properties.

44. Dornier, *Catholiques*, 199; Marcille, "Printemps," 7–9; and Victor Guérin, *La France Catholique en Tunisie, à Malte et en Tripolitaine* (Tours: Alfred Mame, 1895), 18–25.

45. Planel, "De la nation," 1: 117.

46. Morsy, *Essai*, 16. See also Paul Sebag, *Tunis: Histoire d'une ville* (Paris: L'Harmattan, 1998), 271–80.

47. Some anticlerical colonial authorities discouraged proselytizing among Muslims, claiming that it would excite their "fanaticism," which left Algeria's immigrant Catholic flock as the missionaries' target population, a group reputed for its utter lack of faith and morals. Only later during the terrible 1868 cholera and typhus epidemics, accompanied by an unprecedented famine that carried off hundreds of thousands of Algerians, did the colonial state soften its attitude toward Catholic missions, particularly in the Kabylia. Direche-Slimani, *Chrétiens*.

48. Béclard to Ahmad Bey, October 19, 1854, carton 64, dossier 755, ANT.

49. Dornier, *Catholiques*, 399–401; and Marcel Gandolphe, "La vie à Tunis, 1840–1881," in *Histoire de la ville de Tunis*, ed. Charles-Henri Dessort (Algiers: Pfister, 1926), 168–69.

50. Mgr. Baunard, *Le Cardinal Lavigerie*, 2 vols. (Paris: J. De Gigord, 1922), 1: 493; and Dornier, *Catholiques*, 400–403. Of the women entering the novitiate between the 1840s and the century's end, roughly two-thirds—out of a total of about ninety-six novices—were characterized as French, although the French community was relatively small. Prior to the Protectorate, many were Maltese, Sicilian, or Sardinian; six women in Tunisia had come from houses in Greece, Syria, and Tripoli.

51. Dornier, *Catholiques*, 406, 411.

52. Julia Clancy-Smith, "Envisioning Knowledge: Educating the Muslim Woman in Colonial North Africa, 1850–1918," in *Iran and Beyond: Essays in Middle Eastern History in Honor of Nikki Keddie*, ed. Beth Baron and Rudi Matthee (Los Angeles: Mazda Press, 2000), 102–8; Souad Bakalti, "L'enseignement féminin dans le primaire au temps de la Tunisie coloniale," *IBLA* 53, 166 (1990): 249–73; and Curtis, *Educating*, 86–87.

53. Planel, "De la nation," 1: 119, note 87.

54. Personal correspondence, Box 1, RW. In 1862 Count Raffo accompanied Cecil Wood to Paris to enroll him in the international Collège de Notre Dame; Cecil eventually studied Arabic at university, the result of his upbringing in Tunis.

55. Dornier, *Catholiques*, 529–42; and Jann Pasler, "The Utility of Musical Instruments in the Racial and Colonial Agendas of Late Nineteenth-Century France," *Journal of the Royal Musical Association* 129, 1 (2004): 24–76.

56. Raoul Darmon, "Cent années d'enseignement en Tunisie," extrait d'une causerie faite le 19 novembre 1953 à la Société l'Essor, *Bulletin Economique et Sociale de la Tunisie* (May 1954), 73–94; and Gandolphe, "La vie," 169, quote p. 163.

57. Dornier, *Catholiques*, 529–30; Mgr. A. Pons, *La nouvelle église d'Afrique ou le Catholicisme en Algérie en Tunisie et au Maroc depuis 1830* (Tunis: Librarie Louis Namura, n.d.), 206.

58. Abdelhamid Hénia, *Propriété et stratégies sociales à Tunis (XVIe–XIXe siècles)* (Tunis: Publications de l'Université de Tunis, 1999), 311–16.

59. L'Abbé A. F. Leynaud, *Hadrumète: Sousse* (Sousse: Imprimerie Française, 1903), 76; and Dornier, *Catholiques*, 47, 400.

60. Dennis H. Phillips, "The American Missionary in Morocco," *The Muslim World*, 65, 1 (1975): 1–20, notes that American evangelicals were particularly disliked because of their untoward behavior, not only by Moroccans, but also by fellow English missionaries.

61. Béclard to Ahmad Bey, July 4, 1854, carton 64, dossier 760, ANT.

62. Béclard to Bogo, July 4, 1854, carton 64, dossier 760, ANT.

63. Cavasino, *Vialar*, 67–117.

64. Ibid., 128–29. See also Rebecca Rogers, "Telling Stories about the Colonies: British and French Women in Algeria in the Nineteenth Century," *Gender and History* 21, 1 (2009): 39–59.

65. Richardson, "Account," 29.

66. Christian Windler, *La diplomatie comme expérience de l'autre: Consuls français au Maghreb (1700–1840)* (Geneva: Droz, 2002), 425; and for the quote, Béclard to Count Raffo, January 1853, carton 64, dossier 755, ANT.

67. Cavasino, *Vialar*, 119, 138–40.

68. Lady Herbert, *A Search After Sunshine, or Algeria in 1871* (London: Bentley, 1872), 251.

69. Ibid., 250.

70. Edward Suter, *History of the Female Education Society* (London, 1847) whose principal publications was the *Female Missionary Intelligencer*, 1853–1899.

71. The history of Protestant churches and communities in Tunisia awaits its historian. R. Graff, "Le Protestantisme en Tunisie: Données historiques et statistiques," *CT* 3, 10 (1955): 235–46.

72. Nathan Davis, *Tunis or Selections from a Journal during a Residence in That Regency* (Malta: Muir, 1841), 45–46.

73. Dornier, *Catholiques*, 166.

74. Davis, *Tunis*, 45–46.

75. Planel, "De la nation," 1: 119–42, offers the most perspicacious analysis of Bourgade's religious and social thinking; according to Sarah A. Curtis, little is known with any certainty regarding Vialar's personal views on Islam (private communication).

76. Testas, *Vie*, 126–30; and Camps, "Bourgade," 74–75.

77. Marcille, *Printemps*, 7.

78. Gandolphe, "La vie," 164.

79. Pierre Soumille, "Les multiples activités d'un prêtre Français au Maghreb: L'Abbé François Bourgade en Algérie et en Tunisie de 1838 à 1858" in *Histoire d'outre-mer: Mélanges en l'honneur de Jean-Louis Miège*, 2 vols. (Aix-en-Provence: Publications de l'Université de Provence, 1992), 1: 233–72.

80. E. Vassel, "Un précurseur, l'Abbé Bourgade," *RT* 16 (1909): 107–15.

81. Laroussi Mizouri's "La pénétration de l'enseignement Européen dans la Tunisie précoloniale: Origines et répercussions," *CT* 44, 157–158 (1991): 177–96, is emblematic of flawed approaches to precolonial schooling, because the cross-fertilization among institutions is ignored.

82. Planel, "De la nation," 3: 580, contains a copy of Esther's baptismal certificate and authorization of marriage from Ménard's mother, who demanded conversion to Catholicism.

83. Jean Ganiage, *Les origines du Protectorat Français en Tunisie (1861–1881)* (Tunis: Maison Tunisienne de l'Édition, 1968), 139; and Gandolphe, "La vie," 164.

84. Rachel Simon, "Education," in *The Jews of the Middle East and North Africa in Modern Times,* ed. Reeva Spector Simon, Michael Laskier, and Sara Reguer (New York: Columbia University Press, 2003), 148–52.

85. Paul Sebag, *L'évolution d'un ghetto nord-africain: La Hara de Tunis* (Paris: Mémoires du Centre d'Études de Sciences Humaines, 1959); and Paul Sebag, *Histoire des Juifs de Tunisie: Des origines à nos jours* (Paris: Editions L'Harmattan, 1991); Susan Gilson Miller, "Gender and the Poetics of Emancipation: The Alliance Israélite Universelle in Northern Morocco, 1890–1912," in *Franco-Arab Encounters: Studies in Memory of David C. Gordon,* ed. Leon Carl Brown and Matthew S. Gordon (Beirut: American University of Beirut Press, 1996), 229–52.

86. *La Presse,* November 25, 1845; and *La Gazette du Midi,* November 17, 1845, BNF.

87. Abbé François Bourgade, *Au sujet du Collège et de l'Hôpital St. Louis à Tunis: Appel à la charité* (Paris: Imprimerie de Vrayet de Surcy, 1846). On page 2, the tract stated that "donations will be accepted by the *curés* of Saint Thomas d'Aquin and Saint-Louis-d'Antin or by the member of the Association de St. Louis," indicating that Bourgade had set up a fairly extensive marketing network; the 1848 revolutions halted this enterprise for a while.

88. French consul to Bishop de Rosalia, December 2, 1851, carton 483, CADN; and Cavasino, *Vialar,* 135.

89. The quote is from Planel, "De la nation," 1: 119–20. See also Dornier, *Catholiques,* 43.

90. *L'Aigle de Paris,* Microform MICR D-1189, BNF. The publisher Challamel served as the donations center for the Association de Saint Louis resurrected by Bourgade after his definitive return to Paris. See Ganiage, *Origines,* 578–80, for the biography of Rochaïd Dahdah, a Lebanese Maronite and collaborator in the *L'Aigle de Paris.*

91. *L'Aigle de Paris,* December 10, 1859, 1–2, Microform MICR D-1189, BNF.

92. Baunard, *Lavigerie,* 1: 493.

93. Shorter, *Cross,* 144.

94. Bourgade's books included *Les soirées de Carthage* (1847), *La clef du Coran* (1852), *Passage du Coran à l'Évangile* (1855), and *Mémoires sur trois tombeaux d'évêques.* Renault, *Lavigerie,* 89–90.

95. The notion of the civilizing mission, largely associated with French colonialism in Africa, began with sixteenth-century Jesuit missionary activity in port cities such as Naples. Jennifer D. Selwyn, "'Procuring in the Common People These Better Behaviors': The Jesuits' Civilizing Mission in Early Modern Naples, 1550–1620," *Radical History Review* 67 (Winter 1997): 4–34; and Camps, "Bourgade," 86.

96. Mohamed Kerrou, "Les débats autour de la visibilité de la femme et du voile dans l'espace public de la Tunisie contemporaine (milieu XIXe–début XXe siècles)," in *Chronos: Revue d'Histoire de l'Université de Balamand* 12 (2005): 47–50.

97. Planel, "De la nation," 1: 119–20.

98. Abdelhamid Larguèche and Habib Kazdaghli, "Elia Finzi, imprimeur de père en fils," in *Mestieri e professioni degli Italiani di Tunisia/Métiers et professions des Italiens de Tunisie,* ed. Silvia Finzi (Tunis: Editions Finzi, 2003), 278–84.

99. Leynaud, *Hadrumète,* 69–70. See also François Bourgade, *La toison d'or de la langue Phénicienne* (Paris: B. Duprat, 1852).

100. O'Donnell, *Lavigerie,* 56–59.

101. J. N. Hays, *The Burdens of Disease: Epidemics and Human Response in Western History* (New Brunswick: Rutgers University Press, 1998), 135–53, quote p. 135; Asa Briggs, "Cholera and Society in the Nineteenth Century," *Past and Present* 19 (1961): 76–96; Frank M. Snowden, *Naples in the Time of Cholera, 1884–1911* (Cambridge: Cambridge University Press, 1995); and Steven Johnson, *The Ghost Map: The Story of London's Most Terrifying Epidemic—and How It Changed Science, Cities, and the Modern World* (New York: Riverhead Books, 2006). See also Kim Pelis, *Charles Nicolle, Pasteur's Imperial Missionary: Typhus and Tunisia* (Rochester: University of Rochester Press, 2006).

102. Reade, September 7, 1835, FO 77/26, NAUK.

103. The quote is from Briggs, "Cholera," 83. See also Sheldon Watts, *Epidemics and History: Disease, Power and Imperialism* (New Haven: Yale University Press, 1997), 167–212.

104. Daniel T. Reff, *Plagues, Priests, and Demons: Sacred Narratives and the Rise of Christianity in the Old World and the New* (New York: Cambridge, 2005), argues that during devastating epidemics in the New World, missionaries created new physical spaces where indigenous communities shattered by disease, conquest, and violence could regroup.

105. Bin Diyaf, *Ithaf,* 4/6: 143–44.

106. O'Donnell, *Lavigerie,* 163.

107. Gallagher, *Medicine,* 45–59, 110–13; and Dornier, *Catholiques,* 43.

108. Joel Montague, "Notes on Medical Organization in Nineteenth-Century Tunisia: A Preliminary Analysis of the Materials on Public Health and Medicine in the Dar El Bey in Tunis," *Medical History* 17, 1 (January 1973): 75–82.

109. Planel, "De la nation," 3: 459–68.

110. Ibid., 3: 462–65.

111. Ibid., 3: 459–68.

112. Dornier, *Catholiques,* 402–3; and Guérin, *France,* 71. Guérin's brother, Charles, was a White Father, which influenced Guérin's books.

113. Dornier, *Catholiques,* 404–5.

114. Planel, "De la nation," 3: 463. See also Curtis, "Vialar," 280–91.

115. Le Cardinal Lavigerie, *Instructions aux missionnaires* (Alger: Maison-Carrée, 1939), 194–95.

116. Curtis, "Vialar," 285.

117. Quoted in Richardson, "Account," 171.

118. Rousseau to Ahmad Bey, October 17, 1848, carton 206, dossier 88, ANT.

119. Cubisol, December 29, 1870, carton 413, CADN.

120. Ibid.

121. In "The Decivilizing Mission: Auguste Dupuis-Yakouba and French Timbuktu," *FHS* 27, 3 (Summer 2004): 541–68, special issue, *Writing French Colonial Histories,* ed. Alice Conklin and Julia Clancy-Smith, Owen White raises issues of missionary behavior and appearance and "going native," which has not been adequately problematized by historians. For example, a member of the White Fathers, Père Dupuis saw himself as simultaneously African and European, as did the local Muslim Songhay society in Timbuktu.

122. Louis Créput, rapport no. 1, "Notice sur le Contrôle Civile de Nabeul," May 1892, recueil 5, bobine 5, ISHMN.

123. Herbert, *Search*, 244.

124. Dornier, *Catholiques*, 43.

125. Valérien Groffier, *Héros trop oubliés de notre épopée coloniale* (Paris: Librarie Catholique Vitte, 1928), 108; and Leynaud, *Hadrumète*, 94.

126. Shorter, *Cross*, 144.

127. Dornier, *Catholiques*, 47, 400–401.

128. The quote is from Paul Melon, *L'Alliance Française et l'enseignement français en Tunisie et en Tripolitaine* (Paris: Dentu, 1885), 12–13. See also Paul Melon, *Problèmes algériens et tunisiens: Ce que disent les chiffres* (Paris: Challamel, 1903), 131.

129. Renault, *Lavigerie*, 58–60.

130. Reade, 1846, PRO/FO 335/93/1, NAUK. See also Adrianus Koster, *Prelates and Politicians in Malta: Changing Power-Balance between Church and State in a Mediterranean Island Fortress, 1800–1976* (Assen: Van Gorcum, 1984).

131. The petition dated December 1846 is found in PRO/FO 335/92 (6), NAUK.

132. Fr. Salvatore Maria, "L'église de Tunisie en 1882," 9–12, quote p. 9, unpublished ms., BDT. Snowden, *Naples*, 233–34, notes that fishermen were also unwelcome as they brought diseases; during the 1910 epidemic, they introduced cholera to the Apulia. See also Dornier, *Catholiques*, 276.

133. Leynaud, *Hadrumète*, 62–73. Father Agostino repeatedly contacted benefactors in Malta to request financial assistance.

134. Eugène Poiré, *La Tunisie française* (Paris: Plon, 1892), 215; Planel, "De la nation," 3: 738; and Dornier, *Catholiques*, 403–5.

135. Leynaud, *Hadrumète*, 72, 87, 95, quote p. 94.

136. Poiré, *Tunisie*, 215.

137. Irving, August 29, 1867, carton 417, CADN.

138. See Engin Deniz Akarli, "Daughters and Fathers: A Young Druze Woman's Experience (1894–1897)," in *Identity and Identity Formation in the Ottoman World: A Volume of Essays in Honor of Norman Itzkowitz*, ed. Baki Tezcan and Karl K. Barbir (Madison: University of Wisconsin Press, 2007), 167–84, on a young Druze woman, Najla, who took refuge in 1894 with a convent of French Catholic nuns at Mount Lebanon to escape an arranged marriage. The Druze patriarch blamed missionaries for her rebellion; under European treaties with the Porte, missionaries were not necessarily subject to Ottoman or local laws.

139. Poiré, *Tunisie*, 215; Dornier, *Catholiques*, 400–401; and Maria, "L'église," 9–12.

140. Dornier, *Catholiques*, 401.

141. Georges Weill, "Les débuts de l'alliance israélite universelle en Tunisie: 1862–1882," in *Juifs et Musulmans en Tunisie: Fraternité et déchirements*, ed. Sonia Fellous (Paris: Somogy, 2003), 169–80.

142. See O'Donnell, *Lavigerie*, 49–58, 75, for Lavigerie's arguments advanced in 1881, when the anti-Italian nun campaign was in full swing, that another Catholic girls' school was not needed since the SSJ already ran such an establishment—in other words, Italians need not apply.

143. Roustan to Lavigerie, September 3, 1876, quoted in Baunard, *Lavigerie,* 1: 493.

144. Marcille, "Printemps," 126.

145. The shelter on La Marsa *jabal* (hill), built in the neo-Moorish style, dated from 1885–1886, but Lavigerie provided the funds to purchase it. In 1919, the sisters opened one of the first embroidery workshops for Muslim girls in the same building that stands today in a state of advanced disrepair. Pierre Soumille, "Les religieuses Catholiques et la formation professionnelle des Tunisiennes au temps du Protectorat," in *Histoire des femmes au Maghreb: Culture matérielle et vie quotidienne,* ed. Dalenda Larguèche (Tunis: Centre de Publication Universitaire, 2000), 287–317; and Dornier, *Catholiques,* 439–63, quote p. 439.

146. Jane Schneider, *Italy's "Southern Question": Orientalism in One Country* (New York: Oxford, 1998). See also Edmund Burke, III, and David Prochaska, eds., *Genealogies of Orientalism: History, Theory, Politics* (Lincoln: University of Nebraska Press, 2008).

147. Geoffrey A. Oddie, "'Orientalism' and British Protestant Missionary Constructions of India in the Nineteenth Century," *South Asia* 17, 2 (1994): 27–42.

148. Dornier, *Catholiques,* 52–53. On the December 1905 law of church-state separation, see Jean-Marc Regnault, ed. special issue of *Outre-Mers* 93, 346–347 (2005): 5–135.

149. Julia Clancy-Smith, "L'éducation des jeunes filles musulmanes en Tunisie: Missionnaires religieux et laïques," in *Le pouvoir du genre: Laïcités et religions 1905-2005,* ed. Florence Rochefort (Toulouse: Presses Universitaires du Mirail, 2007), 127–43.

150. Ellen Fleischmann, "The Impact of American Protestant Missions in Lebanon on the Construction of Female Identity, c. 1860–1950," *Islam and Christian-Muslim Relations* 13, 4 (2002): 411–26.

CHAPTER 8

Epigraph: Philippa Day, ed., *At Home in Carthage: The British in Tunisia* (Tunis: Trustees of St. Georges Church, 1992), 14. Special thanks to my La Marsa family, the Rostoms, for initiating me long ago into the social rituals of summer.

1. The ruined building, once a bathing house and currently used by fishermen, still belongs to a member of the Husaynid family, Raouf Bey, a descendant of Moncif Bey, who resides in La Marsa.

2. Joëlle Bahloul, *The Architecture of Memory: A Jewish-Muslim Household in Colonial Algeria, 1937-1962* (Cambridge: Cambridge University Press, 1996), 51. For a comparative view, see Kenneth M. Cuno, "Ambiguous Modernization: The Transition to Monogamy in the Khedival House of Egypt," in *Family History in the Middle East: Households, Property, and Gender,* ed. Beshara Doumani (New York: SUNY, 2003), 247–69; and Alan Duben, *Istanbul Households: Marriage, Family, and Fertility, 1880-1940* (Cambridge: Cambridge University Press, 1991).

3. Mary S. Hartman, *The Household and the Making of History: A Subversive View of the Western Past* (Cambridge: Cambridge University Press, 2004). Hartman's principal thesis, however, revolves around the historical uniqueness of northwestern European family structures and households, with scant attention to other types of households; nevertheless, placing the household at the center of historical analysis represents a major conceptual advance.

4. Omar Carlier, "Le café maure: Sociabilité masculine et effervescence citoyenne (Algérie XVIIe–XXe siècles)," *AESC* 45, 4 (1990): 975–1003; and Jean Boutier, "Un autre Midi: Notes sur les sociétés populaires en Corse (1790–1794)," *Annales Historiques de la Revolution Française,* no. 268 (1987): 158–75.

5. The literature on Orientalist representations of women is too vast to cite. See Antoinette Burton's review essay in *Signs* 25, 1 (Autumn 1999): 243–46; Nadi Maria El Cheikh, "Revisiting the Abbasid Harims," *Journal of Middle East Women's Studies* 1, 3 (Fall 2005): 1–19; and Julia Clancy-Smith, "The Intimate, the Familial, and the Local in Trans-National Histories of Gender," *Journal of Women's History* 18, 2 (2006): 174–83.

6. At worst, Muslim households were portrayed as impeding the development of social institutions, social progress, refinement of manners, culture of the spirit, and art, literature, and science, according to the Saint-Simonian theorist and politician Michel Chevalier, writing in 1865 about Algerian Muslim society in which household, family, and harim were conflated for polemical purposes. Julia Clancy-Smith, "Le regard colonial: Islam, genre et identités dans L'Algérie Française," *Nouvelles Questions Féministes* 25, 1 (2006): 25–40. The nineteenth-century discourse on modernity and the family was contradictory. On the one hand, the middle-class family was constructed as a refuge from the stresses and strains of the modern world. On the other, the family was viewed by Third Republic French liberals as the site par excellence for social engineering and thus potentially as the crucible of modernity, or major obstacle to it, when predominant kinship structures were non-European and/or nonbourgeois.

7. The Tunis elite and European residents or travelers generated what little documentation exists, and lack of evidence only allows cursory treatment of important topics. Regrettably, Tunisian women in this period did not write about themselves, nor did they produce anything akin to the memoirs penned by Huda Shaarawi, the Egyptian feminist, *Mudhakkirat* (Cairo: Dar al-Hilal, 1981). On "leisure," a concept demanding problematizing for nineteenth-century Tunisian society, see Dalenda Larguèche, "Loisirs, sociabilité et mutations culturelles dans la Régence de Tunis à l'époque Ottomane," in *Mélanges méditerranéens d'amitié et de reconnaissance à André Raymond,* 2 vols. (Tunis: Fondation Temimi, 2004), 1: 155–65.

8. Arnold H. Green, *The Tunisian Ulama, 1873–1915: Social Structure and Response to Ideological Currents* (Leiden: E. J. Brill, 1978), 50. On the Husaynid family, see El-Mokhtar Bey, *Les beys de Tunis (1705–1957): Hérédité, souveraineté, généalogie* (Tunis: Serviced, 2002); and Mohamed El Aziz Ben Achour, *La cour du bey de Tunis* (Tunis: Espace Diwan, 2003). Fayçal Bey's *La dernière odalisque* (Paris: Éditions Stock, 2001), a somewhat fanciful novel, contains nevertheless historically sound information.

9. Leila Temime Blili, *Histoire de familles: Mariages, repudiations et vie quotidienne à Tunis, 1875–1930* (Tunis: Script, 1999), 86–87.

10. Richardson, "Addenda," account of Miss Smith, p. 58.

11. Ernst von Hesse-Wartegg, *Tunis: The Land and the People* (London: Chatto & Windus, 1882), 85–86. The Austrian baron Ernst von Hesse-Wartegg (1854–1918), one of the nineteenth century's foremost travel writers, published over twenty works devoted to his treks from the Americas to North Africa and East Asia. In Tunis he was received with honors by the ruling family due to his noble rank and reputation.

12. It is useful to compare Egypt under Khedive Tawfiq (1879–1892), where the suburb of Helwan became a winter retreat for the palace and urban elites. A theater, casino, and gardens graced the town; but more importantly, location outside the capital allowed upper-class women more freedom. The Ottoman family moved in summer from Istanbul to the Bosporus, where Ottoman Egyptian elites maintained vacation palaces as well.

13. Ahmed Abdesselem, *Les historiens tunisiens des XVIIe, XVIIIe et XIXe siècles* (Paris: Klincksieck, 1973), 93.

14. Jacques Revault, "Résidences d'été à Sidi Bou Saïd," *Cahiers des Arts et Techniques d'Afrique du Nord* 6 (1960–1961): 153–203; and author's interview with Madame Hasiba Agha, Dar Agha, Kram, November 3, 2007.

15. Charles Lallemand, *Tunis au XIXe siècle* (Paris: Maison Quantin, 1890), 149.

16. Taoufik Bachrouch, *Le saint et le prince en Tunisie: Les elites tunisiennes du pouvoir et de la dévotion* (Tunis: Faculté des Sciences Humaines et Sociales de Tunis, 1989), 387.

17. Mohamed Bergaoui, *Tourisme et voyages en Tunisie: Les années de la Régence,* 3rd ed. (Tunis: Simpact, 2005), 76. Albert Malinas, *Notice sur le groupe hydro-minéral de Korbous (Tunisie)* (Tunis: Imprimerie Rapide, 1909), 3, claims that Muhammad ibn Hassan Bayram's manuscript was a translation done in 1756 from Latin to Arabic of a study written by Yusuf al-Guir, a Christian physician converted to Islam who resided in Tunis.

18. Raymond, *Chronique,* 2: 57, 92.

19. Raymond, *Chronique,* 2: 57. See also Bin Diyaf, *Ithaf,* 3/4: 207.

20. J. Henry Dunant, *Notice sur la Régence de Tunis* (Geneva: Jules Fick, 1858), 122–23.

21. Nadia Sebaï, *Mustapha Saheb Ettabaa: Un haut dignitaire beylical dans la Tunisie du XIXe siècle* (Carthage: Éditions Cartaginoiseries, 2007), 23; and Bin Diyaf, *Ithaf,* 4/6: 156–57.

22. Sonia Slim, "Palais Ahmed Bey: Entre splendeur et décadence," *Archibat: Revue Maghrébine d'Aménagement de l'Espace et de la Construction* 17 (Decembre 2008).

23. Mohamed El Aziz Ben Achour, *Catégories de la société tunisoise dans la deuxième moitié du XIXème siècle* (Tunis: Institut National d'Archeologie et d'Art, 1989), 31, 37.

24. Louis Créput, rapport no. 1, "Notice sur le Contrôle Civile de Nabeul," May 1892, recueil 5, bobine 5, ISHMN.

25. Alain Corbin, *The Lure of the Sea: The Discovery of the Seaside in the Western World, 1750–1840,* trans. Jocelyn Phelps (Cambridge: Cambridge University Press, 1994), 187–281.

26. Ben Achour, *Cour,* xxi.

27. Reade, December 23, 1831, FO 77/22, NAUK.

28. Major Sir Grenville T. Temple, *Excursions in the Mediterranean: Algiers and Tunis,* 2 vols. (London: Saunders and Otley, 1835), 1: 116–17.

29. Richardson, "Account," 20.

30. A number of resident Europeans commented upon this; for example, Le Comte Filippi, Sardinian consul in Tunis, *Fragmens historiques et statistiques sur la Régence de Tunis (1829),* in *Relations inédites de Nyssen, Filippi et Calligaris (1788, 1829, 1834),* by Charles Monchicourt (Paris: Société d'Éditions Géographiques, Maritimes et Coloniales, 1929), 86.

31. Yvan Debbasch, *La nation française en Tunisie (1577–1835)* (Paris: Sirey, 1957), 243.

The fact that Europeans and other foreigners were confined to their nation's funduqs explains the importance of offers of high-end housing.

32. Bin Diyaf, *Ithaf,* 3/2: 147.

33. Day, *Carthage,* 14; Logbook, July 1828, FO 77/21, NAUK; and Monchicourt, *Relations,* 86, note 4.

34. Hesse-Wartegg, *Tunis,* 46.

35. Mgr. A. Pons, *La nouvelle église d'Afrique, ou, Le Catholicisme en Algérie, en Tunisie et au Maroc depuis 1833* (Tunis: Namura, 1930), 228.

36. Pierre Grandchamp, "Autour du Consulat de France à Tunis (1577–1881)," *RT,* nos. 53–54 (1943): 18, note 2.

37. David Blackbourn, "'Taking the Waters': Meeting Places of the Fashionable World," in *The Mechanics of Internationalism: Culture, Society, and Politics from the 1840s to the First World War,* ed. Martin H. Geyer and Johannes Paulmann (Oxford: Oxford University Press, 2001), 435–57.

38. Christina Wood, July 5 and July 29, 1861, WD269–271, RW.

39. Ibid., for a Mardi Gras costume party at the British consulate in Tunis where Le Vicomte Alfred de Caston composed a long French poem, in exceedingly bad verse, dedicated to Christina Wood and had it printed for the guests—which gives us an idea of how the creoles and the diplomatic corps spent their leisure time.

40. Jean Ganiage, *Les origines du Protectorat Français en Tunisie (1861–1881)* (Tunis: Maison Tunisienne de l'Edition, 1968), 447–61; and Paul Cambon, "Lettres de Tunisie," *Revue des Deux Mondes* 3 (May 1931): 127–50, 373–98.

41. André Martel, *Luis-Arnold et Joseph Allegro: Consuls du bey de Tunis à Bône* (Paris: Presses Universitaires de France, 1967), 128–30.

42. Christina Wood regaled her husband with the latest summertime gossip: "Madame Elias has arrived at Goletta, it is officially announced that she is in an interesting state, a most interesting fact for us, also Madame Mascaro (don't laugh)." Unfortunately, we never hear Luigia speak for herself. Christina Wood, July 5, 1861, WD269–271, RW; and Joseph Dean O'Donnell, *Lavigerie in Tunisia: The Interplay of Imperialist and Missionary* (Athens: University of Georgia Press, 1979), 61–62.

43. Reade, December 5, 1834, FO 77/25, NAUK.

44. The princess ʿAziza ʿUthmana funded a large number of public and private charities in Tunis during the seventeenth century, including hospitals and poor shelters. Dalenda Larguèche, "Femme et don pour la ville: ʿAziza ʿUthmana entre histoire et mémoire," in *Femmes en villes,* ed. Dalenda Larguèche (Tunis: Éditions du Cérès, 2005), 35–53.

45. Bin Diyaf, *Ithaf,* 3/4: 202–3.

46. Bin Diyaf, *Ithaf,* chapter 6, *Reign of Ahmad Bey,* edition by Ahmad ʿAbd al-Salam (Tunis: al-Jamiʿa al-Tunisiya, 1971), 212. Amy Aisen Elouafi, "Being Ottoman: Family and the Politics of Modernity in the Province of Tunisia" (PhD dissertation, University of California, Berkeley, 2007), makes a considerable contribution to our understanding of the palace's women. See also Douglas Scott Brookes, *The Concubine, the Princess, and the Teacher: Voices from the Ottoman Harem* (Austin: University of Texas Press, 2008).

47. Julia Clancy-Smith, "A Visit to a Tunisian Harim," *Journal of Maghrebi Studies* 1–2, 1 (Spring 1993): 43–49.

48. Richardson, "Addenda," 60, 62.

49. Ibid., 63.

50. Ibid., 53–54.

51. Ibid., 53–55.

52. Ibid., 56–57.

53. Ibid., 64.

54. Mary Roberts, *Intimate Outsiders: The Harim in Ottoman and Orientalist Art and Travel Literature* (Durham: Duke University Press, 2007), 59–79. The interiors of the Husaynid residences seem to have been furnished à l'européen slightly earlier than was the case in Istanbul. Was this the influence of the local creole class, the Italian mamluk connection, or the fact that the Husaynids maintained closer ties with Europe than other Muslim princes? See Christian Windler, *La diplomatie comme expérience de l'autre: Consuls français au Maghreb (1700–1840)* (Geneva: Droz, 2002), 485–535, on the political significance of gift giving. For a detailed list of the astonishing quantity of valuable items exchanged between Tunis and Paris, see Henri Hugon, "Une ambassade tunisienne à Paris en 1825 (Mission de Si Mahmoud Kahia)," *RT*, nos. 13–14 (1933): 108–14.

55. Reade, August 18, 1825, FO 77/16, NAUK.

56. Hugon, "Ambassade," 111.

57. Windler, *Diplomatie*, 268–69.

58. Lady Mary E. Herbert, *A Search After Sunshine, or Algeria in 1871* (London: Bentley, 1872), 248–63; and Camille Roches, February 8, 1860, carton 207, dossier 96, ANT.

59. Hesse-Wartegg, *Tunis*, 82–83.

60. Fayçal Bey, "Le 1er decembre 1846: Le bey de Tunis chez le roi des français," *Histoire*, March 19, 2004, 68–69. Ahmad Bey was received in the king's private family salon.

61. C. A. Bayly, *Empire and Information: Intelligence Gathering and Social Communication in India, 1780–1870* (Cambridge: Cambridge University Press, 1996), 18–19, 38–39.

62. Reade, April 29, 1835, FO 77/26, NAUK.

63. Richardson, "Addenda," 59.

64. Hesse-Wartegg, *Tunis*, 82–83.

65. Herbert, *Search*, 94–5, 258–59.

66. Ibid., 242–64, quote p. 3.

67. Heinrich Matthias Marcard, *A Short Description of Pyrmont, with Observations on the Use of Its Waters* (London, 1788); and Paul Gerbod, "Une forme de sociabilité bourgeoise: Le thermalisme en France, en Belgique et en Allemagne, 1800–1850," in *Sociabilité et société bourgeoise en France, en Allemagne et en Suisse (1750–1850)*, ed. Étienne François (Paris: La Documentation Française, 1986), 105–22.

68. Maturin M. Ballou, *The Story of Malta* (Boston: Houghton, Mifflin and Company, 1893), 90–91.

69. The quote is from Thomas W. Gallant, *Experiencing Dominion: Culture, Identity, and Power in the British Mediterranean* (Notre Dame: University of Notre Dame Press, 2002), 67. See also Corbin, *The Lure of the Sea*, 254–57.

70. Temple, *Excursions*, 1: 117.

71. Carleton, July 21, 1834, FO 77/25, NAUK.

72. Agnès Cavasino, *Emilie de Vialar, fondatrice: Les Soeurs de Saint-Joseph de l'Appa-*

rition, une congrégation missionnaire (Fountenay sous Bois: Congrégation des Soeurs de Saint-Joseph de l'Apparition, 1987), 123–24; and Dornier, *Catholiques*, 401.

73. Dunant, *Notice*, 99.

74. Cubisol to Rousseau, July 29, 1858, and letter in Arabic by Khayr al-Din, AH 1274, carton 413, CADN.

75. Christina Wood, July 5 and July 29, 1861, WD269–271, RW.

76. Luigi Demech, *The British Consulate in Tunis: Critical Remarks* (Malta: Albion Press, 1868), 24.

77. Christina Wood, July 5 and (for the quote) July 29, 1861, WD269–271, RW.

78. Dunant, *Notice*, 122–23.

79. Planel, "De la nation," 3: 667.

80. Christina Wood, July 5 and (for the quotes) July 29, 1861, WD269–271, RW.

81. There is not much evidence of European governesses serving the great beylical or baldi families of Tunis; in Istanbul and Cairo, on the other hand, educated women found ready employment. Barbara Petzen, "'Matmazels' nell'harim: Le governanti europee nell'impero ottomano," *Genesis* 1, 1 (2002): 61–84.

82. Louis Gaspary, April 15, 1824, and May 24–26, 1824, carton 407, CADN.

83. Eric T. Jennings, *Curing the Colonizers: Hydrotherapy, Climatology, and French Colonial Spas* (Durham: Duke University Press, 2006), 154–77.

84. "Beylical decrees relating to Hammam Korbous," 1787–1885, E-377-3, ANT.

85. Wood to Roches, November 7, 1858, carton 382, CADN.

86. Cubisol to De Vallat, January 31, 1874, carton 413, CADN.

87. Leprieur, *Essai analytique des eaux thermales d'Hammam Korbous* (Tunis, 1858); Dr. Guyon, *Etude sur les eaux thermales de la Tunisie* (Paris, 1864); and Louis Geslin, *Korbous: Histoire d'une station thermale d'Afrique* (Tunis: Société Anonyme de l'Imprimerie Rapide, 1913). Geslin's work was a thesis defended in 1913 for his doctorate in medicine in Paris, inspired by his internship at Sadiqi Hospital in Tunis, where "the affection that the natives held for the thermal waters in Korbous, the virtues attributed to them, and the great use made of those waters for numerous illnesses awakened my interest in this question" (5).

88. Raymond-Joseph Matignon, *L'art médical à Tunis* (Bordeaux: Paul Cassignol, 1901), 80, lauds the properties of Tunisian thermal waters. Ute Lotz-Heumann spoke of German spas at a public lecture at the University of Arizona in 2008, based upon her forthcoming study, "The German Spa: A Heterotopia of the Long Eighteenth Century." The Egyptian ruler Khedive Tawfiq had European doctors as personal physicians and spent forty days annually in Helwan seeking thermal cures. Margot Badran, ed. and trans., *Harem Years: the Memoires of an Egyptian Feminist (1879–1924) by Huda Shaarawi* (New York: The Feminist Press, 1987), 142, note 19.

89. Jennings makes this observation about healing cycles in *Curing*, 164–65. See also Peregrine Horden, "Travel Sickness: Medicine and Mobility in the Mediterranean from Antiquity to the Renaissance," in *Rethinking the Mediterranean*, ed. W. V. Harris (Oxford): Oxford University Press, 2005), 177–99.

90. Le Docteur J. Arnaud, *Les eaux thermales de Korbous près Tunis (Tunisie)* (Paris: Levé, 1912), 3.

91. Muhammad Bayram V traveled to France and Italy in 1875 for a serious nervous disorder, undergoing experimental treatments with electricity by the well-known physician Dr. Charcot in Paris. Ahmed Abdesselem, *Les historiens Tunisiens: Essai d'histoire culturelle* (Pairs: Klincksieck, 1973), 392; and Muhammad Bayram V, *Safwat al-i'tibar bi-mustawda al-amsar wa-l-aqtar* (Beirut: Dar al-Sadir, 1974), 1: 96–103.

92. Khayr al-Din, *Mémoires*, 42, in *Kheredine: Homme d'état; Documents historiques annotés,* ed. Mohamed-Salah Mzali and Jean Pignon (Tunis: Maison Tunisienne de l'Edition, 1971).

93. Dane Kennedy, *The Magic Mountains: Hill Stations in the British Raj* (Berkeley: University of California Press, 1996).

94. Alice L. Conklin and Julia Clancy-Smith, eds., introduction to *FHS* 27, 3 (2004): 497–505.

95. The hefty dossier, Korbous, E-377-3, ANT, contains numerous heart-wrenching petitions from villagers appealing for social justice; for example, on March 30, 1906, "the shaykh of the Sidi 'Ammara complains that their lands were expropriated." See also Jennings, *Curing*, 166–67; and Colette Zytnicki, ed., *Le tourisme dans les colonies (XIXè–XXè siècles): Un outil de domination coloniale?* (Paris: Société Française d'Histoire d'Outre-Mer, 2009).

96. Arnaud, *Eaux*, 6.

97. Jennings, *Curing*.

98. Mary Lynn Stewart, *For Health and Beauty: Physical Culture for Frenchwomen, 1880s-1930s* (Baltimore: Johns Hopkins Press, 2001), 56–74.

99. On French colonial identification with, and glorification of, things Roman in North Africa, see also Patricia Lorcin, "Rome and France in Africa: Recovering Colonial Algeria's Latin Past," *FHS* 25 (2002): 295–329.

100. Thinking about the Korbous situation under the Protectorate from a world historical perspective leads to intriguing differences from, as well as similarities to, the British hill stations in India—despite the problems inherent in comparing a fully colonized land with a precolonial society. In the Indian case, facsimiles of Cotswold villages, where colonials retreated at a comfortable distance from the natives, virtually eradicated South Asian ritual, spatial, and architectural practices.

101. Créput, "Notice."

102. Donald M. Reid, "Consuming Antiquity in the Twilight of Empire: Western Tourism in Egypt, 1914-1959," paper presented at the annual meeting of Middle East Studies Association, 2006, quoted with permission of author.

103. Kenneth J. Perkins, "So Near and Yet So Far: British Tourists in Algiers, 1875-1914," paper presented at the annual meeting of Middle East Studies Association, 2006, quoted with permission of author.

104. *Le Petit Tunisien Indépendant,* Friday, March 12, 1886, 1.

105. Khelifa Chater, *Dépendance et mutations précoloniales: La Régence de Tunis de 1815 à 1857* (Tunis: Publications de l'Université de Tunis, 1984).

106. Roberts, *Outsiders*.

107. C. A. Bayly, *The Birth of the Modern World, 1780-1914: Global Connections and Comparisons* (Oxford: Blackwell, 2004).

108. Julia Clancy-Smith, "L'école rue du pacha, Tunis: L'enseignement de la femme arabe et 'la plus grande France,' c. 1900–1914," special issue, *Clio: Histoire, Femmes et Sociétés* 12 (2000): 33–55; and Ben Achour, *Cour*, v.

109. Author's interview with Naila Rostom, July 1999, La Marsa.

110. Thanks to Professors James A. Miller and to Laurence O. Michalak for oral information on Bourguiba's visceral hatred for the dynasty. As soon as Tunisia was declared a republic, the president alerted the press that he would publicly evict Amin Bey—the last ruler—from his Carthage palace early in the morning. Bourguiba wanted photographers to take pictures of the old man, aged seventy-three, in an undignified state to further humiliate him. In his speeches, Bourguiba frequently claimed that the Husaynids and the political class of mamluk origins were not really Tunisians, often referring to them as Greeks. For these reasons, the history of the Husaynid family was taboo until recently.

CHAPTER 9

Epigraph: Khayr al-Din al-Tunisi, *Aqwam al-masalik fi ma'rifat ahwal al-mamalik: al-muqaddima* (Tunis: al-Dar al-Tunisiya lil-Nashr, 1972), 83.

1. Khayr al-Din sat for a number of portraits that merit closer scrutiny. Mongi Smida, *Khereddine: Ministre réformateur, 1873–1877* (Tunis: Maison Tunisienne de l'Edition, 1970), 38, 47, 87, provides reproductions but without analysis or even attribution. Khayr al-Din's choice of Napoleonic poses was not surprising, given his fascination with the empire's history.

2. Miriam Fuchs, ed., "Autobiography and Geography: Introduction," *Biography* 25, 1 (Winter 2002): 1–8.

3. Khayr al-Din, *Aqwam*, 82, 85. On spatial-temporal compression and modernity, see Stephen Kern, *The Culture of Time and Space, 1880–1918* (Cambridge: Harvard University Press, 1983); critical for Khayr al-Din's generation was the "simultaneity made possible by the telegraph" (68–69). The notion of a communication order—more dense and complex than a system, and more heterogeneous than communications narrowly construed—is advanced by C. A. Bayly in *Empire and Information: Intelligence Gathering and Social Communication in India, 1780–1870* (Cambridge: Cambridge University Press, 1996).

4. Among the first to appreciate Khayr al-Din's intellectual originality was André Demeerseman, a White Father from Belgium, who spent much of his life in Tunis, publishing studies of Khayr al-Din in the journal of the Institut des Belles Lettres Arabes from 1956 on; see Brown, *Surest Path*.

5. G. S. Van Krieken's *Khayr al-Din et la Tunisie (1850–1881)* (Leiden: E. J. Brill, 1976) is the most comprehensive biography; see also G. S. Van Krieken, "Khayr al-Din Pasha," *EI2* 4: 1153–55.

6. Mohamed-Salah Mzali and Jean Pignon, eds., *Kheredine: Homme d'état* (Tunis: Maison Tunisienne de l'Edition, 1971), 5–12. The title—"*homme d'état*"—sums up earlier assessments of Khayr al-Din and his generation. 'Abd al-Jalil al-Tamimi, ed., *Murasalat wa watha'iq al-wazir al-akbar Khayr al-Din: al-tarikh al-tunisi* ('Ayn Zaghwan: Tamimi Foundation, 1999), 267–72, contains an exhaustive bibliography. Some of Khayr al-Din's private papers were destroyed or lost; others were unavailable to researchers until recently.

See also Ahmad 'Abd al-Salam, *Risa'il Husayn ila Khayr al-Din,* 2 vols. (Carthage: Bayt al-Hikma, 1991).

7. Theodor Menzel, "Khair al-Din Pasha," *EI₁* 4: 873. Henri Cambon portrayed him as a Turkophile in *Histoire de la Régence de Tunis* (Paris: Éditions Berger-Levrault, 1948), 127. Other interpretations are found in Mzali and Pignon, *Kheredine,* 7; and Ahmed Abdes-selem, *Les historiens Tunisiens des XVIIe, XVIIIe et XIXe siècles* (Paris: Klincksieck, 1973), 315–31.

8. The best example is Albert Hourani, *Arabic Thought in the Liberal Age, 1798–1939* (London: Oxford University Press, 1962). On the difficulties of defining modernity, see David Scott and Charles Hirschkind, eds., *Powers of the Secular Modern: Talal Asad and His Interlocutors* (Stanford: Stanford University Press, 2006); and Michael Saler, "Moder-nity and Enchantment: A Historiographic Review," *AHR* 111, 3 (June 2006): 692–716.

9. Ilham Khuri-Makdisi, "The *Nahda* Revisited: Socialism and Radicalism in Beirut and Mount Lebanon, 1900–1914," in *Liberal Thought in the Eastern Mediterranean: Late 19th Century until the 1960s,* ed. Christoph Schumann (Leiden: Brill, 2008), 147–74.

10. Venita Datta, *Birth of a National Icon: The Literary Avant-Garde and the Origins of the Intellectual in France* (New York: SUNY Press, 1999).

11. Virtually nothing is known of his childhood; see Khayr al-Din's memoirs, *A mes enfants: Ma vie privée et politique,* in *Kheredine,* ed. Mzali and Pignon, 17–19. He did attempt to locate family members in Egypt but without success.

12. Nadia Sebaï, *Mustapha Saheb Ettabaa: Un haut dignitaire beylical dans la Tunisie du XIXe siècle* (Carthage: Éditions Cartaginoiseries, 2007)

13. Khayr al-Din's first wife is also referred to as Jeannette or Janette as well as by the honorific Lalla Kabira. Under Islamic law, Khayr al-Din could have taken more than one wife. Mzali and Pignon, *Kheredine,* 13.

14. Le Père André Demeerseman discussed the central role of marriage in a series of articles, "Catégories sociales en Tunisie au XIXème siècle d'aprés la chronique d'A. Ibn Abi d. Diyaf," *IBLA* (1967–1970). See also Alessandro Triulzi, "Italian-Speaking Commu-nities in Early Nineteenth Century Tunis," *ROMM* 9, 1 (1971): 13; and 'Ali Chenoufi, intro-duction to *Al-wazir Khayr al-Din wa mu'asiruhu* (Carthage: Bayt al-Hikma, 1990), 18.

15. Mustafa Khaznadar had served the rulers from the 1850s through the 1870s; ex-tremely avaricious, he amassed a huge personal fortune through corrupt business deals with European investors that led to state bankruptcy.

16. On the mamluk system, see Raymond, *Chronique,* 2: 38–40; Mohamed El Aziz Ben Achour, *Catégories de la société tunisoise dans la deuxième moitié du XIXème siècle* (Tunis: Institut National d'Archéologie et d'Art, 1989); and Brown, *Tunisia,* 41–53.

17. Raymond, *Chronique,* 2: 82.

18. Brown, *Tunisia,* 45. See also Bin Diyaf, *Ithaf* 7, no. 332, 105–6; and Triulzi, "Com-munities," 159.

19. Raymond, *Chronique,* 2: 39.

20. Brown, *Tunisia,* 294; Bin Diyaf, *Ithaf,* 4/6: 41–42.

21. Van Krieken, *Khayr al-Din,* 9–17; and Khayr al-Din, *Vie,* 17–19.

22. Van Krieken, *Khayr al-Din,* 12–15. See also Arnold H. Green, *The Tunisian Ulama, 1873–1915: Social Structure and Response to Ideological Currents* (Leiden: E. J. Brill, 1978), 110.

23. Planel, "De la nation," 1: 99–137; and Muhammad Rashad al-Hamzawi, *Mu'jam al-mafahim al-hadariya min khilal "al-Ra'id al-Rasmi" (1860–1900)* (Tunis: al-Wizara al-Ula, 1998), 5–25.

24. Eva Hanebutt-Benz, Dagmar Glass, and Geoffrey Roper, eds., *Middle Eastern Languages and the Print Revolution: A Cross-Cultural Encounter* (Mainz: Gutenberg Museum, 2002), 188–90; G. Zawadowski, "Richard Holt, pionnier de la presse tunisienne," *RT* 41 (1939): 127–31; Muhammad Hamdan, *Dalil al-dawrayat al-sadira bil-bilad al-tunisiya* (Carthage: Bayt al-Hikma, 1989); and Silvia Finzi, ed., *Memorie italiane di Tunisia/Mémoires italiennes de Tunisie* (Tunis: Finzi Editore, 2000), 180–81. Algeria acquired French and Arabic presses in 1830.

25. Muhammad Salih Mzali, introduction in *Min rasa'il Ibn Abi al-Diyaf* (Tunis: Al-Dar al-Tunisiya lil-Nashr, 1969), 18.

26. *L'Aigle de Paris,* December 1859, p. 1, Microform MICR D-1189, BNF.

27. Khayr al-Din, *Aqwam,* 170–71.

28. The British vice-consul Santillana observed in 1861 that "Sy Kiar Edden [Khayr al-Din] is preparing to go to Holland, Belgium, and Sweden with decorations from the Bey for the sovereigns of those countries." May 26, 1861, file folder no. 4, box 5, RW.

29. Triulzi, "Communities," 161. See also Brown, *Tunisia,* 325–34.

30. Fayçal Bey, "Le bey de Tunis chez le roi des Français," *Histoire,* March 19, 2004, 69.

31. Béchir Tlili, *Études d'histoire sociale tunisienne du XIXe siècle* (Tunis: Publications de l'Université de Tunis, 1974), 103; Moncef Charfeddine, *Deux siècles de theatre en Tunisie* (Tunis: Les Éditions Ibn Charaf, n.d.), 16–18; and the *Moniteur Universel,* Paris, December 16, 1846.

32. Bin Diyaf, *Ithaf,* 4/6: 104–24. Interestingly enough, Khayr al-Din did not discuss the first Paris trip in his memoirs. Bin Diyaf's promotion of travel is seen in his biographical notice on Muhammad Siyala (d. 1832), who accompanied Muhammad Khuja to London and other cities where "the trip educated him." Bin Diyaf, *Ithaf 7,* no. 189, 162.

33. Magali Morsy, ed., *Essai sur les réformes nécessaires aux états musulmans* (Aix-en-Provence: Édisud, 1987), 20–21.

34. Khayr al-Din, *Vie,* 19–21; and Van Krieken, *Khayr al-Din,* 22–30. Van Krieken did not consult French diplomatic—above all, the Quai d'Orsay—or other archives in Paris, which would yield additional documentation on Khayr al-Din's experiences.

35. From this period came the letters, *Min rasa'il Ibn Abi al-Diyaf,* exchanged between Bin Diyaf and Khayr al-Din.

36. Richard L. Chambers, "Notes on the *Mekteb-I Osmani* in Paris, 1857–1874," in *Beginnings of Modernization in the Middle East,* ed. William R. Polk and Richard L. Chambers (Chicago: University of Chicago Press, 1968), 313–29. During Khayr al-Din's stay in the French capital, Turkish educators organized the Ottoman Imperial School in Paris.

37. Van Krieken, *Khayr al-Din,* 73; Khayr al-Din, *Vie,* 42, note 69; and Tamimi, *Murasalat,* 2.

38. Khayr al-Din, *Vie,* 23. See also Van Krieken, *Khayr al-Din,* 168.

39. Khayr al-Din, *Vie,* 22–23.

40. Louis Jean-Baptiste Filippi, "Fragmens historiques et statistiques sur la Régence

de Tunis," 103, in *Documents historiques sur la Tunisie. Relations inédites de Nyssen, Filippi et Calligaris (1788, 1829, 1834)*, by Charles Monchicourt (Paris: Société d'Éditions Géographiques, Maritimes et Coloniales, 1929).

41. Khayr al-Din, *Aqwam*, 146–47.

42. Triulzi, "Communities," 168–69.

43. Chenoufi, *Khayr al-Din*, 17.

44. In *Vie*, 23, 39, Khayr al-Din refers to Tunisia as "my adopted country." Sadok Zemerli, in *Les précurseurs* (Tunis: Editions Bouslama, 1979), 66, agrees.

45. Khayr al-Din, *Vie*, 44–45. The perils were outlined in Richard Wood's draft memo marked private and confidential: "The annexation however of Tunis to Algeria would give France an immense extension of Seaboard in the Mediterranean. She could acquire Ports in Africa which she does not possess at present and the spacious Bay of Tunis would be speedily converted by her engineers into an arsenal for her fleet which would then be within 24 hours navigation of Malta." January 25, 1859, file no. 4, box 5, RW.

46. Van Krieken, *Khayr al-Din*, 31–36; Tamimi, *Murasalat*, 13; and for the quote, Baynes to Ahmad Bey, October 26, 1853, carton 227, dossier 411, ANT.

47. Mimi Hellman, "Furniture, Sociability, and the Work of Leisure in Eighteenth-Century France," *Eighteenth-Century Studies* 32, 4 (1999): 415–45.

48. Krieken, *Khayr al-Din*, 31–36, 166–68; and Nabil ben Khelil, *Maisons de Carthage* (Tunis: Dar Ashraf, 1996), 100–108.

49. Ernst von Hesse-Wartegg, *Tunis: The Land and the People* (New York: Dodd, Mead & Company, c. 1881), 80–81.

50. Charles Matrat, "La Société Pastre Frères Agence Commerciale de Sidi Mustapha Khaznadar à Marseille," in *Études d'histoire contemporaine tunisienne (1846–1871)*, by François Arnoulet, Charles Matrat, and Jean-Louis Miège (Aix-en-Provence: Université de Provence, c. 1970), 29. In *Vie*, 46, Khayr al-Din lists his properties, most gifts from the Husaynids in gratitude for state service. The impact of Haussman's rebuilding program on Khayr al-Din's thinking about urban environments and social order is worth pursuing.

51. J.S. Woodford, *The City of Tunis: Evolution of an Urban System* (Cambridgeshire: Middle East and North African Studies Press, 1990), 120.

52. Khayr al-Din's letter of June 3, 1860 concerning La Goulette's Catholic Church and another conflict over use of space; he presided over the "Commission mixte pour les propriétés de la Goulette" and formulated an open letter, "Address to the European Colony in Tunis," regarding property rights; carton 207, dossier 96, 1859–1861, ANT.

53. *L'illustration, journal universel* (Paris), vol. 37 (March 23, 1861): 181–82.

54. Abdesselem, *Historiens*, 357.

55. Van Krieken, *Khayr al-Din*, 48–92.

56. Khayr al-Din, *Vie*, 27–45.

57. Bin Diyaf, *Ithaf*, 5: 37–44; and Khayr al-Din, *Vie*, 22–23.

58. There was universal agreement that Khayr al-Din was of incorruptible morals. Richard Wood expressed the prevailing view in a letter to Sir Austin Layard in Constantinople in 1878: "He [Khayr al-Din] has the reputation of being thoroughly honest; and during my long residence here [in Tunis], I have never heard him accused of corruption in any single instance." File number 3 [5/3], RW.

59. The European expositions, world's fairs, and various Orientalist conferences in 1889 and 1890, exerted a tremendous impact. The Paris trade fairs of 1866 and 1890 inspired several Arabic accounts, including Muhammad al-Tunisi al-Sanusi's *al-Istitla'at al-barisiya,* published in Tunis in 1891.

60. Khayr al-Din, *Aqwam,* 89.

61. Ibid., 85.

62. See Wasti, "A Note," 18, note 50, for the Arabic edition in Istanbul. The French edition's full title reads *Essai formant la première partie de l'ouvrage politique et statistique intitulé: "La plus sûre direction pour connaître l'état des nations"* (Paris: Imprimerie Paul Dupont, 1868).

63. Tamimi, *Murasalat,* 14.

64. Van Krieken, *Khayr al-Din,* 106–36.

65. Brown, *Surest Path,* 47; and Khayr al-Din, *Aqwam,* 187, 202

66. Syed Tanvir Wasti, "A Note on Tunuslu Hayreddin Paşa," *Middle Eastern Studies* 36, 1 (January 2000): 5.

67. Correspondence on conversions is in H series, carton 63, dossier 722, ANT. See also Mohamed Kerrou, "Logiques de l'abjuration et de la conversion à l'Islam en Tunisie aux XIXe et XXe siècles," in *Conversions Islamiques: Identités religieuses en Islam méditerranéen,* ed. Mercedes García-Arenal (Paris: Maisonneuve & Larose, 2001), 325–65.

68. Khayr al-Din, *A mes enfants,* 37. The first public lending library was organized in Tunis in 1840 by Ahmad Bey. Adrien Berbrugger, "La bibliothèque publique de Tunis," *RA* 6 (1862): 222. The first archivist to organize state records in modern fashion, Mohamed El-Karoui (1842–1922), had been trained at the Bardo military school and served as Khayr al-Din's aide-de-camp.

69. Khayr al-Din, *Vie,* 36–37; Noureddine Sraïeb, *Le Collège Sadiki de Tunis, 1875–1956: Enseignement et nationalisme* (Tunis: Alif, 1990); Béchir Tlili, "Eléments pour une approche de la pensée socio-économique de Kheredine (1810–1889)," *ROMM* 9 (1971): 119–52; and Green, *Ulama,* 115–34. It would be important to know to what extent, if at all, Khayr al-Din was aware of the other schooling experiments underway in Tunis, such as the Sisters of Saint-Joseph de l'Apparition girls' schools.

70. Green, *Ulama,* 103–28; Sraïeb, *Le Collège,* 13–64; and Abdesselem, *Historiens,* 99–146. L. Poinssot, "Notes et documents: Une intaille à retrouver," *RT,* nos. 9–12 (1932): 245–46, documents the 1835 theft of a stunning stone carving depicting Neptune's triumph.

71. Green, *Ulama,* 113.

72. Julia Clancy-Smith, "L'école rue du pacha, Tunis: L'enseignement de la femme arabe et 'la plus grande France,' c. 1900–1914," special issue, *Clio: Histoire, Femmes et Sociétés* 12 (2000): 33–55.

73. L.-Charles Féraud, "Notes sur un voyage en Tunisie et Tripolitaine," *RA* 20 (1876): 493–96, quote p. 493.

74. Ibid., 495. School clothing demands study; Sadiqi's uniforms were patterned on those worn by Muslim students in Algeria.

75. Daniel Grasset, "L'instruction publique en Tunisie: Rapport à M. Le Gouverneur Général de L'Algérie," *RA* 22 (1878): 184–201.

76. Ibid., 196. Arabic in Algeria held the status of a foreign language; literary Arabic

was only taught once a week in some establishments. For a contemporary critique of language, see Gustave Dugat, "Des établissements d'instruction publique," *RA* 13 (1869): 279–87; and A. Cour, "Notes sur les chaires de langue arabe d'Alger, de Constantine et d'Oran (1832–1879)," *RA* 65 (1924): 20–64.

77. Hesse-Wartegg, *Tunis*, 55. See also Mohammed Bencheneb, "Notions de pédagogie musulmane: Résumé d'éducation et d'instruction enfantine," *RA* 41 (1897): 267–85. Bencheneb, a student of the Orientalist scholar Fagnan, represented Islam and Muslims in the 1904 international congress held in Algiers. David Robinson, *Paths of Accommodation: Muslim Societies and French Colonial Authorities in Senegal and Mauritania, 1880–1920* (Athens: Ohio University Press, 2000), noted that French colonial authorities in Senegal dispatched Muslim students to study at Sadiqi College.

78. Tlili, *Études*, 97. Bin Diyaf's treatise is printed in *Hawliyat al-jami'a al-tunisiya*, no. 5 (1968): 66–109. See also Mohamed Kerrou, "Les débats autour de la visibilité de la femme et du voile dans l'espace public de la Tunisie contemporaine (milieu XIXe–début XXe siècles)," *Chronos: Revue d'histoire de l'Université de Balamand* 12 (2005): 47–50.

79. Hesse-Wartegg, *Tunis*, 79.

80. Mzali and Pignon, *Kheredine*, 13; Mzali, *Min rasa'il*, 9; and Chenoufi, *Khayr al-Din*, 18. See also Hesse-Wartegg, *Tunis*, 79–81, 83–91.

81. Wasti, "A Note," 19, note 63.

82. Khayr al-Din, *Vie*, 39.

83. Van Krieken, *Khayr al-Din*, 271–78.

84. Sir Austin Layard, September 24, 1878, file no. 3 [5/3], RW.

85. Andreas Tunger-Zanetti, *La communication entre Tunis et Istanbul, 1860–1913* (Paris: L'Harmattan, 1996), 48–49.

86. In *Istanbul: Memories and the City* (New York: Knopf, 2005), 26–28, Orhan Pamuk notes that his family residence abutted the ruins of Khayr al-Din's mansion in the hills overlooking Dolmabahçe palace and that collective memory about him persisted.

87. Wasti, "A Note," 19, note 64.

88. Morsy, *Essai*, 23–24.

89. Chenoufi, *Khayr al-Din*, 26–29. Independent North Africa's need to lay claim to the nation's mythical forefathers, or expel the remains of individuals associated with the colonial past, resulted in a number of exhumations and returns. Amir 'Abd al-Qadir was brought back from Damascus to Algiers; the Tunisian labor leader Muhammad 'Ali left his resting place in Arabia for Tunis; and Charles-Martial Lavigerie was sent from Carthage to Rome.

90. Chenoufi, *Khayr al-Din*, 21.

91. Natalie Zemon Davis, *Trickster Travels: A Sixteenth-Century Muslim between Worlds* (New York: Hill and Wang, 2006).

92. Brown, *Surest Path*, 40.

93. Morsy, *Essai*, 19.

94. Alex Owen, *The Place of Enchantment: British Occultism and the Culture of the Modern* (Chicago: University of Chicago Press, 2004), maintains that a defining characteristic of modernity in the late nineteenth century was openness to esoteric ideas and practices, such as Theosophy. This line of argument applies to precolonial Tunisia and

colonial Algeria where Masonic lodges and ideas attracted some Muslims; the Algerian leader 'Abd al-Qadir was reputedly a Mason for awhile.

95. How do contemporary Web-based communities of thought evaluate Khayr al-Din? A Google search shows that his ideas have attracted some attention. Web sites, such as the Ibn Rushd Fund for Freedom of Thought, the Centre for the Study of Democracy, and the online Library of Liberty Inc., all claim Khayr al-Din as their own.

96. Mikhail Bakhtin, *The Dialogic Imagination: Four Essays,* trans. Michael Holquist (Austin: University of Texas Press, 1981), 243.

97. Hachem Karoui and Ali Mahjoubi, *Quand le soleil s'est levé à l'ouest: Tunisie 1881-impérialisme et résistance* (Tunis: Cérès Productions, 1983).

EPILOGUE

Epigraph: Michel Auguglioro, *La Partenza: La saga d'une famille sicilienne de Tunisie, première partie, 1887-1909* (Tunis: Éditions Cartaginoiseries, 2008), 7.

1. "Tunisie: 26 disparus dans le naufrage d'une barque de migrants clandestins," *Tunisia Watch,* January 19, 2009; Agence France Presse, January 19, 2009; and the Associated Press, January 19, 2009. Today's unskilled workers in Tunisia continue to come from the interior and Libya, but many clandestine laborers, particularly on construction sites, are from Mali and other regions of sub-Saharan Africa; these are the fortunate. Many others end up in small boats navigating the Mediterranean.

2. *Le Monde,* Friday, September 4, 2009, 8.

3. Gerald M. MacLean, *The Rise of Oriental Travel: English Visitors to the Ottoman Empire, 1580-1720* (New York: Palgrave Macmillan, 2004), xiii, reminds us for the early modern period that, "by linking crusading rhetoric with millennial literalism, a powerful tradition of Protestant thought has perpetuated the belief that there can be, and indeed must be, only conflict with Islam."

4. As seen, many consulates could not locate copies of diplomatic agreements, and some communities of long residence in Tunisia, notably the Greeks, were unaware of being subject to a special legal regime. Habib Kazdaghli, "Les communautés dans l'histoire de la Tunisie moderne et contemporaine," in *Les Communautés méditerranéennes de Tunisie: Actes en hommage au Doyen Mohamed Hédi Chérif* (Tunis: Centre de Publication Universitaire, 2006), 59-75.

5. In Effy Tselikas and Lina Hayoun, *Les lycées français du soleil: Creusets cosmopolites du Maroc, de l'Algérie et de la Tunisie* (Paris: Éditions Autrement, 2004), 201, Claudia Cardinale, who was born in La Goulette, observed that the Hollywood director Francis Coppola's family first went to Tunis from Sicily and later to the United States.

6. Julia Clancy-Smith, "Ruptures? Expatriates, Law, and Institutions in Colonial-Husaynid Tunisia, 1870-1914," in *Changes in Colonial and Post-Colonial Governance of Islam: Continuities and Ruptures,* ed. Veit Bader, Annelies Moors, and Marcel Maussen (Amsterdam: University of Amsterdam, 2010); Nada Auzary-Schmaltz, ed., *La justice française et le droit pendant le Protectorat en Tunisie* (Paris: Maisonneuve & Larose, 2008); and Faiza Matri, *Tunis sous le Protectorat: Histoire de la conservation du patrimoine architectural et urban de la médina* (Tunis: Centre de Publication Universitaire, 2008).

7. Frederick Cooper, *Colonialism in Question: Theory, Knowledge, History* (Berkeley: University of California Press, 2005).

8. Recall that the vast majority of Catholic immigrants were impoverished—a reliable figure from 1884 noted that "18,000 live in a state of poverty." Jean Marcille, ed., "Le printemps de Carthage: Souvenirs et images sur les collines de Carthage (période 1841 à 1925)," 48, unpublished ms., BDT.

9. Kenneth J. Perkins, *A History of Modern Tunisia* (Oxford: Oxford University Press, 2004), 44, quoting the Italian Prime Minister at the time, Francesco Crispi, who proclaimed more than once that Tunisia was an "Italian colony occupied by France." See also Daniela Melfa, *Migrando a sud: Coloni italiani di Tunisia (1881–1939)* (Rome: Aracne, 2008).

10. De Lanessan report, 1885, Memoires et Documents, Tunisie, vol. 14, AMAE.

11. After World War I, a number of international congresses on Mediterranean issues were convened, including the 1932 Congrès Méditerranéen de Défense Féminine, held in Constantine. Colonial scholarly journals, such as the *Revue de la Méditerranée* published in Algeria, demonstrate that perspectives beyond national/imperial configurations had taken hold, but these, as well as the international meetings, were mainly the work of elites in the metropoles. Nevertheless, there are few, if any, studies of a variety of cosmopolitanism informed by a mutual awareness of "Mediterranean-ness," since the obsessive concern with Tunisian or North African nationalism has marginalized this question. Jerrilynn D. Dodds, María Rosa Menocal, and Abigail Krasner Balbale, *The Arts of Intimacy: Christians, Jews, and Muslims in the Making of Castilian Culture* (New Haven: Yale University Press, 2009).

12. Béchir Yazidi, *La politique coloniale et le domaine de l'etat en Tunisie de 1881 jusqu'à la crises des années trente* (Tunis: Editions Sahar, 2005), 79.

13. Population figures are found in Martin Thomas, *The French Empire between the Wars: Imperialism, Politics, and Society* (Manchester: Manchester University Press, 2005), 74; Charles-Robert Ageron, *Modern Algeria: A History from 1830 to the Present* (Trenton: Africa World Press, 1991), 82; and Perkins, *Tunisia*, 82–84.

14. Valérie Esclangon-Morin, *Les rapatriés d'Afrique du Nord de 1956 à nos jours* (Paris: L'Harmattan, 2007); and Laurie A. Brand, *Citizens Abroad: Emigration and the State in the Middle East and North Africa* (Cambridge: Cambridge University Press, 2006).

15. So the *New York Times* claimed in "Marseille Sways to a Maghreb Rhythm," July 26, 2009, Travel Section, p. 1. See also Caitlin Killian, *North African Women in France: Gender, Culture, and Identity* (Stanford: Stanford University Press, 2006).

abu	Father
afaqi	Literally, those coming from the "horizons" or from the provinces; contrasts with the urbane inhabitants of Tunis, the baldi
'alim/ 'ulama' (ulema)	A religious scholar or savant
aman	An assurance of protection or clemency; a pardon
amin	Chief, head, or master of a guild
amir/umara'	Prince, emir, or tribal chief; also governor of a province
a'yan	Notables
baldis/baldiya	Urbane, sophisticated inhabitants of Tunis
barrani/ barraniya	Outside or foreign; by extension, recently arrived immigrants or temporary laborers residing in Tunis who were Muslims from elsewhere in the country or the Maghrib
bash hanba/ hamba	A beylical office; a sort of gendarme
bey	In Husaynid Tunisia, the reigning prince of the dynasty ruling in the name of the Ottoman sultan; elsewhere, a military rank
bint	Daughter
burnus	A hooded wool cloak
dabtiya	The urban police; police station
daftir/dafatir	A notebook, roster, dossier, or file

dar/bayt	House
Dar al-Islam	The abode of Islam; the Islamic world
dey	In Ottoman Algeria, a title designating the ruler of Algiers and Algeria, a subordinate to the sultan; also a Turkish military rank
diwan	Council, administrative office, chancellery
fallah/fallahin	Peasant or farmer
faqih	Expert in *fiqh,* a legist or jurisprudent
fatwa	An authoritative legal opinion regarding Islamic law, usually rendered by a mufti
fiqh	Muslim jurisprudence
funduq	Hotel or inn; a poor man's urban hostel, normally for those from outside Tunis; also used to designate the compounds in Tunis where the foreigners resided and worked
hadith	A prophetic tradition; narrative relating the deeds and utterances of Muhammad and his companions
ha'ik	An outer garment usually made of a long piece of woolen material and covering the head and body
hajj	Pilgrimage to Mecca incumbent upon all able Muslims at least once in a lifetime
hara	A neighborhood in Tunisian Arabic designating the indigenous Jewish quarter
Haramayn	The two holy cities, Mecca and Medina
hawma	In North African cities, a neighborhood or urban quarter
Hijaz	The western coast of the Arabian Peninsula on the Red Sea where Mecca and Medina are located
hubus/ahbas	A charitable or religious foundation; property of inalienable legal status whose revenue serves pious purposes (in the eastern Arab world, *waqf/awqaf*)
hurma	Holiness, sacred, sacrosanct
ibn	Son
imam	A leader in prayer
Jama'a	A tribal or village assembly or council of elders
jihad	"Struggle"; by extension, a religious or holy war in defense of the Muslim community
kahiya	Government official or chief officer of an administrative district
katib	A writer, scribe, or secretary
khalifa	Caliph; also a deputy of a ruler or a senior official
khassa	The elite, notables, upper class
khaznadar	State treasurer; keeper of the state's revenues

kuttab	A Quranic school
madrasa	A religious school or college, often attached to a mosque
mahalla	In Algeria and Tunisia, the annual military expedition by the central government to collect taxes, punish rebellious subjects, and render justice
majba	In Tunisia during the Ottoman era, a poll tax
majlis al-shari'a	An Islamic court or tribunal.
Mashriq	The eastern Arab world as opposed to the Maghrib
masjid	Mosque
milk (mulk)	Private property
mufti	An expert in Islamic law authorized to issue *fatwa*-s
na'ib	A representative, agent, or deputy
nishan al-iftikhar	The medal of glorious achievement, a Tunisian state decoration
nizami	Refers to regular troops in the bey's new army
qadi	A Muslim judge or magistrate
qa'id	Chief or leader, tribal or provincial administrator, also governor
qasba	Fortress or citadel; often the highest point in the city
qubba	Dome; a domed building or shrine commemorating a saint
ribat	A fortress or fortified place; also one of the two suburbs of Tunis
safsari	A very fine white cloak or mantle often using wool and silk
shari'a	Literally, the "path to be followed"; the holy law of Islam
sharif/shurafa'/ashraf	A descendant or descendants of the Prophet Muhammad or of his lineage; a noble person
shashiya	Red wool cap worn by Muslim males; akin to the fez
shaykh	An elder, chief, head of a tribe, master of a Sufi order
shaykh al-madina	A sort of city manager responsible for law and order in Tunis
Sufi	An Islamic mystic; a member of a mystical order or brotherhood
suq	A market, bazaar, or fair
tadhkira/teskéré	Permit or license; written authorization
Tanzimat	Reorganizations, meaning specifically the Ottoman state-sponsored reforms of the nineteenth century beginning in 1839
umm	Mother
umma	The community of Muslims
'urf	Customary law
zawiya/zawaya:	Literally, a "corner": a religious building enclosing a saint's tomb; a small mosque or prayer room; a Sufi center often including a mosque, hospice, and educational facilities

SELECT BIBLIOGRAPHY

'Abd al-Salam, Ahmad. *Risa'il Husayn ila Khayr al-Din.* 2 vols. Carthage: Bayt al-Hikma, 1991.

Abdesselem, Ahmed. *Les historiens tunisiens des XVIIe, XVIIIe et XIXe siècles: Essai d'histoire culturelle.* Paris: Librairie Klincksieck, 1973.

Abulafia David, ed. *The Mediterranean in History.* London: Thames & Hudson, 2003.

Alexandropoulos, Alex, and Patrick Cabanel, eds. *La Tunisie mosaïque.* Toulouse: Presses Universitaires du Mirail, 2000.

Anghie, Antony. "Finding the Peripheries: Sovereignty and Colonialism in Nineteenth-Century International Law." *Harvard International Law Journal* 40, 1 (Winter 1999): 1–80.

Arditti, R. *Recueil des textes législatifs et juridiques concernant les Israélites de Tunisie de 1857 à 1913.* Tunis: Borrel, 1915.

Arnaud, J. *Les eaux thermales de Korbous près Tunis (Tunisie).* Paris: Levé, 1912.

Auguglioro, Michel. *La Partenza: La saga d'une famille sicilienne de Tunisie, première partie, 1887–1909.* Tunis: Éditions Cartaginoiseries, 2008.

Auzary-Schmaltz, Nada, ed. *La justice française et le droit pendant le Protectorat en Tunisie.* Paris: Maisonneuve & Larose, 2008.

Bahloul, Joëlle. *The Architecture of Memory: A Jewish-Muslim Household in Colonial Algeria, 1937–1962.* Cambridge: Cambridge University Press, 1996.

Bavoux, Evariste. *Alger: Voyage politique et descriptif dans le nord de l'Afrique.* 2 vols. Paris: Chez Brockhaus et Avenarius, 1841.

Barbera, Serge La. *Les Français de Tunisie, 1930 à 1950.* Paris: L'Harmattan, 2006.

Bayly, Christopher A. *Empire and Information: Intelligence Gathering and Social Communication in India, 1780–1870.* Cambridge: Cambridge University Press, 1996.

Benton, Lauren. *Law and Colonial Cultures: Legal Regimes in World History, 1400–1900.* Cambridge: Cambridge University Press, 2002.

Bordas, Jeannine. *Le peuplement algérien: Essai démographique*. Oran: Fonque, 1958.

Ben Achour, Mohamed El Aziz. *Catégories de la société tunisoise dans la deuxième moitié du XIXe siècle*. Tunis: Institut National d'Archéologie et d'Art, 1989.

———. *La cour du bey de Tunis*. Tunis: Espace Diwan, 2003.

Bey, El-Mokhtar. *Les beys de Tunis (1705–1957): Hérédité, souveraineté, généalogie*. Tunis: Serviced, 2002.

Bono, Salvatore. *Schiavi musulmani nell'Italia moderna. Galeotti, vu' cumpra', domestici*. Napoli: Edzioni scientifiche italiane, 1999.

Braudel, Fernand. *La Méditerranée et le monde méditerranéen à l' époque de Philippe II*. Paris: A. Colin, 1976.

Bridgman, Frederick Arthur. *Winters in Algeria*. New York: Harper & Brothers, 1890.

Brown, Leon Carl. *The Surest Path: The Political Treatise of a Nineteenth-Century Muslim Statesmen; A Translation of the Introduction to "The Surest Path to Knowledge Concerning the Condition of Countries" by Khayr al-Din al-Tunisi*. Cambridge, Mass.: Harvard University Press, 1967.

———. *The Tunisia of Ahmad Bey (1837–1855)*. Princeton: Princeton University Press, 1974.

———. *"Consult Them in the Matter": A Nineteenth-Century Tunisian Argument for Constitutional Government; The Muqaddima to Ithaf Ahl al-Zaman bi Akhbar Muluk Tunis wa 'Ahd al-Aman*. Fayetteville: University of Arkansas Press, 2005.

Burke, Edmund, III, and David Prochaska, eds. *Genealogies of Orientalism: History, Theory, Politics*. Lincoln: University of Nebraska Press, 2008.

Cavasino, Agnès. *Emilie de Vialar, fondatriçe: Les Soeurs de Saint-Joseph de l'Apparition, une congrégation missionnaire*. Fontenay sous Bois: Congrégation des Soeurs de Saint-Joseph de l'Apparition, 1987.

Çelik, Zeynep. *Empire, Architecture, and the City: French-Ottoman Encounters, 1830–1914*. Seattle: University of Washington Press, 2008.

Çelik, Zeynep, Julia Clancy-Smith, and Frances Terpak, eds. *Walls of Algiers: Narratives of the City through Text and Image*. Los Angeles: Getty Research Institute; Seattle: University of Washington Press, 2009.

Çelik, Zeynep, and Leila Kinney. "Ethnography and Exhibitionism at the Expositions Universelles." *Assemblage* 13 (1990): 34–59.

Chater, Khelifa. *Dépendance et mutations précoloniales: La Régence de Tunis de 1815 à 1857*. Tunis: Publications de l'Université de Tunis, 1984.

Chérif, Mohamed-Hédi. *Pouvoir et société dans la Tunisie de H'usayn Bin 'Ali, 1705–1740*. 2 vols. Tunis: Publications de l'Université de Tunis, 1986.

Choate, Mark I. *Emigrant Nation: The Making of Italy Abroad*. Cambridge, Mass.: Harvard University Press, 2008.

Clancy-Smith, Julia. *Rebel and Saint: Muslim Notables, Populist Protest, Colonial Encounters (Algeria and Tunisia, 1800–1904)*. Berkeley: University of California Press, 1994.

———. "The Maghrib and the Mediterranean World in the Nineteenth Century: Illicit Exchanges, Migrants, and Social Marginals." In *The Maghrib in Question*, ed. Kenneth J. Perkins and Michel Le Gall. Austin: University of Texas Press, 1997.

———, ed. *North Africa, Islam, and the Mediterranean World: From the Almoravids to the Algerian War*. London: Frank Cass Publications, 2001.

——. "Locating Women as Migrants in Nineteenth-Century Tunis." In *Contesting Archives: Historians Develop Methodologies for Finding Women in the Sources*, ed. Nupur Chaudhuri, Sherry Katz, and Mary Elizabeth Perry. Urbana: University of Illinois Press, 2010.

Clancy-Smith, Julia, and Frances Gouda, eds. *Domesticating the Empire: Race, Gender, and Family Life in French and Dutch Colonialism.* Charlottesville: University Press of Virginia, 1998.

Colley, Linda. *Captives: Britain, Empire and the World, 1600–1850.* London: Jonathan Cape, 2002.

Colonna, Fanny, and Zakya Daoud, eds. *Etre marginal au Maghreb.* Tunis: Alif, 1993.

Crespo, Gérard. *Les Italiens en Algérie, 1830–1960: Histoire et sociologie d'une migration.* Calvisson: J. Gandini, 1994.

Curtis, Sarah A. *Civilizing Habits: Women Missionaries and the Revival of French Empire.* New York: Oxford University Press, 2010.

——. *Educating the Faithful: Religion, Schooling, and Society in Nineteenth-Century France.* DeKalb: Northern Illinois University Press, 2000.

Dakhlia, Jocelyne. *Lingua Franca: Histoire d'une langue partagée en Méditerranée.* Paris: Actes Sud, 2008.

Day, Philippa, ed. *At Home in Carthage: The British in Tunisia.* Tunis: Trustees of St. Georges Church, 1992.

Debbasch, Yvan. *La nation française en Tunisie (1577–1835).* Paris: Sirey, 1957.

Deguilhem, Randi. *Individual and Society in the Mediterranean Muslim World: Issues and Sources.* Aix-en-Provence: Paul Rouboud, 1998.

Demech, Luigi. *The British Consulate in Tunis: Critical Remarks.* Malta: Albion Press, 1868.

Denis, Léon. *Tunis et l'île de Sardaigne: Souvenirs de voyage.* Tours: Imprimerie E. Arrault, 1884.

Dornier, François. *La vie des catholiques en Tunisie au fil des ans.* Tunis: Finzi, 2000.

Dougui, Noureddine, ed. *Les relations tuniso-françaises au miroir des elites (XIXè, XXème siècles).* Tunis: Publications de la Faculté des Lettres, Manouba, 1997.

Dwyer, Philip. *Napoleon: The Path to Power.* New Haven: Yale University Press, 2008.

Esclangon-Morin, Valérie. *Les rapatriés d'Afrique du Nord de 1956 à nos jours.* Paris: L'Harmattan, 2007.

Ewald, Janet J. "Crossers of the Sea: Slaves, Freedmen, and Other Migrants in the Northwestern Indian Ocean, c. 1750–1914." *AHR* 105, 1 (2000): 69–91.

Finotti, Guglielmo. *La Reggenza di Tunisi.* 2nd ed. Malta: F. Cumbo Tipografo, 1856.

Finzi, Silvia, ed. *Memorie italiane di Tunisia/Mémoires italiennes de Tunisie.* Tunis: Finzi Editore, 2000.

——, ed. *Mestieri e professioni degli Italiani di Tunisia/Métiers et professions des Italiens de Tunisie.* Tunis: Editions Finzi, 2003.

Frank, Louis. *Histoire de Tunis.* Introduction and annotation by J. J. Marcel. 2nd ed. Paris: Firmin-Didot, 1851.

Gabaccia, Donna, R. *Italy's Many Diasporas.* Seattle: University of Washington Press, 2000.

Gabaccia, Donna R., and Franca Iacovetta, eds. *Women, Gender, and Transnational Lives: Italian Workers of the World*. Toronto: University of Toronto Press, 2002.

Gallagher, Nancy E. *Medicine and Power in Tunisia, 1780–1900*. Cambridge: Cambridge University Press, 1983.

Ganiage, Jean. "Les Européens en Tunisie au milieu du XIXe siècle." *CT* 3, 9 (1955): 389–421.

———. *La population européenne de Tunis*. Paris: Presses Universitaires de France, 1960.

———. *Les origines du Protectorat Français en Tunisie (1861–1881)*. Tunis: Maison Tunisienne de l'Édition, 1968.

García-Arenal, Mercedes, ed. *Conversions Islamiques: Identités religieuses en Islam méditerranéen*. Paris: Maisonneuve & Larose, 2001.

Geslin, Louis. *Korbous: Histoire d'une station thermale d'Afrique*. Tunis: Société Anonyme de l'Imprimerie Rapide, 1913.

Geyer, Martin H., and Johannes Paulmann, eds. *The Mechanics of Internationalism: Culture, Society, and Politics from the 1840s to the First World War*. Oxford: Oxford University Press, 2001.

Greene, Molly. *Catholic Pirates and Greek Merchants: A Maritime History of the Early Modern Mediterranean*. Princeton: Princeton University Press, 2010.

Gregory, Desmond. *Sicily: The Insecure Base: A History of the British Occupation, 1806–1815*. London: Associated University Presses, 1988.

Grandchamp, Pierre. "Autour du Consulat de France à Tunis (1577–1881)." *RT*, nos. 53–54 (1943): 1–268.

Greaves, Joseph. *The Journal of Mr. Joseph Greaves, on a Visit to the Regency of Tunis*. In *Christian Researches in Syria and the Holy Land 1823 and 1824 in Furtherance of the Objects of the Church Missionary Society*, by Rev. William Jowett. London: Seeley & Son, 1825.

Hamzawi, Muhammad Rashad al-. *Mu'jam al-mafahim al-hadariya min khilal "al-Ra'id al-Rasmi" (1860–1900)*. Tunis: al-Wizara al-Ula, 1998.

Helms, Mary W. *Ulysses' Sail: An Ethnographic Odyssey of Power, Knowledge, and Geographical Distance*. Princeton: Princeton University Press, 1988.

Hénia, Abdelhamid. *Propriété et stratégies sociales à Tunis (XVIe–XIXe siècles)*. Tunis: Faculté des Sciences Humaines et Sociales de Tunis, 1999.

Henssen, Jens. *Beirut: The Making of an Ottoman Provincial Capital*. Oxford: Clarendon Press, 2005.

Herbert, Lady Mary E. *A Search After Sunshine, or Algeria in 1871*. London: Bentley, 1872.

Hesse-Wartegg, Ernst von. *Tunis: The Land and the People*. New York: Dodd, Mead & Company, 1881.

Hoerder, Dirk. *Cultures in Contact: World Migrations in the Second Millennium*. Durham: Duke University Press, 2002.

Hourani, Albert. *Arabic Thought in the Liberal Age, 1798–1939*. London: Oxford University Press, 1962.

Hughes, J. Donald. *Pan's Travail: Environmental Problems of the Ancient Greeks and Romans*. Baltimore: Johns Hopkins University Press, 1994.

Ibn Abi al-Diyaf, Ahmad. *Ithaf ahl al-zaman bi-akhbar muluk tunis wa 'ahd al-aman*. 8 vols. Tunis: al-Dar al-Tunisiya lil-Nashr, 1989.

Jennings, Eric T. *Curing the Colonizers: Hydrotherapy, Climatology, and French Colonial Spas*. Durham: Duke University Press, 2006.

Keddie, Nikki R., and Beth Baron, eds. *Women in Middle Eastern History: Shifting Boundaries in Sex and Gender*. New Haven: Yale University Press, 1991.

Keller, Richard C. *Colonial Madness: Psychiatry in French North Africa*. Chicago: University of Chicago Press, 2007.

Kenbib, Mohammed. *Les Protégés: Contribution à l'histoire contemporaine du Maroc*. Rabat: Faculté des Lettres et des Sciences Humaines, 1996.

Kerrou, Mohamed. "Les débats autour de la visibilité de la femme et du voile dans l'espace public de la Tunisie contemporaine (milieu XIXe–début XXe siècles)." *Chronos: Revue d'Histoire de l'Université de Balamand* 12 (2005): 37–77.

Khater, Akram. *Inventing Home: Emigration, Gender, and the Middle Class in Lebanon, 1870–1920*. Berkeley: University of California Press, 2001.

Khayr al-Din al-Tunisi. *Aqwam al-masalik fi ma'rifat ahwal al-mamalik: al-muqaddima*. Tunis: al-Dar al-Tunisiya lil-Nashr, 1972.

Khelil, Nabil ben. *Maisons de Carthage*. Tunis: Dar Ashraf, 1996.

Khuri-Makdisi, Ilham. *Levantine Trajectories and the Making of Global Radicalism, 1860–1914*. Berkeley: University of California Press, 2010.

Koster, Adrianus. *Prelates and Politicians in Malta: Changing Power-Balance between Church and State in a Mediterranean Island Fortress, 1800–1976*. Assen: Van Gorcum, 1984.

Lallemand, Charles. *Tunis au XIXe siècle*. Paris: La Maison Quantin, 1890.

Langlois, Claude. *Le catholicisme au féminin: Les congrégations françaises à supérieure générale au XIXe siècle*. Paris: Cerf, 1984.

Larguèche, Abdelhamid. *L'abolition de l'esclavage en Tunisie à travers les archives, 1841–1846*. Tunis: Alif, 1990.

———. *Les ombres de la ville: Pauvres, marginaux et minoritaires à Tunis (XVIIIème et XIXè siècles)*. Tunis: Centre de Publication Universitaire, 1999.

Larguèche, Dalenda, ed. *Histoire des femmes au Maghreb: Culture matérielle et vie quotidienne*. Tunis: Centre de Publication Universitaire, 2000.

———. *Territoire sans frontières: La contrebande et ses réseaux dans la Régence de Tunis au XIXe siècle*. Tunis: Centre de Publication Universitaire, 2001.

Larguèche, Dalenda, and Abdelhamid Larguèche. *Marginales en terre d'Islam*. Tunis: Cérès Productions, 1992.

Larson, Pier M. *Ocean of Letters: Language and Creolization in an Indian Ocean Diaspora*. Cambridge: Cambridge University Press, 2009.

Lobban, Richard A., ed. *Middle Eastern Women and the Invisible Economy*. Gainesville: University of Florida Press, 1998.

Loth, Gaston. *Le peuplement italien en Tunisie et en Algérie*. Paris: Colin, 1905.

MacLean, Gerald M. *The Rise of Oriental Travel: English Visitors to the Ottoman Empire, 1580–1720*. New York: Palgrave Macmillan, 2004.

Makdisi, Ussama. *Artillery of Heaven: American Missionaries and the Failed Conversion of the Middle East*. Ithaca: Cornell University Press, 2008.

Martel, André. *Luis-Arnold et Joseph Allegro: Consuls du bey de Tunis à Bône*. Paris: Presses Universitaires de France, 1967.

Matar, Nabil. *Turks, Moors, and Englishmen in the Age of Discovery*. New York: Columbia University Press, 1999.

———, ed. and trans. *In the Lands of the Christians: Arabic Travel Writing in the Seventeenth Century*. London: Routledge, 2003.

Matignon, Raymond-Joseph. *L'art médical à Tunis*. Bordeaux: Paul Cassignol, 1901.

Matri, Faiza. *Tunis sous le Protectorat: Histoire de la conservation du patrimoine architectural et urban de la médina*. Tunis: Centre de Publication Universitaire, 2008.

McNeill, John R. *The Mountains of the Mediterranean World: An Environmental History*. Cambridge: Cambridge University Press, 1992.

Melfa, Daniela. *Migrando a sud: Coloni italiani di Tunisia (1881–1939)*. Rome: Aracne, 2008.

Michel, Ersilio. *Esuli italiani in Tunisia (1815–1861)*. Milan: Instituto per gli Studi di Politica Internazionale, 1941.

Miège, Jean-Louis et al. *Le café en Méditerranée: Histoire, anthropologie, économie, XVIIIe–XXe siècles*. Aix-en-Provence: Université de Provence/Éditions du CNRS, 1981.

Melon, Paul. *L'Alliance Française et l'enseignement français en Tunisie et en Tripolitaine*. Paris: Dentu, 1885.

———. *Problèmes algériens et tunisiens: Ce que disent les chiffres*. Paris: Challamel, 1903.

Moatti, Claudia, and Wolfgang Kaisers, eds. *Gens de passage en Méditerranée de l'antiquité à l'époque moderne: Procédures de contrôle et d'identication*. Paris: Maisonneuve & Larose, 2007.

Moatti, Lucien. *La mosaïque médicale de Tunisie, 1800–1950*. Paris: Éditions Glyphe, 2008.

Moch, Leslie Page. *Paths to the City: Regional Migrations in France*. Beverly Hill: Sage Publications, 1983.

Moreau, Odile. *L'Empire Ottoman à l'âge des réformes: Les hommes et les idées du "Nouvel Ordre" militaire, 1826–1914*. Paris: Maisonneuve & Larose, 2007.

Mzali, Muhammad Salih, ed. *Min rasa'il Ibn Abi al-Diyaf*. Tunis: al-Dar al-Tunisiya lil-Nashr, 1969.

Naylor, Phillip C. *North Africa: A History from Antiquity to the Present*. Austin: University of Texas Press, 2009.

Nicolet, Claude, Robert Ilbert, and Jean-Charles Depaule, eds., *Mégapoles méditerranéennes: Géographie urbaine rétrospective*. Paris: Maisonneuve & Larose, 2000.

Noiriel, Gérard. *The French Melting Pot: Immigration, Citizenship, and National Identity*. Trans. Geoffroy de Laforcade. Minneapolis: University of Minnesota Press, 1996.

Perkins, Kenneth J. *Historical Dictionary of Tunisia*. 2nd ed. London: Scarecrow Press, 1997.

———. *A History of Modern Tunisia*. Oxford: Oxford University Press, 2004.

Planel, Anne-Marie. "De la nation à la colonie: La communauté française de Tunisie au XIXe siècle d'aprés les archives civiles et notariées du consultat général de France à Tunis." 3 vols. PhD dissertation, École des Hautes Études en Science Sociales, Paris, 2002.

Poiré, Eugène. *La Tunisie française*. Paris: Plon, 1892.

Price, Charles A. *Malta and the Maltese: A Study in Nineteenth Century Migration*. Melbourne: Georgian House, 1954.

Raymond, André, trans. *Commentaire historique d'Ibn Abi l-Diyaf. Présent aux hommes de notre temps. Chronique des rois de Tunis et du pacte fondamental. Chapitres IV et V*. 2 vols. Tunis: Alif, 1994.

Renault, François. *Lavigerie, l'esclavage africain, et l'Europe, 1868–1892*, 2 vols. Paris: E. de Boccard, 1971.

Revault, Jacques. *Le fondouk des français et les consuls de France à Tunis, 1660–1860*. Paris: Editions Recherche sur les Civilisations, 1984.

Roberts, Mary. *Intimate Outsiders: The Harem in Ottoman and Orientalist Art and Travel Literature*. Durham: Duke University Press, 2007.

Robinson-Dunn, Diane. *The Harem, Slavery and British Imperial Culture: Anglo-Muslim Relations in the Late Nineteenth Century*. Manchester: University of Manchester Press, 2006.

Rogan, Eugene, ed. *Outside In: On the Margins of the Modern Middle East*. London: I. B. Tauris, 2002

Saada, Emmanuelle. *Les enfants de la colonie: Les métis de l'empire français entre sujétion et citoyenneté*. Paris: La Découverte, 2007.

Salem, Lilia Ben, ed. *Consommations et consommateurs dans les pays méditerranéens (XVIe-XXe S.)*. Special issue, *RTSS* 42, 129 (2005).

Samrakandi, Mohammed Habib, and Jean-Pierre Poulain, eds. *Horizons maghrébins: Le droit à la mémoire*. Special issue, *Manger au Maghreb*. Toulouse: Presses Universitaires du Mirail, 2006.

Schendel, Willem van, and Itty Abraham, eds. *Illicit Flows and Criminal Things: States, Borders, and the Other Side of Globalization*. Bloomington: Indiana University Press, 2005.

Schneider, Jane. *Italy's "Southern Question": Orientalism in One Country*. New York: Oxford, 1998.

Scott, James C. *Seeing Like a State: How Certain Schemes to Improve the Human Condition Have Failed*. New Haven: Yale University Press, 1998.

Sebag, Paul. *Tunis: Histoire d'une ville*. Paris: L'Harmattan, 1998.

Sraïeb, Noureddine, ed. *Pratiques et résistance culturelle au Maghreb*. Paris: Éditions du CNRS, 1992.

Taraud, Christelle. *La prostitution coloniale: Algérie, Tunisie, Maroc (1830–1962)*. Paris: Payot, 2003.

Temime, Émile. *Migrance: Histoire des migrations à Marseille*. 2 vols. Aix-en-Provence: Édisud, 1990.

Temple, Major Sir Grenville T. *Excursions in the Mediterranean: Algiers and Tunis*. 2 vols. London: Saunders and Otley, 1835.

Torpey, John. *The Invention of the Passport: Surveillance, Citizenship and the State*. Cambridge: Cambridge University Press, 2000.

Tuchscherer, Michel, ed. *Le commerce du café avant l'ère des plantations coloniales: Espaces, réseaux, société (XVe–XIXe siècle)*. Paris: Institut Français d'Archéologie Orientale, 2000.

Valensi, Lucette. *On the Eve of Colonialism: North Africa before the French Conquest, 1790–1830*. Trans. Kenneth J. Perkins. New York: Africana, 1977.

———. *Mardochée Naggiar: Enquête sur un inconnu*. Paris: Éditions Stock, 2008.

Vassallo. Carmel. *Corsairing to Commerce: Maltese Merchants in XVIII Century Spain*. Msida: Maltese University, 1997.

———. *The Malta Chamber of Commerce, 1858–1979: An Outline History of Maltese Trade*. Valletta: Malta Chamber of Commerce, 1998.

Windler, Christian. *La diplomatie comme expérience de l'autre: Consuls français au Maghreb (1700–1840)*. Geneva: Droz, 2002.

Woodward, Jamie. *The Physical Geography of the Mediterranean*. Oxford: Oxford University Press, 2009.

INDEX

1816 expedition to the Maghrib, 1–3, 109,
296, 351n1; depictions of, 72–73
expulsion, 94–97, 220, 225–29; "boat people
crisis," 226–27; political, 70, 83–84, 369n75;
the Sisters of Saint-Joseph, from Algeria,
246, 253–54

famine, 103, 153–54
Fassy, Dominique (French sailmaker in La
Goulette), 154–55
Fatima, Baya Lalla (wife of Husayn Bey), 110, 299
Fedriani, Gaetano (Genoese expatriate), 84, 117
Feise, Godfrey (Englishman in Tunis), 28, 107
Féraud, L. Charles (Algerian interpreter), 333–34
Ferriere, Louis (British consul in Tunisia), 53,
80, 210, 216–17, 302
Filippi, Count Louis Jean-Baptiste (Sardinian
consul in Tunis), 104, 216, 327–28
financial debt, 129–30, 155, 214–15, 355n44
Finzi, Giulio (Italian expatriate), 84, 136, 323,
379n13
fishermen, 40, 51–52, 82–83,165–68, 385n20
French, 53, 61, 266, 278, 325, 334
French consulate: in Algeria, 234–37, 160, 166,
182, 256; carte de sûreté in Tunisia, 235–39,
245, 395n116; charitable assistance of, 154–
56; as employment bureau, 127; and "French
military law" over Algeria—Tunisia border,
233–39, 245; and legal jurisdiction, 208, 210,
212, 220–21, 225, 228, 240–41; policing La
Goulette port, 31–32, 151, 305; relations with
Husaynid dynasty, 297–98. See also Cubisol,
Charles; Gaspary, Pierre; Roches, Léon
French empire, 8; Algeria, invasion of (c. 1830),
1, 5–6, 75, 204; Algiers, repopulation of,
57, 74, 86–90, 93–97, 311; and Algerian—
Tunisian border, 127–29, 339–40; colonialism in North Africa, 14, 345–47; in Egypt,
71–72; female immigration restrictions and
incentives, 94–96; Franco-Italian conflict,
242, 266–68, 278–79, 283, 298, 347, 404n142;
missionaries, 250–56, 261–72, 275–86; Muslim travel and immigration to France, 68–
70, 72, 302, 324–27, 328, 414n32; nationals
in Tunis, 32, 40, 49, 55, 57, 62, 282; relations
with the British empire, 181–82; relations
with the Ottoman Empire, 70, 281
French Protectorate, 16, 240–242, 249–50, 286,
310, 340–42
Frères des Écoles Chrétiennes (FEC), 261–62,
267, 282

Fundamental Pact ('Ahd al-Aman) (1857), 137,
240–41; and Khayr al-Din, 315–16, 330
funduqs (hostels), 34, 55–56, 147

Gabes, 172–73
gambling and cafes, 143–45
Gandolphe, Pascal, 58
Gandolphe, Joseph (French protégé), 213
Garibaldi, Giuseppe, 83–84, 136
Gaspary family, 48, 308, 357n35
Gaspary, Pierre (French vice-consul), 31, 32, 33,
62, 141; conflicting jurisdiction of, 220, 240;
charitable assistance of, 154–56
Gay, Laurent (French physician to the bey),
110–11, 116
Germany, 91, 304–5
gender: and gift giving, 302; and legal plural-
ism, 202; norms, 191, 194; and pursuit of
leisure, 298, 311–12; and urban spaces, 37–
38, 103, 144–7, 276, 303, 305–6, 358n50. See
also women
Genoa, 61, 83
Georgia, 42–43, 47, 109
Ghadaham, 'Ali ibn (Tunisian revolt leader), 242
Ghar al-Milh. See Porto Farina
Gibraltar, 1, 46, 387n54
Gibson, John (British vice-consul), 298
Gibson family, 51–52, 141
gift giving, 290, 299, 301–2; of housing, 296–97
governance, 4; abolition, 114–15; alcohol pro-
curement and consumption, 141–47, 381n58;
clothing regulations, 58–59; contraband
trade, 161, 168, 170–71, 179–81, 193, 197; droit
de résidence (right of residence), 54–55, 205;
municipal council (majlis), 137, 330; prostitution and the mizwar, 89–90, 184, 188–89;
policing urban spaces, 135–37, 167, 177–78,
186–87, 201; public baths, 293, 305–6; Tourism Committee, 152–53; travel regulations,
29–30, 88, 96–97, 216–19. See also identification; law
Greaves, Joseph, 61–62, 83
Greece, 80, 141; Greek community in Tunisia,
59, 84–86, 143, 215, 219–20; Ottoman-Greek
Wars, 57, 79, 86, 219
Greek Orthodox, 40, 84–85, 255

Halq-al-Wad. See La Goulette
Hammam Lif, 288, 293, 307, 309
Hammuda Bey, 27, 44, 49, 138, 296, 357n40
Hanafi (Sunni legal school), 40, 44, 77, 202, 291

282; antagonism toward, 281–82, 404n138; civilizing mission, 256, 270, 402n95; Catholic, 247–49, 270, 298; Catholic female, 19–20, 51, 246, 247–64, 266–86, 305, 400n50; and conversion, 151, 250, 252–55, 270, 274–75, 398n20, 400n47; "going native," 276–78, 403n121; and imperialism, 249–51; Missionaries of Our Lady of Africa (White Fathers), 251, 271, 277, 278, 283; Missionary Sisters of Our Lady of Africa (White Sisters), 248, 251, 278, 283–84; Oeuvre des Écoles d'Orient, 254–55; Protestant, 264–65; scholarship on, 251. See also Sisters of Saint-Joseph de L'Apparition

Missionaries of Our Lady of Africa (Missionaires de Notre-Dame d'Afrique or White Fathers), 251, 271, 277, 278, 283, 403n121

Missionary Sisters of Our Lady of Africa (Soeurs Missionnaires de Notre-Dame d'Afrique or White Sisters), 248, 251, 278, 283–84

mizwar, 184–85, 188–89

Moch, Leslie, 65

modernity, 289–90, 319, 324, 345

monopolies, 40, 46, 103, 141, 161, 168; diplomatic postings, 46–54; tobacco, 140, 174, 177, 193

moral anxiety and women, 106, 145, 184–88, 228, 260, 305

Morocco, 89–90, 111, 235, 263, 347, 365n22

Muhammad 'Ali Pasha, ruler of Egypt, 71, 108, 250

Muhammad al-Sadiq Bey, 142, 233, 241, 297, 307, 330; and teaching missionaries, 262, 267; subordinate to the Ottoman sultan, 327

Muhammad Bayram V, 309, 331, 411n91

Muhammad Bey, 105, 135–36, 241, 296, 306, 327; and Sisters of Saint-Joseph, 247, 266

Munastir, 187–88, 238, 385n20, 392n49

al-Murali, Hassuna, 30, 64, 68, 86, 165, 212, 325

Mussalli, Elias (Tunisian interpreter), 71–72, 297–98, 366n30

Mussalli, Madame Luigia Traverso (wife of Elias Mussalli), 297–98, 408n42

Muslims: and charity, 154; clothing of, 58–59, 169; concept of Muslim Mediterranean, 10–11; conversion to Islam, 19, 42, 49, 229–33, 250, 332; elites, 40, 54, 107, 292–93, 312; and Husaynid dynasty, 44–45; Islamic law, 202–4, 213, 224, 234, 237–38, 241, 331; relations with Catholics, 51, 55, 57, 66–68, 76–78, 256, 258, 270, 280–83; relations with Jews, 41, 256; relations with missionaries, 247–86; slaves, 76–77, 364n9, 367n46, 374n24; and

sex trade, 184–88, 388n85; Sunni, 40; in Tunis, 39–41; women, 37–38, 202, 213, 270, 292–93, 312. See also Husaynid dynasty

Mustafa Bey, 3, 110, 132, 209, 272; forced conscription, 108; abolished mizwar, 184–85; "boat people crisis," 64, 226–27

Mustafa Khaznadar, 118, 127, 129, 154, 413n15; father-in-law of Khayr al-Din, 320, 329, 330, 332

Mzab, 103

Nabeul, 146, 293–94, 311

Naples, 69, 80–83, 270

Napoleon III, 84, 95

Napoleonic Wars, 1–3, 71–72, 76, 78, 85, 87

networks: informational and assistance, 18, 56, 74–75, 91; employment, 101–2, 106, 124–25, 136, 155–58; contraband trade, 160, 177–78, 190, 192, 195. See also sociability

Nicholson (American consul to Tunis), 51

Nishan al-Iftikhar, 247, 281, 397n3

Noiriel, Gerard, 14; The French Melting Pot, 245

North Africa: consular elite in, 53–54; demythologizing of, 72–74, 285–86; French colonialism in, 14, 345–47; Italian movement to, 82; -Mediterranean maritime trade, 162; missionaries' impact on, 250, 285–86; north-south Mediterranean migration to, 11–15, 71–74, 76; as population dump, 65, 95–97, 179, 225–26; scholarship on colonial history of, 14–15, 353n21; transversal movement across, 69–70; travel from, to Europe, 67–69

Oeuvre des Écoles d'Orient, 254–55

Onoffre, Juan (Spanish tobacco merchant in Bougie), 175

Oran, 91, 92, 95

Otth, Adolphe, 73–74

Ottoman empire: borders, 8, 12–13; conquest of Tunis (1574), 23, 40; consular elite in, 53; Ottoman-Greek Wars, 57, 79, 86, 219; relations with Europe, 3, 161, 196–98, 205, 243, 326, 328, 355n2, 361n91; relations with Tunisia and the Husaynid dynasty, 42–43, 45–47, 205, 226, 241, 326–27; slavery and the mamluk system, 42–43, 47, 98, 109–10, 196, 320–21

Pantelleria, 12, 343

Paris, 68–70, 302, 319; Bourgade, François, in, 269–70; as haven, 69, 95–96; Khayr al-Din in, 325–28, 331

TEXT

10/12.5 Minion Pro

DISPLAY

Minion Pro

COMPOSITOR

BookMatters, Berkeley

INDEXER

Sandra Kimball